THE **BROADCAST JOURNALISM**
HANDBOOK

Visit *The Broadcast Journalism Handbook* Companion Website at
www.pearsoned.co.uk/practicaljournalism to find valuable
learning material including:

- Updates on the latest developments in news
  broadcasting
- Audio interviews
- Links to relevant online resources

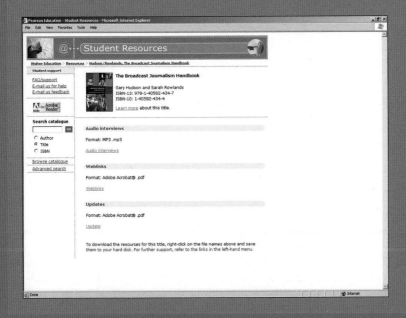

THE **BROADCAST JOURNALISM** HANDBOOK

GARY HUDSON & SARAH ROWLANDS

PEARSON

Longman

Harlow, England • London • New York • Boston • San Francisco • Toronto • Sydney • Singapore • Hong Kong
Tokyo • Seoul • Taipei • New Delhi • Cape Town • Madrid • Mexico City • Amsterdam • Munich • Paris • Milan

Pearson Education Limited
Edinburgh Gate
Harlow
Essex CM20 2JE
England

and Associated Companies throughout the world

Visit us on the World Wide Web at:
www.pearsoned.co.uk

First published 2007

ISBN: 978-1-4058-2434-7

British Library Cataloguing-in-Publication Data
A catalogue record for this book is available from the British Library

10 9 8 7 6 5 4 3 2 1
11 10 09 08 07

Typeset in 9.5/12.5pt Din Regular by 35
Printed and bound by Graficus Estella, Bilbao, Spain

The publisher's policy is to use paper manufactured from sustainable forests.

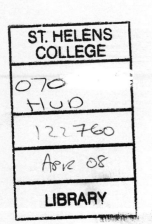

CONTENTS

Supporting resources

Visit **www.pearsoned.co.uk/practicaljournalism** to find valuable online resources

Companion Website

- Updates on the latest developments in news broadcasting
- Audio interviews
- Links to relevant online resources

For more information please contact your local Pearson Education sales representative or visit **www.pearsoned.co.uk/practicaljournalism**

FOREWORD

How do you learn to broadcast? I've never worked out the answer to that question. When I was a teenager, engrossed in the idea of being on the radio because of a fleeting visit I'd paid to Capital at the age of 12, I thought you needed a Physics O Level. That would give me an understanding of the way a transmitter worked, I reckoned; what caused feedback; why speakers have magnets.

'Nonsense,' said a friend. 'You don't need to know any of that.'

So I bought a book instead. In those days, there was only one book. I remember the title as *Being a DJ* by Emperor Roscoe. A great read it was too – all about how to avoid losing records on your way to a gig. Presenters were gods when I was young. They did not write books. DJs did not talk about how to broadcast. Maybe nobody did.

Spool on a few decades. London is making a claim to be the media capital of the world, and now your digital dial shows up, not only Capital, but a score of other stations. The TV has 250 channels! The media hoover up thousands and thousands of young and aspiring journalists, presenters, producers and technicians (now with Physics GCSEs). There is, more than ever, a need for a book that does quite a bit more than Roscoe could, that takes us deep into the jungle of politics, ethics and the law. Well, here it is.

Good luck.

Jeremy Vine
March 2007

PREFACE

A few weeks back I had lunch in Dublin with one of my former students, Richard Hannaford. We had last met over 20 years ago. Since then he had risen to be BBC Health Correspondent, but left the Corporation some years ago and is now one of Ireland's most successful periodical publishers, with a stable of magazines which includes the country's highest selling women's magazine. We took the opportunity to reminisce about his fellow alumni, and it was impressive to realise how well they had done. I even managed to retrieve my 1984 assessment notes from a dark corner of our loft and was impressed to find that some of those who had been quite moderate performers as student broadcasters had nonetheless enjoyed major success on the business side of the media. Like Richard and me, few were still active frontline broadcast journalists, yet many are still using the core journalism skills they have learnt and developed over the years. And I guess that, in the finest tradition of the Blairite nanny state, is the point at which we ought to state the almost mandatory caveat.

The clear factual evidence provided by the regular Skillset media industry surveys shows that there are relatively fewer active broadcast journalists over 40 and even fewer who make it through the fifties to a comfortable retirement living off anecdotes of derring-do with nothing but a microphone to protect them from the wild elements or an even wilder mob.

Yet the growth in demand for professional, accredited training as a broadcast journalist is starting to outstrip more traditional disciplines.

At the time of writing the Broadcast Journalism Training Council already accredits 32 courses, and that number will rise steeply over the next two or three years, with yet more degree and other courses set to launch after that. We are repeatedly asked where are all the graduates of these courses going to find jobs – yet no one ever asked in the past where the graduates from the various traditional academic courses like history, politics and philosophy were going to find work – after all there's hardly ever been a point in history when there's been a burgeoning bull market in philosophers.

For a start, the best graduates will enter the industry, fully and far better equipped to take rapid advantage of the many emerging career opportunities than journalists of my generation could ever have imagined. We learnt 'on the job' and believe me, it's an often painful and embarrassing process.

As this book so powerfully and entertainingly demonstrates, with so many enlightening real-life examples and anecdotes, you will learn how to go straight to the heart of a story, of an idea or a concept; you will learn how to write clearly, succinctly and, hopefully, all in good, properly spelt and grammatical English.

You will learn about presenting what you have written in print, sound and vision across an ever widening range of platforms; about interviewing people and allowing them to present themselves and their views persuasively. Not only that, you will also learn to speak to a microphone, to a camera and even to a live audience in a clear and confident manner. You will learn technical skills and how to use a range of computer software and, on a personal level, you will learn how to organise yourself and your time and to work as part of a team and, in time, to lead those teams. You might even learn shorthand, the most traditional of journalism skills, but evermore relevant even in this hi-tech post-Hutton world, though Hutton should be the least of your reasons for so doing.

I believe there can be few people who could argue that these are not highly valuable and highly transferable skills, with a far wider and longer-term application than many other traditional academic degrees – and there is little danger that journalism and communications skills will ever become obsolete, because they are at the core of the burgeoning information society. But this book is just a beginning. You will need to ensure that you continue to refresh, upgrade and broaden those skills through a continuing programme of personal and professional development. Again, this is a concept largely alien to previous generations of journalists – after all, in nearly 25 years as a print, radio and finally a television journalist, I refreshed my skills in a properly structured way only twice, which is why I have become so committed to high quality, fully accredited training and continuing personal and professional development.

The broadcast and media environment is changing at a faster pace than I can ever recall. We are entering a third age of broadcasting, where traditional linear models, both print and electronic, are starting to look creakingly obsolete. There are newer, smarter technologies and software – digital TV, Wi-Fi, broadband, iPods, DAB, DRM – simply too many to remember, let alone name.

Such is the pace of change that even as I write I feel a second edition of this book coming on, but however good this book is, it ultimately rests with you to make the best of your skills, your abilities and your opportunities. Best of luck.

Steve Harris
Accreditations Secretary
Broadcast Journalism Training Council
November 2006

AUTHOR ACKNOWLEDGEMENTS

This book is the product of a year and a half's research and two lifetimes in broadcasting. It would not have been possible without the enthusiasm and support of all the professionals who welcomed us into their workplaces and homes, and generously shared their ideas, experiences and working practices. We have tried to distil as much as possible of their expertise into its pages. Any mistakes are entirely the authors'.

We particularly thank Vin Ray and Helen Boaden at the BBC, Rob Kirk and Pete Lowe at Sky News and Deborah Turness at ITN for facilitating our visits to their organisations. Except where otherwise stated, quotes come from interviews conducted by the authors. We are grateful to all who gave permissions to reproduce copyright material.

The panel of referees, assembled by Pearson Education from the broadcast industries, educational institutions (Jan Whyatt at City University, Jennifer Brown at Leeds, Carole Fleming at Nottingham Trent and others who wished to remain anonymous) and the BJTC (especially Steve Harris), improved our work immeasurably. Particular gratitude must go to Roy Saatchi and Mike Henfield, whom we knew to be great news editors from the time we worked with them, and who have brought the same sharp insight and good humour to their suggestions for the text.

We could not have completed this project without the support of colleagues at Staffordshire University, who covered for us whenever we were away from the day job, and shared our excitement as the book came together.

Andrew Taylor and the team at Pearson, and Lissy Kowalski, who made sense of more than a thousand photographs and helped edit them down to what you see in the book, shaped the finished product.

Final thanks to our families, who tolerated the late nights in the office and the days away from home.

Gary Hudson
Sarah Rowlands
November 2006

PUBLISHER ACKNOWLEDGEMENTS

We are grateful to the following for permission to reproduce copyright material:

P8 (main), p160, p174 (2nd main) p323, p324 (2nd) and p324 (3rd) photos and graphics reprinted by permission of BBC Worldwide; p8 (t) & 252, p300, p324 (2nd from top) & p324 (b) and p327 photos reprinted by permission of BSkyB Ltd.; screenshots on p305(b), p308 and p352 (b) screen shot frames reprinted with permission from Microsoft Corporation; p122 © Horace Whetton (Staffordshire University); p305 (b) screenshot from RadioMan® Quick Edit Pro reprinted by permission of Jutel Oy; p308 screenshot from Avid Xpress DV reprinted courtesy of Avid Technology, Inc.; graphics on p326 (top 5) Curious World Map images from www.curious-software.com reprinted by permission of Vizrt Ltd.; p385 screenshot from BBC News at bbc.co.uk/news reprinted by permission of BBC News Interactive.

We are grateful to the following for permission to reproduce text material:

Chapter 2, Theories of news production, adapted extract from *Investigating the Media*, reprinted by permission of HarperCollins Publishers Ltd. © Paul Trowler 1988 (Trowler, P. 1988); Chapter 3, Chapter 4, Chapter 6 and Chapter 15 extracts from BBC Editorial Guidelines, reproduced by kind permission of the BBC; Chapter 6 abridged extract from *Guidelines for MPS staff on dealing with media reporters, press photographers and television crews*, produced by the Directorate of Public Affairs, © 2006 Metropolitan Police Authority, reprinted by permission of Metropolitan Police Service; Chapter 9 The INSI Safety Code from www.newssafety.com/safety/index.htm, © International News Safety Institute, reprinted by permission of International News Safety Institute; Chapter 9, Case Study: Explaining the world – a foreign reporter at work, Laurence Lee's report from Russia prior to the presidential elections of 2004, broadcast on Sky News, reprinted by permission of BSkyB Ltd.; Chapter 11, Case Study: Pulling it together – using actuality, Rachel Harvey's report on the Indonesian earthquake, broadcast on BBC Radio 4 18:00 bulletin, 31 May 2006, reproduced by kind permission of the BBC and Rachel Harvey; Chapter 11 Robin Punt's interview with Noel Martin, broadcast on BBC Midlands, June 2006, reproduced by kind permission of the BBC, Robin Punt and Noel Martin; Chapter 11 Case Study: War Artist, Rob Perry's story broadcast on BBC local TV West Midlands, reproduced by kind permission of the BBC and Rob Perry; Chapter 13 Case Study: Working with blue screen – the virtual reality graphic, Chris Evans interview with Jeremy Vine and Peter Snow, broadcast on BBC Radio 2, Chris Evans Show, 4 May 2006, reproduced by kind permission of the BBC, Chris Evans, Jeremy Vine and Peter Snow.

In some instances we have been unable to trace the owners of copyright material, and we would appreciate any information that would enable us to do so.

GUIDED TOUR

A closer look box – focuses on a key topic or issue from the main text in more detail

Remember – a quick summary/revision aid of the key points at the end of each section

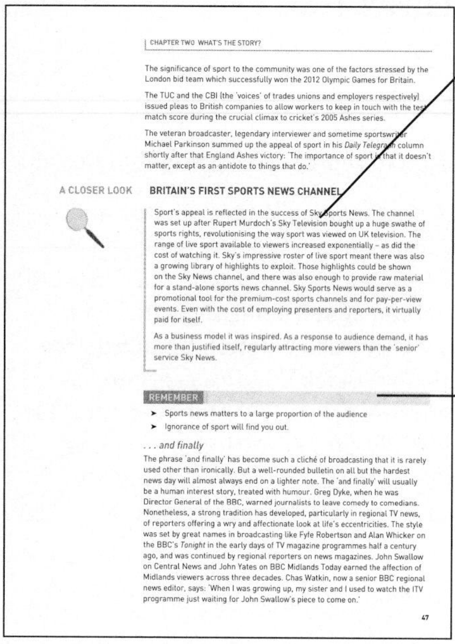

CHAPTER TWO WHAT'S THE STORY?

The significance of sport to the community was one of the factors stressed by the London bid team which successfully won the 2012 Olympic Games for Britain.

The TUC and the CBI (the 'voices' of trades unions and employers respectively) issued pleas to British companies to allow workers to keep in touch with the test match score during the crucial climax to cricket's 2005 Ashes series.

The veteran broadcaster, legendary interviewer and sometime sportswriter Michael Parkinson summed up the appeal of sport in his *Daily Telegraph* column shortly after that England Ashes victory: 'The importance of sport is that it doesn't matter, except as an antidote to things that do.'

A CLOSER LOOK **BRITAIN'S FIRST SPORTS NEWS CHANNEL**

Sport's appeal is reflected in the success of Sky Sports News. The channel was set up after Rupert Murdoch's Sky Television bought up a huge swathe of sports rights, revolutionising the way sport was viewed on UK television. The range of live sport available to viewers increased exponentially – as did the cost of watching it. Sky's impressive roster of live sport meant there was also a growing library of highlights to exploit. Those highlights could be shown on the Sky News channel, and there was also enough to provide raw material for a stand-alone sports news channel. Sky Sports News would serve as a promotional tool for the premium-cost sports channels and for pay-per-view events. Even with the cost of employing presenters and reporters, it virtually paid for itself.

As a business model it was inspired. As a response to audience demand, it has more than justified itself, regularly attracting more viewers than the 'senior' service Sky News.

REMEMBER

- Sports news matters to a large proportion of the audience
- Ignorance of sport will find you out.

. . . and finally

The phrase 'and finally' has become such a cliché of broadcasting that it is rarely used other than ironically. But a well-rounded bulletin on all but the hardest news day will almost always end on a lighter note. The 'and finally' will usually be a human interest story, treated with humour. Greg Dyke, when he was Director General of the BBC, warned journalists to leave comedy to comedians. Nonetheless, a strong tradition has developed, particularly in regional TV news, of reporters offering a wry and affectionate look at life's eccentricities. The style was set by great names in broadcasting like Fyfe Robertson and Alan Whicker on the BBC's *Tonight* in the early days of TV magazine programmes half a century ago, and was continued by regional reporters on news magazines. John Swallow on Central News and John Yates on BBC Midlands Today earned the affection of Midlands viewers across three decades. Chas Watkin, now a senior BBC regional news editor, says: 'When I was growing up, my sister and I used to watch the ITV programme just waiting for John Swallow's piece to come on.'

47

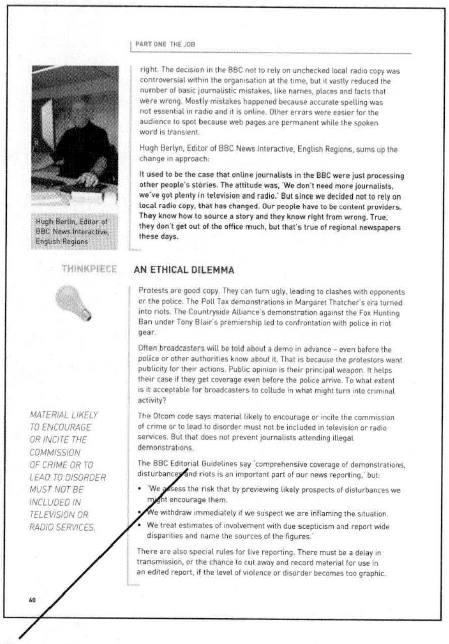

PART ONE THE JOB

Hugh Berlin, Editor of BBC News Interactive, English Regions

right. The decision in the BBC not to rely on unchecked local radio copy was controversial within the organisation at the time, but it vastly reduced the number of basic journalistic mistakes, like names, places and facts that were wrong. Mostly mistakes happened because accurate spelling was not essential in radio and it is online. Other errors were easier for the audience to spot because web pages are permanent while the spoken word is transient.

Hugh Berlyn, Editor of BBC News Interactive, English Regions, sums up the change in approach:

It used to be the case that online journalists in the BBC were just processing other people's stories. The attitude was, 'We don't need more journalists, we've got plenty in television and radio.' But since we decided not to rely on local radio copy, that has changed. Our people have to be content providers. They know how to source a story and they know right from wrong. True, they don't get out of the office much, but that's true of regional newspapers these days.

THINKPIECE **AN ETHICAL DILEMMA**

Protests are good copy. They can turn ugly, leading to clashes with opponents or the police. The Poll Tax demonstrations in Margaret Thatcher's era turned into riots. The Countryside Alliance's demonstration against the Fox Hunting Ban under Tony Blair's premiership led to confrontation with police in riot gear.

Often broadcasters will be told about a demo in advance – even before the police or other authorities know about it. That is because the protestors want publicity for their actions. Public opinion is their principal weapon. It helps their case if they get coverage even before the police arrive. To what extent is it acceptable for broadcasters to collude in what might turn into criminal activity?

MATERIAL LIKELY TO ENCOURAGE OR INCITE THE COMMISSION OF CRIME OR TO LEAD TO DISORDER MUST NOT BE INCLUDED IN TELEVISION OR RADIO SERVICES.

The Ofcom code says material likely to encourage or incite the commission of crime or to lead to disorder must not be included in television or radio services. But that does not prevent journalists attending illegal demonstrations.

The BBC Editorial Guidelines say 'comprehensive coverage of demonstrations, disturbances and riots is an important part of our news reporting,' but:

- 'We assess the risk that by previewing likely prospects of disturbances we might encourage them.
- We withdraw immediately if we suspect we are inflaming the situation.
- We treat estimates of involvement with due scepticism and report wide disparities and name the sources of the figures.'

There are also special rules for live reporting. There must be a delay in transmission, or the chance to cut away and record material for use in an edited report, if the level of violence or disorder becomes too graphic.

60

Thinkpiece box – encourages the reader to consider some of the issues – perhaps ethical, practical or legal - central to working as an informed broadcast journalist

Case study box – looks in more detail at a particular (often real) case or scenario in broadcast journalism

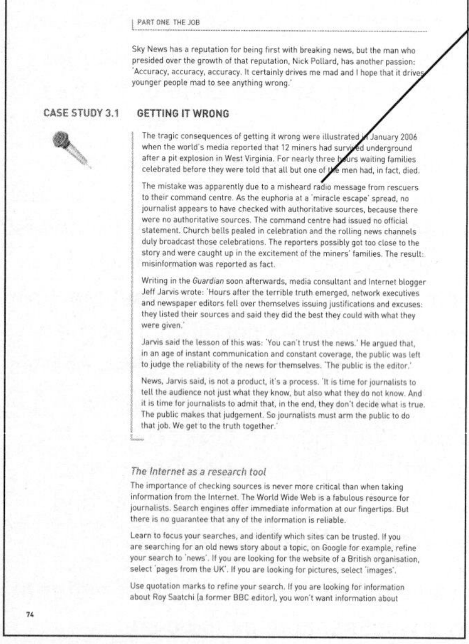

PART ONE THE JOB

Sky News has a reputation for being first with breaking news, but the man who presided over the growth of that reputation, Nick Pollard, has another passion: 'Accuracy, accuracy, accuracy. It certainly drives me mad and I hope that it drives younger people mad to see anything wrong.'

CASE STUDY 3.1 **GETTING IT WRONG**

The tragic consequences of getting it wrong were illustrated in January 2006 when the world's media reported that 12 miners had survived underground after a pit explosion in West Virginia. For nearly three hours waiting families celebrated before they were told that all but one of the men had, in fact, died.

The mistake was apparently due to a misheard radio message from rescuers to their command centre. As the euphoria at a 'miracle escape' spread, no journalist appears to have checked with authoritative sources, because there were no authoritative sources. The command centre had issued no official statement. Church bells pealed in celebration and the rolling news channels duly broadcast those celebrations. The reporters possibly got too close to the story and were caught up in the excitement of the miners' families. The result: misinformation was reported as fact.

Writing in the *Guardian* soon afterwards, media consultant and Internet blogger Jeff Jarvis wrote: 'Hours after the terrible truth emerged, network executives and newspaper editors fell over themselves issuing justifications and excuses: they listed their sources and said they did the best they could with what they were given.'

Jarvis said the lesson of this was: 'You can't trust the news.' He argued that, in an age of instant communication and constant coverage, the public was left to judge the reliability of the news for themselves. 'The public is the editor.'

News, Jarvis said, is not a product, it's a process. 'It is time for journalists to tell the audience not just what they know, but also what they do not know. And it is time for journalists to admit that, in the end, they don't decide what is true. The public makes that judgement. So journalists must arm the public to do that job. We get to the truth together.'

The Internet as a research tool

The importance of checking sources is never more critical than when taking information from the Internet. The World Wide Web is a fabulous resource for journalists. Search engines offer immediate information at our fingertips. But there is no guarantee that any of the information is reliable.

Learn to focus your searches, and identify which sites can be trusted. If you are searching for an old news story about a topic, on Google for example, refine your search to 'news'. If you are looking for the website of a British organisation, select 'pages from the UK'. If you are looking for pictures, select 'images'.

Use quotation marks to refine your search. If you are looking for information about Roy Saatchi (a former BBC editor), you won't want information about

74

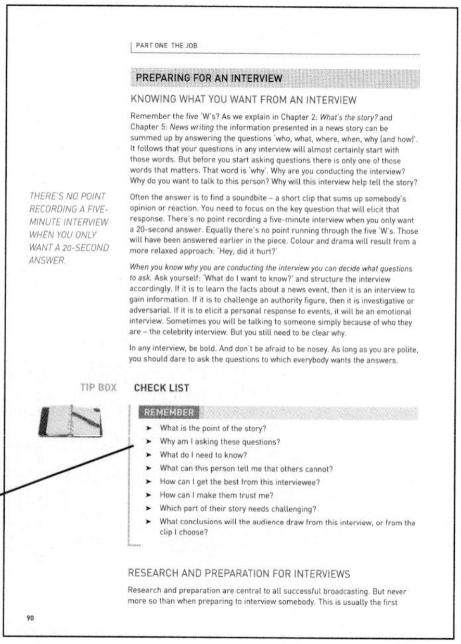

PART ONE THE JOB

PREPARING FOR AN INTERVIEW

KNOWING WHAT YOU WANT FROM AN INTERVIEW

Remember the five 'W's? As we explain in Chapter 2: *What's the story?* and Chapter 5: *News writing* the information presented in a news story can be summed up by answering the questions 'who, what, where, when, why (and how)'. It follows that your questions in any interview will almost certainly start with those words. But before you start asking questions there is only one of those words that matters. That word is 'why'. Why are you conducting the interview? Why do you want to talk to this person? Why will this interview help tell the story?

THERE'S NO POINT RECORDING A FIVE-MINUTE INTERVIEW WHEN YOU ONLY WANT A 20-SECOND ANSWER.

Often the answer is to find a soundbite – a short clip that sums up somebody's opinion or reaction. You need to focus on the key question that will elicit that response. There's no point recording a five-minute interview when you only want a 20-second answer. Equally there's no point running through the five 'W's. Those will have been answered earlier in the piece. Colour and drama will result from a more relaxed approach: 'Hey, did it hurt?'

When you know why you are conducting the interview you can decide what questions to ask. Ask yourself: 'What do I want to know?' and structure the interview accordingly. If it is to learn the facts about a news event, then it is an interview to gain information. If it is to challenge an authority figure, then it is investigative or adversarial. If it is to elicit a personal response to events, it will be an emotional interview. Sometimes you will be talking to someone simply because of who they are – the celebrity interview. But you still need to be clear why.

In any interview, be bold. And don't be afraid to be nosey. As long as you are polite, you should dare to ask the questions to which everybody wants the answers.

TIP BOX **CHECK LIST**

REMEMBER

- What is the point of the story?
- Why am I asking these questions?
- What do I need to know?
- What can this person tell me that others cannot?
- How can I get the best from this interviewee?
- How can I make them trust me?
- Which part of their story needs challenging?
- What conclusions will the audience draw from this interview, or from the clip I choose?

RESEARCH AND PREPARATION FOR INTERVIEWS

Research and preparation are central to all successful broadcasting. But never more so than when preparing to interview somebody. This is usually the first

90

Tip box – pithy advice showing key techniques and practices in broadcast journalism

PART ONE THE JOB

REMEMBER

➤ Online story-telling can be non-linear – the user chooses a way through the content
➤ Combine text, stills, graphics, video, audio and user content
➤ Online packages can appeal to different target audiences at the same time
➤ Use graphics programmes like Flash
➤ Make your package interactive for users

CONCLUSIONS

The traditional TV or radio package is probably as good a way of telling a linear story as has ever been devised. All the elements can be edited and crafted into an easily digested form that's convenient for viewers and listeners to understand.

But there are new horizons and new challenges. The limits of non-linear story-telling have yet to be explored. There is clearly an appetite for the new form. Many young people prefer playing video games to watching TV. They still use TV, but fewer are engaged by scheduled news programmes. Interactive journalism offers a way to attract that audience, and the opportunity to expand the limitations of traditional broadcast journalism.

FURTHER READING

Chantler, Paul and Stewart, Peter (2003) *Basic Radio Journalism*, Oxford: Focal Press. Expertise on producing wraps and features for radio.
McAdams, Mindy (2005) *Flash Journalism: How to create multimedia news packages*, Oxford: Focal Press. The definitive guide to using Macromedia's Flash in web journalism.
Ray, Vin (2003) *The Television News Handbook*, London: Macmillan. TV reporting explained with many examples from senior practitioners.

WEB LINKS

www.flashjournalism.com. Mindy McAdams' site.
www.newsday.com. A first-class example of Flash Journalism.
www.viewmagazine.tv. David Dunkley Gyimah's web-based magazine *The View* with examples of packaged TV reports.

302

Newsdays sections – show the excitement, pressure and key events of days in real-life newsrooms

Sky News

Sky News was the UK's first rolling 24-hour news channel. Part of Rupert Murdoch's News Corporation, it has regularly won awards as Britain's top rolling news channel. It is on satellite, cable and digital terrestrial TV. It has interactive and mobile phone services too.

In late 2005, Sky News moved to a purpose-built studio complex across the road from its original base on a trading estate in Osterley, West London. The move coincided with a redesign of the channel, and a switch to widescreen broadcasting. The programme schedule was refreshed, with dedicated shows aimed at different audience demands throughout the day.

The channel's unique selling point (USP) is that it is first for breaking news. Channel head Nick Pollard, who ran the operation for ten years, asserted: 'We can't afford to go on background or analysis when there's a breaking story.' So, each programme was constructed so it could be broken into at any time to deliver major news.

The programmes changed when John Ryley took over from Pollard in summer 2006, but the commitment remained to build on the reputation for breaking news with specialist correspondents delivering more original journalism.

When we visited Sky, ITV had announced the closure of its rolling news channel, leaving Sky News and BBC News 24 competing head-to-head. According to a senior Sky News manager, the two big players had their tanks parked on each other's lawns.

Sunrise, Sky's breakfast programme, goes on air. It is co-presented by Eamonn Holmes, one of the UK's most popular broadcasters, famous as the host of GMTV's breakfast show and of the lottery, quizzes and factual light entertainment on the BBC. Lorna Dunkley co-hosts, with Jacquie Beltrao on sport.

The opening story is a Sky exclusive about the rescue of a Midlands woman from a forced marriage in Pakistan. The film, following a foreign office rescue team backed up by armed police, is the result of nine months' investigation, research and persuasion by reporter Eve Richings.

At the home news desk next to the studio, Senior Home News Editor Kirsty Thomson has just come on shift. She's been briefed about overnight developments on stories the channel is covering. She'll keep track of crews and reporters across the UK, and keep an eye on what the opposition is doing on a multi-screen display on her desktop. Nick Toksvig is on the foreign desk, co-ordinating input from correspondents around the world.

End of chapter – weblinks and further reading encourage you to look further

---

THE LAW AND BROADCAST JOURNALISTS

Broadcast journalists operate within a legal framework, regulated by the statutory bodies which govern broadcasting (in the UK, Ofcom) and the laws of the land (which differ in Scotland from the rest of the UK).

This is a guide to the areas of law and court practice of which journalists have to be aware. It is not a substitute for the law modules run within accredited broadcast journalism courses, or the information found in specialist books (*McNae's Essential Law for Journalists*, the core text, runs to over 500 pages).

Law comes from a variety of sources:

• Custom – established practice (known as common law)
• Precedent – the application of earlier decisions to a current case (case law)
• Statute – Acts of Parliament (statutory instruments)
• European Union regulations
• The European Convention on Human Rights.

In Scotland, there are also 'writers', institutional texts from respected writers on Scots law, mostly from the seventeenth, eighteenth and nineteenth centuries. Equity, the concept of natural justice and fairness, informs all the UK's legal systems.

DEFAMATION

Defamation is probably the biggest risk faced by working journalists. Whenever you write about someone, there is a danger you will damage their reputation, sometimes unwittingly. A spoken defamatory statement is slander, except where it is spoken in a broadcast (or in a public performance of a play). Then it has the same status as a statement in print and is defined as libel.

Civil actions for libel in pursuit of damages may be taken out against a broadcaster by anyone who considers they have been defamed. There is also, much more rarely, a risk of criminal libel, where the publication might lead to a breach of the peace.

Juries have to decide if reasonable men and women would consider a statement defamatory. Does it:

1 expose the person to hatred, ridicule or contempt?
2 cause him (or her) to be shunned or avoided?
3 lower him in the estimation of right-thinking members of society generally? or
4 disparage him in his business, trade or profession?

Essential Guide section – provides the tools the broadcast journalist needs

---

DVD – explains and demonstrates radio and television recording techniques

---

Workshops section – gives opportunities to practice key skills

WORKSHOPS AND EXERCISES

CHAPTER ONE: INTRODUCTION

• Track the progress of a news story on different platforms from the same news organisation (the BBC and Sky News offer TV, radio, online and mobile phone services). How do the length and treatment of the story differ on:
1 Terrestrial television news
2 Rolling news
3 Radio bulletins
4 The website
5 Broadband services
6 Mobile phones.
• Visit the website of a major news provider. How many different types of job do they offer in broadcast journalism? Find out the roles of:
1 A field producer in TV
2 A foreign news editor
3 A TV researcher
4 A regional TV programme producer
5 A radio reporter in commercial radio.
• Prepare a background file on a running story – e.g. conflict in the Middle East, the next US presidential election, the London Olympics. Select stories that are new developments or related to the same issue. Order them in a folder (preferably electronically as downloads or weblinks, or, if not, in the form of newspaper cuttings). Whenever there is a new angle on the story, consult your files and see how that helps your understanding of the story.

CHAPTER TWO: WHAT'S THE STORY?

• Who do you think is the typical listener to the radio station nearest to your home? Now do a bit of research into the profile – average age and social background.
• Ask somebody at the station if they have an imaginary listener in mind when they broadcast.
• Imagine a commercial radio station playing your favourite music. What might be the profile of the imaginary listener?
Now think of a station playing your parents' favourite songs. Would the target audience just consist of older

people? Or would they have to broaden the appeal to attract advertisers?
• Think back over your lifetime. Can you recall five big stories and remember where you were when you first heard the news? How did you receive the news? Were you on your own or in company? How did you react?
• Look at the table on *Theories of News Production* (page 23) and decide which model most closely represents the way news is produced on:
1 BBC News 24
2 Sky News
3 Your local commercial radio station
4 A tabloid newspaper
5 A Sunday broadsheet newspaper.
• Consider the **news values**, as defined by Harcup and O'Neill (pages 24 and 25). Watch a TV news bulletin, listen to news programmes on radio, or consider a half-hour segment of any rolling news programme – Radio Five Live or Sky News, for example. Now ask:
› Did all the stories fit into the categories outlined by Harcup and O'Neill?
› If not, what were the factors that made other stories newsworthy?
› Does the requirement for balance and impartiality in broadcast news affect the news agenda?
› Where does sport fit into this list?
› Is broadcast news becoming more or less like newspaper news?
• How could you make the following stories relevant to the core audience for an independent local radio station in Scotland:
1 House prices in the Home Counties are rising by 20 per cent a year.
2 London's congestion charge is going up again.
3 A budget airline has announced more flights from Edinburgh airport.
4 Andrew Murray is promoting tennis for young people at a photo-call in a Central London car park.
5 Firemen in Cardiff have rescued an iguana from a chimney.
• Consider whether you would want to use any of these stories at all. Then imagine it is a slow news day – and you have to use them. How would you treat them? And what order would you put them in?

Website – keeps you up to date with the latest developments in news broadcasting and provides interviews with experts

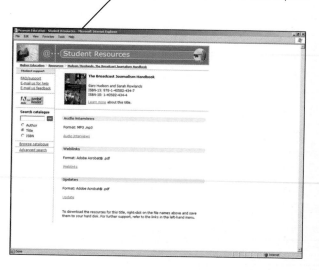

PARTONE THE JOB

CHAPTER ONE

INTRODUCTION

WHY BROADCAST JOURNALISM MATTERS

We live in the digital age. News bulletins and programmes that used to be available only on television and radio sets are now available on your computer or mobile phone. News reports that were presented to viewers and listeners in a running order decided by editors and producers are now available on demand at the click of a mouse or a remote control, whenever the consumer wants them.

Andrew Marr, the TV and radio presenter, and a former national newspaper editor at the *Independent*, said in the 2006 Hugh Cudlipp lecture (named after the great editor of the *Daily Mirror* in the 1950s and '60s) that we are witnessing 'the replacement of a largely written culture – the Gutenberg-Caxton culture, if you like – by a culture largely composed of spoken words and moving images.'

Marr said the change was happening because of 'the convergence of television and the Internet delivered to tiny portable screens'.

'All kids download film clips and television clips, they quite like the newspaper that is delivered to the front door, but they find it increasingly weird. They find it old-fashioned and nostalgic. They are used to manipulating pictures themselves on computer screens.

'We've all observed how television and even newspapers are adapting the aesthetic and the style of broadband Internet culture. Digital television has the red button, the drop-down menu, the familiarity of moving images in one part of the screen, words in another part of the screen, and perhaps a moving banner at the bottom as well.'

Never before have so many people had access to the means of producing video and audio content that was once the preserve of professional broadcasters. The media has become more fragmented. Most of the World Wide Web's content has tiny audiences. Andy Warhol's idea that everyone will be famous for 15 minutes has been modified by the idea that anyone can be famous for 15 people (a phrase, incidentally, that was coined in 1991 by Momus, a Scottish punk techno artist, talking about the fragmentation of the music industry). The digital revolution means almost anyone can produce a video report and put it on a website for anyone to view. It's a great way to spread opinion and information, but it should not be confused with journalism.

This is where broadcast journalism comes in. Nick Pollard, the Head of Sky News for ten years, who stepped down less than a year after the channel relaunched in a new state-of-the-art centre, sums up the impact of change: 'You shouldn't mistake the advance of technology for journalism. It's not. All it does is allow you to get stuff on air quicker, perhaps in better quality and more cheaply, in a way that you just couldn't possibly years or decades earlier, but you still have to have people who understand what the story is, and ideally who've been around the block a bit and can put it in context.'

His successor John Ryley sums up how that affects their output: 'People need to view Sky News as a brand that offers dynamic news content on television, radio and Internet across a variety of platforms, however and wherever they want it.'

Journalism is gathering, writing and publishing news and factual information. How that information is published – in print or electronically – changes with the times. But there's no sign in the modern media landscape that there will be any less demand for professional journalists. Instead, the number of outlets for the work of broadcast journalists is multiplying. Andrew Marr describes journalism as 'the industrialisation of gossip'. The industry is now global. These are exciting times.

Andrew Marr delivers the Hugh Cudlipp lecture

REMEMBER

➤ We live in a culture of spoken words and moving images
➤ The media has become increasingly fragmented
➤ The advance of technology is not journalism
➤ Journalists gather and publish news and information.

Millions of people – many of them the same people who will access occasional online content or put their own work on the Web – still want professionally produced news content. They want journalists to interpret the world around them and tell them what's going on, because they don't have time in their busy lives to work it out for themselves. That is why the role of the broadcast journalist is more important than ever. It's why the traditional skills of the journalist – uncovering information, interpreting it, and presenting what is truthful and relevant to as many people as possible – are more valuable than ever.

Presenters, reporters and correspondents are supported by researchers, producers and editors. There are many jobs in broadcast journalism other than broadcasting.

JOURNALISTS . . . HAVE TO COLLECT, CHECK AND ORDER FACTS. THEY WEIGH ARGUMENTS. THEY MAKE JUDGEMENTS. AND THEY TELL STORIES.

The professionals are no longer the gatekeepers – the only people who have access to the means of distributing news. But they have become the arbiters, the ethical guides and the role models for the many amateurs using the new technology. Journalists have to be authoritative content providers for the multiplicity of delivery platforms available for news and factual information. They have to deliver compelling information to engage audiences. They have to collect, check and order facts. They weigh arguments. They make judgements. And they tell stories.

Story-telling is at the heart of good journalism. The stories journalists tell are true stories, not fantasy. Journalists present factual information in a way that audiences can relate to and understand. They do it in an ethical, moral and legal framework.

To suggest that bloggers and video diarists, or people who take video shots of news events, are replacing broadcast journalists is like suggesting anyone with a pen can write like Shakespeare or Dickens. The technology of story-telling should not be confused with the art of story-telling.

The growth of so-called 'citizen journalists' – people putting their own news online – is a challenge to professional broadcast journalists. Our skills distinguish us from others in the online community who have access to the means of digital production. Access to a microphone or camera crew has never been the defining characteristic of a professional broadcast journalist.

Chris Vallance, who produces a weekly radio feature for BBC Five Live, using podcasts and blogs from around the world, says being a journalist is not about qualifications: 'There's probably a mindset, an attitude and a commitment to a certain set of practices that makes you a journalist.'

The American TV producer Michael Rosenblum, who has trained thousands of people in video journalism, including hundreds of BBC staff, has a broad view of what makes a journalist: 'Anybody who's a cameraman is a journalist. Anybody who came to work for the BBC is a journalist. This notion of separating journalists from craft people is entirely specious and a misnomer.

'Most of what you see on most news organisations is incomprehensible pap, filled with facts sometimes – sometimes not – but generally it has very little to do with journalism.'

Rosenblum says multi-skilling is the only way ahead, and established broadcasters with only one skill – traditional journalism – are in a fight for their lives: 'There's a whole wave of people out there who are young, bright, creative, willing to work for nothing, and can do this with their eyes closed, slam it together and make it really cool. They can sample music through MP3 off the Internet, use a lot of graphics. They make stuff you really want to watch, and at the end of the day they will win out. It's do or die.'

Michael Rosenblum: 'Anybody who's a cameraman is a journalist.'

So multi-skilling is essential for *all* journalists. But what makes a *good* broadcast journalist is probably easier to define. Getting to the truth of a story and telling it in a way that engages wide audiences – within ethical and legal guidelines – will always be more important than mastering the latest technology. The professional journalist will want to learn the technical requirements of each new development as it supersedes the last. But the core story-telling and writing skills never become redundant. They apply across all platforms.

It's a cliché of journalism that you're only as good as your last story. But it's not true. Yes, you should always try to deliver a performance better than your last. Over time, however, you develop a reputation that is about more than your performance on a given day. A commitment to reliability and accuracy will be recognised by your peers and potential employers. These qualities distinguish the professional from the enthusiastic amateur.

Andrew Marr says these are good times to be a journalist: 'It's time to reassert the need for verbal clarity and to champion good writing. We are in a strong position to do it. We are in a democratic culture of a kind we haven't had before.

At a time when journalism seems to be growing a little stronger again we have comparative freedom of speech. Only the means of delivery is in doubt and that is a second order matter.'

The BBC Director General Mark Thompson, speaking in 2006 about the corporation's Creative Future plan, said: 'The BBC should no longer think of itself as a broadcaster of TV and radio and some new media on the side. We should aim to deliver public service content to our audiences in whatever media and on whatever device makes sense for them, whether they are at home or on the move.'

Senior editors in broadcasting organisations – and people teaching broadcast journalism in colleges and universities – will remember a 1972 hit by Slade, *Mama Weer All Crazee Now*. The quirky spelling wasn't obvious to radio listeners – they were hearing rather than reading the title – but it amused record buyers. Nowadays, even radio journalists have to know how to spell correctly, because their work may be re-versioned for websites and headline straps on digital radio sets. Today's broadcast journalist provides content for many different platforms. Mama, we're all content providers now.

REMEMBER

- ➤ Story-telling is at the heart of good journalism
- ➤ Journalists make judgements based on professional experience
- ➤ All journalists are content providers.

A CLOSER LOOK

There are two essentials. Be fair and be right. And if you want a third one – be bold. It's the job of all journalists to be fair and be right, but be bold too and don't be manipulated.

Greg Dyke, former BBC Director General

Former BBC Director General Greg Dyke with the authors

THE PLEASURES AND PITFALLS

Michael Buerk, the BBC reporter and newsreader, introduced himself on a celebrity edition of *University Challenge* as 'sometimes described as a "distinguished journalist", one of the great oxymorons of our time'. Journalists do not have a good reputation, often appearing just above estate agents and politicians when opinion polls ask 'who do you trust?' But when the same polls are more specific, it becomes clear that tabloid newspaper journalists are the most distrusted, and broadcasters, in particular newsreaders, are well regarded by their audience.

And broadcasting seduces many of those who work in it.

Five Live late night presenter Anita Anand says: 'There is something so charming and immediate and honest about radio. It's the voice. It's the story, and it's hopefully the truth if you do it properly.'

Many are attracted to the job from an early age. BBC Radio Two's Jeremy Vine, who has also presented *Newsnight*, *The Politics Show* and the swingometer on election specials on TV, says: 'I was intoxicated with the idea of radio when I walked into Capital Radio at the age of twelve and saw Roger Scott sitting in a tiny studio talking to all these people, and I just thought that looks amazing – this is magical. Gradually, as I went through my teenage years, I thought being a DJ is a bit of a kid's thing to do, so I went for journalism.'

Vine's advice to young people: 'When you're studying, just think broadly, read broadly, because the whole business of being in a profession is a narrowing experience. We meet fewer and fewer people; we do a very small number of things. So the wider we can keep our minds at a young age the better.'

His BBC colleague George Alagiah grew up steeped in the values of the BBC World Service: 'I grew up in Africa to the strains of BBC News, and being clipped round the earhole by my dad if we were making a noise, because it was a kind of revered half-hour. Then when I was a foreign correspondent, literally the guns would fall silent in Africa around seven o'clock when Focus on Africa came on. Rebel leaders on both sides would tune in and try to work out what the hell was going on.'

Alagiah's co-presenter on the Six O'Clock News, Natasha Kaplinsky, is frequently asked how she got to 'be on the telly.' She says: 'Anybody who just wants to be on the telly would be rooted out pretty early on, because it just doesn't work like that. You have to be completely, firmly immersed in journalism to survive five minutes in a regional newsroom let alone a highly competitive national one.'

She has sympathy with anyone trying to get their first job in broadcast journalism: 'My main message is not to give up. The people who will survive in this industry are the people that won't give up because they'll have so many rejection letters. I literally have a file, and I keep it under my bed and I keep it there as a reminder, for one reason. When I've had a rubbish day, just to remind myself how difficult it was to get the jobs, and how easily they go, and how many people can fill your shoes and probably do your job a lot better than you can do it.

'It is so hard to break in, but if you accept rejection first off, frankly, you know what? You shouldn't be in the business. If you are absolutely determined to not let "No" be an answer, that's what makes a good journalist.'

BBC Radio Five Live presenter Anita Anand: 'Radio is the truth if you do it properly.'

Jeremy Vine of BBC Radio Two and TV: 'I just thought that looks amazing. This is magical.'

George Alagiah and Natasha Kaplinsky on the BBC Six O'Clock News

Sky News reporter Laurence Lee: 'You'd never go to any of these places unless you were completely mad.'

Ian Woods of Sky News: 'Somebody else is paying for me to see the world.'

Among the joys of journalism are travel and meeting people. Laurence Lee, of Sky News, visited thirteen countries across Eastern Europe and Asia during his two and a half years as Moscow correspondent: 'I just think I'm really lucky. You'd never go to any of these places unless you were completely mad – countries nobody's ever heard of. It's really interesting and I'm getting paid for this.'

His colleague Ian Woods echoes that thought: 'The biggest attraction of my job is that somebody else is paying for me to see the world. That's something to tell your grandchildren.

'The world is shrinking. We can go to all sorts of exotic places on holiday, but nobody goes to Iraq or Afghanistan unless they're going to kill people or going to report on people killing people.

'I like the idea of being a foreign fire-fighter. There's always a buzz when you get sent on a breaking story. I get excited by spending a couple of weeks in a country I've never been to before.'

A CLOSER LOOK THE NEWSMAKERS

We all talk about events and people that 'make the news.' But the real newsmakers are journalists. They set the news agenda. In the language of social scientists they 'frame' the news. They determine how audiences will perceive issues and stories. They portray groups in society in certain ways.

Broadcast journalists, in particular, present information in a way they believe will appeal to the widest possible demographic. They do this to maintain and increase the number of viewers and listeners for their output, because they operate in a competitive commercial environment. Stations dependent on advertising need to maintain the appeal to advertisers; publicly funded broadcasters (in the UK the BBC) need to justify their public funding (the licence fee). In doing this, they inadvertently write for 'the majority.' And so the dominant view in society is well represented in news coverage. Minority views are sidelined, and often silenced. People with opinions outside the political discourse typified by the two-party system (with occasional contributions from the Liberal Democrats) are under-represented. In this way, the concept of 'balance' in reporting has come to mean a balance between differing views that reflect an assumption of the mainstream divide in public opinion.

Because journalists usually opt for preferred sources of news (the so-called primary definers) the idea that broadcast news is politically impartial (as required by UK law) is questionable. 'Spin doctors' and PR agents play their part to try to influence news coverage. Resisting the influence of 'spin' often means falling into the trap of responding to the agenda set by the spinners.

Journalists need to be aware that a truly objective account is rarely possible. The search for 'truth' is a worthy one. But selecting stories for inclusion in a news bulletin means making a value judgement that excludes other stories; adopting the objective position of the 'outsider' risks criticism that you approach the story from the assumptions of your own background.

Journalists need to be aware of these critical observations. They need to acknowledge that 'dominant values' – the conventions of global capitalism and traditional ideas of race, religion and gender – are not the only way to interpret events. News *is* constructed, but not necessarily because of a dominant set of values that must be followed. The modern broadcast journalist has access to traditional and new media. It is an opportunity to challenge convention and develop new audiences for news. A public with access to an increasing number of platforms of information needs the signposting and the judgement professional journalism can provide.

Nick Pollard, former Sky News boss

ESSENTIAL SKILLS

It can be argued that the most basic journalistic skills are writing and story-telling. But the modern multi-media journalist has to learn a lot of technology along the way to do the job well.

Although we've heard from former Sky News boss Nick Pollard that technology should not be confused with journalism, a straw poll of workers on Sky News Interactive found that they were using 23 different software programs to get content on air or online. Adam Harding, their deputy editor, says nobody can expect to be an expert in all these programs, but you will need to be good at a number of them to do the job. So the modern broadcast journalist has to be a 'jack of all trades, and master of some.'

Helen Boaden, Director of BBC News

Helen Boaden, the Director of BBC News, sums up what those 'trades' should be: 'You're hoping that someone will come with basic law, basic writing skills, particularly for broadcasting, how to ask a question properly and ideally some skills around the technology. But actually what you're asking for as much as that is a kind of mindset. You want curiosity. You want the capacity to challenge, to see stories laterally, to ask difficult questions of everybody. You want people who are interested in the people they're likely to be interviewing but also the issues of the wider world.'

Kevin Bakhurst, the controller of BBC News 24, emphasises the starting point for all aspiring journalists: 'An interest in news and current affairs – and not a sudden interest! I do think it's important that people take a long-standing interest and watch TV programmes, listen to the radio, use online and read the papers.

'It is actually increasingly difficult to get people who have a real general knowledge of news and current affairs. I do find that quite worrying and disappointing. I know people are young, but you start asking people in their early twenties about the Callaghan government and even Margaret Thatcher's first government. I've done interviews with people who've been applying for jobs in the newsroom, and they didn't even know who Callaghan was. I wasn't alive during Macmillan, and certainly don't remember any of that, but I know who he was, who was in his government and what the big issues were of the day.

'A lot of the most successful journalists have had a very long interest [in news and current affairs] and have got a good hinterland.'

He says attitude is important. You should enjoy the job: 'It is a genuinely interesting, often exciting, stimulating job. There are so many people who'd like to come and work here. If you don't enjoy it, leave and someone else will come and work here who would enjoy it.

'When people in the newsroom are up for it, excited and confident, that translates directly onto screen.'

Deborah Turness, Editor ITV News

Deborah Turness, the Editor of ITV News, also stresses the importance of 'hinterland': 'I always prefer to have people coming to ITV News who have got hinterland, and who have done interesting things in their lives, and who probably haven't just come out of college. Those people are transparent in their vapidity. They've been nowhere, they've done nothing . . . Bring something else to the party. Have you travelled round the world on a unicycle? Have you launched a charity, or do you speak languages, or have you got great passions in your life? Because I think there's a danger that we're creating a whole generation of identikit journalists, who think it is enough to get that degree and then they're going to be a TV star somehow. For me there is greater value placed on writing skills than ever before, and visual creativity.'

Kirsty Young: 'Get your on-air miles.'

Most experienced professionals emphasise the value of starting in local radio. TV presenter Kirsty Young talks of getting your 'on-air miles' – the experience of being on air frequently so that you are comfortable in front of a mic. Rachel Burden of BBC Radio Five Live says: 'I don't think anything substitutes for working in a local environment and having to knock on doors, and dig around for stories. For your credibility as a journalist, that's massively important.'

Five Live's Rachel Burden: 'I don't think anything substitutes for having to knock on doors and dig around for stories.'

Helen Boaden expands on that theme: 'Local radio reporting is fantastically valuable. It's like newspaper reporting once was (and still is in some places). You learn the basics. You learn to ask the right basic questions; you learn to handle yourself in a lot of very different and sometimes difficult situations; you learn to talk to people on the phone; you learn to get into people's houses in a subtle and careful way without being exploitative; and you learn law and writing. You'll come with some of that from college, but actually this is where you get to practise it. And you learn from people who've done it before, and who've done it very well.

'It's about being hard-working, connecting to the team, sticking up for yourself where you can, and being confident – knowing what you know and, as importantly, knowing what you don't know and being prepared to ask for help. It's important to realise that most people don't mind. So there's a sort of slight humility – knowing what you don't know and trying to do something about it.'

Broadcast journalists work to tight deadlines. Precise time-keeping is essential to the point of obsession. John Sergeant, a senior political correspondent with the BBC and then political editor with ITV News, says: 'It's extremely important to make sure you stick to time. It's one of the things that becomes obsessive for a broadcast journalist in ordinary life. It's amazing how people are invited to a party, and if they're broadcasters they'll turn up on time, and find it very difficult to have people turning up five or ten minutes late. It does become an obsession and it ought to. Broadcasters who don't keep to time don't stay in their jobs.'

Many broadcast journalists are used to working long hours, travelling to foreign locations, working throughout the day, barely sleeping, grabbing food when it's available, and not having a day off until the story is over. At home, too, people make sacrifices to gain experience and get on. Natasha Kaplinsky commuted from London to Southampton to present the regional evening news before landing a job at Sky News.

REMEMBER

➤ Writing and story-telling are core skills in journalism
➤ You need to be a 'jack of all trades and master of some'
➤ You should have a long-term interest in news and current affairs
➤ 'On-air miles' help you become comfortable in front of the mic
➤ Precise time-keeping is essential
➤ Expect to work long hours.

AMBITION

You will need ambition and determination to succeed in broadcast journalism. That should be coupled with a consuming interest in news and current affairs.

Huw Edwards, presenter of BBC's *Ten O'Clock News*

Huw Edwards, presenter of the BBC's *Ten O'Clock News*, says: 'It's a very difficult area to get into. I'm not sure why lots of people try to get into journalism. Lots of them don't seem to have an interest in actual journalism – it's wanting to be on television, to be on radio or to be performing.'

Shelagh Fogarty, a presenter on BBC Radio Five Live, says she never had a great drive to be a presenter, but she was always interested in news: 'I didn't give a great deal of thought to what job I wanted to do until I was near the end of university [she studied foreign languages]. But I'd always been interested in news. I met an old school friend recently. She said: "You once gave up watching the news for Lent." So I must have been a right news junkie even then! I think I was, because my family's very news-oriented, very political, into watching politics and that kind of thing.'

Deborah Turness, the Editor of ITV News, says she looks for that kind of enthusiasm: 'I'm looking for people who've got more than just a knowledge of how to do process journalism. I'm looking for people who have got a lively mind, who are inquiring, who have strong opinions and passions – who actually feel the news.'

Shelagh Fogarty, presenter on BBC Radio Five Live

Frank Gardner says a lot of obstacles were placed in his way before he got a BBC job as a foreign correspondent. He was told he was too late to enter journalism at 33, that he hadn't been through the graduate training system and that his voice was too posh to be on national television: 'A lot of people at the BBC were very unimaginative when I said I wanted to be a foreign correspondent. They're so blinkered, and the only way to break that is to go out and do it yourself. If necessary, borrow the money, get out there and do it. If the BBC hadn't offered me some freelance shifts [in 1995] I would have gone to Afghanistan with a cameraman, carried his bags for him, paid my own way, seen how he'd done his job and perhaps sold a few stories for print, on the back of that. And that's the way to do it. Just tag on to people.'

BBC Security Correspondent Frank Gardner: 'Just tag on to people.'

The then unknown Natasha Kaplinsky tagged on to Jill Dando, who was the presenter of the news, *Crimewatch* and the *Holiday* programme. Kaplinsky had been signing on and trying to gain as much work experience as possible. She says: 'I just wrote to Jill and said, "Look, please can you help. I don't know how to get into the industry." And she said, "Come and meet me for a cup of tea," which I did. She was unbelievably elegant. I'd given her a showreel which I'd done, and she was very kind and gave me some constructive criticism, and then she introduced me to her agent and somebody else and that kind of started things off for me.'

Five Live's Anita Anand says: 'Don't sit on your bottom wishing you could be in the industry. Do something. I was working in local newspapers from the age of 14. I worked at the *West Essex Guardian and Gazette*, and I cleared paper jams out of photocopiers, just so I could be around people who were working and see what it was like. You have to love it. It's a hard slog. It's such a boring thing and I used to hate it when old farts used to tell me in newsrooms that you have to pay your dues, but they're right. You have to learn everything from the ground up.'

Juliette Ferrington, a sports reporter with BBC Radio Five Live, who's covered two World Cups and the Olympic Games, says you can only succeed if you learn to cope with rejection: 'I was told I'd never be a broadcaster by a BBC local radio station. They just didn't rate me.'

She also had to deal with being a woman in the mostly male world of professional sport and sports reporting. Interviewing footballers presented particular problems: 'They'd try and trip you up. It was a challenge. "See if we can get her

Natasha Kaplinsky, BBC News presenter

on the offside rule, or who our next opponent is or what position I play." It was a learning experience, but once I got through that it was fine and they treated me as maybe a little bit special and they liked me being around.'

She says a lot of women succeed in television because of the way they look: 'In radio it's ten times harder, because you don't see faces, you don't see pictures, you've got to describe what you're doing, and it's bloody hard work. You need a lot of grit and determination and a thick skin.

'It's a piranha pool. There are not many female sports broadcasters on radio, but you're competing with the men as well.'

Juliette Ferrington of BBC Radio Five Live: 'It's a piranha pool. You need a lot of grit and determination and a thick skin.'

REMEMBER

➤ You will need determination and persistence to succeed
➤ Tag on to people – learn from experience
➤ Don't be afraid to start at the bottom and work your way up.

THE FREELANCE MENTALITY

Many outlets will employ journalists on a freelance basis or on short-term contracts. Freelances are paid for what they do on a day-to-day basis – either for a particular story or for a day's work at a time. Contract workers may be engaged by a programme for a week or a few months. The job-for-life is almost a thing of the past in current affairs journalism. Ask most journalists about the 'freelance mentality', and they'll say it means never being able to say no. This requires a particular dedication from those who chose the lifestyle, but the versatility of the work on offer means life is often exciting, never dull and often richly rewarded.

Many freelances have a policy of never turning work down. You might not get asked again. Paul Ross, whose career spans serious journalism and the light entertainment shows for which he's now best known, has an answerphone message that says: 'I'll do it!'

Freelance Steve Lee: 'I'm fascinated by what's going on in the world.'

Ross is affable and popular with everyone he works with. A successful freelance can't afford to upset anyone.

Steve Lee, a sports reporter who's worked for most of the major TV networks, might work for a BBC network sports programme, regional ITV and Sky Sports all in the same week. He's not a star name, but he's a trusted professional, respected for his contacts and knowledge of his subject. He says it's not a matter of never switching off. It's just about keeping your wits about you: 'You're always aware of what's going on. You look at the fixtures at the weekend to know what's coming up in the next week. When you visit a town you buy the local paper. You buy the regional papers too. And then a lot of it is reactive day-to-day.

'Most of my work is in sport, but I read the front pages as well as the back pages. I love the excitement of turning on the radio in the morning and finding out what's happened overnight. I'm fascinated by what's going on in the world. I have been since I was a teenager.

'You develop your contacts over the years and you keep in touch with those contacts and keep adding new ones.'

Natasha Kaplinsky underlines the value of keeping up your contacts. She worked for personalities like Esther Rantzen and Ruby Wax when she was on the BBC's production panel – a kind of typing pool: 'These people come back into your life at various points. Keeping in touch with people is very important.'

REMEMBER

➤ Never turn work down

➤ Don't upset anyone

➤ Develop contacts.

DIVERSITY

Broadcast journalism recruits from all sections of society. You only have to watch your TV screen to realise that it is a microcosm of multi-ethnic Britain. But therein lies the problem. The on-screen talent does not reflect the industry as a whole.

Few people in senior editorial and management positions in the industry are from ethnic minorities. The BBC and commercial television have a good record of recruiting from minority groups. Commercial radio does not.

This was highlighted, appropriately, by Trevor Phillips, the Chair of the Commission for Racial Equality, who is a former presenter and a television executive. At the CRE's Race in the Media Awards in June 2006, he said: 'Yes, staff in broadcast organisations are more representative of modern Britain, but the change doesn't go very high in the food chain, and it hasn't penetrated the top management or the boardrooms.

'It hasn't significantly stretched to national radio where actually your colour shouldn't matter. One major radio station, I have been told, cannot count a single non-white presenter amongst its regular voices. In print, especially locally and regionally, the preferred flavour is still vanilla. The fact is that none of this will change by itself.

'Eight years ago, Sir William Macpherson added the term "institutional racism" to our media lexicon. Today, we face an added challenge – deep, institutional complacency.'

The BBC Director General Greg Dyke coined the phrase 'hideously white' to describe the corporation. He made the comment after a management Christmas lunch in 2000. He said: 'As I looked around I thought, "We've got a real problem here." There were 80-odd people there and only one person who wasn't white.'

Dyke wasn't in office long enough to oversee major cultural change, but his successor Mark Thompson summed up the BBC's commitment to diversity in a keynote speech in June 2004. He said they planned to 'foster audience understanding of differences of ethnicity, faith, gender, sexuality, age and ability or disability, by accurately and sensitively reflecting modern Britain's diversity across our programmes and opening up the BBC itself to talent from every community.'

Anita Bhalla is the BBC Head of Political and Community Affairs for the English Regions. When she joined the corporation in 1987, she says she had to cope with a male-dominated newsroom culture that was hard to penetrate.

She shares Trevor Phillips' (and Dyke's) concern about the lack of executives from minorities: 'While the BBC is not "hideously white" any longer and there are more opportunities, there are still issues. We have managed to get an on-screen presence with presenters and reporters from black and ethnic minorities.

'We are also getting more people into the organisation, but we are still not getting enough people into key executive, editorial and managerial posts. This is something we need to work harder at. There is a school of thought which suggests that given enough time it will happen naturally, but when? Perhaps we need to be a lot more proactive in nurturing talent.'

In the meantime, the involvement of people like Bhalla as reporters and correspondents has helped build trust in minority communities. She says: 'When I joined the BBC, its reputation in black and Asian communities was nil. As a correspondent I had to do a lot of footwork before people started ringing me and coming to us with stories. I had to prove I could deliver and get stuff on air.'

Other successful broadcast journalists have come from socially diverse backgrounds. Freelance Ashley Blake, a presenter on regional television in London and Birmingham and a reporter on network shows like *Watchdog*, *Restoration* and the *Holiday* programme, grew up in Lozells in Birmingham. He says: 'If you wanted to make money the options were there – nicking cars, selling drugs, burgling houses. But my mum was a good Yorkshire lass and said, "You can either work hard, or win it, and you don't look lucky enough to win it." I've always been a grafter, so that was the way to go.'

Blake worked as an airline steward, and then did a couple of days' work experience at the *Birmingham Evening Mail*, where he was excited by going to press conferences and seeing people from television. He did a postgraduate course at University College, Falmouth, and worked for cable television in Coventry, Liverpool and Birmingham, before winning a short-term contract with the BBC: 'The Coventry job was expenses only – 9p a mile. But it was enough to get me from Erdington [in Birmingham] where I was living to Coventry. And I learned television.'

Disability is not a bar to working in broadcast journalism, sometimes at the highest level. BBC Radio and TV's disability affairs correspondent Peter White has been blind since birth. He has worked in local and network broadcasting for over 35 years. He says: 'Don't let anybody say it's impossible for you to work in broadcasting. Most of the problems are not technical, they're human.

'You are only ever discriminated against by people who are no good at their jobs. People who are insecure don't like the idea that disabled people can do their jobs as well as they can.

'Broadcasting is about telling stories in an engaging and exciting way, and you have to convince people that you are the right person to do the job. If they have the right attitude then the technical problems won't be a problem.'

Disability legislation has made it unlawful to discriminate against disabled people, but White warns: 'We may have legislation and pompous statements about mentors, but people don't have the time these days to help. There's a bad life–work balance. You have to want to do it more than other people want to stop you.'

Anita Bhalla: 'We are still not getting enough people into key executive, editorial and managerial posts.'

Ashley Blake: 'I was on work experience, and I went to a police press conference and saw all these people off the telly, and I thought, "I want some of that."'

➤ Broadcast journalism is a career open to all sections of society

➤ Ethnic minorities are under-represented in senior editorial positions

➤ Broadcasters have been accused of institutional complacency

➤ Disability should not prevent you getting a job in broadcast journalism.

TRAINING COURSES

In the last decade of the twentieth century broadcast journalism training moved from being almost exclusively in-house within the larger broadcast organisations to being delivered in higher education. Recruitment is no longer exclusively from print journalism (the traditional route), but often direct from colleges and universities.

The bigger broadcasters still offer bursaries for people on selected university training courses and have graduate training programmes. The BBC set up its own virtual College of Journalism in 2005. It is for BBC staff and is not an alternative to higher education courses.

The Broadcast Journalism Training Council (funded by broadcasters like the BBC, Sky, ITV, Reuters and the independent radio contractors and by training courses) accredits dozens of courses around the UK. BJTC accreditation is a benchmark of quality, guaranteeing a high level of practical content, including a regular number of 'newsdays' when you will replicate newsroom practice, working in teams to produce your own bulletins and even rolling-news programmes.

You may want to apply for an undergraduate Broadcast Journalism or Multimedia Journalism course and study for three years. Or you can take another subject you are interested in at undergraduate level and move on to a one-year Postgraduate (MA) Broadcast Journalism course. There are specialist Online and Sports Broadcast Journalism courses at some institutions.

Details of undergraduate courses are available through UCAS, the university applications body, and on university websites. A list of courses can be found on the BJTC website (www.bjtc.org.uk).

The BBC presenter George Alagiah says: 'People write to me and ask me what degree should I take, and I don't think what you study matters. The one-year postgraduate course is worth doing, but I don't think there's any particular degree that prepares you for journalism more than any other.'

That view is backed by News 24 controller Kevin Bakhurst: 'You don't need to do a journalism degree to do journalism. If you want to do journalism fine, but I'll certainly give equal weight to people who've done other subjects. I often think people who've done a language degree or a science degree are a rounded person, and they will come and contribute a lot.'

BBC Security Correspondent Frank Gardner studied Arabic and it helped in a first career in merchant banking in the Middle East: 'What I learned after graduating is that Arabic on its own is not much use. You have to combine it with an actual skill such as being qualified in insurance, accountancy, photography, journalism, or whatever. You've got to have a core skill.'

He switched to broadcast journalism at the age of 33: 'I wanted adventure. I wasn't completely new to journalism. I'd been writing articles for magazines and newspapers on a freelance basis since I was 24. I knew how to write but I was completely new to broadcast journalism, so I found out what courses were available – just short one- and two-week courses in TV and radio production – so I understood, or thought I did, how to put together a radio package, a combination of your voice and sound effects, and I did a filming course which, unfortunately, I didn't remember enough of.

'I managed to talk my way into a Latvian women's prison – the first journalist to be allowed in. It was atrocious conditions. There were all these tough, shaven-headed, tattooed women there, broken teeth. There was no hot water, the winter was coming and there was no heating. They were having babies born in the prison. It was really rough. But I didn't know what I was doing with the camera at the time, and I completely squandered this great opportunity. After that I resolved to learn how to do it.'

Huw Edwards, who's involved in training at the BBC and has been an external examiner on university courses at Cardiff, has this advice to students wanting to study broadcast journalism: 'You will do yourselves an enormous favour if you question yourself quite rigorously as to why you think this is a good course for you to take. Why do you want to be in this kind of area of work? Is it because you're influenced by friends? Is it because you quite fancy being on telly? All sorts of things. And the earlier you go through that process of self-analysis the better it is. The thing you really want to do may, quite frankly, be something you're not really suited to.

WANTING TO 'BE ON TELLY' IS NOT A GOOD ENOUGH REASON FOR ENTERING BROADCAST JOURNALISM.

He explains why wanting to 'be on telly' is not a good enough reason for entering broadcast journalism: 'There were eight of us on my BBC training course years ago. All eight of us wanted to broadcast and perform. I'm the only one who's broadcasting. The other seven, I have to say, are far more powerful than me. They're all executives. There was no question on the course. Everyone wanted to be on television; everyone wanted to be on camera. That was the attraction. But one by one they all quite correctly came to the view that they weren't properly geared to that. They were actually much better at the production and much better behind the scenes.'

If, however, you have a passion for being a creative power away from the microphone there may be numerous opportunities that open up while your counterparts are struggling to be recognised as broadcasters.

The better university courses will include work placements in a broadcast newsroom. BJTC courses have formal arrangements for placements with the major broadcasters. These placements are a chance to make a good impression, to network and make contacts. They can lead to jobs. Mark Austin of ITV News has good advice: 'Young trainees, if they come here, have just got to be prepared to get on with it. Pick up the phone, make calls, and realise that news stories can be got by anybody. It's that enthusiasm you really look for in someone, and an ability to write, which sounds obvious, but it's amazing how few people that come into this business can write. There's a very big difference between writing for newspapers and writing for television.

'You get a lot of people who come in here and don't really give the impression that they are passionately interested in journalism. If you've got that and an inquiring

COMING TO WORK AT ITN OR SKY OR THE BBC IS A HUGE OPPORTUNITY FOR SOMEONE WHO'S YOUNG AND COULD MAKE THEIR MARK.

mind and an understanding of current affairs and the determination to get on and do things on your own when you're in here, then coming to work at ITN or Sky or the BBC is a huge opportunity for someone who's young and could make their mark just breaking one story or helping to break one story, or doing particularly well on one story. There's nothing to stop you doing that. Someone who can appreciate that will do very well.'

REMEMBER

➤ There are dozens of broadcast journalism training courses

➤ Look for BJTC accreditation

➤ You don't necessarily need a broadcast journalism degree to enter the business

➤ Many people prefer to take a fast-track one-year postgraduate course after studying a different subject at undergraduate level

➤ Work placements are a chance to make a good impression with potential employers.

CAREER OPPORTUNITIES

How do you knock on the door of opportunity and make sure you get an answer?

The answer is persistence and determination. No two people at the top of broadcast journalism will tell the same story about how they achieved success. But nobody who ever made it will deny that they were persistent, and didn't take no for an answer.

FURTHER READING

Branston, Gill and Stafford, Roy (2006) *The Media Student's Book*, London: Routledge. A comprehensive look at media theory and practice.

Marr, Andrew (2004) *My Trade*, London: Macmillan. Part-history/part-autobiography – journalism explained by a leading modern practitioner in newspapers and broadcasting.

Randall, David (2000) *The Universal Journalist*, London: Pluto Press. What journalists do and how to do it.

Ray, Vin (2003) *The Television News Handbook*, London: Macmillan. A brilliant hands-on guide to success in TV journalism – including how to get through job interviews.

WEB LINKS

www.bjtc.org.uk The website of The Broadcast Training Council, listing all the accredited courses in the UK.

CHAPTER TWO

WHAT'S THE STORY?

'What's the story?' That's what a news editor asks a reporter offering a new item for the bulletins. And the reporter will try to respond as concisely as possible, 'selling' the story to the editor. They judge the story against a set of **news values** – the criteria by which all stories are measured, though often subconsciously.

Finding and telling stories are fundamental to journalism. They are the arts that distinguish the bulletin writer from the gossip in the launderette and the professional content provider from the rambling blogger.

We'll also look at different types of story, and how each should be tackled. We'll consider conventions in broadcast reporting. Why do TV and radio not follow the same agenda as newspapers? And has online news bridged the gap between print and broadcast media?

Along the way we'll try to answer that trickiest of questions, 'What is news?'

WHO DECIDES WHAT IS NEWSWORTHY?

There's a common belief among old-school hacks that there's such a thing as a 'nose' for news. They know what a story is and they don't need somebody from outside – particularly somebody who's 'not a proper journalist' – coming along and telling them the stories they should be covering in their programmes. Those dismissed as not knowing what they're talking about can include TV executives, radio station managers and almost certainly any member of the public who has the temerity to phone in. In this world, even presenters are not immune to criticism. One senior correspondent was overheard observing of a colleague: 'He wouldn't know a story if it hit him on the head wrapped round a house brick!'

There's also a view, from sociologists, that agreed news values are somehow passed on from one group of mostly white, mostly middle-class men to other groups of mostly white, mostly middle-class men, who create programmes according to their own tastes and judgements and then impose them on the audience. The journalists are telling the public: 'We know what you want.'

Maybe there's not much difference between these two models. The only real difference is that the academics have analysed what the journalists do not bother to analyse because they thought it was instinctive.

In reality neither version does full credit to the way the modern news agenda is drawn up. The traditional assessments of 'newsworthiness' – the qualities that make

DEBORAH TURNESS: 'EVERY SINGLE NEWS ITEM THAT WE DO SHOULD PERFORM SOME KIND OF EMOTIONAL FUNCTION . . . THERE HAS TO BE A REASON FOR EVERY STORY TO BE IN OUR RUNNING ORDER.'

a story worth telling – are based on the news values we outline below. They are adapted from newspaper practice, as are concepts of relevance, immediacy and an appreciation of the diversity of modern culture, and therefore of modern audiences.

But the practical implications of this are straightforward. Does the story excite you? Do you want to know more? Will your friends and family want to hear it?

Deborah Turness, the Editor of ITV News, says: 'Every single news item that we do should perform some kind of emotional function. So it either absolutely clarifies something and makes the penny drop; it reassures; it explains; perhaps it shocks; perhaps it inspires fear; or perhaps makes you laugh. Perhaps it's delivering some consumer information that makes your life easier to live, or you are informed by it and you might base your decisions on that. There has to be a reason for every story to be in our running order.'

KNOW YOUR AUDIENCE

What the audience wants – or has come to expect – is probably the biggest factor in determining whether an item is suitable for a particular programme. You need to know what the audience expects. So you will need to know who they are. Many local radio stations invent typical listeners.

1 *The Local Radio Group*, with more than two dozen stations reaching nearly a million listeners a week, imagined their typical listener as Jane, a married mother of two children, in her mid-thirties. Jane watches more ITV than BBC, and reads the *Daily Mail*. Because of her children she is interested in health and education stories. The Jane in Winchester and Macclesfield is more likely to be better off than the Jane in Darlington or Portsmouth (all towns where the group had stations).

2 *BBC Local Radio* imagined a middle-aged couple, Sue and Dave. He's self-employed; she's a school secretary. They are on their second marriages and have grown-up children. They are saving for a conservatory – or a holiday in Australia.

   The average age of the audience for BBC Local Radio is over 55, according to the corporation's own research. The average age of people working in BBC Local Radio is 30, which means most members of staff have to tune in to the values and expectations of their parents' generation.

3 *Heart FM* told staff their audience was mainly women, home-owning, intelligent, professional, interested in soaps, gossip, showbiz and up for a laugh at weekends. They read tabloid papers and 'brain-drain fodder' like *Heat* magazine and *TV Quick*. Some have settled down with children; others are Bridget Jones types. They aspire to escape, be it on holidays or just a night out.

4 *Century FM* in the north east of England had a similar target listener – known as Debbie – but they warned their staff not to become too 'Debbie-centric', particularly as one of their most popular programmes was a football phone-in.

Market research refines the data. Statistics have shown that 'main shoppers' – what used to be called housewives – tune in to commercial radio for an average of 15 hours a week; business people for 12 hours. Commercial radio accounts for 69 per cent of the listening of 4–15 year olds – an average of nine hours a week.

Most Independent Local Radio (ILR) stations have a younger audience profile – more under-thirties and more women than their rivals. But the network is growing and diversifying (Saga is a brand that has identified and pursued the 'grey pound' – older people with money to spend). So an ILR station with a target audience of young to middle-aged women won't report stories about senior citizens unless they can make them relevant to their own audience – 'Is your granny going to be feeling the cold this winter . . . ?'

REMEMBER

➤ Learn who makes up your audience

➤ Work out what they want to know

➤ Make stories relevant to your audience.

INCREASING YOUR AUDIENCE

Whoever makes up the audience now, you will want to increase it. Every TV programme, every radio station and every website wants to grow its audience wherever possible. Commercial stations need bigger audiences to prove more attractive to advertisers. The BBC needs viewers, listeners and users of web content to justify the licence fee.

GROWING AN AUDIENCE IS ABOUT MORE THAN JUST NUMBERS; IT IS ABOUT GETTING THE RIGHT AUDIENCE.

Growing an audience is about more than just numbers; it is about getting the right audience. People in the wealthier socio-economic groups (the ABC1s) are more appealing to advertisers because they have more disposable income to spend on consumer goods. Advertisers also like young audiences, because they are more likely to change brands or be receptive to new ideas than older people, who are more set in their ways. Channel Four has a higher proportion of young affluent ABC1s in its audience than ITV1 and its profits reflect this. Another success in attracting the 'right' audience is BBC Radio Four's *Today* programme. It is not the most-listened-to breakfast show by any criteria, but it prides itself on being listened to by opinion formers and decision makers in government.

Word of mouth is a good way to increase audiences. 'Talkability' is a word coined to express how much the content of a station is being discussed at work, in the pub, the supermarket or at the bus stop. UTV Radio invites its journalists to ask which stories pass 'the Bingo Hall Test' – which one will their core listeners be chatting about when they go out at night.

Even a station with a minority target audience is in the business of broadcasting – not narrowcasting.

LOCALNESS

In local radio, one of the biggest factors in deciding the importance of a story and its place in the running order is localness. 'This is a local station for local people', as a character in BBC TV's *The League of Gentlemen* might have put it. This leads to the localising of national and international stories: 'Local man feared missing in tsunami.'

Localness, as we shall see, is an overriding consideration for local broadcasters, and hugely important in attracting audiences and keeping them loyal. Audience focus is at the core of all successful broadcasting.

REMEMBER

- ➤ All channels want to increase their audience
- ➤ Write stories so they will be talked about
- ➤ 'Localise' stories if you can.

See Workshops and Exercises.

PUBLIC SERVICE COMMITMENTS

Many UK broadcasters have statutory commitments to Public Service Broadcasting – programmes that are for the public benefit rather than commercial gain. All the terrestrial analogue TV stations (BBC1, BBC2, ITV1, Channel Four (S4C in Wales) and Five) have a public service remit, as do the BBC's digital TV channels and BBC radio. The minimum amount of local speech content on independent radio stations (including news) is set out in their licence from the regulator Ofcom.

The PSB requirement includes a commitment to covering a diversity of interests and tastes, including minority interests. In the case of S4C, there is a commitment to the national identity and community of Wales.

Notions of public service inform the way news is covered. Broadcasters present what they believe to be in the public interest as well as what is of interest to the public.

WHO SETS THE NEWS AGENDA?

The audience may be the ultimate judge of news content – they'll switch off if they don't like what they hear – but they don't decide what is newsworthy. Some groups in society have more say in what is broadcast than others.

The education charity the Sutton Trust, which aims to provide educational opportunities for people from non-privileged backgrounds, reported in June 2006 that more than half Britain's top journalists went to private schools. A further third went to grammar schools. One danger of this is that senior journalists might be out of touch with their audience's concerns.

There has been a lot of academic study of the relationship between journalists and their sources. Some cultural critics argue that dominant groups in society like politicians and the police are 'primary definers' of events. They set the parameters for discussion, and journalists are 'secondary definers,' passing on the interpretations of the elite groups. Tony Harcup says in *Journalism: Principles and Practice*: 'The question of power relations between journalists and sources has been explored at length by academics while journalists have been more concerned with the practicalities of getting the story.'

We shall look at the many ways of getting the story. But, first, have a look at these simplified theoretical models of how news is spread.

THEORIES OF NEWS PRODUCTION

The Big Brother model (Manipulative)	The Dominant View model (Hegemonic)	The Audience Knows Best model (Pluralist)
The mass media are controlled by the owners of broadcasting and the press. This model is based on the Marxist position which divides society into capitalists and the proletariat.	One set of ideas dominate society – what we call 'common sense'. The media consider these ideas normal and true.	There is a plurality of media outlets, each offering different perspectives to different audiences.
The media owners manipulate the audience. They tell them what they want them to know.	The news agenda is set by journalists and editors trained according to a shared set of values – largely because they are recruited from the same section of society – historically, white, middle-class and male. They pass on their values to new recruits, whatever their backgrounds.	The audience gets what it wants. And if it doesn't like it, it can look somewhere else.
They get news from official sources and diary events: the government, the church, royalty and capitalist press agencies, which all but monopolise the news agenda. They promote big business and capitalist interests.	News comes mostly from official and diary sources, because they are considered reliable and have the resources to offer information quickly.	News comes from a variety of sources: all the *official* ones, but also journalists' contacts and investigative reporting, 'ordinary' people contacting news organisations with their grievances, 'stringers' other than the main news agencies, pressure groups and 'axe-grinders'.
Conscious bias in the system means the rich get richer and powerful people get more powerful. Social conventions are reinforced. The notion of 'common sense' is a cultural concept that impinges on the selection of stories.	Most news organisations are based in London, so Metropolitan (London) bias occurs because of the constraints of time, money and technical resources.	Broadcast organisations try to report the news impartially. Any bias is determined by what the audience wants, and one set of views is usually balanced by an opposing set of views.

See Workshops and Exercises.

WHAT MAKES A STORY WORTH COVERING?

Broadcasters no longer slavishly follow the news agenda set by newspapers. Our bulletins would be out-of-date as soon as they appeared if we did. The Independent Television Commission (whose role is now performed by the regulator Ofcom) found in a 1998 survey that more than 70 per cent of the UK population relied on television as their main source of national and international news.

In 2006, a survey for the BBC and Reuters, the news agency, found national television in the UK was trusted by 86 per cent of people compared with 75 per cent who trusted national newspapers. Almost one in five 18–24 year olds preferred online news sources.

The most trusted specific news brand in Britain was BBC News, mentioned by 32 per cent, compared with 3 per cent for the *Daily Mail* and 2 per cent each for *The Times* and *Daily Telegraph*.

Nonetheless, broadcasters are still in debt to the news values established by the print media. They form the basis for a lot – but not all – of the judgements made in broadcast newsrooms.

THINKPIECE

TEN NEWS VALUES (BASED ON A SURVEY OF NEWSPAPERS)

The following is a list of the types of stories which conform to the traditional news values of modern newspapers. Consider it in the light of the typical news agenda of broadcasters.

Tony Harcup and Deirdre O'Neill studied nearly 1,300 cuttings from 'page leads' in newspapers and published a list of ten categories that describe what is selected as 'news':

- **The power elite**

Stories concerning powerful individuals, organisations or institutions

- **Celebrity**

Stories concerning people who are already famous

- **Entertainment**

Stories concerning sex, showbusiness, human interest, animals, an unfolding drama or offering opportunities for humorous treatment, entertaining photographs or witty headlines

- **Surprise**

Stories with an element of surprise/and or contrast

- **Bad news**

Stories with negative overtones such as conflict or tragedy

- **Good news**

Stories with positive overtones such as rescues and cures

- **Magnitude**

Stories perceived as sufficiently significant either in the numbers of people involved or in potential impact

- **Relevance**

Stories about issues, groups and nations perceived to be relevant to the audience

- **Follow-ups**

Stories about subjects already in the news

- **Newspaper agenda**

Stories that set or fit the news organisation's own agenda

> Harcup, T. and O'Neill, D. (2001) 'What is News? Galtung and Ruge Revisited', *Journalism Studies,* 2(2): 261–80.

'Galtung and Ruge' were, and are, widely cited in academic studies of news media. Norwegians Johan Galtung and Mari Ruge, who published their research in 1965, were concerned with how overseas events were reported – or not – in newspapers in Norway. Tony Harcup and Deirdre O'Neill, who have both been working journalists and academics in the UK, set out to find out whether the Norwegians' list of values applied to British national newspapers at the end of the twentieth century. They approached it from a different angle: 'Their concern was with events and how they did or did not become news. Our concern has been with published news items and what may or may not have led to their selection.'

Not surprisingly, given their very different approach, Harcup and O'Neill concluded: 'the much-cited Galtung and Ruge list of news values should be regarded as open to question rather than recited as if written on a tablet of stone: the same critical scepticism should also be applied, of course, to the set of contemporary news values we propose . . .'

Importantly for broadcasters, Harcup and O'Neill say: 'It would be illuminating to compare our findings with the categorisation of news values, operating at local, regional and international levels; in broadcasting and online media as well as print; to explore changes over time; and to take the process further through interviews with working journalists.'

This book doesn't set out to redefine news values for broadcasters, though it does contain many examples of the criteria they apply, and it does include plenty of comment from working journalists.

See Workshops and Exercises.

A CLOSER LOOK

NEWS – SOME DEFINITIONS

'When a dog bites a man, that is not news, but when a man bites a dog, that is news.'

> Charles A. Dana, 19th century editor of the *New York Sun*

'News is something somebody somewhere wants to suppress; all the rest is advertising.'

> Lord Northcliffe, 19th/20th century newspaper proprietor

'News is the first rough draft of history.'

> Ben Bradlee, Executive Editor, *Washington Post*

'News is what a chap who doesn't care much about anything wants to read. And it's only news until he's read it. After that it's dead.'

> The hack reporter Corker in Evelyn Waugh's *Scoop*

'News is anything that makes a reader say "Gee whiz!"'

> Arthur MacEwen, editor of the *San Francisco Examiner*

'It's stuff I care about, and stuff I want to pass on.'

> Anonymous, quoted in the *Guardian*, 19 June 2006

NEW VALUES FOR BROADCASTERS

When a reporter is asked 'What's the story?', he or she will have a rough idea how the item will sound or what pictures will be needed. But in a busy newsroom the editor or producer wants a swift response, so the answer will probably be one sentence. That sentence will summarise the key elements of the story. Journalists don't resort to formal check lists, but it is worth considering the factors that can be said to be the news values by which all stories are (usually subconsciously) judged. Most journalists agree that the best stories are those that have a combination of several of the following elements.

RELEVANCE

The relevance of a story to the audience is a result of both its cultural impact and its political importance. If petrol taxes go up in the budget, that's a political decision that affects the finances of all drivers, and the families of all drivers, which means almost everybody. In the long term rising fuel costs might change people's driving habits, affecting all road users, which means almost everybody. According to the balance of contemporary scientific opinion, levels of fossil fuel consumption are changing the global climate, which definitely affects everybody. By these criteria this is a big story.

On the other hand a reduction in corporation tax for small businesses would interest the proprietors of small businesses, but not other people. The importance of the tax cut might need to be explained in terms of how it will

boost the economy and create job opportunities. It does have relevance to a wider audience, but it's a harder story to sell.

The trial of Michael Jackson for alleged child abuse had no impact at all on the audience's pockets – except perhaps in their decision whether or not to buy any more Michael Jackson albums. But it was a massive story because it had enormous cultural resonance. Almost everybody has heard Michael Jackson's music and his records can be found in almost every household. He'd been the biggest pop star on the planet. And in an age where celebrity culture dominates the tabloid agenda, and even the mundane details of the lives of minor television personalities sell newspapers, here was a global star in crisis. Most of us had invested in Michael Jackson, financially – through album or concert ticket sales, and emotionally – through his music. The allegations were serious in their own right, but more than that the court proceedings opened the doors on one of the most bizarre lifestyles ever reported. Most of the information in the public domain was known to be highly suspect. Now the rigours of a judicial process were to be applied to his lifestyle.

Jackson's story has relevance to us because it informs our relationship with those around us. Everybody was talking about it. It was good gossip.

If the relevance of a story is not clear to the audience, you need to tell them why it matters: like explaining the role of small businesses in the economy. Hurricane Katrina in the Gulf of Mexico caused petrol price rises in the UK and panic buying, because US oil production was affected.

REMEMBER

➤ Ask how a story impacts on the audience

➤ Explain why stories matter

➤ Value 'good gossip'.

See Workshops and Exercises.

INTEREST

News has to be interesting. It goes without saying that anything that takes up valuable air-time on radio or television, or even space on a website, should be of interest to the audience.

If a story interests you, the journalist, it should interest the audience. You need to detach your personal interests from your professional judgement. Judgement is one of the most valued qualities in any journalist.

The idea of what is interesting forms the basis of extensive debate. Rupert Murdoch runs the biggest news organisation in the world. He is much more powerful than any twentieth-century press baron. And he says of his global empire: 'We are in the entertainment business.'

News as entertainment

So where do news and entertainment meet? Is something news just because it is new and entertaining? Clearly, newspapers, which have lost their role as providers of fresh news, have to offer entertainment (and analysis) as an alternative to traditional news. Tabloid papers unashamedly run stories because they are entertaining in their own right. The sex lives of soap stars are not traditional news. The broadcast news agenda is defined more by the public-service ethos of the need to 'inform, educate and entertain'.

Telling stories in an entertaining way is not the same as choosing entertainment over information – and certainly not the same as 'infotainment', a term frequently used as a criticism by those accusing the media of 'dumbing down'. There are stories that we call 'human interest' – stories about people. And there are other stories where we show their impact on one person or group of people to make them relevant to other people. An entertaining treatment can make a complicated story interesting and accessible. 'Worthy but dull' remains a damning indictment of any report.

THINKPIECE

THE PUBLIC INTEREST V. INTERESTING TO THE PUBLIC

The 'public interest' is a very different idea from simply being 'of interest to the public', as judges and politicians are quick to point out to journalists. Lurid stories about the private lives of celebrities may be of interest to lots of people, but their publication is rarely in the public interest.

The public interest is an important legal concept – the justification for the publication of material of social importance even when it infringes other legal rights of individuals or organisations. That is why the Ofcom Code allows secret filming or recording to be used by investigative journalists when 'there is prima facie evidence of a story in the public interest'.

In 2000, a judge ruled that a BBC *Panorama* programme was in the 'public interest'. *Who Bombed Omagh?* was about the 1998 atrocity in which 29 people died, and it named the suspects. The Northern Ireland Human Rights Commission tried on the day of the programme to stop its broadcast, because it would be a breach of the human rights of nearly everybody involved – the police, the suspects, the survivors and the relatives of the dead – and the show was condemned as a 'trial by media'. Ninety minutes before transmission, Mr Justice Kerr accepted the BBC's argument that a ban would mean no *prima facie* evidence of criminal conduct should ever be exposed in public for fear of prejudicing something or someone. That would have put an end to newspapers and broadcasters exposing corruption. Similar public interest arguments won *Panorama* the right to show *The Corruption of Racing*, an exposé of alleged horse race fixing, two years later.

There is also a public interest test enshrined in the Communications Act of 2003 after extensive lobbying by pressure groups and the Labour peer and film producer Lord Puttnam. This means viewers and listeners have to be treated as citizens as well as consumers of commercial services.

A public interest test is developing too in libel cases. After the *Sunday Times* accused the Irish Prime Minister Albert Reynolds of misleading the Irish Parliament, he sued. The paper lost the case, but for the first time judges ruled that the media had a duty to inform the public and engage in public discussion of matters of public interest. This is known as the 'Reynolds defence', and, as more media organisations use it in court, their duty to the public is being more closely defined by the judges.

It is important that broadcast journalists are aware of the debate about public interest and the legal precedents being set in the courts. It is equally important that we know how to interest an audience and engage them in often-complicated issues.

SHOCK VALUE

The very 'newness' of something – its shock value – can make something news. Rarely has an event had such an impact on the British public as the death of Diana, Princess of Wales. It was shocking to wake up on a summer Sunday morning in 1997 and discover that one of the most famous women in the world had died in a car crash; so shocking that most us spent the rest of the day in front of our televisions.

Diana's funeral attracted a TV audience of many millions worldwide. The funerals of ordinary people caught up in extraordinary events also feature on news programmes. In April 2006, in Leek, Staffordshire, TV cameras were out in force for the funerals of three children killed in an explosion at their home. The funeral of a man who died in the same incident – their mother's boyfriend – was also covered. It was a domestic tragedy that shocked a rural community. The news media transmitted the shock to a wider audience, and the audience shared the mourning at the funeral. The initial event was clearly shocking. Does that make the funerals newsworthy?

DRAMA

Certain stories grab audiences because they are dramatic in their own right. Strangely, real-life stories often have the kind of plot twists found in novels and plays. Look at the events in the life of MP, novelist, mayoral candidate, adulterer, perjurer and convict Lord Archer – every episode could have come straight from a soap opera, complete with cliff-hanging will-he-won't-he endings.

The English novelist and essayist G. K. Chesterton famously said: 'Journalism largely consists of saying "Lord Jones dead" to people who never knew Lord Jones was alive.' It begs the question, would people have been interested to know who Lord Jones was if we'd told them? If Lord Jones had a life like Lord Archer's, we probably would have.

When encouraging journalists to write in a conversational style, editors will often suggest: 'How would you tell it to your mates in the pub?' or 'Can you explain this to the receptionist at the gym?' It's also worth asking: 'Would your mates in the pub or the receptionist at the gym be interested in this?'

'HOW WOULD YOU TELL IT TO YOUR MATES IN THE PUB?'

'CAN YOU EXPLAIN THIS TO THE RECEPTIONIST AT THE GYM?'

REMEMBER

➤ News has to be interesting – to you and the audience

➤ News can be presented in an entertaining way

➤ Shock value and drama are important elements in choosing stories.

PICTURES

In television and online, the level of interest is often determined by the pictures available. The drama of the floods in Boscastle in 2004 was captured in home video footage later shown around the world. Exceptional rainfall caused two rivers to overflow their banks. Cars and trees were swept down the main street. Later, the footage from helicopters as people were lifted to safety from rooftops added to the spectacle.

Great pictures – from your own camera people, from the emergency services, or from people with home video footage, camera phone stills or video – can turn an ordinary story into exciting television.

People will talk about great pictures. The biggest stories are remembered through powerful images: smoke billowing from the World Trade Center on September 11, 2001; a lone protester in front of a tank in Beijing's Tiananmen Square in 1989; Zinedine Zidane's head-butt in the 2006 World Cup Final. And smaller stories can become more memorable if pictures are available: an air-sea rescue; a factory fire; a spectacular goal.

REMEMBER

➤ Great pictures can turn an everyday story into a memorable one.

THINKPIECE

THE IMPACT OF NEWS – THE PUBLIC'S CHOICE

When ITV News asked viewers to vote for *The Shot that Shook the World* as part of the fiftieth anniversary celebrations of independent television in the UK in 2005, the poll showed how public perceptions of what is newsworthy are affected by time and distance. This was the result of the vote for the best news pictures in 50 years:

1   The second aeroplane hitting the World Trade Center, 2001
2   Man landing on the moon, 1969
3   Tsunami, 2004
4   President Kennedy assassinated, 1963
5   England's World Cup win, 1966
6   The death of Princess Diana, 1997
7   Ethiopian Famine, 1984
8   Tiananmen Square protests, 1989
9   Liverpool's Champions League comeback, 2005
10 The fall of the Berlin Wall, 1989

Most commentators would agree that the running order would be very different if the poll had been taken in another country or at another time. Diana's death might well have topped a UK poll in late 1997. England's World Cup win would be unlikely to feature in any other nation's top ten. And in any other year or any other country, Liverpool's comeback, remarkable though it was, would probably not have featured at all. There's a sporting chance Manchester United's Champions League Final comeback might have been mentioned if the vote had taken place in 1999.

The moon landing would almost certainly have topped any poll of the late twentieth century. Is 9/11 a more significant event? Journalists – and ITV viewers – would be better off leaving that judgement to historians.

IMMEDIACY

NEWS HAS TO BE NEW. WHEN IT IS NO LONGER NEW, IT'S NOT NEWS.

It is stating the obvious – but news has to be new. When it is no longer new, it's not news.

They don't even wrap fish and chips in yesterday's newspapers any more. But at least newspapers have the virtue of being available to read again if you need to refer back to them.

Much time and effort is expended in newsrooms bringing stories up to date and finding new angles to make them as immediate as possible. An editor will dismiss a story that has already been reported elsewhere as a 'history lesson'. But sometimes a story that has appeared elsewhere is so important that it can't be dismissed lightly. In these instances reporters will search for a new 'nose' or 'peg' to give the story 'new legs'. Don't worry about the mixing of metaphors in the last sentence: just remember that the job is about giving people up-to-date information.

Broadcast news is of the moment or it is nothing. That's one reason why so much emphasis is placed these days on reporting live from wherever the news is happening. If you can't go live, then you have to tell the very latest on a story.

WHAT COUNTS AS 'NEW'?

Journalism is about more than just reporting events. So, what happened may not be new, but the information must be. Terrorists know this. They will release a video of a suicide bomber's last message weeks after the bombing, or even on the anniversary of the event. It revives the story. Anniversaries of major events can be the 'peg' (or reason) for running any story.

Often facts emerge about events many months or even years after the events themselves, or details come to light that make a previously unreported event newsworthy. For example, the former Prime Minister John Major became newsworthy again when ex-MP Edwina Currie revealed they'd had an affair.

There are formal inquiries into events which also make them news again:

- **Court cases** give an opportunity to relate information that has previously been out of the public domain. It is a principle of the law (both the law in Scotland and the law in the rest of the UK, which have many differences) that reporting restrictions apply until a case reaches trial, so that a jury is not unfairly influenced (see the *Law* section at the back of this book). This means there's a chance for the whole story to be told when the case is heard. Once it is told in open court, in front of either the magistrates or a judge and jury, the story can be reported. The bonus for reporters is that accurate, contemporaneous court reporting is covered by absolute privilege in law. In other words, contentious and otherwise potentially libellous material can be included without fear of legal redress. What you are not allowed to do in the UK is to record and broadcast proceedings in magistrates' and crown courts. It is also unlawful to take pictures within the precincts of the court – and that word 'precincts' is defined by the magistrate or judge, not by you as a reporter. It could include the steps of the court, the street or a lawn outside: the very places where camera crews want to put their tripods.

A CLOSER LOOK

REPORTING RESTRICTIONS

The law on contempt of court is designed to allow defendants a fair trial. The idea is that a jury should only hear the evidence in court, rather than through the newspapers or on a TV or radio bulletin.

Restrictions apply as soon as a case is active. This means when a person has been arrested; a warrant for arrest or a summons has been issued; or a person has been charged orally.

At a preliminary hearing in a magistrates' court of a case that's likely to go to crown court and be tried by a jury, reporters are only allowed to report the bare details of the case. These include the name, age, address and occupation of the accused and witnesses, the charges, bail conditions, and the time and place to which proceedings are adjourned. You can name the lawyers in the case and whether legal aid was granted. The Magistrates' Court Act 1980 sets out these reporting restrictions. They can be lifted at the request of the defence. The guiding principle behind the 1980 Act is that anything that might later be presented as evidence before a jury cannot be reported at preliminary hearings because it might prejudice the jury's deliberations.

- **Inquests** are another forum where new facts – often about tragic deaths – come to light. An inquest is held whenever someone dies in unusual or suspicious circumstances. The opening of an inquest will hear evidence of the identity of the deceased and the cause of death. How they died is determined later, at a full hearing after the police and investigating agencies have gathered all the available evidence. In most cases a coroner sitting alone will record a verdict. Occasionally a jury is needed to hear the evidence and return a verdict. Misadventure, unlawful killing, suicide and accidental death verdicts usually mean there is a story to tell. Death by natural causes does not normally provide good copy, unless there were circumstances causing wide public interest – the death of a celebrity, for example. An open verdict means there is still cause for doubt.

Coroners also hold inquests into treasure trove – to determine the ownership of hidden or lost valuables. These hearings are rare, but almost always make fascinating copy.

- **Accident and planning inquiry reports** are also sources of new stories about old events. Formal hearings (into major accidents, such as plane crashes, or plans to build motorways or redevelop town centres) are followed by the release of a report, usually months later. The hearing and the outcome will be reported separately, meaning there are several chances to tell the story.

Just occasionally a story is so remarkable, it doesn't matter that it has grown a few whiskers. Britain's news media reported to most people's astonishment on 6 July 2005 that a teenage sleepwalker had been rescued after being found asleep on the arm of a 130 ft crane. Incredibly she had climbed the crane and crossed a narrow beam before curling up on top of a concrete counterweight. The story had no relevance to listeners, other than that it was an amazing tale. The fact that it had happened 11 days earlier did not stop its being news on the day it came to public notice.

WHAT'S NEW? – A CHECK LIST

The criteria for judging what is new (rather than what is news) are clear:

- Is the story being told for the first time?
- Is new information being made public?
- Has the story changed?
- Are key people talking for the first time?
- Are there new sound clips or moving pictures?

If the answer to *any* of the above is 'yes', then you have a new story.

REMEMBER

➤ News has to include new information
➤ The event itself need not be new.

Keeping it fresh

For broadcast journalists, yesterday's news – most of what appears in newspapers – is not news. But sometimes yesterday's news is so big that it demands to be retold for a fresh audience. Typically this applies when a story happens late in the day, and only makes the late bulletins. In radio, breakfast

FOR BROADCAST JOURNALISTS, YESTERDAY'S NEWS – MOST OF WHAT APPEARS IN NEWSPAPERS – IS NOT NEWS.

is the biggest audience, so the station wants to be able to retell the story to the largest available number of listeners the next morning.

Moving a story on is an important skill. Updates are the most obvious way of doing so. New information gives the story a new lead. When a new line is available it is fairly straightforward to use that as the top of the story for future bulletins. Occasionally there is little new information, but it is still vital to give the audience news in a way that sounds immediate.

Different treatments can also make a story sound fresh. In bulletins, you might start with a copy story, then use a voicer, an interview clip or a wrap in later bulletins.

In news programmes, stories can be treated in different ways too. You might send a links vehicle (radio car or satellite truck) to a location for live interviews, or invite people into the studio for a discussion. On a crime story, you might want to talk to a victim of crime or an expert on criminal behaviour.

TIP BOX   UPDATING – TECHNIQUES

The simple way to update a story is to ask, after an event, what happens next? Usually the answer is fairly straightforward.

After a road accident the police investigate it. So 'Two people have died in a road accident' becomes, for the next day's bulletins: 'Police are investigating a road accident in which two people died.'

After an election result, the parties assess the consequences of victory or defeat. So, 'Labour have won an historic third General Election victory' becomes, in later bulletins: 'Tony Blair says the Labour party will learn the lessons of its reduced majority in the General Election.' And other events follow: 'After his party's defeat in the General Election, Michael Howard says he'll stand down as Conservative leader.'

The day after violent clashes between police and anti-capitalist demonstrators in Edinburgh, radio and TV reported: 'Dozens of protestors are due to appear in court this morning.'

'Liverpool have come from three goals down to become champions of Europe' becomes, the next day: 'Huge crowds are expected in the streets of Liverpool for the return of football's European Champions.'

Many local radio stations will deliberately withhold information to use as a fresh line for later bulletins. Veteran local radio broadcaster Stuart Linnell OBE used to stretch one interview with Coventry City's football manager across at least three days of Mercia Sound's output. It is difficult to make your material sound fresh these days, if viewers of Sky Sports News have already heard the same soccer boss saying the same thing two days earlier.

Nonetheless, the guide issued by the radio company the Wireless Group to its journalists in 2003 recommended that interviews should be long enough to take several cuts out to update bulletins and for overnights. When the story is not being reported widely elsewhere this is sound advice.

When you're listening to the radio, you expect different things depending upon what time of day you're listening. First thing in the morning you probably want a digest of the day's news, a summary of what's happened overnight, things that have come to light in the morning's newspapers, and what's going to be happening during the day. If you're on your way to work, you'll want travel information too. But by the end of the rush-hour, or 'morning drive-time' as radio schedulers call it, you'll probably have relaxed into wanting to be entertained or informed in a less frenetic form. It follows that you won't expect to hear the same information in the news bulletins as you have already heard.

A lunchtime audience will expect a summary of events during the day so far and a look ahead to what is likely to happen during the rest of the day. Courts sit in the morning, but not before ten, and early sessions can often be taken up with legal argument. By lunchtime there is usually something to report. The House of Commons' business is conducted mostly in the afternoon and evening, so parliamentary stories generally break after midday. The agenda is set well beforehand, though, and bulletins can include details of what is to come. By mid-afternoon, Parliamentary announcements will have been made. Reaction is gathered, either from the floor of the House, using clips from the Parliamentary broadcasting service shared by all broadcasters, or in interviews. These are conducted outside, usually on College Green, the stretch of lawn opposite the public entrance to the Commons, or in Millbank, where the broadcasters have their offices.

By the end of the working day, during the evening drive-time, the second highest number of listeners during the radio day will be expecting a round-up of the day's events. Traditionally television news bulletins are scheduled at a time when they can be watched by people who have just returned home at the end of the working day or late in an evening's viewing.

AS PEOPLE GET USED TO THE IDEA OF HAVING NEWS ON TAP . . . THE TRADITIONAL BULLETIN MAY BE UNDER THREAT. WE NO LONGER HAVE TO MAKE A CONSCIOUS DECISION TO LOOK FOR NEWS. ONLINE AND MOBILE PHONE TEXT SERVICES WILL DELIVER IT TO US.

Online news and rolling news stations have changed the audience's expectations. The idea of an 'appointment to view' the news may still be popular in many households, but as people get used to the idea of having news on tap – and even being able to filter the kind of news they receive – the traditional bulletin may be under threat. We no longer have to make a conscious decision to look for news. Online and mobile phone text services will deliver it to us.

Audiences at different times of the day have different expectations. You need to update stories, look for new angles and keep your output fresh. Sometimes you can withhold information to use later in the day or the next morning.

REMEMBER

➤ Updating stories to keep them fresh is an important journalistic skill
➤ In local radio, exclusive information can be withheld to freshen up later bulletins
➤ Audiences expect the latest.

CONTROVERSY

It's hard to believe today, but the BBC – when it was still the British Broadcasting Company and not a Corporation – was prohibited from broadcasting 'controversial' material. Today controversy is one of the most obvious values contributing to newsworthiness. Many 'rows' are created by journalists seeking an angle for a story, but there is still a place for genuine political debate.

The news agencies which compiled the first radio bulletins were acknowledged on air. In the early 1920s, the BBC did not want to be seen as a provider of information in its own right. Indeed, so timid was the national broadcaster that they did not air news bulletins until after seven in the evening. The news agencies had done a deal with the newspaper proprietors, who did not want to see their sales damaged. It's no wonder that Marxist analysts reckon the news agenda is determined by a controlling economic elite.

Even more remarkable to those of us used to a diet of 24-hour news, a BBC announcer on Good Friday 1930 told the nation: 'There is no news tonight.' That wasn't the only time that happened. Three quarters of a century later, the *Guardian* newspaper could joke in an ad for its web services: 'Isn't it amazing that the amount of news that happens in the world every day always just exactly fits the newspaper?'

Much modern news content is controversy generated by journalists. They invite comment on issues from politicians or people already in the news, and then report their comments as a new story. Politicians and other opinion formers vie to be quoted in this way. In 2005, in the days leading up to the Parliamentary vote on a bill to detain terrorist suspects without trial for up to 90 days, the Prime Minister, Tony Blair, the Metropolitan Police Commissioner, Sir Ian Blair, and the Home Secretary, Charles Clarke, seemed to be competing to see who could make the latest statement on the issue and so lead the bulletins.

Responsible journalists will be wary of presenting every new statement on an issue as if it were a dramatic development. But a balanced presentation of the arguments can involve focusing on different viewpoints in different bulletins.

> *RESPONSIBLE JOURNALISTS WILL BE WARY OF PRESENTING EVERY NEW STATEMENT ON AN ISSUE AS IF IT WERE A DRAMATIC DEVELOPMENT.*

REMEMBER

➤ Controversy is an important factor in public debate
➤ Some controversy is a product of the way journalists select information rather than a true reflection of events.

PROXIMITY

Controversy on its own is not enough unless the story fits other news criteria. It has to be relevant and interesting to the audience. Another factor which might make it relevant is proximity – or closeness to home. This is different from localness, which we'll discuss later. It's a concept that is defined by people's perception of themselves and how they fit into the world around them.

In the Second World War, television broadcasts were suspended and the British nation relied on BBC radio for the most immediate information about the progress of the war. The reputation of the BBC for authoritative news coverage was established during this time. Since then, many more wars have been reported but they were always overseas events. During the Second World War, British civilians were at risk. There can be no greater demonstration of the proximity of news to the audience; national security, and more specifically the very life and death of the listeners, was at stake. When the IRA bombed targets in England from the 1970s onwards, similar considerations affected the coverage. The success of terrorism is measured politically not in terms of lives taken, but in its effect on public opinion through the news media.

The coverage of subsequent wars – particularly those in the Falklands, Afghanistan and Iraq – focused on the involvement of British troops: sons, daughters, brothers, sisters, fathers, mothers and lovers of those watching at home. Meanwhile there have been wars in Africa, largely unreported in the British media, because of the lack of British involvement.

A senior executive of ABC in the United States, Av Westin, used to ask these questions to decide what was newsworthy:

- Is my world safe?

- Are my city and home safe?

- If my wife, children and loved ones are safe, then what has happened in the past 24 hours to shock them, amuse them or make them better off than they were?

A more flippant version of the same idea – that the closer to home news happens, the more important it is – is found in the so-called McLurg's Law. There are various versions, though none should be taken seriously by modern journalists. The British one used to run along the lines of one dead Briton is worth five dead Frenchmen, 20 dead Egyptians, 500 dead Indians and 1,000 dead Chinese. It is the kind of attitude that led to *The Times* newspaper headline 'Small Earthquake in Chile – not many dead.' It was a joke – but a sick one.

Some listeners to Radio Five Live were disappointed by the high level of coverage given to the death of 12 miners in an underground explosion in West Virginia in January 2006. One e-mail (read out on-air) said: 'The US is not the centre of the universe. Where was the in-depth coverage the last time this happened in China or South Africa?' Another said: 'It's bad enough having US news rammed down our throats every day. Why is it that British and American lives are more valuable than anybody else's?' A caller to Victoria Derbyshire's morning phone-in said the coverage reflected modern news values. Simon, a former teacher of American history in the US, now living in Cambridgeshire, said: 'Where communications are good and where the media are situated, you are going to get more coverage. The closer it is to home the more likely it is to be covered – you know – "Earthquake in south-east Asia, Cambridgeshire man survives." That's one of the truisms of news.'

A story may be more important to some members of the audience than others. The safety of home and family are the first concerns of almost everyone. A story on the other side of the world can impact on that safety.

REMEMBER

➤ Audiences consider their own and their family's security to be of prime importance

➤ The geographical location of news organisations and their crews can distort news coverage.

See Workshops and Exercises.

CASE STUDY 2.1   PAKISTAN EARTHQUAKE

When a genuinely horrific earthquake occurred in the Kashmir region in October 2005, it failed to make the front page lead on any of the next day's national Sunday newspapers. One critic, a Labour peer, remarked that the newspapers seemed to think England qualifying for football's World Cup (which happened on the same day) was more important than the devastation in Pakistan. Not for the first time, broadcasters saved the reputation of the British media with extensive coverage that brought home not only the horrors of events in the earthquake zone but also the impact on people at home. Thousands of British Asians had relatives in the affected area. The BBC reported that 70,000 people in Bradford had links to the earthquake zone; a man in Swindon lost 17 members of his family; and there were British people who had lost up to 600 members of their extended family. Correspondent Mark Easton reported from Luton that among the town's Pakistan Kashmiri community hardly any family was unaffected. Rozina Sini of radio's Asian Network told BBC News 24 that all their listeners knew someone in the region, and many were desperate both to find out more about the casualties and to offer help.

As a result, many people went to airports immediately to fly out to Islamabad. Such was the clamour to assist the rescue operation that charities and official rescue agencies appealed for people to stay at home, fearing they would hamper the relief effort.

LOCALNESS

In its 'news mission statement', the commercial radio company UTV Radio (formerly the Wireless Group) insisted that at least one of the top three stories in any bulletin should be local, with 70 per cent local content in breakfast bulletins . . . 'more if you can with localised national stories. The more local people/places mentioned in your bulletin, the more "talkability" the station gets.'

'THE IDEA IS TO WIN THE TRUST AND RESPECT OF YOUR LISTENERS. YOU ARE THE ONE WHO TELLS THEM IF SCHOOLS ARE CLOSED WHEN IT SNOWS, IF ROADS ARE BLOCKED OR IF POWER IS DOWN.'

They talk too about 'owning your patch'. The idea is to win the trust and respect of your listeners. You are the one who tells them if schools are closed when it snows, if roads are blocked or if power is down.

Local radio stations will aim to provide an 'addictive service of vital news and information people can use in their everyday lives', but it's often the filler stories – a missing parrot, for example – that get people talking.

Localness is what makes local radio – and local TV – distinctive.

REMEMBER

➤ Make sure local stories are near the top of the bulletin
➤ Own your patch.

A CLOSER LOOK

A CLOSER LOOK   **LOCAL STORIES WITHIN THE BIGGER PICTURE**

Events that have no significance internationally can be hugely important to national or local audiences. The closer to home, the more newsworthy it is. Britain's first toll motorway the Birmingham Northern Relief Road, later named the M6 Toll, was the result of an important transport policy decision in the 1990s, aimed at reducing traffic congestion by using private sector finance. It was a significant political debate – and therefore a national story – as the road went from planning application to public inquiry. But to those living along the route the political dimension was overshadowed by a local environmental story. Large swathes of agricultural land were being covered in concrete. Peaceful demonstrations and lobbying of politicians followed, reported mostly by local and regional rather than national media. Then protestors occupied woodland and a house due for demolition on the route; the conflict with bailiffs and police brought wider attention to the problem – with mostly regional but some national coverage.

Now the road is in use, a rise in tolls is news to its users, but is unlikely to be reported much beyond the pages of the *Birmingham Post* and *Mail*, or the bulletins of Radio WM and BRMB.

WHAT'S THE ANGLE?

The angle is the approach a journalist takes to a story. Sometimes there are several possible approaches to the same story. Recognising the different angles available not only helps focus on the best way to tell the story, it offers the option of featuring different approaches in later bulletins, updating and freshening the coverage without necessarily relying on new information.

A question editors ask soon after deciding to cover a story is: 'What's the angle?' Some stories are straightforward: Princess dies in car crash; terrorists kill thousands by flying planes into New York landmark; tsunami kills more than a quarter of a million people.

However, other stories are more complicated and can be subject to any number of interpretations. Sometimes that means journalists get it wrong. In September 2005, there was panic buying at Britain's petrol stations. Long queues formed and many pumps ran dry. The chaos was a direct result of media hype – journalists predicting that a shortage was likely because demonstrators were going to blockade supplies from oil terminals in protest at rising prices. In fact, the protestors, who turned out only in very small numbers, had already promised they would not disrupt supplies, and the government had announced it had contingency plans if they did. But newsdesks responded on the basis of previous protests in 2000 which had cut off petrol deliveries. In 2005, broadcasters and newspapers misled the public by sloppy journalism.

New angles

The angle chosen will almost always rely on the criteria of newsworthiness outlined earlier. Usually a fresh angle, or new *top line*, is obvious; it is the latest development. It is common practice though to save secondary or less important information for inclusion in later bulletins, to provide a new 'nose' in the absence of new developments. In a breaking story – one that is developing through the day – new angles emerge as events occur.

The breaking story may become a *running story* – one that has repercussions over the following days, months, weeks and years. It is important for journalists in a newsroom to stay abreast of running stories. Often expertise in a running story will be a factor in getting a new and better job if a journalist wants to move from one news organisation to another.

Journalists should always ask *the five 'W's – who, what, where, when, why* – and sometimes how. The 'what' is almost always the most important: a plane crash, a political agreement, an election result, a royal marriage, a sports result. Often the 'who' gives the story its significance, but we still want to know what they've done: Prince Harry has announced his engagement; Bob Geldof is planning another rock concert; Murray is out of Wimbledon.

When a story breaks, *what* has happened is the most important thing to report. *Who* is involved is also important – remember that people want stories about people.

As the story changes and new information is available, it is important to present the latest information to the audience. Usually the latest information comes first. This is the new 'nose' for the story – the new angle.

CASE STUDY 2.2   NEW ANGLES – A TIMELINE

Remember where you were on September 11, 2001. Many people heard that a plane had crashed into the World Trade Center in New York. To start with, that was the story. That was the angle. It happened at 8.46 a.m. local time.

9.02 a.m. A second plane crashes. *New angle.*

The twin towers are alight. *Newer angle.*

9.17 a.m. The Federal Aviation Authority shuts down all New York City area airports. *Newest angle.*

9.30 a.m. President Bush, at a school in Florida, speaks of 'an apparent terrorist attack' and 'a national tragedy'. *Another new angle.*

People are trapped on the upper floors and some are jumping to their deaths. *Newer angle.*

9.37 a.m. American Airlines Flight 77 hits the Pentagon. *Newest angle.*

9.59 a.m. The South Tower of the World Trade Center collapses. *Another new angle.*

10.28 a.m. The North Tower of the World Trade Center collapses. *Newer angle.*

10. 48 a.m. The police confirm the crash of a large plane in Pennsylvania. *Newest angle.*

And so it continued, hour after harrowing hour. The loss of fire crews, the death toll, the political fallout, the War on Terror, Afghanistan, Iraq. Events that shaped the early part of the twenty-first century. All new angles on the biggest story in a generation. A story this big is covered by teams of reporters around the world.

Local angles

Big national and international stories generate local angles. Local radio stations look for victims or, better still, survivors of global catastrophes, and for local people caught up in world events. This is where citizen journalists – people caught up in events – can be useful, particularly if they have video or audio material. Their blogs and podcasts can be a source for broadcasters.

The Tsunami of Boxing Day 2004 generated hundreds of local stories. There were victims' families to talk to, survivors' tales to hear and widespread charity fund-raising efforts, many of them newsworthy in their own right because of their sheer inventiveness.

The Pakistan earthquake of 2005 had a huge impact on Kashmiri families in England, many of whom had relatives who were involved. And on September 11, 2001, the regional ITV service Central News South went into the centre of Oxford looking for reaction from American tourists and students.

But beware of tagging a local story on to a national one for the sake of it. The attempt to broaden the appeal of the local event may achieve the opposite effect. It can make something that otherwise might be included on its own merit look trivial by comparison with the national event. Here's an example from *BBC Midlands Today:*

In less than 48 hours we'll know if London has been successful in its bid to hold the 2012 Olympic Games. At the same time over one thousand of the world's young sporting stars will be arriving in the Midlands for the International Children's Games.

BBC Midlands Today, 4 July 2005

This approach seems rather patronising, and undersells a good local story.

REMEMBER

➤ Journalists always look for a new angle

➤ Local angles can make a national story relevant to a local audience.

CASE STUDY 2.3   ON THE HOME FRONT

The role of local combatants in overseas wars always provides copy and story ideas. These can be expanded into longer features.

The BBC in the Midlands took advantage of a facility trip to visit soldiers of the Staffordshire Regiment preparing for the Gulf War of 1991 to produce a documentary *The Gulf Between* featuring local soldiers in the desert and their families, both at home in the UK and at the regiment's German base in Fallingbostel. After the war, some of the same people were revisited in a second documentary *After the Gulf*, which included a young soldier's first sight of his child born while he was at war, and his wedding. The programme included the return to their base in Germany of two pilots held hostage in Iraq. One of them was native to the Midlands.

REGIONAL NEWS

As well as considering the news values of individual stories, the producers of bulletins on regional radio stations and regional TV have to consider how their programmes reflect the region they serve. News does not happen to order. So, stories may be dropped simply because there are already other stronger stories from the same part of the patch.

Mike Henfield, a former local radio news editor and managing director, says a not infrequent instruction in the north west of England is: 'We haven't had a story from Preston for weeks – drop that Liverpool protest story.'

'MOST PEOPLE COULDN'T GIVE TWO FIGS ABOUT WHAT HAPPENS IN SHROPSHIRE IF THEY LIVE IN CHELTENHAM, AND VICE VERSA.'

Regional television was based on the areas covered by the analogue transmitters. Commercial pressures mean independent TV has cut back on many of its regional opt-out programmes. In the digital age, programmes based on regions may be an anachronism. Tim Burke, the Community Content Editor of the BBC's Local TV Pilot in 2006, says: 'Most people couldn't give two figs about what happens in Shropshire if they live in Cheltenham, and vice versa.'

For now, regional considerations are all part of the 'news mix' – the choice of stories for a programme.

REMEMBER

➤ Covering a region may mean dropping stories from one place in favour of another.

THE NEWS MIX

Most journalists acknowledge a difference between *hard* and *soft* stories, but few will agree just where the line between the two lies. Critics of the journalistic trade will often remark that there's too much bad news. In the 1990s, TV newsreader Martyn Lewis publicly declared there should be more good news – and was far from universally applauded by his colleagues. The following comment from James Naughtie on the *Today* programme in 2005 was a slip of the tongue rather than a statement of the BBC's core values:

There's news coming in from Russia of a gun battle that's said to be taking place between police and armed men in Nalchik, which is the regional capital of Kabardino-Balkaria. One report from the French news agency, and it's pretty unconfirmed, says armed men entered a school. We don't know any more at the moment, but if it turns out to be something pretty awful, we will let you know.

You might ask whether audiences really do prefer to hear about things that are 'pretty awful'?

HARD NEWS

Hard stories are those with importance, significance and relevance to the audience. Almost always they are told as and when they break, so they can also be said to have immediacy. It is almost unthinkable to have a news bulletin without hard stories. Types of hard stories include events (war, conflict, disaster,

emergencies, crime); international, domestic and local politics; and public affairs
(health, education, housing, transport, the environment).

Events

Some events are of such immediate significance that no-one would dispute their
news value: September 11, the Tsunami, war in Iraq.

The significance of outbreaks of BSE and foot and mouth disease in Britain took
longer to emerge. Trends in crime have a political dimension and therefore fall
within the hard news agenda. And some serious crimes make it into national
bulletins. But many crime and emergency stories fulfil the same role as soft
stories. They don't impact on the social or political agenda, but they do interest
the audience on an emotional level: a multiple murder within a family; a child
rescued from a pothole. The Soham murders of schoolgirls Holly Wells and
Jessica Chapman in August 2002 had emotional and political repercussions.
The crime was shocking. The investigation into police checks on school staff
had implications for parents everywhere.

Politics and public affairs

People may be cynical about politicians and apathetic about the political process,
but policy decisions by government affect people's wealth, welfare and the way
they conduct their lives.

Broadcasters are required by law to be impartial and balanced. This law does not
apply to print journalists, who are often required by their papers to take sides
and campaign actively for one party or another. The rules on the time allocated
to party political opinion on radio and TV are particularly strict at election times.
A stopwatch will be applied to the output to ensure fair play – although nobody
judges the quality of the politicians' comments except the voters.

According to the Ofcom Broadcasting Code, due impartiality may be achieved
during a programme or over a series of programmes taken as a whole.

*POLITICAL ISSUES
HAVE TO BE
POPULARISED
AND HUMANISED
FOR MOST PEOPLE
TO WANT TO
WATCH THEM.*

Political debate is a mainstay of news bulletins. But there has been a growing
recognition among news organisations that top-down politics – reporting the
minutiae of political debate – does not engage the audience. Political issues
have to be popularised and humanised for most people to want to watch them.
Broadcasters get criticised for reducing politics to the conflict between
personalities. But often that is the best way to introduce the arguments.

Mick Temple, a professor of journalism and politics at Staffordshire University,
argues, in praise of 'dumbing down', that those of the population generally
uninterested in formal politics – the majority – need at the very least to be
informed about basic issues. He says engaging and entertaining political
coverage can encourage further examination of the issues at a more
informed level.

In news reporting, when a matter of public policy can be illustrated with a real-
life example – somebody's personal experience – it is usually considered a better
way of telling the story than simply using soundbites of politicians' views. As
an American publisher once put it, journalists can't congratulate themselves
on having got at the facts impartially by quoting at length from two uninformed
idiots on opposing sides of an issue.

➤ Hard stories make up most of the content of news bulletins
➤ Political stories need to be popularised
➤ There are laws about political balance in broadcasting.

SOFT NEWS

Soft stories do not usually have a direct impact on people's day-to-day lives. But they are what the US newspaperman Arthur McEwen called stories that make the reader go 'Gee whiz!' They include *human interest* stories, like the sleepwalking girl found on top of a crane, animal stories, sport; and, finally, the *'and finally ...'*.

Human interest

Human interest is a broad term that barely does justice to the range of stories it covers. Stories have to be about people or to affect people to attract interest. So, almost all stories could be classified as human interest. But the term usually refers to emotional stories about people or lighter, quirkier stories about human beings – and animals. These stories may offer little more than 'bread and circuses' to the audience, but the editor who ignores them risks losing viewers or listeners. That means the audience for so-called 'serious' stories will be much smaller. Human interest stories are an essential part of the news mix.

HUMAN INTEREST STORIES ARE AN ESSENTIAL PART OF THE NEWS MIX.

Celebrities

The word 'celebrity' has become devalued in recent years. There are two types of celebrity nowadays: the 'elite' celebrities with whose fame no-one could disagree, and the 'vogue' celebrities famous for the moment but soon to be forgotten. Elite celebrities include presidents, prime ministers and world statesmen, like John F. Kennedy, Margaret Thatcher and Nelson Mandela. Musical figures from Mozart to Frank Sinatra and Bob Dylan are also part of an elite. The vogue celebs are often created by the media that reports on them. They are 'famous for being famous'. Jade Goody springs to mind. Bienvenida Buck and Antonia de Sancha do not – but they were once heavily reported on, particularly in newspapers.

Celebrity stories, mostly of 'vogue' celebrities, fill so much space in top tabloids, it's hard to find hard news. The *News of the World* became Britain's biggest-selling paper with a steamy mix of sex and scandal. Broadcast news has always occupied a higher moral ground, from the Reithian values of the early BBC – the Scots Presbyterian approach of the first Director General Lord Reith – to today's carefully regulated multi-channel environment. Arguments about 'dumbing down' and 'tabloidisation' are familiar territory to media commentators. Whatever the trend, the huge audiences attracted by network broadcasting – far bigger than any newspaper's sales – mean that broadcast news is a popular medium. That means it has to offer coverage of popular culture. Broadcast journalists need to be aware of the latest movies, the best-selling music, and plotlines in *Coronation Street* and *EastEnders*.

Pop and movie stars feature heavily in news stories. How newsworthy they are depends on their star quality – that elusive combination of charisma and mystique. The presence of a big name is usually enough to justify coverage on local and regional bulletins.

Royals

Royal stories too fall into the human interest category. The survival of Britain's constitutional monarchy has been assisted by favourable press coverage. Queen Victoria projected her image as a dutiful widow through the British newspapers and was apparently popular in an age sandwiched between the French and Russian revolutions, when royals were put to death. The influential press barons of the late nineteenth and early twentieth centuries used their newspapers to support the Establishment, including the monarchy. The Abdication Crisis of 1936 went unreported in the British press until it became inevitable that Edward VIII would relinquish the throne over his love for the American divorcee Wallis Simpson.

Nowadays the press can be highly critical, particularly of the younger royals. Broadcasters are traditionally less censorious, and they are criticised by newspaper editors when they follow up stories in the papers they might otherwise have ignored. So, it was the *Sun* that sent an undercover reporter into Sandhurst military college where Prince Harry was being trained for life as an army officer. The 'security breach' was covered by all the broadcasters, as was the story which appeared first in newspapers of the young prince wearing Nazi uniform to a fancy dress party.

THE ROYALS AND OTHER CELEBRITIES NEED THE MEDIA TO BOOST THEIR POPULARITY – WHETHER THAT'S MEASURED IN BOX-OFFICE RECEIPTS, ALBUM SALES OR AVOIDING THE GUILLOTINE.

The Royals and other celebrities need the media to boost their popularity – whether that's measured in box-office receipts, album sales or avoiding the guillotine. So, they will collude with newspapers and broadcasters to secure favourable coverage. The prime exponent of this was the late Diana, Princess of Wales, who frequently tipped off tabloid reporters and dramatically aired her marital difficulties in a *Panorama* interview.

Children

The involvement of children in a story always makes it more newsworthy. Most adults are horrified by any injustice done to children, and are shocked by the corruption of innocence. Whenever children are caught up in tragedy or disaster, the story can be upsetting but compelling.

Television images of starving children have inspired international fund-raising campaigns – the most famous being Bob Geldof's Band Aid/Live Aid charity in 1984–5, which raised £150 million for famine relief in Ethiopia.

More health stories about children are covered than those that affect the elderly. Children are seen as being more appealing to audiences.

The appeal of children in news extends to stories of children's achievements – child prodigies, children involved in charity fund-raising, children's success in school exams. The annual debate about whether exams are getting easier is always accompanied by shots of youngsters hugging as they learn their marks and sometimes stilted radio interviews with young people who are not used to being in front of a microphone.

Animals

Animal stories have always been popular with viewers and listeners. The Tamworth Two – two pigs who 'escaped' from an abattoir – captivated viewers for days before they were recaptured . . . and sent to live out their days in an animal sanctuary.

The importance of animal stories was lampooned in the title of a cult comedy series about a TV newsroom, *Drop the Dead Donkey*. And in newsrooms, the 'skateboarding duck' became a generic term for a great animal story. The original duck in question, Herbie, appeared on the BBC's early evening current affairs show *Nationwide* in the 1970s. Such was his fame that the *Mail on Sunday* felt it was of sufficient importance to report some 30 years later that – horror of horrors – the trick had been achieved by *nailing* the duck to the skateboard. The newspaper report – splashed across half a page – was untrue, as anyone who had seen the original footage of the duck jumping on and off the skateboard could have told them. Letters of correction duly appeared in the newspaper, from the duck's owner Jacqueline Randall and the retired *Nationwide* reporter Alan Towers.

Why are animal stories popular? You might as well ask why the British are described as 'a nation of animal lovers'. Animals are cute, cuddly, scary, funny and entertaining. All human life is there.

REMEMBER

- ➤ Human interest stories attract audiences
- ➤ Celebrity news is an accepted part of the news mix
- ➤ Animal stories are always popular.

Sport – and why it's important

Do you read the back pages of the newspaper first? If you don't, you'll know somebody who does. For a vast proportion of the population, sports stories are the most important thing on the news.

IF YOU NEVER READ THE BACK PAGES, YOU MIGHT WANT TO KISS GOODBYE TO A CAREER IN BROADCASTING.

If you never read the back pages, you might want to kiss goodbye to a career in broadcasting. It may sound harsh, but no broadcast journalist can expect to stay long in the job if they don't understand sport. In a local radio or regional television newsroom, you may be the only news writer on shift in the evening when the late football or 20–20 cricket results come in. You will have to write those results for a late evening bulletin or for breakfast news the next day. Sky News foreign affairs correspondent Ian Woods started his career as a student compiling late sports results at Mercia Sound, the ILR station in Coventry.

A CLOSER LOOK

MAKING A FOOL OF YOURSELF

Misinterpreting sports news makes you look foolish, because so many of the audience are passionate about it. Rick Thompson was editing a national television news programme when the newsreader said England's opening batsman had been dismissed 'One-B-W'. He says she was rapped on the pads later.

The significance of sport to the community was one of the factors stressed by the London bid team which successfully won the 2012 Olympic Games for Britain.

The TUC and the CBI (the 'voices' of trades unions and employers respectively) issued pleas to British companies to allow workers to keep in touch with the test match score during the crucial climax to cricket's 2005 Ashes series.

The veteran broadcaster, legendary interviewer and sometime sportswriter Michael Parkinson summed up the appeal of sport in his *Daily Telegraph* column shortly after that England Ashes victory: 'The importance of sport is that it doesn't matter, except as an antidote to things that do.'

A CLOSER LOOK

BRITAIN'S FIRST SPORTS NEWS CHANNEL

Sport's appeal is reflected in the success of Sky Sports News. The channel was set up after Rupert Murdoch's Sky Television bought up a huge swathe of sports rights, revolutionising the way sport was viewed on UK television. The range of live sport available to viewers increased exponentially – as did the cost of watching it. Sky's impressive roster of live sport meant there was also a growing library of highlights to exploit. Those highlights could be shown on the Sky News channel, and there was also enough to provide raw material for a stand-alone sports news channel. Sky Sports News would serve as a promotional tool for the premium-cost sports channels and for pay-per-view events. Even with the cost of employing presenters and reporters, it virtually paid for itself.

As a business model it was inspired. As a response to audience demand, it has more than justified itself, regularly attracting more viewers than the 'senior' service Sky News.

REMEMBER

➤ Sports news matters to a large proportion of the audience
➤ Ignorance of sport will find you out.

. . . and finally

The phrase 'and finally' has become such a cliché of broadcasting that it is rarely used other than ironically. But a well-rounded bulletin on all but the hardest news day will almost always end on a lighter note. The 'and finally' will usually be a human interest story, treated with humour. Greg Dyke, when he was Director General of the BBC, warned journalists to leave comedy to comedians. Nonetheless, a strong tradition has developed, particularly in regional TV news, of reporters offering a wry and affectionate look at life's eccentricities. The style was set by great names in broadcasting like Fyfe Robertson and Alan Whicker on the BBC's *Tonight* in the early days of TV magazine programmes half a century ago, and was continued by regional reporters on news magazines. John Swallow on Central News and John Yates on BBC Midlands Today earned the affection of Midlands viewers across three decades. Chas Watkin, now a senior BBC regional news editor, says: 'When I was growing up, my sister and I used to watch the ITV programme just waiting for John Swallow's piece to come on.'

Chris Tarrant says that when he was 'interviewing nutters' as a reporter on *ATV Today* he had found his broadcasting home. It led to an illustrious career via *Tiswas* to *Who Wants to be a Millionaire?*

➤ A well-crafted bulletin will finish on a high – usually a quirky or lighter story.

WHO DECIDES WHAT TO COVER?

With so many types of story vying for a place in news programmes, who decides what makes the cut? That depends on the news organisation, of course. But whether the decision is to be made by the editor of the day at the BBC's *Ten O'Clock News* or the early reporter on shift at Signal Radio in Stoke-on-Trent, the stories are subject to the process of copy-tasting.

Copy-tasting

At its simplest, copy-tasting involves assessing stories, or copy, as they come into a newsroom and deciding whether they are worth running. That can be as simple as the on-shift reporter taking the story off the wires as it appears in front of them, and reading it on air in the next bulletin. Or it can mean the intake editor in a larger organisation passing the copy to a researcher or reporter to investigate further.

OFTEN . . . YOUR EFFORTS WILL COME TO NOUGHT. NOT BECAUSE THE STORY DIDN'T STAND UP. BUT SIMPLY BECAUSE BIGGER STORIES HAPPENED.

Larger newsrooms split the roles of intake and output. That can mean a story will be accepted by the intake desk, and time will be expended on it, only for the output editor or programme producer to decide they don't want to carry it. Producers still talk of stories being 'spiked', the old newspaper term for sticking copy on a spike on the desk. Other stories will be developed as standbys, just in case bigger stories don't make it to air.

Newcomers to a broadcast newsroom find it hard to accept, but often all your efforts will come to nought. Not because the story didn't stand up. But simply because bigger stories happened, and there was not enough room in the programme.

➤ All stories are subject to copy-tasting
➤ Some stories will be dropped for lack of space.

CONCLUSION

We've seen in this chapter the factors that determine if a story is worth telling. Most news organisations still choose stories according to traditional criteria. But there is a growing emphasis in news on allowing witnesses to tell their own stories, and on enabling people to use new technologies to engage in the news-making process.

We'll move on to explain how to find stories worth telling – the traditional and modern sources of news – and how to tell them, across all media.

In the digital age, where the availability of news is limited only by the imagination of software designers, any webmaster will tell you that content is king. In news broadcasting, content almost always means the story.

FURTHER READING

Harcup, Tony (2004) *Journalism: Principles and Practice*, London: Sage. An innovative split–page layout makes this a unique blend of theory and practice.

Randall, David (2000) *The Universal Journalist*, London: Pluto Press. Strong on how to find good stories.

WEB LINKS

www.nationalstudent.tv/docs/BestPractices.Westin.pdf. An online book from US experts about best practice in newsgathering – worth a look.

CHAPTER THREE

FINDING THE NEWS

WHERE DOES NEWS COME FROM?

Most broadcast reporters are fed up with being asked the question: 'Where does the news come from?' It's definitely the question asked most often by any first-time visitor to a newsroom.

The answer is simple: news is everywhere. The answer is also complicated: there are dozens of sources of news – many of them tried and tested over years of newsroom practice; others unexpected; some the product of new technologies; still more probably yet to be discovered, as the means of disseminating information multiply in the digital age.

All journalists need to know the main sources of news.

We'll begin with the best way of finding original stories – those that are known as off-diary.

NEWS SOURCES

CONTACTS

Most reporters recognise that the best way of finding new and exclusive stories is through personal contacts, people who've become reliable sources of news and information. All journalists keep a contacts book. After a pen it is probably the most important tool of the trade. A contacts book is usually laid out alphabetically and contains names, addresses, phone numbers – particularly mobiles – and e-mail addresses of anyone who might be a source of news.

Who might they be? Well, almost anyone, from politicians and captains of industry to market traders, pub landlords, policemen and members of voluntary organisations. A contacts book might include a particularly chatty milkman or waiter, or local church leaders.

Organise your contacts

Despite the growth of electronic organisers, it is probably still a good idea to keep your contacts in a traditional book (possibly loose leaf like a Filofax), because, as your career develops, any electronic means of storage will undoubtedly be superseded by new technology. If you don't mind the hassle of transferring data to the next best thing every couple of years, try both. Cross-reference your entries, so that you can find people easily, according to their expertise.

But whatever form your contact book is in, make sure your name and your own contact details are clearly marked on it. You may wish to offer a reward if it is lost.

A GOOD IDEA FROM THE PAST

Weekly newspapers used to allow reporters out on 'district calls' at least one afternoon a week, simply to chat to people in a neighbourhood and to call on community leaders in the hunt for stories. It was an investment by the newspaper proprietor in generating original off-diary material. The BBC had a similar policy when it introduced specialist correspondents into their regional newsrooms during the 1990s. They were 'ring-fenced' from the demands of contributing to day-to-day news. The idea was that they would be able to work their contacts and come up with exclusive stories.

Some BBC local radio stations have revived this idea of 'district calls' with 'no e-mail' weeks – when reporters shun their most familiar form of communication and take to the streets in search of stories, armed only with a microphone and recorder. These special days have produced some original journalism. But it only works if you have enough staff to send out 'on spec'. Most commercial radio stations do not.

Journalism educator F. J. Mansfield wrote that the good reporter is able to find at least two good stories during a twopenny bus ride. You can work out how long ago he said that from just how far you would get on a bus today for tuppence (less than a penny in 'new' money). It was in the 1930s. But the principle holds good today. One freelance working in the Midlands reckons he never pays for a holiday, because every time he goes away (to destinations all over the world) he comes across a story or two which he then sells, covering the costs of the family trip. If anybody has a 'nose for news', then he does.

Mixing the professional and the personal

THE BEST JOURNALISTS ARE NEVER OFF-DUTY. REGULAR CONTACTS BECOME GOOD FRIENDS.

The best journalists are never off-duty. Regular contacts become good friends. And friends become good contacts. Separating the professional and social relationship is not as difficult as it might appear. Good contacts know what you do for a living. They recognise when information might be valuable. Equally, no sensible reporter would jeopardise the relationship with a contact, or a friend, by treating them unfairly.

Maintaining contacts is the same as maintaining any relationship. Keep in touch, socialise when possible, and remember to give and take. Some information is best kept private in return for trust.

Some contacts offer information anonymously. It may need to be checked with other sources before it can be broadcast. Others will be only too willing to be interviewed as an on-air source. And some will be public relations (PR) people, or press officers, whose job it is to contact the press on behalf of a commercial client. PR people may not sound like great contacts. After all, it is their job to give you and everybody else stories. They are not paid by you, the journalist, but by an organisation that may want them to apply 'spin' to the information they give you.

But a trusting relationship can lead to preferential treatment and a steady flow of inside information about major businesses or local authorities.

Sometimes, like any other friendship or business deal, the relationship may break down. Roy Greenslade wrote in the *Guardian* how he'd been friends with Jonathan King, who became known to the tabloids as a 'paedophile pop pervert'. Greenslade was assistant editor of the *Sun* when King wrote a column for the paper, and he'd appeared on King's radio shows. But after the former pop star was jailed for offences against teenage boys, Greenslade said he felt duped by King, who'd repeatedly told him he was innocent. He refused to answer King's letters and e-mails.

Martin Brunt was recruited from the *Sunday Mirror* when Sky News started. He's the station's crime correspondent, and says the value of contacts can never be underestimated:

Contacts are the most important thing. It's not complicated or very clever. It's a simple question of doing what I learned in newspapers; talking to people, never throwing away a phone number, going to see people and ringing them up from time to time.

It's not sitting in cellar bars getting drunk with coppers. You still do that a little bit but it's not like crime reporters used to work, where you lived in the press room at Scotland Yard, and slept there, and a policeman would come down at three in the morning with a story.

Most newsrooms don't do enough to keep track of contributors to the rest of their station's output. A database of their interests and expertise can be invaluable. Even phone-in callers can provide news content. Just be aware that under the Data Protection Act people's details shouldn't be used without their permission.

'CONTACTS ARE THE MOST IMPORTANT THING. IT'S NOT COMPLICATED OR VERY CLEVER. IT'S A SIMPLE QUESTION OF . . . NEVER THROWING AWAY A PHONE NUMBER.'

THINKPIECE

THE ROLE OF PRESS OFFICERS

Press officers are potential contacts. They'll be the source of many stories. But it is also important to recognise the different roles of journalists and PR people.

Columnist Cristina Odone, writing in the *Guardian* in April 2006, responded to a PR professional's assertion that there was a 'moral equivalence' between the two professions: 'Journalists are in the business of exposing the truth, PRs are in the business of twisting it. Journalists want nothing more than to strip away the protective layers with which the powerful camouflage their objectives or their achievements; PRs are paid by the powerful to prevent precisely this. So, no, there is no moral equivalence between journalism and PR.'

REMEMBER

➤ Anyone can become a good contact

➤ Stay in touch with your contacts – cultivate them

➤ Back-up your contact information – always keep a hard copy

➤ Don't compromise your impartiality

➤ Never throw away a phone number.

ROUTINE CALLS

Every newsroom carries out routine check calls to the emergency services: police, fire, ambulance, coastguards. A radio station might make them every hour; TV might make them before each bulletin with just enough time to spare to write the story and despatch camera crews if needed.

The calls are often carried out by junior members of staff, which is probably a false economy given how important the result can be. A warm telephone manner and incisive, but never rude, questioning used to be the keys to unlocking information from occasionally reticent control room personnel. Nowadays police and fire services are more likely to offer the increasing number of news organisations a recorded message service – the voice-bank. This is essentially second-best. There's no substitute for talking to a real person. Even when a police inspector was restricted for operational reasons from giving too much information about, for example, a fatal stabbing, other facts could be gleaned from other sources – the ambulance service, perhaps – and a story could be written.

THERE'S NO SUBSTITUTE FOR TALKING TO A REAL PERSON.

The information on voice-banks can be limited and the journalist relies on police or fire service personnel, usually in a press office rather than an operational officer, to update the information. Follow-up calls will be directed through the organisation's press office, rather than straight to the senior officers in charge of an incident. Police press offices in particular can now control an important part of the news agenda – that relating to criminal activity.

The use of voice-banks and press offices underlines the increased importance to the emergency services of managing their relationship with the media. It also means old-fashioned contacts with serving staff in those services are even more important for journalists. The reporter who has a trusting relationship with senior detectives can steal a march on his or her rivals.

REMEMBER

- ➤ Call regularly
- ➤ Never assume recorded information is up-to-date – or complete
- ➤ Always try to speak to a real person
- ➤ Adopt a friendly telephone manner and develop a rapport with the person on the other end of the line
- ➤ Remember that the calls are just the start of the news-gathering process.

FREELANCES AND AGENCIES

Freelance reporters, either self-employed or working for agencies, are an important source of news copy and story tip-offs for most news organisations. These 'stringers' or correspondents, will cover court cases, for example, when broadcasters can't afford to send their own reporters. The origin of the word 'stringer' is obscure. The *Oxford English Dictionary* suggests it may be because they string words together.

Freelance photographers provide 'stills' (photographs) of people in the news to TV stations. These may be photos they have taken themselves or 'pick-ups', pictures they have collected from family members. Freelances who also work for the print media are unlikely to sell their best or exclusive stories to broadcast newsrooms because newspapers and magazines pay considerably more.

Many people working for broadcasters are themselves freelance, of course, but they won't be asked to come back for another shift if they start selling the story they're working on to an immediate rival.

WIRE SERVICES

National and international news stories come into newsrooms on 'the wires'. They are called 'wires' because they used to be teleprinter services; now they are delivered by the Internet or satellite. The information available includes everything from share prices to racing results, and the full range of news and sports stories. There are diary subscription services too which provide advance notice of news events – with contact numbers for reporters to get in touch with PR agencies and press offices.

The main UK news agency is the Press Association (PA). Associated Press (AP) is a US equivalent. Reuters is an international name in news gathering and now has a division specialising in electronic news media, as do Associated Press Television News (APTN) and United Press International (UPI).

IN A LIVE BROADCAST, THE WIRE SERVICE MAY BE CREDITED AS THE SOURCE OF INFORMATION IF IT IS NOT CONFIRMED BY ANOTHER SOURCE.

These are services that broadcast organisations subscribe to; they are paying for information, pictures and sound. There was a time when newsrooms trusted the wires implicitly. PA was thought to be the ultimate arbiter of truth. Nowadays wire services are not revered in quite the same way, but are still considered reliable. In a live broadcast, the wire service may be credited as the source of information if it is not confirmed by another source. A conscientious journalist will check information whenever possible. Two sources are always better than one.

TIP BOX

Remember that freelance agencies and wire services are not just working for you – everybody else will have the same information, unless you pay to keep it exclusive.

PRESS RELEASES

Every newsroom receives a steady supply of press releases, either electronically or in the post. Releases come from pressure groups, politicians, government and community organisations, sports clubs – in fact, anyone who has a story to tell.

Each contains a potential news story. Whether the story is worth telling depends on the judgement of copy-tasters (see Chapter 2) and intake desks. Not all will be worth following up.

Many are just thinly veiled attempts to gain free advertising. Some will provide filler material or short copy stories. Others will be the starting point for investigations or will provide big stories in their own right. Press releases always include contact details and usually offer the chance to speak to people the organisation is 'putting up' for interview. A press release is, by its nature, only one side of the story. Following up a press release may mean challenging the information it contains and approaching people whose views oppose those of its writers. This is an essential part of balanced and impartial journalism. It would be a naïve lobbyist who did not recognise that you will need to do this.

Many news releases will be subject to an **embargo**. This is a request that the news is not published or broadcast until a certain date and time: e.g. 'embargoed until 0001 hrs, Friday 28 July'. It helps forward planning. The news organisation is able to gather information and conduct interviews ready for publication. It ensures the story is released on all media at the same time. No-one gets the exclusive. Embargos have no weight in law, but they are almost always worth observing. *To break an embargo is to risk losing the trust of the organisation that provided the information.* The embargos on the New Year's and Queen's Birthday Honours Lists and the content of the Queen's Christmas message are almost always observed. But embargos can be used to manipulate news media, and editors often argue that they should run the story early. If one organisation breaks an embargo, the gloves are off and others will follow.

Electronic press releases

Some organisations use new technology for their media releases. Video news releases – containing footage and interviews to enable journalists to cover a story without leaving the office – sound like a good way for organisations to ensure coverage. Pressure groups use them to get their message across. There are also EPKs – electronic press kits – often used to promote film releases. They will contain clips from the movie and interviews with the stars – Hollywood 'A-listers' who are never likely to visit your neck of the woods.

MOST NEWS ORGANISATIONS ARE RIGHTLY SUSPICIOUS OF USING THIRD-PARTY MATERIAL TO TELL A STORY.

But most news organisations are rightly suspicious of using third-party material to tell a story. To do so surrenders editorial control. The Hollywood stars won't answer the questions you want to ask; they'll just talk about their film role. And the campaigner is unlikely to be responding to the challenges you would make if you were face-to-face over a microphone. Agencies that supply this sort of material are offering a service to commercial clients, who see it as an alternative to paying for advertising.

AGENCY INTERVIEWS FOR RADIO SHOULD ONLY BE USED WHEN IT SUITS YOU.

Agency interviews for radio should only be used when it suits you. If they want their material used, manipulate them to your advantage. Insist on local content in the interview.

VIDEO FROM A PRESSURE GROUP WILL NORMALLY ONLY BE USED AS A LAST RESORT AND WITH A STRONG ON-SCREEN DISCLAIMER EXPLAINING WHERE THE PICTURES HAVE COME FROM.

Video from a pressure group will normally only be used as a last resort *and* with a strong on-screen disclaimer explaining where the pictures have come from. That's because the broadcaster cannot guarantee they present an unbalanced view of events.

Some video footage is so graphic you will want to use it anyway. But you must tell the audience its source. The environmental pressure group Greenpeace now insists that journalists on their payroll write impartially as if they were working for an independent news gatherer. In January 2006 Greenpeace vessels clashed with Japanese whalers in the southern oceans off Antarctica, and the dramatic pictures were shown worldwide. It would have been hugely expensive for broadcasters to follow the Greenpeace ships as they tried to find the whalers in hostile seas. But there was footage freely available – from Greenpeace's own video crews. Broadcasters could present the political arguments about whaling by using the Greenpeace footage and conducting their own interviews to create a balanced report.

REMEMBER

➤ Maintain your objectivity when considering press releases

➤ Try to find the best angle for your audience

➤ Beware of 'spin' – there might be a better story they don't want you to hear

➤ Tell the audience if audio or video does not come from your own organisation.

A CLOSER LOOK

LIVING WITHOUT PRESS RELEASES

Is it possible for newsrooms to operate without press releases and a steady flow of e-mails from pressure groups and regular contacts? Undoubtedly, yes, as experiments in BBC local radio have proved.

Radio WM, in the West Midlands, banned press releases and e-mail for a week. Only the news editor and bulletin editor were allowed access to them. Radio Cambridgeshire went a step further, banning press releases and e-mail in a 'non-rota' week. All the usual shift patterns – except those of programme presenters and newsreaders – were scrapped.

Stuart Ratcliffe, one of the journalists in the Cambridgeshire trial, says: 'The producers and reporters just went out and we did some fantastic stuff. All our microphones, all our radio cars were out. It was exhausting, because we were never sure if we had enough, but it worked.

'After that, from what we'd learned, we re-jigged all our rota patterns. There was a whole reappraisal of the way we worked.'

Sue Owen, the Managing Editor of BBC Radio Stoke

Sue Owen, the Managing Editor of Radio Stoke, says it's harder work than relying on press releases, but stations running these experiments get more and better stories than if their staff are desk-bound: 'They get more original stories and meet more normal people – more people that aren't the "voices on sticks" we use all the time.

'We've had some of the best stories by saying, "Grab your Nagra [a portable recorder] and go out and find your story." '

NEWS CONFERENCES

Press conferences are set-piece events staged by organisations wanting to make news. These days they're also known as news conferences or media conferences because they are open to all media, not just the press. Journalists often call them *pressers*. They range from government announcements and lobbying by pressure groups to opportunities to interview celebrities and sports stars.

Football clubs will call a news or media conference every time they sign a new player or appoint a new manager. But it is rare indeed for a club to announce at a news conference that they have sacked their manager. This illustrates the problem with news conferences. They are controlled by the organisation that stages them. Access to the conference is restricted to invited members of the media. But as long as everybody gets equal access to all the interviewees, the conferences are at least fair to all news organisations.

You need to assess the amount of interest in a story before you go to a news conference, because that determines how early you need to turn up to get a good place. You will need to know where the main speaker will be sitting so you can position your microphone for the best sound quality. If hundreds of press are likely to be there you may need to arrive several hours ahead of the start if possible. If the event is of only local interest, 20 minutes to half an hour will be enough time to set up.

WILL THERE BE AN OPPORTUNITY FOR ONE-TO-ONE INTERVIEWS BEFORE OR . . . AFTER THE MAIN CONFERENCE, OR WILL YOU HAVE TO MAKE DO WITH THE MATERIAL RECORDED DURING THE 'PRESSER'?

It is important to establish the ground rules before a news conference. Will there be an opportunity for one-to-one interviews before or (more usually) after the main conference, or will you have to make do with the material recorded during the 'presser'?

Whether they are well organised or not, press conferences are a good place to meet new contacts and establish relationships with press officers and others who can assist you. If there is an opportunity for individual interviews with footballers and managers, for example, that is the time to try to earn their trust – and ask for their personal contact details.

Photo-calls

Photo-calls are stage-managed media events similar to news conferences with the emphasis on the picture opportunities they offer the media. They sometimes take place before or after a formal news conference.

The traditional accompaniment to the announcement of a new manager or player at a football club is the photo-opportunity on the pitch, where the new signing is paraded with club scarf and a shirt with his name on it. It's a TV and newspaper cliché. Politicians' election visits are carefully planned so that the 'right' pictures appear on the evening news – the would-be Prime Minister with nurses/teachers/people from ethnic minorities, for example. Camera crews and reporters look for the slip-ups amidst the spin.

Sometimes what happens at a photo-call becomes the story. When Prince Charles appeared with his sons William and Harry on the ski slopes prior to his 2005 wedding, the brief question and answer session began with an inquiry from BBC Royal Correspondent Nicholas Witchell about how the young princes were looking forward to their father's wedding. The microphones picked up the Prince of Wales muttering: 'Bloody people. I can't bear that man. He's so awful, he really is.'

REMEMBER

➤ Always arrive in plenty of time for news conferences
➤ Establish the ground rules – will there be one-to-one interviews?
➤ Find a good position for recording

> ➤ Try to find the story behind the 'spin'
> ➤ Use media events as a chance to network and improve your contacts.

PROTESTS AND DEMONSTRATIONS

DEMOS FOCUS ATTENTION ON ISSUES, BUT THEY HAVE TO BE CONSIDERED IN CONTEXT. TO WHAT EXTENT ARE THE ORGANISERS SETTING THE NEWS AGENDA, AND THEREFORE MANIPULATING US AS JOURNALISTS?

Some pressure groups and campaigners will tire of lobbying through press releases and letters to the local papers. They'll stage a protest or demonstration. Others will go for the grand gesture from the off. Bob Geldof did not send out press releases before he urged people to march on Edinburgh during the 2005 G8 summit. Demos focus attention on issues, but they have to be considered in context. To what extent are the organisers setting the news agenda, and therefore manipulating us as journalists? There is a trade-off between the drama these events provide and the threat to the independence of the news organisation.

The BBC used to have a rule about not previewing demonstrations. It was felt that publicising the event gave the organisers free advertising to attract bigger crowds than they would otherwise get. Current practice suggest the rules have changed. Geldof's comments came at the press conference announcing the Live8 series of concerts – such a momentous event that it attracted worldwide coverage (or at least coverage throughout the major part of the world where rock'n'roll is a cultural force). Consequently, the call to march on Edinburgh had a huge audience. In the event, the greatest publicity on the march itself attached to breakaway 'anarchist' elements who clashed with police. Geldof and Bono were welcomed by the G8 leaders and won what they claimed to be significant concessions over the cancelling of debt in Africa.

In another example, the pressure group Fathers 4 Justice, campaigning for the rights of absent fathers to have access to their children, achieved public notoriety and no little sympathy by dressing as superheroes and climbing public landmarks including Buckingham Palace, the Foreign Office and the Severn Bridge. Many of their protests caused widespread disruption to traffic, and could not have been ignored by local media. When Fathers 4 Justice threw flour-bombs at the Prime Minister, Tony Blair, from the public gallery of the House of Commons in May 2004, it was international news. And four months later, no editor could resist Batman scaling the Queen's balcony.

But there is a limit to such activity. When the *Sun* reported early in 2006 that Fathers 4 Justice were planning to kidnap the Prime Minister's son, the leader of the group said that would be going too far. Matt O'Connor said: 'If our position is constantly undermined by extremists, we will shut down the Fathers 4 Justice campaign.' And he did.

REMEMBER

> ➤ Don't be manipulated
> ➤ Remember the need for impartial, balanced reporting
> ➤ Consult editorial guidelines if you are concerned that the protestors, or even you, might be breaking the law.

THINKPIECE

NEWS PROCESSING

There is a problem for people working in modern broadcast newsrooms, particularly those in the larger organisations where journalists are working for numerous outlets, including online and interactive services. The problem is that many journalists (often very capable people who have either had or will have great careers as producers, reporters and presenters) find themselves in the role not of news gatherers but of news processors. They rewrite press releases or make new versions of stories that other people have gathered and written. The news processors could be forgiven for asking if what they are doing is proper journalism.

They are certainly one step removed from most of the sources outlined in this chapter. But successful broadcast journalists – those who hope to lift themselves above this bottom rung of the career ladder – will question the information they are processing, and check it out with primary sources wherever possible.

Paul Chantler and Sim Harris were prescient in their 1997 book *Local Radio Journalism* (Focal Press) when they warned that new technology was leading to one of the biggest dangers of all: 'There could be a tendency to think of news as that which simply appears on the screen or the printer. Never forget that real news is what you go out and find through your own efforts.'

The printer – in the sense of the machine in the corner of the newsroom that provided a landline feed of copy and 'rip and read' bulletins, rather than the printer linked to your computer – is now old technology. And it is simplistic to suggest that what you find out for yourself is the only 'real news'. But the warning is sound more than a decade on. It can be argued that 'proper journalism' is still the craft of finding new stories.

Nonetheless, journalists have always reworked material collected by others. The sub-editor on a newspaper and the producer in radio or television take others' work and where possible improve it.

In television, where team work is so important, several reporters can work on one package. The senior correspondent will usually write and present the item, but interviews and sequences of shots within the finished film may have been collected by others. A producer will have been assigned to co-ordinate the different ingredients and supervise the assembly of the final product. Any member of the team may need to check the facts, or other people's written copy, as they go along. It is a poor researcher who accepts others' data unquestioningly, and a poor reporter who sticks to the research brief when events in the field suggest the details he has been given are wrong.

WHEREVER POSSIBLE GO TO PRIMARY SOURCES.

Wherever possible go to primary sources. That became the mantra of the BBC's local online news services after a series of users complained about inaccuracies in stories based on local radio copy. Radio journalists in the pre-digital age did not have to worry about accurate spelling. Some spellings – of names, for example – might be deliberately spelled differently to aid pronunciation.

Now, online journalists are involved in re-sourcing – not just re-versioning – material, and in finding fresh stories. They are content providers in their own right. The decision in the BBC not to rely on unchecked local radio copy was controversial within the organisation at the time, but it vastly reduced the number of basic journalistic mistakes, like names, places and facts that were wrong. Mostly mistakes happened because accurate spelling was not essential in radio and it is online. Other errors were easier for the audience to spot because web pages are permanent while the spoken word is transient.

Hugh Berlyn, Editor of BBC News Interactive, English Regions, sums up the change in approach:

It used to be the case that online journalists in the BBC were just processing other people's stories. The attitude was, 'We don't need more journalists, we've got plenty in television and radio.' But since we decided not to rely on local radio copy, that has changed. Our people have to be content providers. They know how to source a story and they know right from wrong. True, they don't get out of the office much, but that's true of regional newspapers these days.

Hugh Berlin, Editor of BBC News Interactive, English Regions

THINKPIECE

OFCOM:
'MATERIAL LIKELY
TO ENCOURAGE
OR INCITE THE
COMMISSION
OF CRIME OR TO
LEAD TO DISORDER
MUST NOT BE
INCLUDED IN
TELEVISION OR
RADIO SERVICES.'

AN ETHICAL DILEMMA

Protests are good copy. They can turn ugly, leading to clashes with opponents or the police. The Poll Tax demonstrations in Margaret Thatcher's era turned into riots. The Countryside Alliance's demonstration against the Fox Hunting Ban under Tony Blair's premiership led to confrontation with police in riot gear.

Often broadcasters will be told about a demo in advance – even before the police or other authorities know about it. That is because the protestors want publicity for their actions. Public opinion is their principal weapon. It helps their case if they get coverage even before the police arrive. To what extent is it acceptable for broadcasters to collude in what might turn into criminal activity?

The Ofcom code says material likely to encourage or incite the commission of crime or to lead to disorder must not be included in television or radio services. But that does not prevent journalists attending illegal demonstrations.

The BBC Editorial Guidelines say 'comprehensive coverage of demonstrations, disturbances and riots is an important part of our news reporting,' but:

- 'We assess the risk that by previewing likely prospects of disturbances we might encourage them.
- We withdraw immediately if we suspect we are inflaming the situation.
- We treat estimates of involvement with due scepticism and report wide disparities and name the sources of the figures.'

There are also special rules for live reporting. There must be a delay in transmission, or the chance to cut away and record material for use in an edited report, if the level of violence or disorder becomes too graphic.

COURTS AND TRIBUNALS

Courts and the judicial process have been a mainstay of news reporting since the first modern newspapers were published. The reason for attending courts is not simply because the institutions themselves are important parts of our constitution – even though they are. Nor is it because 'justice has to be seen to be done' – even though that is a fundamental principle of British law. We cover courts because they provide great stories. Murder, rape, robbery and massive fraud all end up in the courts. That's why it's important that journalists understand the rules governing the various courts – juvenile, magistrates', crown, civil, courts of appeal, coroners' – and tribunals.

The law on contempt of court is designed to prevent evidence that could prejudice a fair trial appearing on the media before it has been presented in court. There's more on the law that applies to journalism and broadcasting later in this book.

Crown court and higher court listings are available online at www.courtserve2.net. Magistrates' court lists are available from the court clerks. You will need to make regular checks about forthcoming cases, because preliminary hearings are often postponed or adjourned, and there are many potential delays in the judicial system.

When a case comes to court, you need to make the same assessment as you would for any media event. Will there be so many media there that you will need to turn up especially early to get a place on the press bench? It's normally 'first-come-first-served', although access to some large trials is by ticket only, or a special pass arranged with newsrooms in advance. Sometimes an electronic feed of events in the court will be relayed to a separate press room.

COURT REPORTING PRESENTS SPECIAL PROBLEMS FOR BROADCASTERS BECAUSE TO DATE THERE IS NO ACCEPTANCE THAT ELECTRONIC RECORDING MEDIA SHOULD BE ALLOWED INSIDE COURT ROOMS.

Court reporting presents special problems for broadcasters because to date there is no acceptance that electronic recording media should be allowed inside court rooms. The Criminal Justice Act 1925 makes it an offence to take pictures in court and to publish those pictures. It means that broadcast journalists have to be imaginative in telling court stories, while sticking to the legal requirements to be fair, accurate and contemporaneous.

Television has particular problems. How do you tell a story with no pictures? Courtroom artists are one solution. Pastel sketches show the accused or witnesses in the dock, usually being cross-examined. It may surprise viewers to know that artists are not permitted to sketch inside the court itself. Their remarkable work is done at speed and from memory. Computer graphics, placing figures in virtual courtrooms, are a more recent and often more time-consuming alternative. Graphics artists will visit courts and make notes of the interior layout to create a virtual representation of the scene. The faces of defendants and witnesses, taken from stills or video taken outside court, will be added to the digital image to replicate the scene inside.

The option favoured by Sky News during the Hutton inquiry and the child abuse trial of Michael Jackson is the most elaborate, ambitious and expensive – a full re-enactment of the court proceedings using actors.

The O. J. Simpson trial and that of the British nanny Louise Woodward were seen worldwide because they took place in US states where TV cameras were allowed in court. This version of justice being seen to be done does not yet extend to TV cameras in British courtrooms. There is a fear that witnesses would play to the camera or would be afraid to appear if they could be widely recognised by TV viewers. The idea that people would play to the camera was also used as an argument against the televising of Parliament a couple of decades ago.

➤ Learn where to find information about forthcoming court cases

➤ Check court listings regularly

➤ Prepare for a court visit as you would for any media event

➤ Know the law on court reporting and contempt

➤ Be aware of the problems broadcasters – and in particular TV – face when reporting court proceedings.

GOVERNMENT BODIES

Every government department has its own teams of press officers, many of them regionally based. The Central Office of Information used to be an apolitical source of information working within civil service guidelines. After the 1997 election of New Labour, there was growing concern among media commentators about the politicisation of the civil service – and, in particular, government press officers. When dealing with them, you need to be aware of the risks of 'spin' – the manipulation of journalists by the political parties' marketing specialists or 'spin doctors'.

There are also dozens of public bodies set up by government, sometimes known as quangos. They include regional development agencies, and everything from the Design Council to the Health and Safety Executive. There is a list of these bodies on the Cabinet Office website www.knowledgenetwork.gov.uk/ndpb. Most have press officers looking for publicity, and are able to help when stories about their area of expertise are in the news.

POLITICIANS

Broadcast journalists spend an inordinate amount of time persuading newsworthy people with a story to tell, or a valued opinion to express, to talk into a microphone. We also talk to politicians. Elected representatives thrive on what one of their number famously called 'the oxygen of publicity'.

MPs and councillors will issue press releases and call newsrooms either in person or through their press representatives. Anyone with a political cause to promote will want to appear on the media. Some develop a reputation as 'dial-a-quote merchants'. Whether what they have to say is worth reporting depends on the story. If the purpose of their involvement appears to be self-publicity, you may prefer to ignore them.

Council leaders, their opposition counterparts, local cabinet members and nowadays elected mayors, who may have considerable power, are worth cultivating as contacts.

Whenever a journalist deals with a politician, the journalist must be aware of the political agenda and the need for impartial reporting. At election times, this is especially important and there are specific, legally enforceable guidelines on the interviewing of candidates. These have been drawn up to ensure impartiality in the electoral process, and are available online, in section six of the Ofcom Broadcasting Code (www.ofcom.org.uk).

If you are looking for fringe or minority political opinion, just type the specific area of minority interest plus 'blog' into a search engine. The blogs will lead you to news sources and potential interviewees.

COUNCILS

Local government is a prime source of controversy, a mainstay of local news reporting. Planning rows, controversial policy decisions and occasionally corruption all make headlines. These days, most broadcast organisations do not consider it worthwhile covering council meetings and they certainly don't bother with council committees. But professional relationships with council press officers are worth fostering. And it is worth remembering that debate in council chambers can often be filmed or recorded when newsworthy decisions are being made. This is the stuff of local democracy and can lead to lively actuality. The conflict between New and Old Labour politicians in Walsall provided regular fireworks on regional TV in the Midlands in the 1990s.

Trading standards departments offer a steady flow of consumer stories. Raising public awareness of citizens' rights is part of their brief. So, they often enlist the help of reporters to expose wrong-doing. Such stories can offer two bites at the same cherry: the exposé followed by the court case. The reporter earns the kudos of helping to uncover law-breaking. And where suspected criminality has been exposed by investigative reporting, trading standards can be offered the evidence to support a prosecution – and a follow-up story.

REMEMBER

➤ Don't be manipulated – beware of 'spin'
➤ Cultivate national and local politicians and government officials as contacts
➤ Remain politically impartial
➤ Remember the need for balanced reporting
➤ Know the guidelines on election coverage.

COMMUNITIES

Schools, churches, voluntary and residents' associations, clubs, societies and special interest groups often welcome coverage of their affairs. Trades unions and business organisations can provide interesting copy. Consumer watchdog groups, both statutory and voluntary, also have stories to tell.

MANY BROADCASTERS ARE CONCERNED THAT THEY DO NOT FULLY REFLECT THE COMMUNITIES THEY SERVE.

Beyond the reporting of organised groupings, many broadcasters are concerned that they do not fully reflect the communities they serve. The quest to represent those who are traditionally under-represented in the news continues, and it is at a local level that it can be most effective. Winning the confidence of potential news sources is no more or less difficult be they cabinet ministers or costermongers, successful rappers or suspected rapists.

The growth of local radio and the BBC's development of local TV have been presented by the corporation as attempts to engage local communities. Campaigners for community broadcasting argue that the top-down approach from a national corporation is the wrong way to go about this. Community radio stations, some of which are not on air permanently but granted short-term restricted service licences (RSLs) by Ofcom, are usually run by local people. They attempt to encourage contributions from anyone in the community with a story to tell.

REMEMBER

➤ Cultivate local contacts
➤ Try to find stories from groups who are not normally represented in the media.

TIP-OFFS

Tip-offs to journalists take many forms. A tip might be information from trusted freelances, for which they will expect to be paid an appropriate fee when the story has been investigated and (hopefully) confirmed. Or it might be a call from a member of the public. Radio stations and regional TV encourage listeners and viewers to call in with stories. It is a cheap way of finding exclusive material, and is always worth the effort of discounting those stories that don't make it to air. It is also a way of engaging groups who otherwise feel excluded from the media. The BBC's local television pilot in the Midlands, between December 2005 and August 2006, focused on encouraging contributions from people and communities not given a voice by traditional media.

There are also anonymous tip-offs. Sometimes they offer an immediate lead to a story. Someone has noticed armed police surrounding a house. A siege is in progress. The caller doesn't want to get involved, but thinks the story should be on the news. At other times, anonymous tips need to be treated with a healthy scepticism. The call could be malicious, a hoax. It could come from someone with an unfounded grievance, or be well-intentioned but inaccurate.

For example, a radio reporter was once hoodwinked into broadcasting that a gorilla had escaped from a local zoo, and was a danger to the public. The source was the zoo owner, who was known to the reporter and had been interviewed by him before. He made a series of calls reporting on the primate's progress. The station duly reported that a gorilla was on the loose. It wasn't until the reporter rang the zoo back, suggesting he might come out to report on the growing crisis, that the source admitted he'd made the story up. Was he trying to drum up trade on a slack Sunday afternoon? Or just playing a practical joke?

IF YOU RECEIVE AN ANONYMOUS CALL, ALWAYS ASK FOR EXTRA INFORMATION THAT WILL HELP CHECK IT OUT.

The only way to avoid being hoaxed is to find a second source for the story. If you receive an anonymous call, always ask for extra information that will help check it out. If someone says there's an MRSA outbreak at a hospital, ask for as many details as you can of who has been affected and on which wards. If you then approach the hospital with a series of facts, even unsourced ones, it is much harder for them to deny the story. It is more likely that they will correct any mistakes in your information, and you will end up with what you hoped for – an accurate story.

Off the record

When a tip-off is from a trusted source who doesn't want to be named, the question of *off-the-record* information arises. It's important both parties understand what this means. There are varying interpretations and the ground-rules have to be made clear in any relationship. It might be that the informant did not mind the information being broadcast so long as they were not identified as the source. It might mean the story should only run if it can be confirmed by somebody else. Or it could mean that the information should be merely guidance to the reporter in the pursuit of the story.

> *A SOURCE CANNOT TURN ROUND AFTER REVEALING SOME JUICY TITBIT OF INFORMATION AND SAY: 'OH, BY THE WAY, THAT LAST BIT WAS OFF THE RECORD.'*

There is a useful guiding principle of the off-the-record briefing, used by the *Washington Post* reporters Bob Woodward and Carl Bernstein in *All the President's Men*, the story of the Watergate scandal that brought down US President Richard Nixon. They made it clear to sources that nothing could be placed off-the-record after it had been said. This means that a source cannot turn round after revealing some juicy titbit of information and say: 'Oh, by the way, that last bit was off the record.' The *Post*'s style guide says: 'We do not allow sources to change the ground-rules governing specific quotations after the fact. Once a quote is on the record it remains there.'

In investigative stories, you may be dealing with *whistleblowers*, insiders prepared to give you information about an organisation for which they work. They may lose their job if they are identified. If you promise to protect a source, the responsibility for that decision is yours. It is a fundamental ethical principle of journalism that you should not reveal sources. UK case law has not automatically protected journalists who want to keep information secret, and reporters have faced imprisonment. But the 1998 Human Rights Act incorporated the European Convention on Human Rights into English law. Article 10 upholds freedom of expression, which includes journalists' right to protect their sources, particularly when the story is in the public interest.

These niceties are important, but not much use to the reporter defending a libel action, when the story has to be justified by witnesses prepared to give evidence in court.

REMEMBER

➤ Beware of anonymous sources

➤ Question the motives of people offering tip-offs

➤ Seek a second source where possible

➤ Understand what you and others mean by 'off-the-record'

➤ Protect your sources.

A CLOSER LOOK

PROTECTING SOURCES – THE LEGAL POSITION

The right of journalists to protect their sources was established in English law after a six-year legal battle. In the case of Mersey Care NHS Trust against Robin Ackroyd, the High Court decided – in accordance with Article 10 of the European Convention on Human Rights, which gives a right to freedom of expression – that a journalist could only be ordered to reveal a source if there was a 'pressing social need'.

Ackroyd, a freelance journalist, was ordered by the High Court to say who gave him medical information for a *Daily Mirror* story about the Moors murderer Ian Brady. The trust which ran Ashworth secure hospital took the paper to court to find out who had leaked confidential medical records. The *Mirror* had fought the case all the way to the House of Lords, but lost, and had to reveal that Ackroyd was their source.

The trust then pursued Ackroyd through the courts. Mr Justice Tugendhat delivered the ruling in Ackroyd's favour in the High Court in February 2006. The journalist had been supported by the National Union of Journalists. The union's general secretary Jeremy Dear told the trade journal *Press Gazette* it was a fantastic verdict for all journalists: 'The fundamental point of principle – that there is a strong public interest in upholding journalists' right not to reveal their sources – has been maintained.'

The issue of journalists naming their sources was also highlighted when Dr David Kelly was identified by the government as the source of a BBC report that the government 'sexed up' a dossier about the reasons for going to war with Iraq (see Case study 3.3 later in this chapter for further details of the case and the subsequent Hutton Inquiry into Dr Kelly's death).

The Foreign Affairs Committee chairman, Donald Anderson MP, accused reporter Andrew Gilligan of changing his story when he gave evidence to them. The chairman said journalists should have to name their sources if they were making allegations under Parliamentary privilege (the committee's hearings are covered by privilege, which means accusations made during their business cannot be subject to a libel action).

Jeremy Dear, of the NUJ, told BBC News Online that 'whistleblowers' must be protected as they 'will not come forward if they think they are going to be grassed up at a later stage'.

He said one of the roles of journalists was to expose wrong-doing and bad practice by public institutions and big corporations: 'For that reason it is the golden rule of journalism that we don't betray our sources and are prepared to go to prison to uphold that principle.'

Ackroyd told the BBC at the time: 'Journalists protect their sources because they have a professional duty of confidence to them. It is not a standpoint we take because we are being difficult or precious. I do not reveal confidential sources of information as an overriding matter of conscience.'

When Ackroyd won his case on appeal, Mr Justice Tugendhat said that there must be a 'pressing social need' before an intermediary [the journalist] will be required to disclose her or his source. The judge concluded that Ackroyd was 'a responsible journalist whose purpose was to act in the public interest'.

The ruling depended on a series of competing factors – the right to medical privacy against the right to protect sources. The judge said courts should apply a test of 'proportionality' to such conflicts. One fact which helped Ackroyd win was his proven track record as a responsible investigative journalist. But during the six-year battle, none of his contacts could be sure they would remain confidential as a source, and his career suffered.

ROBIN ACKROYD: 'JOURNALISTS PROTECT THEIR SOURCES BECAUSE THEY HAVE A PROFESSIONAL DUTY OF CONFIDENCE TO THEM. IT IS NOT A STANDPOINT WE TAKE BECAUSE WE ARE BEING DIFFICULT OR PRECIOUS.'

OTHER NEWS MEDIA

No matter how good your news organisation, you are not going to get every story first. There are other journalists in other organisations trying just as hard to find stories. So, it is vital to check other media organisations. That means reading newspapers, watching TV, listening to radio, checking news blogs and subscribing to podcasts.

In large cities there may be several local or regional radio stations, and they will all be listening to each other, hoping they haven't been beaten to an item of news. If they have, common sense dictates that the listener will not have been listening to both stations at once, so an item will be lifted, checked out and run in the next bulletin by the station that missed it first time round. *Checking the information is vital. Just because somebody else reported it first does not give you legal immunity from libel or other legal actions.*

Spoilers

Rival regional TV stations monitor each other's output and are fiercely jealous of the other's exclusives. The 'exclusive' may not be a whole story – a key interview on a story everybody's covering will inspire just as much envy.

Tabloid newspapers are famous for running 'spoilers' – stories designed to spoil the impact of their rivals' scoops or cheque-book sign-ups. The spoilers will often take the form of a story written to suggest the beaten party has a story just as good as or better than their rivals'. This practice is not common in broadcasting, partly because cheque-book journalism (paying for stories) is not common in broadcast news, but there are versions of it. For example, at the end of the trial of kidnapper and murderer Michael Samms, reporter Keith Wilkinson of Central TV in the West Midlands secured an exclusive interview with Stephanie Slater, the key witness in the case. She was the estate agent Samms kidnapped and kept prisoner in a wheelie bin. Central's BBC rival Midlands Today put together a background report using extensive clips of on-camera comments by Ms Slater taken from a press conference she'd given when she was released months earlier. It was a poor second to Central's coverage, but at least BBC viewers had been told the story.

A different agenda?

The newsroom of the Independent Local Radio (ILR) station in Coventry, Mercia Sound, prided itself in the early 1980s on never being beaten to a major story by the local newspaper the *Coventry Evening Telegraph*. Few radio stations can make that claim today. Newspapers often have ten times as many journalists as radio stations covering the same patch. So, radio stations end up following newspapers – not a proud boast for a medium that has immediate access to the means of broadcasting information.

But that should not stop the drive to be different. Sue Owen, the Managing Editor of BBC Radio Stoke, has the confidence to say: 'Newspapers simply do not set our agenda. We set our own. We should be doing something different.'

BBC2's *Newsnight* reports the front pages of the next day's papers, and most breakfast programmes feature a review of the morning's papers. A healthy respect for other journalists' output should not detract from the drive to be first with the news.

➤ Know what the competition is doing – check them out regularly

➤ Never use other media organisations' information without checking it

➤ Be confident – don't let other media set your agenda

➤ Always aim to be first – and accurate.

FREEDOM OF INFORMATION ACT (FOI)

Being first to report the news doesn't necessarily mean racing round chasing ambulances. Patience and a cool head are virtues, particularly if you are using the Freedom of Information Act 2000 as a research tool. Information released under the Act, often at the request of journalists, can take months to emerge because of the appeals procedure built into the Act. But when it finally comes into the open, that information may be dynamite.

You can make an application, in writing, for information to any public authority. They have 20 days to respond. They may charge a fee, according to a published scale of charges. They may be able to argue that collecting the information will be too costly. If they can't or won't respond, they may issue a Refusal Notice. Then the appeal process starts. Under the Act, authorities have a duty to provide advice and assistance to applicants.

The Act covers government departments, councils, NHS bodies, schools, colleges and universities, and the police. It also applies to the Houses of Commons and Lords, the Northern Ireland Assembly and the National Assembly for Wales. The Freedom of Information (Scotland) Act 2002 covers Scottish public authorities.

The *Daily Mail* requested details of an exchange of letters between the Metropolitan Police Commissioner Sir Ian Blair and a senior civil servant written in the immediate aftermath of the shooting by armed officers of Brazilian Jean Charles de Menezes at Stockwell tube station in 2005. The letters showed that the Commissioner had tried to block the Independent Police Complaints Commission's inquiry into the killing. He said he should be allowed to suspend the section of the Police Reform Act that requires information to be supplied to the IPCC. The *Mail*'s headline asked if the Met Chief had become a 'law unto himself?' The *Mail* heard about the letters during Sir Ian's evidence to a Parliamentary committee, on 13 September 2005. The FOI request resulted in a story on 1 October. That was quick work. The Act is a valuable tool for investigative journalists, but don't expect a story on the same day.

Here's another interesting example, bearing in mind what we said earlier about police voice-banks. In August 2006, the *Press Gazette* reported that 'a reporter found out via an FOI request that more than 5,000 incidents (5,083 to be precise) took place over a weekend when a police voice-bank reported nothing had happened.'

Anyone can request information under the Act. The Information Commissioner's Office will rule on requests that are refused. It is an independent public body set up to promote access to official information – though it is also charged with protecting personal information.

Details of how to make an application under the Act are explained on the Information Commissioner's website www.ico.gov.uk.

Often, a contact will make the initial inquiry and journalists can act on the results. When the government decided against a blanket ban on smoking in public, the charity Cancer Research UK made an application under the Act. They knew that research in Northern Ireland showed more than 90 per cent of the public supported a total ban, and they wanted the results of the consultation exercise in England. Three months later – in February 2006 – the government line changed and Parliament voted for a total ban.

Responses to the Act, by government departments for example, are officially 'made public'. That doesn't mean issuing a press release: it may just mean publishing the information on a website. *So, it is a question of knowing where to look, and then interpreting the information. Just because it is available to everyone doesn't mean everyone will be looking for it.*

There is a very good guide to using the Act written by investigative journalist Heather Brooke (with a foreword by *Private Eye* editor Ian Hislop). *Your Right to Know: A Citizen's Guide to the Freedom of Information Act* explains how the Act can be used by reporters. It includes advice on the law in practice (including in Scotland) and even a chapter on business reporting showing how to get hold of contracts, tenders and performance evaluations. Heather Brooke's website www.yrtk.org has links to examples of FOI reporting and tips on how to prevent public authorities trying to block journalists' requests for information.

INTERACTIVE NEWS AS A SOURCE

The Internet is so popular that viewers of digital television are invited to click through pages as if they were surfing the Net rather than switching TV channels. The growth of TV content on the Internet means viewers can select which stories they want to watch, or even tailor their viewing to news about subjects they have pre-selected. The RSS system (Really Simple Syndication or Rich Site Summary) means web users choose topics they want to know about and are alerted when stories on those topics are available to view. News and sports content was the 'driver', in the Net jargon, for this type of video on demand. Interactivity means more feedback from viewers – and more story ideas.

INTERACTIVITY MEANS MORE FEEDBACK FROM VIEWERS – AND MORE STORY IDEAS.

Viewers of interactive news services click on a mouse or press the red button on their remote control and choose the story they want to watch. These viewers feel they have more control of the broadcast process than they could ever have imagined in the pre-digital age. Many broadcasters hope the red button is more than just another level of public service. They think it encourages viewers to be more involved in the news making process. Viewers will get in touch by text and e-mail with comments and opinions on stories and their treatment. They might also offer new stories. Still others will be bloggers – with their own sites offering information and opinion.

Citizen journalists

The opportunity for viewers, listeners and Net users to share their experiences of breaking news stories means witnesses – to terrorist attacks, police operations and natural disasters – are easier to find than in the days when tracking down

BBC News Interactive

Gary Duffy

sources relied on journalistic legwork and phone-bashing. These **citizen journalists** are a valuable news source, and may provide eye-witness accounts, via Have Your Say boxes on websites, and pictures, from mobile phones, digital video and stills cameras.

Gary Duffy, UK Editor of BBC News Interactive, says: 'If there's a sudden explosion, oil refinery fire or terrorist attack, or anything like that, within minutes now we expect to have user-generated content on BBC output.' A specialist hub within News Interactive, staffed by at least six people throughout the day, is responsible for getting content to the websites and to television and for passing on contacts to radio stations.

Matthew Eltringham, an assistant editor within the unit, says material from the public has proved its value on all types of stories: 'There's obviously the breaking news, where you want immediate eye-witness accounts of what's happening around you, but we use user-content in lots of different ways. We ask people to talk about their own experiences – whether it's pension funds, drugs or sexual harassment in the army. If it's a particularly strong case study, we'll use them in our coverage across television, radio and online. In a way it's a shortcut to finding the human aspects of the stories, but it's incredibly effective.'

The BBC said in April 2006 new photo supplied of Gary Duffy after a year-long review called Creative Future: 'Increasingly, audiences of all ages not only want the choice of what to watch and listen to when they want, they also expect to take part, debate, create and control. Interactivity and user-generated content are increasingly important stimuli for the creative process.'

Blogs

Blogs are a fantastic way to track down first-person testimony and witnesses to stories and events. There are news-based blogging communities, many offering 'citizen journalists' the chance to report their own news. Some have payment systems, although the business models for successful blogging are in their infancy.

Shayne Bowman and Chris Willis, who run the Hypergene.net weblog, offered a definition of 'participatory journalism' as early as 2003. In *We Media: How Audiences are Shaping the Future of News and Information*, they defined citizen journalism as the act of citizens 'playing an active role in the process of collecting, reporting, analyzing and disseminating news and information'.

They described 'a bottom-up, emergent phenomenon in which there is little or no editorial oversight or formal journalistic workflow dictating the decisions of a staff'. Their book is available online.

On almost any running story, you can enter the story subject and the word 'blog' into a search engine and find someone commenting on the story or, better still, involved in it. Blogs are less use on breaking news because the blogger is most frequently an amateur, who can't keep updating the site as news develops.

The ethical questions about the use of these amateur reporters are still being debated. Editors agree they should never be in the position of asking a member of the public to endanger themselves to get original material for broadcasters. Health and safety considerations apply just as they would to your own staff.

The National Union of Journalists has its own code of practice for what it calls 'witness contributors'. The code – aimed mainly at protecting the livelihoods of the union's members and preventing the abuse of members of the public by cost-cutting editors – is available on their website nuj.org.uk.

The union argues that 'the integrity and reliability of material and the safety of bona fide newsgatherers may be challenged and compromised by the use of "witness contributions"'.

They say that organisations using them should 'accept that appropriate and agreed payments will be made to witness contributors for all uses of their material and that the terms of licensing will be easily available and clear'.

Contrast that with the disclaimer on the ITV news website in 2006: 'By sending us your video footage/photographs/audio you agree we can broadcast, publish and edit the material and pass it on to others for similar use in any media worldwide, without any payment being due to you.'

ACCESS TO THE MEANS OF DISTRIBUTING NEWS MATERIAL IS NO LONGER THE EXCLUSIVE PRESERVE OF PROFESSIONAL JOURNALISTS.

The reality is that access to the means of distributing news material is no longer the exclusive preserve of professional journalists. But there are potentially millions of people who are now able to contribute to news media with or without payment.

BBC News 24's Home Affairs Correspondent Andy Tighe offers a word of caution: 'It's fantastic in so far as it enables us to get information and perspectives from a much wider range of people, and they find it much easier to tell us what they're doing. So it's an important advance in news gathering. It does make our journalism more responsive and more democratic. The downside is if we open the gates completely, without any mechanism to check what we're being told.

BBC News's Andy Tighe: 'Don't always take things at face value.'

'We have to be pretty careful we don't throw the baby out with the bathwater. It's great to involve more people and make them part of the story-telling. On the other hand, there's a reason so many of us go to journalism college, spend a lot of time in local television and radio, or whatever it might be, getting trained so that we develop these skills, this ability to be a little bit careful, a little bit cautious and to really not always take things at face value. That's what journalism's all about, and we mustn't forget that.'

When an oil depot in Hemel Hempstead caught fire in December 2005, BBC News 24 was evangelical in its requests for viewers' contributions. A caption beneath the headline OIL DEPOT BLAST read: 'Send footage to yourpics@bbc.co.uk', a presenter repeated the request, and, to assist those who might be struggling with the technology, a message on the on-screen streamer, or tickertape, advised: 'For help in sending pictures 0208 576 8200.'

Greater rigour needs to be applied to checking pictures from your audience than to input from trusted professionals. Sky News fell for a hoax when it broadcast a picture sent in by a viewer in March 2006. The shot purported to show heathland fires raging in Dorset in the west of England. It wasn't until the picture was printed in the *Guardian* that a reader pointed out there were two North American elk in the middle of the shot.

But checking the authenticity of pictures – or any information – is part of basic journalism. The technology hasn't changed that.

Pictures are difficult to fake at short notice. Information is not, so there's still a need for caution. When a tornado struck Birmingham in 2005, causing millions of pounds of damage, one eye-witness account posted on a BBC website was from Dorothy worried that her dog Toto had been swept away. Fans of *The Wizard of Oz* will recognise the reference.

REMEMBER

- ➤ Extra caution is needed when using information from the public
- ➤ Check facts wherever possible
- ➤ Check the health and safety implications
- ➤ Beware of hoaxers.

BLOGS BY JOURNALISTS

Many broadcast journalists – and some in newspapers – produce their own blogs. It means they get feedback from readers, viewers and listeners. This is a way of gauging public opinion, and can provide story ideas. But there is a danger that responding to the blogging community can be time-consuming, and a risk that the journalist loses sight of the wider audience of which the bloggers may be only a tiny part.

Some people inside the BBC, where blogging was successfully practised by political experts Nick Robinson and Mark Mardell, think there is a danger of 'over-cooking' the idea. Not every story nor every reporter needs a blog. Used wisely though, blogs help you stay in touch with your audience and help the audience engage with the medium that serves them.

THINKPIECE

CITIZEN JOURNALISTS – THE CHALLENGE

Hugh Berlyn, of BBC News Interactive, says that when a big news event happens: 'Probably the first pictures we get are submitted by our readers and we use them. But what responsibility do we have for that person being near the bus bomber or whatever? I don't know. It's a big question.'

And who takes legal responsibility for the content of these contributions? Emily Bell, writing in the *Guardian* in December 2005, noted that 'the realities of mainstream media and citizen journalists living together have begun to bite'. She highlighted the *Daily Telegraph*'s 'snap and send' initiative, asking readers with a 'front row view of some major event' to send in a picture. The *Press Gazette* reported concerns by the Chartered Institute of Journalists that the terms and conditions applied to senders of photographs included an agreement 'to indemnify Telegraph Group Ltd against all legal fees, damages and other expenses that may be incurred . . . as a result of a breach of the above warranties'.

The copyright in such pictures usually remains with the contributor, while their agreement to terms and conditions licenses the newspaper [or broadcaster] to use them. This is the arrangement the BBC introduced for viewers' videos shown on local TV. Contributors signed a licence agreement, but received no payment.

In the *Telegraph* case, Bell, the editor of *Guardian Unlimited*, points out that, if the newspaper were sued as a result of printing or uploading to its website a picture that breached copyright, privacy or libel laws, then one would expect the newspaper to fight the case and pay the costs. She wrote: 'Pursuing a reader would be a marketing disaster for the paper.'

There's also a concern, voiced among other places in *Journalist*, the magazine of the National Union of Journalists, that the contributions of unpaid members of the public might be used in preference to the work of professional journalists.

Photographer Pete Jenkins wrote that an NUJ member arriving at the scene of the tornado in Birmingham in 2005 was 'surrounded by locals waving their fashion accessories and demanding money in exchange for (very) dodgy smudges'.

Emily Bell, writing in March 2006, asked: 'Is there a difference then between the professional journalist and the citizen contributor? By the very definition there is – one is casually contributing their expertise, the other is paid for an ability to make judgements on how to convey stories or content in the most effective way. But the idea that what the professional journalist can provide will always in all circumstances be qualitatively better than a citizen journalist is not true anymore – if it ever was.'

The ethical and legal issues are in their infancy. What do you think?

- Why shouldn't a broadcaster use any material they can to tell a story?

- What checks should be applied to viewers' or listeners' material to ensure it is safe to broadcast?

- Should members of the public charge a professional rate for their contribution to news programmes?

- Are TV stations exploiting viewers' goodwill when they use their video or photographs? If so, how does this differ from newspapers filling column inches with readers' letters?

- Is the NUJ's Witness Contributors' Code of Practice a sensible response to the issues raised by the use of citizen journalists? Or is it a Luddite reaction to new technology?

MARK BYFORD, THE BBC DEPUTY DIRECTOR GENERAL: 'NEWS IS ABOUT IMMEDIACY, BUT IT'S ALSO ABOUT BEING ACCURATE AND BEING RIGHT. IT'S BETTER TO BE RIGHT AND SECOND THAN FIRST AND WRONG.'

Whatever the source – if in doubt, check it out

News editors are fond of saying it's important to be first and it's important to be right, but it's more important to be right first.

Mark Byford, the BBC Deputy Director General, explained their approach in an interview in the *Guardian* in June 2005, announcing the corporation's 'virtual' College of Journalism. He said: 'News is about immediacy, but it's also about being accurate and being right. It's better to be right and second than first and wrong. To be almost right or broadly right is not good enough for the BBC.'

Sky News has a reputation for being first with breaking news, but the man who presided over the growth of that reputation, Nick Pollard, has another passion: 'Accuracy, accuracy, accuracy. It certainly drives me mad and I hope that it drives younger people mad to see anything wrong.'

CASE STUDY 3.1   GETTING IT WRONG

The tragic consequences of getting it wrong were illustrated in January 2006 when the world's media reported that 12 miners had survived underground after a pit explosion in West Virginia. For nearly three hours waiting families celebrated before they were told that all but one of the men had, in fact, died.

The mistake was apparently due to a misheard radio message from rescuers to their command centre. As the euphoria at a 'miracle escape' spread, no journalist appears to have checked with authoritative sources, because there were no authoritative sources. The command centre had issued no official statement. Church bells pealed in celebration and the rolling news channels duly broadcast those celebrations. The reporters possibly got too close to the story and were caught up in the excitement of the miners' families. The result: misinformation was reported as fact.

Writing in the *Guardian* soon afterwards, media consultant and Internet blogger Jeff Jarvis wrote: 'Hours after the terrible truth emerged, network executives and newspaper editors fell over themselves issuing justifications and excuses: they listed their sources and said they did the best they could with what they were given.'

Jarvis said the lesson of this was: 'You can't trust the news.' He argued that, in an age of instant communication and constant coverage, the public was left to judge the reliability of the news for themselves. 'The public is the editor.'

News, Jarvis said, is not a product, it's a process. 'It is time for journalists to tell the audience not just what they know, but also what they do not know. And it is time for journalists to admit that, in the end, they don't decide what is true. The public makes that judgement. So journalists must arm the public to do that job. We get to the truth together.'

The Internet as a research tool

The importance of checking sources is never more critical than when taking information from the Internet. The World Wide Web is a fabulous resource for journalists. Search engines offer immediate information at our fingertips. But there is no guarantee that any of the information is reliable.

Learn to focus your searches, and identify which sites can be trusted. If you are searching for an old news story about a topic, on Google for example, refine your search to 'news'. If you are looking for the website of a British organisation, select 'pages from the UK'. If you are looking for pictures, select 'images'.

Use quotation marks to refine your search. If you are looking for information about Roy Saatchi (a former BBC editor), you won't want information about

Saatchi and Saatchi the advertising agency, Roy Keane, the former footballer, or the Scottish hero Rob Roy. So type "Roy Saatchi" and only the exact phrase will be found.

Official sites of recognised organisations, such as universities and government bodies, can usually be relied on to give the official views of those bodies, and to store information. The name of a government website will have the suffix .gov; universities and other academic organisations have .ac.uk in the United Kingdom; non-profit organisations have .org, or .org.uk.

So much official information is now available online that 'computer-assisted reporting' is an important discipline within journalism. The phrase is a misnomer, because, as some practitioners have pointed out, nobody talks about 'telephone-assisted reporting'. The computer is just another tool for the journalist. You need to investigate what information it can give you access to, and analyse that information to see if it is worth presenting to the public.

CASE STUDY 3.2   THE INTERNET – A WARNING

Perhaps the most dramatic example so far of the unreliability of the Internet came in December 2004, on the twentieth anniversary of the Bhopal chemical disaster in India. A producer on BBC World was asked to find a spokesman from Dow Chemical, the company involved. An interview with Jude Finisterra followed. Mr Finisterra admitted the company's responsibility for the disaster and offered $12 billion compensation.

But Finisterra was not a Dow official. He was a hoaxer from a group calling themselves the Yes Men, online political activists, who had electronically hijacked part of the Dow website. His interview ran on BBC News 24 and Radios Two, Four and Five Live. The hoax was soon uncovered, but the BBC's only consolation was that its response and apology was 'speedy, frank and open'. Worldwide headlines suggested the corporation's reputation for accuracy was damaged.

The constant flow of information into newsrooms from viewers and listeners via text messaging and e-mail, and journalists' access to blogs and podcasts mean there has never been so much research material available to reporters. It is instant information, but little of it can be treated as instantly authoritative. Everyone and anyone has access to the Web and mobile phones. Few websites can be treated as reliable sources of information; text messages even less so.

'BBC ONLINE CONTENT . . . HAS BECOME AN IMPORTANT PLACE OF RECORD FOR NEWS IN THE UNITED KINGDOM AND BEYOND.'

BBC online content is widely used as a journalistic resource. Gary Duffy, of BBC News Interactive, sums up the organisation's influence and responsibilities: 'I don't think there's a news organisation in the United Kingdom whose journalists don't go out clutching print-outs from our website. One PR man from the nuclear industry was trying to get us to correct something he disputed. He said to me: "If we don't get it changed on your website, lazy bastards for years will be reprinting this as fact."

'It has become an important place of record for news in the United Kingdom and beyond.'

Is it new?

A serious problem with web pages is that there is often no way of telling if they are up to date. BBC web pages usually include a date when the material was posted. Most websites do not. Unless whoever posted the information keeps it updated or removes it when it is no longer current, the misleading page just hangs around in cyberspace waiting to undermine future researchers. It's as if you went into the newsagent and were sold last year's paper – with the date removed.

The BBC, by expanding its licence-fee-funded online empire, has provided an impressive volume of news background material online, and opportunities for non-broadcasters to respond to news items. Because it is produced within BBC guidelines of fairness and accuracy, this information is among the most reliable of any web resource.

But mistakes still occur. There are fewer checks before web content is aired than for most other broadcast outlets. BBC News online content is always checked by two journalists, but that is not true of all the corporation's websites. Web surfers may not recognise the distinction. On 22 November 2005, the front page of Radio Five Live's website (not a BBC News site) proclaimed 'George Best dies' and invited surfers to 'click here' for coverage of 'the death of the Manchester United legend'. Those surfers would have had some difficulty finding what they were looking for. George Best was still alive. Apparently someone preparing obituary material had pressed the wrong button. The mistake – a bit of 'finger trouble' by someone who was uploading other information from Five Live at the same time – was rectified within about 20 minutes. The legend died three days later.

Most reliable news sites (and the BBC is *usually* reliable) offer links to external sites, with warnings that the host of the main site can't be held responsible for other sites' content. Follow these links and you are in uncharted and dangerous waters. But you can use a selection of sites to cross-reference information and make a judgement about what is to be trusted.

CASE STUDY 3.3   GETTING IT RIGHT – THE IMPORTANCE OF NOTE-TAKING

The importance of checking facts and the accuracy of sources was highlighted by the Hutton Inquiry into the death of civil servant Dr David Kelly in 2003. Dr Kelly killed himself after being named as the source of a BBC story about the reliability of the intelligence information on which Tony Blair took Britain to war in Iraq. Hutton cleared Tony Blair's government and damned the BBC.

The government had been accused of 'sexing up' the dossier claiming Iraq had weapons of mass destruction. Reporter Andrew Gilligan said in an early morning two-way on Radio 4's *Today* that the government probably knew the claim that weapons of mass destruction (WMDs) could be deployed in 45 minutes was wrong or questionable. He said the 45-minute claim had not appeared in the first draft of the document because intelligence agencies did not believe it was necessarily true. Hutton said: 'The allegations reported by Mr Gilligan . . . were unfounded.'

Hutton pointed out that Gilligan's notes of his conversation with Dr Kelly did not fully support the most serious of the allegations that he had reported.

It wasn't just the reporter who came under fire. The editorial controls of the BBC were criticised by Hutton: 'The editorial system which the BBC permitted was defective . . . in that Mr Gilligan was allowed to broadcast his report at 6.07 am without editors having seen a script of what he was going to say and having considered whether it should be approved.'

The BBC's Chairman Gavyn Davies, the Director General Greg Dyke and Gilligan resigned. Dyke and the reporter still believe the essential truth of the story. No WMDs have been found in Iraq.

The corporation commissioned its own report into the consequences of Lord Hutton's criticisms. Ron Neil, a former Director of BBC News and Current Affairs, and his team, concluded that the BBC should improve the training of its journalists. Spending on training was doubled and a new 'virtual college' of journalism was set up.

THE NEIL REPORT: 'ACCURATE AND RELIABLE NOTE-TAKING IS AN ESSENTIAL AND PRIME JOURNALISTIC CRAFT.'

The Neil Report stressed the importance of good note-taking: 'Accurate and reliable note-taking is an essential and prime journalistic craft.' Neil said that, where practicable, interviews with sources should be recorded on tape, and if that might inhibit the source, full shorthand or longhand notes were the best alternative.

One consequence of Neil is that it highlighted shorthand (always an essential skill for print journalists) as a valued skill for broadcasters. There are many places where electronic recording is not allowed (courts and tribunals, for instance). The journalist with the best shorthand note is always popular among colleagues and rivals. At the adjournment or conclusion of any high-profile court case, there is a huddle of reporters trying to agree the exact words used by a key witness or a judge summing up or sentencing.

Andrew Marr, the BBC's political editor at the time of Hutton, wrote in *My Trade* that shorthand is 'invaluable to anyone in journalism'.

The BBC did not go so far as to insist that it would only recruit journalists with a knowledge of shorthand. But senior managers confirmed at meetings of the Broadcast Journalism Training Council that shorthand was a desirable skill for job applicants. And Neil concluded that note-taking should be part of all BBC journalists' training.

Details of the evidence to the Hutton Inquiry can be viewed at www.the-hutton-inquiry.org.uk.

CASE STUDY 3.4   GETTING IT RIGHT – REACTING TO INFORMATION

The speed with which breaking stories change offers massive challenges to 24-hour news operations. The desire to get it first has to be balanced by the need to get it right. The credibility of any news organisation depends on its accuracy. Cynics coined a slogan for CNN, the US station that was the first to offer 24-hour news: 'Never wrong for long.' Getting something wrong and then correcting it quickly just isn't good enough.

The rush to be first does not always lead to inaccuracy, but it can cause confusion. To the viewer that may be almost as bad. Research by the BBC shows, however, that viewers of rolling news are sophisticated consumers. They want to be told as much as the broadcaster knows. If it is properly sourced, they can then make up their own minds.

Here's an example of Sky News responding to new information as it became available.

Two weeks after the suicide bombings in London on 7 July 2005, there was a second series of attacks, this time unsuccessful. Three tube trains and a bus were again targeted, but the bombs did not go off. The day after the second attacks, the police released four CCTV pictures of the suspected bombers and a man was shot dead by armed police at Stockwell tube station.

At 4.55 p.m. Sky News carried the headline on its Sky News Flash lower third caption SUSPECTED SUICIDE BOMBER SHOT BY POLICE AT STOCKWELL.

The *Live at Five* sequence carried the headline: 'Marksmen shot dead a suspected suicide bomber as he boarded a train at Stockwell.' During the lead report a new caption appeared under the strap 'Breaking News': SOURCES: SHOT MAN NOT CONNECTED TO BOMBINGS.

At 5.05, at the end of the first package, newsreader Anna Botting linked live to crime correspondent Martin Brunt at Scotland Yard who reported: 'I can only tell you what I'm picking up from security sources. It's believed that the man who was shot this morning wasn't one of the four bombers that police are still hunting.'

By 5.07 the News Flash caption had changed to SOURCES: SHOT MAN NOT CONNECTED 4 ON CCTV (*sic*).

A minute later (5.08) reporter Nicola Hill, in a separate live two-way from Stockwell, said: 'Sir Ian Blair [the Metropolitan Police Commissioner] said he thought the gentleman shot here was directly connected with yesterday. Martin's just told us he wasn't.'

Martin Brunt explains what had been happening:

The key to it was being stood outside Scotland Yard. I just saw an awful lot of people, some I knew and some I half knew – people of all ranks. Four chief constables stopped and said hello – not all of whom I knew – and between them all, right down to the lowliest PC, I got little bits of information, like bits of a jigsaw. That helped me put together what was going on so I could confirm it by putting it to somebody senior later on.

At 5.10, presenter Anna Botting was talking about the 'shooting dead . . . of a suspected, or perhaps not, suicide bomber'. The caption had changed to SOURCES: SHOT MAN NOT ONE OF FOUR CCTV SUSPECTS.

At 5.12, Martin Brunt was live again, offering new information from his sources: 'Although they believe, and this isn't confirmed, they believe this man that was shot by police this morning wasn't one of the four bombers from yesterday, he was a terrorist suspect, and the police's interest in him did emerge after yesterday's bomb attack, and I think it's important, I'm told, to make that plain. Although he wasn't, they believe now, one of the four bombers from yesterday, he was somebody who emerged of interest to them yesterday and was considered a terrorist suspect.'

The BBC *Six O'Clock News* stuck to the suspected suicide bomber line. Security correspondent Gordon Corera said in a live two-way: 'The police are being very clear that the individual who was shot in Stockwell this morning was directly linked to the attacks yesterday.'

The dead man was Brazilian. He was unarmed. And innocent of any involvement in the bombings. The fact that he was not a terrorist was not confirmed by the police until the next day (Saturday). The weekend's news agenda was dominated by apologies and statements of regret from Sir Ian Blair and senior politicians, and by the political, diplomatic and legal repercussions. The story continued to run for months afterwards.

The early reporting of events had been subject to police 'spin' – an attempt to sanitise a very serious mistake. The best of the reporting emphasised the attribution of sources – where the information came from: 'what I'm picking up from security sources'; 'the police are being very clear'; 'they believe, and this isn't confirmed'.

Healthy scepticism – never cynicism – aids good reporting. In this case it also meant Sky News were first to suggest the enormity of the story – that the police had shot an innocent man.

REMEMBER

- ➤ Check every fact
- ➤ Use secondary sources where possible
- ➤ If in doubt, leave it out
- ➤ Use your contacts to challenge 'official' sources
- ➤ Maintain your objectivity – don't get caught up in rumour
- ➤ Learn which Internet sites you can trust
- ➤ Record conversations with sources if possible
- ➤ Always keep accurate notes, preferably using shorthand.

FORWARD PLANNING

While news programmes give the impression of being responsive to events on the day, much of their content has been planned in advance. This can be anything from pre-recorded interviews to packages telling embargoed stories or illustrating stories that are in the news that day. There are also features on newsworthy issues that have no *peg* to a particular moment in time, and exclusive stories – the product of investigations for example – that can be aired whenever the broadcaster feels they will have most impact – usually as soon as possible, but on a 'slow news day'.

THERE CAN BE NO GUARANTEE THAT ENOUGH NEWS WILL 'BREAK' ON A GIVEN DAY TO FILL NEWS PROGRAMMES.

The importance of forward planning cannot be over-emphasised. There can be no guarantee that enough news will 'break' on a given day to fill news programmes.

Most editors will tell you that usually about half of any day's output is pre-planned. This changes if big stories break. Coverage of those stories takes over, and the planned material is dropped. If it's a slow news day, the proportion of pre-prepared content increases. Items are taken off the *shelf* and used to fill programmes.

Larger newsrooms will have a *planning desk* with dedicated teams of journalists reporting to a planning editor. Planning departments within BBC Newsgathering prepare material that can be accessed by all the corporation's newsrooms. In any organisation, all reporters, researchers and producers are encouraged to contribute to the *diary*.

The newsroom diary

The most important tool for collating information from all the different news sources, and planning coverage of news, is the newsroom diary. It contains all the stories that news planners and field reporters know will be happening on each day. On a typical day almost half the stories covered will be from the diary.

Larger organisations will maintain their own diary of key national events. Smaller stations can subscribe to online diary services – listing everything from court cases to football fixtures. These will have contact names and numbers so the sources can be asked for details, localised information or interviews.

The diary is kept up to date by the forward planning teams. In a small local radio newsroom that may mean the editor keeps a watching brief, while anyone else can add to the diary if they have useful information.

Stories that break during the news day, or exclusives uncovered by correspondents, are known as **off-diary** stories.

Nowadays the diary will be in electronic form but years ago it would literally have been an A4 page-per-day diary with handwritten entries. Newsroom management software, such as ENPS (Electronic News Production System), allows the information to be presented to different people in the production process in the form that is most useful to them. A TV producer will want to know where his reporters and camera crews are being sent. A sports producer will want to know that day's fixtures. The camera desk will want to know the whereabouts of crews and an estimate of how long each job is likely to take. The programme editor will need to know what stories will be available in time for the bulletin.

The diary file

It is also good practice to keep a hard copy file of all forthcoming events. This should include copies of **press releases**, whether they arrived in the post or had to be printed from e-mail. Reporters need their own copies of releases to take on location and they need to know where to find them at short notice.

The same filing cabinet can contain **press passes**. An increasing number of events – including royal visits and sports fixtures – require special passes issued by the organisers. Sometimes these are issued to news organisations, but on other occasions accreditation of the individuals who will be attending is required.

Without accreditation journalists and any technical crew are unlikely to be admitted to the event. Sometimes accreditation is needed for legitimate security reasons, particularly at high-profile events where senior politicians are involved.

Frequently, accreditation is arranged by PR companies so the organisers of an event know who has turned up. That makes it easier for them to assess the coverage they receive. Ethically, it can be argued that an NUJ (National Union of Journalists) Press Card or Sky News security pass should be enough to prove the credentials of a bona fide representative of the news media. Operationally, having to apply for accreditation is a nuisance. Practically, if you can't get in, you can't do your job.

Press passes. Without accreditation journalists and any technical crew are unlikely to be admitted to the event

REMEMBER

➤ Forward planning is essential to any news operation

➤ The diary is the central point of reference for the newsroom

➤ Keep the diary up-to-date

➤ Apply early for accreditation to events

➤ Know where to find your press passes.

CASE STUDY 3.5   WORKING 'OFF-DIARY'

Eve Richings, journalist, Sky News

Eve Richings works on special projects for Sky News. It is her job to come up with story ideas and issues that nobody else is doing – completely off the diary. Her investigations have included sensitive subjects like child soldiers, child trafficking and living with HIV. But her most difficult assignment came in 2005.

Early in the year she had a story idea. She can't even remember where she first heard about a special government unit that helped young Britons forced into marriages abroad against their will. The story was transmitted only after nine months of in-depth investigation: building trust at the highest level of the governments of two countries thousands of miles apart; establishing personal relationships with senior diplomats and victims; and considerable financial investment by Sky News. The delicate permissions involved meant that right up to the final day of filming there was no guarantee the story would ever be aired.

Eve knew no-one else had covered the story of rescues by the Foreign Office, but she found it fascinating. She says: 'I have to admit I had all these sort of James Bond ideas; men in black hurtling through the night and abseiling down mountains.'

She decided not to approach the government press office. Instead she found the number of the forced marriages unit and called them direct. This was a shrewd move. They invited her in for a cup of coffee. They mentioned that they were planning a media briefing to raise awareness of the problem of forced marriage, and to launch a set of guidelines for teachers in schools. Eve's timing was perfect.

She went to the launch and was surprised that no-one picked up on the angle of the rescue missions. 'They didn't make anything of these rescues, and

I was amazed that other people hadn't picked it up, because I thought, to a journalist, it was amazing.'

After the briefing, she asked if she could cover a rescue. 'I said people will be fascinated that you're doing this, and they said: "Absolutely not, it's far, far too sensitive, far too difficult. We can't allow anyone to do that."'

Eve was convinced there must be a way round the problem. Also at the briefing was the head of the British consular division in Islamabad, Pakistan. 'They'd told me she was coming over to the briefing. I knew who she was and nobody else did. I ended up hanging around at the end of the briefing and started talking to her. I was saying: "Let us cover one of these rescues," and she said: "No way."'

Eve didn't give up, and was eventually told: 'What you can do is come along in the car and there'll be a point where we'll tell you to wait, and we'll go off and do the rescue. If it happens you can talk to the victim with their permission.'

Eve knew Sky News would never invest in the story on those terms. But she persisted. While she was trying to agree a way to cover a rescue, she continued to investigate wider aspects of the story, contacting pressure groups and campaigners. 'I got lots of footage of women and girls in the UK; some who'd been rescued; some who hadn't; building up trust and building up contacts – lots of contacts. I think it really helped, because they thought I wasn't just jumping in and jumping out again. I was trying to build their trust and confidence in me so we could actually make the package.'

One of the sticking points was the suggestion that if anyone saw a camera during the undercover operation, that would inflame the situation and jeopardise the mission. Eve suggested using hidden cameras. That was a breakthrough.

She now had the support of the Foreign Office team in Islamabad – the head of the consular division and their press office. But to get the government approval she needed, she had to submit a formal proposal. 'The proposal was sent to the Foreign Office and it had to be approved at ministerial level. Then it had to go to the Pakistani government because the British government has a very good working protocol with the Pakistani government. It went backwards and forwards because we had to agree various things. The Foreign Office was very concerned about the human rights of the victims.'

Sky News had to agree to use hidden cameras, to guarantee the victim's anonymity (because women who leave forced marriages can become targets for reprisals), and there was a final condition which meant that, even after filming, there was a danger the story might not run. 'We had to get – retrospectively – the victim's permission. There was no question of us being able to run a frame without the victim's permission.'

After nine months of perseverance and hard work, the ideal case came up. Eve and her camera team joined a mission in Pakistan to rescue a young woman from the Midlands. They called her Sadia.

Series of stills taken from the film about Sadia

'The rescue team hadn't met her. It was all done over the phone. They have to ascertain the person wants to be spoken to. They'll think of an excuse to ring. They say: "There's an irregularity with your passport" or whatever. Her family were around her. She could only answer yes or no. If they found out, there's a risk of the family spiriting her away, never to be found.'

Eve and her team filmed as the rescuers were joined by what she describes as a 'posse' of armed police. 'It really is dangerous because households in Pakistan tend to have guns. They were lucky because male members of the household were away at a funeral.

'On the rescue, it literally is diplomacy at work. They won't say: "Here you go, young lady, come with us." The choice is hers. They try to build up trust in a very short time.

'We had to keep everything hidden. The undercover camera guys went in and I didn't because I would have been in the way. It would not have been as good as what you saw.'

The secret cameras captured the deliberations and the victim's dilemma as diplomats informed her of her rights, and offered to explain to the family that they have no right to force a British national to get married against her will. 'It's not bish, bash, bosh, "Come on we'll grab you by the hair." It's her decision – freedom or family.'

Sadia decided to leave with the rescue team. Eve already had interviews with other victims: a woman who'd been shunned by her family for eight years for walking out of a forced marriage; the story of a father banging on the window threatening to kill his own daughter. But she needed 'Sadia's' permission to show the rescue itself. Without that, there would be no pictures to tell the story.

Eve's own diplomacy came into play. She had to gauge exactly the right moment to explain to Sadia why she was with the rescue team.

'I travelled back with her in the car. The bottom line is sticking to the truth. We were following the forced marriage unit and we need to see a rescue. There came a point where I got on well with her. A diplomat actually explained it: "Eve is a journalist, and she's spent nine months trying to follow this story, but if you don't want your rescue shown, it won't be."

'I was thinking: "I hope she agrees. So much work has gone into this."

'I spent the next three days building a relationship with her. I explained about other work I'd done, and how we'd agreed with the Foreign Office that we wouldn't identify her. The Foreign Office showed her the agreement we'd drawn up.'

Eve explained to Sadia that the report would highlight the issue of forced marriage, and could help other women. The two got on well. Sadia agreed to an interview, and also agreed to be filmed at the airport when she returned to Britain, which Eve thought would be a 'wonderful last shot'. As the crew waited at Heathrow, after obtaining special permissions to film, Eve was told by an airport official that Sadia was exhausted by the long flight and had changed her mind.

'You can't push people in these extreme emotional situations. So we put the camera down. We won't film. What does she do? She comes out to us. It was all hugs and kisses, "how lovely to see you," and then she said: "I will do it." So she walked back, bless her heart, and we filmed her.'

Sky News allowed Foreign Office officials to see the film before transmission, but there was no question of surrendering editorial control. The diplomats were happy with the programme. *Finding Sadia*, a half-hour documentary, was shown on Sky News in the week before Christmas 2005. A three-and-a-half minute version led the news on the Monday morning of that week, and another cut of 13 minutes ran on the early evening *Sky Report*.

The story of how Eve Richings researched and reported the story of *Finding Sadia* is an object lesson in developing a long-term project, and in overcoming practical and ethical problems as they arise.

- The story would not have been possible without guaranteeing anonymity to the victim. In this case, that was achieved by a combination of pixilating some of the action shots of the rescue, and by the use of a back-to-camera interview where the reporter's face rather than that of the interviewee is seen.

- Secret filming was essential to tell the story. The Ofcom Code prescribes that surreptitious filming is warranted if 'there is *prima facie* evidence of a story in the public interest' and 'it is necessary to the credibility and authenticity of the programme.' These criteria appear to apply here, but the decision is always taken at a senior editorial level – not by the reporter.

- Special arrangements had to be made with the Foreign Office. In this story, the deal with the Foreign Office went further than the Ofcom Code. The Code says that, when secret filming has been used: 'If the individual is not identifiable in the programme then consent for broadcast will not be required.' Since 'Sadia' was to remain anonymous, her consent would not appear to have been necessary according to the code. Given the intensely personal nature of the story, however, most editors would consider Sky News' approach to have been the right one.

- Sky News had to maintain editorial control, while entering a relationship of trust with the Foreign Office. Allowing Foreign Office officials to view the finished film reinforced that trust, without giving them a right of veto over the content of the report. What would have happened if they didn't like it? Experienced documentary producers say that, when a long-term relationship of trust has been established with contributors, this rarely happens.

- The Foreign Office were concerned about the victim's human rights. By disguising Sadia's identity, and seeking her informed consent to show the film, there was no breach of her right to privacy. By agreeing those editorial guidelines early in the process, there was no conflict later on. The long-term trust and respect Eve won from government officials helped reassure Sadia about her intentions.

- The best-laid plans, guidelines and protocols would have been of no use without Eve's warmth and personal charm. At each stage of the investigation, she was able to persuade people – from consular officials to Sadia herself – that her film was not just good television, but a way of highlighting the problems of forced marriages and helping other young women.

CONCLUSION

So how does the information you've gathered from your sources become a news story? You need to assess it according to the criteria we've discussed in Chapter 2. You need to talk to the people involved and work out how the raw facts can be turned into a story for your station and made relevant to your audience. And you need to do that in time to meet deadlines.

Editors and producers give a lot of thought to the best way to treat stories. In the news broadcasters' ideal world, cameras would record every newsworthy moment, there would be great pictures to show on TV and actuality sound for radio. Despite the spread of CCTV and the ease of video recording on phones and camcorders this rarely happens. Cameras, both professional and amateur, record many events, but news is much more than pictures of things happening.

Much of what we call news depends on the interpretation of journalists. How to tell a story, in words, sound and pictures, and present it on air is the subject of the rest of this book.

FURTHER READING

Brooke, Heather (2007) *Your Right to Know: A Citizen's Guide to the Freedom of Information Act*, London: Pluto Press. An up-to-the-minute handbook from a journalist who uses the FOI every day in her work.

Chantler, Paul and Harris, Sim (1997) *Local Radio Journalism*, London: Focal Press. A comprehensive look at BBC and commercial radio practice.

Harcup, Tony (2004) *Journalism: Principles and Practice*, London: Sage. Practical advice on finding stories and how to treat them.

WEB LINKS

www.courtserve2.net. Details of forthcoming court cases.

www.google.com. The world's favourite search engine.

www.the-hutton-inquiry.org.uk. All the evidence presented to the inquiry.

www.hypergene.net/blog/weblog.php. Blogs from journalists and the continuing citizen journalism debate.

www.ico.gov.uk. The information commissioner's website.

www.nuj.org.uk. The journalists' union site, including codes of practice.

www.ofcom.org.uk. The site of the regulatory body Ofcom.

www.yrtk.org. Heather Brooke's site with details on using the FOI and other investigative journalism.

CHAPTER FOUR

THE INTERVIEW

Journalism is about asking questions. Lots of them. And the right ones. Journalists need an inquiring mind. We want to know more about the world about us, even if it means uncovering awkward truths. From conversations with friends and relatives to confrontations with prime ministers, the interview is the most important means by which journalists gather information. In the world of broadcasting, the interview is also one of the most important ways of providing information to viewers and listeners.

We also look at the different types of interview you will use, and show you how to get the most out of every one you do.

WHAT IS AN INTERVIEW?

An interview is a structured conversation. But it's not a conventional conversation in which both people are interested in what the other has to say. It is a series of questions and answers, where only one party – the interviewer – is asking the questions. It follows that an interview is only as good as the questions that are asked. We'll explain how to ask the right questions in differing situations. And how, sometimes, interviewing is not about asking questions at all.

Some interviews will be live on air; others will be recorded and used in future broadcasts, probably as part of an edited report or a documentary. By far the majority will be neither on-air nor recorded electronically. All these types of interview form part of the news-gathering process.

We will look in detail at the broadcast interview: those conducted to provide information and those designed to challenge authority figures. We'll pay particular attention to the need for preparation.

We look too at specific types of interview – including the studio, down the line, the two-way, when one journalist questions another, and the doorstep. And we consider how to approach different types of interviewee, from senior politicians, rock stars and top sportsmen to the recently bereaved.

A television interview on the street. BBC Midlands Political Editor Patrick Burns questions a political expert for *The Politics Show*

A CLOSER LOOK

A BRIEF HISTORY OF THE INTERVIEW

The interview is the most important news-gathering weapon in the broadcast journalist's armoury. It is also a way of challenging opinions and orthodoxies, and at its purest can become an entertaining or informative programme in its own right. Political discussion programmes have been a mainstay of the schedules since the early 1950s. Chat shows came along a little later, and so did Michael Parkinson.

It may come as a surprise to those of us who have enjoyed the verbal joustings of John Humphrys on BBC Radio Four and *Newsnight*'s Jeremy Paxman that it was not always so. The journalistic interview is a relatively modern invention – the broadcast interview even more so.

There's a famous bit of black and white footage from 1955, where the Labour Party leader Clement Attlee is approached by an eager but ever-so-polite chap with a microphone who asks if he'd like to say anything about the coming election. The great statesman's reply? 'No.' That was in an age before television became the most important medium of political information. Can you imagine a modern party leader refusing the same opportunity?

Attlee himself was described (by Labour cabinet minister Douglas Jay) as a man who never used one syllable where none would do. Indeed, he once answered all the questions prepared for a 15-minute broadcast in five minutes. Barely three years later, Robin Day on ITV conducted a confrontational interview with Prime Minister Harold Macmillan.

A hundred years before Mr Attlee's famous reply, the idea of the interview as a journalistic tool had yet to be established. The first 'modern' interview with a public figure was apparently the *New York Tribune* editor Horace Greeley's verbatim account of a discussion with the Mormon Church leader Brigham Young in Salt Lake City in 1859.

INTERVIEWS ARE THE MAINSTAY OF STORY-TELLING IN BROADCAST JOURNALISM – FIRST-HAND EYE-WITNESS ACCOUNTS FROM PEOPLE AT THE HEART OF THE STORY.

Now interviews are the mainstay of story-telling in broadcast journalism – first-hand eye-witness accounts from people at the heart of the story. Not everybody loves them though. The journalism trainer Michael Rosenblum says bluntly: 'Interviews are boring.

They make better radio than television, but the really good radio, Radio Four documentaries, are full of natural sound and events and have an arc of story to them. Mediocre people rely on interviews to carry them. Obviously, Jeremy Paxman is an exception, but people look at him and rationalise their own crap interviews.'

So, even if you have secured the key interview, you have to do it well and use it well.

PREPARING FOR AN INTERVIEW

KNOWING WHAT YOU WANT FROM AN INTERVIEW

Remember the five 'W's? As we explain in Chapter 2: *What's the story?* and Chapter 5: *News writing* the information presented in a news story can be summed up by answering the questions 'who, what, where, when, why (and how)'. It follows that your questions in any interview will almost certainly start with those words. But before you start asking questions there is only one of those words that matters. That word is 'why'. Why are you conducting the interview? Why do you want to talk to this person? Why will this interview help tell the story?

THERE'S NO POINT RECORDING A FIVE-MINUTE INTERVIEW WHEN YOU ONLY WANT A 20-SECOND ANSWER.

Often the answer is to find a soundbite – a short clip that sums up somebody's opinion or reaction. You need to focus on the key question that will elicit that response. There's no point recording a five-minute interview when you only want a 20-second answer. Equally there's no point running through the five 'W's. Those will have been answered earlier in the piece. Colour and drama will result from a more relaxed approach: 'Hey, did it hurt?'

When you know why you are conducting the interview you can decide what questions to ask. Ask yourself: 'What do I want to know?' and structure the interview accordingly. If it is to learn the facts about a news event, then it is an interview to gain information. If it is to challenge an authority figure, then it is investigative or adversarial. If it is to elicit a personal response to events, it will be an emotional interview. Sometimes you will be talking to someone simply because of who they are – the celebrity interview. But you still need to be clear why.

In any interview, be bold. And don't be afraid to be nosey. As long as you are polite, you should dare to ask the questions to which everybody wants the answers.

TIP BOX

CHECK LIST

REMEMBER

➤ What is the point of the story?

➤ Why am I asking these questions?

➤ What do I need to know?

➤ What can this person tell me that others cannot?

➤ How can I get the best from this interviewee?

➤ How can I make them trust me?

➤ Which part of their story needs challenging?

➤ What conclusions will the audience draw from this interview, or from the clip I choose?

RESEARCH AND PREPARATION FOR INTERVIEWS

Research and preparation are central to all successful broadcasting. But never more so than when preparing to interview somebody. This is usually the first

Jeremy Vine

point at which your professional expertise comes into contact with the outside world. Suddenly there's someone in the story-telling process that isn't part of your team. And sometimes – in the case of politicians, captains of industry and other public figures who've been trained in media presentation – they're on the opposing team. They have skills to challenge your own. More about them later – but, remember, most of them have been on a course lasting a few days at most, whereas this is your lifetime career choice.

BBC Radio Two's Jeremy Vine says: 'The most important thing about an interview is to be briefed, and briefed, and briefed, because you don't want to be discovering key facts that everybody else knows during the interview.'

Research need not mean hours of back-breaking work. In a newsroom, you will be unconsciously researching breaking stories all the time simply by being aware of what's going on in the world and watching your own and others' news bulletins. But if you don't know enough about a story before you are sent to interview somebody, you must know where to find information fast. The Internet is the first port of call these days. It is almost entirely full of nonsense, so you need to know which websites can be relied upon.

For example, if the Chancellor of the Exchequer is coming to town and you have the opportunity to interview him, you may already know which aspects of government financial policy are proving the most controversial, whether economic growth forecasts are living up to Treasury predictions, what impact fuel prices or interest rates are having on local people and businesses, and which social groups in your patch are most affected by changes in the benefits system. But you will want to look up facts and figures. You need to know where to find them. Government websites are a good starting point. The whole process of 'researching' a brief news interview with one of the most powerful men in the country should take less than 20 minutes.

Research is the key to longer interviews. A specialist correspondent will be expected to have detailed knowledge of their subject. The health correspondent, for example, must know government health policy, the administrative structure of the health service, the performances of local hospital trusts and the waiting lists for operations. They must also have a range of specialist contacts, providing access to the people – usually patients, doctors and nurses – who can be interviewed to provide the human stories that illustrate the issues of the day.

General reporters need to know how to access specialist information quickly. Contacts are vital. So too is knowing how to use search engines. When you make notes, jot down the source of the information in case you are challenged. The successful interviewer wins the respect of their subject by being well-informed. The journalist who wins that respect gets better answers.

REMEMBER

➤ Keeping abreast of the news is a shortcut to informed interviewing
➤ Learn which websites can be relied upon
➤ Know how to use search engines effectively
➤ Note the source of all information.

CASE STUDY 4.1

CHALLENGING THE PRESIDENT

Irish journalist Carole Coleman told RTE radio she was nervous for days before a ten-minute TV interview with US President George W. Bush: 'Immediately I settled into this intense preparation period. I thought about nothing else for five or six days, even in my sleep.

'When you're given an opportunity like that you hope in your heart you're going to be the one that cuts through the fudge. Otherwise there's no point being there. You really have to challenge him. Otherwise the interview's a waste of time.'

Coleman revealed that before the interview the White House had requested a list of topics she would cover. On the day, officials mentioned some things they didn't want discussed – including Michael Moore's documentary *Fahrenheit 911*. Coleman had never intended mentioning the film. But she did say during the interview that people were angry about the invasion of Iraq. It started a lively exchange, with the President repeating the phrase: 'Let me finish, please.' He gave what Coleman later described as 'a daggers look'. The confrontation made headlines in the US and back in Ireland.

President Bush was used to a more deferential approach from American reporters. Coleman, RTE's Washington Correspondent for two years, said: 'I had to challenge him. It wasn't that I didn't like him. I was just doing my job. My personal attitude to Bush was neither here nor there.'

REMEMBER

➤ Coleman's experience illustrates the need for the journalist to maintain control of an interview

➤ Don't be overawed by people in positions of power. Most politicians expect tough questioning and have been schooled to deal with it. They are ordinary people in extraordinary positions who have been given power temporarily

➤ Ask the questions the audience expects to hear

➤ Don't allow your personal feelings to colour your professional judgement.

See Workshops and Exercises.

INTERVIEW TECHNIQUES

PUTTING PEOPLE AT THEIR EASE

1 People speak more fluently if they are relaxed. It is always in your interests to put your interviewee at ease. If that means spending time with them and making them feel special, then do it. If it means paying a compliment to someone you find obnoxious, so be it.

Making people feel comfortable starts even before the moment you enter their home, welcome them to the studio or meet them on location. You need to reassure people when you first contact them (if not in person then on the phone or by e-mail) that they will be treated fairly and your intentions are sincere. Explain what programme the interview is for, if it's likely to be edited, and how much will probably be used. They need to have confidence that you are professional and know what you are doing.

2   They will also want to feel they have some control over what happens next. This may be difficult when you and your crews are re-arranging the furniture in their living room. One BBC cameraman used to joke that he ought to work for Pickfords, the removal company. Be courteous throughout and remember that this is someone's home, their personal space. Don't comment adversely on the décor.

3   You need to remain calm and unruffled even if you are only five minutes from your deadline. Any signs of anxiety will be picked up by your interviewee, and result in a weak performance by both of you.

4   Take care how you address people. An elderly person might prefer to be called Mrs Jones rather than Hilda, which she might consider too familiar. A celebrity would be used to people calling them by their first name. Even before he was knighted, not many people would have called Sir Paul 'Mr McCartney'.

5   Lead people through the technicalities. 'Look at me, not the camera.' 'Don't worry about the microphone.' 'We'll be live when that red light goes on at the end of the adverts.' Explain that you need to take a sound level by asking them to tell you a little about themselves (see also Chapter 7: *Location video and sound*).

6   Before a TV interview, tell people how much of them the camera can see. Show them a monitor if possible. It stops them worrying about dirty shoes. If it's someone you're likely to want to interview again, it also assures them that they can look good on television. Demystifying the process usually helps people relax and give their best performance. The BBC's Jeremy Vine says of interviewing people who aren't experienced interviewees: 'I do think that as professional broadcasters we underestimate the extent to which coming into a studio and talking to somebody and having five minutes to say your bit – and you're never going to get that five minutes again, and it's live – we underestimate how frightening that is.

'It's easier to help them on radio because if they're sitting there in front of you, you can look really encouraging, nod and smile, and all of that. Television's slightly more difficult, because a person who wilts on television almost can't be reached. They're really on their own. It creates a great deal of loneliness when you're at the front end of a camera. They need to know we're not going to trap them – we just want to hear the story.'

7   Your conversation before recording starts can touch on the subjects you'll cover, but don't rehearse the interview in full. It kills the freshness you're looking for, and leads inexperienced guests to fill their conversation with lines like 'as I said earlier' and 'like I already mentioned'.

John Sergeant, with more than 30 years' experience in TV and radio, much of it confronting senior politicians, says the easiest interviews are those with people used to being interviewed: 'What's the hardest interview? It's someone who has no experience being interviewed, who can't concentrate on the question and who rambles on, and you've got to bring them back to the main point – people who are inarticulate for all sorts of reasons and are not thinking in a sensible way and you're trying to grapple with their thought processes.'

8 Always respect your interviewees and don't judge them. Chris Tarrant says his early days in regional television were spent 'interviewing nutters', but he would not have achieved respect within the industry if he had gone round insulting members of the public. Don't bully or patronise people, just because their communication skills are not as accomplished as your own. Jeremy Vine says: 'I just don't think the interviewer needs to try to look clever-clever or superior or to blindside the interviewee or make them look silly. The purpose is just to get them to say as cleanly and as clearly as possible what they want to say.'

9 Sometimes you don't have time for introductory niceties. Someone may be brought into a radio studio while you are live on air. Give them an encouraging smile.

10 Your duty of care to your interviewees doesn't end when you turn off the mic. If you got what you wanted from them, thank them and compliment them on their performance. Reassure them it sounded great. Take contact details if you haven't already done so. Don't switch off the charm until you've parted company. You might need them again.

REMEMBER

➤ Relaxed people make better interviewees
➤ Explain technicalities
➤ Don't patronise people
➤ Take contact details of all interviewees.

EYE-CONTACT

Always try to maintain eye-contact during an interview. It shows you are interested and encourages the speaker.

For television, you also want your interviewee to keep looking at you. If they are uncertain or embarrassed they may look away, perhaps to somebody else, or straight into the camera, which looks unnatural.

For radio, conducting an interview face-to-face is much easier than down a line or over the phone because of the eye-contact. Victoria Derbyshire of BBC Radio Five Live says: 'It makes a huge difference. The eye-contact is really important. You can also pick up things by their facial expressions, which give you a clue as to something that perhaps they're not telling you. Or something that they want to share but don't have the confidence to share. You can see it in their eyes.

'You also can see if they're not happy with the question because of their body language, and you can share that then with the listeners.'

If it's appropriate, you will want to appear friendly and considerate. Eye-contact and an open posture – that's keeping your arms and (if sitting) your legs

Victoria Derbyshire

uncrossed – will help somebody relax. But be sensible. Don't stare. People don't like it, and it's rude.

You're probably wondering how you can maintain eye-contact if you're operating a recorder or writing notes. Technical operation shouldn't be a problem, because you will have set your recording levels before you start, and then you can concentrate on the content of the interview. Writing notes does not prevent you looking up frequently. Note-taking is not a calligraphy class.

REMEMBER

➤ Maintain eye-contact whenever possible, but don't stare
➤ It helps to be friendly.

TAKING NOTES

Taking notes is just as important for broadcast journalists as it is for their newspaper counterparts. Not everything you witness will be recorded on tape, disc or hard-drive. This is especially true of court reporting, inquests and other hearings where electronic recording is not permitted. But it also applies as you go about the business of collecting facts about a story. And a written note of what somebody said when the tape was rolling will help you as you edit.

SHORTHAND IS AN INVALUABLE SKILL FOR BROADCASTERS.

An unrecorded interview has much in common with the work of print journalists, where the interviewer takes notes. Some print journalists use small recorders (usually not of broadcast quality), but their traditional tool is shorthand. It's an invaluable skill for broadcasters too.

The importance of note-taking was stressed in the Neil Report, the BBC's internal response to the criticisms of the Hutton Inquiry into the death of Dr David Kelly in 2003 (see Case study 3.3). Dr Kelly took his own life after being named as the source of Andrew Gilligan's report that the dossier on Iraq's weapons of mass destruction had been 'sexed up'. Gilligan, when pressed, could not produce notes from his interview to substantiate his claims. The implication of the Neil Report was that the BBC would have been in a stronger position to defend itself if the reporter had a full note – preferably in shorthand – of the content of his private meeting with his source.

TIP BOX

We must take accurate, reliable and contemporaneous notes of all significant research conversations and all other relevant information.

We must keep records of research including written and electronic correspondence, background notes and documents. Research should be kept in a way that allows double checking, particularly at the scripting stage, and if necessary by another member of the team.

We must keep accurate notes of conversations with sources and contributors about anonymity. A recording is preferable where possible.

BBC Editorial Guidelines

Shorthand is as valuable a tool for broadcast journalists as for their print counterparts. It takes time to learn and longer to get up-to-speed, but many reporters swear they could not do their jobs without it. Teeline is the preferred system of shorthand for most journalism students. It's easier to learn than the older Pitman method, although harder to achieve the really high speeds an old-fashioned secretary would have needed. You will only be able to keep up-to-speed if you use your shorthand every day.

The BBC recognises the value of electronic note-taking, even recording people without their consent, using small cameras, over the telephone or using discreet digital audio recorders. But the intention of unauthorised recordings is to ensure accuracy and avoid legal challenges rather than for broadcast. Permission to broadcast these recordings is only granted in exceptional circumstances.

REMEMBER

➤ Accurate note-taking is a vital journalistic skill

➤ Learn shorthand and keep up-to-speed

➤ Use recording equipment when allowed, but make it clear to contributors if the recording is likely to be broadcast.

ASKING THE RIGHT QUESTIONS

If you are a 'news junkie,' as most journalists have to be, interviewing people in the news is relatively straightforward. You are asking the questions any reasonable member of the public wants answered. The skilled professional does so with courtesy and impartially. Playing Devil's Advocate is an acceptable ploy – challenging the interviewee with their opponents' views – but not at the expense of objectivity. Nobody should be interested in your opinions, and you should not express them.

An interview may appear to be a conversation, but it is not a discussion. One person is asking questions and the other answering them. You are the facilitator. *Your job is to elicit information and opinions, not offer your own.* Sometimes an interviewee will try to gain control by turning the question back on the interviewer. To avoid being intimidated, you need to have stock responses to hand. If you are asking an anti-drugs politician if he ever dabbled in soft drugs during his university days, he might respond: 'We all did things in our youth. Have *you* ever taken cannabis?' It would be reasonable to point out: 'I'm not standing for public office. Would you answer the question, please?'

THE JOURNALIST HAS TO BE A 'FIVE-MINUTE EXPERT ON EVERYTHING, BUT A TEN-MINUTE EXPERT ON NOTHING'.

Nobody is an expert on everything in the news. It has been said that the journalist has to be a 'five-minute expert on everything, but a ten-minute expert on nothing'. From your professional experience and knowledge of news and current affairs, you will have gleaned enough to be able to discuss – or interview someone – on any topic for five minutes. But a longer conversation would require serious research.

Former political correspondent John Sergeant has good advice on preparing your questions: 'You should have a pretty good idea how the person's likely to respond, because no-one is so quick on their feet that they can get a reply from someone and then immediately think of the perfect follow-up question. What is the standard argument against this? What are they going to say? Why on earth wasn't this done? Or why was this prisoner released early?

'You've got to have, if you can, some idea how the official, the person in authority, is going to respond to that because it usually leaves open an enormous series of questions and you've got to get to that very quickly. If it's live, that's even more important.

'The great interviewer is the person who could certainly answer the questions themselves, and who certainly knows the subject very well. The idea that the great interviewer is some sort of ingénue, or some innocent who goes forward and says, "I don't know much about this, but tell me what's happened," that's ridiculous, and it just does not work.'

DON'T THINK TOO HARD

A successful interview – from the journalist's point of view – is one where you maintain control. That means asking the right questions. How do you think of the best questions? That's easy. Don't think too hard. What would any sensible person want to know: your friend in the pub, the shopper in the supermarket queue, or your next-door neighbour? What would they ask if they had the chance? That's the question you ask.

Remember the five 'W's: *Who, what, where, when, why?* And perhaps *how?*

When gathering eye-witness accounts at breaking news events, a simple 'What happened?' may be enough. Or even 'Please, just tell me about it.' Follow up with: 'What happened next?' or just 'And then . . . ?'

John Sergeant says if you know your questions won't be used on air, it doesn't matter how you put them: 'If it's recorded, you just want the quote. So it's a question of how you achieve that. You can say, "Oh come off it", "What do you mean?" or "Do you really mean that?" It doesn't matter how it's phrased.'

Occasionally a less obvious approach will be necessary. You may want to wrong-foot a politician to expose hypocrisy or inconsistency. That might involve setting up one predictable answer so that the follow-up has more bite.

Here's Peter Allen of Radio Five Live pressing home his advantage in an interview with Liberal Democrat MP Sarah Teather. The party leader Charles Kennedy had admitted he had a drinking problem – something he'd repeatedly denied in public. He was under pressure to resign.

> **Allen:** Was it all about the drinking for you, or was it the way he was running the party?
>
> **Teather:** For myself it was the former, erm . . .
>
> **Allen:** The drinking?
>
> **Teather:** Yes. It was.
>
> **Allen:** But you knew all about that.
>
> **Teather:** Yes, I did. We all encouraged him to . . .
>
> **Allen:** So you don't mind him drinking [but] you don't want us to know about it.

John Sergeant, former political correspondent: 'The great interviewer is the person who could certainly answer the questions themselves.'

Teather: Well, I think he had a right to try and deal with the matter privately. However, when we first, you know, we first raised this with him, after there was a number of major events about 18 months or so ago, not long actually after I was first elected, was when I first became aware of the problem. We sought reassurance that this was something he was going to take treatment [for], and he was going to take the matter seriously.

Allen: How long ago was that?

Teather: Oh, it's been in the public domain. This was around April of 2004.

The interview took place on 6 January 2006. Allen succeeded in establishing just how long Lib-Dem MPs had known of their leader's problem, and that they tried to keep it from the public. Teather's interview was among many by disaffected MPs. Charles Kennedy resigned as party leader the next day.

REMEMBER

➤ Ask what the audience wants to know

➤ Be courteous and impartial

➤ An interview is not a discussion – your views are unimportant

➤ Maintain control of the interview.

HOW TO STRUCTURE AN INTERVIEW

Every interview has a structure. Longer interviews have a more obvious beginning, middle and end, and take the audience on a journey of discovery.

You will want your questions to flow from the previous answer. It is often suggested that each question should contain a separate, distinct idea to avoid confusion. As a broad rule, this is good advice. But sometimes a double question will be more use if both parts are related. It does away with the need for the reporter's voice interrupting the interview clip.

'What's your favourite school dinner, and why?'

'What about Andrew Murray's performance? What does that say about his chances for Wimbledon?'

Don't be afraid to repeat the question, or ask it in a slightly different way, if the first response is disappointing or evasive. When you get a good answer, don't rest on your laurels; follow through with another strong question.

Most recorded news interviews operate on a different principle. You are after a soundbite for use in a package. It's like a football match that's decided by a Golden Goal. When you've got it, game over.

THE OPENING QUESTION

It is good practice to inform interviewees of the topics on which they will be questioned and helpful to let them know how long the interview will last. We are not in the business of ambushing or trapping people. The exception is when we are exposing criminal wrong-doing.

It is never a good idea to provide a list of questions in advance. It restricts the opportunity to challenge what has been said. If you have agreed you will only ask pre-arranged questions, the interviewee is at liberty to offer an incomplete answer and refuse to expand on it in a supplementary inquiry. 'I've answered the question we agreed. I didn't agree to answer that. Please move on.'

The BBC's guidelines say we can only give a broad outline of question areas because the direction the interview takes will be dependent on what is said. But it sometimes helps to let your interviewee know what the opening question will be. It helps them relax, because it offers them the chance to mentally rehearse their first response. For this reason, professional media trainers suggest to their customers that they should always ask what the first question is going to be.

This tactic doesn't have to work. You may decide to stay in control. The late Tony Maycock, of Central TV News, was once interviewing a senior Staffordshire policeman, who asked what the first question was going to be. Maycock replied: 'You've been on one of those courses, haven't you? To tell the truth, sunshine, I haven't a clue what my question will be till that camera starts rolling.'

Given that the police officer knew why he was being questioned, this was perfectly acceptable practice, and would comply with today's Ofcom Code, which requires only that interviewees are informed of the area of questioning. Being too prepared can destroy spontaneity.

DON'T READ YOUR QUESTIONS

MAKE A LIST OF QUESTIONS BEFORE AN INTERVIEW, IF YOU MUST, BUT DON'T FEEL YOU HAVE TO STICK TO IT . . . A CRIB SHEET OF KEY WORDS IS MORE USEFUL.

Make a list of questions before an interview, if you must, but don't feel you have to stick to it. Before a longer interview, it may help you order your thoughts. That may be important if your newsdesk has asked you to cover a series of points. But if you write out a list verbatim, it will probably sound as if you are reading, and the pretence of a conversation has gone.

Interviewees will notice if you are reading questions, and will not be flattered. In a Channel Four programme in 2006 *Ricky Gervais meets . . . Larry David*, the writer and performer of *The Office* and *Extras* and the man who created *Seinfeld* and *Curb Your Enthusiasm* were in fits of laughter recalling interviewers who had confronted them with a list of written questions. They mimicked the way the interviewers looked down at their notes, without making eye-contact with their subject.

> **Larry David:** I say to them sometimes: 'Put that away. Talk to me.'
>
> **Ricky Gervais:** You wanna hear [*laughs*], you wanna hear: 'That was an amazing answer.'

Others who see you reading questions may not see the funny side. Either way you lose. You need to maintain control of the interview and the respect of your interviewee.

A crib sheet of key words is more useful. You can refer to it as the interview comes to a close to check that you've covered all the ground. Shelagh Fogarty of BBC Radio Five Live says: 'Sometimes if I really want to set out a couple of points before I ask the question, I'll formally write it out. But by and large I just add little notes that remind me of the point I aim to get at.'

BBC Radio Five Live's
Peter Allen: 'Listen to
the answer.'

You should be listening to the answers, and taking into account what has been said as you formulate your next question. This maintains the natural flow and stops you asking something that has already been answered. Asking something the audience already knows the answer to makes you look stupid.

Peter Allen of BBC Five Live says: 'Listen to the answer. Listen to what the guy or woman is saying, and then you probably won't have to write down a second question, because the second question will occur as you're really listening to what they're saying.'

He says he frequently hears interviewers failing to pick up on points because they've moved on to the next written question. 'The more important the person the greater the tendency to think "I must write down the six questions I've got to ask here" and not follow your head. A little bit of briefing obviously helps, but you should know enough to ask a few intelligent questions.'

'LISTENING IS AS IMPORTANT AS ASKING THE QUESTION.'

Helen Boaden, Director of BBC News, says: 'Sometimes it drives me mad when I hear or see interviews where they've obviously got their ten questions and this person has just said something completely riveting or unexpected, and they just go on to question number eight. Listening is as important as asking the question.'

If you don't understand an answer, seek clarification. Don't be embarrassed. Ignorance is not the same as stupidity. If you don't know something, there's a good chance most of the audience won't. Have confidence in your judgement.

It's an old lawyer's trick, beloved of politicians, to try to gain control by quoting numbered paragraphs from obscure statutes. Don't be fooled, and don't fall into the trap of using the technique yourself.

Keep your questions simple, clear and concise. They are not an excuse to show off your knowledge of a subject, or to showcase the longest words in your vocabulary. Even if they are to be edited out of the final broadcast, long-winded questions can lose the interviewee's attention. In a confrontational interview, they will give the interviewee more thinking time than you would ideally want them to have.

KNOWING WHEN TO SHUT UP

The biggest mistake during a broadcast interview is to talk over the answer. In conversation it is natural to punctuate somebody's comments with encouraging verbal tics – 'Yes', 'That's right', 'OK', 'I see', 'How interesting', and, almost unconsciously, lots of 'Mmms'. It encourages the person you are talking to and is considered polite. But in a recorded interview, whenever you are not asking questions – shut up! That doesn't mean you can't encourage somebody to talk more. Nodding in agreement works well. So does the simple device of maintaining eye-contact. That's polite too.

If someone is fluent and interesting, you won't want them to stop talking. A simple 'and?', 'so?' or 'why?', or a gesture of encouragement from the interviewer should work better than a lengthy follow-up question.

The silent question

Sometimes silence is better than asking a supplementary question. Most people take their cues to speak from pauses in conversation. Silences are awkward. People like to fill them. If you don't speak, they may feel obliged to. This is a useful technique with shy or inexperienced interviewees. They may feel they have done enough by providing the shortest possible answer, but what *you* want is for them to open up more.

Non-verbal communication is vital in all interviews. Nod encouragement. Smile when appropriate. Look quizzical if you need further explanation. But don't give away too much of your excitement if in the middle of a draining emotional interview your subject comes up with a killer soundbite. Read the interviewee's facial expressions and body language.

Repeating part of somebody's answer – reflecting the thought back to them – usually results in an expanded answer.

To take an example, the doyen of US reporters Ed Murrow, featured in the George Clooney film *Good Night, and Good Luck*, had a technique he shared with younger colleagues. According to his biographer Joseph E. Persico, Murrow told juniors that a direct question often results in the same answer the interviewee has given dozens of times before: 'Then begins the waiting game. He thinks he has given you the definitive answer. You manage a slightly uncomprehending, puzzled expression, and you can watch his mind work. "You stupid oaf, if you didn't comprehend that, I'll put it in language you can understand" and proceeds to do so. Then, in the course of editing, you throw out the first answer and use the second one.'

REMEMBER

- ➤ Explain areas of questioning but don't give the questions in advance
- ➤ Listen to your interviewee's answers
- ➤ Don't rely on written lists of questions
- ➤ Know when to shut up
- ➤ Don't be afraid to repeat or reword questions to get a different answer.

TIME REFERENCES

When you are recording an interview, bear in mind when it is going to be heard. If you interview a football manager on a Friday about Saturday's game, it doesn't matter if he refers to 'tomorrow's match' in a clip broadcast on the Friday. But if you want to take a grab for Saturday morning's bulletins, it's better if there is no reference to 'tomorrow'.

Often you will be required to record preview material for future bulletins and you will need to explain to the interviewee how it is going to be used. Most people won't mind talking about 'today's event' in a cut to be used on the day of an event, even if the interview is recorded several days in advance.

Similarly, it is worth asking interviewees not to use phrases like 'as I said earlier' or 'like I told you before' because they will have to be edited out if only a short clip is to be used. Nervous interviewees may not be able to comply with that request – it's another detail to think about while concentrating on getting a message across. But it's worth asking, as it can save you time in the edit.

REMEMBER

➤ When recording, think when the interview will be heard
➤ Avoid confusing time references
➤ Explain to interviewees when their contribution will be broadcast.

TYPES OF INTERVIEW

It helps to differentiate between the types of interview broadcast journalists conduct and what they are for.

In an attack on the language of PR people, John Humphrys joked that Radio Four's flagship morning programme should bear the catchline 'Arguing and interrupting . . . for a better *Today*!' Humphrys could start an argument in an empty room. He says arguing is fun. And important. He points out that interviewing is part of the process whereby political leaders argue things out in front of the rest of us. Then we decide who has the better case and deserves our vote. It's a vital part of democracy. So is a free flow of information. The kind of interviews conducted to gather information do not always have to be argumentative, aggressive or even – to use what Humphrys calls a 'limp-wristed' word – robust. They can be friendly, chatty even.

INTERVIEWING IS PART OF THE PROCESS WHEREBY POLITICAL LEADERS ARGUE THINGS OUT IN FRONT OF THE REST OF US.

RECORDED INTERVIEWS

Recorded interviews follow clear patterns. Hard news interviews need to be short and to the point as a deadline approaches. Feature interviews can be longer and more relaxed, but are still restricted by the need to turn the material round in a limited time. Your ear will, with experience, become attuned to selecting sound clips as people talk, and remembering them ready for the edit. During a reply you will hear your 'in' – the first words of the clip you will use – buried within an answer, and then you will hear your 'out' – the last words of the clip – shortly afterwards. You get used to mentally calculating the gap between them – between ten and 20 seconds is usually about right. When you've heard the clip you can relax. Provided you've asked the right questions, you can draw the interview to a close.

Much of the time you will have to listen back to what you have recorded, making notes of in and out points, time-codes and durations. All this takes time, and it takes a lot more time if you have recorded 20 minutes when five would have been enough.

IT TAKES EXPERIENCE AND CONFIDENCE TO KNOW WHEN TO STOP RECORDING.

It takes experience and confidence to know when to stop recording. Think back to your preparation. Is there anything else you would have expected them to say? Has the interview raised new questions you still want answered? If the answer is 'no' on both counts, stop recording. The chances are, of course, that this is when the interviewee comes out with a cracking soundbite. Don't worry. Just press record again and ask them to repeat it. It may not be as spontaneous, but at least you've got it, and even your editor won't know they said it better the first time.

Documentary makers have the luxury of taking more time over interviews. Longer programmes require more material, and editing schedules are less fraught than on news. But the discipline learned in news reporting is invaluable to journalists making longer-form programmes.

REMEMBER

➤ Hard news interviews tend to be short and to the point
➤ Interviews for features can take longer
➤ Get used to listening for usable clips
➤ Learn when to stop recording.

INFORMATIONAL INTERVIEWS

An informational interview may take place live as an interviewer tries to find out what has happened in a breaking news story, or it may be recorded, so that an authoritative source of information other than the journalist can be presented on air.

Subjects for news interviews have a natural pecking order. Eye-witnesses are vital in any hard news story: fires, bombings, shootings. They will tell the personal experience of people caught up in a news event and its emotional impact. The interviewee may have only limited knowledge of the bigger picture, but first-hand accounts are highly prized and will usually be the first clips used in packaged versions of the story.

The spontaneous live interview most often takes place as news first breaks. An eye-witness may be the first person spoken to: the caller to the radio station; one of the first people approached by a reporter on the scene. The interview may start by seeking information – 'What happened?' – but it soon becomes an *emotional* interview – 'How has this affected you?' (hopefully, not the hackneyed 'How do you feel?', which usually sounds crass and begs the answer, 'How do you think, dimwit?').

Even as the quest for more detailed eye-witnesses continues, there will be a need for an authoritative informed source, perhaps from the emergency services or the government. They may have information which gives the viewer or listener the bigger picture. If there is a matter of public policy involved – like the government's spending on rail or road safety – this type of informational interview may develop into an *adversarial* interview.

In a developing story, the presenter or reporter apparently knows as little as the audience. Sometimes this is true, but often a producer or researcher will have spoken to the interviewee before they go on air. The presenter will be told through their headphones or earpiece what the interviewee should be able to say on air. Lines of questioning or even particular questions will be suggested.

TIP BOX

> Eye-witnesses and informed sources – like official spokespeople – add colour, immediacy and authority to reporting. They also save the reporter the need to summarise what is better told as first-hand evidence or expert opinion.

Interviewing experts

Experts will often be used to interpret information, particularly where the facts are sketchy or require specialist explanation. When interest rates are raised by the Bank of England, a financial expert may be asked to explain the likely impact on the economy. A mortgage expert may be asked to speculate on the likelihood of the interest change affecting house prices. The idea is that a large proportion of the audience will be home-owners, or live in mortgaged homes, and the expert can make the story relevant to them.

Former senior police officers are often asked to comment on policing. What was the Metropolitan Police's 'shoot-to-kill' policy after the terrorist bombings of July 2005? It led to the death of Jean Charles de Menezes on the London tube. If ever there was a case where reporters should stick to the facts and leave opinions to others, this was it. The ex-police experts could attack or defend the policy without damaging the news organisation's impartiality.

WHEN TALKING TO EXPERTS, ASK THEM TO AVOID USING JARGON . . . OTHERWISE YOU WILL HAVE TO EXPLAIN IT TO YOUR AUDIENCE.

When talking to experts, ask them to avoid using jargon – the specialist language of their trade. Otherwise you will have to explain it to your audience.

The choice of experts and opinions that are given air-time leaves the broadcaster open to criticism. Impartiality and even-handedness should apply to the selection of expert interviewees as much as to the content of reporters' and presenters' scripts.

When choosing experts, try to avoid 'dial-a-quote merchants' – people who promote themselves relentlessly on radio and TV. Former radio news editor Mike Henfield says: 'Regional radio and TV is full of them. Many an expert wheeled in by TV newsrooms isn't able to say more than a well-informed viewer. We used to have "China watchers" but now that country is more accessible, we appear to have self-proclaimed terror experts in the studio instead.'

It may seem obvious, but make sure the expert is who you think they are. In May 2006, there was much hilarity in media circles when BBC News 24 interviewed completely the wrong man as an 'Internet expert'. The hapless victim had been rushed into the studio from the BBC's reception area by mistake. He obligingly bluffed his way through the interview, even though English was not his first language. It later transpired the interviewee was an applicant for a job at Television Centre. He *was* there for an interview – but not that kind.

REMEMBER

➤ Eye-witnesses are essential in hard news stories

➤ Learn how to react to breaking news as part of a team

➤ Experts can add authority to your reporting, but choose them carefully.

EMOTIONAL INTERVIEWS

Often the emotional impact of an interview will be the most important element. The facts can be explained by the presenter or reporter. What the interviewee offers is the human impact or drama of the story.

This is true of eye-witness accounts of news events, or first-hand testimony in human interest stories, including the reporting of sporting triumphs and failures. Asking hard and fast questions will not always elicit the best response from someone who is in a state of anxiety, shock or even elation.

The most successful approach to any emotional interview involves winning people's trust. Sometimes that is as simple as sharing their enthusiasm at a time of great elation – the successful sports team on its victory parade, for example. They want to talk, so interviewing them is easy. Sometimes the hardest part of the job is getting them to shut up.

FOR SOME VICTIMS THE PROCESS OF BEING INTERVIEWED CAN BE CATHARTIC – IT HELPS THEM COME TO TERMS WITH WHAT HAS HAPPENED.

But dealing with people in distress requires great sensitivity. For some victims the process of being interviewed can be cathartic – it helps them come to terms with what has happened. It may be the first time they have been able to express their feelings. But for others, the idea of talking publicly about private matters is abhorrent.

The initial approach should involve some expression of sympathy and an acknowledgement that they might not want to talk. This might seem obvious, but it is amazing the number of people who go in feet first. The BBC advises that requests for interviews with people who are injured or grieving should normally be made through friends, relatives or advisers.

Longer reflective interviews – particularly with people who've undergone great physical or mental trauma – depend on building a rapport with the subject. This can take time, and can be emotionally draining for the reporter.

At a time of grief, great care needs to be taken. Media intrusion and insensitivity are not generally welcomed by audiences. But most people want to know how people respond to tragedy and misfortune. There may be hypocrisy in this, but it is not the journalist's job to second-guess the audience's response.

Instead, it is advisable to be aware of these mixed emotions and take account of them.

Emotional interviews can illustrate political issues, or be at the heart of human interest stories. The following examples work because they bring the stories to life and create an emotional response in the audience.

1   BBC Midlands' health correspondent Michele Paduano reported on a 33-year-old cystic fibrosis patient's hopes of a transplant. Mark Allen, struggling for breath, offered his thoughts on what the operation would mean: 'It will change my life. It would mean I could be how I used to be. I could go out with friends. I could not be on oxygen. I could go more than twenty minutes away from the house. I could live independently again. I could go out to work again. I could just have a normal life that everyone else takes for granted.'

His mother Maureen: 'Nothing's worse than seeing your own child suffer, and that I find heart-breaking, when I can hear him coughing and being sick . . . I know that every morning he dreads actually getting out of bed, because that's such an awful time . . . you can't put things right, and, as a mother, obviously that's what you always want to do is put things right.'

2   An 85-year-old Burma Star veteran, Norman Auld, was interviewed on the sixtieth anniversary of the end of the Second World War on BBC News. He was visiting a primary school to share his experiences. One of the children asked how he'd felt about being at war. His understated reply was that it was 'disappointing – I'd been told to go so I had to go.' But during an interview by reporter Denise Mahoney, he was near to tears as he recalled his unit being shelled and the death of a friend: 'And we had to take him down the track and bury him, and that's the worst thing I've ever done [puts hand to face] . . . and it still gets me.'

3   And a stroke patient campaigning against hospital ward closures in Evesham, Worcestershire, emphasised the human impact: 'They gave my life back to me, and I feel very, very strongly about this. We've got to save our hospital.'

REMEMBER

➤ Approach interviewees with sensitivity

➤ Use intermediaries (friends, relatives, advisers) if necessary

➤ Avoid the question 'how do you feel?'

➤ For longer, reflective interviews, invest time in your subject.

ADVERSARIAL INTERVIEWS

Challenging, or adversarial, interviews can be among the most entertaining parts of any broadcast. The BBC's *Newsnight* has a fine band of reporters, many working on investigative or in-depth accounts of stories behind the news, but few viewers would deny that the programme's unique selling point is the lively confrontations between its presenters and senior politicians. The most successful presenters are well-briefed and will have done enough research to counter any challenges from their interviewees. They will often appear to know more than the interviewee.

In adversarial interviews, a broadcasting convention about always asking 'open' rather than 'closed' questions does not apply. The open question seeks to get the interviewee talking. 'What happened in the meeting?' 'Why does the government want to introduce this policy?' 'How can you justify your attack on the Prime Minister?' A closed question can be answered very briefly, often with the single word 'yes' or 'no'.

Closed questions are obviously useless for uncovering information about a news event or for providing soundbites. 'Were you on the tube?' 'Yes.' 'Did you see the explosion?' 'No.' 'Did you hear it?' 'Yes.' 'I suppose people panicked?' 'No, not really.' And so on.

CLOSED QUESTIONS ARE . . . USELESS FOR UNCOVERING INFORMATION ABOUT A NEWS EVENT OR FOR PROVIDING SOUNDBITES.

But a closed question can have a dramatic effect in an adversarial interview. It was a closed question, 'Did you threaten to overrule him?', that Jeremy Paxman famously asked the Home Secretary, Michael Howard, 12 times. The topic was the political fallout over the dismissal of the Head of the Prison Service, Derek Lewis, in 1997. After repeating the question eight times, Paxman even pointed out: 'It's a straight yes or no answer.' But the Home Secretary refused to offer anything so straightforward.

Paxman later said he kept repeating the question because the producer told him the next item wasn't ready. If he'd thought of an open question, there might have been no reason to repeat himself, and we would have been denied a memorable television moment. The Paxman interview and Ann Widdecombe's observation that the Home Secretary had 'something of the night' about him came to haunt Mr Howard, who went on to become Conservative party leader but lost the 2005 General Election.

Jeremy Vine, a former *Newsnight* presenter, says: 'Political interviewing is a particular art form and it may be that it's becoming more and more of a minority sport. I've learnt through bitter experience that embroidering questions to politicians is a bad idea. The thing to do is to really sharpen them, to have the facts right and the attitude right, and to chase them down when they don't respond.'

Vine says interviewing politicians should not be all about conflict: 'We've been through a period where political interviewing has become very gladiatorial, and it probably needs to get a bit shrewder. There probably need to be rather fewer fireworks in it, because we've ended up in a situation where they seem to have clammed up and they're not telling us anything.'

'YOU SHOULD ONLY BE COMBATIVE WHEN IT BECOMES PLAIN THEY'RE NOT PREPARED TO ANSWER THE QUESTION.'

If you are recording what you expect to be an adversarial interview, it can be worth asking a soft question to start with, so that at least you have something to work with if your adversary walks out. Peter Allen of BBC Radio Five Live says: 'I think you should only be combative when it becomes plain they're not prepared to answer the question. Give them a chance to say what they've got to say. Don't launch straight into the aggression.'

CASE STUDY 4.2 OLD ADVERSARIES

Here's Jeremy Paxman interviewing George Galloway, newly-elected MP for Bethnal Green and Bow, on BBC1's election night programme, 6 May 2005. Standing for the Respect party, Galloway, a former Labour MP, had defeated Labour's Oona King.

Paxman: Mr Galloway, are you proud of having got rid of one of the very few black women in Parliament?

Galloway: What a preposterous question! I know it's very late in the night but wouldn't you be better by starting by congratulating me for one of the most sensational election results in modern history?

Paxman: Are you proud of having got rid of one of the very few black women in Parliament?

Galloway: I'm not . . . Jeremy . . . move on to your next question.

Paxman: Are you proud . . .

Galloway: 'Cos I've got a list of people who want to speak to me.

Paxman: Ah, are you pr . . .

Galloway: If you ask that question again, I'm going. I warn you now.

Paxman: Don't you threaten me, Mr Galloway, please.

Galloway: You . . . you're the one who's trying to badger me.

Paxman: I'm not trying to badger you. I'm merely asking you whether you're proud of having . . . (*Galloway is talking, saying* 'I've actually got. I've actually got . . .') having driven out of Parliament one of the very few black women there.

Galloway: You are actually conducting one of the more, even by your own standards, one of the most absurd interviews I have ever (*cutaway of Paxman looking skyward*) participated in. I have just won an election. Can you find it within yourself to recognise that fact? Can't you find it within yourself even to congratulate me on this victory?

Paxman (*sarcastically*): Congratulations, Mr Galloway.

Galloway: Thank you very much indeed.

Paxman: How do you propose to . . . ?

Galloway: Thank you very much (*waves and goes to remove mic*).

Paxman: Oh, I see. It's another occasion when you're not wanting to talk to someone who doesn't agree with you.

Galloway (*in background*): No . . . no, no, no, no . . . no no no no. Actually, Jeremy . . .

Paxman: All right. (*turns to studio guest*) David Lammy, what do you make of Mr Galloway?

[David Lammy, the Labour MP for Tottenham, is black.]

See Workshops and Exercises.

Jon Snow in his autobiography *Shooting History* describes his frequent encounters with the Iron Lady herself, Margaret Thatcher. He says it was 'sometimes akin to an execution'.

'Well, Jon, how are you?' she would ask, not apparently wanting an answer, but delighting you that she remembered your name. 'I do find these European sessions perfectly frightful,' she would go on, then there would be some small talk, and then we would start. The moment the camera rolled, the iron would return to her demeanour. Some harmless question would issue from my lips, and she'd sit bolt upright. 'How can you ask such a stupid question?' she'd bellow.

'Damn me,' I'd think, 'have I said something silly? What a fool I am . . . I'm so sorry.' Then I'd pull myself together and remember, for an inadequate moment, that it was *I* who was supposed to be shaping the questions, and *she* who was supposed to be answering them.'

Snow's example, written to amuse, nonetheless illustrates the key question – who is in control of the interview? Both parties can be fighting for that control. It usually leads to the kind of fireworks that make for entertaining broadcasting. Some attempts to control the agenda involve interviewees trying to take the heat out of the situation, by blocking or stonewalling. These interviews are invariably less entertaining.

Prepared statements

Some interviewees will want to read from prepared statements, usually agreed with their lawyers before they face the media. In extreme circumstances that may be inevitable – perhaps with the lawyer reading the statement on the courtroom steps. But whenever you have the chance to challenge somebody who wants to read from a script, point out how artificial and contrived it looks.

Lawyers, their clients, and any other potential interviewees who think prepared statements are a good idea are rarely able to read from a script and make it sound sincere. You've seen it on TV. You know it always sounds like they have something to hide. Tell them there is no reason why they shouldn't take legal advice first about how they should answer, but they would be better off answering questions spontaneously.

WHENEVER YOU HAVE THE CHANCE TO CHALLENGE SOMEBODY WHO WANTS TO READ FROM A SCRIPT, POINT OUT HOW ARTIFICIAL AND CONTRIVED IT LOOKS.

Consulting notes

Interviewees who want to consult notes during an interview should also be discouraged. If it is a TV interview, looking down at their papers will make them look shifty. If it is radio, they will sound hesitant as they scan the notes. It's best to advise interviewees to put their notes to one side. They will feel comfortable that they are there – as a safety net – and probably won't need to look at them. Don't simply take their notes away. That will make your interviewee feel insecure.

'No comment'

Some people – usually celebrities – will say they are only prepared to answer questions on certain subjects. Explain that a polite, non-committal response to controversial questions serves them better than a blanket refusal. The formula phrase 'no comment' always sounds like a euphemism for 'I've got something to hide.'

Nobody has to take part in your programmes. Broadcasters faced with restrictions on interviews are within their rights to inform their audience, but only if it's relevant to the story. In the interests of accuracy, you should make the distinction between refusing to comment, refusing to answer questions, refusal to take part in a programme and not being available for interview.

Press officers

Some people will insist that a press officer or other associate is present during an interview. It happens frequently during political and showbusiness interviews. The advice from Jim Beaman, a university lecturer and former BBC trainer, in *Interviewing for Radio*, is: 'Agree, but on condition that they do not interrupt or interject during the interview.'

You then have to decide whether you will allow the interviewee to stop the recording to consult their adviser. Beaman says you should, within reason, allow this to happen. We suggest that you should never allow politicians such an opportunity.

The doorstep

THE DOORSTEP . . . SHOULD ONLY BE USED WHEN OTHER ATTEMPTS TO SECURE AN INTERVIEW HAVE FAILED.

The doorstep is an unannounced interview. The term can apply to any approach to someone without giving them prior notice, not just those that literally happen on their doorstep. Clearly this breaches the normal ethical convention of arranging interviews with consenting people and telling them what they are going to be asked about. It should only be used when other attempts to secure an interview have failed, only with prior approval from a senior editor, and only in accordance with the professional guidelines outlined in Chapter 6: *Location reporting and production*.

The practicalities of the doorstep are that you will normally be recording as you approach the subject, and you will probably have only one chance to ask your question. So, you should have that question very clear in your mind. This is rarely the time for a subtle approach.

When you are reduced to knocking on a door in the hope of catching your interviewee unawares, expect the unexpected. Many people in the news will refuse to come to the door. But others have been known to answer the door with a paper bag or even a fruit basket over their head, or to cover their face with a newspaper or umbrella. In the multi-award-winning feature length documentary *Capturing the Friedmans*, a suspect in a child abuse case confronts a TV crew with a pair of underpants on his head – Fruit of the Loom, we're informed. More aggressive interviewees (particularly those being accused of criminal behaviour) may attack a reporter or camera crew, or pour water – or worse – on them from an upstairs window. Discretion is the better part of being attacked by a Rottweiler.

REMEMBER

➤ Know your facts and be thoroughly briefed
➤ Anticipate the likely answers
➤ Closed questions can be useful in adversarial interviews
➤ Always stay in control
➤ Discourage interviewees from reading their answers or consulting notes

➤ Challenge restrictions on interviews

➤ Seek editorial permission before doorstepping

➤ Prepare for the unexpected.

VOX-POPS

Vox-pops – a series of comments from a variety of people – are a great way to include a sample of public opinion in your programmes and to add colour to reports that would otherwise suffer from a lack of lively soundbites.

They should be approached in the same way as all other forms of interview – the difference is that, instead of asking one person several questions, you are usually asking several people one question.

The term *vox-pop*, or these days even *voxes*, comes from the Latin *vox populi* or *voice of the people*. Americans used to call them *man-in-the-streets*, though *person-in-the-street* has taken over. Americans also call them *triple As* – which stands for 'Ask Any Asshole'. That's no way to talk about your audience.

THREE OR FOUR PITHY EIGHT-SECOND COMMENTS WILL HAVE MORE IMPACT THAN HALF A DOZEN LONGER ONES.

Stand-alone vox-pops are still popular on some stations, but most of the time you will use them as part of a wider feature. Then the key is to keep them snappy. Three or four pithy eight-second comments will have more impact than half a dozen longer ones.

Don't kid yourself that vox-pops represent a true reflection of public opinion. Any sample taken in a shopping centre during the daytime, for example, cannot be representative of the population at large, because many people will be at work. Also, it is essentially self-selecting, consisting only of those people who choose to be interviewed by a stranger with a roving mic. So, be careful how you use them on sensitive issues and at sensitive times – like during an election campaign.

None of this means, however, that you should not strive to show a diverse cross-section of people. If your selection includes young and old, an ethnic mix, disabled people, and even a sample of well-dressed and scruffy individuals (for TV), you will give the audience the quite correct impression that you have tried to canvass a broad range of views.

Of course, not all vox-pop sequences need to represent everybody's viewpoint. Sometimes the story dictates the type of person you want to speak to – an education story might lead you to conduct vox-pops with parents outside a school; a story about Islamophobia might require a vox-pop outside a mosque. If you are looking for memories of the 1950s, there's no point talking to teenagers.

Here are some tips for carrying out vox-pops:

1 Make sure that, wherever you go, you have permission to be there. Public places – on the street and in parks – are fine. Many shopping centres are privately owned and you must seek the management's permission. Airports, bus and railway stations, schools and hospitals and their car parks are also no-go areas without official consent. If you are refused admission, wait outside on the public highway and approach people there. As long as you are not causing an obstruction, you are well within your rights.

2 Be polite – nobody is obliged to talk to you, even if you do represent the mighty BBC or Sky News. Explain that they will be doing you a big favour by helping

Grabbing them at a bus stop – radio reporter Charlotte Foster conducts a vox-pop

with your report. One trick is to approach people who cannot escape – at a bus queue or taxi rank, for example. The potential 'victims' might be grateful of a way of passing the time. Remember, though, that everybody in a bus queue is a public transport user, so it might not be a great idea to ask their opinion of a rise in petrol prices. For that you might get a livelier response on a garage forecourt.

3 It can also help to approach groups of people who appear to know each other. One friend will egg on another. Sometimes a conversation or disagreement will emerge. These may be useful, but think how they will sound in the final edit. Will you be able to reflect the spontaneity of the moment in an eight-second extract? And if it's television, are all the speakers on camera at the same time? A good cameraman will try to show who's speaking, but won't jeopardise the shot to chase actuality from someone outside the viewfinder, because they may stop speaking at any moment. You must maintain as much control as possible of what you are filming. It may be better to pair people off before you turn the camera on them, but you might risk losing that special moment.

4 Usually there is little need to ask more than one question, so you need to have prepared that question well. How you phrase the question is crucial. It must be instantly and clearly understandable to everyone.

If the same question is asked of each interviewee then the answers should cut together nicely. It is usually best to avoid the reporter's voice – so the question needs to elicit a self-contained response, preferably not one that requires an elaborate set-up in the preceding voice-over or studio link. Avoid closed questions (those that lead to a yes/no response), and don't be afraid to stay silent; if you keep looking at someone encouragingly, they'll probably keep talking.

5 Some questions can assume knowledge on the part of the interviewee, particularly if it's a subject 'everybody' is talking about. In February 2005, 'What do you think about the Queen missing Charles' and Camilla's wedding?' would guarantee a response on the streets. In May of that year, did the hordes of happy Scousers celebrating Liverpool's return from an historic comeback in the Champions League final even need to be asked a question before they volunteered their views?

6 But sometimes you need to inform people before you can ask their opinion. When the Food Standards Agency announced the withdrawal of hundreds of products containing the banned colouring Sudan 1, Radio Five Live had a reporter outside a supermarket within half an hour. He had to tell people about the scare – and then record their reaction. Most were shocked when they learned the reason for the ban – the risk of cancer. It made lively radio.

Vox-pops have been a mainstay of TV coverage of controversial or amusing issues for years. Esther Rantzen's *That's Life* programme always used to feature an extended vox-pop near the top of the show. Often the same crowd would gather at the same location (usually a local market) and the same faces would feature in successive weeks. They became micro-celebrities in their own right. But for news and current affairs coverage, it looks lazy if the same person repeatedly appears – particularly in the same programme. You are not on the lookout for television regulars – you need a variety of opinions. If you come across a genuinely famous face, consider whether they are worth a separate interview. A *Midlands Today* crew found the comedian Harry Enfield in a queue at Alton Towers. And students from Staffordshire University spotted Nick Hancock, the presenter of shows like comedy sports quiz *They Think It's All Over*, buying a ticket at Stoke-on-Trent railway station.

ALWAYS REMEMBER TO THINK HOW THE CLIPS WILL EDIT TOGETHER.

Throughout the process of gathering vox-pops – approaching people, persuading them to talk on mic, suffering rejection, coaxing a response, monitoring your sound levels – always remember to think how the clips will edit together. It's a tall order, and it's no surprise that many seasoned reporters don't like doing vox-pops at all.

In a (mostly light-hearted) ITV show *It Shouldn't Happen to a TV Reporter*, the usually fearless and intrepid BBC war correspondent and presenter Jeremy Bowen said: 'They're totally humiliating and awful to do I think, because you have to go up to people – complete strangers – and ask them a daft question.' Another of Britain's most respected war reporters, Jon Snow, the presenter of Channel Four News, said: 'There is something absolutely devastatingly grim about it.' And the distinguished Sir Trevor McDonald called vox-pops 'fairly useless'. But he didn't explain why he thought so, and it has never stopped ITV News using them.

Vox-pops are here to stay, and all this offers an opportunity to aspiring broadcasters. They are one of the tasks that local radio news editors regularly entrust to students on work experience. And in bigger newsrooms they can provide a chance for newcomers not yet on the reporting roster to pace the streets with a microphone. The senior reporter is putting a story together which the editor thinks will benefit from vox-pops. The junior can offer to do the voxes, gaining experience while sparing the senior journalist the trouble.

If you're the lucky junior sent to do voxes, there are some technical matters you need to consider:

1 Location is important because background noise will set the scene on radio and the background is always an important part of telling the story on television.

   In radio, the greatest barrier to a good edit is background noise. If background sound levels jump too harshly, clips may sound ugly when joined together. Roadworks and traffic noise are intrusive. Music is particularly distracting as only a short snatch will be heard behind each interview and the snatches will not join together.

2 For television, watch the sound levels too, but also vary the picture background to avoid jump-cuts (the appearance of one person miraculously changing into another against the same background). Keep the shot sizes the same (a medium close-up – MCU – works best) and try to alternate which side of the camera the reporter is standing, so that the eye-lines of the interviewees vary from left to right. When you edit the pictures it is aesthetically more pleasing if a person looking camera right is followed by a person looking camera left and vice versa. Also it gives the impression of a conversation or debate (in the same way that alternate eye-lines are used for cut-away questions in longer interviews).

3 When introducing vox-pops in your script try to avoid the stale old formula of 'We went into the street to find out what people think,' or 'So what do people on the streets of Paisley think?' Better would be 'It's divided public opinion . . .' or 'People are really angry/confused/happy about it . . .' and then cut straight to the vox-pops.

ALWAYS END A VOX-POP SEQUENCE ON A PARTICULARLY STRONG COMMENT.

4 Always end a vox-pop sequence on a particularly strong comment, and, if appropriate to the tone of the story, a funny one. It is not always a good idea to start on your strongest clip, because it may make those that follow look weak by comparison.

Let's say you are asking about the law banning smoking in public places, and the point of the vox-pop is to demonstrate public confusion over the legislation.

The cue reads:
'People are confused by the law.'

Someone says:
'It's a complete dog's breakfast and whoever thought of it should be strung up.'

Somebody else says:
'I'm not really sure. I haven't been able to understand it. It's all a bit confusing.'

The second clip would work perfectly well at the top of the sequence, even though it is clearly the less dramatic of the two. If it were placed second it would appear weak even though it is a perfectly valid opinion, and probably more representative of people as a whole than the 'stronger' clip.

5 The visual demands of television mean that more samples are needed for a TV vox-pop than for radio. For example, you might talk to ten people and get four great answers. That might be enough for a radio vox-pop. But if all four people are facing camera left, you have a problem. It's usual to alternate the direction in which interviewees are facing. As mentioned earlier, it is visually more satisfying to the viewer, because it conveys the impression of a conversation between your contributors. So, you need to do more interviews for a television piece – this time with everyone facing camera right – until there are enough to choose from.

6 Sometimes you can 'flip' a TV picture in the edit – reversing the image so that someone looking left is now looking to the right. But you can't always do that. Any writing on screen will appear back to front. So company logos, writing on tee shirts, or shop signs in the background will immediately look wrong. To the perceptive viewer so will the buttons on a man's shirt. But don't worry too much about reversing somebody's hairstyle. If you flip a shot of a man with a side parting, the parting will be on the wrong side. But he probably won't notice. The television image will look the same as he sees himself every day in a mirror. His friends and relations might notice though.

Beware. Vox-pops are not an easy option or a quick fix for a dull story. They have to be included in the piece on merit – often because of their entertainment value, but also because they shed new light on the topic.

REMEMBER

➤ Relevant vox-pops can liven up a story

➤ Ask people the same question

> ➤ Try to get a diverse mix of interviewees
> ➤ Approach people in queues – they can't escape!
> ➤ Be aware of background music and noise levels
> ➤ For TV, keep shot sizes the same, but alternate the direction interviewees are facing.

LIVE INTERVIEWS

Live interviews hold no fear for well-prepared interviewers. But they can be daunting for beginners. To stay within the 'comfort zone' you need to be disciplined and stick to the areas you have researched.

1 Stay in control of the interview. If you are live, you can't edit out your gaffes.

2 You need to concentrate and choose your words carefully. An RTE radio presenter, Ryan Tubridy, asking Carole Coleman about her controversial interview with George Bush, said: 'What was happening with all the people round George Bush – his courtesans?' We think he meant courtiers.

3 A strong beginning and end are important. Think hard about your first question. It must be one that will elicit a fluent response and preferably not cause the interviewee to clam up. If you appear too aggressive and put them on the defensive, you will struggle. Prepare plenty of follow-up questions.

4 An interview should end on a high. Save a good question till last, and rehearse your closing comments. If you are in a studio, you will know what comes next and be ready to link to it. If you are on location, think how you will hand back to the studio.

5 Timing is vital in all broadcasts. In a live interview, sticking to time requires collusion with the interviewee. Arrange hand signals so they know when to stop talking. If your subject is proving awkward and tries to keep talking, you need to take control by interrupting politely and firmly.

6 Occasionally you will run out of questions. The late Barney Bamford, a BBC reporter, had a solution to this: 'It's easy. I just lean forward, look intense and ask: "Just how serious *is* the situation?" Works about 90 per cent of the time!'

7 Talking over someone to end an interview can sound messy, but should never be rude. You, the broadcaster, are in charge, because you control the microphones and sound levels. A simple 'thank you' is usually enough. A phrase like 'that's all we have time for' is not a good idea. It begs the question, 'Who says?' You can't expect audiences to respect your running orders.

The pressure of live broadcasting adds an extra frisson to an interview. As you listen, assess the relevance of the answer and whether it is interesting or not. You may need to interrupt even if there is plenty of time left. Look out for people who start listing points, 'Firstly, let me say . . .' Can you afford to let them go on to 'fourthly' and 'fifthly'? When you know there are 30 seconds left, it should be the time to ask a final question with an answer that's likely to be quite short. It's good practice when briefing the interviewee to warn them what the closing question is going to be, and ask them to answer it concisely. Experience will help you judge how much more needs to be said when timings are shouted in your earpiece.

A live radio interview on location. Freelance Mick Tucker talks to an allotment holder

Shelagh Fogarty: 'Edit with your ears, not with your eyes.'

Cutting an interviewee short can sound rude. Watching the clock is important, but not as important as the output. Provided you don't crash into what's coming up next, bring things to a natural close. BBC Radio Five Live's Shelagh Fogarty has good advice: 'Edit with your ears, not with your eyes.'

REMEMBER

➤ Structure a live interview so you can begin and end powerfully

➤ Practise ways of interrupting without appearing rude

➤ Stay in control

➤ Practise timing your closing comments.

DOWN-THE-LINE AND TELEPHONE INTERVIEWS

Radio

Down-the-line interviews (or DTLs), where the interviewee is in a remote location, offer particular difficulties. The subject may be in another studio or on an outside broadcast (OB) unit. The connection with the studio may be via microwave or satellite link, ISDN (a broadcast quality phone line) or landline.

Telephone interviews are a form of down-the-line interview. They are an almost instant way of covering breaking news. You are unlikely to have enough reporters to send out on every story. Even in a well-staffed newsroom, you almost certainly won't have the time to get out, record an interview, and play it back or return to the studio in time for the bulletin on the next hour. The *phoner* is the staple of local radio bulletins.

The sound quality of telephones, even 3G mobiles, is never as good as that of a broadcast line or face-to-face chat. But this is not a serious problem. Paul Chantler and Peter Stewart in *Basic Radio Journalism* say:

Research shows that the listener does not mind phone cuts at all. In fact, he or she thinks the story is actually more 'immediate' if it is done on the phone. It sounds to them as if you have reacted fast to a story . . . So phone audio not only makes use of radio's greatest strength – its immediacy – but also makes good economic sense for small stations with few staff and limited resources.

EDITORIAL GUIDELINES INSIST YOU SHOULD TELL SOMEONE IN ADVANCE IF THEY ARE BEING RECORDED.

Editorial guidelines insist you should tell someone in advance if they are being recorded. Even before they consent, though, it is good practice to make the call on the line you will be recording. Calling from the newsroom and transferring to a studio or, worse, having to call back later wastes your time and theirs. The longer you take, the greater the risk of someone saying no. 'I'd like to record your comments. Is it OK if I press the button now?' is rarely refused.

When you are recording, remember to 'ride' the sound levels – close your mic while they're speaking and drop the interviewee's level while you ask your questions. The audio will be clearer without interference from the other end of the line.

If you are after a simple soundbite (as is usually the case with interviews for radio news bulletins), listen for the 'in' and 'out' – the start and finish of the cut you will use. When you have what you want, politely end the interview.

Longer confrontational interviews require a slightly more aggressive tone on the telephone than if you are speaking to someone face to face. They can't see your body language.

BBC Radio Five Live presenter Shelagh Fogarty has a useful tip for signalling to an unseen interviewee (or a co-presenter) that she wants to ask a question: 'I just take a little breath in – not massive but audible – as though I'm about to ask them something. So what you haven't done is start your question and had that awful radio moment when you half-interrupt a guest and then they carry on speaking. Your breath indicates to them that you have something else to say.'

Fogarty reckons it works with most contributors unless they're nervous or so focused they carry on regardless. If they won't stop, she says, you just have to wade in. The audible breath trick works too on outside broadcasts when you don't have your co-presenter's eye.

TV

It's obvious that someone on the phone or in a remote radio studio cannot see the person asking them questions, but many viewers do not realise that the same applies to most remote television interviews. The vision link goes only one-way – from the remote location back to the studio. It would be too expensive (and too much trouble) to provide a television picture from the studio back to the remote location.

This means all the visual signals you give your subject in a face-to-face encounter are no longer available, which is disconcerting. If they are on an outside broadcast (OB), listening to you through an earpiece, there will be all the distractions of their own environment and an uncertainty about when to expect the next question.

The interviewee should be told clearly where to look, usually straight into the camera. In a live interview, when the interviewee is within the broadcast's transmission area, they may be provided with an off-air monitor, so they can see their interviewer. But it may be a distraction to viewers if the interviewee keeps looking at the monitor.

IF YOU ARE BEING INTERVIEWED VIA SATELLITE LINK . . . THERE WILL BE A DELAY IN THE SOUND REACHING YOU.

If you are being interviewed down the line as a location reporter, you may want a monitor. If you are linking within the interview to a video clip or package you may want to introduce it by looking down at the monitor. Even if you don't have one, it is a convention to look down to where it would be. It's easier than looking blankly at the camera.

If you are being interviewed via satellite link, be aware that there will be a delay in the sound reaching you because of the time it takes the signal to reach the satellite and return to earth.

REMEMBER

➤ Down-the-line interviews are like talking on the telephone
➤ Be aware of time delays caused by satellite links
➤ For TV, advise your interviewee where to look.

BBC Radio Stoke's
Stuart Fear awaits
his cue on a two-way

The two-way

The two-way, when a reporter is questioned by a presenter to provide extra information or analysis of a story, is a type of interview. But it follows very different rules from the interview with a guest contributor. For a start you should know all the questions in advance. You will have agreed them with the programme producer or the presenter in person. Usually you will have written or suggested them yourself. It follows that there is no excuse for not knowing the answers.

The two-way is an artificial device, scripted to create the impression of a conversation. It became increasingly common during the 1990s when live location broadcasting became cheaper and easier to do, and is now a staple of television and radio coverage of major stories.

You will hear questions, and instructions from the studio, via an earpiece or headphones. The producer's comments can be distracting. It's like trying to hold a conversation with someone on the telephone while somebody in the same room is speaking to you. Concentration and practice are the only ways to master this art.

BBC *Ten O'Clock News* presenter Huw Edwards has this approach from the studio end: 'I will talk to every correspondent about the questions. We will agree questions quite often. One or two correspondents have been very happy not to agree a specific question. Andy Marr [former political editor], for example, because we were two fairly political animals, former lobby correspondents, he'd be happy to say, "I kind of want to talk about what Blair's up to on this." He didn't mind what the question was as long as I was driving towards that area, which actually made for a better exchange, because the form of words I used would trigger him off.

'Sometimes the danger is,' Edwards explains, adopting a staccato voice, 'you-ask-a-question-and-they-answer. A bit unavoidable I'm afraid, especially if you've got an inexperienced correspondent (and I've been there myself) very worried about form of words, maybe on a difficult legal story where you have to get the form of words absolutely right, they don't want to be involved in some kind of cosy exchange. They want to just deliver what they've got. In which case, I've got to just say "Let's join her now." They don't want to be waylaid by any other considerations.'

Being interviewed on a two-way makes you realise what it is like to be on the receiving end. You might feel you are not in control, which is very disconcerting. You will have more control than most of your interviewees, however, because you know what questions are coming.

The experience is proof that both parties in an interview must feel comfortable. The best interviews are those where both people feel they have some control.

> ### REMEMBER
>
> ➤ You can agree the questions for a two-way in advance
> ➤ Interviewer and interviewee should be on the same 'side'.

TIP BOX

IN SEARCH OF THE SOUNDBITE

If you are recording an interview – whatever the style or subject – you will almost certainly want to edit it. That may mean cutting your own words out, or cutting the interviewee's words down. But most often it is to find a soundbite – a short clip expressing the key point made by the interviewee. The clip may be used in another reporter's package, or even on another medium. Audio clips from TV interviews regularly appear on radio or the Internet. Radio interviews are a mainstay of websites; if they are the words of someone who is not available for TV interviews on the same day they are often used on TV bulletins.

The key to securing a good soundbite is to frame your question so the answer will sum up the respondent's position – their view, reaction or account of what they have witnessed.

'What did you see?'

'What happened?'

'What's your opinion?'

'What do you think?'

'How did it affect you?'

But preferably not: 'How do you feel?' You should structure your questions to help the interviewee express their answer in the best way they can.

It's good practice to advise interviewees not to use your name in their answers. You may have to edit it out later, and that may not be possible if the vocal inflection (whether the voice goes up or down) makes the clip sound odd without the missing name. It's flattering to think you are on first name terms with celebrities, but not very helpful in the production process.

If you are preparing a packaged news report, you will know what you want from each of your interviewees. You are looking for the ten- or twenty-second clip that sums up their contribution to the story. You learn to listen for 'in' and 'out' points, the beginning and end of the cut you will use.

If somebody is close to saying something clearly but messes up the answer, tell them not to worry and ask the question again. Sometimes you may wish to phrase the question differently to help them. If *you* make a mistake during a question, pause long enough to make an edit, and ask it again.

John Sergeant offers a final question you need to ask yourself after the soundbite interview: 'Have I actually got them to say on tape what I want them to say? Have I actually got on tape the quotes that I need, and the bits that I need to work into the programme, or the item, or whatever it is I'm interviewing the person for.'

YOU ARE LOOKING FOR THE TEN- OR TWENTY-SECOND CLIP THAT SUMS UP THEIR CONTRIBUTION TO THE STORY.

CHILDREN

Children can be a fantastic source of lively comment. But Ofcom and BBC Guidelines say they should not normally be interviewed without the permission of a parent, guardian or other person of 18 or over *in loco parentis*.

The guidelines say that under-16s should not be asked for views on matters likely to be beyond their capacity to answer properly, without such consent.

The child's age, stage of development and degree of understanding should be taken into account when deciding whether consent is essential.

The BBC suggests an exception may be vox-pops on non-controversial subjects such as pocket money or favourite singers. If a child tells you their mother is the meanest in the school and should be shamed into coughing up more cash right now, you may decide the guidelines need to be interpreted less liberally.

CASE STUDY 4.3   INTERVIEWING CHILDREN

We've all heard the warnings about appearing with 'children and animals'. Steve May, a sports presenter on Radio Four's *Today* programme could see the funny side when he attempted a live interview with a seven-year-old football prodigy. It's also a priceless example of the dangers of asking closed questions.

May: Hallo, Jack.

Jack: Hallo.

May: Hi, Jack. How you doing?

Jack: Good.

May: Excellent. Now you want to sign for Manchester United, I know, don't you?

Jack: Yeah.

May: But you can't until April the fourth, because that's when you're eight years of age, because football regulations mean that you can't sign until eight. But that's what you really want to do, isn't it?

Jack: Yeah.

May: Yes. Are you a big Man U fan then, obviously?

Jack: Yes.

May: Right, and your speciality is scoring double hat-tricks, isn't it?

Jack: Yes.

May: Tell us about that.

Jack: Mmm, what did you say?

May: Your speciality . . . (starts to laugh)

John Humphrys (interrupting): How many goals have you scored?

May (still laughing): Something like that. You scored 37 goals last season, didn't you?

Jack: Yeah.

May: And what your speciality is is scoring six goals at a time, isn't it?

Jack: Yeah.

May: Right, and what's your ambition in football? (*laughter in studio*) What's your ambition in football? Why do you want to be a professional footballer?

Jack: Because I like football.

May: Yeah, yeah, absolutely. I suppose that's a good answer. Your favourite player?

Jack: What did you say?

May: Who is your favourite player?

Jack: Cristiano Ronaldo.

May: Absolutely. For Man U, and I've got a note here to say that your ambition is to buy a fast car and a big house for your parents. Is that your dad's ambition for you?

Jack: Yeah.

May: OK. Lovely. Jack, thank you very much indeed for joining us. Good luck with your career.

Jack: OK.

May: You take care.

Jack: Yeah.

May: Yeah. Absolutely. There you go.

Humphrys: Well done, Steve.

May: Never work with children and John Humphrys. That's the idea.

Humphrys: He got direct answers, didn't he? Which is more than we get most of the time. Give a lot for a one-word answer occasionally here we would.

The interview made it on to the *Today* website for the amusement of fans of the programme and students of how not to do it. Steve May proved himself a sporting presenter in more ways than one.

VULNERABLE PEOPLE

'Meaning of vulnerable people':

This varies, but may include those with learning difficulties, those with mental health problems, the bereaved, people with brain damage or forms of dementia, people who have been traumatised or who are sick or terminally ill.

Ofcom Broadcasting Code

Ofcom says persons under 16 and vulnerable people should not be questioned about private matters without the consent of a parent, guardian or other person of 18 or over *in loco parentis* (in the case of persons under 16) or a person with primary responsibility for their care (in the case of a vulnerable person), unless it is warranted to proceed without consent.

REMEMBER

➤ Don't expect children to understand the interview process

➤ Be aware of the guidelines about interviewing children and vulnerable people.

CELEBRITY INTERVIEWS

Many young people entering journalism want to interview famous people. The reality of the celebrity interview is that it can be the toughest test of the integrity of the interviewer. Political spin is but a pale imitation of the control freakery beloved by most 'stars'.

Press agents will attempt to dictate the areas of questioning that are allowed: the plot of the movie, but not their private life. Film stars are stationed in hotel rooms, and interviewers are corralled into ante-rooms awaiting their five minutes (or less) 'exclusive' access to the star. You meet famous people, but what follows has precious little to do with journalism.

Two cameras are set up (by the film company) awaiting the conveyor belt of interviewers. One is on the star, and you can request the other is on a 'two-shot' (proving you were in the same room together). Alongside the star may be a personal assistant, furnishing them with a glass of water or applying make-up, and someone with a stopwatch. The star may be willing to talk for hours but the minder with the stopwatch does the dirty work, calling time on the interview. But they won't interrupt the star, so shrewd interviewers will save a question they know the star will want to answer at length until the end.

Nina Nannar has interviewed numerous 'A-list' Hollywood stars as Arts and Media Correspondent for ITV News. She's done 'junket' interviews with everyone from Brad Pitt and Angelina Jolie to Britney Spears. Miss Spears' publicist (at an interview before her marriage) insisted: 'Miss Spears will not answer questions about Justin Timberlake, virginity or September 11.'

Nannar says: 'If there's something personal you want to ask, you save it till about the third question. Two questions about the latest film, then in with the one you really want an answer to. Even if they say, "I don't really want to answer that question," you've got something.'

'The really big stars like Tom Cruise and George Clooney can be absolutely charming, really gracious – and they remember you.'

When Tom Cruise agreed to a truly 'exclusive' interview – he'd requested that Nina was the only journalist he spoke to – Nannar says she was treated 'like a queen.' 'They couldn't do enough for me because I was the one the star had asked for. It was just before I got married and he was great, hugging and congratulating me.'

David Braithwaite, a specialist in organising film star interviews for BBC Radio Five Live, says his job is about developing personal relationships with people from film studios and specialist PR companies: 'It's about being professional, not about meeting stars, but about knowing this is someone we can get on air, they'll say something good or controversial and they'll be a good interview.

'Most film companies prefer junkets, because they have control. You're split up in terms of regional and national press, radio and television. They also have another group for ethnic press, all treated differently. If you're national and you have a big audience you get treated better than if you're a regional journalist.

'When I go along to an interview and they tell me I've got ten minutes, I arrive and I say, "So how long have I really got?" And they say eight minutes, and then as the junket goes on it can go down to six minutes.'

Nina Nannar, ITV News: 'If there's something personal you want to ask, you save it till about the third question.'

At film company junkets, BBC Five Live likes to use ISDN lines or radio cars with wireless links, leaving the presenter in the studio. 'Every director and A-list film person who's been in London, we've done.'

When a guest comes into the studio, it's a bonus, a tribute to Braithwaite's persistence, and to the status of the film slot on Simon Mayo's show. 'Sometimes we get people on an ISDN line for great lengths of time and that's as good as coming in. [Film director and former Monty Python star] Terry Gilliam was the ultimate professional. He sat there, had his headphones on and held his own mic.'

Braithwaite says there's sometimes a trade-off with PR companies to secure big names: 'I'll put on a guest that I don't think is overly great for five minutes at the top of the film slot, so that I'm going to get somebody else later. We don't just do A-list stars. We will do a director of obscure documentaries. We can say we do everyone.

'It's about what gets on air. The people I meet – I've met Nicole Kidman, seven or eight minutes in a room, shake hands, do the interview and go – I meet them but I don't really meet them. They're like press conferences. You've got to treat them like a news item.'

David Braithwaite with film director Spike Lee. A result! Lee came into the Five Live studio, complete with Thierry Henry Arsenal shirt

CASE STUDY 4.4   THE CELEBRITY INTERVIEW – A LESSON FROM HISTORY

There is nothing guaranteed to make experienced journalists cringe more than hearing a fawning celebrity interview. You know the sort of thing: reporters, who act like the longest-serving paid-up member of the artist's fan club, rather than an informed, reflective observer, asking questions to which the wider public – not just fans – want answers. Giveaway questions include:

'Tell me about your latest album.'

'What attracted you to the part?'

'Have you a message for your British fans?'

This type of questioning takes place frequently in an age when politicians are shown little or no deference. As long ago as 1982, Mrs Thatcher's Defence Secretary John Nott walked out on interviewer Sir Robin Day when he was described as a 'here-today-gone-tomorrow' politician. John Nott is best remembered – by journalists at least – for that incident alone.

And yet pop and film stars, who more than any others in the media are part of a here-today-gone-tomorrow celebrity culture, are given undue respect by reporters. Sometimes the reporter acts like an adolescent fan. At other times the reporter's critical faculties appear to have deserted him or her, and the resulting questions are just plain embarrassing.

Bob Dylan, more than most pop performers, can be said to have stood the critical test of time. There are many examples of what can only be described as silly questions from Dylan's mid-sixties press conferences. And we all know what happens when you ask silly questions.

'Why do you sing?'

'Why? Just because I feel like singing.'

'How many people who labour in the same musical vineyard in which you toil, how many are protest singers, that is people who use their music, use the songs to protest the social state in which we live today; the matter of war, the matter of crime, or whatever it might be?'

'How many?'

'Yes.'

'I think there's about 136.'

'You say about 136 . . . or do you mean exactly 136?'

'Either 136 or 142.'

'Do you care about what you're singing?'

'How can I answer that if you've got the nerve to ask me? You've got a lot of nerve asking me a question like that. Do you ask the Beatles that?'

And in the perfect rejoinder to a journalist in Stockholm who hides behind others' opinions, and – a greater sin – hasn't done his research:

'They've said that you must be the ultimate beatnik.'

'What do you think . . . I won't tell anybody what you say, what do you think?'

'Not your personal comment?'

'No. What do you think?'

'I have no opinion about that.'

'Well, why?'

'Because I haven't heard you sing . . .'

'You've never heard me sing, and yet here you are sitting here asking me all these questions!'

It's been said that there's no such thing in journalism as a stupid question, only stupid answers. No. There are stupid questions.

SPORTS INTERVIEWS

The approach to interviewing sporting personalities and administrators should be no different from any other interview. The same journalistic rigour and integrity should apply. But, as with the celebrity interview, modern professional sport can be controlled by agents and press officers, who want to insist on what their clients will be asked and what they will not answer. Nowhere is this more true than in the 'big business' that is football. The idea of football as 'big business' pervades modern journalism, largely because of the large sums involved in the sale of sports rights to broadcasters, and the transfer fees and wages for players. But football clubs are not truly 'big' businesses in a FTSE 100 sense.

Sports clubs earn their money from broadcasters, who collude in promoting their image, and from the fans, who pay at the ticket office, the club shop and in Sky subscriptions. Therefore, sports organisations are hugely conscious of their public image. They try to control the way their sport is reported. The following advice is based on the way major sports clubs, and in particular Premiership football teams, control access to their personalities.

SPORTS ORGANISATIONS ARE HUGELY CONSCIOUS OF THEIR PUBLIC IMAGE. THEY TRY TO CONTROL THE WAY THEIR SPORT IS REPORTED.

Previews

Sports personalities need the media – not least to add value to their lucrative sponsorship deals. Football managers' pre-match press conferences, usually on a Thursday or Friday before a weekend game, are part of the process of keeping the fans informed and involved in events at the club. But modern football managers are trained in how to avoid answering questions. They are media-savvy and wary of the press. They know, for example, that unguarded comments in the heat of the moment can mean charges of bringing the game into disrepute, and disclosing which players they want to sign can lead to inflated prices on the transfer market.

You must aim for trust and honesty in your dealings with high-profile figures. But that trust can only be won over a period of time. And in an age when there are sackings within the first few weeks of a season, time is the one thing football managers don't have much of. Regional reporters often get to know managers at one club and develop the relationship at another. After parting from Leicester, Micky Adams found a new job at Coventry City. Harry Redknapp left Portsmouth only to resurface at Southampton.

From the club's viewpoint, the preview press conference is free publicity, a promotional device to provide upbeat messages ahead of the match. In practice, managers may be working to their own agenda. Apparently unguarded comments may have been carefully thought through, sometimes to put pressure on the club chairman or board, or to give messages to their own players or those they might want to sign from other clubs. It's up to you to interpret those messages. Don't be afraid to ask the question the supporters want asked.

Radio Five Live and BBC TV's Garry Richardson told a Good Practice training workshop for BBC local radio reporters that they should not be nervous about the big question: 'Never think you can't get the interview you actually want. Always ask – you never know – always aim high.'

There are rich pickings for reporters prepared to ask provocative questions. But the need for fairness and impartiality applies just as much to highly paid

*THE NEED FOR
FAIRNESS AND
IMPARTIALITY
APPLIES JUST AS
MUCH TO HIGHLY
PAID SPORTSMEN
AS TO ANY OTHER
WALKS OF LIFE.*

sportsmen as to any other walks of life. Knowledge of their sport and an understanding of the difficulties of their job are always appreciated. So too is good time-keeping.

Think of your audience. If you are working for a local station that is part of a network, that means thinking of the network's needs too. Some of the personalities you meet will be big names whose opinions can make headlines. In October 2005, Wolverhampton Wanderers had an important Championship game against Sheffield United. But the same week England had just finished their qualifying campaign for the 2006 World Cup. The Wolves manager Glenn Hoddle was a former England manager. As local radio and newspapers reported the club's team and injury news ahead of the top-of-the-table match, BBC Five Live and Sky TV homed in on another of Hoddle's comments. He said that Wayne Rooney could be to England what Platini was to France and Maradona to Argentina. 'Rooney the new Maradona' led the sports bulletins on Five Live and Sky News for most of the day.

After-match

Barely a week goes by without a football manager being hauled before the FA for 'bringing the game into disrepute' in comments he made in an after-match interview. Media trainers now tell soccer managers that the first interview after the game is not the place to vent your frustration at a referee's shortcomings. They are advised to take their time, calm down and if possible speak to a trusted assistant before going before the cameras. Nonetheless, getting it off your chest publicly can be more satisfying than getting it off your chest privately. Some managers may consider the FA fine a price worth paying.

Some football interviews have become the stuff of legend. Kevin Keegan's 'I'd love it if we beat them. Love it!' rant, against Manchester United, and his on-air resignation as England manager left interviewers almost speechless. Be ready for the unexpected when passions are running so high.

Veteran manager Ron Atkinson once told reporters he never commented on referees' performances, 'and I'm not going to break the habit of a lifetime for that prat'. Big Ron, of course, often found his tongue led him into trouble.

Mark Bosnich, the Chelsea goalkeeper, launched an astonishing attack on his club after a UEFA cup defeat to Hapoel Tel Aviv. The trip came barely a month after the 9/11 terrorist attacks. Players had been told it was up to them whether they made the journey, because they could be terrorist targets in Israel. A weakened Chelsea lost 2-0.

Bosnich complained – live on Channel Five TV – that whatever he did at the club he wasn't given a fair chance. He worked hard in training, he said, but when the team sheet was posted he wasn't on it. Interviewer Steve Lee remembers the studio director in London telling him, through his earpiece, to get Bosnich to say more of this. Bosnich obliged. He played barely half a dozen more games for Chelsea. Within a year he had tested positive for cocaine. Soon afterwards the club sacked him.

The most successful manager in English football Sir Alex Ferguson avoided some of the flak of confronting the after-match interviewer by refusing to talk to the BBC at all for years on end. But his comments were available online, on Sky and on MUTV, the club's own TV channel. His words could be reported by the BBC, even if they could not always use the audio.

CONCLUSION

How many interviews have you read with minor celebrities, or even the latest person to be evicted from the *Big Brother* house, where they say their ambition is to have their own 'chat show'? The implication is that interviewing people on radio or television is easy. Anyone can do it. Well, they can't. High-profile TV personalities, like Davina McCall, and even the former Prime Minister Harold Wilson met with critical condemnation as TV interviewers. Interviewing is a specialist skill, and a very important one for broadcast journalists. You should prepare for every interview, and treat every interviewee with respect.

Few people master every kind of broadcast interview. With practice you will find your niche. With more practice you will develop your talent to become an all-rounder. The more you do, the more you will feel comfortable with approaching any type of interviewee. But practice never makes perfect in this game. Experienced professionals can all point to recent failures. There is always more to learn.

FURTHER READING

Adams, Sally (2001) *Interviewing for Journalists*, London: Routledge. A useful introduction, though weak on broadcast techniques.

Beaman, Jim (2000) *Interviewing for Radio*, London: Routledge. The most detailed guide to the types of interview you'll conduct in radio.

Chantler, Paul and Stewart, Peter (2003) *Basic Radio Journalism*, Oxford: Focal Press. Sound advice on interviewing alongside other radio practice.

Harcup, Tony (2004) *Journalism: Principles and Practice*, London: Sage. Practical advice on finding stories and how to treat them.

Snow, Jon (2004) *Shooting History*, London: Harper Perennial. His career in journalism, including his account of interviewing Margaret Thatcher.

CHAPTER FIVE

NEWS WRITING

INTRODUCTION

Broadcast journalists write words that have to be spoken and sound natural. Their words must not sound as if they are being read out loud. In that sense broadcasters have more in common with the dramatist than with newspaper reporters. Unlike the dramatist though, the journalist deals in fact rather than fiction. But in any form of story-telling, it is essential to communicate immediately and directly and to engage the listener in your narrative thread.

It's possible to re-read a newspaper story if the meaning is not clear, but nobody watches the TV news with their hand poised on the remote control ready to play back a recording of what they've just heard. The audience needs to understand the story immediately – on first hearing.

A CLOSER LOOK

ODD FACT

It seems odd today, but in the days of 'steam radio' BBC bulletins were read 'first at normal speed, then at dictation speed so that listeners can take notes.'

This idea developed a venerable history. In World War Two, American short-wave stations and the BBC World Service offered 'dictation speed news', so that servicemen in remote camps and even on ships could jot it down and report it to their comrades. The Shipping Forecast on Radio Four is still delivered at 'dictation speed.'

In this chapter, we'll explain that the most important thing to remember when writing news is to use good conversational English, whether you are writing for television, radio, online or text services. This is because it is easy to understand. We are in the communications business, and anything that detracts from communicating gets in the way of the story.

Most news organisations have a *style guide* – summing-up the in-house conventions for script writing. We'll explain the reasons for them and look at examples.

We'll round the chapter off by looking at sports writing; the differences between radio and TV scripting; and how the writing skills of the broadcast journalist have to be adapted for online work, where the words are, for a change, meant to be read rather than spoken.

Good journalism begins – and ends – with good standards of English. The BBC newsreader Huw Edwards says: 'Standards of writing are rather depressing – I could put it much more strongly. It is a growing problem.

'When I go to mark external papers [for university courses and others] I'm horrified by what people consider to be acceptable news writing. I'm not looking for great style. I'm really talking basics – 'O' level English. I preach this when I go to schools and I see teachers vigorously nodding at the back of the hall.'

Edwards, who writes all his own scripts for the *Ten*, wonders why the education system isn't, in his view, working: 'I get the results of it in front of me every day. Why should I sit there using my time correcting basic grammar and basic punctuation mistakes which can really cause trouble for me on air? It really irritates the hell out of me.'

John Sergeant, best known as a political correspondent with BBC and ITV News, stresses the importance of consistent grammar: 'You've got to decide, for example, whether collective nouns are going to be "is" or "are". So "the government is" or "the government are", but once you've decided that, you obviously must be consistent within your piece. You can't say, "The government is considering this. They want to do that," because that's a grammatical howler. You're moving away from the structure of the English language and that has an integrity of its own which you may not be able to get back to if you're sloppy about these things.'

BBC news correspondent and presenter George Alagiah says: 'You've got to write as if you're talking. I came into this business because I like to communicate; I like to write.

'When you're reaching between five and six million people, accessibility is absolutely key. The writing has to be engaging and it has to be rooted in experience. You need to know your audience. Succinctness and accessibility are quite hard things to do.'

Huw Edwards says good writing helps people get jobs: 'If people turn up here for jobs, submit an application form (which I will often see), and it's written nicely – good English, nothing fancy, nice clear concise English, grammatically watertight – it will stand out from the rest of the crowd and that person will be interviewed.'

George Alagiah, BBC news correspondent and presenter

ADVICE FOR EFFECTIVE NEWS WRITING

GOOD CONVERSATIONAL ENGLISH

If you invite someone into your home, you are almost certainly hoping they will be good company. You expect good conversation on subjects that interest you, presented in a way you understand, even if the topic is quite complicated. It wouldn't be a bad thing if your guest was witty and entertaining, but above all they must never be boring. It's a tall order for any visitor to fulfil all those requirements, and yet this is exactly the pact we make with broadcasters every time we switch on the radio or TV news.

We expect the news to be interesting, understandable and sometimes entertaining, expressed in a familiar way. We expect the news readers and reporters to know what they are talking about. We don't expect them to sound as if they are reading something they don't quite understand.

A news script must sound like natural conversation. The advice from the BBC's Peter Elliott, author of their style guide back in 1979, holds good today: *Write as you would talk. Better still, write as you would hear.*

PEOPLE GET UP TO ALL SORTS OF THINGS WHILE THEY LISTEN TO THE RADIO: THEY DRIVE, DO THE HOUSEWORK, FIX THE CAR, COOK, HAVE SEX.

You have to attract the listeners to what you are telling them. People get up to all sorts of things while they listen to the radio: they drive, do the housework, fix the car, cook, have sex. And surveys have shown, perhaps surprisingly, that they do many of those things while they're watching television too. Each of those potential listeners is alone in their thoughts, if not necessarily alone in physical space. You have to connect with those thoughts. You talk to the listener one-to-one.

When a broadcaster's words have been spoken they disappear into the ether. They are not available for clarification. They must make sense on first hearing. And the words must hold the listeners' interest, so that they will want to hear more. In the 1931 Hollywood classic *The Front Page*, a newspaperman says: 'Who the hell's gonna read the second paragraph?' The suggestion is that a headline and the first paragraph are all most readers bother with. In broadcasting, if the listener doesn't stay with you beyond the first paragraph, you haven't just lost them to another story on the same page. You've lost them to another station.

REMEMBER

➤ Write as you would hear
➤ Speak to one person
➤ Make immediate sense.

TELL IT TO YOUR FRIENDS

The advice of editors to reporters offering a story in the newsroom applies to journalists writing copy: 'How would you tell it to your friends?'

The idea of telling a story to a group of friends works well because everyone can imagine themselves in a social situation: in a pub or café, at a party, round the dinner table. Various people may be contributing to a conversation, and within the bounds of politeness you have to earn your right to be heard. In broadcasting, the competition is not other people's jokes and anecdotes, but the other things the listeners could be doing and the other stations they could be listening to.

Peter Allen of BBC Radio Five Live says most people can tell a story, without notes, but they complicate things by writing it down: 'It's a good exercise to be given a microphone and told to "Go". They'll be amazed at just how good they are at telling a story without any notes because most of us can.

Peter Allen, presenter, BBC Radio Five Live

'The other thing that people do without a script is they tell it simply. They say: "I've just seen a car crash. I think three people were killed. It was terrible. There was a bloke coming down the road and the other one went head on. One was a Jaguar, the other was a Mercedes, I think. They were obviously going too fast."

'And they think, "Oh I've just told a story," whereas if they tried to put that into a script it wouldn't have the immediacy or the power. When you just tell it as it comes into your head, it comes out in an immediate, easily communicated way.'

A CLOSER LOOK

THE ORAL TRADITION

Broadcast journalism is part of a long tradition of the spoken word as the medium of story-telling. Ancient civilisations relied on word of mouth communication. The Greek poet Homer spoke his epics or sang them to a lyre – a primitive stringed instrument (think Bob Dylan without the harmonica). Scholars have worked out that the *Iliad* and *Odyssey* were probably not written by one man. It was probably hundreds of years before they were written down. The rhythm of verse helped poets through the centuries remember the flow of the narrative. Songs served mediaeval balladeers in much the same way.

The stories in the Bible belong to an oral tradition. Most of the New Testament stories about Jesus were not written down until decades after his death. Shakespeare wrote his plays to be performed, to be spoken on the stage, long before scholars decided they were the finest examples of written English.

The essayist and critic William Hazlitt said in 1819: 'To write in a genuine, familiar, or truly English style is to write as anyone would speak in common conversation.' Hazlitt was encouraged to take up journalism by Samuel Taylor Coleridge, a poet.

The critic and author Cyril Connolly rather pompously observed that 'Literature is the art of writing something that will be read twice, journalism what will be read once.' Broadcast journalism isn't read at all; it is heard once. As BBC radio news's style guide points out, who reads Cyril Connolly any more?

Broadcast speech belongs in the long oral tradition – a lineage with a proud history and important lessons for us:

• Write as anyone would speak
• Remember that it will only be heard once.

BE CONCISE

IN A NEWS SCRIPT, THERE IS NO PLACE FOR PADDING OR SUPERFLUOUS WORDS.

People who can communicate perfectly well in casual conversation and in some cases write perfectly good essays, or even newspaper copy, become afflicted by all manner of verbal tics when they write for broadcast. For young people entering the profession it is probably a hangover of school or university days when they were asked to write essays of a certain length. In an essay, every word is a step nearer the target; more words mean less work yet to be done. In a news script, there is no place for padding or superfluous words.

People speak an average of three words every second – that's 180 words a minute. In a half-hour news programme, if every second were taken up with speech (which it is not) that would be a total of 5,400 words. A single story on the front of a broadsheet newspaper might contain 500 words. So you can see that words are at a premium in broadcasting. Each word in a news script not only has to be used precisely, it has to justify its inclusion. Concise writing is essential.

BBC Five Live's Peter Allen says: 'Most writing is just too complex; too many sub-clauses; too much thought; too much trying to compress lots of facts into a single sentence. A sentence should have a thought in it, I think. Just one idea. Bump. Full stop.'

READ WORDS OUT LOUD WHEN YOU HAVE WRITTEN THEM . . . IT IS AN INVALUABLE DISCIPLINE.

A script has to sound right. The rhythms of natural speech must be followed. The best way to check this is to read words out loud when you have written them. In modern computerised newsrooms, the clatter of typewriters no longer covers the chatter of journalists. Writers have to overcome their self-consciousness to speak the words they are writing. It is an invaluable discipline.

Make sure you know the meaning of every word you use, and understand how it fits into the grammar of the sentence you are writing. If you don't understand it, what chance does the listener have?

REMEMBER

➤ Use each word precisely
➤ Cut out superfluous words
➤ Read your scripts out loud.

KEEP IT SIMPLE

Complicated sentence structures and long words are difficult to listen to and understand. We could warn here against dangling participles, passive verbs and stacked modifiers. But we'll do so without engaging in too much grammatical analysis because that would be contrary to the best advice in this chapter: KISS – Keep it simple, stupid!

Simple sentences means active sentences. Subject, verb, object in that order. It is a direct and strong way to deliver information. The subject is usually a person or people doing something. It is better to say somebody did something than to say something was done *by* somebody. 'Rooney scored the first goal just before half time' rather than 'The first goal was scored just before half-time by Rooney.' The audience wants to know who scored. So tell them. Beware of other structures that delay the important information: 'It was just before half-time that Rooney scored the first goal.'

Some passive sentences sound plain wrong. 'Father Christmas was believed in by the children' or even 'Father Christmas was the object of the children's belief' are both horrible constructions. They sound awkward, and are not how you would speak. When you start a sentence with his name, you expect Father Christmas to be doing something.

Usually it is as well to have just one idea in each sentence. Consider this: 'After arriving in Singapore to support London's campaign to host the Olympics, the

Prime Minister said the bid is fantastic and the country is right behind it.' It is clumsier and more difficult to read than using two sentences. 'The Prime Minister has arrived in Singapore to support London's bid to host the Olympic Games. He said the bid is fantastic and the country is behind it.'

Sir David Nicholas, former editor of ITN, the provider of ITV News in Britain, said every sentence must stand on its own legs with no hanging thoughts or subordinate clauses.

CLARITY IS ALL. IT MAY BE NECESSARY TO LOSE SOME DETAIL TO CLARIFY WHAT IS BEING SAID.

Clarity is all. It may be necessary to lose some detail to clarify what is being said. As long as none of the accuracy of the statement is lost, that is usually worth doing. Here's a link to a radio report as it appeared on the BBC's national news service:

A spokesman for Tony Blair has indicated that the Government's Health Improvement Bill – which restricts smoking in enclosed public spaces in England – will be published tomorrow as planned. The Cabinet has so far failed to come to an agreement about the extent of a smoking ban – it's likely that there'll now be more discussion on the issue. From Westminster, here's Mike Sergeant.

And this is how BBC Radio Stoke rewrote the same link, losing none of the sense and only a little of the detail:

The Government's plans to ban smoking in enclosed spaces will be published tomorrow as planned. The Cabinet has so far failed to agree on the extent of the ban. From Westminster, here's Mike Sergeant.

We no longer have the source of the information (the rather vague 'spokesman for Tony Blair'), we've lost the name of the bill (who cares?) and we are no longer told the ban will apply specifically in England, but that would surely be understood by a listener to an English radio station. The shorter version has to be preferable for the purposes of broadcast journalism. It is certainly easier to understand.

REMEMBER

➤ Use simple, active sentences

➤ Stick to one idea per sentence

➤ Clarity is all.

TIP BOX **GREAT WRITING**

Great writing is a matter of opinion. One man's idea of great journalistic writing is another person's idea of pretentious drivel. But few can fail to be impressed by the words that capture an idea or a moment so that others can only say: 'I wish I'd said that.'

Your favourite might be Brian Hanrahan during the Falklands War in 1982, ad-libbing on BBC radio to fill a hole in the script because the government censors wouldn't allow him to report the numbers of aircraft on a mission: 'I counted them all out and I counted them all back.'

Or the simple use of the word 'biblical' in Michael Buerk's description of the Ethiopian famine in 1984, in a report that inspired Bob Geldof's Band Aid and Live Aid fund-raising campaigns: 'Dawn – and as the sun breaks through the piercing chill of night on the plain outside Korem, it lights up a biblical famine – now, in the twentieth century.'

Or Martin Bell on Soviet troops leaving Czechoslovakia in 1990: 'They outstayed a welcome they never had . . .'

The lessons of good style can be learned from those whose plaudits have been earned in spheres of writing beyond broadcast news. The great sports writer Hugh McIlvanney described the British boxer Joe Bugner as having 'the physique of a Greek statue but fewer moves'. Alan Bennett, who wrote the hugely acclaimed series of TV monologues *Talking Heads*, said of his own mother: 'A sausage had only to be hoisted on a stick to become . . . an emblem of impossible sophistication.'

Pithy, terse and brilliant. Witty too. Learn from the experts, and don't restrict your influences to other broadcast journalists.

LEARN FROM THE EXPERTS, AND DON'T RESTRICT YOUR INFLUENCES TO OTHER BROADCAST JOURNALISTS.

HOW TO TELL YOUR STORY

When you sit down to write your copy, you should ask yourself how you are going to tell the story to a friend. What do you want to tell them? What will they want to know? And what do they need to know? You want to grab their attention. But there is a world of difference between being the girl who makes everyone laugh in the pub and being a successful stand-up comedian. Similarly, to be a successful broadcast journalist, there are rules that will help you apply your story-telling skills accurately and concisely. We'll now consider some of the guidelines and techniques that will help you write well. Many have trodden this path before you, and their expertise is readily available.

STYLE GUIDES

There is a big difference between the language suitable for a BBC Radio Four bulletin and that of the local commercial radio station. Within the BBC, Five Live is less formal than Radio Four. ITV News has adopted a more tabloid style than the BBC. But the BBC Radio News Style Guide, which is available online, warns writers that there is no such thing as 'trying to be a bit more Radio Four'. That is just an excuse for flabby prose. The difference between networks is one of tone, not the way stories are told: 'The same species of clear, straightforward English will stand you in equally good stead whichever outlet you are writing for.'

Each organisation will have its own style guide – a useful book or online resource to be consulted by news writers, setting out the preferred usage of the language.

Many style guides have a lot of material in common, pointing out frequent mistakes. Most will recognise that the spoken language evolves and what was common usage for one generation may not have the same meaning for the next.

THE SPOKEN LANGUAGE EVOLVES AND WHAT WAS COMMON USAGE FOR ONE GENERATION MAY NOT HAVE THE SAME MEANING FOR THE NEXT.

Here's an example of what's considered correct modern usage from the the Sky Sports News Writing Style Guide:

Effectively/in effect

Effectively means *with (good) effect;*

Don't use it to mean *in effect*, for example:

. . . the game was effectively over by half time . . .

But the right-winger was used *effectively*.

And from the BBC News Style Guide:

Effectively is often confused with *in effect*. If something is effective, it produces a satisfactory result, so *effectively* means with *a satisfactory outcome. The outbreak of plague in Skegness has been effectively contained* means the rest of us are safe. *In effect* means *in practice*, and often indicates an unplanned outcome, as in *The new tax has in effect made it more sensible for Geoff to remain on benefits*.

Another adverb often used wrongly is **literally**. It is literally the opposite of 'metaphorically,' so it should never be used before a metaphor. Don't say: 'Walcott literally flew down the wing.'

Be careful how you use simple everyday words. You often hear 'on either side of the road' or 'either side of half-time' when the speaker really means on 'each' or 'both' sides.

There are many more examples in style guides online.

See Workshops and Exercises.

ACCURACY

You will notice a theme running through a lot of this chapter – and a lot of this book – the need for accuracy, both in the reporting of facts and the use of language.

KEITH WATERHOUSE: 'WORDS ARE FACTS. CHECK THEM (SPELLING AND MEANING) AS YOU WOULD ANY OTHER.'

The credo of Joseph Pulitzer who gave his name to the US renowned journalism prize was: 'Accuracy, accuracy, accuracy.' That was echoed by the Head of Sky News for ten years, Nick Pollard. Keith Waterhouse, a great British newspaper columnist *and* writer of fiction, advises journalists: 'Words are facts. Check them (spelling and meaning) as you would any other.'

Mistakes slip into copy under the pressure of deadlines. They occur too when you are writing about something unfamiliar. There will be many in your audience who do not know what you're talking about, but also some who care passionately about the subject. For example, the two-hundredth anniversary of the Battle of Trafalgar produced a series of inaccuracies and howlers.

A reporter on BBC Breakfast News commented (twice) on flags being 'risen'. Christ is risen – it's biblical language. Flags are raised.

A BBC Radio Four report spoke of HMS *Victory* being 'anchored' in Portsmouth Harbour. It is in dry dock.

The BBC's *Ten O'Clock News* referred to 'the HMS *Victory*'. HMS stands for Her Majesty's Ship. Would you refer to the Queen's shoes as 'the her shoes?'

And most confusing of all, a link from Independent Radio News for their network reported: '*Lord Nelson was fatally wounded and supposedly said to his right-hand man: "Kiss me, Hardy." '*

Nelson did not have a right hand – he lost most of his right arm in Tenerife – so the phrase 'right-hand man' is confusing. Is it meant to imply that Hardy was some sort of gofer for the admiral? Hardy was the captain of HMS *Victory*. He was with the Admiral when he was shot. Hardy continued to command his ship and visited the wounded Nelson twice before he died. Nelson was attended below deck on the *Victory* by the ship's surgeon, a steward, a chaplain and a purser. He had a secretary, who was killed in the early stages of the battle. And then there was Admiral Collingwood, who commanded the right-hand column of British ships of the line at Trafalgar. To describe Hardy as Nelson's 'right-hand man' is simplistic, to say the least. It may work as a newspaper headline (where the 'joke' is implicit) but does not suit broadcast style.

If it's any consolation to modern reporters, the very first newspaper account of Nelson's death – in the *Gibraltar Chronicle* of 24 October 1805 – was also riddled with inaccuracies, claiming the Admiral was shot once, had his wound dressed and returned to the deck, was shot again and then survived till the evening. His last words, in this account, were: 'Thank God! I have outlived this day, and now I die content!' Sloppy journalism from two centuries ago!

UTV Radio's news mission statement says: 'We don't deal in half-truths or speculation . . . We check facts and source our stories.'

The Ofcom Broadcasting Code says: 'News, in whatever form, must be reported with due accuracy and presented with due impartiality.'

ACCURACY IS OFTEN MORE THAN A QUESTION OF GETTING THE FACTS RIGHT. FACTS AND INFORMATION SHOULD BE WEIGHED TO GET AT THE TRUTH.

The BBC's policy is that it considers accuracy more important than speed. There is no justifiable argument for inaccuracy in journalism, but the BBC's position is not merely a statement of the obvious. According to its Editorial Guidelines, accuracy is often more than a question of getting the facts right. Facts and information should be weighed to get at the truth.

The BBC reported riots in the Lozells area of Birmingham in October 2005, but failed to mention the racial element of the disturbances. The violence followed a rumour on a pirate radio station that a gang of Asian youths had raped a 14-year-old black girl. Newspapers reported that there were rival gangs of black and Asian youths fighting in the street. The BBC was criticised by viewers for not reporting the race of those involved. TV News editor Marek Pruszewicz admitted on News 24's *NewsWatch* that they probably could have been clearer than they were, and that they had learned a lesson.

He said: 'There are times when you can tell viewers things you don't know as well as things you know for sure. If you don't do that you can find yourself losing trust from the viewer. You can find yourself in a position where the viewer thinks: "Are they holding something back?"

'I think the lesson we've learnt is let the viewer in on the information you're party to. Journalists at the BBC want to report fact. They want to be accurate. They don't want to be in a position where they report any rumour that springs from the rumour mill.'

Caution in the BBC's reporting led to a lack of accuracy.

Evan Davis, the BBC Economics Editor, explained in an online article that it is not the case that 'comment is free and facts are sacred', as he had always supposed. 'Far from being precious nuggets of valuable information to be cherished, most facts are left discarded and unused.'

Davis argues that the audience wants the journalist to make judgements on their behalf, about the significance of the available facts and the pattern that fits them together.

So how do you avoid inaccuracy?

REMEMBER

> ➤ Check every fact
> ➤ Only use words you understand
> ➤ Check the spelling and meaning of unfamiliar words
> ➤ Don't report rumour
> ➤ Be bold – if you are sure of your facts, use them.

See Workshops and Exercises.

KEEP IT UP-TO-DATE

PEOPLE EXPECT TO HEAR ABOUT WHAT IS HAPPENING NOW, NOT WHAT HAPPENED YESTERDAY.

Precision also applies to any references to time in your script. Broadcasting has supplanted newspapers as people's main source of news because it is immediate, and not subject to printing and distribution deadlines. People expect to hear about what is happening now, not what happened yesterday.

We know from Chapter 2: *What's the story?* that immediacy is one of the factors that makes a story newsworthy. News has to be new. We've also mentioned that when you record interviews you should be aware of when the recording is likely to be broadcast, so that there are no misleading references to time and dates. It is equally important to write stories in a way that keeps them bang up to the minute. That means using the present tense where possible.

In the aftermath of Hurricane Katrina in August 2005, there was widespread looting in New Orleans. It would have been accurate to lead a news bulletin with the phrase: 'lawlessness continued this morning', or 'lawlessness has continued'. But it had much more impact to say: 'lawlessness is continuing'. This underlines the fact that the law-breaking was not under control. It keeps the audience wanting to know more.

Even after an event, it is important to keep the information as immediate as possible. 'Two people have been killed and seven injured in a road accident,' rather than 'two people were killed . . .' And if the information is being reported the morning after the event, consider updating it by saying: 'The police are investigating a road accident which killed two and left seven people injured.'

You might even want to project forward to future events: 'The police will begin interviewing witnesses today . . .'

➤ Report what's happening now, not what happened yesterday
➤ Use the present tense where possible
➤ Think of ways to keep stories fresh.

USE SHORT WORDS NOT LONG ONES

NEVER USE A LONG WORD WHERE A SHORT ONE WILL DO.

Never use a long word where a short one will do. That advice was one of the rules from English novelist George Orwell in *Politics and the English Language*, written in 1946. The man who gave us 'Big Brother' and 'Room 101' (both from his novel *1984* and both the titles of twenty-first-century TV series) is still relevant today.

So use:

• Start *not* instigate
• Dead *not* deceased
• Cut *not* eliminate
• Fire *not* conflagration
• Truth *not* veracity
• End *not* terminate.

Another word that creeps into scripts all the time is *however.* The BBC presenter John Humphrys got it right in his *Lost for Words*, aptly subtitled *The Mangling and Manipulating of the English Language*. He wrote: ' "However" instead of "but" is clumsy. Any word that requires a pair of commas to surround it before it is allowed out in public should stay at home.'

And don't feel the need to replace the perfectly serviceable 'said' with its many alternatives: affirmed, announced, asserted, claimed, commented, observed, stated, and so on. Phrases like 'expressed the view that' are ugly and unnecessary. 'Had this to say' is a broadcasting cliché.

USE SHORT PHRASES RATHER THAN LONG ONES

Many of the phrases in everyday speech are fillers used to buy the speaker thinking time. Just as you wouldn't expect to hear 'you know' or 'if you see what I mean' in a broadcast script, you shouldn't use 'at this moment in time' or 'at present' when the perfectly serviceable 'now' will do. Similarly, 'more than' is more concise than the rather pompous 'in excess of'. Some common phrases can be replaced by a single word.

So use:

• Although *not* in spite of the fact that
• To *not* in order to
• During *not* in the course of
• Scarce *not* in short supply
• Thought *not* was of the opinion that
• Because *not* owing to the fact that
• If *not* in the event of.

You will find your own examples as you think harder about the language you use.

➤ Use short words instead of longer ones
➤ Use short phrases or single words where they can replace longer phrases.

USE SHORT FORMS

In everyday speech we shorten common phrases. 'I will' becomes 'I'll', 'we will' becomes 'we'll', 'you are' is 'you're', 'they are' is 'they're'. These short forms, or contractions, are the best form to use for broadcast scripts. They are conversational and concise. If you speak it that way, then write it that way. You'll find we do it in this book all the time. It may not be the best written English style, but, hey, we're broadcasters!

Many natural contractions are pronoun–verb combinations like those above. There's never any harm in using the short form. Others have to be used more judiciously, particularly when they involve a negative. It's usually acceptable to say *isn't*, *aren't*, *hasn't*, *haven't*, *don't* and *won't*. But if you want to emphasise the negative, avoid the contraction. 'The Prime Minister said he will not resign,' is stronger than 'The Prime Minister said he won't resign.' That is because you can put emphasis on the word *not* when you read it.

Contracting *has* or *is* into '*s* at the end of a noun also usually works. So 'The President's appointed a new Secretary of State' or 'The President's on his way to Camp David' are fine and work well.

Contraction doesn't work though when it becomes an excuse for sloppy speech. Don't use 'wanna' instead of 'want to'. And if you use 'could've', be aware it's short for 'could have' and not 'could of'. Most broadcasters frown on the use of slang expressions, but some commercial radio stations aimed at younger audiences encourage the kind of street language an older generation would frown upon. Offensive language remains taboo.

IF IT SOUNDS RIGHT, CONTRACT AND USE THE SHORTENED VERSION, BECAUSE IT IS HOW WE ALL SPEAK.

The general rule is: If it sounds right, contract and use the shortened version, because it is how we all speak and what the listener's ear is attuned to.

➤ Contract words and phrases where it sounds natural to do so
➤ Avoid slang – unless it's part of your house style
➤ Leave out the contraction if you want to emphasise something – particularly a negative
➤ Make your scripts sound like everyday speech.

WHO SAID WHAT – ATTRIBUTING STORIES

Good journalistic practice requires information to be properly sourced. The listener needs to know who is responsible for what they are hearing. In newspapers the attribution often comes at the end of the paragraph, after the reader has read the main point of the story. Here's an example from a newspaper:

Tony Blair has issued a furious dressing-down to Charles Clarke, the Home Secretary, for going soft in the fight against crime, a secret Downing Street memo has revealed.

Sunday Telegraph, front page, 3 July 2005

This is strong stuff – the newspaper had apparently seen the minutes of a meeting between the PM and Home Secretary. But the story would not work well as a broadcast script in this form. For a start it is not a natural way to speak.

The man at the bar wouldn't say: 'My dinner will be in the dog if I don't return soon from the pub, a mobile phone call from my wife has revealed.' He might say: 'My wife tells me . . .' etc.

A broadcast version of the *Sunday Selegraph* story might read:

A leaked Downing Street memo reveals that Tony Blair has accused the Home Secretary Charles Clarke of going soft in the fight against crime.

There is another problem with giving information before it is attributed. Your newsreader or reporter becomes the person offering the information to the listener. Contentious statements can be given authority because they are heard first from the mouth of a trusted newsreader.

Consider this example: 'The Prime Minister took the country to war on the basis of a lie and must pay the price by losing his job, according to . . .'

Listeners need to know who's saying something before they know what they said. They can then judge the authority of the information.

REMEMBER

➤ Make the source of your information clear.

Avoid direct quotes

Direct quotes appear all the time in newspapers. What somebody says appears between sets of inverted commas. It's the nearest readers of newspapers can get to hearing somebody saying something. Radio has the advantage of being able to use the actual sound of somebody saying something, and on television we can see them saying it.

There are still times when we want to quote what somebody has said – in the intro to a story for example – and that's when dangers arise. On radio in particular it is difficult to tell whether you are reading your own words or somebody else's. Direct quotations should only be used sparingly.

'Bob Geldof said the Live 8 concerts had been "full of hope and possibility and life".'

BBC News, 3 July 2005

This works because the quotation is short and easy to follow. Any longer though and it might be difficult for the listener.

Look at this example from the BBC TV interactive service just before the G8 summit in Scotland where the cancellation of debt in Africa was to be announced:

The Chancellor Gordon Brown told the BBC: 'It is a lifetime's work where we empower the people of Africa and the developing countries to make decisions for themselves.'

If this sentence were to be broadcast on radio it would be difficult to work out to whom 'we' refers. Is it the British government, all the governments of the G8, citizens of developed countries, the BBC? Using *indirect* speech would make it clearer. 'The chancellor said it was a lifetime's work where the G8 countries empower the people of Africa and the developing countries to make decisions for themselves.'

So, *it's usually better to use indirect or reported speech.* The tense as well as the person linked to the verb changes in reported speech: 'I am' becomes 'he was'.

Direct speech: Jaldeep said: 'I'm going to the concert in Hyde Park.'

Reported speech: Jaldeep said he was going to the concert in Hyde Park.

The word 'that' could be included in the second example: 'Jaldeep said that he was going to the concert in Hyde Park.' But what's the point? It is a superfluous word. Strike it out. The word 'that' is almost always unnecessary in this type of sentence and should usually be omitted.

PUNCTUATION

Punctuation in a broadcast script should be kept to a minimum, to make it easy to read. Full stops are essential, but inverted commas are almost always unnecessary and colons are impossible to express in speech.

We speak in phrases rather than perfectly formed sentences. So there is no harm in writing that way.

REMEMBER

➤ Use short words instead of long ones
➤ Use short forms (contractions) of phrases such as can't, don't, won't
➤ Attribute your stories – make the source clear
➤ Avoid direct speech.

If you follow these simple rules, you will develop a clear concise way of expressing yourself. Many people master these techniques, and then allow all manner of sloppy expressions to cloud the clarity of their writing. When you know how to spot these intrusive phrases, though, they are easy to avoid.

CLICHÉS

A cliché is a hackneyed and over-used expression, and, boy, are they over-used in journalism!

Julia Cresswell, the editor of the *The Penguin Dictionary of Clichés* defines a cliché as 'an expression that does your thinking for you: an expression so well established in the language that you know exactly how it is going to end once someone has started saying it, and which conveys instant meaning without your having to work out anything for yourself.'

Aha, you're thinking. That's handy. Phrases I can use so that everybody knows what I mean. Really useful if I'm up against a deadline. And that's fine. If you want to produce turgid and predictable copy.

Andrew Boyd, in *Broadcast Journalism: Techniques of Radio and Television News*, summed it up brilliantly: 'Cliches and journalese are devils disguised as angels. They lie in wait for the moment Inspiration turns her back, before overpowering her, stealing her clothes and sneaking up on the reporter as a deadline approaches.

'Hapless hacks are usually so intent on beating the clock that they fail to see through their disguise and welcome these saboteurs as saviours.'

Let's have a look at some examples of cliché (and journalese) from just one *hour* of broadcasting in July 2005:

. . . a huge security operation – BBC News

. . . a huge boost to the economy – BBC News

. . . in a comfortable condition – BBC News

. . . scientific studies – BBC News

. . . will add some time to your journey – BBC London News

. . . on your supermarket shelves – BBC News 24

. . . quiet confidence – ITV News

. . . flying the flag for Britain – ITV News

. . . singing London's praises . . . hot contenders . . . top of an exclusive pile . . . so good they named it twice – Sky News

. . . face a major hurdle – Sky News

. . . a battle of wills – Sky News

. . . fears are growing – Sky News

. . . all-time highs – Sky News

. . . the best sporting action from all around the globe – Sky Sports News

. . . Jack Nicklaus rolled back the years – Sky Sports News

. . . trained negotiators – BBC Radio One

. . . enjoyed a huge boost – BBC Radio Two

. . . keeping a very close eye on – BBC Radio Four

. . . ring of steel – BBC Radio Four

. . . cut up rough – BBC Radio Four

. . . walking tall – BBC Radio Five Live

. . . sales have rocketed – BBC Radio Five Live.

All those phrases were used by news readers and reporters. People turn on the news to hear fresh information – not stale and predictable phrases. A fun test which can help you avoid some of these pitfalls is to apply the opposite word to a phrase. You'd never say '<u>un</u>trained negotiators' or 'walking small'.

It has become a cliché of books on news writing that they all seem to offer the old joke: avoid clichés – yes – like the plague. Better to avoid them like any nasty disease.

Be realistic though. Mike Henfield, a seasoned radio news writer, says: 'When the chips are down (there's a cliché for you), there's often very little alternative when you need a shorthand way of telling a story. By all means avoid really obvious ones – but sometimes they're a necessary evil (another one!).'

REMEMBER

➤ Avoid clichés if you possibly can.

JARGON

Journalism is all about interpreting events and information in everyday language – language people understand. Every business has its jargon, language specific to the job in hand. For those in the know it can be, though isn't always, the best way of communicating. There's a lot of jargon from the world of broadcast journalism in this book. But you wouldn't expect your mother, your sister or the bloke in the pub to understand 'voicers', 'two-ways' and 'pressers'.

DON'T EXPECT YOUR VIEWERS AND LISTENERS TO UNDERSTAND THE JARGON.

So, don't expect your viewers and listeners to understand the jargon of the legal or medical professions, or that of the emergency services.

If someone is pronounced *dead on arrival* at hospital or *DOA* that means death was certified at that point because someone was available to do so officially. It doesn't always mean they died on the way to hospital. If they died in a road accident, say so.

If a policeman tells you an HGV and a private motor vehicle were involved in a fatal RTA it means someone died in a crash involving a lorry and a car. We don't all watch *The Bill*.

Presenter Jeremy Paxman on *Newsnight* debunked the jargon, and indeed the mixed metaphors, of international diplomacy by quoting BBC Radio News coverage of the Middle East peace process. The radio reported: 'The road map was derailed before it got off the ground.' Paxman's sardonic tone said it all. Incidentally, 'road map' is defined in Nick Webb's *The Dictionary of Bullshit* as a noun meaning 'a plan, but a little more vague.'

A conservationist on BBC *Breakfast News* spoke of the 'Cotswold Water Park biodiversity plan in its action statement'. He was talking about the reintroduction of beavers into the wild.

REMEMBER

➤ Learn to recognise jargon – the specialist words and phrases used by specific professional groups

➤ Even if you understand the phrase, don't assume your audience will

➤ Try to dissuade interviewees from using jargon – you will end up interrupting them to explain their meaning.

Journalese

Journalism has its own ugly jargon – a form of the English language beloved of many newspaper journalists and abhorred in almost equal measure by most broadcasters. Former BBC news editor Rick Thompson says in *Writing for Broadcast Journalists*: '. . . the language of broadcast news is infected by the virus of so-called journalese. It is rampant. And there seems to be no known cure.'

JOURNALESE IS THE JARGON OF BAD JOURNALISM . . . THE PROBLEM WITH JOURNALESE IS THAT PEOPLE DON'T SPEAK LIKE THAT.

Journalese is the jargon of bad journalism. Dozens of journalese words infect the pages of newspapers, many of them chosen because they are short and fit neatly into headlines. Shock. Bid. Probe. Clash. Plea. Blast. Slam. Row. Short words are always preferable to longer alternatives, but only where their meaning is precise and not sensational.

Another type of journalese is the use of the stacked phrase, cramming adjectives and nouns into unwieldy phrases that are difficult to say on air and often look ridiculous, even in print: five times Olympic gold medal winning oarsman Sir Steve Redgrave; the Bob Geldof-inspired global series of Live 8 concerts; double-oscar winning actor Tom Hanks. 'London mayor Ken Livingstone' is more clearly expressed as 'the Mayor of London, Ken Livingstone' or 'Ken Livingstone, the London Mayor'.

Newspapers also seem to have an obsession with age: the 30-year-old mother-of-two; the 20-year-old soul-singing sensation; the 30-year-old midfield maestro. Better to say 'Angela Johnson, who's 30 and has two children; the soul singer Joss Stone, who's 20; David Beckham, who's 30. That's if you consider age an important part of the story. It probably isn't. In January 2006, the *Daily Mirror* described the Education Secretary Ruth Kelly, who was under pressure to resign, as a '37-year-old mum-of-four'. You should never hear that phrase in a broadcast.

The problem with journalese is that people don't speak like that. Nobody says: 'Drinks probe cheat makes shock eleventh hour bid to end row.' They say: 'OK, I'll get my round in!'

REMEMBER

➤ Learn to recognise journalese

➤ Treat it like any other jargon – leave it out

➤ Don't be obsessed by people's age unless it's relevant to the story

➤ Journalese might work in a newspaper headline, but not in the spoken word.

Officialese

Politicians and businessmen have their own languages – often employed to disguise the real meaning of what they are saying. *Downsizing* means people lose their job. *Human Resources* or *HR* means people. And the word *issue* has become a euphemism for *problem*. But the two words do not mean the same thing. If there's a problem, that's part of the story.

You should avoid euphemisms in all your writing. For clarity, always say 'died' rather than 'lost their life' or 'passed away'. When you are trying to get to the meaning of officialese, cutting out euphemisms is equally important.

Here's an intriguing one from John Clare, the chief executive of DSG International (that's the electrical shops Dixons and Currys to you and me). He told an interviewer on Radio Five Live's business news: 'We're putting some exciting new executions into the marketplace.'

The idea of exciting new executions surely whetted the appetites of any horror fans in the breakfast audience. What did he have in mind? Celebrity disembowelling? What do you think he really meant?

Also on Five Live, when commuters were trapped in London after the terrorist bombs of July 2005, many complained of being charged up to three times the normal rate for hotel rooms. A spokesman for the hotel trade was asked to explain this apparent exploitation. He said it was an example of 'yield management'. Now, yield management is a perfectly respectable term for dealing with supply and demand, notably in the airline and hotel businesses. In this context, though, the jargon seemed callous.

And in another business bulletin, Sir Nigel Rudd, the chairman of Boots, commenting on a proposed merger with the pharmacy chain, Alliance Unichem, said there was 'complementarity' between the two companies. Faced with a light-hearted challenge about whether there really was such a word, Sir Nigel laughed and confessed: 'I don't honestly know. I probably just invented it!'

REMEMBER

➤ Officialese should always be challenged

➤ Avoid euphemisms

➤ Where possible, convert official language into plain English.

HYPE

THERE'S A TEMPTATION TO MAKE STORIES SOUND MORE IMPORTANT THAN THEY ARE BY USING EXAGGERATED LANGUAGE. RESIST THAT TEMPTATION.

Professional rivalry means most journalists want to impress their editors and colleagues, and excite audiences. So, there's a temptation to make stories sound more important than they are by using exaggerated language. Resist that temptation.

According to BBC Radio Four the French President Jacques Chirac committed a 'monumental' blunder with a comment in July 2005 that the only thing the British have ever given European farming was mad cow disease. Napoleon won monumental victories – they built the Arc De Triomphe because of them. Nelson won a monumental victory at Trafalgar – otherwise there would be no column in Trafalgar Square. Nobody is planning a monument to M. Chirac's bad taste jokes.

The spread of early man into the Americas was described on BBC Radio Five Live as 'a hugely controversial area'. But it isn't. Are they talking about it in your supermarket? We doubt it.

A BBC TV regional breakfast bulletin reported: 'Crucial talks between West Midlands fire service and union leaders take place this week in a last-ditch attempt to avoid strike action.' The sentence has all the hallmarks of a hastily written Sunday overnight filler. The clichés 'crucial' and 'last-ditch' add little to the sense.

A reporter on ITV News in the Scottish village nearest the G8 summit in Gleneagles in July 2005 said: 'Nearly every vehicle is packed with police.' There were empty cars behind her.

And street demonstrations in Scotland the previous day were described on Sky News as 'violent battles with police'. As opposed to those 'battles of wills' which are presumably non-violent?

The UTV Radio mission statement – for radio stations with a style they themselves describe as 'tabloid, punchy and to the point' – makes it clear that they avoid 'tabloid excesses'.

REMEMBER

➤ If a story is worth reporting, there is no need to use hype

➤ Exaggerated language runs the risk of appearing ridiculous.

NUMBERS

Numbers present real problems for broadcasters, particularly on radio. Television can explain with a graphic. Charts or simple figures on screen let the eye take in what the ear is hearing. It is important the words match the picture – don't say *one in five* if the graphic says *20 per cent*.

RADIO IS A POOR MEDIUM FOR DEALING WITH NUMBERS.

But radio listeners will struggle to take in big or complicated figures. The BBC News Style Guide says bluntly that radio is a poor medium for dealing with numbers. A story with too many figures numbs the listener.

Psychologists have proven there's a limit to how many numbers people can retain. The art is to simplify. Round up or down where appropriate. And always start a story by identifying a trend or somebody's reaction, rather than getting bogged down in the numbers. So:

There's been an increase in the number of people unemployed and claiming benefit.

Or:

The Prime Minister says he's disappointed by the rise in unemployment.

Rather than:

The unemployment figures have risen by 37,000.

Be particularly wary of percentages. A rise in interest rates from 4 per cent to 5 per cent is not a 1 per cent increase. It's a 25 per cent increase, although to say so in those terms would be confusing.

Doubling a figure is an increase of 100 per cent, not 200 per cent. If something goes up 200 per cent, it triples in cost.

Try not to mix decimals, fractions and percentages in the same story. Listeners do not have the opportunity to sit back and ponder the figures. A bulletin is not a mental arithmetic test. A bemused audience will certainly switch off mentally, and may switch off physically.

When writing about figures, be careful about the use of words like 'number' and 'amount' and their close relatives 'fewer' and 'less'. It's 'the number of people on hospital waiting lists' not 'the amount of people'. Fewer means smaller in number (fewer coins, for example); less means smaller in quantity or a smaller amount (less money).

Even if you get the numbers right, watch how they fit into the sense of what you are saying. Avoid nonsense like this from BBC Midlands Today, reporting on improvements at a secondary school: 'Exam results have rocketed from 11 to 34 per cent.' No, they haven't. It's likely that there were results for 100 per cent of the exams taken, both this year and last. The meaning was probably that the pass rate improved.

REMEMBER

➤ Simplify numbers where possible

➤ Round up or down if appropriate

➤ Don't mix decimals, fractions and percentages

➤ On television and online use graphics to explain numbers.

USING GOOD ENGLISH IN YOUR COPY

If you take the advice above, you will already be able to construct clear, understandable broadcast sentences. Think what you want to say. Work out how you want to say it. Then consider how each strand of information, clearly expressed, should come together in the finished copy.

A GOOD STORY IS MORE THAN A COLLECTION OF FACTS. IT HAS A NARRATIVE STRUCTURE.

A good story is more than a collection of facts. It has a narrative structure. That structure will be designed to attract and keep the attention of the audience. The facts must be assembled in a logical sequence to tell the story. You need to understand the story before you begin to tell it. You should marshal all the information into a structure that tells people what they need to know in a sequence they can easily listen to, follow and comprehend. What you tell them should make sense to the listener. They might want to find out more about the story – that's a good sign, because it shows you have interested them in the subject – but they should not be left asking questions you should have answered.

PUTTING THE STORY TOGETHER – THE FIVE 'W'S

The key ingredients of most news stories can be summed up in the five 'W's – who, what, where, when, why.

- Who was involved?
- What happened?
- Where did it happen?
- When did it happen?
- Why did it happen?

Some textbooks on journalism suggest 'How' is important too. It depends on the story. How something happened is often complicated. In the case of a train or air crash, it's best left to the accident inquiry. In any case, 'how' or 'why' will rarely be the main point of the story.

Telling the story depends on marshalling the ingredients into a coherent structure. It is not necessary to have all the 'W's near the top of the story. But what happened and who was involved are almost always in the introduction.

If the 'who' is well known you may name the person or give them their title, or both, straight away.

'The former Prime Minister Ted Heath has died.'

In this example, to say 'a former Prime Minister has died' would be unduly vague. To say 'Ted Heath has died' would not deliver enough information to younger people who don't remember or have not been told about Mr Heath's premiership. He died 31 years after leaving power, so we can't assume everybody knew who he was.

HEADLINE WRITING

Opening with impact

They're the first thing the audience hears, but often the last thing to be written. The headline has to capture the attention, sum up the key point of the story, and tell people why they should want to stick with the bulletin. Teasers midway through the programme serve the same purpose. They trumpet why this story is news.

HEADLINES NEED A SENSE OF URGENCY. THEY NEED TO BE BRIEF AND PUNCHY.

Headlines need a sense of urgency. They need to be brief and punchy. To achieve these effects they are often written in the present tense.

The government is urging GPs to improve their service to patients, by keeping their surgeries open for longer.

A teenage girl is in hospital after being repeatedly stabbed at school.

Here are the headlines for a typical Radio Four bulletin:

A rush for flu vaccines means supplies have almost run out.

Concern about cheating is leading to a review of exam coursework.

Kenya has voted 'no' to a new constitution.

Angela Merkel is about to take power in Germany.

And here's an example of a headline sequence from BBC TV News, suggesting that sports news can and should be given – on merit – the same treatment as hard news:

After the best series ever, England's cricketers regain the Ashes – for the first time in eighteen years.

A superb century from Kevin Pietersen wrecks Australia's chances on the final day of the fifth test.

We'll have the full story of the day's play and the celebrations at the Oval.

*POWERFUL
ACTUALITY AND
PUNCHY INTERVIEW
CLIPS SHOULD BE
INCLUDED IN
HEADLINE
SEQUENCES TO
ADD IMPACT.*

Also tonight, after the violence in Belfast local leaders are told to back the security forces.

In Niger, food is still not getting through to many of those who need it.

Motorists are told not to panic buy at the petrol pumps.

And President Bush in the centre of New Orleans, on the day one of his top officials resigns.

Powerful actuality and punchy interview clips should be included in headline sequences to add impact.

REMEMBER

- ➤ Headlines need a sense of urgency
- ➤ Be brief and punchy
- ➤ Use actuality to add impact.

Closing heads

Many programmes close with headlines. They are a summary of the day's top stories, and are written in a different style from the opening heads. The purpose is to inform, not to tease. Similar sequences occur in the middle of longer programmes, perhaps after an ad break. Again the language is different from the opening menu.

You're watching the Sky Report, our top stories tonight:

More than two thousand people have attended a memorial service in Saint Paul's Cathedral for the victims and survivors of the London bombings in July.

David Blunkett says he won't resign despite new evidence that he's breached the ministerial code of conduct. It's emerged that he failed to seek advice over a third job despite being warned three times.

And the Prime Minister's met energy ministers from around the world as part of discussions to tackle climate change and global warming.

REMEMBER

- ➤ Closing heads inform rather than tease
- ➤ They should summarise the whole of the story.

The menu

A headline sequence is known as a menu – it tells what is on offer and whets the appetite. The example above from the day England regained the Ashes was followed by two regional headlines. Viewers would be in little doubt they were to get comprehensive coverage of the cricket story – but not at the expense of the international or local news agenda. That didn't stop some viewers complaining to the BBC's *NewsWatch* programme that the cricket was given too much prominence.

WHY HEADLINES ARE EVEN MORE IMPORTANT IN THE DIGITAL AGE

Streamed video on demand means viewers can choose their own news agenda to suit their interests. You might assume headlines are no longer important, and that they are a hangover from newspapers and traditional media. Perhaps you consider they are only important to broadcasters working on traditional 'appointment to view' bulletins, and on rolling news. Think again.

Headlines have never been more important. Vin Ray, founding head of the BBC's Virtual College of Journalism, says headline writing skills are at a greater premium than ever before. That's because it is the headline – summarising the story – that determines what people will watch. The headline is the only thing many viewers of interactive digital TV or news websites will see. Just as key words determine the web content that appears on an Internet search, the words in headlines will determine which stories are available to viewers who have pre-selected their viewing options. And the headlines in menus offered on interactive TV and the Net are the basis for the choices made by all users of those media.

The buzz phrase for successful interactive operations is that 'content is king'. But nobody will access the finest content in the world if the headlines that lead to it are not compelling.

NOBODY WILL ACCESS THE FINEST CONTENT IN THE WORLD IF THE HEADLINES THAT LEAD TO IT ARE NOT COMPELLING.

INTROS AND OUTROS

Hooking the listener

The introduction to a story is known as an *intro* or a *link* in most UK TV newsrooms. Americans prefer to call it the *lead*. In radio, the words that introduce an item may be known as a *cue*.

Whatever you call it, the idea of an intro is to hook the viewer or listener. And as any angler will tell you, that's the hardest part of the game. The best way to tell a story is almost always to give the main facts first. But how you do it can vary. The intro might be a dramatic or exciting sentence in its own right. It could include a telling quote, an amazing statistic or a witty turn of phrase.

Here's the lead to ITV News' 10.30 p.m. programme in February 2006:

Forget the Great Train Robbery. Forget the Northern Bank in Belfast. Britain's biggest ever robbery took place in the early hours of this morning in Kent. Sources have told ITV News tonight that as much as 40 million pounds in bank notes was taken. A security manager and his family were abducted by men pretending to be police officers. They told them unless they co-operated their lives would be in danger. Tonight the man's employer Securitas said it was a brutal crime. Our reporter Harry Smith is live in Tonbridge tonight. Harry . . .

The first sentence can be as short as those above, but should not be more than 20 or at the outside 30 words long. People speak at an average of three words per second (a useful guide when calculating the length of your script).

So 20–30 words is roughly between seven and ten seconds – a comfortable time span for the listener to take in your meaning.

Here's an example from Radio Four:

The American Secretary of State Condoleezza Rice has arrived in Iraq on a surprise visit. (15 words)

This addresses the questions *who, what* and *where* and the use of the word 'surprise' tells you it was unexpected, and therefore newsworthy. Here's another intro from the same edition of the *Today* programme. It's longer because the story is more complicated:

The Health Secretary, Patricia Hewitt, is calling for GPs to do more to meet local demands – if necessary by extending surgery hours into the evenings and weekends. (27 words)

Again the *who* and *what* questions have been answered. We also know *how* GPs are expected to meet local demands.

Sometimes the content of two stories is connected. The lead will draw them together. This is known as an *umbrella* lead because it covers more than one story.

Michael Brown, the official in charge of organising the response to Hurricane Katrina, has resigned tonight. Mr Brown has come under severe criticism for his performance, and President Bush has now acknowledged that mistakes were made.

As the recovery work goes on in New Orleans, 45 bodies have been found in a hospital there. Reports suggest that the bodies were those of some of the hospital's patients.

(BBC TV News)

The stories about an official's resignation and the discovery of bodies in a hospital are both aspects of the aftermath of the hurricane. You might want to consider whether the political angle is more important than the hospital deaths. How might the story have been written if you judged the deaths more significant?

NEVER *REPEAT THE INFORMATION FROM A LINK IN THE OPENING LINE OF A PACKAGE.*

When a cue or link introduces a package, it should be written first. The information in the package then flows from what the presenter has said. *Never repeat the information from a link in the opening line of a package.* It sounds clumsy, wastes time and makes the audience think the reporter hasn't been listening to what has just been said. The reality is, of course, that the package was most likely pre-recorded, and the reporter probably wrote the link for the presenter to read. The reporter has made himself sound foolish. In larger newsrooms, the correspondent in the field will have suggested material for the cue and left it to a producer back at base to write. It's important they liaise to avoid repetition.

When writing your story, never raise questions that can't be answered. If in doubt, check it out. If still in doubt, leave it out.

REMEMBER

➤ Hook the listener

➤ Write the intro first

➤ Include the vital facts – cut out the merely interesting

➤ Never repeat information from the link at the top of a package.

The pay-off

The last words of a programme are the lasting impression with which you leave the audience. The final words of a news story or report are your final chance to make an impact. It is usually considered weak to close a report without some sort of pay-off. Tagging a standard out cue (e.g. 'Gary Hudson, BBC News, Birmingham') on to the last interview clip or piece of actuality is lazy. Ending on an interview – unless it is a particularly dramatic and punchy clip – rarely works, and it runs the risk of leaving the final say to one party in an otherwise balanced story.

HOW A STORY ENDS IS AS IMPORTANT AS HOW IT BEGINS.

Most newspaper reports are not read in full. In the traditional inverted pyramid construction less important information comes lower down the story. But the broadcaster wants the listener to keep listening. So, how a story ends is as important as how it begins.

The well-crafted pay-off is an opportunity to tie up loose ends, to summarise, or to project forward to future developments. It is possible to look forward to potential future outcomes without speculating or being bland. Variations of 'What happens next remains to be seen' or 'This story will run and run' aren't good enough.

Possibly the laziest example of any of this occurred in a BBC Midlands Today report about a metal sculptor Len Clatworthy. The talented Len was asked, towards the end of a lengthy feature, about his future plans. His reply was a non-committal 'who knows'. The reporter provided a pay-off (mainly because the editor had recently issued an edict insisting that reports should not end on interviews). The reporter's words: 'Len Clatworthy, a man with an uncertain future. Who knows what the future holds? Certainly not Len himself.'

REMEMBER

➤ A pay-off can summarise the story

➤ It can tie up loose ends

➤ It can project forward

➤ Avoid obvious or bland statements

➤ It's the last thing the listener hears, so make sure it has impact.

TIP BOX   **THE INVERTED PYRAMID AND THE CHRISTMAS TREE**

The Conservative MP Boris Johnson was accused in 2004 by a posse of tabloid reporters over an alleged affair. He told them their stories were an 'inverted pyramid of piffle'. He'd borrowed a phrase from the teaching of journalism. As a journalist and columnist, Johnson knows about journalism, and he was the editor of the *Spectator* magazine at the time. But most of the readers of the well-reported comment in the next day's papers would have been mystified by the phrase.

In traditional newspaper writing, the facts are organised so that less important material is at the bottom of the story and can be cut by a sub-editor if necessary so the story fits the space on the page. The construction is known as an inverted triangle or pyramid. It works as a model for newspaper writing because, as we've heard, people often don't reach the end of a story before moving on to something else in the paper. It almost doesn't matter if the sub cuts out the summarising paragraph at the bottom of the story. For broadcasters it is as important to end well as it is to begin well, because you need to hold the audience's attention throughout a programme.

So let's suggest another model. What about a Christmas tree? Not a luxuriant Norwegian spruce but the type a child would draw – a simple diagrammatic representation.

Think of the intro as the top of the tree. If it's bright enough you can put a star on it! Below the intro the branches flare out and then there's another narrow bit. This is the second place you have to put emphasis, the second opportunity to grab the audience. It's the start of the package or edited report.

In radio, a package needs to start with powerful actuality, an audio clip or a telling introductory phrase in the voice-over. In television, it would be a strong opening picture, perhaps with dramatic actuality sound.

Here the Christmas tree broadens to a wider base. This is where your story blossoms and fills out.

And the Christmas tree needs a solid base. That's your pay-off or outro – the final summarising thought or phrase that rounds up the item or projects the story forward.

Remember, it's one Christmas tree. The link and the report, the top and the branches, are part of the same story. Nothing grates on the listener quite as much as hearing the same information repeated. We've all heard this sort of thing:

Newsreader: Three people have been injured in a fire at a house in the Llandaff area of Cardiff. It broke out in the early hours of this morning. Jeffrey Walsh has the details.

Reporter: The fire broke out in the early hours at a house in the Llandaff area. Three people were injured . . .

The Sky Sports News writing style guide sums it up well, taking into account that the intro may be prepared by newsroom subs while the reporter is preparing their script on location:

Don't give the whole story away in the intro – save something for the reporter. Ensure that the last line of the link is different to the opening line of the package. Reporters should think what the top line of the intro is likely to be and avoid that as their top line.

When you are writing your own intro, write it first. The rest of the report follows from it. If it's a feature item, you may even be able to write your cue before you leave the newsroom. It saves time when you file your report or edit your package later.

intro or cue

start of package

sound bite

link

soundbite

pay-off

The Christmas tree structure of broadcast stories

Almost all of what we've learned so far applies across the whole range of broadcast output. Wherever the spoken word is the means of communicating – that's all TV and radio, and much online content – the rules of good conversational English and well-structured story-telling should be followed. We'll take a look now at how this advice can be applied to specific contexts.

APPLYING THE ADVICE

SPORTS REPORTING

If ever there was an area of broadcasting where the conventions of good news writing seem to be in danger of falling into misuse it is sports reporting. Sport is hugely important to audiences. Watching and playing sport are massive sectors of the leisure industry. Sport is entertainment as well as information. Sports reporters tell people what they *want* to know rather than what they *need* to know. So it's up to us to tell them in the best way our journalistic skills will allow. That means avoiding jargon and cliché just as we would in a well-crafted news report.

Some sports reporters believe there is a language specific to their trade, and which sports fans expect. The argument goes that we as broadcasters are giving the fans what they want. The fact that half the audience switches off mentally as soon as they hear that 'Shearer made no mistake from the spot' doesn't occur to them. They're proud to be hacks, and it's probably a long time since they consulted a dictionary, which would point out that a hack is 'a literary or journalistic drudge'.

THE SPORTS REPORTER HAS TO SPEAK TO SOME PEOPLE WHO SWITCHED ON TO LEARN ABOUT THE LATEST WORLD EVENTS AND OTHERS WHO ARE WAITING FOR THE WEATHER REPORT.

There could be an argument made, though it would be a pretty poor one, that the only people who read the sports pages of newspapers are sports fans, so it is perfectly acceptable to use sporting clichés in newspaper copy. But news broadcasting must be different. Mainly because it is *broad*casting not *narrow*casting. We are not talking to narrow interest groups. We are addressing a wide audience. Just as the political correspondent has to make politics relevant to people who say they are not interested in politics, the sports reporter has to speak to some people who switched on to learn about the latest world events and others who are waiting for the weather report.

Even though its audience is probably made up exclusively of sports fans, Sky Sports News, the most watched all-sports channel in the UK, has no time for cliché merchants. Its style guide is quite specific. It has a banned list of phrases it doesn't want to hear. Among them:

- Denied by the woodwork
- Writing on the wall
- History was made
- Gifted them a goal
- Marching orders
- Outfit – as in Hungarian outfit/Spanish outfit etc.
- Just what the doctor ordered
- On the stroke of
- Nothing more than a consolation
- International duty
- Winning ways

- Have it all to do
- Top flight
- But they hadn't read the script – and other variations on the theme
- Unveil – statues and plaques are unveiled – managers are appointed
- Headed home
- Long range effort.

And of course:

- No mistake from the spot.

Sky Sports News bans these phrases because it is more professional to avoid clichés. As we said earlier, audiences want lively content not dull and predictable phrases.

The *Football Lexicon* by John Leigh and David Woodhouse is hugely entertaining – both to football fans and to lovers of the English language. It is also recommended reading for any sports reporter, as a warning against resorting to phrases so hackneyed that these Cambridge University academics put them in their book. It's the first alphabetical glossary of the language of football, mostly that of reporters and commentators but also players and managers. The authors pass no judgement but there is a gentle humour in their analysis. Here's their entry for the simple word *effort*:

Effort: Perhaps surprisingly, an *effort* **can also be a goal: 'Notts County have pulled one back, another** *effort* **from McSwegan.' But more typically, when a goal fails to materialise, an** *effort* **will be described as long-range or speculative.**

In a recommendation of the book in his column in the West Bromwich Albion matchday programme, *Match of the Day Two* presenter Adrian Chiles asked: 'Why is a successful penalty taker always said to have "made no mistake"? Nowhere else in sport, or indeed life, are you said to have "made no mistake" when you accomplish something relatively straightforward: "Well done for paying the gas bill, darling, you made no mistake there."'

The authors of *Football Lexicon* sum up the attitude of fans to the way players speak: 'The clichés and set phrases – sick as a parrot, over the moon, game of two halves – to which players and managers seem to turn at every juncture have indeed been echoed so gleefully and frequently by the public that the mockery of these commonplaces has itself become commonplace.'

'Sick as a parrot' and 'over the moon' have been parodied to extinction. But 'game of two halves' enjoyed a form of post-modern revival in 2005, when Liverpool came from three down at half-time to win the Champions League Final.

REMEMBER

- ➤ Address the whole audience
- ➤ Try to broaden your audience
- ➤ Avoid clichés.

WRITING FOR RADIO

It's a cliché beloved of people who've worked all their lives in radio that it's a superior medium to television because the pictures are better. Think about it.

Every picture conjured up by a radio script exists in the mind of the listener. It's their personal version of events. The film version of a beloved novel fills fans of the novel with dread. Will the hero be as attractive as I've imagined him? Will the heroine be as feisty and gorgeous? Will the locations match those in my imagination? The 2005 movie remake of *Pride and Prejudice* drew comparisons not only with the novel, but with the earlier TV version. When J.K. Rowling told Harry Potter fans 'That's my Hogwarts,' they were reassured that the school they saw in the movies was what the author had in mind.

So, description is the key to evocative radio scripts.

Introducing audio

Voice reports and interviews add colour to radio reporting. Their use should not be blunted by predictable introductions. The tried and tested 'Laurence Lee reports' should not be overused. 'From Moscow, here's our correspondent Laurence Lee' is similarly unimaginative. Try to vary it.

'Laurence Lee explains.'

'Laurence Lee has been following the story.'

'Laurence Lee has the background.'

'. . . as Laurence Lee, who's been following the story, now explains.'

Similar variety should be applied to the introduction of audio clips, either in bulletins or within reports. Never include your question at the start of an audio insert. Equally, 'I spoke to Jose Mourinho and asked him . . .' is amateurish and unacceptable. Instead, you should write into the clip. Assess what has been said in the interview and write accordingly. 'Mourinho was angry at the suggestion that his side are feeling the pressure . . .' 'Why was Mourinho angry?' 'So what makes the Chelsea manager so upset?' 'Mourinho rounded on his critics . . .'

Pick up on a previous clip to introduce the next one. 'While the Chelsea manager was in belligerent mood, his Arsenal counterpart was more reserved . . .'

IT IS ALMOST ALWAYS ESSENTIAL ON RADIO TO INTRODUCE SOMEONE BY NAME BEFORE WE HEAR THEM SPEAK.

It is almost always essential on radio to introduce someone by name before we hear them speak. The audience needs to know who is speaking. In a longer feature, it may be acceptable to hear a short clip before the speaker's identity is revealed. The clip can then continue.

I absolutely refute that view. Conservative spokesman Andrew Mitchell. *We believe the government has . . .*

WRITING FOR TELEVISION

Writing for television follows the same broad guidelines as writing for radio – good conversational English is paramount. But the added dimension of pictures requires changes to vocabulary and syntax – the grammatical structure of your sentences.

Write captions rather than narrative sentences – but captions that move the story along.

The biggest difference between TV and radio is that there is much less need in television to be descriptive. People can see things for themselves on screen.

The worst television scripts fail to fit the words to the pictures, but it is almost as great a mistake to describe what is already there.

ACTUALITY GIVES VIEWERS A SENSE OF AUTHENTICITY, OF 'BEING THERE'.

Sometimes 'writing' for television means not writing at all. Pictures with natural sound – the sound recorded at the scene – may be more effective in helping tell a story than the same pictures with a voice-over. Actuality gives viewers a sense of authenticity, of 'being there'.

Interviewees do not have to be named in a script before they speak. That is a radio technique. An on-screen caption can supply the name and a brief description of the speaker.

TELEVISION INTERVIEWEES DO NOT HAVE TO BE NAMED IN A SCRIPT BEFORE THEY SPEAK. THAT IS A RADIO TECHNIQUE.

Here are some guidelines:

- Let the pictures tell the story
- Use as few words as possible to deliver the information
- Try to be conversational rather than declamatory
- Make the words fit the pictures, but . . .
- Don't describe what people can see for themselves
- Allow the pictures to 'breathe' using natural sound
- Don't name interviewees to introduce them when a caption will do the job
- Never use 'wallpaper', i.e. pictures that are simply there to cover the narrator's words. This isn't proper television; it's radio with pictures.

Read back your script – out loud – for accuracy and ease of delivery. Do so without looking at the pictures. Obviously, no journalist should simply make things up, but it is surprising how often errors creep into scripts simply because the writer is concentrating on making the words fit the pictures.

REMEMBER

➤ If in doubt, check it out
➤ If still in doubt, leave it out.

TIP BOX   **NEWSWRITING FOR BROADCAST: SOME DO'S AND DON'T'S**

What do I want to say?

How can I say it naturally?

DO

- Write clear, concise sentences
- Use short rather than long words
- Start with the most important/most recent fact(s) of the story
- Make sure all the vital points are included
- Follow a narrative thread (*beginning, middle, end*)

- Stick to the facts

- Avoid unnecessary adjectives

- Avoid clichés

- Avoid repetition

- Avoid confusion

- Keep sentence structure simple

- Use active – not passive – sentences whenever possible

- Cut out any words that can be cut out

- Check the meaning of words

- Check facts

- While doing all this, avoid complicated, compound sentences with too many subordinate clauses, dangling participles, conjunctions and other bits added to them, just to make them sound more important, while still trying to keep to the sense of what you are trying to write, notwithstanding the difficulty of maintaining the audience's interest despite your periphrasis and obfuscation!

- Remember the rules of story-telling – who, what, where, when, why

- Learn to *edit yourself* – read out loud what you have written to ensure it makes sense

- Count the words (three to a second) to check how long it is.

DON'T

- Use jargon or journalese

- Use clichés

- Use foreign words or phrases when there is an everyday English equivalent

- Use words you don't understand

- Write sentences that are too long or too complicated to understand on first hearing

- Invent or assume anything

- Use lengthy direct quotes (reported speech, e.g. *He said: 'I am not happy being here because I don't like being told what to do by that rascal Hudson.'*)

- Offer opinions by inserting unnecessary adverbs (e.g. *Luckily, they escaped from the fire . . . Fortunately, a local postman spotted smoke . . .*)

- Use unnecessary adjectives

- Use words like 'stated' or 'commented' or phrases like 'expressed the opinion that' when the simple word 'said' will do instead

- Hype up the story – just stick to the facts

- Write a story you don't understand. If you don't understand it, how can you expect the audience to?

A CLOSER LOOK   **THE ART OF WRITING 'SLIGHTLY OFF THE PICTURES'**

The following passage is not from a textbook. It is from a blockbuster novel, but is the best description we have read of the art of writing a television news script.

It was a specialist art form, difficult to learn, and some in television news never quite succeeded. Even among professional writers the talent did not receive the recognition it deserved, because the words were written to accompany pictures and seldom read well alone.

The trick . . . was not to describe the pictures. A television viewer would be seeing . . . what was happening on the screen and did not need verbal description. Yet the spoken words must not be so far removed from the pictures as to split the viewer's consciousness. It was a literary balancing act, much of it instinctive.

Something else TV news people recognised: the best news writing was not in real sentences and paragraphs. Fragments of sentences worked better.

Extract from *The Evening News* by Arthur Hailey

WRITING FOR ONLINE

Does the online work of a broadcast journalist suddenly have to be written in newspaper style? Not exactly. But it's true that online writing is probably the only time broadcast journalists write to be read rather than heard.

IT IS NOT GOOD ENOUGH TO SIMPLY UPLOAD YOUR BROADCAST SCRIPTS ONTO THE WEB.

It is therefore not good enough to simply upload your broadcast scripts onto the Web. Otherwise you get this, from Staffordshire-based Signal Radio's website:

The search is on for a mum after a baby boy was dumped on a Staffordshire doorstep.

The little boy, thought to be three weeks old was left at a house in Post Office Lane in Rugeley (pronounced Rouge . . . lee).

Apart from anything else, it begs the question: why don't Signal Radio's journalists know how to pronounce the name of Rugeley, a town in Staffordshire?

Some commercial local radio stations can upload their scripts to the Web at the touch of a computer key. But it does not mean their web users get the full benefit of an interactive service. The full range of online skills for writers includes preparing headlines, single paragraph summaries, longer stories, and cross-heads. There are also picture captions to write and interactive boxes to prepare.

Online journalists also learn the technical skills to import still pictures, graphics, audio and video, and have to write the links to these, and to related stories and other sites on the Web.

The BBC – with licence fee cash to invest in the project – has pioneered online news in the UK. Its sites are the most visited news websites in the world (four million unique users a day by mid-2006), and it is the UK's biggest employer of online journalistic talent. A clear house style has developed, which would-be online journalists need to know.

But the rules about grabbing an audience are the same as for all forms of broadcasting. Hugh Berlyn, Editor of BBC News Interactive, English Regions, sums it up: 'Content is king. If you haven't got a fresh, interactive, easy-to-use site, the punters will just go away.'

Headlines

Online headlines differ from newspaper headlines, because the number of characters (or letters and spaces) is not so strictly limited. You have more freedom on the Web to write good English. Web pages usually have a standard font size for headlines. Sometimes a main headline will be larger, but most will be of the same size, big enough to attract the reader's attention.

This means the number of letters available does not restrict what you can say. You don't need to use those journalese words like *probe*, *clash* and *row* to fit the length of the line. Online writing does not have to follow a tabloid style.

An exception is the BBC News service where headlines are written to a length of 31 to 33 characters, so that they fit the Ceefax text pages on television. The online version can be over-typed later to make it shorter, but it is more efficient to make the same wording fit both media.

A page from a BBC website, showing headlines and navigation tools

Summaries

It is common to have a brief summary of the story on the front page of a website. The BBC has title pages – or index pages – for each of its local news sites. A one-paragraph (or par) summary of the story appears underneath the headline. The BBC style is to write the summary in the present tense. This version also appears on digital radio scrolling text and on BBC 'big screens' around the country.

The story

Most stories on BBC sites are written in just four paragraphs. All but the biggest stories will have a maximum of 250 words. Those four pars will also appear on Ceefax, on digital text and be sent to mobile phones.

Hugh Berlyn says: 'Young people today don't watch traditional news bulletins or sit and read long newspaper articles as their parents did. They are reluctant even to scroll down text on a web page. All our indications suggest our users read the top four paragraphs. Only if they are thoroughly engaged will they read much more. We are breeding a *four-par generation*. Stories need to be told in a maximum of four pars. We as journalists have to live with that or die.'

Longer stories can be used, but they will be sub-divided by newspaper-style *cross-heads*, one or two words in bold splitting up the text.

Maurice Blisson, an experienced freelance journalist who's written for BBC News online in Leeds, says: 'You put in cross heads just like a newspaper after every four pars or so. You rarely write more than eight pars, though you might for a lengthy court case. The cross head is a visual thing. You can also liven it up by putting a *quotebox* in. There's a place on the template to put the quote and another place for the name and it does it automatically.'

He sums up the tone of his online work: 'I write in a fairly light newspaper style. I think of it as traditional *Daily Express* or *Daily Mirror* style without the clichés and the journalese. There are specific things you have to do. You have to tell the story in the first four paragraphs so that it automatically goes onto Ceefax. You must fit your facts and your location into those four pars. There's a template that tells you if you're going to bust.'

Maurice concedes that a lot of online work is re-versioning other people's original material: 'It's 95 per cent re-hashing what others have written.'

When those others are broadcast journalists more used to writing for radio, there can be a lot of work to do. Hugh Berlyn explains: 'We're definitely looking for writing skills. Newspaper journalists have those skills. People from local radio take longer to retrain. Spelling is obviously important, but a lot of people trained in radio don't think it matters, for obvious reasons.'

Sky News Interactive uses stories of between eight and 12 paragraphs, usually with three headlines (for different pages on the site) and two pictures. Their red-button Sky News Active service (on satellite TV) has ten text sections and eight mini video screens.

Writing online copy means ignoring those guidelines about broadcast writing that relate to the spoken word, but not the principles of concise and accurate use of English.

REMEMBER

- ➤ Online writing has to be read not spoken
- ➤ Check spellings
- ➤ Don't use contractions like *isn't, aren't, hasn't, don't*
- ➤ Direct quotes *can* be used online – perhaps in a separate box
- ➤ Use graphics to explain numbers.

WRITING FOR SMS

Text (SMS) news flashes to mobile phones have become one of the most popular ways for people to keep up with the latest news. They are a quick way to find out what's happening so you can watch fuller coverage later, without breaking into what you are doing.

Writing text flashes is a tight journalistic discipline, because you don't want to bombard subscribers with more information than they want. Sky News sends out up to three flashes a day. On quiet news days there will be none at all. Adam Harding, Deputy Editor of Sky News Interactive, sums up the writing style: 'One story. One sentence. One chance to get it right. 140 characters maximum.'

Look at today's top stories online. Decide which, if any, would be worth a news flash to mobile phones. Now try writing those stories in less than 140 characters (that's letters and spaces). It's not easy.

A CLOSER LOOK

WRITING FOR CHILDREN

Writing for children is a particular skill. The BBC's *Newsround* is targeted at nine-year-olds. Presenter Lizo Mzimba says they cover two types of story – things that children are interested in, and things they might not be interested in at first glance, but really ought to know about.

'It's all about language and presentation. We use simple, straightforward language and put everything into context. We'd never talk about the Middle East Peace Process, but we would explain what's happening now and what has been happening for more than 50 years, and what's likely to happen in the future.'

The rule about knowing your audience is rarely more important than when addressing this group of viewers. 'Kids are interested in entertainment (Harry Potter and *Lord of the Rings*, that sort of thing), sport, mostly, and they're interested in the environment. They're worried about the planet and what we're doing to it.'

Mzimba says nine-year-olds will never say they're interested in politics: 'But if you say to a nine-year-old: "How big is your class in school? Is it too big?" or "Are you interested in the threat to the planet from what people call global-warming," a lot of that's related to politics.

'We'd never start a story: "The government has issued a White Paper on education," but we would say: "Schools are being offered millions of pounds to improve the standard of education." '

He says you have to be reassuring and honest with children. 'Children get worried after a terrorist attack. You can't say: "No, don't worry. There won't be any more." But you can say: "The police and security services are working very hard to make sure things like this don't happen again." You have to be honest with children.'

Explaining 'adult' news to children is a challenge. Done well, it is one of the most satisfying jobs in journalism. Mzimba says: 'We get a lot of mail from adults saying *Newsround* is the only news programme they really understand.'

Newsround presenter Lizo Mzimba: 'You have to be reassuring and honest at the same time.'

CONCLUSION

Once you've read this chapter, you should have an understanding of the guiding principles of good broadcast writing. You will be aware of the range of writing skills you may need in your career to produce everything from snappy radio headlines to online copy.

The only way to become fast and fluent as a writer is to practise. If you're not working in a newsroom yet (or on a course that involves a lot of writing every day), do it in your spare time. Take a newspaper and re-write the stories in it for broadcast. That is an easy way to start because the key news points should already have been picked out for you. Then go online, or better still out into the community where you live, and try to find original stories to write.

Much of broadcast journalism involves teamwork. Most writing does not. Writing well is one of the most satisfying aspects of the job because what you create is all your own work. Learn to enjoy it.

FURTHER READING

Boyd, Andrew (2001) *Broadcast Journalism: Techniques of Radio and Television News*, Oxford: Focal Press.

Ford, Simon (2006) *Writing News for Local Radio*, Nottingham: Booklaw. A comprehensive look at the art from an experienced BBC practitioner.

Hicks, Wynford (1998) *English for Journalists*, Oxford: Routledge. A clear and accessible guide to grammar and usage in all types of journalism.

Hicks, Wynford, with Sally Adams and Harriett Gilbert (1999) *Writing for Journalists*, Oxford: Routledge. One of the definitive works on writing for all journalists, although aimed at print specialists.

Humphrys, John (2005) *Lost for Words: The Mangling and Manipulating of the English Language*, London: Hodder & Stoughton.

Thompson, Rick (2005) *Writing for Broadcast Journalists*, Oxford: Routledge. Lively, often witty and always definitive – an invaluable guide.

WEB LINKS

www.bbc.training.com. A wealth of BBC training resources, including their news writing style guide.

CHAPTER SIX

LOCATION REPORTING AND PRODUCTION

Getting out and about and meeting people are among the greatest joys of being a reporter. Foreign correspondents speak of the thrill of being eye-witnesses to history. But even a murky morning outside Middlesbrough magistrates' court beats being stuck at a desk in front of a computer screen. The best reporters prefer being out on a story to the glamour and big salaries of presenting in the studio, or climbing the greasy pole of management.

Military strategists will tell you that no plan survives contact with the enemy. The same is true of broadcast journalism. So, who are our enemies? We're not talking about those (often-powerful) people who may have good reason – in their own terms – for not wanting your story broadcast. Very few of them will take to the streets to prevent you doing your job; they're more likely to try taking out an injunction. We're talking about, to quote Harold Macmillan: 'Events, dear boy, events.' Those events – beyond your control – include hanging around in the cold and wet for hours on end, the mic going dead, or the satellite link going down; and when it comes to children and animals, the old actors' adage applies – you might as well raise the white flag.

This chapter examines the practical considerations of news gathering in the field.

THE BEST WORKING PRACTICES

BE PREPARED

When Robert Baden Powell wrote *Scouting for Boys* in 1908, there was no such thing as broadcast journalism. But the motto 'Be Prepared' could have been written for us. There's no substitute for preparation. That means research and forward planning. A *recce* (short for reconnaissance) or site visit lets you work out where you should position your microphones and cameras. It helps you find locations for the *pieces-to-camera* or *stand-ups* by a reporter. Sometimes there will be a *pre-shoot*, a chance to shoot material that helps tell the story before the day on which it is broadcast. If you are covering an awards ceremony, for example, you might want to film the nominees at home or at work. You would not be able to do that on the day of the ceremony itself, because they will be busy getting ready for and travelling to the event.

You will almost certainly want to talk to potential interviewees on the phone before visiting them. You can check their availability, and what they are likely to say, and explain what the story involves. Seeking written permissions, printing off location maps and drawing up realistic shooting schedules are all part of good newsroom practice on diary stories. For breaking news, you might have to forget all of these and rely on one thing – *experience*. But it doesn't have to be your own experience.

News gathering is a team effort. The experience of the whole team is brought to bear on big stories – editors, producers and reporters will discuss the way to cover a breaking event, and each will perform their duties to achieve the best results possible within the organisation's capabilities and budget. A small radio station with limited resources has to make compromises on big stories. Staff find themselves working hard for long hours.

NEVER BE AFRAID TO ASK OLDER COLLEAGUES HOW THEY HAVE COVERED SIMILAR STORIES IN THE PAST.

There is expertise to be tapped into on any story. Never be afraid to ask older colleagues how they have covered similar stories in the past. It may seem a surprising admission by people who are used to dealing with what is new and often surprising – otherwise it wouldn't be news – but most journalists will agree there's no such thing as a new story.

There have been natural disasters, terrorist attacks, political scandals and almost every imaginable form of criminal activity before – and people who have covered those stories. This is not a recipe for formulaic or predictable reporting. But it is a reminder that there is no point in re-inventing the wheel, if you'll excuse the cliché.

NEWSROOM MEETINGS

Most newsrooms will have at least one planning meeting a day – usually at the earliest opportunity in the morning after most staff have come on duty. The morning meeting sets the agenda for the day. The stories that are likely to be covered are known as the *prospects*. This will include diary items and breaking stories to which reporters and producers have yet to be assigned. In a well-staffed newsroom, some reporters will be assigned researching duties, on the understanding that, if new stories break during the day, they are available to go on the road. They are in 'coiled spring' mode – waiting to be unleashed on 'the big one'.

There will also be *forward planning* meetings in which ideas for future use will be discussed. These might include diary stories, new developments in *running stories*, embargoed material and ongoing investigations. Planning desks are at the heart of all successful newsrooms. On a 'quiet' or 'slow' news day, almost all the bulletin content will be a result of their efforts. Planners fix technical facilities and feed-points, transport and accommodation, and arrange any special passes that are needed to cover events.

See Workshops and Exercises.

The main bulletins on terrestrial TV and longer, speech-based radio programmes will also have *production meetings* in which editorial and technical staff discuss the logistics of getting the programme on air. These meetings are important in providing an operational framework, but, inevitably, on most days the running order will change several times as new stories break and some of those which looked likely to make it to the bulletin fall by the wayside. Often the running order changes while the programme is on air. Stories break, items overrun, edited packages miss their feed time, live links go down. Anything can happen in the next half hour – and probably will.

In the midst of all this, you, the reporter or producer, are planning to go out and cover your story. And you know that there's a more than even chance that what can go wrong will go wrong. So, how do you play the percentage game, and reduce the chances of letting down your editor, your station, your audience and yourself?

Below are some tips. Every one is based on the bitter experience of not one, but hundreds of broadcasters. Show us a broadcast journalist who denies falling prey to any of these pitfalls, and we'll show you a liar.

Everyone has a story of when they messed up. Helen Boaden is the Director of BBC News, a former controller of Radio Four, producer, presenter, reporter and executive producer in television: 'The worst thing I ever did, I was so excited about a story I drove off in my car and only halfway to the story did I realise I'd left the tape recorder behind, which, given the fact that it was radio, was a bit of a problem.'

BEFORE YOU LEAVE THE NEWSROOM

Do your research

The best way to cover any story is with more background knowledge than you are ever likely to need. When you write the story, your hardest decision will be knowing what to leave out. Check the Internet and your cuttings library for information. Read all the newspapers. Research the station's archive. In television, find out what pictures are available on related stories. Larger broadcasters will have dedicated library services with a willing librarian to help.

WHEN YOU ARE ARCHIVING YOUR OWN MATERIAL, REMEMBER THAT THE INFORMATION YOU PROVIDE WILL PROBABLY BE RETRIEVED BY SOMEBODY ELSE WHO DOESN'T KNOW THE STORY AS INTIMATELY AS YOU DO.

TIP BOX

A NOTE ON ARCHIVING

Most library systems these days will have a computerised search facility. The old principle of 'rubbish in: rubbish out' applies. When you are archiving your own material, remember that the information you provide will probably be retrieved by somebody else who doesn't know the story as intimately as you do. Label your images clearly. Cross-referencing helps.

The first TV report of a murder might include pictures of the victim, the murder scene and a police press conference, with interviews. The pictures of the scene might be valuable in future reports about police resources. Do they include the activities of scenes of crime officers, police photographers, door-to-door inquiries, patrol cars, fingertip searches, incident control rooms and plain clothes officers? All could be useful. Armed police are increasingly commonplace on Britain's streets. But it is still worth noting shots of police officers with pistols drawn or using Heckler and Koch machine guns. Be specific.

Permissions

Before you record or film at any location you need to make sure you have permission. As soon as you have a microphone or camera in your hand you are not treated like a member of the public, even though you are one. It's a shock to newcomers to the business, but you cannot always expect special treatment because you are part of the media. And you are often prevented from going places everybody else can wander through with impunity.

NEVER ASSUME – JUST BECAUSE SOMEBODY TELLS YOU IT WILL BE OK – THAT YOU HAVE THE AUTHORITY TO ENTER PRIVATE PROPERTY.

Never assume – just because somebody tells you it will be OK – that you have the authority to enter private property. Private, in this case, includes public buildings like schools and hospitals and their car parks, and places that encourage most other people to enter, like shopping centres. You will need permission from the head teacher, the hospital's chief executive (or communications department) or the shopping centre manager respectively. It's not enough that a doctor or shop-worker says you're welcome to record what's happening. It is your responsibility, not theirs, to get the proper permissions. That usually means a verbal agreement from the right person, but, if they are not likely to be around, a written note or e-mail will help satisfy over-zealous security staff.

Here's an example of how inexperience led to two student journalists losing their exclusive video. A young mother in Stoke-on-Trent, who did not know she was pregnant, went to bed one night unaware that next morning she would have two extra children. She gave birth to twins in the family bathroom in the middle of the night. A few days later, she agreed to an exclusive interview with the two students.

The twins had been taken to a hospital's baby care unit and the mother asked a nurse if the students could film them there. The nurse agreed, so the students thought they had permission. It wasn't until they had all the footage they wanted of mother, father and the surprise arrivals that a hospital official arrived and confiscated their tape. The students lost all their footage of the babies.

Nobody has a right to take away your tapes. But if you don't have the proper permissions it's much more difficult to argue your case. On a practical note, if you are in danger of somebody wanting to take your material, have a blank tape in your pocket and practise a little sleight of hand. Camera crews in politically sensitive parts of the world do this all the time.

THERE IS USUALLY NO PROBLEM WITH RECORDING OR FILMING FROM THE PUBLIC HIGHWAY.

There is usually no problem with recording or filming from the public highway, but you may be accused of causing an obstruction. If the police ask you to move on, there is usually no alternative but to comply. There's more on police guidelines about dealing with the media later in this chapter.

Health and safety

Health and safety considerations come into play every time you leave the newsroom. Health and safety training for reporting in the field is a legal requirement for all journalists. As a reporter or producer it is your responsibility to assess the safety of a location before you leave the newsroom, and to update that assessment as circumstances change.

Generic health and safety assessments will apply to day-to-day news assignments. Workplaces will insist on the completion of hazard assessment forms for particular high-risk situations. How these situations are defined depends on the organisation. Some stories present obvious dangers. Journalists and technical crews will be given hostile environment training before they are sent to war zones, for example. But there are also rules that need to be observed every time you record or film in public locations. Cables laid in public places present particular hazards. If a passer-by trips over unattended cables, the broadcaster is liable. If a radio reporter or camera person walking backwards to grab an interview bumps into somebody, the broadcaster is liable. If a lighting rig or a radio car gets in the way of people going about their everyday business, the broadcaster may be liable.

You have a duty of care to your station's staff too. A radio engineer in the West Country was killed when the telescopic mast of a radio car hit overhead power lines.

Nobody can predict everything that might go wrong on a location recording or shoot, but the *risk assessment forms* available in all well-ordered newsrooms cover most eventualities and repay the time spent filling them in. Completing one before you go out on location shows that you have considered all the possible risks. If anything does go wrong, and you can't prove you made every effort to prevent it, your personal insurance and that of your organisation will be invalidated.

Foreign assignments often include exposure to hostile environments. So hazard assessment is vital. These can include operating in countries at war or prone to civil unrest and terrorism. Many regions have extreme levels of crime and lawlessness. This can include banditry and the kidnapping of foreign nationals, particularly those from Western nations. A responsible news organisation will also require the completion of risk assessment from its workers in places with extremes of climate or terrain. Mountains and deserts are as great a danger to the inexperienced as war zones. So is the reporting of severe floods, hurricanes, earthquakes and volcanic eruptions.

High-risk events in domestic reporting, where completing a hazard assessment is essential, include riots and civil disturbance, serious public disorder, firearms incidents like hijackings and sieges, and terrorist attacks – suspected or real. Where there's a bomb threat, or the suspicion of chemical, biological or radiological substances, extreme caution must be exercised.

ONE OF THE GUIDING PRINCIPLES OF COVERING RIOTS AND DISORDER IN THE STREETS IS TO FIND A SAFE VANTAGE POINT.

One of the guiding principles of covering riots and disorder in the streets is to find a safe vantage point, usually above the action. For radio reporters this provides a commentary position. For TV, it is a secure place from which cameras can view what happens. This may involve reporters and producers negotiating with householders, shopkeepers or landlords for access to an upstairs window or balcony. The delicate conversations that precede such arrangements, occasionally involving payment of a facility fee, are more often than not repaid with quality coverage.

REMEMBER

- ➤ News does not just happen on the day
- ➤ Forward planning is essential to broadcast journalism
- ➤ Research and set up as much of the story as you can before you go out

➤ Make sure you have permission to record or film

➤ It is almost always OK to film in the street

➤ Consider health and safety, and complete a risk assessment if appropriate.

You are what you wear

We'll leave fashion tips to the experts (though, trust us, there will be plenty of comments about appropriate dress in Chapter 14: *Presentation*). Dressing to do the job well is about more than looking good. Sports producer Mitch Pryce, a veteran of World Cups and Champions League football for ITV, says his first piece of advice to young journalists is: 'Get a decent pair of shoes.' You'll spend a lot of time walking, and a lot of time hanging around out of doors. High heels are rarely a good idea – even for women! Comfort is all-important.

Decent waterproof clothing is a must. A warm, weatherproof jacket can be kept in the car. Make sure it's one that won't look out of place in front of a court or in the middle of a field. And when you're choosing your life-saving, and perhaps expensive, winter warmer, don't just admire yourself in the mirror. Listen too. If the fabric rustles, the sound may be picked up on the mic, and the coat will be useless for broadcasting.

Select a jacket with lots of pockets – for pens, notebooks, briefing sheets and your mobile. Female reporters may find handbags a hindrance on location.

Keep a hat handy – not necessarily to be worn on camera, but to avoid that drowned-rat look. Wellingtons are a must for those muddy country lanes and fields. Fishing waders are handy if you have to cover flood stories. Keep them in the boot of the car along with an umbrella. If you're a TV reporter, make sure the design of your brolly is not a distraction. Company logos should be avoided (there are rules against product placement and advertising within programmes). Some programmes will provide you with an umbrella decorated with the show's own graphics. During a downpour, though, heavy raindrops may be heard on mic, sometimes even drowning out an interview or live report. You may have to put the brolly down just before you go on air.

WHEN POSSIBLE, A REPORTER'S CLOTHING SHOULD SUIT THE LOCATION AND THE STORY.

When possible, a reporter's clothing should suit the location and the story. In the city, reporters should look businesslike. On a farm, casual country clothing is in keeping with the environment. In a war zone, helmet and flak jacket are not a question of style; they are essential for health and safety.

Reporters are better off avoiding blatant fashion statements. It is a distraction from the news. BBC newsreader Michael Buerk's comment that Oscars correspondent Rosie Millard was due an award for 'best-supporting dress' drew attention to Ms Millard's low-cut outfit rather than her news report.

If the idea of 'appropriate' dress is a little vague, then think about the clothing that will help you do the job more easily. That would obviously mean wellies or waders for floods, and a weatherproof coat for anything outdoors in winter. But it is not just a question of comfort. The way you dress can also make the job easier, because your clothes give strangers messages about you. If you want to be treated as an equal when you go to interview a business executive, wear a suit. If you are visiting an eco-warriors' protest camp, dress casually and practically, and avoid designer labels. It sometimes helps not to be seen as an 'establishment' figure; on other occasions you will want to present yourself as the very model of conventional respectability.

Know where you're going

Obvious. Yes, but if you're in the West Midlands and somebody tells you there's a fire in a street in Willenhall, where do you go? Well, Willenhall's between Walsall and Wolverhampton, isn't it? Maybe. Unless they're talking about the Willenhall in Coventry, 20 miles away.

There were riots in the streets of Wood End in the 1990s. BBC Breakfast News duly showed a map of the village of Wood End in North Warwickshire. Unfortunately, the incident was nowhere near that village, but on a council estate in a suburb of Coventry. It's easy to pick on Coventry (check out the pronunciation of Styvechalle and Cheylesmore if you want to know the dangers *that* city presents to broadcast journalists), but these quirks occur throughout the British Isles. And street names will often get confused in transmission from newsdesk to reporter. Hagley Road and Hagley Street may be miles apart. One may be a main thoroughfare, the other a sidestreet. Check it out online or in an A–Z street map. Use websites like theaa.com for routefinder facilities. They will not only find the street, but tell you how to get there.

SATELLITE NAVIGATION IS A GREAT TOOL IF YOU CAN AFFORD IT. BUT SO IS COMMON SENSE.

Satellite navigation is a great tool if you can afford it. But so is common sense. On entering a strange town, stop at a service station to buy a local street map. Keep maps of places you regularly visit in the car. And if you are travelling on a strange road in what might be the wrong direction, remember that the sun rises in the east and sets in the west. At night you can find north by locating the Pole Star from the Plough constellation. If it's cloudy, stop and ask for directions. If it's raining and nobody's on the streets, try petrol stations, pubs or shops.

Be punctual

'Be punctual, be polite and ask questions' – that's the advice newspaper feature writer and interviewer Lynn Barber offers beginner journalists in Tony Harcup's *Journalism: Principles and Practice*. She's quite correct that reporters need good manners and the ability to interview. But it is equally obvious that punctuality has to come first. If you're not there on time – or better still before time – you can't cover the story.

The importance of punctuality is not unique to journalism of course. In the movie *The Fabulous Baker Boys*, a down-at-heel piano player says to a singer who turns up late for an audition: 'Punctuality – the first rule of showbusiness.' Michelle Pfeiffer's character replies sarcastically: 'This is showbusiness?' You may feel the same about broadcast journalism on a wet, winter weekend shift at Radio Rubbish. But you still have to be there on time.

Sports reporters will have their own personal horror stories of when they missed the kick-off. It might have been because their car broke down, because of traffic congestion or because their train or flight was delayed. Whatever the excuse, there's no justification for not building a reasonable margin for error into your travel plans. Britain's roads are congested. Trains get delayed. Flights are subject to weather and air traffic controllers. The important thing to recognise is that a lie-in or a little more time at home reading the newspaper may be tempting, but you're better off getting to the location, and then relaxing. Take a newspaper or book, or listen to the radio.

REMEMBER

➤ Dress appropriately for the weather conditions and for the job

➤ Keep waterproofs and an umbrella in your car

➤ Plan your journey

➤ Be on time, or better still early.

RADIO ON LOCATION

The best radio reporting has strong *actuality* – sound recorded on location. First of all, a radio reporter looks for strong interviews: first-hand eye-witness accounts in the case of a breaking event; the words of the key news makers in other stories. Next there are the background noises that draw the listener into the scene. These are the sounds that separate the event being covered from our normal world.

Most of us operate in a sound landscape so bland we don't think about it. *It's worth taking the time to shut your eyes and listen – to recognise the ordinary so you become attuned to the extraordinary and the newsworthy.*

Our workaday world takes place against a backdrop of traffic noise, birdsong, perhaps aircraft passing overhead or music blaring from somebody's home or car. In a city or large town these elements are rarely far from our ears. A dog might bark or children shout. We take little notice. But there are other sounds which clearly place us in a location, and which can transport our listeners there too. The echoes and splashes of the swimming baths. The excited chatter of schoolchildren at playtime. Some sounds relay their own drama: police sirens during a terrorist alert; the roar of the crowd at a football match; loudspeaker announcements from a water company's vans during a hosepipe ban; leather, willow, chants from the Hill.

THERE REALLY IS NO SUBSTITUTE FOR ACTUALITY SOUND IN NEWS REPORTING. YOU CAN'T FAKE IT BACK IN THE STUDIO.

There really is no substitute for actuality sound in news reporting. You can't fake it back in the studio. And if you try to – by spending considerable time and effort mixing in sound effects – you are cheating your audience. That would be dishonest and would not be journalism. It would be fiction.

DESCRIPTION

Painting pictures with your words is one of the delights of radio journalism. Some of your description may be scripted. You can also try ad-lib commentary 'on the hoof'. This works in both recorded and live situations.

Peter Allen of BBC Five Live says: 'Some of the best radio is when you go to the scene of a train crash or an earthquake, and just paint pictures, just tell people what you can see. In a way you can do it more powerfully than a television camera ever can. It's a fantastic medium, radio. I really do believe in its power.

'It's the time I really feel a buzz, when I get out of the studio. You haven't got a computer screen, you haven't got anything written down, and you simply have to make it up.'

➤ Listen for background sound that helps set the scene

➤ Record and use actuality sound

➤ Describe what you can see.

PERSONAL SPACE AND MIC TECHNIQUE

Recording a radio interview is an intimate experience. You will need to be close to your interviewee, and you need to explain why. Most mics work best about 25 cm from the sound source – roughly a hand's span from the mouth of the subject. Stand at right angles to your subject to avoid staring them in the face. Face-to-face confrontation usually makes people back away, and you will find yourself chasing them across a room.

If you are sitting, you may need to position yourself alongside the interviewee on a sofa, or on chairs angled so your knees are almost touching. This might be embarrassing, and not how you would naturally sit, but the important thing is to get good quality sound. Television interviewers suffer similar unnatural posture to get the shot right. If you are not relaxed though, how can you expect your interviewee to be at ease? A radio interview will probably not be part of their everyday routine. You are the expert; you need to take the lead. Charm and confidence come into play here, making your subject comfortable while invading what they are unconsciously aware of as their personal space. Just remember to use a decent deodorant, brush your teeth and don't have a Balti the night before.

Seated interview position for radio

Your charm should also help entice executives away from their desks. People like to be on familiar territory. Sitting behind a desk is a way to feel secure or assert power. It can also produce stilted and pompous, predictable dialogue. Besides, it is very difficult to operate a microphone across an expanse of wood and piles of papers. Use that as an excuse to invite your interviewee to another location – perhaps the factory floor (which has background sounds to help tell the story).

Interviews can take some time, so it's vital you are in a comfortable position. It's no use fidgeting once the interview's under way. You will lose concentration and start thinking about your aching arm or sore bottom instead of the next question. And make sure your interviewee is comfortable too.

Closeness to the interviewee removes the need for excessive movement of the mic and the danger of handling noise. Grip the mic firmly but not too tight, taking up any slack in the cable with your fingers. Don't tug at or stretch the cable, as strain on the connections can cause clicks on the recording.

Grip the mic firmly but not too tight, taking up any slack in the cable with your fingers

Beware of jewellery and coins rattling. A ring may click against the mic as you hold it. A bracelet may jangle. And interviewees, particularly if they are standing up, may jingle coins in their pocket. It's a common nervous reaction. Be aware of it and politely ask them to take their hand from their pocket. Even clothing can rustle or brush against a mic causing distracting noises. And trailing leads can bump against furniture.

➤ Make sure you are relaxed

➤ Put your interviewees at ease

➤ Position yourself so you get good sound

➤ Avoid handling noise on the mic

➤ Be aware of distracting sound.

SENDING MATERIAL BACK TO BASE

Radio reporting used to involve some live work – probably via a radio car or phone line – and a lot of driving back to base to edit tapes. But not any more.

Broadcasters use portable links, technically called wireless audio codecs, but known in the newsroom by trade names. The full name of the 'Comrex box' is Comrex Matrix Portable – a device for doing cheap outside broadcasts over phone lines. Programme and off-air cues (a conversation between the studio and reporter) can be sent over the same phone line.

A pocket computer phone revolutionised radio news gathering across the BBC local network in 2007. It became possible to record quality audio, edit a simple package in the field and send it back to base without going anywhere near a radio car or an ISDN line.

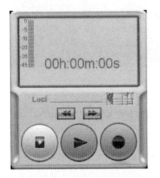

Luci edit program on a
Mobile phone

Unusually the system was developed not by BBC engineers in London, but by journalists at Radio Lincolnshire. Senior broadcast journalist Andy Roche, who had a background in computers before joining the BBC, recognised the potential of the software in a new PDA phone from O2, the XDA. He contacted the company behind the recording software – a small specialist operation in Maastricht. The Dutch team was in almost daily contact with the Lincolnshire journalists as the pilot scheme developed.

They discovered that the input sockets on the phones were not robust enough to use external mics, but the internal mic was more than good enough for most everyday journalistic applications. The phones have manual level control and simple single-track editing, with a familiar wave form display. The audio can then be sent back to the radio station over the mobile phone network or on broadband from wi-fi hotspots.

Files can be transferred in MP2 format which plays on the local radio Radioman playout system (and is a higher quality audio format than MP3). Or they can be sent as .wav files.

The phones also take pictures for use on websites and video, which can be used for television on breaking news stories.

Andy Roche, the senior
broadcast journalist
who directed the
computer phones
project

The pilot scheme started with the XDA phone but other models have now been tested which do the job even better. Project Director Andy Roche says: 'These phones have now become standard issue for all our journalists. Most people always have their phone with them, and now they can produce quality audio for a radio report. A minute of audio takes six minutes to send on the mobile phone network, but that's just the start. You can send a minute of audio in 30 seconds

The Comrex box – a portable reporting device in action

A PC phone, running Windows mobile, complete with windsock. It can be used to record, edit and transmit audio

BBC Radio Lincolnshire's William Wright interviews celebrity chef Jamie Oliver on a PC phone

on a wireless broadband link, and we're working on quality live stuff through the 3G network.'

The quality of the audio can be adjusted to reduce the transfer time. When Radio Lincolnshire gave phones to its freelance non-league football reporters they reduced the transfer rate to half that used by news reporters. Even with reduced audio quality, Roche says it made a huge difference to the station's reports: 'Previously you got them on crackly mobile phones, and sometimes you could hardly hear them, with all the crowd noise at the grounds. Suddenly you could actually hear what they were saying.'

The station gave the phones to Red Arrows pilots, based at nearby RAF Scampton, when they went on their annual training trip to Cyprus. The pilots produced audio diaries of their training schedule.

And the phones can also be given to other contributors with a story to tell. For ME Awareness Week, a sufferer produced a compelling audio diary, explaining how she became tired after performing simple household tasks: 'I've been gardening for five minutes, and I've got to sit down now because I'm totally exhausted.'

She admitted she would not have been able to explain the effect of ME so well in a conventional interview. Roche recognised the advantages of using the new phones over the older approach of lending a contributor a MiniDisc recorder: 'The simple reason this works better than giving somebody a MiniDisc is feedback. We've all given people recorders for a week, and then had hours of material to listen to, and not had the time. But this way, they can record a short piece and send it to you, and you can give them instant advice and encouragement. They send you one or two minutes and you ring them immediately. You can tell them if the background noise was too loud, for example, and ask them to do it again.'

TELEVISION ON LOCATION

USING THE LANGUAGE OF FILM-MAKING

A TV reporter is like a film director. You use the camera to tell a story. The difference is that the movie director has control over almost every part of the action. He might have planned a location shoot where the only variable is the weather. Rain or cloud might determine whether the scene can be filmed or not. That's why the movie industry flourished in Hollywood, California, where it's usually sunny. For the film director, sets have been built, lighting planned, focal lengths measured, microphones positioned and actors rehearsed. In the modern blockbuster, he might be filming actors against a green screen, with the wizards of computer-generated imagery waiting to insert the action. The TV reporter has hardly any of that control. The trick is to take as much control as you can, but to be flexible and to respond to the events around you.

Whether you are working with a crew or shooting material yourself, it is essential to understand the language of filming. That includes its grammar. It helps you choose your shots and to appreciate what is and is not possible (see Chapter 7: *Location video and sound*).

The grammar of film making is the same for film and television, and for online packages. And the vocabulary people use is the same too. You need to know how to describe what you want to the subject and to the camera person. We're in the communication business, after all. 'Can you get a shot of that over there?' usually isn't good enough.

The hugely experienced BBC foreign correspondent Brian Barron reckons filming a location report is like doing a jigsaw. You compose the story in your head as the day unfolds, mentally moving the pieces of the jigsaw around until you're settled on your final structure.

PIECES TO CAMERA

Ian Woods filming a PTC

On location you will almost certainly want to do a piece-to-camera (PTC) or *stand-up*. If there's time. And if it's essential to tell the story. They're not compulsory.

Of course, it's good to see your face on the telly – that's probably one of the reasons you became a TV journalist. And it's true that audiences like to see who's talking to them. But the stand-up must serve a purpose within the piece. Think hard about how you are going to use it.

Placing the reporter at the heart of the action is a legitimate reason for a stand-up. It lets the audience know you were there, which gives you authority. Make sure there is plenty of action in the background as you film. There is no excuse for a PTC against a blank wall. It looks as if you are about to be shot by a firing squad rather than a camera.

Experienced, and bold, reporters may want to place themselves in the action at the key moment in the narrative – the finish of a race, the arrival of the Prime Minister, or as the winning captain lifts the cup, for example. But remember, if you fluff your lines at that point, you won't be able to use the shot. And unless you have another camera angle available, you will have no pictures of that moment for use in headlines or as archive.

Another good reason for the stand-up is to explain part of the story for which there are no pictures. For example, if a public body issues a statement, but will not offer anybody for interview, a stand-up outside their headquarters explaining their position may be a quicker option than a graphic.

Make sure you're not trying to say more than you can comfortably memorise. If you are having trouble recalling all your words, the piece-to-camera is probably too long. As a guide, 15 to 20 seconds is usually about right.

Among the clichés of TV reporting are stand-ups at the start and end of reports. The opening stand-up can set the scene, but may not be the best visual image to open your piece. The closing stand-up allows you to sum up the story and sign off – useful in some stories but not all.

EVER THE SHORTEST STAND-UP IS LIKELY TO BE THE LONGEST SHOT IN YOUR PIECE, SO IT'S WORTH TAKING TIME TO GET IT RIGHT.

On a complicated legally sensitive story, you will need to be word perfect. Write the words down first and learn your script like an actor. At other times you can ad-lib around key words and phrases.

Whenever possible, try to introduce movement – of yourself, the camera or both – into your PTCs. Even the shortest stand-up is likely to be the longest shot in your piece, so it's worth taking time to get it right.

LOCATIONS FOR TV INTERVIEWS

Television interviews can be spoilt by a poor choice of location or background. The best talker in the world shot against a distracting or irrelevant backdrop will appear less interesting.

Try to talk to people in their natural environment – a bus driver in her cab, a builder laying bricks, a businessman in his factory (usually better than an office).

You should obviously avoid excessively noisy scenes, but if the audience can see the cause of the noise, background sound is much less of a problem on TV than on radio. A lawnmower off camera could be an annoying distraction, but if you are interviewing a cricket groundsman and the mower can be seen on the other side of the pitch, the shot may work.

Choosing a background for interviews is particularly difficult when you are indoors and space is limited. Don't shoot against blank walls or windows if you can help it. If the room, or what's going on in it, is relevant to the story, take people to one end of the room or even into a doorway if it is the only way of getting the room in shot.

Often in documentaries you will see people interviewed with an attractive fireplace (and perhaps even a vase of flowers) behind them. The next time you do, ask yourself how many rooms are arranged so that you sit with your back to the fireplace.

➤ Pieces to camera should help tell the story

➤ Introduce movement into your stand-ups

➤ Choose your backgrounds carefully

➤ Make sure there is space between the subject and the background.

RECORDING VOICE-OVER ON LOCATION

You may have to record voice-over (V-O) for a package on location. The pictures and V-O will be sent back to your edit, where they'll be assembled. You need to be aware of what shots you have and how the story fits together.

You also need to find a suitable location to record, preferably with as little background noise as possible. A quiet room, preferably without echoing walls, and inside the car are favourites. Use the mic close to your mouth with the gain (level control) turned down, so that less ambient sound is picked up. Use headphones to monitor the sound quality and make sure there is no 'popping' on the mic.

If you are using tape and have to send it back for someone else to edit, record the V-O over colour bars (on the stripe, as it's known), so that it can be found easily when the editor is spooling through.

➤ Choose a quiet spot to record location V-O

➤ Record over colour bars to make it easier for an editor.

USING VIEWERS' VIDEOS

The growing number of so-called 'citizen journalists' – people reporting events for online sites – has highlighted the contribution of 'user-generated content' to modern broadcast journalism. Finding contributors is exhilarating. The simplest ways to find them are on-air pleas and captions requesting phone pictures and video. Reporters in the field also join the quest for the material usually captioned on screen as 'viewer's video'. The radio equivalent might be an audio recording of a dramatic event. Radio reporters should remember that video cameras record sound too.

It's not too many years since domestic camcorders were a luxury. Nowadays every home seems to have one. But cries of 'get the video, Mavis' are less common than you might think when disaster strikes on the doorstep. If a terrorist bomb explodes, an aircraft crashes or armed police break into the house next door, self-preservation is the first instinct, rather than 'I wonder if the TV would like shots of this?'

There was extensive home video footage of the 2004 Tsunami, because it affected coastal areas packed with holidaymakers. Taking holiday pictures is one of the main reasons people buy video cameras, so hundreds of people caught up in the tragedy were able to take pictures later seen on news bulletins around the world.

The chances of someone recording moving pictures of an event other than in a holiday resort increased exponentially when video on mobile phones became commonplace. Almost all modern phones have some sort of picture facility, and many have video. Many digital stills cameras can take short clips of video. While moving pictures are highly prized, camera-phone stills can also help tell a story. The quality of moving pictures from mobiles is usually poor by normal broadcast standards, but the newsworthiness of an event will determine what is and is not acceptable.

CASE STUDY 6.1　　WITNESS VIDEO

The first major use of mobile-phone video in mainstream broadcasts in the UK came during the July terrorist bombings in London in 2005. There was enough material from commuters caught up in events to fill a separate package within the BBC's coverage. Sky News too made extensive use of shots taken on the tube within seconds of the bombs going off. Both organisations were well equipped to handle these pictures prior to transmission, as they had been experimenting for several years with ways of using camera-phone technology to enhance their own reporting. The idea that a TV journalist can be live on air at the scene of a breaking news story, even before the camera crew arrives, is hugely attractive to editors. Broadcasters are prepared to accept poorer picture quality in the short term in the race to tell the story first.

ALMOST ALL MODERN PHONES HAVE SOME SORT OF PICTURE FACILITY, AND MANY HAVE VIDEO.

Just as television reporters will seek out domestic video of news events, radio can accept poorer quality recordings where the content is newsworthy. BBC Five Live ran a recording from a listener's Dictaphone when police raided terrorist suspects in the aftermath of the July 2005 London transport bombings. The man, whose home overlooked the flat on the Peabody Estate in West London where two of the men were arrested, had recorded loud bangs and the shouting of armed police officers to the men inside the flat. The recording was crackly and distorted but dramatic – and made compulsive listening.

The same episode led to one of the scoops of the year for ITV News. When pictures of the arrest of the two suspects appeared on their 6.30 and 10.30 bulletins, they were captioned 'EXCLUSIVE: ITV News/Daily Mail'. ITV News secured the pictures from a man who'd taken them, according to first reports, with his girlfriend's DV camera. A bidding war had already started when ITN decided they needed to increase their financial clout. News Editor Deborah Turness called the *Daily Mail* newspaper, because she had shared stories with them before. The joint bid helped stave off a late attempt by Sky News to win the rights. Turness brokered the deal with the amateur cameraman and the *Mail* without even seeing the moving pictures. The man was trapped within a police cordon, but a grabbed frame sent by e-mail convinced her she must have the footage.

Turness told the *Independent* newspaper shortly afterwards that the deal broke new ground in the kind of deals television can do with newspapers. The *Mail* had exclusive stills of the arrests. ITV News had exclusive TV pictures without having to pay the full asking price. Crediting the newspaper on screen – as part of the large 'EXCLUSIVE' caption on the top left of the picture – helped prevent other newspapers from lifting the pictures for their own editions. Otherwise there would be little incentive for a newspaper to work with a TV programme that could show the pictures the evening before the paper came out. The graphics department of ITV News sent the paper 25 high-quality stills from the ten minutes of rushes on the DV tape. Despite legal warnings, other TV channels lifted the pictures complete with the 'exclusive' logo. The BBC report acknowledged that the scenes had been 'sold to a commercial broadcaster'.

Broadcasters like to think of themselves as being at the cutting edge of audio and video production, but the newest technology can catch us out. The highly dramatic pictures of cars being swept down a flooded main street in Boscastle in Cornwall in 2004 were taken on a new hard-disk domestic camcorder. The first TV crews on the scene did not have the software to download the shots on to their edit systems. The first use of those pictures on air came after a cameraman pointed his own lens at a playback monitor. Later BBC engineers worked out how to retrieve the pictures in all their glory, rather than off a flickering screen.

The debate about what constitutes 'broadcast quality' is an argument engineers have had with journalists since broadcast news began. It continues, but the engineers have lost! There was a time when pictures taken by professional cameraman would be rejected if they didn't show the correct wave pattern on an oscilloscope – never mind that they showed a perfectly comprehensible picture on a television screen. The quality argument has been reduced to this: do the pictures or sounds tell a really important story? If the answer is 'yes', then they will be used, no matter how shaky, grainy, fuzzy or distorted. This is not an excuse for subjecting viewers to second-rate images. Too many wobbly or badly focused shots will quickly make the audience queasy. These shots have to be used sparingly. The duration on screen is directly proportional to the news value of the pictures. If the pictures are exclusive, that adds a little extra to what will be tolerated.

Release forms

COPYRIGHT NORMALLY RESTS WITH THE PERSON WHO TOOK THE PICTURES, SO IT IS BEST – TO BE LEGALLY COVERED – TO GET THEIR WRITTEN PERMISSION TO USE THE MATERIAL.

You may have charmed the video tape from the hapless home video enthusiast. You may have transmitted the video clip from the mobile phone back to your newsroom. You may have the camcorder in your hand ready to wire it up to your mobile edit. But that doesn't mean you can use the pictures. Copyright normally rests with the person who took the pictures, so it is best – to be legally covered – to get their written permission to use the material. Most organisations have a standard release form to be filled in by those contributing material. It's a good idea for reporters and producers to keep a handful in the car. This document will also act as a receipt and a legal contract if money changes hands.

It is usual to arrange for all rights in material gathered in this way to be transferred to the broadcaster. This allows unlimited future transmissions, and for the news organisation to sell on the pictures to other broadcasters. The Boscastle flood pictures mentioned above were sold worldwide. The BBC made so much from them they felt obliged to go back to the original cameraman and offer him more money. He declined, asking instead that a contribution be made to the town's relief fund.

Exceptionally, other arrangements will be made. The nationally known motorcycle stunt rider Eddie Kidd was seriously injured in an accident at the Bulldog Bash, a huge gathering of bike enthusiasts in Warwickshire, organised by Hells Angels. One of the crowd caught on video the moment Kidd's bike leapt the track at Long Marston airfield. It appeared to be slowing down after landing, but toppled over the edge of a steep embankment. Eddie Kidd's back was broken; he was lucky to be alive, and his stunt career was effectively over. As a fellow biker, the amateur cameraman did not want to profit from the stunt man's injuries, but he allowed the BBC to use the pictures on condition that a donation to a bikers' charity was made every time they were shown.

Every time you use somebody else's pictures, remember the law of copyright. Copyright belongs to the person who took the pictures (or if they were a professional contractor the person who commissioned them). You can't use anyone else's pictures without their permission.

GIVING PEOPLE CAMERAS

'User-generated content' is not just about waiting for people to send in material or seeking it out after an event. Ever since lightweight DV cameras came on to the market, journalists have been lending them to people to make their own video diaries and to report stories from their own viewpoints. This can make compelling television.

The authored report (a first person narrative from a contributor) has an important place in the modern news balance. It enfranchises groups who might otherwise not have a chance to air their views on mainstream media.

Cameras producing pictures of broadcast quality are so cheap that within the budgets of big news organisations they are almost disposable. But that doesn't mean you should give them to everybody.

Ask whether what anybody can produce (with a little basic camera training) will provide exclusive or otherwise unavailable footage that enhances the story-telling. The key question is one of access – the secret of much good documentary making. A homeless person with a camera may give a better account of their plight than a homeless person being followed by a video crew, where the presence of the team prejudices the authenticity of the material. There's an example of the results of giving a contributor a camera in Chapter 11: *The package.*

> ### REMEMBER
>
> ➤ More people than ever are carrying video and stills cameras, often on their phones
> ➤ Video cameras also record sound that might be useful for radio
> ➤ Check copyright and ask for a written release
> ➤ Make use of authored reports
> ➤ Consider lending lightweight cameras to contributors.

PRESSERS AND PRESS PACKS – REGULAR SCENARIOS

No two stories are the same but the situations you find yourself in often will be. You will often find yourself at a news conference – or 'presser' – or in a pack of other reporters chasing the same tale. The first time these situations are daunting, but you very soon get used to them and will know how to prepare.

At times you may need to co-operate with other journalists from rival organisations. In practice, reporters are not lone wolves – they often hunt in packs. Many on-the-road reporters spend more of their working day with their rivals than with colleagues from their own newsroom. They trade favours, information and occasionally audio and video material. Sometimes their editors never get to know about these arrangements, which can make life easier working in the field.

THE NEWS CONFERENCE

Always arrive in good time for press conferences, so you can set up your equipment and find a seat where you will have good eye-contact with the people at the top table when you ask your questions. The pressures of a small radio newsroom mean you will not have the luxury of being first to arrive and claiming the best position. You will be covering many stories in the day. So time-management is the key. Can you bag your seat at the presser and then continue writing the earlier story you were working on? Can you make those vital calls on the mobile while you are waiting? Can you set up at the presser and *then* file the earlier story in time for the bulletin.

It's helpful to establish the ground rules with the press or media liaison officer at the conference. Can you plead early deadlines so you are in and out swiftly without missing anything? Do the speakers have to leave at a certain time? Is there a photo-call and if so what form will it take? Most importantly, is there an opportunity for separate one-to-one interviews? If there is, that's good news, but you should record the presser anyway, in case the plan changes. If the conference overruns, separate interviews may be cancelled.

If you arrived early, there is a better chance of being first in the queue for the one-to-one, but bear in mind that, deadlines permitting, it can be better to go second. The interviewee will have been warmed up and had a chance to order their thoughts. But you never want to be late in the pecking order. Interviewees will have become bored, and will rush their answers to get away.

In large set-piece news conferences, like the Presidential-style monthly gatherings Tony Blair introduced at 10 Downing Street, there are standard procedures and favoured reporters will get priority.

The press conference: arrive in good time to set up your gear

High-profile news conferences raise a contentious point about how to cover them. Editors will differ on this question. Does it really matter who asks the questions as long as you get the answers? Everybody ends up with the same material from the conference itself. If you have an exclusive point to pursue, a one-to-one interview after the main event is the best time to reveal your hand. Interviewers' questions are included in coverage of news conferences from time to time. *The next time you see that happening, ask yourself whether the reporter's question was really necessary to tell the story. Or was it a case of the reporter and the news organisation giving themselves a pat-on-the-back for getting their question in?*

➤ Arrive early at press conferences

➤ Ask if there will be one-to-one interviews

➤ Everybody gets the same material from a 'presser'.

MEDIA SCRUMS

You may find yourself involved in a media scrum. We've all seen them on television. The bigger the story, the bigger the scrum. Hordes of TV and stills cameras. Radio reporters shoving microphones into people's faces. Print reporters brandishing mini-recorders and notebooks. They're not an easy place to record sound and video. Often they follow a *stake-out* of somebody or somewhere in the news. They can be great fun, or they can degenerate into fist fights.

But they can also be intimidating and intrusive. That may depend on who is at the centre of the mêlée. Is it a public figure who can expect this level of attention? Is it a criminal who cannot reasonably expect privacy? Or is it an otherwise innocent member of the public who does not deserve to have their privacy invaded and might even be frightened?

The BBC guidelines suggest it will sometimes be appropriate to make pooling arrangements with other media organisations, and at other times we may judge it proper to withdraw.

So, there are times when it is right to pull out, but when should we get stuck in? A Sky News crew edged their way into one scrum live on air. Gerard Conlon, one of the Guildford Four who were wrongly jailed for IRA pub bombings in the 1970s, emerged from the House of Commons after an historic meeting with Tony Blair. The Sky reporter was live on air at a different entrance to the House. The camera was transmitting to the satellite truck via microwave link. So, the team had the freedom to march down the street, still broadcasting, and edge their way into the pack. It was exciting and innovative television.

And there's another incentive for getting stuck into the scrum. Many local radio stations will consider it a job well done if you manage to shove your microphone so close to the interviewee that it can't help but appear on the TV news. Indeed, in the early days of commercial radio, reporters were paid a bonus if their mic, with its prominent station logo, made a TV appearance. Station managers still consider it part of the reporter's job to get this free publicity. It helps the station's profile.

➤ Media scrums can be exciting, but don't expect top quality recorded material

➤ They may be intrusive.

DOORSTEPPING

In an age where cold-callers are invading most of our homes via phone and e-mail with sales patter for everything from double-glazing to Viagra, it may be a surprise that broadcasters are so sensitive about the rights and wrongs of doorstepping.

Doorstepping is not just any interview on a doorstep, and the term doesn't apply to journalists knocking on doors in the normal course of inquiries. The term is defined in the Ofcom Broadcasting Code as:

The filming or recording of an interview or attempted interview with someone, or announcing that a call is being filmed or recorded for broadcast purposes, without any prior warning.

It doesn't include people in the news being recorded in public places, or vox-pops, where opinions are sought from random members of the public.

The Ofcom code says:

Doorstepping for factual programmes should not take place unless a request for an interview has been refused or it has not been possible to request an interview, or there is good reason to believe that an investigation will be frustrated if the subject is approached openly, and it is warranted to doorstep.

DOORSTEPPING SHOULD NOT TAKE PLACE UNLESS A REQUEST FOR AN INTERVIEW HAS BEEN REFUSED OR IT HAS NOT BEEN POSSIBLE TO REQUEST AN INTERVIEW.

The BBC guidelines say that all proposals to doorstep people, whether or not they have been approached for an interview beforehand, have to be 'referred up'. If there has been a prior approach, a senior editorial figure, or for independent programme makers the commissioning editor, must give approval for the doorstep. Where there has been no prior approach, Controller Editorial Policy must give approval (there is an exception for daily news gathering). The Controller will normally only give permission for a doorstep if there is clear evidence of crime or significant wrong-doing, or good reason to believe an investigation will be frustrated or allegations avoided if the individual is approached openly.

Notwithstanding these very strict rules, doorstepping has become a staple of consumer reporting. The reporter or camera being attacked has become a cliché of this type of television. Central Television's *Cook Report* set the standard through the 1990s. Programmes were structured to lead to a confrontation with a wrong-doer.

APPROACHING THE BEREAVED

Most reporters dread the *death-knock*. It is an insensitive but commonly used term for calling on the recently bereaved to request interviews, or to ask for home video or photos of someone who has just died. It is an uncomfortable experience, and difficult to avoid guilt at intruding on grief. But people react differently in times of distress. Some may want to talk – to unburden their own emotions or to pay tribute to a lost loved one. Others may react angrily. The sensible rule of thumb for reporters and producers is to learn when to take no for an answer – which should, in these circumstances, be the first time it is said to you.

The BBC has a reputation among journalists for being among the more timid organisations at times of bereavement. Most BBC journalists will defend the corporation's policies as the most sensitive and appropriate way to treat people. Its *Editorial Guidelines* are clear:

We should normally request interviews with people who are injured or grieving following an accident or disaster by approaching them through friends, relatives or advisers. We should not:

- **put them under pressure to provide interviews**
- **harass them with repeated phone calls, e-mails, text messages or knocks at the door**
- **stay on their property if asked to leave**
- **normally follow them if they move on.**

The Ofcom Broadcasting Code is more succinct: 'People in a state of distress should not be put under pressure to take part in a programme or provide interviews, unless it is warranted.' The definition of 'warranted' has yet to be defined in law.

REMEMBER

➤ Learn when to take no for an answer
➤ Before doorstepping or approaching the bereaved, you should know the relevant sections of the Ofcom code.

MORE ON EDITORIAL GUIDELINES

WHENEVER LEGAL AND ETHICAL JUDGEMENTS HAVE TO BE MADE, EDITORIAL GUIDELINES CAN BE CONSULTED. THERE IS NO GREATER RESERVOIR OF EXPERIENCE TO DRAW UPON.

Whenever legal and ethical judgements have to be made, editorial guidelines can be consulted. The BBC's Editorial Guidelines – almost 200 pages of them in the 2005 edition – are the best known example. They used to be called Producers Guidelines, but now include the relevant sections of the Ofcom Broadcasting Code. They are available online at: www.bbc.co.uk/guidelines/editorialguidelines. The Ofcom code, which is also available on the Internet at www.ofcom.org.uk, replaces the regulatory codes of the Independent Television Commission (which governed independent television), the Radio Authority (commercial radio's regulator) and the Broadcasting Standards Commission, which controlled taste, decency, fairness and privacy.

These guidelines are the result of years of experience and case studies, drawn up by senior editorial figures, many of whom have had to make critical and controversial decisions in their own careers. The BBC guidelines are approved by the BBC Trust, a body appointed by the government to regulate the corporation. The guidelines are constantly reviewed by the corporation's Editorial Policy team of senior managers. Ofcom maintains a similarly rigorous regime of review and control.

The guidelines are not just a sop to viewers' and listeners' pressure groups. They are a working tool, consulted by broadcasters every day.

Just as there is no such thing as a truly new story, there should be no contentious issue that isn't covered by the guidelines. If one arises, be assured there will soon be a policy about it. In short, there is no greater reservoir of experience to draw upon.

The guidelines, either those of the Ofcom code or the BBC, are more than just a legal framework. They are a one-stop shop for any reporter worried about the appropriate way to approach a delicate story. They cover accuracy, fact-checking, impartiality, fairness, consent, privacy, crime and anti-social behaviour, the use and treatment of children in broadcasts, politics and public policy, war, terror and emergencies, religion and the editorial integrity and independence of the broadcaster. They also tackle the conflicts of interest brought about by the modern broadcast environment, in which co-production and content bought in from independent producers are an important part of the mix.

A CLOSER LOOK

THE REPORTER'S ROLE – A POLICE VIEW

Ofcom sets out a legal and ethical code for the work of broadcasters, including reporters in the field. But journalists are not above the other laws of the land, and will often find themselves dealing with those who have to uphold those laws – the police.

The interests of the police and reporters are not mutually exclusive. Often the police will want help from the media. The most obvious examples of this are appeals for witnesses to crime or accidents. Reporters cultivate police contacts and they are a valued source of information. But there may be conflict too.

Police constables maintain traffic flow and crowd control at major incidents. They are on duty at crime scenes to prevent anyone interfering with evidence. But they are not allowed to give ad-hoc media interviews.

The police have their own guidelines for police–press relations. The Metropolitan Police drew up ground rules after consultation with media representatives including the National Union of Journalists.

The Met's guidelines say:

1 Members of the media have a duty to report from the scene of many of the incidents we have to deal with. We should actively help them carry out their responsibilities provided they do not interfere with ours.

2 Where it is necessary to put cordons in place, it is much better to provide the media with a good vantage point from which they can operate rather than to exclude them, otherwise they may try to get around the cordons and interfere with police operations. Providing an area for members of the media does not exclude them from operating from other areas to which the general public have access.

METROPOLITAN POLICE GUIDELINES: 'ONCE IMAGES ARE RECORDED, WE HAVE NO POWER TO DELETE OR CONFISCATE THEM WITHOUT A COURT ORDER, EVEN IF WE THINK THEY CONTAIN DAMAGING OR USEFUL EVIDENCE.'

3 Members of the media have a duty to take photographs and film incidents and we have no legal power or moral responsibility to prevent or restrict what they record . . . Once images are recorded, we have no power to delete or confiscate them without a court order, even if we think they contain damaging or useful evidence.

The Met's guidelines go on to cover issues including dealing with bereaved and distressed people who are subject to media attention, and advice that the media must obtain recorded permission to enter private property while accompanying police officers. The BBC's advice on 'tag along raids' echoes this.

West Midlands Police produced an A4 folder with no fewer than 12 inserts covering everything from media training courses to an A–Z guide on subjects from 'accidents' to 'young offenders' (an A–Y guide).

Staffordshire Police's media unit produced a pocket guide for their officers. It also included advice which is helpful for reporters to know:

- The presence of a photographer or a reporter at an accident, crime or disaster scene does not of itself constitute an unlawful obstruction or interference.

- The taking of pictures or the asking of questions should not be restricted, even if the police officer disagrees with the nature of the pictures or questions.

- If a distressed or bereaved person requests an officer to ask the media to leave them in peace, the officer can pass that request on to journalists, in the spirit of 'victim support'. This is advice on which journalists and editors can base their own decisions, unless there is an identifiable Breach of the Peace, when journalists, like any citizens, have a duty to disperse.

- Journalists should carry press credentials and produce them if requested by an officer.

- Journalists have a right to photograph and report events that take place on public property.

- The police can invite journalists onto private property where an event of public interest has occurred, but the journalists have to respect the rights of the owner of the property and may have to leave.

- Access to crime scenes can be denied for evidence gathering and forensic examination, but the reasons for denying access should be explained.

- As long as a journalist does not break the law or interfere with an investigation, a police officer should not impede the journalist.

- It is reasonable for a police officer to ask a journalist to move his or her vehicle – even if it is legally parked – if it could obstruct the movement or parking of emergency vehicles.

Awareness of this range of advice leaves you better equipped to cover big stories with a heavy police presence – and to deal with individual officers as you go about your day-to-day business. Remember that courtesy is more productive than confrontation.

JOURNALISTS HAVE A RIGHT TO PHOTOGRAPH AND REPORT EVENTS THAT TAKE PLACE ON PUBLIC PROPERTY.

CONCLUSION

Reporters and producers on location are under a lot of pressure. In radio, you will almost certainly be alone. That is why it helps to prepare as well as you can before you leave the studio, where others, like the planning desk or your editor, will have been able to help you.

It is almost always a good idea to arrive early for a story. That's a piece of good advice that may be impossible to follow. We're well aware of the pressures of busy newsrooms. So, perhaps it's better to offer another platitude. Don't panic. Think on your feet and respond to changing circumstances. Remember, no plan survives first contact with the enemy.

FURTHER READING

Beaman, Jim (2000) *Interviewing for radio*, Oxford: Routledge. Practical advice on dealing with interviewees and how to structure interviews in different locations.

Chantler, Paul and Stewart, Peter (2003) *Basic Radio Journalism*, Oxford: Focal Press. The role of the reporter on location.

Frost, Chris (2001) *Reporting for journalists*, Oxford: Routledge. Useful on the preparations you need for working in the field – not broadcast-based though.

Ray, Vin (2003) *The Television News Handbook*, London: Macmillan. Strong advice based on the experience of television practitioners.

WEB LINKS

www.bbc.co.uk/guidelines/editorialguidelines. The code by which BBC journalists operate.

www.luci.eu/eng/pages/manual.html. More on the use of PDA phones for newsgathering.

www.ofcom.org.uk/tv/ifi/codes/bcode/. The site of the regulatory body Ofcom.

www.theaa.com. The routefinder facility can be invaluable.

CHAPTERSEVEN

LOCATION VIDEO AND SOUND

Getting out of the office to cover a story – any story – is one of the joys of broadcast journalism. There's an excitement and an expectation – the thrill of not knowing exactly what might happen or how people will react to you. And you have to capture the essence of it all in sound or on video. Unless you are very familiar with the recording kit you're using, the job becomes extremely difficult.

AS ALWAYS – BE PREPARED

HEALTH AND SAFETY

The risk assessment of any location must include a consideration of how safe it will be to operate your equipment. Clearly, in a war zone or a riot a video journalist is at greater risk than a three-person TV crew. A reporter and a sound recordist can keep watch for danger while the camera operator concentrates on filming. But even routine domestic stories present dangers – not just for yourself, but more importantly for members of the public. Trailing cables can trip people up. Is there somewhere to park your radio car or satellite truck, legally, without it causing an obstruction?

As we explained in Chapter 6: *Location reporting and production*, newsrooms have risk assessment forms for you to fill in whenever you identify hazards beyond the routine of daily news gathering. When you are taught how to use a new piece of kit, the health and safety aspects of using it should be explained to you.

BEFORE YOU LEAVE THE NEWSROOM

Newsroom planning involves working out what equipment you need to cover a story and the logistics of how the story will be transmitted. What distances have to be travelled? Will a reporter be able to return to base to edit, or will they be on location feeding output for several hours or even days? Do you need live links, location editing, and feed points for audio and video? Do you need to book overnight accommodation?

Local radio newsrooms cover a small patch. Reporters spend much of their time travelling to and from base. They edit and voice most of the material collected in the field back at the studio. National news gathering relies on reporters based around the country in regional centres. Travel times are an important part of the calculation of how long it takes to cover a story.

Foreign news operations have correspondents based around the world, but the stories which occur in their geographical region often mean lengthy flights or overland journeys to locations that are not necessarily served by regular transport links. The technical resources available vary hugely, particularly in developing countries, and news crews have to take all the equipment they need with them.

Whoever you work for, making sure the equipment is up to the job is the first step before you go out on the road. If you are using unfamiliar equipment, try it out before you leave the newsroom. Always ask how new kit works, and have a look at the instruction manual if you get the chance. Being caught out in front of an interviewee or when you arrive in a foreign hotel room is embarrassing and unprofessional.

CHECK YOUR BATTERIES

IN ANY NEWSROOM, MAKE SURE YOU KNOW WHOSE JOB IT IS TO MAKE SURE BATTERIES ARE CHARGED, AND, IF THEY'RE NOT AROUND, DO THE JOB YOURSELF.

Most electronic recording devices use batteries. Do you have batteries ready to use? Are they fully charged? It's almost incredible how many interviews have been lost because the reporter left the newsroom with dead batteries or, worse, no batteries at all. Bear in mind that pieces of kit you may use only occasionally – radio mics, for example – need their own batteries. It's always handy to carry spares.

The biggest problems occur with shared equipment. In any newsroom, make sure you know whose job it is to make sure batteries are charged, and, if they're not around, do the job yourself. On foreign assignments make sure you have an international adapter so you can plug in the battery charger – and your mobile phone.

CHECK YOUR TAPES

You might be using audio or video tapes, hard-disk recorders or memory cards. Whatever the medium, do you have enough recording capacity for the job in hand? Always carry spares in case the unexpected happens. There are few more depressing feelings, professionally speaking, than watching events unfold in front of you that you can't record because you've used all your tapes.

If you are on a big story, don't think simply in terms of how much recording time you have available. You may need to send a tape or memory card back to base or to a satellite truck with only a few shots, or a single key interview on it.

A classic how-not-to-do-it documentary *Stalking Pete Doherty*, broadcast on Channel 4 in 2005, recorded the moment when the interviewer, who had been trying to document the life of the rock star *du jour*, Pete Doherty of the Libertines and Babyshambles, found himself alone with his subject at last. Doherty suggested this was the time to do the interview. The tape ran out.

REMEMBER

➤ Prepare the logistics of your shoot

➤ Check batteries (make sure they're charged) and carry spares

➤ Make sure you have enough recording capacity (take spare tapes).

RADIO ON LOCATION

RADIO REPORTING ON LOCATION – THE HISTORY

The technical challenge of radio reporting has always been how to capture location audio – interviews, actuality, the reporter's voice – in the highest sound quality with the least physical effort.

Technological advances have transformed radio reporting within the lifetimes of many working in the industry today. The legendary Richard Dimbleby, the father of David and Jonathan the television presenters, was the first BBC war correspondent and, according to the US Museum of Broadcast Communications, the virtual founder of broadcast journalism. During the Second World War, he reported from Allied bombing raids; from the Normandy beaches; was the first radio reporter to reach the concentration camp at Belsen, and the first to enter Berlin.

The BBC developed portable 'midget' disc recorders to be operated by reporters in the field without an engineer. The terms *portable* and *midget* were misnomers by modern standards. The machines weighed 40 pounds – about the same as a soldier's rucksack – and the reporter had to carry his personal kit as well. The Riverside Portable recorded on to double-sided ten-inch disks. It got its name from the gramophones taken on picnics in the 1930s. Under fire, it was no picnic to operate one.

Magnetic tape was a German invention, copied by the Allies after the war. For radio programmes, it was a revelation and dominated the medium for half a century. Programmes could be recorded and edited very simply. A classical music performance that lasted an hour and ten minutes could be condensed into an hour's transmission slot. Or a long-winded interview with a politician could be cut down.

The Uher – heavy as a housebrick, but at least you could see your tape going round

For several decades the most reliable portable recorder for news reporters was the Uher – pronounced 'ewer'. Many people working in news today recall the Uher fondly – it was the size of a large handbag and heavy, but trusty and rarely broke down. If your batteries lost their charge you could buy replacements at any corner shop. And you could see, through the Perspex lid, that your tape was in place and turning at the right speed.

The Uher also had record level meters the same size as the ones back in the studio, so it was clear to see whether the sound you were recording was too quiet or, worse, too loud and therefore likely to distort on playback.

Elderly relatives may have told you about the first video recorders. They were four times the size of most DVD recorders in the shops today and could only record up to one hour's programming. The picture was comparatively fuzzy, whereas a modern domestic recording is an exact digital copy of whatever was broadcast. Similar advances have been made in audio recording and for a while it looked as if domestic and professional news recording equipment would converge.

THE DIGITAL REVOLUTION

As early as the 1980s radio reporters were using cassette recorders, the 'professional' equivalent of the Sony Walkman – the personal stereo that was everywhere before the advent of iPods and MP3 players.

A MiniDisc recorder, professional kit at a high-street price

Then the digital system MiniDisc was developed, and it looked like the answer to a station manager's prayers: a professional piece of kit at a high-street price. Reporters went out with domestic recorders and a high-quality professional microphone that probably cost twice as much as the tiny recording deck. The controls are fiddly, and the record level meter a little awkward to see, but used properly MiniDisc gives results of the highest quality.

Digital recording means you only record the electrical signal from your microphone or line sound source. That signal is converted into a binary code, and once encoded it will not change. You are not recording the tape hiss or distortion typical of analogue copies. And each copy will be as good as the original, not subject to increasing amounts of tape noise. MiniDisc players have never matched the robustness and longevity of the Uher, but, at a fraction of the cost, they are virtually disposable. That doesn't help the reporter on location when bits fall off his MiniDisc player, but it pleases the accountants. One advantage of MiniDisc is that it is possible to perform simple edits on location. A reporter can select in and out points on an interview clip by adding inaudible markers to the recording. The resulting soundbites can be played back instantly. The separated tracks can also be shuffled, and played back in any order. A simple package can be produced in the field. Other digital recording devices can do the same.

The more recent advance – solid-state recording on to removable media cards, of the type found in digital stills cameras – is fast becoming standard. Equipment is again being developed with professionals in mind. Radio news reporters need no longer take to the streets carrying the equivalent of an upmarket personal hi-fi.

Modern machines will have *automatic level control (ALC)*. What ALC does is to flatten out the incoming signal to a consistent level that is neither too low nor too high. It should guarantee no distortion on playback. It would appear to be a useful tool, but the problem for professionals is that because *all* the recorded sound is at the same level, as soon as there is a pause in what you mean to record, any background noise may be boosted to fill the gap. You might be on a pavement, interviewing a fire officer outside a house fire. When he pauses at the end of a sentence, or to collect his thoughts, traffic noise swoops in to fill the gap. You might think his next comments would be drowned out by the cars and lorries. But no, as soon as he starts speaking again the din subsides. It is a most unnatural effect and disconcerting for the listener. Radio professionals call it *surge* or *pumping*, and they hate it, because it is an unnatural distortion. Domestic tape decks have had ALC for years. But there is rarely any circumstance in which it should be used by broadcast professionals.

You might get away with using automatic level control in perfectly quiet conditions, but it is better to set the levels manually and alter or *ride* them as you monitor what you are recording. Cheaper equipment has pre-set ALC, but on more sophisticated kit it is possible to adjust threshold settings and attack and release times. Trust us, it is simpler to use manual level controls.

REMEMBER

➤ Digital recording means you can make multiple copies without reducing the sound quality

➤ Avoid automatic level settings

➤ Be prepared to ride the levels.

MICROPHONES

Whatever you are recording onto, the sound will only be as good as the microphone you are using. And the mic will only be as good as the person using it. If you move the mic around too much, there will probably be handling noise: the cable may rattle, causing scratching effects on your recording. If you use the wrong type of mic, you may record sound from the wrong direction or sound that is horribly distorted by wind noise or electrical interference.

If you work in a radio newsroom, the chances are the options will have been taken away from you. There will be a standard piece of kit taken out by every reporter on news jobs. The mic will have been chosen according to its fitness for the job, its reliability based on the chief engineer's past experience, and almost certainly its cost. But you still need to know what type of mic it is to get the best results from it. And if you fancy producing outside broadcasts or covering sports events, it's worth knowing a little about the other microphone types.

Microphones are described according to the way they pick up the sound and according to the direction from which the sound is recorded. All pick up sound waves, vibrations in the air, in a similar way to your eardrum.

The standard news-gathering mic for radio can be an *omni*, short for omni-directional. It picks up sound from any direction, and is useful for interviews and close-up sound recording.

The gun mic used by TV reporters can be held further away from the interviewee and kept out of camera shot because it is directional; in other words it only picks up sound from the direction in which it is pointed. It will be a *capacitor* or *moving coil* type. The capacitor or *condenser* type has an electrically charged capacitor plate, and needs an electric current to work. The electricity can be supplied by a battery in the mic itself, or from the recorder. You need to know if you are using this type of microphone because you will have to make sure the battery is charged for it to work. If it is operating from the power in the recorder, known as *phantom power*, then it will be a small extra drain on the recorder's battery.

The moving coil, or *dynamic*, mic has a wire coil attached to a diaphragm vibrating in a magnetic field.

There are also *ribbon* mics, where the vibrations are picked up by a diaphragm of foil, usually a thin strip of aluminium, vibrating in a magnetic field. These are

Omni mic

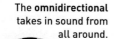

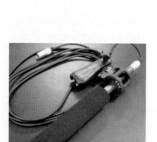

The **omnidirectional** takes in sound from all around.

Gun mic

Ribbon mic

Lip mic

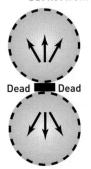

The **cardioid** has a heart-shaped area of pick-up.

The **hypercardioid** is more directional than the cardioid.

Dead   Dead

The **figure-of-eight** takes in sound from front and back but not from the sides.

Dead   Dead

Personal mic (a.k.a. clip-on mic or tie mic)

expensive and most often found in studios, where they are used for high-end music recording. They are hardly ever used in the open air because they pick up wind noise, which distorts and crackles. An exception is the *lip mic*, a type of ribbon mic which, as the name suggests, is held close to the lips.

These are the microphones favoured by many sports commentators, and are also used in TV edit suites for recording voice-over. They only pick up sound at very close range. So, they cut out crowd noise while relaying the commentator's voice. Effects mics will be placed around the ground to pick up sound from the crowd and the pitch to be mixed in on transmission. Nowadays many commentators use mics attached to headsets. These are likely to be dynamic or condenser types.

We mentioned that the standard TV news-gathering mic is likely to be directional. Technically its *polar pattern* (or polar diagram) – the direction from which it picks up sound – is known as hypercardioid. The *gun mics* used by TV news crews are covered in fluffy wind covers, which trap a layer of air through which the sound travels, preventing wind noise and *'popping'* on the recording. It's not an original joke – but they are often referred to as a dog. Prince Charles used to ask sound recordists: 'Does it bite?' Longer guns are even more directional – you'll have seen them in documentaries about the making of wildlife films, and in spy movies.

Hypercardioid is a more extreme version of the polar pattern known as cardioid, or heart-shaped. Sound is collected from a heart-shaped area around the front of the mic.

Some mics record in a figure-of-eight, receiving sound from the front and rear but not the sides. They're sometimes called bi-directional. These are handy in studios for recording an interview where interviewer and subject are sitting either side of the mic.

Apart from strongly directional mics, the type of most use to broadcast journalists is the omni-directional, which as the name suggests collects sound from all directions. It's not much use if you want to eliminate heavy background noise, but can be effective if used close to the subject. They're commonly used by radio reporters. The tiny personal mics used by TV crews are usually omni-directional. They can be attached to the recorder or camera by cables or by radio link.

For lengthy radio interviews on location, personal mics attached to yourself and your interviewee do away with the need to stretch across chair arms and coffee tables. If you are using two mics, be aware of how you are going to mix the sound into the recorder. A small mixer might be the answer, or else you could record onto separate stereo tracks and adjust the balance and levels in the edit.

A useful tip when recording in a noisy area is to hold the mic very close to the speaker's mouth and turn down the record level accordingly. The mic will pick up the voice and cut the background noise to acceptable levels.

PROTECTING YOUR MIC OUTDOORS

Just as the fluffy 'dog' protects TV gun mics from wind noise, a foam windshield is usually provided for reporters' stick mics. It fits on top of the mic and keeps some wind noise at bay, though not as much as the dog. What it won't protect the equipment against is pouring rain. The BBC advises its radio reporters to carry a

Fluffy dog wind shield

condom . . . to slip over the end of the mic in a downpour. The windshield can be placed over the top of the protected mic, so that the makeshift waterproofing doesn't alarm interviewees.

REMEMBER

➤ Different mics record sound in different ways
➤ Try to choose the best mic for the job
➤ Protect your mic from wind and rain.

RECORDING INDOORS

Wherever you record sound it is important to take control of the environment. Normally that is easier indoors than outside. You might not be able to halt the traffic on the M6 or divert the 1030 flight from Manchester to Malaga, but you can, politely, ask for a quiet room in which to conduct an interview.

Listen to the acoustics of the room. Clap your hands if necessary to hear any echoes. Bare walls, tiles and wooden floors will echo. Soft furnishings help dampen reflected sound. Avoid bathrooms and kitchens. Standing or sitting next to curtains can help.

The trend for laminate flooring played havoc with sound recording. One radio producer, confronted with an interviewee's newly modernised home – all wooden floors and no curtains – had to hire a room in a local B & B to ensure sound without echo. She said hiring a room at an hourly rate during the daytime did nothing for her reputation.

Often, you will want background sound to add colour to your interview: to prove you are on location, and haven't just invited everyone into the studio. Then you might be faced with the opposite problem to those above. For example, you might have to persuade the managing director who has set aside a nice quiet room for the interview that it will be better conducted on a noisy shop floor.

'TURN IT OFF' – THE PROBLEMS OF DISTRACTING SOUNDS

Indoors it's easy to unplug telephones so they don't interfere with your recording. It's also important to remember to switch off mobile phones – your own and your interviewee's – while you are recording. If other people are in the room, ask them to switch theirs off too.

Clocks, fridges, freezers, air-conditioning units and other electrical equipment can also be picked up on your recording. You have to ask if they can be turned off. And remind people to turn them back on again. You won't be popular if you've left somebody's freezer full of food to defrost.

SETTING A LEVEL

It is normal practice to set your sound level before you start recording. Exceptionally, if there is a danger you would otherwise miss something, you can start recording first and then adjust the levels immediately. If your settings are as they were the last time you recorded in that location, there is a fighting chance you will have usable sound. Recording on-the-fly like this happens more frequently than you might expect. The demands on the radio reporter are such that you may have just completed a live two-way or returned from feeding material via the radio car to find that a press conference has already started. Or you may be outside a court as the key witness emerges and starts talking to a television camera ten yards away.

Usually you have control over the situation and can take your time to do things properly. The recorder has a pause mode and, while it is in pause, you set the record levels by directing your microphone at the sound source and monitoring it. If the sound source is a human voice, make sure the speaker is talking at the same level when you come to record. A shy interviewee may be reluctant to speak up before the interview proper. It used to be thought good practice to ask an innocuous question like: 'What did you have for breakfast?' These days many people say: 'I didn't have any breakfast', which adds up to less than two seconds – barely time to look at the audio meters, never mind adjust them. A more imaginative approach may be needed. 'Tell me about your holidays.' 'Tell me what your job involves.' Sometimes it's best to ask people to identify themselves with their name and title, spelling out any difficult words. You may wish to record this as an audio note.

Some reporters have problems monitoring their own levels. They sound check at one level – usually sotto voce because they don't want to be overheard. Then, as they launch into the report proper their voice booms out much louder. Avoid this temptation. If you're happy for thousands of people to hear your words over the radio, it shouldn't matter that a few people within 20 yards or so can overhear you. Counting into the microphone – 'one, two, three, four, five' or even, like a rock show roadie, 'one-two, one-two' – is a poor way to take your own level. You will probably count in a monotone, all at the same level, whereas your voice report will contain many ups and downs, just like a normal conversation. So it's better to sound check with the words you will be using.

USE HEADPHONES

It is surprising how many radio reporters conduct interviews without wearing headphones. The headphones or *cans* are your quality control. Your ears are the best judge.

Monitor the sound through your ears

Monitor the sound going into your recorder and you can ensure that the levels will be correct when it is played back. In news gathering with tight deadlines it is not good enough to assume you can boost the level on playback if it's a bit quiet. There may not be time to play with the levels before your recording is on air.

Worse still, if sound has been recorded too high it will distort, or on some digital systems disappear altogether. This is irretrievable. Distorted sound cannot be restored. Recording it is wasted effort. If it was a key interview with a witness who has left the scene, you will never be able to recapture the moment. You have failed to do your job.

You wouldn't take a photograph without looking in the viewfinder. Don't record sound without monitoring it. Some radio reporters prefer a small earpiece – it's less intrusive, but not as reliable as cans, which should encase your ears and eliminate the sounds you are not recording.

USEFUL EXTRAS

There are a few accessories worth taking out with any microphone kit. These are a small desktop mic stand, lengths of extra cable and gaffer tape. Leave them in the car until you need to use them. They come in handy for formal news conferences. The mic can be mounted on a desk and the cable laid to where the reporter is sitting. The tape helps keep it out of the way of fumbling hands and feet. The reporter can then operate the controls on the recorder in comfort, and concentrate on what is being said.

You may have seen, on television coverage of major news stories, radio reporters crouching under a desk with their microphone hand held aloft to record press conferences. This is a bad idea for a number of reasons. Firstly, it makes your arm ache and after ten minutes or so it is unbearable. You can't concentrate on your recording if you are engaged in an endurance test. Secondly, it is hard to earn the respect of your interviewee if you are crawling around on the floor at their feet. Thirdly, even if you don't ask questions, it is decidedly undignified and does your reputation and that of your radio station no good at all.

REMEMBER

- ➤ Control the recording environment
- ➤ Remove the source of distracting sounds if you can
- ➤ Set your levels before you start recording
- ➤ Always monitor your recording – preferably with headphones
- ➤ Don't forget the extras (cable and mic stands).

TELEVISION ON LOCATION

ON THE ROAD WITH A CAMERA CREW

IF IT IS POTENTIALLY UNSAFE FOR ONE PERSON TO BE RESPONSIBLE FOR TECHNICAL OPERATION AND WATCHING THEIR OWN BACK, A SECOND PERSON IS VITAL.

Most television news reporting is carried out by a reporter with a camera crew. In domestic reporting the crew is usually one person, who's responsible for operating the camera and recording sound. In more dangerous locations, and that includes many foreign assignments, there will be a sound person too. If it is potentially unsafe for one person to be responsible for technical operation and watching their own back, a second person is vital.

It wasn't always so. Early BBC news reporting, on film, used two-person crews: one for the camera, the other for sound. In ITV there was a third person, a lighting electrician. Greg Dyke tells a story of when he was a young researcher on an ITV programme. A car pulled up on location with no-one in the back. The future Director General of the BBC asked why.

'He's the electrician's driver.'

'So where's the electrician?'

'He prefers to use his own car so he can claim the mileage.'

That was an example of the infamous 'Spanish practices' when trade union rules dictated ITV crewing policy. But Margaret Thatcher's government of the 1980s, with its determination to limit trade union power, and the advent of ENG – electronic news gathering – changed that.

ENG – or PSC (portable single camera), as it was known in the BBC – was the first major technical advance. Video took over from film as the medium for recording news events.

Then the Betacam system replaced U-Matic. In the U-Matic tape system, the camera was attached by an umbilical cable to the recorder, carried by the sound person. It would have been impossible for a camera operator to carry the heavy recorder. To this day, sound recordists who carried those recorders slung over one shoulder complain of back problems.

Gary Darfield, experienced cameraman working with Patrick Burns of BBC Midlands

Betacam introduced the camcorder to television news. It also brought us the *one-man-band* – the camera person who did sound. The economic advantages are obvious. The practical problems of one person carrying camera, tripod, and often lights are harder to justify. Carrying the 'sticks' or tripod certainly endears a reporter to the crew. But always ask first. Don't just pick up a camera person's kit. These are the tools of their trade.

The introduction of single-person crews had another benefit – cameramen or women became used to working in tight two-person teams, not with a sound recordist, but with a reporter. People who had previously seen their responsibilities as purely technical became part of the journalistic process. They helped to tell the story, contributing filming ideas and adding an extra pair of critical eyes to the news-gathering process.

The value of a good camera person can never be overestimated. They will suggest shots that help tell the story, and will often pick up pictures or story-lines you miss. There may be times though when you are expected to operate the camera yourself. Increasingly, the video journalist is a key player in television news gathering.

OPERATING THE CAMERA YOURSELF – THE VIDEO JOURNALIST

Video journalism is not just a way of news operations saving money. Journalists can bring greater intimacy and authenticity to their reports by operating their own cameras. Because the technology and the manpower (one person instead of two or three) are cheaper than traditional crews, the reporter can spend longer on the story, get closer to the people involved and uncover much more detail.

Lightweight, low-cost digital cameras producing pictures almost up to the quality then considered acceptable for broadcast came on the scene in the 1990s. Debates followed about the technical quality of the pictures and about who could and should use them. The ground rules are still being drawn up, but so far the only practical restrictions on journalists 'one-man-banding' seem to be health and safety and human imagination.

BBC Security Correspondent Frank Gardner, an Arabic speaker and Middle East expert, emerged as a leading video journalist after he was based in the Gulf in 1997: 'By then I'd picked up a lot of tips by watching how cameramen work. I did all my own films after that, and just shot everything for the BBC, because it was the right thing to do, rather than hiring a crew who didn't really understand what a sequence is (which you need to be able to do to make a film really watchable). So I've been pretty much a one-man-band most of the time.'

There are obviously situations where it would be folly for one person to act as reporter and camera operator. In riots, war zones and natural disasters, it is dangerous not to have someone watching your back while your eye is to the viewfinder. It's physically impossible to report from inside a courtroom, film witnesses going in and out, and have the camera ready for a stand-up outside at the end of the session. Frank Gardner, incidentally, was not alone when he was shot in Riyadh in 2004. The attack left him disabled. His cameraman Simon Cumbers died.

But there are stories where the portability of lightweight cameras and the intimacy of being a single person rather than a cumbersome crew can be assets. Many of the short news features produced under the BBC's PDP (Portable Digital Production) programme showed these advantages. They were mini observational documentaries, benefiting from intimate access to their subjects. Hundreds of journalists – and technical staff – have been trained to operate DV cameras and to use laptop editing systems. The confusing 'PDP' label was dropped from BBC training in 2006 in favour of the clearer description 'video journalism'.

REMEMBER

➤ It has never been easier to take your own broadcast-quality pictures

➤ Lightweight cameras give access to situations where a crew might be intrusive

➤ Video journalism enables you to control a story from beginning to end

➤ There are some situations where, for health and safety reasons, it is impossible to work alone.

THE LANGUAGE OF FILM-MAKING

When you shoot pictures, you need to understand the language of film-making. It helps you to think in pictures – to work out what you want to say televisually.

COMPOSITION

You will want every shot in your piece to look beautiful – but in news coverage events do not unfold to suit the camera. You have to do your best with what happens in front of you. But there are rules you can apply which help.

The rule of thirds has been used by artists and photographers for centuries to produce pleasing compositions. Mentally divide your viewfinder into thirds vertically and horizontally, like a noughts-and-crosses grid. The horizon or a distinct horizontal line in the landscape (a river or road, perhaps) should be a third of the way up or a third of the way down the screen.

The rule of thirds: in a landscape, and a shot of a vehicle

People should be a third of the way across frame – looking into or walking into the two-thirds space, rather than walking out of frame. If you are walking alongside somebody, allow space in front of them for them to walk into. Stop and allow them to clear the frame at the end of the shot. It makes a good edit point.

Look at the lines; the lines in the picture draw attention to the subject

Another technique is to have a point of interest in the foreground and strong action in the background – for example, the flashing lights of a police car in the foreground with police in riot gear behind. Strong foreground action against an imposing backdrop also works – think of the television coverage of the London Marathon, where runners are frequently shown against a background of familiar landmarks. Shots with both foreground and background interest give depth to the flat image.

Some people have a natural eye for a good shot. They're usually the people who were good at art in school. But you can learn composition. Whatever the subject, try to look at the lines in the frame. Are there lines, perhaps created by a row of trees or buildings or a stack of shelves, that are drawing your eye to one part of the picture? If there are, can you place your subject in that part of the picture? The effect is visually satisfying.

REMEMBER

➤ Use the rule of thirds
➤ Strong foreground and background give depth
➤ Look at the lines.

SEQUENCES

Each shot in a news report should be there for only one reason – to help tell the story. But isolated shots will not tell the story very well. The pictures need to flow from one to the next. The best way of making your story flow is to film sequences – collections of shots that fit together. A sequence is usually an event filmed with different shot sizes and from different angles. You will often need to film the same action repeatedly to get enough shots for an edited sequence.

With a single camera you can create the illusion of a multi-camera shoot by shooting the same event several times from different angles. Make sure though that you maintain *continuity* – the appearance of continuous action – between shots. There's more on continuity later in the chapter.

Shooting sequences also helps you edit your pictures, because you can shorten or lengthen the action to fit your story. If you take a single shot of a top athlete running 100 metres, it will take just over ten seconds. If you shoot the same thing three times (each time on a different shot size or angle), you have 30 seconds of rushes to play with. So you could create a sequence much longer than ten seconds. Or, by cutting from the athlete starting the run to a close-up, and then back to the finish of the run, you could condense all of the action into six or seven seconds.

You may find it helpful to sketch out your ideas on a *storyboard*. The storyboard is a standard tool for feature film makers and for many documentary directors. Divide a piece of paper into squares. Sketch roughly what you want to see in each shot in a separate square. Add notes about camera moves.

In news, you will rarely have time for a storyboard. But it is useful for longer features and for designing graphics sequences.

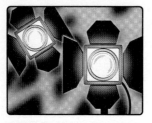

Lights on   CU

Band on Stage   WIDE

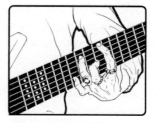

L. hand   CU

R. hand   CU

Singer   CU

Drummer   MCU

Band   WIDE

Crowd   WIDE

Example of a storyboard

REMEMBER

- ➤ Shoot sequences, not single shots
- ➤ Think of the edit
- ➤ Use a storyboard if it helps and you have time.

SHOT SIZES

Different sizes of shot perform different functions in our story-telling. The diagram below shows a summary of them.

Illustrating shot sizes

These are filming conventions which you will recognise from TV, movies and news coverage. Shots of people are graded from the long shot to the big close-up. A long shot shows the whole body; the big close-up shows detail of the face.

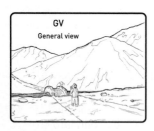

GV
General view

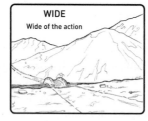

WIDE
Wide of the action

LS
Long shot

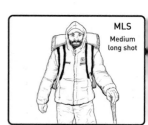

MLS
Medium long shot

MS
Mid-shot

MCU
Medium close-up (the interview shot)

CU
Close-up

BCU
Big close-up

MCU

The interviewee needs to look at the reporter and not at the camera

The interviewee should be framed so that their eyes are looking into free space at the side of the shot

MCU – the interview shot

The most important shot in your arsenal is the medium close-up – the standard shot for television interviews. It enables the viewer to see the subject's face clearly, their clothing, body language and the setting in which they are being filmed. It also allows enough space at the bottom of the screen to superimpose a caption giving their name and title without obscuring their features.

A reporter asking questions will stand directly alongside the camera, as close as possible. This has the effect of drawing the subject's eye-line round just away from the camera without their looking directly into it. *Always advise interviewees to look at you and not at the camera.*

The effect of the standard interview shot is that we see three-quarters of the face. It is important the viewers can see both eyes. It keeps them interested in the face. A face in profile is a face partly turned away from you – and therefore a face that is talking to somebody else. You, the viewer, do not feel part of the conversation.

So, why does the interviewee address the reporter rather than talking directly to the camera? It's a convention from documentary film-making that helps assert the authority of the narrator's voice. The reporter is the mediator of the story. When the reporter does address the camera, he looks straight into the lens. His eye-contact is with the viewer, not a third party.

When you accept material from contributors or lend a video camera to someone to make their own film, you will probably want them to address the camera like a reporter. They are telling their own story.

Experienced interviewees, particularly politicians who may have done down-the-line interviews from remote studios, will ask: 'Where do you want me to look?' It's probably one of the things they were told to ask on a media training course.

The interviewee should be framed so that their eyes are looking into free space at the side of the shot. If the centre line of the head were to be exactly in the middle of frame it would look as if the subject were looking away from the interviewer. This gives the impression that they are trying to avoid the questions, and also that they don't really want to be there. It's unfair on a willing interviewee if poor framing gives a misleading impression of their motives.

The shot should also give the interviewee a little, but not too much, headroom – space above the head. Too little headroom and they may look unnaturally tall; too much and they appear too short. Camera operators will spend time adjusting the height of the tripod so that the eye-line of the interviewee is level, irrespective of their height relative to the interviewer. Their eyes will then be more than halfway up the screen. If someone's nose is almost at the exact centre of the screen, and they are looking neither up nor down, they are in the right position.

You may have heard stories of Hollywood leading ladies having to stand in a trench so they would be level with a particularly short leading man. Or of a leading man standing on a box for the *two-shot*. On a news shoot, you don't have time to dig trenches, but a little manipulation of the topography may be permitted (stand the shorter person on a box or a step, for example). The idea is not to mislead the audience – that should never be tolerated – but to present people as naturally as possible. The heights of your contributors are rarely part of the story (unless you're covering basketball), so there is no point confusing the viewer by filming somebody looking up or down. They'll be wondering what or who they're looking at, and miss what they're saying and the point of the story.

It's worth remembering that, when you are facing the camera, your left and right will be the opposite of the camera operator's. So give instructions to move out or in as 'camera left' or 'camera right', the way events are seen in the viewfinder. It is usually considered good practice to alternate the direction in which interviewees are looking during a piece. So, you need to remind the cameraman: 'We're probably using this after the first one we did, who was looking right, so can we do this one looking camera left, please?'

You will always want the background to an interview to help tell the story (see Chapter 6: *Location reporting and production*). It's a useful shorthand for the viewer, adding extra information while the interviewee is saying their piece. The leader of an industrial dispute may be interviewed in front of a picket line. The spokesperson for a protest movement stands in front of banner-waving demonstrators. A winning golfer chats in front of the packed gallery around the eighteenth hole.

Beware, though, of being manipulated by those with a political or commercial agenda. Is it appropriate to film a protest leader in front of the half dozen people who bothered to turn up when he is claiming massive support for his cause? Would it not be more accurate to show the wider picture – with most of the street empty? And just because somebody represents a particular commercial concern, you don't have to film them in front of their advertising hoarding. Product placement is not allowed in British-made news programmes, and there is a ban on 'undue prominence' for commercial services.

Anyone who has ever seen after-match interviews with football managers and players will know that every professional football ground has an interview room with a board behind the interviewee filled with sponsors' logos. There may be separate boards for different broadcasters: one with a Sky Sports logo plus the sponsors; the other with BBC Sport, perhaps, and the same sponsors' logos.

The interview room

This is part of a commercial arrangement involving the clubs, the competition's organisers (UEFA, the FA or the Premier League, for example) and the broadcasters who have paid for the rights to the event. There is no obligation on news crews to use these interview rooms, although in the real world you have to go where your interviewees are.

Close-up (CU) and big close-up (BCU)

The close-up (CU), in which the picture cuts off just below the subject's neck, offers a more intimate look at the subject and is appropriate when the speaker is intense, emotional or under pressure.

The big close-up, or BCU, cutting off the top of the head and chin and concentrating on eyes and mouth, is rarely used in news except for the most emotive content. It used to be standard practice for the camera to zoom in if someone started crying. But audiences are more aware of the techniques of film-making these days. Caution should be exercised. Does the camera appear to have been too intrusive?

(a) Close-up (CU)
(b) Big close-up (BCU)

The two-shot

When two people are featured in a shot, it's known as a two-shot. It has a variety of uses.

It can be a shot of two interviewees.

The two-shot –
two people being
interviewed

Or it can be a shot of the interviewer and the interviewee. A static two-shot taken from behind the interviewer used to be a common way of introducing the interviewee. These days you are more likely to see a walking two-shot, sometimes with the interview starting on the move, using radio mics.

It is rarely a good idea to conduct a lengthy interview on a two-shot. If two people are in frame all the time, the shot will be so wide that there will not be enough detail in the face of the speaker to keep the interest of the viewer. Another problem with the static two-shot is that the interviewer and interviewee are likely to be facing each other and will therefore be in profile. There is no eye-contact with the viewer and, again, not enough of the speaker's facial expression can be seen. Interviews conducted on a two-shot are also difficult to edit.

If you must start an interview on a two-shot – in a live or 'as live' situation perhaps – try this common technique. After your introductory comments and first question, the camera zooms in to a single shot of the interviewee – a conventional MCU. At the same time the reporter steps round alongside the camera, into the same position as for a regular interview. This draws the eye-line round so the speaker is no longer in profile and the viewer can see both the speaker's eyes. As the interview closes – and on a pre-arranged signal or instruction from the gallery – the reporter steps back round in front of camera as the operator zooms out, widening the shot. The reporter thanks the interviewee and delivers his or her closing lines to camera.

Over-the-shoulder two-shot

The over-the-shoulder two-shot is useful for editing. It enables you to jump from one point in an interview to another. The back of the reporter's head is towards the camera, so the movement of their mouth is not visible. This means the shot can be dropped over any question. When filming these shots it is vital to be aware of how they might be used in the edit. It is tempting to relax at the end of the interview and, while the cameraman concentrates on the shot, interviewer and interviewee share a joke. This will not work if the subject of the interview has been a serious one. You will need to advise the interviewee what's going on so they adopt a suitable expression.

The over-the-shoulder
two-shot

The reverse two-shot

By moving the camera you can take a *reverse* two-shot, over the shoulder of the interviewee favouring the interviewer. You may wish to record *cutaway questions*, or *reverses* as they are also known, repeating questions you have already asked. Or you can do listening shots. They're sometimes known as *noddies*, but the temptation to nod during them should be resisted as it gives the impression you agree with everything being said. These shots can be edited in later if needed.

Most news reports rely on short soundbites and there is no need for reverse questions or even two-shots. Up against tight deadlines, it's easy to ignore them. But the day will come when you are in an edit truck and you wish you had them available to help edit your piece. It is worth developing the discipline of doing them every time you film, or at least every time you have time to.

CUTAWAYS

The reverse: a useful editing device and an opportunity to ask cutaway questions

Over the shoulder and reverse two-shots are known as cutaways because you cut away to them during the edit. Close-ups – of hands for example – serve the same purpose. These shots are not dependent on *sync* sound, the term for any shot where the picture has to match the sound, usually because we can see someone's lips moving. A cutaway is a picture that can be used over the sound from another picture.

Cutaways can disguise an edit point in an interview. The sound may flow seamlessly but the picture will not. Without a cutaway, the viewer would see a *jump-cut*. The jump-cut is where the action jumps from one part of a scene to another. It happens all the time in really old newsreel where film stock has degenerated and frames are missing. It also happens if you cut a section out of someone's answer. All of a sudden their head jumps from one position on the screen to another. There are ethical considerations in all this, because the cutaway disguises the edit. You should not set out to deliberately mislead the audience. Alternatives are discussed in Chapter 12: *Editing*.

When shooting sequences, you may wish to cut away to details of the action. For example, when shooting someone painting a picture, you will want to cut to the close-up of brush on canvas. Be conscious though of *continuity*, the need to make the action appear continuous when you edit. If you cut back to a wide shot, the brush must appear to be in the same position and not to have jumped across the canvas.

Annette Martin, a director on factual programmes from *Top Gear* to *Countryfile*, says: 'You can never have enough cutaways. Do your shoot. Get your cutaways. And then get more.'

Dozens of websites and chat rooms are devoted to pointing out continuity mistakes in multi-million dollar Hollywood epics. So, on location on your own or with a camera person, you will have your work cut out making sure your shots fit together.

SET-UPS

Every time you interview someone think how you will introduce them into your film. The best way is with set-ups – a shot or preferably a sequence of shots of them doing something, and preferably something exciting or at least with bold movement. The advantage of a sequence is that the length can be adjusted in the edit depending on how much you need to say to introduce the interviewee. You will not normally need to say somebody's full name and title – that can be done with a caption – but you may need to lead in to what they are about to say.

A set-up shot – let the interviewee clear shot to assist the edit

Some set-up shots are so tired from overuse that they have become visual clichés. Regular viewers of television news will recognise these examples. The academic takes a book from a shelf and thumbs through it. The MP walks across College Green (outside the Houses of Parliament) or down the stairs in Millbank.

To avoid crossing the line, the subject in the close-up should be facing the same direction as in the wide shot

The elderly woman makes a cup of tea. The chief constable/government minister/football manager is seen in a wide shot at the head of a table during a press conference.

Like all clichés, these shots save time because they save the need to think. That doesn't mean you have to do the same.

Paul Myles, a senior trainer at the BBC's Centre for Video Journalism, says: 'The politician on College Green and the man taking a book off the shelf are exactly the kind of set-up, staged television the BBC is so keen to get away from. But sometimes there's no time for anything else. The politician comes out of his office and will only give you two minutes.'

Myles and his colleagues encourage video journalists to spend time with their subjects, filming people as they go about their daily business, rather than directing them for the camera. Snatches of comment or interview from the subject can be grabbed as you go along, rather than inserted from a set-piece interview. This style of filming leads to very naturalistic, highly watchable results.

REMEMBER

➤ Learn the names of different shots and what they're for
➤ Get cutaways
➤ Try to film imaginative set-ups
➤ Spend time with your subjects.

CROSSING THE LINE

You will hear camera crews and directors talk about the *line* and warn about not crossing it. At first it sounds like warning children about stepping on cracks in the pavement. Watch out for the bears! In practice it is a very useful way of making sure that what you film does not confuse the viewer.

If the close-up is from the opposite side to the wide shot, viewers are left wondering in which direction the cyclists are travelling

The line is best explained by looking at the way a football match is televised. The main cameras are on one side of the pitch. As the director cuts between them, perhaps to go from a wide shot to a close-up of the player on the ball, play continues in the same direction. Chelsea are kicking left to right, Arsenal right to left. If the second camera were on the opposite side of the pitch, the teams would appear to be kicking the other way when the director cut to the close-up. If he then went back to the wide shot, the teams would appear to be attacking the opposite goals again. Very confusing. This is because the action has *crossed the line.*

In all film-making, directors do not want to confuse the viewer so they try not to cross the line. If you have only one camera you need to be especially aware of this. Make sure any action continues in the same direction. If someone clears shot left of frame they should enter the next shot right of frame. If a golf ball is played from right to left of screen we need to see it arriving on the green from the same direction.

The only time crossing the line does not seem to jar in the mind of the viewer is when pictures are set to music. This means pop videos can cross the line several times a second. You may use music in features, but you will rarely be able to in hard news.

The imaginary line in an interview runs between interviewer and interviewee. The camera stays on one side of it, so that a reverse angle or cutaway question will show the interviewer facing the opposite direction on screen to the interviewee. This gives the impression of two people talking to each other. It is this final impression that is the most important thing. If it looks right, it is right. The *line* is a useful tool, but like all tools it can be discarded if it is not helping you to do the job. And you *can* cross the line if you take the viewer with you. You can move the camera across the line as you shoot, or track around the subject, and use the shot in your piece.

The reverse angle in an interview shows the interviewee facing the interviewer

REMEMBER

- Keep the camera on one side of the action
- Film interviewer and interviewee facing in opposite directions
- Crossing the line doesn't matter in music sequences
- You can cross the line if you track round the action, 'taking the viewer with you'.

CONTINUITY

Crossing the line on a single-camera shoot kills the illusion of continuous action. Similarly you should aim for continuity in the content of what you shoot. For example, if you cut from a wide shot of a chef chopping vegetables with the knife in his right hand, to a close-up of the knife in the left hand, it will look odd. If the first shot showed carrots but the second shot has leeks, that too will jar with viewers. A wide shot of the chef wearing his hat followed by a close-up without it will not work either.

You need to be aware of the possible breaks in continuity as you film. If you are alone, this is difficult. Feature film crews have a member of the team whose only job is to ensure continuity between takes. And still there are continuity mistakes in the biggest-budget Hollywood blockbusters.

If you get it wrong, both parties will be looking the same way, and the illusion of a conversation is lost

The easiest way to ensure continuity in news features is to enlist the aid of your subjects. Tell the chef, 'Make sure you keep your hat on'. And explain why.

One of the biggest mistakes is to take a break in mid-sequence and return to filming later. 'Now where were we? Did you have your hat on?' Finish the sequence, and *then* have your cup of coffee.

Whenever you shoot a set-up sequence, think what will come next in the finished piece. What exactly are you 'setting-up'? If you are cutting to an interview, then make sure the set-ups of that person are in the same location. In particular, make sure that you don't jump from indoors to outdoors or vice versa. Watch enough TV news, and it won't be long before you see a shot of someone walking into a building followed immediately by an interview of them outdoors. We know why it was done: the lighting was easier outdoors for the interview (no need for fiddly artificial lights); the easiest set-up was to film the subject going into the building (no need to ask them to go in, come out again, and walk past the camera without looking at it). The result is lazy television and it looks odd.

The skateboarder is wearing a hat.

Spot the mistake!

- Concentrate between shots to ensure continuity
- Enlist the help of your subjects
- Don't break from shooting mid-sequence
- Do set-ups and interviews in the same location.

TRACKING

When the camera moves over the ground it is known as tracking. In news coverage, tracking usually means the cameraman is walking. When the budget allows, it will be mounted on a *dolly*, which runs along a track, like a narrow gauge railway line. Again, bigger-budget productions might allow for a stabilising device like Steadicam, a harness with a counterweight. You see them all the time on the touchlines at televised football matches. In news, you will probably be relying on your own (or the camera person's) expertise to achieve a wobble-free shot.

Where action is unfolding in front of the camera there is rarely a need for tracking. 'Point and shoot' (with the minimum of camera movement) is the best approach to news events. But tracking shots – and other camera moves – help when there is a shortage of action to film. Crime and court reporting are good examples. If it is known that an attacker fled down an alleyway, a tracking shot down the alley will illustrate this.

Tracking shots can also be *POV* shots. POV stands for *point of view* – what somebody sees as they are walking along. It's another useful technique in crime scene reconstructions.

Tracking with a subject can also add movement to a story that would otherwise be a series of static scenes. If you want to demonstrate how busy someone is, it is better to film them racing between meetings than sitting in a series of meeting rooms.

PANS AND TILTS

The pan (short for panoramic shot) is a camera move on a horizontal plane – left to right or right to left (but never both in the same shot). The tilt is a vertical move – up or down. Both pans and tilts can be achieved using the pan handle on the tripod. The pan handle is not so-called because it looks like the handle of a frying pan (although it might). It is the handle that helps you pan.

The most important things to remember about pans and tilts are that these shots must have a purpose and they must have a beginning, middle and end. One of the most common and annoying faults of people using a home video camera for the first time is that they pan and tilt (often at the same time) aimlessly and endlessly. This is known as 'hose-piping' because the camera is being waved around at random like an uncontrollable garden hose. It might be fun for the kids, but most adult gardeners will tell you it's not the best way to water the lawn.

If you must pan, decide what you are panning from and to. If it's a view across typical English countryside, start with a landmark like a church tower left of frame then pan right to reach another landmark or natural feature, such as a copse. Make sure the pan lasts no more than the three or four seconds you would reasonably expect to use, and record enough at the beginning and end of the pan – say four or five seconds – to use as separate static shots if needed.

Pans and tilts may last longer in features and documentaries, where the pace of story-telling will be affected by the director's choice of shots. In news, stick to the guidelines above and you won't go far wrong.

THE ZOOM

The zoom lens – a lens that can make far-away objects appear closer to the camera – is one of the most useful and also the most abused controls on any video camera. The best thing the zoom does is enable you to change the shot size without moving the camera. The worst thing it does is to encourage inexperienced operators to zoom in and out of shots to the annoyance of the viewer. That's a favourite trick of holiday camcorder users, and is particularly irritating when the camera is hand-held. There is a time and place for hand-held shots but, whenever you use them, the zoom should be as wide as possible. As soon as you zoom in, you magnify the effect of any camera shake. Even experienced camera operators using tripods will be unable to prevent some shake on shots of distant action if they are working 'at the end of the zoom'.

Only ever use optical zoom. Modern cameras have a digital zoom facility, beyond the range of the optical zoom. It is an electronic enhancement of the picture – blowing up the available pixels to fill the screen. It results in a loss of picture quality and is not suitable for most professional purposes.

The shot we call a zoom – the act of zooming in or out of the action – also has to be approached with caution. You see zooms all the time in news coverage – usually on regional programmes when not much is happening in front of the lens. Exterior *GVs* (general views) of buildings will often include a pull-out from a window to see the whole of a house or office block. Occasionally a zoom-in will highlight an interesting architectural feature.

Mostly though, zooms are a boon to lazy reporters because they fill time and can cover sloppy scripting. Great film-makers rarely use zoom shots, however, unless it is for dramatic effect. Watch any feature film and it will be rare to see a zoom at all. John McLeod, a senior news correspondent, who worked for both ITV and BBC, refused to use them in his reports. His argument was that they were 'unnatural'. They were the only movement the camera made that did not replicate the way our eyes see the world. We can look up and down objects (the tilt), turn our heads to look along the horizon (the pan), look at things in detail (the close-up), or take in a broad view (the wide), but nobody, unless they are a T-1000 Terminator sent back from the future to kill the mother of a resistance leader, has eyes that zoom in and out.

A pan from left to right: The shot moves from the landscape to show a campsite
(a) The tree is the start point for the pan. The wheelbarrow provides foreground interest
(b) As the camera moves, it reveals the tent
(c) The camera settles on the tent

(a) The wide shot
(b) Zoomed in

REMEMBER

➤ Camera moves can make shots more interesting

➤ There has to be a start and an end point for any camera move

➤ Moves should rarely last more than three or four seconds

➤ Use zooms rarely, if at all

➤ If you are hand-held, keep the zoom as wide as possible.

A CLOSER LOOK

PRESSERS AND PRESS PACKS – REGULAR SCENARIOS

Many news-gathering situations occur frequently and it's possible to prepare for them. Not every news conference or press briefing is the same – but there are similarities.

The news conference

When you are sent to cover a news or press conference, plan what equipment you will need. If it is indoors, as most are, TV crews may need lights. Some press conference rooms, at police headquarters buildings for example, are in regular use for the purpose and have their own TV lighting built in. Ask your producer or researcher, or better still the organisers of the conference, before you leave the newsroom.

You will definitely need enough mic cable to run from the top table to the camera or to where you are sitting as a radio reporter. Alternatively, use radio mics. They are a better option on health and safety grounds too. No-one will trip over your cable.

In large set-piece news conferences, larger radio stations will have more than one microphone and TV will have more than one camera. If you have the option of more than one audio channel, one will be a mic on the main speaker (or a feed from an audio desk of a mic on the lectern), the other a mic you can use for your questions. Similarly, one camera will be on the main speaker; the other will take wide shots, cutaways and a shot of you as you ask your question. Make sure you sit where the second camera can see you clearly.

Media scrums

FOR A LONE PERSON WITH A HAND-HELD CAMERA, THE SCRUM IS THE WORST OF WORKING ENVIRONMENTS . . . ASK YOURSELF IF YOU NEED TO BE IN THE THICK OF IT.

It is easy for reporters to operate effectively in media scrums. Just shove your microphone to the front and start recording. For a lone person with a hand-held camera, the scrum is the worst of working environments. You will have no protection against being jostled as you try to maintain focus and framing. The chances of securing steady usable shots are not high. The chance of recording quality sound (without an undue emphasis on the grumbles and complaints of those around you) is minimal. Ask yourself if you need to be in the thick of it. Might you be better off dropping back and getting a steady, wide shot that tells the story just as well? Here are some tips:

- Don't zoom in – as we've said, the zoom magnifies camera-shake and makes steady shots almost impossible

- Use your ears – listen, preferably through your headphones, for the actuality sound you want to hear. When the subject at the centre of a scrum has said something relevant and usable, consider whether you can then drop back and get the wide shot of the scene

- Stand your ground. Don't be intimidated, but resist the temptation to fight for position. When you are operating equipment you are more vulnerable than a reporter with a notebook who may be trying to elbow their way past you.

THE CAMERA

The growth of video journalism has been made possible by the reduced costs of cameras that can produce a broadcast quality picture. The gulf between home video equipment and professional cameras has all but disappeared in the last decade.

The cameras used most often by video journalists are at the top end of the domestic camcorder market. They will be similar to the ones used by students on broadcast journalism courses, which means today's graduates have an advantage over the journalists of earlier generations. They are more likely to be multi-skilled when they start the job.

Cameras using MiniDV tape are capable of producing High-Definition widescreen pictures – as good as anything on most TV news stations worldwide and of a higher specification than you'll need for broadband content. The Sony Z1 became the instrument of choice for the BBC's regional video journalists in 2005. Then Panasonic introduced their P2 system – solid state with high-powered memory cards. The cards can be 'hot-swapped' allowing continuous recording, with no gaps while tapes are replaced. Video files are transferred to the edit system at up to 640 megabits per second (Mbps), much faster than the time it takes to *digitise* tapes, which have to be played back in real time.

THE PROFESSIONAL OPERATOR SHOULD ALWAYS USE THE MANUAL SETTINGS.

These cameras may have automatic functions aimed at the domestic user. Mum or dad won't want to bother with lots of tricky buttons to press at family parties. They want something to point and shoot immediately. But the professional operator should always use the manual settings. They ensure you have control over the picture quality at all times.

White balance

Cameras are electronic instruments. They're not as good as the combination of the eye and the human brain at determining colour. A white shirt looks white to you and me whether we are indoors or outdoors. The camera will see it differently because different types of light favour different parts of the colour spectrum. Daylight is mostly blue. Artificial light is more yellow.

These differences can be shown on a scale as *colour temperature*, measured in degrees Kelvin (or K). Daylight in the UK measures around 5,000 K. Overcast skies have a higher colour temperature. Sunrise and sunset are much lower. Ordinary household bulbs are nearer 3,000 K – more yellow on the scale.

Before you take a shot, the camera needs to be white-balanced, or told the colour temperature in the prevailing conditions. If we tell the camera an object is white, it will make it look white and adjust all the colours in the picture in relation to it. *You need to do a fresh white balance every time you move between different types of light, outdoors to indoors, or from fluorescent to tungsten lighting.*

Always do a white balance

The process of white-balancing is usually straightforward. Zoom in on a white object – a white wall, a white shirt or a sheet of white paper – and press the camera's white-balance button. The image in the viewfinder will flash and then set itself at the appropriate colour temperature. What you see in the viewfinder when you zoom out to the wide shot will look the same colour as what you are seeing around you with your own eyes. Pre-set white balances (for outdoor and indoor shooting, for example) allow you to move rapidly from one lighting environment to another.

You can create a warmer, or more orange, picture, by white-balancing on a light blue object. Or make things look blue by white-balancing on something yellow. Such techniques can replace the use of colour filters. They can be practised through trial and error, but are usually best left to experienced operators.

Electronic editing systems can compensate for mistakes with your white balance. But that takes time. It's better to get the white balance right from the start and apply any artistic adjustments in the edit.

Exposure

You can control the exposure – the amount of light let into your camera – by changing the *aperture* and the *shutter speed*, just like on a conventional stills camera. The aperture setting acts like the iris of your eye, controlling the amount of light let in. Smaller aperture settings allow less light in – you can see this on your viewfinder.

A CLOSER LOOK

F-STOPS – MEASURING THE APERTURE

Aperture is measured in f-numbers, and they can be confusing to non-photographers. Because f-numbers are the ratio of the focal length (the distance from the lens to its focal point) to the aperture diameter, smaller numbers mean a larger aperture. As the numbers on the scale increase, the amount of light is halved at each stop. The f-numbers don't double though, because of that ratio formula. Don't worry about this. In practical terms you will see the result of changing the f-stops in your viewfinder.

These are the numbers you'll see on your camera and how they relate to the amount of light being let in.

f-stop	1.4	2	2.8	4	5.6	8	11	16
light entering lens	1	1/2	1/4	1/8	1/16	1/32	1/64	1/128

The shutter speed also affects the amount of light let into the camera. A fast shutter speed allows less light in than a slow one. You will need a larger aperture with a faster shutter speed.

You may want to change the shutter speed depending on what you are filming. A fast shutter enables you to capture fast action without blurring. A very slow speed creates an interesting deliberate blurring effect, which can look good behind graphics sequences or in stylised reports. Adjusting the shutter speed can also get rid of the annoying stripes that appear on video and computer monitors when they are shot by video cameras.

In very bright lighting conditions – outdoors on a sunny day – you may want to use a *neutral density* filter. It is a feature built into many cameras – the equivalent of giving your camera an electronic pair of sunglasses. The neutral density filter is usually applied using a separate control marked *ND*.

Your eyepiece viewfinder should show when pictures are correctly exposed. Flip-out LCD screens are useful, but outdoors in sunlight you won't be able to see the picture clearly enough to check the exposure. The best tool on a professional camera for checking exposure is the *zebra* feature. Zebra stripes are diagonal black and white stripes that appear on the picture in the viewfinder – but *not* on your recording. If you set the zebras to 100 per cent, they will show on areas that are too bright or over-exposed. The most useful setting, particularly when setting up interviews, is 80 per cent. The zebras should appear on the nose, forehead and cheekbones of your subject. The patterns on darker skins will appear smaller than on Caucasian subjects. Adjust the exposure accordingly.

Focus

Only after you have set your white balance and exposure should you worry about the focus. But focus is the most important of your camera settings. Small errors in white balance and exposure can be corrected in the edit – but *when something is recorded out of focus you can never make it sharp again*.

Never leave auto focus switched on. The camera will *hunt* for focus as objects move in and out of the centre of the frame. The result looks decidedly amateurish.

You should usually control focus using the focus ring. This is the best way to change focus when an object is moving towards or away from you. Some cameras have a focus button which switches to auto focus for as long as it takes to sharpen up your picture, which can be useful.

Rotating the focus ring to pull focus

To set focus, zoom into your subject. Choose a part of the subject that has clearly outlined features – not a mass of colour. If it's a person, zoom in on the eyes. Then turn the focus ring until the picture is sharp. When you zoom out to reframe your shot, the subject and everything immediately in front of and behind it will be sharp in the frame.

After you have focused, everything within the lens's *depth of field* will be sharp on screen. The depth of field is the distance from the nearest to the furthest points at which objects appear to be in focus. Manipulating depth of field is a useful device. It enables you to *pull focus* – to change the part of the picture that's sharp, and so switch the viewer's attention from one thing to another. You'll have seen this in drama when two people are talking, or in news and documentaries when an object in the foreground gives way to what's happening behind it, or vice versa.

Reducing the aperture size increases the depth of field. A narrow depth of field, created with a wider aperture, will mean your subject is in sharp focus, but objects in front of and behind it appear blurred or *soft*. If your subject strays closer to or further from the camera, it will go out of focus.

To set up a pull-focus shot, frame your shot so that the two subjects, at different distances from the camera, are in view. Use a wide aperture setting, so that only one of the subjects is in focus at a time. Practise rotating the focus ring so that the plane of focus moves from one to the other, before you start recording. When you're sure just how far to rotate the ring, press the record button. Hold the shot for a few seconds before you pull focus.

The pull focus: the foreground and background are in different planes of focus. Rotate the focus ring to go from one to the other

In bright sunlight the field of focus will be so deep you might not be able to pull focus. Try using the neutral density filter to reduce the light coming into the camera, or move further away from the subjects and zoom in. Operating on the end of the zoom is another way of reducing the depth of field, but you can only do so if you are using a tripod. Otherwise there will be too much camera shake. It's a matter of trial and error. Full-time camera operators take a long time setting up their artier shots, but the results are rewarding. They add a professional gloss to your filming.

Often the problem you face filming in available light (that is, without professional lighting) is that there is not enough light. Indoors in gloomy buildings or at dawn and dusk, you might need to use another electronic trick – the camera's *gain*. Gain boosts the exposure of the picture. It might be added using the flywheel or ring that changes the f-stop settings or with a separate switch on the side of the camera. Gain has a disadvantage. It makes the picture grainier and less sharp. The graininess is known as 'noise' and is measured in decibels (or dB). Video cameras usually offer 9 dB or 18 dB of gain. 18 dB is always noticeable, and you may prefer, if possible, to use artificial light.

REMEMBER

Every time you take a shot you need to check:
- ➤ White balance
- ➤ Exposure
- ➤ Focus

And
- ➤ Don't use autofocus
- ➤ Practise pulling focus.

Only when white balance, exposure and focus are set (and sound levels have been checked) should you press the record button. Make sure the record symbol (usually a red dot in the corner) is showing in the viewfinder. If you are taking lots of shots, it's very easy to get 'out of sync' and think you are recording when you're not. Most professional camera people have fallen into this trap at one time or another. *Follow the red dot.*

LIGHTING

As soon as you start using professional lighting, the quality of your pictures, particularly in indoor locations, steps up a gear.

As well as showing what might otherwise be in the dark, lights can create mood and a sense of depth in your pictures. They can also highlight a particular part of the shot. But for the single-person operator, new considerations come into play – mostly about health and safety.

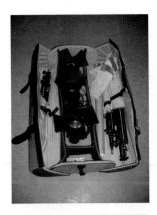

The lighting kit

A small light can be fitted to the top of your camera. It will use a lot of battery power, but the improved picture quality should repay reduced battery life. Switch it off as soon as you have finished a shot. Be careful. If you get too near your subject with a camera light, you may bleach out their features in the recorded shot. A single light source also flattens the image. A camera light will not give any impression of depth.

A portable camera
light with barn doors

To create depth, you need more than one light. You will need to plug your lights into a separate power source, usually the mains, and that means trailing leads. There's always a risk of someone tripping over loose cables, so you can't use mains lights unless you have complete control over your working space. You should also use a circuit breaker to avoid fusing electrical systems. Television lights can take a lot of power. A redhead, so-called because the 'head' of the lamp (not the bulb) is by convention coloured red, offers 1 kilowatt of light. A blond (yellowish in colour) offers 2 kilowatts.

Lights are mounted on their own stands. There are movable flaps, called barn doors, on the front of the lamps to help you direct the light.

THREE-POINT LIGHTING

The traditional TV rig for lighting an interview or talking head is known as three-point lighting. Three lights are used, each with a different function.

- The **key** light, with hard-edged shadows, brings out the main features of the face. It will be placed in front of the interviewee, on the same side as the interviewer.

- The **filler** light, with a softer edge, lightens or 'fills in' the shadows cast by the key on the other side of the face.

- The **back** light is placed behind the interviewee to one side. It gives depth to the picture – a 3D effect – making the subject stand out from the background. It can be very flattering, adding sparkle to a subject's hair.

Three-point lighting for
an interview

When you use artificial lighting indoors, be aware of the obvious light sources in the room. Your lighting scheme should echo what looks natural to the viewer. If there is a window or a lamp in the picture, the viewer expects that to be a source of light. When blue natural light from a window is competing with the yellowish light from your lamps, a transparent blue film or gel can be placed over your lights. Your lights are then complementing the daylight with more blue light, rather than competing with it. This helps achieve an accurate white balance. The gel can be attached to the barn doors with bulldog clips or clothes pegs.

But remember, if you are on your own, lights are heavy to carry around and take time to set up. Keep a lighting kit in the car, if you can, but expect to use it only on pre-planned shoots or when you have plenty of time.

THE TRIPOD

Whenever possible use a tripod to make your shots steady and free from wobble. There's a vogue in reality TV shows and some news coverage for verité-style hand-held camera shots. These can add excitement and a sense of 'being there' to your coverage. But too much camera movement is disconcerting for the viewer. The best hand-held camera shots are those that use the advantages of not being mounted on a tripod to get into situations where a tripod would get in the way. But the operators still keep the camera steady.

The Steadicam – a counterbalance system worn by the operator to keep shots stable – offers steady shots on the move. But Steadicam is a specialist area of camera operation and too cumbersome to use for news coverage.

A tripod is a stable platform for the camera

The tripod is a stable platform for your camera. It's essential if you're shooting something that isn't moving – scenery or buildings, for example. The height can be adjusted, which helps you set up an interview with the camera at eye level whether the interviewee is seated or standing. The tripod should have a spirit level to ensure vertical and horizontal lines are not shown at odd angles in your pictures. There are few sights more upsetting than a shot of a lake that appears to be sloping from one end to the other. It brings new meaning to the old joke about wanting to take up water-skiing, but not being able to find a lake with a big enough slope.

THE ROSENBLUM EFFECT

The American TV producer Michael Rosenblum has been a key figure in the BBC's video journalism training. He says the idea of a TV news operation being planned around the availability of five or six cameras is like a print newsroom having only five or six pencils. He persuaded the BBC's board of governors that, if they didn't embrace the new technology of cheap, lightweight cameras and editing, the BBC had no future as a producer of broadcast programmes.

Rosenblum says traditional broadcasters are reluctant to embrace change: 'Institutionally they're not really prepared to cope with the ramifications of what all this means. They pay lip service to it, and they try, but they're not really psychologically or emotionally prepared to embrace the reality of what has to come.'

Michael Rosenblum's advice to journalists: 'Either understand how to do this, or learn how to sell life insurance.'

He says TV stations don't need studios: 'People are going to work at home, and feed their stuff online with fibre-optic and Wi-Fi. This is all here. The way they work now is extremely cost- and journalistically ineffective. Either they get it or they'll be fundamentally out of business.'

His advice to trainees who don't want to become multi-skilled: 'Either understand how to do this and skill yourself, or learn how to sell life insurance.'

THE FIVE-SHOT METHOD

Any event can be filmed as a series of sequences, and the easiest way to shoot a sequence is to use the five-shot method, based on Michael Rosenblum's teaching.

This is taught on BBC video journalism courses. Rosenblum insists on people-led television. Stories are always about people, and there's no place in his world for exterior shots of buildings. So, this method applies to filming people – but it can be adapted for any shoot. If you are with someone, and they're doing something, these are the shots you need:

1 The **hands**. What is this person doing? Look at their hands. Get a close-up of the hands. Focus. Press record. Hold it for ten seconds.

2 The **face**. Who is this person? What is their expression? Are they concentrating on what they're doing? Are they enjoying themselves? Are they unhappy? Get a close-up of the face. Focus. Record. Hold for ten seconds.

3 The **wide** shot. Where is this person? What is their environment? Are they at home, at work, or at leisure? Step back for the wide. Focus. Record. Hold for ten seconds.

4 The **over-the-shoulder**. What or who are they looking at? This may be a high-angle shot looking down at what the hands are doing, or a shot from behind. Move yourself and the camera. Focus. Record. Hold for ten seconds.

5 The **shot-of-choice**. This can be an alternative wide, or an unusual angle suggested by the setting or the activity, a high (top-shot) or low-level view of the scene, perhaps. Move yourself and the camera. Focus. Record. Hold for ten seconds.

These shots are interchangeable in the edit. When the action is continuous or repeated (working at a desk or bench, for example), they can be taken in any order. Each shot will act as a cutaway between any two others. You will choose the best two or three seconds of each shot to match the others.

The method is flexible. If you're filming someone kicking a ball, the hands shot will be replaced by a feet shot.

You need to monitor the sound as you record, to make sure it is usable throughout. Don't talk over the shot while you are recording. You may decide that to maintain the continuity of sound in the edit, you are better off not switching the camera off between shots.

When you edit, you will not need to use all five shots every time. Some sequences will be more important in the story than others. If you are overlaying the shots over someone speaking (voice-over or interview), the duration of the cut sequence may be determined by the audio.

DON'T MOVE THE CAMERA

When you have framed your shot, don't move the camera. Keep it steady. Steady shots are so much easier to edit. Wobbly shots, or shots where the framing changes midway through, are a distraction to the viewer.

Move the shot to follow the action only if you are sure how the action is developing. It may be better to re-frame and shoot the new action separately, keeping the camera running to capture continuous sound, which will help in the edit. You can link from one shot to the other with a cutaway if there is a continuity break.

The five-shot technique: hands; face; wide; over-the-shoulder; shot-of-choice

SOUND ON VIDEO – A REMINDER

Great sound helps pictures to tell stories. Good actuality sound is better than voice-over at letting the viewer know what's happening on screen. You need to monitor sound whenever you shoot. Wear headphones or an earpiece whenever the camera is running, and watch the levels. You will have two channels of sound on the camera. If you are working with a sound recordist (a rarity in news or video journalism), they can monitor and mix the sound from different sources as it is recorded.

In the absence of a sound recordist (i.e. almost always), use your second audio track as a back-up for the main sound source. For example, you may be filming someone wearing a radio mic. Set their audio level manually and keep an eye on the meter in the viewfinder as you film. Use the on-camera mic on channel two as a back-up, in case the signal from the transmitter or the batteries fail. Set the level on channel two slightly lower, so if there is a sudden loud noise it won't distort on the recording.

➤ The five-shot method helps you shoot sequences

➤ Steady shots are easier to edit

➤ Maintain continuity of sound.

TRANSMISSION – GETTING THE STORY BACK

Technology has revolutionised the way stories can be transmitted from the field. The possibilities of broadband and wireless networks, particularly in built-up areas, are still being explored. As bandwidth increases, live links from anywhere on earth look increasingly possible. We are not yet in a Wi-Fi (wireless Internet) world. Developing countries and remote regions are not wired up for unlimited broadcasting. But the domestic (UK) landscape has been transformed.

Outside broadcasts (OBs) historically relied on microwave links to fixed receivers. The radio car or TV links vehicle needed to be sited within a 'line-of-sight' of the receiving station. Line-of-sight did not literally mean you had to be able to see the receiver – it could be many miles away, and a tall mast would mean the reach would be much further than the eye could see from ground level.

Engineers kept maps of the regions their vehicles covered, showing sites from which a strong signal could be transmitted and also the blind-spots, areas where hills and valleys, or even tall buildings, prevented a signal getting through. Sometimes a chain of vehicles would be needed to deliver a signal. This had obvious disadvantages in time, manpower and expense. There were problems too with permissions for parking vehicles on site (you needed the consent of the landowner). Many stories could not be covered live. Despatch riders – freelance or staff motorcyclists – ferried tapes back to the studio or to the nearest available feed points.

Satellite communications changed news gathering forever in the late twentieth century and continue to do so. The advantage of satellite transmission is that all you need to do is point a satellite dish at the right point in the sky and you can transmit from anywhere in the world.

Early satellite transmission was costly, and the equipment cumbersome. Sandy Gall of ITN became a broadcasting hero, taking a small, diamond-shaped satellite dish by mule into Russian-occupied Afghanistan in 1985.

Now, satellite links vehicles are used every day by regional news operations. They are expensive and have to be used sparingly even in the best-funded organisations, but they mean a 'live' is possible from almost any location (see Part 2: *Newsdays* for how they are used by broadcasters).

As the costs of satellite time came down, more satellite transmissions were possible, and satellite phones became a viable alternative for lower-resolution broadcasting from remote locations. Inmarsat's M4 system, the first of which weighed about seven kilograms, has been used for 'videophone' reports from around the world.

During the invasion of Iraq in 2003, 'vehicular videophone' was used by reporters 'embedded' with US troops. Portable M4 sat-phones and tracking-antenna systems offered live video reports from reporters with troops on the road to Baghdad and on warships in the Gulf. The hardware involved a dish about a metre across and a heavy dome which could be fitted to 4×4s or flatbed trucks.

Inmarsat's BGAN (Broadband-Global-Area-Network) offered another breakthrough less than two years later – better picture quality and a fully mobile base station. The highest bandwidth terminal weighed just over two kilos, was fully portable in a back-pack, and could be operated, the manufacturers said, by 'non-technical staff', anywhere on the planet.

In the developed world, wireless broadband connections (Wi-Fi) are being used to send location reports back to base. The picture quality is improving all the time.

Paul Clifton, the transport correspondent for BBC South, has pioneered Wi-Fi transmission of packages he edits on a laptop: 'The most spectacular use of this was last summer in New York (2005). I flew with Sir Richard Branson on a Virgin twenty-first anniversary flight, just me and my little hand-held camera and a laptop. My ITV opponent brought a cameraman, and also his news editor, who had a small camera to look helpful.

'I shot most of the piece on the plane, edited on the plane, and just picked up a handful of shots and a piece-to-camera on the tarmac at JFK. I then simply squatted down on the tarmac beside the plane, edited in the final shots and hit the "send" button. With a strong wireless broadband signal, the story was on air 20 minutes later in the UK. That was 24 hours quicker than the team from Meridian. It was even quicker than any of the six local New York crews (who'd come to film Branson with Pamela Anderson), because they could not get back through customs quickly.'

Paul Clifton, BBC South Transport Correspondent, claims a world first for shooting, cutting and broadcasting from a moving train

Clifton, working with a camera person, also filmed, edited and broadcast from a moving train – believed to be the first time this had been achieved anywhere in the world. He explains: 'Southern Railway have fitted wireless broadband to the London Victoria to Brighton line. After talking at length to T-Mobile, who fitted it, we reckoned it was just about possible to send a compressed-quality (not as good as normal but much better than videophone) file whilst the train was running at 90 miles an hour. The transmission would be picked up by a succession of base stations mounted along the track, and in theory would automatically be reassembled into a single file. It was, though we only just made it in time. The file was still trickling through as the train pulled into Brighton station, and as passengers started getting off.'

Clifton says that, with Wi-Fi broadband hotspots now pretty much everywhere, we no longer need despatch riders or satellite trucks to send edited packages: 'Any McDonald's, airport lounges, many railway stations, all Café Nero shops etc. etc. are now TV edit suites! I often cut and file from the back of my car sitting in a car park.'

Clifton uses Final Cut Pro on a Mac, and converts the sequence into an H.264 file, a form of QuickTime Movie: 'This is the current "best available" format, essentially a form of MPEG-4 [the broadcast video standard]. That's about as far as my technical knowledge goes. I then send that over a wi-fi broadband link to a computer in Southampton.'

Inevitably, technology is making this sort of transmission simpler all the time. A programme called Snapfeed works out how much material you have to send and how long it will take to send it at varying degrees of picture quality. Senior Broadcast Journalist Phil Simpson, a BBC trainer, explains: 'It assesses the amount of time available, and gives you as much bandwidth as it can. If you have a two-minute story and 30 minutes to send it, it'll assess what bandwidth is needed to get the highest-quality resolution.'

REMEMBER

- ➤ It is possible to broadcast by satellite from anywhere in the world
- ➤ Satellite is no longer the only option for sending material from remote locations
- ➤ Packages can be transmitted by wireless broadband.

CONCLUSION

An increasing number of technical skills are needed by modern broadcast journalists. Many of the new technologies improve our news gathering and make it easier to send stories back from the field.

There is an increasing demand for all journalists to be multi-skilled. That means radio broadcasters, particularly in larger organisations like the BBC, will have to learn video production skills. But you should never let the technology get in the way of the journalism. You should embrace new technologies when they enhance our ability to tell stories to an audience. Video journalism allows a more intimate relationship with your witnesses and contributors. Often, you will not be the story-teller; you will be the facilitator who allows contributors to tell their own story through your technical expertise. It's still broadcast journalism.

FURTHER READING

Chantler, Paul and Stewart, Peter (2003) *Basic Radio Journalism*, Oxford: Focal Press. How radio professionals go about the job.

Ray, Vin (2003) *The Television News Handbook*, London: Macmillan. Experts, many of them household names, on how it's done.

Watts, Harris (1997) *On Camera: Essential Know-how for Programme Makers*, London: AAVO. The first and still among the best – a guide to TV production.

WEB LINKS

www.bbctraining.com. Includes downloadable guides to using equipment in the field.

CHAPTER EIGHT

SPORTS REPORTING AND COMMENTARY

It has to be the best job in the world – watching sports from the best seats in the house and getting paid for it. If you're a sports fan, that is. If you're not, then you'll never make it as a sports journalist, and you won't want to. But many reporters find themselves covering sport as part of their everyday routine. Not every news provider has a separate sports department, even though sport is an important part of the modern news agenda. Sports stories make it on to the front as well as the back pages of newspapers. All broadcast journalists have to be aware of sports stories.

There's no place in the broadcast newsroom for anybody who says: 'I'm not interested in sport.' You may find yourself on shift alone late in the evening, and needing to put together a summary of cricket or football results for a late bulletin or the breakfast news. You need to be familiar with the terminology and even the jargon of sport and write it in a way audiences will understand.

In this chapter, we'll look at the skills and experiences applicable to sports reporting – and the specialist skills of the sports commentator. An understanding of these will also help the general reporter called in to cover sports events. Some people make a distinction between sports journalism (covering sports stories) and sports broadcasting (coverage of live sports events). But journalism skills are essential for both. In 2006, the BBC management brought sport within the remit of its journalism board – a recognition that sports are part of the mainstream news agenda.

There is a strong emphasis in this chapter on football reporting. That is because football dominates sports coverage. Look at any newspaper, or listen to BBC Radio Five Live or Talksport. And the Sky Sports News channel on TV is usually Sky Football News. That doesn't mean broadcasters are not interested in other sports; a specialism in a minority sport can be an invaluable career asset. But the reality of the modern world is that football is a dominant cultural force – and not just on sports programmes.

SPORTS RIGHTS

The broadcast journalist working on sports programmes is covered by different rules from news broadcasters – mainly because of sports rights contracts.

Most top sports events are covered by contracts with strict rules about how the event is covered, and what can and cannot be broadcast. Huge sums change hands, and the contract will be enforced in the courts by the parties to it – usually the event's organiser and the broadcaster that has made the highest bid for the rights to cover it. Separate rights may be sold for radio, TV, Internet and mobile phone updates. Live and recorded coverage will be negotiated separately.

For example, from 1992 to 2006 Sky Sports had the exclusive rights to live Premiership Football on TV. BBC Sport had the TV highlights (*Match of the Day*) from 2003 and BBC Radio Five Live had the network radio commentary rights. Sky's live TV monopoly was broken (at the insistence of European competition commissioners) when the Irish pay-TV company Setanta bid successfully for two of the packages of live Premiership matches for 2007 onwards. TV rights to the English Premiership sold for £1.7 billion in 2006 – a 65 per cent increase on the previous three-year deal. As if to prove football's dominance of broadcast sport, that's more than ten times what Sky paid for all the cricket controlled by the England and Wales Cricket Board, including Test matches.

Rights issues can be confusing in a converged world where more and more traditional broadcast services are available over broadband. In 2006, many BBC Local Radio stations with commentary rights for their local football clubs could not run those commentaries on their streamed radio services because they did not have the Internet rights.

JOURNALISTS WORKING FOR ORGANISATIONS WITH BROADCAST RIGHTS TO A TOURNAMENT GET BETTER ACCESS THAN THE REST OF THE SPORTING PRESS.

Journalists working for organisations with broadcast rights to a tournament get better access than the rest of the sporting press. There are usually obligations for players (and managers) to be interviewed after the event as part of the broadcast deal. While the reporter working for the rights holder is guaranteed an interview, others wait their turn on the off-chance.

The deal will prohibit commentary on the event or the use of extensive pictures of the action by all but the rights holders.

Usually news coverage is allowed outside the terms of the contract. News organisations are covered by the copyright law of 'fair dealing', and by news access agreements, allowing them limited access to show up to a minute's highlights of a football match, for example, within 24 hours of the match taking place. Oddly the news access agreement does not extend to Sky Sports News, because it is not considered a news channel by the regulators, or to sports programmes.

For weekday regional TV news programmes, news access is extended to include the first full-length programme after a weekend's sporting action. Hence the popularity of goals round-ups on Monday evening programmes.

Reporting Saturday afternoon's events on a Monday evening would appear to break most conventions of broadcast journalism. It undermines the immediacy of television as a medium. Defenders of the practice will point out that Monday is the best day to evaluate the full weekend's football programme, now that games are played with various kick-off times between Saturday lunchtime and Sunday evening. The truth is that regional TV has been doing this since all the games kicked off at 3pm on a Saturday. Regional ITV sees itself as the natural home of the Football League, with regional stations covering teams in their patch, and other broadcasters accessing the material under the news access agreement.

The goals round-up has become a habit for TV producers and – to some extent – the audience, although there can be few real fans who have not seen their team's goals on TV before 6.45 on Monday evening. Many will have subscribed to see them on the Internet or their mobile phone. The days of the Monday round-up are surely numbered.

To students of media law it is a mystery why news access agreements exist at all. In 1991, the BBC tried to claim that British Satellite Broadcasting was in breach of copyright for showing the goals from World Cup matches to which the BBC had exclusive rights. But Mr Justice Scott ruled that the goals could be shown under the law of 'fair dealing' for reporting current events. It is a condition of 'fair dealing' that the copyright owner is acknowledged, and the use does not compete commercially with the copyright owner. Fair dealing for the purpose of reporting current events does not apply to photographs, however, and in 2005 the BBC stopped showing the front pages of the day's newspapers on its online news review, because lawyers advised there was a 'considerable risk of litigation' from copyright owners including paparazzi photographers. The advice has not been tested in court.

REMEMBER

➤ Sports rights contracts can determine what you show
➤ News access agreements allow news reports of sporting events.

RULES AND REGULATIONS

A fundamental of reporting any sport is knowledge of the rules of the game(s). Just as court reporters need an in-depth understanding of the risks of contempt of court, sports reporters need to know not just the laws by which a game is played but the rules of the competition and the administrative structure of the sport. Sports Institutions and Regulations are taught on specialist sports journalism degree courses. But you can do much to find out these rules yourself.

Sports governing bodies have their own websites. Many have valuable background information which you can use when you are covering an event. They also explain the rules of the competitions they organise. These can change frequently, and can sometimes be confusing. For example, Twenty20 cricket, the limited-overs County competition drew big crowds from the start, but in its first few seasons the structure of the competition was modified to improve its appeal. When the number of games in the three regional groups was increased to eight, each county played three teams twice and the two other teams once each – an unprecedented arrangement. It's a journalist's job to understand these complicated rules and explain them to the audience.

Sky Sport and BBC Five Live's commentators had to explain cricket's rules (in the complete absence of any official comment) when England's Third Test against Pakistan came to an unprecedented end in August 2006. England were awarded five penalty runs when Pakistan were accused of ball-tampering. The Pakistani players protested by refusing to leave the dressing room after tea. The umpires and batsmen took to the field and then left. Pakistan tried to return, but the umpires said they were too late, and play could not continue. With no play, the crowds at the Oval sat in ignorance of what was happening for over an hour and a half, until they were told play had been abandoned for the day. Eventually – after calls to the International Cricket Council headquarters in Dubai – England were awarded the match. In the meantime, the commentators (and other broadcasters) were left to speculate. Only by researching – live on air – the game's extensive (and sometimes obscure) rule book were they able to keep the audience accurately informed. People at home knew more than the 23,000 paying customers at the ground.

There was less confusion among spectators at Aintree when the 1993 Grand National became 'the race that never was', but the estimated 300 million television viewers worldwide relied on a series of swift decisions by the BBC production team and presenter Des Lynam to interpret events. After a second false start, 30 of the 39 runners in 'the world's greatest steeplechase' carried on running. The race was declared void. Esha Ness came in first, but goes down in history as the answer to a trivia question rather than a Grand National winner. Thanks to information from the broadcasters, punters at home knew they'd be enjoying a refund from the bookies long before the 'winning' jockey. (Lynam also famously ad-libbed through high drama at the National four years later when the race was postponed because of a bomb scare and the evacuation of the course.)

The regulatory framework of sport provides stories in its own right. For example, the World Anti-Doping Agency had to test its strict liability rule (whereby an athlete is automatically disqualified for a positive drugs test) against international law and human rights legislation. That was a complicated story to tell, requiring research into international law. An easier sports administration story to understand was the reinvention of rugby league in Britain as a summer attraction with the establishment of the Super League. The idea was to improve attendances. It worked.

SPORTS JOURNALISM V. SPORTS BROADCASTING

The relationship between sports broadcasting and journalism has always been an uneasy one. Punditry and opinion (often from ex-players) is mixed in with reporting.

THE LEVEL OF OPINION ALLOWED IN SPORTS COVERAGE DIFFERS FROM THAT IN NEWS REPORTING. OUTSPOKEN COMMENT IS ALLOWED.

There is also an element of commercial cross-promotion as channels that have rights to an event report on the build-up to that event. The free-to-air Sky Sports News channel helps promote the subscription-only Sky Sports channels.

The level of opinion allowed in sports coverage differs from that in news reporting. Outspoken comment *is* allowed. BBC Radio Five Live's commentator Alan Green has made it a trademark – to the annoyance of some Premiership managers (and many sports fans). But the sports broadcaster is still governed by the same laws of libel as news reporters. 'Fair comment' is no defence unless you are commenting on provable fact.

THINKPIECE

JOURNALISM OR BROADCASTING

Raymond Boyle of the University of Stirling, in *Sports Journalism: Context and Issues*, says there's an institutional and cultural distinction to be drawn between sports broadcasting and sports journalism. He says some sports broadcasters (notably Henry Blofeld of Test Match Special) don't really see themselves as reporters or journalists, while others (Des Lynam) have insisted that what they do is very journalistic.

Boyle says sport on television is dominated by entertainment rather than journalism values, and points out that, while there are big audiences for sports events, broadcasters perceive there to be less demand for investigative documentaries about sport.

In support of his argument Boyle quotes the former Liverpool striker Michael Robinson, now a popular sports presenter in Spain. Robinson told the *Observer* in 2005 he now sees himself as a journalist who wants to 'invade living rooms'. He despises the way sports broadcasting, and that of football in particular, has been 'hijacked by ex-pros' in England.

Robinson said: 'There is a screaming necessity for a journalist, because they all speak now in a certain argot, they all sit down comfy, comfy – and there's no journalist saying, "Why?" They need to be challenged. It's all happy families. I consider the BBC to be the mother and father of all television but they've become totally prostituted.'

The journalist and author Eamon Dunphy is also a former professional player. He often causes controversy in Ireland with his outspoken views on football and politics. He told Boyle: 'You are very inhibited if you are in a contractual arrangement with an organisation. You do not hear the idiosyncratic voice on television as much as you ought to. It's not cultivated. The media should be working for its readers and viewers. If that leads you into direct conflict with managers and players, then you have got to do that. But of course rights to events are important as well. So there is a fine line to walk on this.'

Sports news is big business, and BBC Sport has the most visited sports web pages in Europe. Sky Sports web presence is popular too. Club websites are often the first to carry breaking stories of injury and transfer news. Other journalists rely on them increasingly.

The BBC remains committed to a strong 'journalistic spine' in its sports coverage and says the news agenda should never be determined by sports rights the corporation holds. The organisation's commitment to strong sports journalism was underlined by the appointment of Roger Mosey as BBC Director of Sport in 2005. He is a former Head of TV News, Controller of Radio Five Live and editor of the flagship Radio Four *Today* programme.

SPORTS NEWS COVERAGE

Larger broadcast organisations will have 'sports news correspondents'. It's an acknowledgement that sports coverage goes beyond reporting events. Sports news correspondents cover more than just sports stars and the activities of sports organisations. Sports stories may find their way into news programmes because of the celebrity of those involved or the controversy an issue is generating: for example, Zinedine Zidane's World Cup Final sending-off and England being awarded the Third Test against Pakistan in 2006. There can be political and social implications of sport too – as in these examples:

1 Governments talk of the importance of widening participation in sport to improve the health of the population.

2 Major sporting events are used to regenerate inner city areas. The Manchester Commonwealth Games of 2002 meant world-class sporting venues were built in the city, to be inherited by local athletes.

3 The continuing delays and rising costs of the new Wembley stadium were a major news story, particularly when the developers ran hugely over-budget and failed to open in time for the 2006 FA Cup Final.

4 The business opportunities offered by the successful London 2012 Olympic bid – and the reluctance of some in the local community to relinquish their homes and businesses for redevelopment projects – are ongoing stories.

5 And then there are sporting drug scandals. The reporter who is well briefed on the characteristics of performance-enhancing drugs will be in heavy demand for two-ways.

Even within the tightly media-controlled world of professional sports, good contacts, sheer tenacity or good luck can produce exclusive stories. BBC Radio Five Live's Juliette Ferrington was the first reporter at the England training camp one morning during the 2006 World Cup. She saw something that was to make headlines throughout the country. The big story in the build-up to the tournament had been Wayne Rooney's metatarsal injury. The broken bone in the foot of England's most talented player had dominated the back – and some of the front – pages for the month before the tournament.

Ferrington says: 'It was the first time we'd seen him kick a ball, run with a ball, turn with a ball, since he was injured. I broke the story and I was everyone's best friend that day – even the dailies [newspapers], a lot of people who missed it, the daily journalists, the Sunday journalists, everyone asked: "What did you see?"'

Rooney went on to play in the tournament, didn't score, and was sent off in England's quarter-final defeat, on penalties, against Portugal.

Juliette Ferrington on getting one of the scoops of the World Cup 2006: 'I was everyone's best friend.'

REMEMBER

➤ Sports news is about more than reporting events

➤ Sporting issues make strong running stories

➤ Traditional reporting skills – tenacity and hard work – can still break sports stories.

REPORTING EVENTS

SPECIALIST EQUIPMENT FOR SPORTS REPORTERS

Radio and TV reporters providing voice-only reports at live sports events normally do so via ISDN – a broadcast-quality phone line. To connect to the line in the press box, you will carry your own outside broadcast unit, packed in a small flight case or shoulder bag. This will be mains-powered, preferably with battery back-up. You may also need to record interviews. It is vital to check equipment before leaving the studio or your home on match day.

- Are all the parts there?
- Are you sure they're working?
- Have you tried a test recording?
- Have batteries been charged?
- Will you need an electrical extension lead? If you're not sure, take one just in case.

At the end of the match there is usually a need to pack equipment away quickly – probably because you need to get to the tunnel area to record interviews with managers and players.

Bizarrely, given how much sports clubs are paid by broadcast companies, the operational needs of the media are often overlooked when stadia are designed. Coventry's Ricoh stadium opened at the start of the 2005–6 football season. The TV gantry is on the opposite side of the pitch to the TV interview room.

It's during the rush to pack equipment away that it is most likely to get broken or lost. The connecting jacks on mic and headphone cables can become detached when they are stuffed hastily into bags.

They may not belong to you, but these are the tools of your trade. Take care of them. And don't blame the station engineers if they go wrong. It is usually not the engineers who abuse equipment.

Press conference at the 2006 World Cup in Germany with England's manager Sven-Goran Eriksson

PREVIEWS

Clubs arrange pre-match press conferences at which journalists have the chance to question managers about forthcoming fixtures.

At some clubs broadcasters may be excluded from the conference itself. TV crews may be allowed to film the opening moments to use as set-up shots. The exclusion of broadcast reporters is at the request of print journalists, who want a chance to pursue their own stories without microphones recording everything. It is an understandable plea because the presence of a mic destroys any chance of exclusivity for the newspapers.

Radio and TV usually have the opportunity to conduct one-to-one interviews either before or after the main press conference. This is the chance to ask your own questions and to try to secure exclusive comments. Players too will be offered for interview. Any one-to-one is an opportunity to get a story that others have missed, or to develop an angle that will provide headlines beyond your own output.

A CLOSER LOOK

KNOW YOUR SPORTING AUDIENCE

The demands of different audiences are rarely better illustrated than at a football club's press conference. The national media want different stories from the local media.

In October 2005, Aston Villa's Premiership derby with Birmingham City took on added significance because the teams were on equal points just above the relegation zone. Local reporters were keen for team and injury news. But the national story was Villa manager David O'Leary ruling himself out of the job of Irish international coach.

Later that season, when it was known that England coach Sven-Goran Eriksson was to step down after the World Cup in the summer, media questions to English managers of Premiership clubs focused on whether they wanted to be considered for the national job. But local reporters still needed to know what was going on at the club itself, and they were often anxious not to antagonise the 'boss' by pressing him about his international ambitions.

When Steve McClaren of Middlesbrough got the job, journalists on Teesside breathed a sigh of relief – they didn't have to ask him about it any more.

MATCH DAY

Reporters attending matches need to prepare with background information and statistics just as if they were a news reporter covering a diary story. Most are fans of the sports they cover, so a lot of the background will already be known to them. But a specialist football reporter can find himself covering a minority sport of which he has little knowledge. When Great Britain's women won gold in curling at the Winter Olympics in Salt Lake City in 2002, there was frantic research into a sport many reporters had previously dismissed as 'housework on ice'.

Steve Lee at home on the computer: 'There's no excuse for not being statted up these days.'

Freelance sports reporter Steve Lee has built a reputation for reliability and always doing his homework. That's why he's used by the BBC, ITV and Sky Sports programmes. He says: 'There's no excuse for not being statted up these days. If it's football you're covering, there's soccerbase.com, which is fantastic, and the various football yearbooks. It's at your fingertips, even in the press box if you want it.'

It's increasingly common for broadcast reporters to have a laptop linked to the Internet sitting on the desk alongside their outside broadcast equipment. If something happens, they tap the player's details into a website like soccerbase (run by the *Racing Post*) and can announce with confidence it's the player's first goal in 18 months or their second booking in ten games. The Internet means that a huge range of statistics is available to you during the match beyond those you had time to research before kick-off.

Sports reporters usually need specialist *press passes* to attend an event. These often have to be applied for in advance. Accreditation may require proof of identity, or photographs to be laminated on to passes. Tickets for regular fixtures like football matches will normally be left at a special press window at the ground, at the club's reception, or at the entrance to the press room. Arrangements differ according to the venue. Before your first visit to a ground, it's worth speaking to someone who's been there before or telephoning the club to ask how to find the press entrance. Match-day stewards and police officers do not always know. Much time and legwork can be wasted getting into a football or cricket match. Walking the entire circumference of a stadium lugging a heavy outside broadcast kit is not the best preparation for great broadcasting.

There can be administrative errors, even at the best run events. Hundreds of media representatives might be expected, so losing one ticket – yours – is not necessarily a sign of the club's gross incompetence. Stay cool and try to resolve the problem. Make sure you carry your Press card or workplace security pass as proof of identity. If the doorman can't help, ask him to find a club official who can.

Contrary to popular myth, a Press card or BBC pass is not a golden ticket to any event. They certainly don't impress the 'Jobsworth' at the gate. But they can help sort out misunderstandings.

Sports reporters also need to pay special attention to travel and parking arrangements, particularly if large crowds are expected at an event. It is usually better to arrive well before the paying public. You will avoid most of the traffic, and the crowds on the way in. Arriving early will allow you time in the press room to check out any late team or transfer news. Time spent at a sports ground on match days is usually of more value professionally than time spent in the newsroom or at home.

Press passes: essential for sports reporting

AFTER-MATCH

Most football clubs have press rooms where the managers will hold after-match press conferences. But first the managers will visit the flash interview room, where a single TV camera provides a feed to broadcasters who have bought the rights to live coverage or recorded highlights of the game. The advertising boards on the wall have the names of the TV company and the competition sponsors on them. There's a separate board for each TV station.

You will probably need a separate *tunnel pass* for the after-match interview area. This will be given to you when you arrive at the ground or in the press room. Pitch-side access will be covered by yet another ticket. Sports clubs are fond of controlling access to their stars. As we've explained, it can be in their commercial interests.

Interviewers await the managers, and also try to grab interviews with players. At most clubs, the interview room is near the players' tunnel and the dressing room, so it may be possible to approach players in person. Usually, though, the request for an interview with a player is made through club press officers. Any time you can spend getting to know sports personalities when the cameras are not rolling is time well spent. These are the moments to establish a rapport, and to ask for mobile numbers.

Radio stations with live broadcasting rights will usually have an ISDN feed point in the tunnel area. In the English Premiership, BBC Five Live has points for live inserts near the players' area at all clubs. Other radio reporters will record interviews to be played down the line from the press box, or persuade interviewees to come to the press box so they can chat to the presenter back in the studio.

THE MIXED ZONE

At bigger sporting events, the mixed zone is an area where sports journalists from organisations that have not bought broadcast rights will wait to get interviews with sportsmen and women and team managers. It's a free-for-all, and those with the best contacts – those who know the players already – will win out.

For the 1999 Rugby World Cup in Wales, ITV Sport contracted former Welsh Rugby Union International Nigel Walker, who'd been freelancing for Eurosport, to cover the Wales team. His personal knowledge of players and coaching staff was invaluable, and a major stepping stone in his career. He later became Head of Sport for BBC Wales.

The mixed zone is usually an area that all the players and coaches have to pass through on their way out of the dressing room. But that doesn't mean they will want to stop and chat, particularly if they've just lost a cup semi-final. The famously enigmatic soccer manager Gordon Strachan wouldn't talk to TV reporters in the mixed zone even when his team had *won* an FA Cup semi-final.

Be bold – and ask the questions the fans want answered.

Mixed zone interview arrangements are not exclusive to match days. They are also arranged at training sessions for major events.

THE LANGUAGE BARRIER

Reporters have to be bold, not only in what they ask and how they ask it, but in tackling the language difficulties at international events.

Steve Lee, who was working for the BBC at the 1998 World Cup, recalls an ITV reporter making the first approach to Romania's star Gheorghe Hagi. The ITV man had insisted: 'I know Spanish. He'll know Spanish because he played for Real Madrid.'

The player obliged and an interview in faltering Spanish followed. Lee's response was to ask: 'Gheorghe, a few words in English please?'

'Why yes, of course, what would you like to know?'

The interview that followed with the multilingual Mr Hagi was not only more fluent than the Spanish version, it was of considerably more use to a British broadcaster. The lesson from this is obvious. If you are working for an English language broadcaster, try to gather your material in English.

BBC Radio Five Live's Juliette Ferrington recalls a similarly helpful Luis Figo of Portugal answering in English at a team press conference at the 2006 World Cup in Germany. But his coach Luiz Felipe Scolari's only English words in response to her question were: 'I don't answer questions in English.' Ferrington concedes: 'He was quite cool, because he would not answer any questions in English, even though you knew he spoke English.'

She'd asked him about taking over the England manager's job. His answer ran – in translation – on Five Live, BBC World Service, in newspapers and on television.

➤ Get to the venue early

➤ Most sports interviews take place under controlled conditions

➤ Make sure you have the correct passes

➤ Be bold – ask the right questions.

COMMENTARY SKILLS

Sports coverage relies on one specific form of journalistic expertise – live commentary. The great commentators grace their sport and become synonymous with it: Richie Benaud on cricket; Henry Longhurst and later Peter Allis on golf; football's John Motson.

Encyclopaedic knowledge and diligent research mark out the best commentators. But they have another thing in common – a passion for their sport, a passion they can transmit to audiences.

Good commentary appears fluent and seamless. But, like all broadcast speech, it consists of different elements combined for effect. An overload of factual information serves the listener as poorly as too little description of what's happening. An over-opinionated commentator, or one who is too partisan, can be seriously annoying.

AN OVER-OPINIONATED COMMENTATOR, OR ONE WHO IS TOO PARTISAN, CAN BE SERIOUSLY ANNOYING.

Description

Americans call it play-by-play or calling the action. Describing what is happening requires knowledge of the rules of the game, its terminology and jargon, and above all the players. In team sports, recognition – preferably instant – is vital. More words are of course required on radio or a webcast than on television, where the words have to complement the pictures.

'Gerrard . . . Owen . . . one-nil.' (TV version)

'Gerrard, right-footed through the middle for Owen to chase. Owen – good first touch – onto his right – beats the keeper. One-nil to England.' (Radio version)

On TV, a caption at the top of the screen will tell viewers the score in a live match. On radio, the question of how often to repeat it is a matter of judgement. It usually depends on the station. It is normal before and after ad breaks on commercial radio, or when returning to coverage from other reports on a BBC station.

Background

The commentator includes what he knows from his background covering the sport. This can include contextual, factual or anecdotal content. In practice it's usually indistinguishable from researched material.

'Ernie Els with a hole-in-one at the Postage Stamp . . . that's the hole where Gene Sarazen hit an ace at the age of 71 in the 1973 Open.'

Research

However good your background knowledge, you need to research and prepare for specific events. This information includes players' names, individual and team statistics, statistical analysis, biographical detail, historic context, and anecdotes gleaned during the research process. To the casual listener these facts appear to be your own background knowledge and add greatly to your credibility.

Research helps fill a lull in the action, or the wait between events. Athletics coverage relies almost exclusively on research and background knowledge. A commentator may describe what the athletes are doing as they warm up, and speculate about their mood, but that is something the audience can usually see for themselves. The expert should add to the audience's knowledge, not simply repeat what they can see.

THE EXPERT SHOULD ADD TO THE AUDIENCE'S KNOWLEDGE, NOT SIMPLY REPEAT WHAT THEY CAN SEE.

In a fast-moving event like a horse race, you are lost without research. You will need to know horses, jockeys, trainers and owners, and the betting odds. You then have to recognise the runners, often as they're bunched together. The colours of the horses and the jockeys' caps and silks need to be memorised. Commentators will note which horses are wearing nosebands, visors, cheek pieces and blinkers. It's a complicated specialism. Few people who are not racing fans can cover a horse race.

Football is a fast-moving sport too, but there are long periods when the ball is out of play, at throw-ins or during injuries, for example. Then you draw on your reserves of research. Typically, a commentator on a live match will have 150 snippets of information – factoids, if you like – at their fingertips. If you have a summariser alongside you – an ex-player, perhaps – there's time to draw breath, consult your notes, or even access the Internet to find new facts.

'That's his seventh goal in as many games . . . and his first for England.'

Opinion and bias

Richie Benaud, the great Australian cricketer and broadcaster, has sound advice for sports commentators: 'First of all get your brain into gear, and when you've got your brain into gear, only add to the picture. What you have to do is not describe to people what has happened, but to explain to them why it has happened.'

In a radio interview about his craft, Benaud singled out as the greatest commentators Henry Longhurst and Dan Maskell, the voices of golf and tennis respectively in their time, because they only ever added to the television picture. And for devotion to research and preparation, Benaud praised racing's Peter O'Sullevan. In his early days at the BBC, Benaud spent a day following O'Sullevan, who advised him to stay quiet, take notes, and ask questions at the end of the day over a beer.

If outright partisanship is usually taboo, expressions of opinion are almost inevitable given the enthusiasm shown by most commentators. Outright bias is best left to summarisers. If an ex-pro from one of the clubs in the game is sitting next to you, you will want him to reflect his passion for the club and provide professional tactical analysis. If he does that, there's no need for you to do the same.

AN ENGLISH AUDIENCE FOR AN ENGLAND FOOTBALL MATCH WILL WANT ENGLAND TO WIN. A UK AUDIENCE FOR THE SAME EVENT WILL BE DIVIDED.

Sometimes, sharing a point of view with the audience is accepted: on a club website or local radio station, for example. But many local radio stations cover more than one club. Aston Villa fans don't want to hear a Birmingham City supporter commentating on BRMB or Radio WM. But they will want information about how their closest rivals are getting on.

An English audience for an England football match will want England to win. A UK audience for the same event will be divided. Experience tells us that most

Scottish international fans support two teams: Scotland and anyone who's playing against England. It's good advice to take the example of the former Australian cricket captain. In his 40-year broadcasting career, Richie Benaud never referred to the Australians as 'we' or 'us'.

Statements of the obvious don't help the listener either: *'I don't believe he wanted to do that!'*

Reaction

There's no harm in a natural response to events. Exclamations and expressions of surprise, wonder and amazement are all part of the mix. The late Dan Maskell, the 'voice of Wimbledon' for 40 years, peppered his tennis commentaries with an expression that became his catchphrase: *'Oh, I say.'*

REMEMBER

➤ Sports commentary relies on extensive research and background knowledge

➤ Radio commentary requires more description of the action

➤ Expressions of your own excitement are acceptable

➤ Consider the audience before expressing any bias.

THE LONE VOICE

Sports commentary is available across all media, and the economics of media businesses mean that, for smaller audiences, commentators work alone. A lone voice covers the event, often in a cramped seat in the press box, alongside others doing the same thing for club websites, Internet services and local radio. The lucky ones are operating with headphones and a mic on an ISDN line; others use a telephone.

Horse racing commentator Gary Capewell working from home

It's possible to earn a respectable living working for the Internet and premium-rate telephone services set up to satisfy the demands of the growing betting industry. Gary Capewell began commentating on horse racing while still a broadcast journalism student. He covers hundreds of miles a week visiting race courses for phone and Internet services (including William Hill radio and Racecall). And he also works from home. Using a Skype link on a PC in the corner of the family dining room in Uttoxeter, he can watch race meetings on TV and broadcast internationally.

Capewell's preparation for a phone commentary is as meticulous as when he's at the racetrack: 'I always have lots of extra snippets of information – bits and bobs I can throw in if there are quiet moments, either before the race or if there aren't many runners and one horse is way out in front. If I'm watching a race from Ireland, say, where they're often covered by just one camera, I need all that extra information to fill if I can't make out exactly what's going on.'

THE COMMENTARY TEAM

Maintaining fluent commentary for 45 minutes or longer at a football match is hard work. That's why bigger stations share the load. BBC Radio Five Live will

have two commentators at a football match, each doing half of each half's play. There will be a match analyst with them – usually a player, ex-player or manager. When the analyst is summarising the action, there's a chance for the commentator to make a brief scribble on their notes, keeping tag of scorers, bookings and sendings-off.

Five Live have also experimented with two commentators together in rugby league: one describes the play when the home side is in possession; the other picks up when the other side has the ball. It's a different and entertaining approach, but would be unlikely to work in sports where possession changes more frequently like association football (soccer).

ITV producer Mitch Pryce

At big tournaments, broadcasters will team their commentators with a regular summariser and a producer. These three-man units will work, travel, and usually eat and socialise together. At the Germany 2006 football World Cup, BBC TV had five of these teams; ITV Sport had three. Producer Mitch Pryce, who worked with commentator Jon Champion and the ex-Liverpool and Republic of Ireland international, Jim Beglin, for ITV, said it was an exciting time but very hard work: 'We covered 17 games in 25 days, taking in 11 of the 12 venues, and 21 of the 32 teams in the tournament. We took 11 internal flights and drove thousands of miles. On our day off we drove three hours to Dortmund to see Brazil v. Ghana.

'Normally commentators spend the best part of a week preparing for a game, but in a big tournament you're doing it day by day, telescoping your normal work schedules to fit everything in. You just don't stop. The most important thing is that you all get on and get on with the job.'

WORKING WITH A CO-COMMENTATOR

Compared with the frenzy of working alone, life is a little more relaxed for the commentator working with an experienced summariser, usually an ex-player or manager. They offer expert opinion, a change of voice for the listener, and a breathing space for the commentator to catch up on their notes. Conversation replaces the need to carry on regardless.

The BBC *Match of the Day* commentator Guy Mowbray says: 'It's much easier with a co-commentator. He's the expert. He's the one who's played the game, so let him give the opinions. You just call the action. You can argue with them at times, but don't get ideas above your station.'

Mowbray also has a guide to when to introduce the summariser after a goal is scored: 'The first replay you can still be talking about what has just happened, but the second replay belongs to my colleague to analyse it. If I'm still talking during the second replay, I'm doing a bad job.'

THE ROLE OF THE PRODUCER

At big events, the location sports producer makes life easier for a commentator and his summariser. He'll locate the stadium media centre and pick up match tickets from the host broadcast service. For ITV's Mitch Pryce, at some games in the 2006 World Cup this meant not only collecting three commentary position seats for his team but also 'observer' seats for reporters from ITV News and the breakfast service GMTV.

The BBC's Guy Mowbray: 'If I'm still talking during the second replay, I'm doing a bad job.'

Mitch Pryce at the World Cup 2006: 'You don't just sit back with your feet up and watch the match.'

Pryce observes: 'Contrary to popular opinion, you don't then sit back with your feet up and watch the match.'

The producer in the press box is an integral part of the commentary team, although you won't hear his voice on air. He's watching the action and has his own input. Pryce says: 'I can talk to the commentator through his headset, but I prefer not to interrupt their flow. I'll usually write something and put a piece of paper in front of him. Sometimes the commentator will slip his headphones off and ask something off mic.'

When Radhi Jaida scored for Tunisia against Saudi Arabia in 2006, Pryce was able to tell Jon Champion that Jaida was the first Bolton Wanderers player to score in the World Cup finals since Nat Lofthouse in 1954. Champion used the statistic – as did the next day's *Daily Telegraph*.

As Champion and Jim Beglin were concentrating on the replays of Wayne Rooney's sending-off for England against Portugal in the quarter-final, Pryce was watching the action on the field and saw Rooney's altercation with Manchester United team-mate Cristiano Ronaldo. That part of the story became a huge talking point in the British media but might have been missed by the ITV commentary team at the time without the producer's involvement.

Pryce says: 'As field producer, I am the link between the studio gallery and the action. It's down to me to pass on to the commentators how long they have to talk about the team line-ups, links to studio and to commercial breaks; also to ensure the right on-air promotions are delivered without interfering with the action. In return I can pass on any editorial issues back to base that might affect the studio discussions. For instance, to confirm that Graham Poll really *did* issue three yellow cards to the same player as happened in the Australia v. Croatia World Cup match in Stuttgart.'

Sports producing at the highest level is a rewarding and exciting job. And occasionally producers get to broadcast too. Pryce interviewed Henrik Larsson live to an audience of eight and a half million people after Sweden's Euro 2004 game with Italy. Pryce says: 'It helped that we were staying in the same hotel as the Swedish team, and I'd said hello to him in the lift!'

REMEMBER

➤ Sports commentators are part of a team

➤ Summarisers are the experts

➤ The producer is a fixer and extra pair of eyes.

CONCLUSION

Sports reporting gets you free tickets for the best events in town – but you have to work long and hard to win the right to be there. Even if Chelsea are playing in the Champions League, someone has to cover the league match on a rainy night in Grimsby. Only the elite of sports broadcasters have any guarantee of being at the biggest events, and there's no guarantee if your organisation hasn't won the broadcast rights.

But if you love sport – all sport at whatever competitive level – a great life awaits in sports broadcast journalism. Like foreign correspondents you will see the world at somebody else's expense. And there's less chance of being shot.

FURTHER READING

Andrews, Phil (2005) *Sports Journalism: A Practical Introduction*, London: Sage. Covers many practical problems – but is light on broadcast skills.

Boyle, Raymond (2006) *Sports Journalism: Context and Issues*, London: Sage. A look at theoretical issues in sports journalism and broadcasting.

USEFUL REFERENCE BOOKS

Most sports journalists will need at least some of these to hand for background and research:

• IRB International Rugby Yearbook.
• Rugby League Yearbook.
• Rules of Golf.
• Sky Sports Football Yearbook.
• The Directory of the Turf.
• Wisden Cricketers' Almanack.

WEB LINKS

The sites of sports clubs and governing bodies and the sports news sites should be bookmarked on your computer:

news.bbc.co.uk/sport

www.iaaf.org

www.cricinfo.com

www.formula1.com

www.golfonline.com

www.racingpost.com

www.rfl.uk.com

www.rfu.com

www.skysports.com

www.soccerbase.com

www.thedirectoryoftheturf.com

www.tennis.com

www.wada-ama.org

CHAPTER NINE

FOREIGN REPORTING

Foreign correspondents are the journalistic elite. Theirs is a world of travel, adventure, excitement and, yes, glamour. It can also be a world of danger – of greater risk than any other job in the modern media.

The risks can be appealing to some people, but for most the attraction of foreign reporting is the chance to witness world events and interpret those events for an audience at home. More than any other group of reporters they are providing 'the first draft of history'. And, of course, they get to travel the world at someone else's expense.

We'll also reflect on the differences between being based overseas and 'parachuting' in to cover stories. Most news organisations have fewer permanent overseas bureaux these days. It is easier than ever to travel around the globe and reach the world's trouble spots. But does that mean the reporter is less aware of local culture, and therefore less able to report with authority on the impact of events on local people?

We'll also consider the role of 'embedded' journalists based with military units in times of war. Does embedding compromise their independence? And is it safer than acting as a 'unilateral' – operating without military assistance?

A JOURNALISTIC ARISTOCRACY

The broadcaster and writer Andrew Marr describes foreign correspondents as an 'aristocracy'. In *My Trade* he says of foreign reporters: 'Though the trade is old, the real glamour of the job reaches back only about 70 years, from roughly the time imperial soldiering and missionary exploration began to decline. Unlike missionaries, foreign correspondents had a moral message not for the natives out there, but for the folks back home. Ever since the first wars involving fascism, in Abyssinia and Spain, the foreign correspondents of the democracies have been bringers of warnings. They have been adventurers who returned not with loot but with information.'

BBC TV Special Correspondent Gavin Hewitt agrees with his colleague about the prestige attached to foreign reporting, although he stresses it's just as important to report well on domestic issues. He says some of the blame lies with the television industry's obsession with awards: 'It is true that time and time again people get recognised on the whole for the work they do abroad. There seems to be greater interest when you're reporting from Afghanistan, Iraq or America or whatever.

'Obviously our principal duty is to reflect what's happening in our own society. It's been a criticism in the past that we reflect what happens around the world with fantastic reports and brilliant cameramen. Why don't we do the same in the UK? I think there's a little bit more of an emphasis on trying to do that.'

In response to Andrew Marr's 'aristocracy' comment, Sky News' Ian Woods, who was based in Washington DC for four years, says he never felt like an aristocrat, but he knows plenty of foreign correspondents who lived like a lord on expenses.

Another inference of Marr's comment is that foreign correspondents are like old-fashioned imperial adventurers, who have little regard or respect for the people whose countries they visit. This was true of newspaper correspondents of the type parodied by Evelyn Waugh in the comic novel *Scoop*, written before the Second World War. Modern broadcasters have to apply journalistic principles of objectivity and cultural neutrality, and will find empathy with the people they report on. Finding the human interest angle in a story is even more important in cultures that differ from what the audience knows. Humanity is the shared bond with the viewer or listener.

The larger news organisations maintain foreign bureaux – permanently staffed offices around the world. They're usually in capital cities – Washington, Paris, Moscow, Beijing – where major political stories will happen and a country's media are based. When big stories break, they serve as regional bases. The North America correspondent will set out from Washington or New York to cover election campaigns in the Mid-West or hurricanes in Florida. When there are not enough staff in that part of the world to cover a major disaster – the Tsunami of Boxing Day 2004, for example – extra reporters and crews will fly in from the UK. These big stories require management and organisation, so producers and fixers will be sent too. There are journalism jobs in foreign news other than those for on-screen talent.

FOREIGN TRAVEL

Travelling abroad is part of the appeal of being a foreign correspondent or producer. Being ready to travel at a moment's notice is part of the job. Keep up-to-date with the jabs you would otherwise need for only the most exotic holiday destinations.

Many reporters keep a bag permanently packed ready for short-notice assignments. It should include the documentation, currency and medical supplies you will need for the first few days in a strange environment. You need to plan for the worst-case – an earthquake perhaps with no fresh water and little shelter. Unless your operational area is restricted to, say, northern Europe, it's difficult to plan what clothing to take, because you won't know what weather or temperatures to expect.

Passports

Keep your passport handy at all times, and up-to-date. Many countries will not let you in unless your passport has at least six months left to run. Newsrooms are full of stories of reporters who were sent to breaking foreign news stories simply because they were the only one in the office who had their passport with them.

Many experienced foreign reporters keep two passports. This makes it easier to travel between countries at war or with strained diplomatic relations, particularly in the Middle East. Many Arab countries will not let you in if you have an Israeli

BIG STORIES REQUIRE MANAGEMENT AND ORGANISATION, SO PRODUCERS AND FIXERS WILL BE SENT TOO. THERE ARE JOURNALISM JOBS IN FOREIGN NEWS OTHER THAN THOSE FOR ON-SCREEN TALENT.

KEEP YOUR PASSPORT HANDY AT ALL TIMES, AND UP-TO-DATE. MANY COUNTRIES WILL NOT LET YOU IN UNLESS YOUR PASSPORT HAS AT LEAST SIX MONTHS LEFT TO RUN.

stamp in your passport, for example. In Syria you will be denied entry if you have a stamp from another country's border crossing point with Israel. There are similar restrictions about travelling between Turkey and Cyprus. The Foreign Office does not keep a list of these 'incompatible countries' but you can check by phoning their individual embassies.

To apply for a second passport you will need a letter of support from your employers explaining that your work will take you to incompatible countries.

Even if you have only one passport, keep a photocopy of the main pages separate from the passport, in case it gets lost or stolen. It's also worth keeping a couple of passport-sized photographs with you. They're sometimes needed for local accreditation.

Visas

Ian Woods reporting from Ground Zero

Working abroad differs from travelling abroad. Countries you can enter freely as a tourist may require a work permit or visa.

The US is a case in point. Most visitors from the UK no longer need a visa to enter the States, as long as they plan to stay no more than 90 days. But working journalists require a special 'I' classification visa. It's granted to people working on news or information programmes, whose work involves the normal news-gathering processes, like interviewing people or covering events. British journalists working for US media, on reality TV programmes or dramatic reconstructions for documentaries will find they need a different category of visa. The details can be checked on the US embassy website (www.usembassy.org.uk).

Visas for India can be obtained in person on the same day from India House in London or the Consulates General in Birmingham or Edinburgh, but you'll need a special permit if you are filming a documentary.

WHEN YOU APPLY FOR A VISA, TRY TO GET ONE THAT WILL BE VALID FOR AS LONG AS POSSIBLE AND FOR MULTIPLE ENTRY TO THE COUNTRY. YOU MAY WANT TO RETURN.

When you apply for a visa, try to get one that will be valid for as long as possible and for multiple entry to the country. You may want to return.

Whichever country you are visiting or planning to work in, the Foreign Office website (www.fco.gov.uk) is a useful first port of call. It has details of entry requirements, and web links and contact details for all countries with embassies or high commissions in the UK. There is also good advice on currencies, customs, medical precautions and the British government's assessment of the current security risks.

Driving licence

Don't forget your driving licence. Keep it with your passport. In many parts of the world you will want to hire a car, or to be able to drive a crew car. There's road safety advice and information about local traffic laws on the Foreign and Commonwealth Office website.

If you are hiring a car abroad, make sure you are fully covered when you sign the contract and that there are no exemptions or hidden costs.

Insurance

If you travel abroad regularly, you will want insurance cover against the usual hazards of travel like lost luggage and unexpected medical bills, but the travel insurance you bought for your holiday will not cover visits to war zones or natural disasters. Larger organisations will have their own cover. Check what's available to you under your conditions of employment. If you are freelance, consider taking out specialist insurance. The National Union of Journalists can advise.

What to pack

Packing for foreign work need not mean taking enough clothes for an indefinite stay. Use hotels or local laundries. Buy cheap clothes on location and discard them at the end of the trip if they won't fit into your travel bag.

Women should be aware of the sensitivities of locals in Muslim countries and wear clothes that cover their arms, legs and chest.

You will need waterproofs and sensible footwear. And emergency medical supplies.

WATER PURIFICATION TABLES ARE ESSENTIAL IN DEVELOPING COUNTRIES AND IN AREAS AFFECTED BY DISASTERS LIKE FAMINE, EARTHQUAKES AND FLOODING.

A basic medical travel pack is available from Boots and other high street chemists. You can add your own extras. Your pack should include sterile hypodermic needles – there's a high risk of infected needles in parts of Africa and the Far East. Water purification tablets are essential in developing countries and in areas affected by disasters like famine, earthquakes and flooding.

You will want good maps of the area where you are operating, and satellite phones for communications.

In war zones, your organisation will provide you with helmets and flak jackets. You should expect to travel in vehicles with some level of armour-plating, and to carry a personal GPS (global positioning system), so your employer always knows where you are.

CASE STUDY 9.1

TSUNAMI 2004 – TRAVELLING LIGHT

Sky News presenter Julie Etchingham took a sleeping bag, mosquito net, water purification tablets, medication and the kit she always had on standby as a reporter when she received the call on Boxing Day 2004 to cover the Asian tsunami. Despite the devastation across many thousands of miles, the damage was restricted to coastal areas. Many reporters found themselves in comfortable hotels just a few miles from scenes of almost unimaginable destruction. She says: 'There were still holidaymakers by the swimming pool. It was bizarre. You'd got this extraordinary disaster unfolding and people still sitting reading Jackie Collins by the pool.'

But the relative comfort didn't make the job easy, as she explains: 'It was 12 hours in the air, an hour on the ground to put your bags down and get your bearings, and then straight down to the feed point and the live point. Then I was live for about 12 hours and I did that for two weeks day in and day out.

'The other anchor who was there was Jeremy Thompson. We literally worked in a shift pattern. He would do ten hours on: I'd do 12 hours off. Then we'd just swap round, and we were also doing it for Five News, because it was just when Sky News took over the Five News contract [from ITN], and I was working as a presenter for them. We had one ridiculous afternoon when Jeremy and I were both on, on different paths to the truck on two cameras. Then I would leap over and do Sky News for the rest of the evening, so it was pretty demanding.'

Currency

Travelling abroad on holiday, you probably take foreign currency or travellers cheques, or rely on the convenience of 'hole-in-the-wall' banking. Some of the places you visit as a journalist may not offer such ready access to your money.

For longer overseas trips, you will usually want a cash advance or 'float' from your employer. Taking large cash sums in US dollars is helpful. The dollar is negotiable almost everywhere (although it's still not welcome in Cuba).

REMEMBER TO KEEP EVERY RECEIPT. YOU WILL NEED TO ACCOUNT FOR THE MONEY LATER . . . DON'T BE TEMPTED TO EXAGGERATE YOUR EXPENSES.

Remember to keep every receipt. You will need to account for the money later. We've already heard that foreign correspondents can 'live like a lord' on their allowances, but don't be tempted to exaggerate your expenses. One correspondent was found out after he claimed for a lawn-mower – he lived in a flat.

The advice to travellers on the Foreign and Commonwealth Office website (www.fco.gov.uk) includes information about foreign currency.

REMEMBER

- ➤ Keep your passport(s) and jabs up-to-date
- ➤ Check visa requirements
- ➤ Take your driving licence
- ➤ Make sure you are insured
- ➤ Keep a bag packed
- ➤ Research your destination before you leave
- ➤ Take a cash advance
- ➤ Make sure you have good communications – satellite phones and GPS.

LANGUAGE

It goes without saying that a knowledge of foreign languages is useful for anyone working abroad. You are unlikely to get a posting to Paris without workaday French. And French is spoken in many former French colonies. Spanish is useful in much of Central and Southern America (although in Brazil they speak Portuguese). In all parts of China the language is written the same, but words are pronounced completely differently in Mandarin and Cantonese speaking areas.

If you are to be based for any length of time in a non-English speaking country, you will want to learn some of the language. But the modern foreign correspondent visits so many countries that only a fanatical linguist could keep up with the demands.

Frank Gardner, BBC's Security Correspondent

The BBC's Security Correspondent Frank Gardner speaks fluent Arabic that has served him in two careers, banking and journalism: 'Almost the only sensible decision I took as a teenager was to embark on a difficult language that would then be useful. I thought, well, I could go and learn Mongolian, but it's not going to be much use outside Mongolia, whereas Arabic is a lingua franca in about 20 countries and a lot of those countries have got oil. So therefore, there should always be a job.

'I could not have done the reporting I did in Yemen or Saudi Arabia without Arabic. I've been detained in both countries several times. I was arrested by the Saudi authorities once, and without Arabic I would not have got out.'

Gardner was able to interview a kidnapper in Yemen. The man spoke no English, and Gardner had nobody with him who spoke English: 'If I hadn't had Arabic, I wouldn't have got the interview.'

Gardner uses a wheelchair after being shot by Al Qaeda in the street in Riyadh in June 2004. His cameraman Simon Cumbers died. 'I honestly thought that having Arabic was like a sort of armour, but the people who shot us were not interested in negotiation or discussion. I did plead for my life in Arabic and they didn't accept it. They decided to just put me away. But these were hardcore psychopaths. There have been many times since, for example covering the intifada in the West Bank in Gaza, where Arabic has been really, really useful.

'And also I don't like having to do journalism with a government minder beside me – a government minder/interpreter – because then you just hear the government version of events, and I prefer to be able to do it myself.

'Arabic has allowed me to do proper journalism, to go on my own to countries with a pack-up camera, that goes in the back of my rucksack, and go and do the interviews myself without having a whole big team of producers, lights and cameramen and interpreters. It's allowed me to do it on my own, which to my mind is the purest journalism.'

REMEMBER

➤   Language skills are useful – but not all languages are equally useful.

LOCAL GUIDES

Ian Woods in Basra

News organisations rely on local guides and fixers to organise their itinerary, set up interviews and smooth the way for reporters and crews. Some do little more than translate; the best are freelance journalists based in the country, with inside knowledge and contacts to help you look good. Some fixers fall into the role by chance: it can be a good source of income in an economy disrupted by war or natural disaster.

The fixers are the unsung heroes of foreign reporting – the ones left behind when the journalists have gone. Larger broadcast organisations will have a global network of them.

The most important quality in a fixer is trust. You must be able to trust them and they should trust you. Your lives may depend on it. You can expect to rely on people your organisation has used before, or trust can be built on a personal relationship. If you are charged with finding a fixer to help cover a foreign event, it is probably the most important part of the job.

Frank Gardner says he learned never to trust Saudi Government minders after he and cameraman Simon Cumbers were shot. The minders had told them the location was safe: 'They weren't dishonest. They were just incompetent, and I've always distrusted going with minders. I've avoided them whenever I can.

'The mistake we made was believing that the Ministry of Information minders knew what they were doing and were an accurate judge of the security situation in Riyadh. They weren't. They misjudged it horribly. My cameraman's dead and numerous lives were ruined because of it.'

Trusted local guides should be your surest guide to any local customs that might affect your newsgathering. For example, you should not try to arrange an interview in a Muslim country at a time that clashes with the call to prayer. And if you are in Japan, there is strong business etiquette associated with the exchange of business cards. If you have time, get some cards printed with your details on one side in English and on the other side in Japanese.

REMEMBER

➤ Only use guides you can trust
➤ Be wary of government minders
➤ Be aware of local customs.

LOGISTICS

Getting pictures and sound back from remote locations is a big headache for broadcast organisations. We've seen in Chapter 7: *Location video and sound* how wireless broadband and satellite connections have made that easier in recent years. But getting people to and from places where things are happening can still be a nightmare.

George Alagiah, of the BBC, says the importance of this was brought home to him as a correspondent in southern Africa: 'I would say television journalism is 75 per cent logistics. How do you get in, and more importantly how do you get out? More than once, in the beginning, I managed to get into places – I was one of the first people to get into Somalia, before 1992, before the invasion – and I hadn't really sorted my way out, and I was beaten on one occasion by the competition, rather annoyingly.'

Alagiah says you can do now, with two or three people, things that ten years ago might have taken five people. But you still have to get them in and out on time, and you have to think of sources of power for your technology: 'There are still large chunks of the world where you do need to take that with you, or organise it.'

Alagiah was presenting the *Six O'Clock News* in July 2006, when the BBC mounted one of its more spectacular logistics exercises. Correspondent David Shukman was live from a tiny boat on the Amazon river with a second camera mounted on a balloon, offering dramatic wide shots over the rainforest.

REMEMBER

➤ Plan the logistics of your trip
➤ Make sure you have a way of getting your story, and yourself, out of the country
➤ Consider power sources for your equipment.

THE DANGERS

Journalism is a dangerous trade in many parts of the world – and not just for foreigners going into war zones. Harassment, physical violence, kidnapping and even murder are occupational hazards for reporters covering domestic news in many countries.

The West Bank, where Israeli troops have targeted news gatherers, topped a recent list of the worst places for journalists to operate. In Colombia the media are targeted by all sides in a civil conflict. Afghanistan, Eritrea, Belarus, Burma (Myanmar), Zimbabwe, Iran, Kyrgyzstan and Cuba completed a bloody Top Ten.

In the first decade of the twenty-first century, according to the International Federation of Journalists, the number of journalists and support staff killed because of their work averaged 120 a year, with at least 150 dying in 2005 alone. Most of these were operating in their own countries – many of them murdered by people who knew they would probably get away with it (94 per cent of the murders of journalists worldwide remained unsolved in 2006).

For those on foreign assignment, there have been few more dangerous places than Iraq during the conflict that followed the US-led invasion. Western journalists were killed by roadside bombs set by insurgents and by the so-called 'friendly fire' of US troops.

And sometimes there is danger despite your own precautions. Frank Gardner says, of being shot in Saudi Arabia: 'We were very unlucky. We had government minders with us. We weren't going off on our own. We asked to film the edge of an area where there'd been trouble in the past, only if it was safe. Our minders from the Saudi Government said: "It's safe. You can come with us. No problem."

'They took us there, and quite clearly it wasn't safe and an Al Qaeda team drove past and happened to see us at that time. If we had finished filming five minutes earlier, we would have gone back to the hotel and nothing would have happened.

'They happened to see us. The cell leader said: "They're infidels. You must kill them." In a way it was a racist killing. If we'd have been brown-skinned they wouldn't have stopped. They shot us because we were white Western Europeans, not because we were journalists, but just because we were infidels, non-believers, in their minds.'

HOSTILE ENVIRONMENT TRAINING

Responsible news organisations will not send reporters or crews to war zones without hostile environment and first aid training (HEFAT). It is part of the employer's duty of care to its employees.

A HEFAT course will typically last a week, and parts of it will be conducted by former military personnel, usually SAS or Royal Marines. It will include:

- First aid, including battlefield dressings
- The use of protective equipment, including body armour
- What to do if you come under fire
- What to do in a minefield
- Dealing with roadblocks and check-points

- Vehicle hijacks
- Using body language to escape an angry crowd
- How to avoid being kidnapped
- What to do if you *are* kidnapped
- How to behave as a hostage.

Much of the course will be about improving your awareness of risk, avoiding confrontation and defusing potentially volatile situations. The experience can be frightening. There will usually be a journalist or two 'shot' during role-play simulations, and people are often reduced to tears.

Details of the organisations running courses can be found on the website of the Dart Centre for Journalism and Trauma, a body of journalists, journalism educators and medical experts. The Dart Centre tries to improve the coverage of conflict and tragedy by giving journalists a better understanding of trauma and emotional distress. They're also concerned about the emotional well-being of journalists themselves.

WAR REPORTING

Edwin Starr sang: 'War! What is it good for?' Few would disagree that the late Motown legend's answer, 'absolutely nothing', is true. But truth is the first casualty of war, and it is an uncomfortable truth that war has been very good for the careers of many broadcast reporters.

NO STORY IS WORTH A LIFE . . . DEAD JOURNALISTS DON'T TELL TALES.

Rodney Pinder, director of the International News Safety Institute, and a former international correspondent, writes on the organisation's website (www.newssafety.com): 'Successful war reporting can enhance a career like little else. But more journalists and bosses are coming around to the view that no story is worth a life. They are reining in some of the wilder impulses that can prompt home desks to drive field journalists deeper into danger to match or outstrip a competitor. Dead journalists, after all, don't tell tales.'

The Channel 4 News presenter and veteran foreign correspondent Jon Snow says in his autobiography *Shooting History*: 'War brings you extraordinarily close to the people you work with. Your team become brothers and sisters, in an intense, almost familial conspiracy both to stay alive and to tell the story of what you have seen more graphically, more coherently, more speedily than anyone else.'

Two British television journalists were killed by a roadside bomb in Iraq in May 2006. They were with American troops and were working for the US network CBS. It brought the total of media staff killed in the conflict to 127, since the invasion of 2003, according to the International Federation of Journalists.

The IFJ General Secretary Aidan White said: 'This was a tragic example of how journalists embedded with occupation forces face the same perilous conditions that have affected many local reporters.'

EMBEDDING

The idea of 'embedding' reporters with troops was not new to the invasion of Iraq. Richard Dimbleby famously flew with the RAF on raids over Germany in World War Two. He and others reported from numerous allied operations.

Gavin Hewitt

But the move by the Pentagon in 2003 to welcome embedded reporters, even laying on 'media boot-camps' (hostile environment training courses) was seen by many media commentators as an attempt by the military to control media coverage.

The BBC's Gavin Hewitt, who was embedded with the US 3rd Infantry during the invasion of Iraq, says he had no problem with the practice: 'It did give us a front row seat at the war. The advantage of embedding on this occasion was that you were right at the heart of the action, but it was always very important to be honest: when people came across to you and said "Well, how is the war going?", not to extrapolate from what you were witnessing that you knew how the war was going. You knew how your unit was going, or you might pick up a little bit from divisional level.

'I think, alongside all the other material that was coming in, embedding provided some very useful material. I would always run an embed in a conflict, but I'd also run everything else that I could as well from all the other sources, and I wouldn't, just because you've got good access, elevate that necessarily.

'I think embedding works absolutely fine. Where it becomes slightly problematical is that, of course, you are dependent on this unit for your safety, and in certain circumstances that does create a bond. But I think you have to be honest with your audience and honest with yourself.

'Nobody censored me either on radio or television. Nobody looked at my reports. So I think it was invaluable in some of the things we were able to point up, and in retrospect turned out to be very important.

'We saw a lot of civilian casualties, and I realised that the way the Americans were fighting the war, which was if they were attacked, they replied with very considerable force, that, and I said this, if the war went on too long, you would alienate the population. And of course as time has gone on, we've seen some of those problems.

'The looting was clearly an issue in the battle for hearts and minds, which I think it's just possible we might have won. The fact they took a decision to stand by as neighbourhoods were ransacked was a huge blunder.'

A US press analyst Mark Jurkowitz, of *The Boston Globe*, described the coverage provided by 'embeds' as like looking through a drinking straw: 'There is plenty of information, but it only allows us to see a narrow slice of the war.'

The ITN reporter Terry Lloyd died with two other members of his team when they were caught in cross-fire near Basra, during the invasion of Iraq in 2003. He was not embedded. Subsequent reports suggested he was killed by a US helicopter gunship.

Lloyd's TV exclusives had included the gassing by Saddam Hussein of 5,000 Kurds in Halabja in 1988, and the discovery of mass graves in Vukovar, in the former Yugoslavia in 1994. In an obituary in the *Guardian*, the former ITN editor Sir David Nicholas wrote: 'One can be certain that he would not have entered into a foolhardy enterprise.' Terry Lloyd's fate, and those of dozens of other journalists worldwide, highlight the risks of operating in a war zone outside military control.

A CLOSER LOOK   **WORKING SAFELY ABROAD – A CODE OF PRACTICE**

The International News Safety Institute – a coalition of media organisations, press freedom groups, unions and humanitarian campaigners – has developed a Code of Practice for journalists working in dangerous parts of the world.

INSI recognises that the work of journalists and media staff can never be completely safe, but says it will strive for the elimination of unnecessary risk, in peace and in war. This is their code.

1   The preservation of life and safety is paramount. Staff and freelances equally should be made aware that unwarranted risks in pursuit of a story are unacceptable and strongly discouraged. News organisations are urged to consider safety first, before competitive advantage.

2   Assignments to war and other danger zones must be voluntary and only involve experienced news gatherers and those under their direct supervision. No career should suffer as a result of refusing a dangerous assignment. Editors at base or journalists in the field may decide to terminate a dangerous assignment after proper consultation with one another.

3   All journalists and media staff must receive appropriate hostile environment and risk awareness training before being assigned to a danger zone. Employers are urged to make this mandatory.

4   Employers should ensure before assignment that journalists are fully up to date on the political, physical and social conditions prevailing where they are due to work and are aware of international rules of armed conflict as set out in the Geneva Conventions and other key documents of humanitarian law.

5   Employers must provide efficient safety equipment and medical and health safeguards appropriate to the threat to all staff and freelances assigned to hazardous locations.

6   All journalists should be afforded personal insurance while working in hostile areas, including cover against personal injury and death. There should be no discrimination between staff and freelances.

7   Employers should provide free access to confidential counselling for journalists involved in coverage of distressing events. They should train managers in recognition of post traumatic stress, and provide families of journalists in danger areas with timely advice on the safety of their loved ones.

8   Journalists are neutral observers. No member of the media should carry a firearm in the course of their work.

9   Governments and all military and security forces are urged to respect the safety of journalists in their areas of operation, whether or not accompanying their own forces. They must not restrict unnecessarily freedom of movement or compromise the right of the news media to gather and disseminate information.

10   Security forces must never harass, intimidate or physically attack journalists going about their lawful business.

➤ Foreign reporting can be dangerous – and not only in war zones

➤ Never visit a risky country without proper hostile environment training

➤ Embedding produces valuable front-line reporting, but you will be unaware of the bigger picture in the conflict.

WORKING IN A FOREIGN BUREAU

Maintaining foreign bureaux is expensive. At the height of the insurgency against the foreign occupation of Iraq, BBC world affairs editor John Simpson said (during a debate in London on Reporting the Middle East) that a quarter of the corporation's foreign news budget went on maintaining its bureau in Baghdad.

Nowadays, correspondents do not merely report from world capitals. They use the bureau as a base for covering a region of the world. Usually the office will be shared with a national broadcaster from the host country, so that technical costs, like lines and satellite feeds, can be shared. There will usually be an arrangement about using the host's audio or pictures.

For example, in Moscow, Sky News used to use the AP (Associated Press) studio. Feeds to the UK from there cost $500 a time. But then they struck a deal with NTV, a Russian commercial station. NTV now has an office at Sky News HQ in Osterley, west London. Sky News built their own small studio in Moscow, and linked it via fibre-optic cable to NTV, so there were no more lines/satellite costs.

Sometimes a bureau will be established in a country which ceases to be as significant politically as when the bureau was set up. One option is to close it down. Another is to use it as a base for covering a region of the world. That was what happened in South Africa in 1994, when the BBC's George Alagiah was there: 'The South Africa story itself had ceased to be a television story. Up to 1994 you had the Mandela factor. Then peace broke out and the story moved into parliament. My job was to turn this into an Africa bureau. It was just another place to be based, and we flew in from there to Kinshasa or Nairobi or Sudan.'

Using his specialist knowledge of African affairs (he'd been Africa Editor of a magazine), Alagiah was able to interpret events across the continent. He says old-fashioned journalistic skills were vital: 'Make the calls and make contacts.'

Informal sources like aid agencies and business people could be contacted on mobile and satellite phones, often with invaluable results: 'I spent the best part of three months [in 1997] watching the Mobutu regime in Kinshasa collapse [in the Democratic Republic of the Congo], and my best source was a businessman. I didn't name him because he didn't want to be known, but he was a trader, and so he had trucks moving up and down the country, he had little shops, offices all over the place, and he was getting information. There were times when CNN was running stuff saying such-and-such a place is surrounded by rebel troops and I'd phone him and say: "Have you got anything?" And three hours later he'd come back and say: "There's nothing. Absolutely nothing."

'So those informal things are really crucial – the information sources – and they're rarely the official ones. Almost by definition the official sources in some of these places are bankrupt. They're just not working. They're institutionally defunct.'

COVERING FOREIGN POLITICS

Covering the politics of a foreign country presents two major problems. First, most of your audience will only be interested if they believe the story is relevant to them. Secondly, the political elite in most countries will have no interest in engaging with the foreign press unless it suits their international policy aims.

We are conditioned in the UK into believing that US politics matters to us. The US is seen as the world's only global superpower. Its economics and politics impact on the world stage. So a lot of US politics is reported in Britain. But, for all the talk, mostly by British politicians, of a 'special relationship' between the two countries, public opinion in the UK is of little interest to American politicians. There is no electoral advantage in talking to the British media.

Ian Woods spent four years as Sky News' Washington correspondent, living on Capitol Hill, about a mile from the office. He says: 'We were painting in broad brush strokes – the big picture – most Sky News viewers wouldn't be interested in the minutiae of American politics.'

Ian Woods with President Clinton and President Bush

But there was a big problem: 'The attitude of the White House to foreign media was summed up during the last presidential election campaign, when one of the people closest to [President George W.] Bush was asked about the demands of the foreign media, and he said: "They're like vermin." That was their attitude. You were treated with complete disdain and you just had to smile through it.

'None of the American government departments will give foreign broadcasters the time of day. They don't see the point. (The exception is the State Department whose job is to deal with foreign affairs.) They won't answer your questions, do interviews or even return your calls. They've got enough on their plate with their own media.'

Ian Woods interviewing President Clinton and President Bush for Sky News

Sky News has the problem of not being shown in the US, so there is little awareness of what it does. Occasionally, Woods said he would introduce himself as being from 'the sister station of Fox News'. Fox News is the notoriously right-wing channel owned by Rupert Murdoch's News Corporation. Sky News is, of course, bound by the British regulatory framework of remaining politically neutral. Nonetheless, Woods says the link with Fox News played well in the 'Bible belt' of middle America. But, on the east and west coasts, where political opinion is more liberal, he would introduce himself as being from 'British TV' – although most people assumed that meant the BBC.

The BBC does have a worldwide reputation, which makes the job of BBC correspondents a little easier than their independent counterparts. BBC special correspondent Gavin Hewitt, who has also spent time in Washington, says: 'We are lucky in so far as when the White House does think about foreign broadcasters we usually are at the top of the heap.'

Ian Woods doing a PTC

But Hewitt, too, acknowledges that getting access to the Bush administration, with its emphasis on tight control and news management, was notoriously difficult: 'It is very important to work hard, and to turn up at press conferences, and to try and see people, and to, as far as you can, get within the bubble.'

Woods says: 'Washington's full of commentators, analysts and pundits so you mostly interview them. You get to know second and third tier people in the hope they'll become first tier people. You find out who talks to the Defence Secretary every day, and you talk to them rather than talking directly to him. It can be a bit frustrating because it's always second and third hand reporting.'

Hewitt says there's so much source material in English in the US that there's a danger for foreign correspondents of living off the wires and the all-news channels: 'You need to go out and realise that, outside of the coasts, middle America is a very different place, and you need to go there frequently.

'It's a challenge. We all know this country's swamped with Americana, offbeat stories about wacky America and those crazies over there and all the rest of it. It's both interesting and a kind of disservice because America's not full of crazies or full of religious fanatics or the stereotype that's developed. There's a lot of impassioned argument over there between pretty sensible people and I sometimes think our reporting is drawn to either the strident or somebody you can say is a nut with a gun. But we do ourselves a great disservice if we go for the caricatures.

'So it's actually a slightly more difficult job than often people think. People think it is more easy than elsewhere because of the language, and the culture seems so accessible. That's one of the challenges in our broadcasting – not just to reinforce the stereotypes.'

Woods agrees that getting out of the office is essential to doing the job properly: 'In four years, the United Nations was the only political story where I could truly report first hand. You were able to grab an ambassador and talk to them, which you can't do in American politics. You had the same access to the key players as the US media. In fact, I felt I was able to be more accurate than the US media, who were so caught up in the White House spin that they were blind to what opponents of the war [in Iraq] were saying.

'I was there for two months in the build-up to the invasion of Iraq [in 2003] and then I was at the Pentagon, in the bunker, covering the briefings and we had a permanent line in there.

'The best stories I did were outside Washington – hurricanes (even before Katrina), and wild fires in California. We were competing on equal terms with American journalists – in Washington you aren't on the same playing field.

'Outside Washington, I found people genuinely helpful and genuinely interested that a British broadcaster wanted to talk to them. I spoke to Arnold Schwarzenegger in California, Jeb Bush in Florida – state governors were happy to see us – and Ray Nagin, the Mayor of New Orleans after Hurricane Katrina. And we did a 15-minute sit-down with Presidents Bush senior and Clinton when they were raising money after the tsunami, because they wanted international help.'

CASE STUDY 9.2

WHEN THE LEVEE – AND THE STORY – BREAKS

Sky News' Ian Woods explains how, when a big story breaks, the correspondent drops everything – including his holiday plans. This is how he covered the aftermath of Hurricane Katrina, which devastated New Orleans and other Gulf Coast communities in August 2005.

Ian Woods and his crew with the Sky News Winnebago – $10,000 a week well spent

Ian Woods at the wheel

I was on holiday in New York to watch the US Open tennis at Flushing Meadows. I went to the theatre to see the Monty Python musical *Spamalot* and Condoleezza Rice was there. She came in for a lot of flak because she was at the theatre while this natural disaster was taking place – and I was at the same show! I'd already realised what a big story it was. We had somebody there and Sky were sending out presenters from London, so I just rang the office and said: 'This is stupid me being on holiday while we've got the biggest natural disaster in this country in years.'

So I left my wife in New York (she had to drive back to Washington), and caught a flight to Houston, which was hundreds of miles away but the nearest I could get. Then I hired a big eight-sleeper Winnebago for $10,000 a week (they were at a premium!) and drove all day to get to New Orleans. It was 300 miles or something like that. Some of the Sky crew that came out ended up sleeping in the Winnebago. All the hotel rooms for miles around were full of refugees. I was on somebody's floor in a sleeping bag in Baton Rouge 80 miles away. So every morning we had to get up at five in the morning, drive 80 miles, work for 15 hours and then drive back to Baton Rouge.

Ian Woods reporting for Sky News during a wild fire in California

FINDING THE STORIES THAT MATTER TO YOUR AUDIENCE

Finding stories is never a problem in the US. The challenge, as Gavin Hewitt says, is to avoid stereotypes. In other parts of the world the correspondent will have to persuade the foreign desk to take an interest in stories from places the audience may not have heard of.

Laurence Lee, who was based in Moscow for Sky News, says: 'You look for hard stories that really press the buttons at home. Stuff that people can relate to even if they're in a country nobody's ever heard of – heroin smuggling into Tajikistan, people trafficking, the big geopolitical stuff about the oil in Central Asia, the use of gas supplies as a political tool – stories that travel well.

Laurence Lee

'First you've got to persuade the foreign desk in London, and then make them relevant to people at home.'

Lee says there were not a lot of big stories in Moscow itself, so, again, the trick was to get out of the office – and all over his part of the world: 'I visited 13 countries. We'd work to a cycle, planning two trips every month. While the producer was planning and finding a fixer in the country where the next story was, we'd knock off a couple of stories in Moscow. I'd tell the desk: "Next week we're going to Kazakhstan, but in the meantime there's this story about a paedophile ring that's been broken up in Moscow."'

Lee says the stories always had to be relevant to Sky News' audience: 'We covered the heroin smuggling out of Afghanistan into Tajikistan and there were all these people swimming across the river that makes up the border – it's 800 km long – carrying this heroin. Then they were stuffing it in their shoes and the chassis of cars and into railway carriages. We saw somebody whose slipper was cut open by security and it was full of heroin. There's evidence that all this stuff that Westerners are shooting into their veins is being sold to drug dealers and the money is going to fund the resurgence of the Taliban in Afghanistan, which I think is pretty interesting to anybody.'

Sometimes the British angle is clear, like when British technology saved the lives of a group of Russian submariners in August 2005. A Priz submersible, with seven crew on board, was trapped by cables on the floor of the Pacific Ocean. A remote-controlled British submarine was sent in an RAF aircraft to help. Lee says: 'Obviously there was lots of interest. I did 28 lives [news reports] in a weekend. Our little studio virtually paid for itself.'

On other occasions the impact of the story took longer to sink in: 'Covering the Orange revolution in Ukraine [in 2004–5] was probably the most satisfying thing I did. It was a piece of history and I was there. But more than that it was the moment I felt I persuaded London that there were things worth reporting in this part of the world.

'It started badly. I could hear the studio in London saying: "Why should we care about Ukraine?" and a presenter says: "Well it's the biggest country in Europe and the inventor of the helicopter was Ukrainian." I'm thinking is that the best they can do – the inventor of the helicopter! And then it's: "Laurence Lee is in Kiev . . ." They've completely undersold the story, and then I've got to build it up again. There were a hundred thousand people on the streets!'

When Lee got hold of video from election monitors, showing the way the election had been rigged, the story took another turn: 'People were going round beating the opposition up, and they destroyed loads of votes and you could see it all happening. That was an exclusive, which we later let the BBC and others have.

'Within two or three days the story had developed such a head of steam that you didn't need to explain it, and it was leading the bulletins for a week.'

Stories that can be linked to events at home also have a good chance of making it. Here's another example from Laurence Lee: 'When there was a cold snap in Britain we decided to do a piece on a place that's statistically the world's coldest town. You know the sort of thing: "If you think it's cold here, have a look at this place."

'It's in Yakutia, which is a region of Siberia and it's bigger than India. So we fly six hours from Moscow to Yakutsk, the capital of Yakutia. Then we drive in a clapped-out minibus for two days to the mountains in the north of Yakutia. This town, Oymyakon, has recorded temperatures down to minus 71. It was minus 41 and people were just going about their daily business. They didn't even think it was particularly cold.

'The schools were still open. There were kids going to school. A bit of frost on the ground in Britain, and schools are closing all over the place, but here it has to be minus 45 before they think about closing them.

'We'd travelled two days to get there, spent three days living with a family, they were reindeer herders, and two days getting back, but you know it's the sort of story that people are just going to go "wow". That's really interesting the way these people live. It's part news, part *National Geographic*.'

REMEMBER

➤ Foreign bureaux are bases for covering large regions of the globe

➤ Don't rely on agency pictures and wire feeds

➤ Build your own contacts

➤ Tell the stories that matter to your audience at home

➤ Get out of the office as much as possible.

CASE STUDY 9.3   EXPLAINING THE WORLD – A FOREIGN REPORTER AT WORK

This is an example of how foreign reporting provides a window on the world. It's one of an award-winning series of five pieces Laurence Lee did for Sky News prior to the Russian presidential elections of 2004. He travelled across the country from Moscow to Vladivostok, explaining how people live and offering amazing facts – 'part news, part *National Geographic*'.

Pictures	Sound – VO and sync
 A series of shots of Lake Baikal, beginning with a wide pan	How big is Siberia? Well, consider for instance Lake Baikal. It's one of those few places to offer statistics so stupendous as to be almost meaningless. The oldest and deepest lake in the world, it's a mile down before you reach some of the hundreds of species unique to its waters. It's bigger than all the American Great Lakes put together. Only in Siberia could its size feel appropriate.

Pictures	Sound – VO and sync
 The shots include close-ups of ice	
 . . . and a hand-held zoom looking through the ice	
 Piece to camera, pointing down	Do you know, there's 20 per cent of all the world's fresh water right under there.
 Reporter's feet	It's just the weirdest place.
 Van driving across lake	During the winter the great lake becomes a road, even if the fact of that makes the mundane appear ridiculous.
 Tracking shot – driver's POV	Every spring when the ice starts to crack they lose about half a dozen cars to the depths.

Pictures	Sound – VO and sync
Driver Sergei	Sergei remained impossibly calm. Up sound of Sergei speaking (calmly)
Motorcycle and sidecar	So, if a ten-ton truck is OK, then these fellows have nothing to worry about. They live on an island, right in the middle of the lake. Up sound 'Good morning,' as they drive past the reporter
Wides of town in lake	It's almost as if they were faced with a life of exile in Siberia and decided they might as well go the whole hog.
Yelena greets her long-lost uncle	Yelena, our guide from the mainland, came in search of an uncle who hadn't surfaced for 30 years. She found him too.
Interview with Yelena's uncle	(voice fades). Translator: The one problem we have on the island is with the electricity supply. Other than that it's fine.
A street scene with electricity poles	They find a way to get supplies through when they can.

Pictures	Sound – VO and sync
Clothes shopping	There's more stuff in the shops. It just depends how much money you have.
Daytime fireworks	(Sound of fireworks) The closest town to Baikal is Irkutsk where two-thirds of a million live in slightly decadent remoteness.
Ice sculpture	
Shots of skiers	They're holding a winter games. Hardly an outsider here. Just a chance to celebrate each other.
Vox-pop	Translator: 'There's nowhere else like Siberia. It's got everything.'
Vox-pop	Translator: 'Siberia may be cold, but it's very beautiful.'

Pictures	Sound – VO and sync
 Wide shot of Irkutsk	(Local music in background) Some of the earliest inhabitants here were former slaves, escaping the Tsarist autocracy of Western Russia.
 People shots	These then are the descendants of Siberia's pioneers, whose exploration of the east mirrored the conquest of the American west.
 Railway tracking shot	The Trans-Siberian railway was built at the turn of the last century to make travel easier for explorers and peasants alike,
 Wide shot of train on mountain pass	
 Interiors of train	. . . and today our carriage is still awash with long-distance human traffic.
 Family in carriage	A family dividing its time between Russia and China – three days from Beijing to Irkutsk.

Pictures	Sound – VO and sync
Businesswomen on train	In the next compartment some local businesswomen who've been buying Chinese clothes to sell to the Siberians.
Getting off the train	(Up sound of footsteps) We got off the train at the southern tip of Lake Baikal. They were already waiting for us.
Trackside fish salesman	This is smoked omul, a relative of the salmon, and it's the staple food and the staple income source for many. (Upsound trading) It's only five minutes till the train moves on. They need this trade to survive. Omul's dirt cheap. They have to sell fast.
Train departs	Siberia has always been synonymous with suffering.
Close-up of local woman	But these people have no-one to complain to.
Wide of woman on fish stall	They seem to feel no self-pity.

Pictures	Sound – VO and sync
Pull focus from woman in foreground to reporter eating omul	And they refuse to submit to the harshness of the place. But they have each other and of course they have the great lake.
Reverse of Lee looking out over the lake	Laurence Lee, Sky News, Lake Baikal in Eastern Siberia.

CONCLUSION

Foreign reporting can occasionally be glamorous. It is often dangerous. It requires a level of professional commitment beyond the routine of turning up at the office every day and being sent out on a story.

Even foreign stories need to justify their place in the bulletin. If you are based in a foreign bureau, you are the eyes and ears of your organisation in that region of the world – not just the city where you are based. You need to identify and report stories from many countries, and work out the logistics of how to cover them. Or you might be 'parachuted' into a big global story, where you will be pitted against not just your own country's but the world's media.

Foreign correspondents are part of a journalistic elite – even an aristocracy. To maintain their position most of them work long hours in difficult and occasionally dangerous conditions. If you aspire to join them, weigh up the impact on your lifestyle. Don't expect a settled home life, or to see much of your children.

FURTHER READING

Many foreign correspondents have written their memoirs. The following are all entertaining and informative.

Adie, Kate (2002) *The Kindness of Strangers*, London: Hodder.

Alagiah, George (2001) *A Passage to Africa*, London: Little, Brown.

Alagiah, George (2006) *A Home from Home: From Immigrant Boy to English Man*, London: Little, Brown.

Hewitt, Gavin (2005) *A Soul on Ice*, London: Macmillan.

Marr, Andrew (2005) *My Trade*, London: Macmillan.

Simpson, John (1998) *Strange Places, Questionable People*, London: Pan.

Simpson, John (2001) *A Mad World, My Masters*, London: Pan.

Simpson, John (2002) *News from No-Man's Land: Reporting the World*, London: Pan.

Simpson, John (2003) *The War Against Saddam: Taking the Hard Road to Baghdad*, London: Pan.

Snow, Jon (2005) *Shooting History*, London: Harper.

Tumber, Howard and Webster, Frank (2006) *Journalists Under Fire: Information War and Journalistic Practices*, London: Sage. An examination through first-hand testimony of the way journalists operate in war zones.

WEB LINKS

www.dartcenter.org. A global resource for journalists covering violent and traumatic events.

www.fco.gov.uk. The Foreign and Commonwealth Office site, detailing the precautions to be taken when visiting foreign countries.

www.ifj.org. The site of the International Federation of Journalists, with updates on the number of journalists and media workers killed worldwide.

www.newssafety.com. The site of the International News Safety Institute.

www. usembassy.org.uk. For details of US visa classifications.

CHAPTERTEN

GOING LIVE

Mark Austin, presenter of ITV News

When Mark Austin took over as the presenter of ITV News' main 10.30 programme at the start of 2006, he said: 'I want to take the programme to the story.' It was a strong assertion of the importance of being live at the scene of events.

As early as the 1980s, there was a saying in the US: 'If it ain't live it don't jive.' It is often true in television that where the US leads Britain follows. That has never been truer than in the growth of live coverage of news events. It predates the advent of multiple 24-hour news channels, and was made possible by new technology that enabled live links to be established quickly and relatively cheaply from remote locations. One of the biggest factors was the widening availability of satellite time, which used to be expensive and only available to national networks. Now satellite links are so commonplace that most people working in regional TV newsrooms in the UK cannot remember the time when they were not a daily feature of their programmes.

When the Americans were setting the trend for going live, broadsheet news values were not in vogue. Even at network level US stations have never majored in foreign news – unless it's news from a country where US troops are fighting a war. What we call tabloid news was believed to be what audiences wanted. So, Rick Sanchez on Channel Seven in Miami earned a reputation for chasing ambulances to report via live links from south Florida's crime scenes. He said: 'I just go where the bodies are warmest.' It led to an undiluted agenda of often sensational crime coverage where the significance or importance of the story itself was valued less than the live drama it produced. Ambulances were highly prized. Bodies even more so.

This approach has definitely crossed the Atlantic, even if its realisation is rarely quite so tabloid. We don't chase ambulances, but editors do appear to value live coverage simply because it is live.

THE ART OF THE TWO-WAY

The ability to talk live on air and unscripted has never been more highly prized. It is no longer the preserve of presenters, but has to be practised by all reporters in radio and TV, usually in the form of live two-ways – question and answer sessions with the studio – or the 'throw', where the studio 'throws' to the reporter who picks up the story and runs with it.

It was a live unscripted two-way that landed Andrew Gilligan and the BBC in such trouble with the Labour government, and led to the resignation of the

BBC's Chairman and Director General (see Case study 3.3). Among the new BBC guidelines arising from the case is this: 'We should not normally use live unscripted two-ways to report allegations.' But that hasn't stopped the widespread use of two-ways on the BBC and elsewhere for all other types of reporting.

The measure of great presenters has always been the ability to ad lib and to cope with changing events – and studio mishaps. Reading an autocue convincingly was never enough, and now reporters too need the same live skills as studio presenters.

You will have an ear-piece through which you can hear studio output. You should hear all the studio sound, including instructions from the gallery, but without your own contribution. This is known as *clean feed*. The clean feed lets you speak naturally in response to questions or instructions from the studio without hearing yourself back.

Without clean feed, a reporter on a satellite link hears their own voice a second or two after they have spoken. The delay is caused by the time it takes for the signal to reach the satellite and return to earth. Hearing your own words coming back at you is most disconcerting. It is almost impossible to broadcast for any length of time under these conditions.

Reporter Steve Lee of Sky Sports News has suffered from this problem several times: 'It's one of the worst things that can happen on a two-way. You almost inevitably stumble over your words because it's impossible to think.'

If an engineer has accidentally flicked the wrong switch and you can hear a delayed feed of your own voice, there are a couple of ways to cope. You can remove your earpiece, or turn it down if you can find the volume control. If you need to listen for the next question there is no choice but to soldier on, or apologise and explain on air. Audiences are more forgiving than you might think; they quite enjoy a glimpse of 'behind the scenes' difficulties.

So, technical hitches can spoil the flow of your report as well as the difficulty of remembering what you need to say. How then do you gain the fluency and confidence to go live? How do you work without a script but still get it right?

ON-AIR MILES

Five's Kirsty Young: 'There's no substitute for on-air miles'

Kirsty Young, the presenter of Five News on terrestrial television and *Desert Island Discs* on BBC Radio 4, has watched the trend for live reporting grow: 'The great thing about 24-hour news and radio stations like Five Live is that there are now some crackingly fluid individuals who can stand and just tell you a story.'

Young advises broadcasters to start in radio where you can learn a lot quickly: 'Don't be seduced by the glamour and apparent big bucks of television. In radio nobody is worried about making hugely expensive mistakes, so you're more likely to be given your head.'

She says the experience she gained at BBC Radio Scotland helped her get used to being live on air, and today's best reporters have done the same: 'They've earned what I call their "on-air miles" because they have been on air, and there's nothing really to substitute for that. I think that one of the great things the 24-hour era is throwing up is people who are very fluent. For me, being on radio for a few years really helped me overcome the idea of simply talking. That's what we do for a living – quite an intimidating thought, when you think about it – communicating. Being on air really helps.'

Hospital radio and community stations are good places to start, because keen volunteers are always welcome. Your ambition may lie in being a news reporter, but don't restrict yourself to just doing the news. Offer to present music or sports shows, anything where you're just talking, mostly without a script. Clock up your own 'on-air miles'.

ENJOY YOURSELF

Simon Cole, Deputy Head of Sky News

Simon Cole, Deputy Head of Sky News, says on-air reporting is about confidence, and he encourages their reporters to enjoy what they do.

He's suspicious of training reporters to perform, and critical of the BBC: 'Sometimes they go through the BBC machine and they come out without a lot of character. They have these trained movements, like the 'behind me wooden move' – like the guy does on *Dead Ringers* when he's doing his Tony Blair impression. They have to do things that way – you have to check this, you have to do that – and you actually inhibit sometimes the reporter's natural effervescence or exuberance.

'What I've always said to my lot is, forget all about the BBC. I don't want you to do BBC. Do Sky, which is go out there and have fun, because if you're enjoying the story, if you're really into it, the viewer will pick up on it.

'Our people are told to just be natural and give it some. I think that's important. The whole image of Sky is of a vibrant throbbing station.'

REMEMBER

> ➤ Talking live and unscripted is an important skill for a broadcaster
> ➤ You can only get better with experience – your on-air miles
> ➤ Act naturally and enjoy it – don't appear wooden.

CASE STUDY 10.1 — THE IMPORTANCE OF GREAT PICTURES

When a series of explosions devastated an oil depot in Hemel Hempstead in December 2005, it was described as the biggest fire ever seen in Europe in peacetime. 24-hour news wasn't around during the Great Fire of London, so that claim may never be proved, but it was certainly the biggest fire ever seen on television. Buncefield was also the biggest news story to break on a Sunday morning since the death of Diana, Princess of Wales.

Sky News' Geoff Meade was at home in bed and awoken by the explosion: 'I thought it was a plane crash. You are at home with your loved ones, and you convince yourself we've just escaped another Lockerbie.'

Professionalism – the urge to find out what was happening and report it – kicked in within seconds: 'When I looked out of my bathroom window it seemed like the whole horizon was on fire.'

He immediately called the newsdesk and was on air in minutes: 'It was a different experience because the story had come to me. It crossed the line between the professional and the personal.'

Meade's telephone reports included vox-pops with guests evacuated from a hotel: 'I just thrust my mobile phone out and said: "Would you speak to Sky News please?" What I'd have done if they'd told me to bugger off I daren't think.'

Duty editor Roger Protheroe recalls: 'Within 45 minutes we had viewers' video off phones. We had so many images we did a whole package on them later in the day. Some of the stills were sensational. It's the biggest response we've ever had on any domestic story.'

BBC TV received their first picture, a still, at 6.16 a.m. – about 13 minutes after the explosion – and the first moving image seven minutes later. There had been no on-air request for pictures at that stage. They received 15,000 images throughout the day.

Once satellite trucks were in place, broadcasters soon had live feeds showing pictures of the blazing depot and the plume of smoke spreading across the Home Counties. Those pictures dominated the next several hours of live coverage to such an extent that viewers rarely saw the people in the studio anchoring the programme. On Sky News, it was over an hour after the live pictures began rolling that the first studio face appeared. It was Political Editor Adam Boulton explaining why his Sunday morning programme would not take place as normal. His studio guest, the cabinet minister Dr John Reid, commented on the incident and said: 'I understand fully why you might leave to nip over for a press conference or whatever.'

Sky News presented viewers with information as they received it, running the latest video in a split screen alongside the live shot. They ran uncut rushes of vox-pops with witnesses, including the reporter asking an interviewee to move so 'we'll just get the flames over your shoulder', and thanking a contributor: 'Cheers, mate, lovely talking to you.' The reporter Enda Brady had been with Sky just three months and did not realise the vox-pops were going to be 'hot-rolled': 'It was an eye-opener for me. When you're doing voxes you think you're just after three lovely clips and nobody will hear the other stuff. I'm still learning the Sky way of doing things. But it worked. It added immediacy to the story.'

Enda Brady

Although the studio presenters were not seen as the story developed, reporters *were* shown, even when what they were reporting was their own predicament. Geoff Meade told the studio – and viewers: 'The police are quite adamant our satellite truck has to relocate, so we might not be able to bring you these pictures for much longer. The police are saying it is hazardous to us to be in this area, so they are evacuating the area around Leverstock Green.' His words added to the drama, and gave viewers a powerful impression of how events develop during a large-scale emergency.

Meade sums it up: 'On a story like that the normal rules of neat and tidiness go out the window.' His own bathroom window perhaps.

The Deputy Head of Sky News Simon Cole was delighted: 'Yes, we were lucky, but, you know, old hack gets out of bed in his pyjamas and does the business. It was fantastic and led the way.'

PUSHING THE LIMITS

Technology is making it easier to report and present from live locations. Mark Austin made good on his promise to take the ITV News programme to the story during Israel's attacks on Hezbollah fighters in Lebanon in summer 2006: 'Part of the job that I took was whenever possible to present the programme from locations. We did it for two weeks in first Beirut and then Tyre. I just think it adds something to the viewer. I am then able to report as well, so I can double up. That would not have happened five–ten years ago. Now we try and do it more often than not, if there's a big breaking story.'

On 24-hour news channels, 'lives' fill time as well as being a quick and easy way to update a story. And if your reporter and satellite truck are already in position, they are cheap too. Sky News has set daring precedents in the use of two-ways. Reporters are often required to speak to camera when important events are imminent, rather than just after they have happened, keeping the audience in a state of heightened expectation even before a crucial court verdict is announced or a key politician walks out of an international conference. Keeping talking like this requires great fluency and huge amounts of confidence.

Jeremy Thompson, a 30-year veteran as a foreign correspondent with ITN and Sky News, is one of the 24-hour channel's most senior presenters. He's not afraid to take risks – to busk it. When US and British troops invaded Iraq in 2003, Thompson showed daring in his approach both to covering the war – and to what he could get away with on air.

I just went in with a truck, crossed the border illegally into Kuwait and just busked it. We weren't embedded. We just busked it, with me and the engineers on the truck, a cameraman and a producer, and we just rock' n'rolled. When we were on the road to Baghdad, as soon as we got across, we started interviewing Iraqis as the British troops were coming in. I heard in my talkback that in London they had Geoff Hoon on, and they were talking to him, and I just shouted down the line: 'Give him to me, give me the Defence Secretary.'

So they said: 'Oh, Defence Secretary, Jeremy Thompson is in Iraq,' and he obviously went: 'Oh dear.'

I said: 'I'm surrounded by Iraqis. You've just sent your troops in to liberate and save them, and they don't seem that pleased . . . so what have you got to say to them?'

ART OR ARTIFICE?

As well as their obvious value in filling time on rolling news, two-ways are a way for correspondents to expand coverage of important stories on terrestrial television's main bulletins. This means facts and analysis should be saved for the two-way, not repeated from the package.

Some viewers, believing themselves 'media-savvy', think the reporters on two-ways are so fluent that they must have autocue. They almost never do. Others wonder whether the questions and answers are rehearsed. The truth is there is rarely time for a full run-through, although the reporter will have suggested the questions to the producer or presenter before they go on air. The pretence of spontaneous questioning is artificial. It is not the same as an interview with a politician or even a regular contributor. The reporter may have written their answers before delivering them live, and it is not uncommon to see reporters pacing alongside satellite trucks trying to remember their lines. But usually there is no time for that.

So it is that reporters are valued today as much for their competence in live, unscripted broadcasts as for their ability to tell a story in a well-crafted package. But this doesn't mean writing skills are any less valuable. The best exponents of the two-way speak as they would write for broadcast. They construct sentences in a way that would sound right on air whether they wrote them down first or not. Most of the best do it well because they have had years of practice at it. Although the growing demand for live contributions is a relatively modern phenomenon, many experienced older hands in TV newsrooms found it a straightforward skill to accomplish. It was almost as if it saved them the trouble of having to bother writing things down.

The BBC's Martin Bell was a master of this art, which is probably why he became effective as a straight-talking politician later in his career. In fact, his preferred method of working on location – even on news packages – was not to commit the words to paper. He would pace up and down collecting his thoughts as the picture editor compiled a sequence. Then on cue he would deliver flowing prose. His words had never appeared on the screen of a word processor nor even the back of a fag packet. The value of Bell's approach was that, if the words were easy to remember and deliver without writing them down, they would be easy for the audience to understand. For a professional with many years in the field this process worked superbly, and the words rarely failed to enliven and enhance the pictures. Bell spoke of his words 'caressing' the pictures. For newcomers it is a difficult skill to master. But worth trying – if only as an exercise in plain speaking.

The growing importance of being available to 'go live' has thrown up another dilemma which Martin Bell summarised, eloquently as ever, in the BBC publication *50 years of BBC Television News*. Despite his 'lucky' white suit, Bell was injured by shrapnel in Sarajevo in 1992. But he looks back fondly on that period in his career as a 'golden age':

I see the war in Bosnia as belonging to a golden age of journalism. It was the last one we could report in the time-honoured way, by going into the field and finding things out, making sense of them and reporting them in a considered but rapid manner. This is hard to do in the age of rolling news, which requires its practitioners to be tethered for long periods to the satellite dish, to answer questions from distant anchors.

Martin Bell, a master of the unwritten script: 'The war in Bosnia belonged to a golden age of journalism.'

Bell admits his comments may be 'an old soldier's prejudice'. But his concerns are supported by another term, probably too inelegant for Martin Bell, used by a lot of industry insiders to describe today's satellite reporters. They are known as 'dish monkeys'. The expression does no justice to the performing skills of the modern TV correspondent, but it underlines how they operate. 'Tethered to the satellite dish', they are fed titbits of information by producers and researchers. Sometimes those other journalists are in the field working alongside them, but often the material is being gathered from wires and other sources thousands of miles away back in the studio. The reporters then repeat what they've just been told by somebody else. Perhaps 'dish parrot' would be a better description than 'dish monkey'.

Sky News's crime correspondent Martin Brunt echoes Bell's fears:

> I spend a lot of time standing outside somewhere reporting the elements of a story that isn't moving at all and sometimes the reason it's not moving is because I'm not able to get away from being on air. I remember [*when the failed London transport bombers were arrested*] monitoring the siege in west London, and they kept me talking, speculating about what was going on. I'd been talking for about 20 minutes and Scotland Yard had sent somebody down to see me. I could tell that they had something to tell me and they were hovering at my shoulder and I just said [*to the studio*]: 'If you can go away for two minutes and talk to somebody else I might have something to tell you.'
>
> It was a very senior guy [*press officer*] from Scotland Yard and he had a piece of paper in his hand. He did enough for me to get a sense he was there. He moved slightly into my eye-line, and I had to engineer myself away from being on air.

The idea of speaking on air unscripted is of course nothing new to those who make a living from sports commentary. The late John Arlott is revered among cricket fans. His informed description, flawless analysis and much-mimicked Hampshire burr helped make radio's *Test Match Special* a broadcasting institution around the world. When he was asked for the secret of his art, he said that even though he was speaking live he always worked out exactly how his sentence would end before he started it. Sound advice to anyone in live broadcasting.

Arlott was of course a fine writer. Imagine the pictures to accompany this description of the day Geoffrey Boycott scored his hundredth first class century. Boycott was the first to achieve that feat in a Test match, and he did so at Headingley in his native Yorkshire in August 1977.

'All Yorkshire knew he would do it, so they came in their thousands, and long before play began the dense, patient crowds in their long crocodiles to the turnstiles ensured that the gates would be closed.'

It could be a good descriptive piece of radio, or the opening of a TV news package. In fact, it is from Arlott's report in the *Guardian*. As we say, he was a good writer.

REMEMBER

➤ Be bold – don't be afraid to push the limits

➤ Use clear, concise language at all times

➤ Beware of being tied to the dish.

A CLOSER LOOK

John Sergeant, former
Senior Political
Correspondent at
the BBC and ITN

THE TWO-WAY – A MASTERCLASS

John Sergeant has been a fixture of British broadcasting for more than three decades. He was a foreign correspondent on BBC radio, the BBC's Chief Political Correspondent and later Independent Television News' Political Editor. He was live on air outside the British Embassy in the final days of Margaret Thatcher's premiership, when he was famously pushed aside by her press secretary Sir Bernard Ingham as she emerged from the building. The British Press Guild voted it the most memorable broadcast of 1990, ahead of footballer Paul Gascoigne's tears at the Italia 90 World Cup.

He remains a popular guest on entertainment shows like *Have I Got News for You* and *Room 101* and on Radio 4 quizzes and chat shows.

He called his autobiography *Give Me Ten Seconds* – a reference to the precise time-keeping needed by broadcasters on two-ways. Here he gives us some tips gleaned from those hundreds of hours waiting outside No. 10 Downing Street and in the corridors of power.

If you tell a professional broadcaster they have ten seconds to go, it isn't a vague discussion. That's it. It's got to be ten seconds. I used to find, if I was doing a two-way for ITN, that I might be given one minute 50 seconds in all. I might be given two minutes, or I might be given one minute ten seconds for the whole thing, and I found it extremely difficult to be counted through all that. Sometimes they give you, 'you've done a minute', and then 'ten . . . nine . . . eight', as if you're some sort of machine. You're not a machine, but it's useful to know when you're about to get to the end, and I used to find it was good if someone just said in my ear, 'ten'. Sometimes they'd say, 'ten, John' or 'John, it's ten', and it was enough for me to realise that I've got to wrap up.

I would try and work out a final sentence, so if you were discussing some particular problem facing the Prime Minister, or some decision that had to be taken, you might then say: 'But whatever happens he must decide by the weekend,' or 'This is the sort of subject that has got to be resolved quickly.' You'd know that was going to be your final thought.

What you can't do is end your interview, your two-way, on some kind of vague or pathetic note. It's got to have something quite firm or definite. It's useful, when you're trying to work these things out in your mind, to have a very solid and strong thought to end on.

You'd usually have the sentences you would need at the beginning of the answer: 'The key thing to remember about this is . . .'

You'd then decide how much history you'd give: 'This is a problem they had to cope with two or three years ago . . .' or whatever it was.

You'd then know as you were moving towards the end of your reply that you had to reach firm ground. So you can go off into the sea, you can do all sorts of strange things, you can have all sorts of diversions, but you then come back to the main point. And that usually is an answer to the question.

So, that's how you work it out. But if you work out every sentence and try and memorise it, then you can't succeed.

So, you've got to allow yourself that quite a lot of that answer is going to be extempore. And why do you do that? Is it out of bravado? No, it's because you want to do really well, and to do really well in a two-way, you can't prepare it. You've got to wing it, because then you might be just surprisingly articulate, and the only way you can do that is to be under a great deal of pressure.

You don't quite know what you're going to say, and the audience sense that you're thinking about what you're going to say, and that you're reaching the main point, like in an ordinary conversation. If you do that, the listeners are following you very closely.

It's a curiosity about my trade, but in newsrooms they tend to be just looking at you on the screen and seeing Big Ben behind you or something, but real listeners are actually listening to your words.

So it's very important that you shouldn't look nervous; you shouldn't look as if you're under terrific pressure; but the words that you're using and the thoughts that you've got are absolutely vital, because, amazingly and wonderfully, the audience stretched across the British Isles are listening very carefully to what you're saying. And that's the fun of it.

The lessons from John Sergeant's masterclass include:

1 Don't look nervous
2 You can't memorise every sentence in advance
3 'Winging it' makes you perform at your best
4 Know how you are going to end
5 Always end on a firm and definite note.

THE THROW

When the studio 'throws' to a reporter on location, the idea is that the reporter will pick up the story and run with it. Usually that involves a live piece to camera, but there can be other elements.

From a radio car, you will be able to report live and play in your own audio clips – an interview perhaps or some actuality at a scene.

Live location mixing of television pictures is available on some satellite trucks and in self-contained, fully portable systems. Usually though, reporters will link to video played in through the gallery back at the studio. This may be rushes, an interview clip or a cut package sent back moments earlier. The reporter needs to give the gallery a cue for them to play in the clip. This will be a form of pre-arranged words ('as he told me a few moments ago . . .' or 'says he's not happy about it . . .', for example).

Sometimes the director will 'float in' pictures of whatever the reporter is talking about. If the reporter has a monitor he will see the shots and be able to talk over them, matching words to the changing shots. If there's no monitor, there'll be an instruction from the gallery ('on pictures' or 'on video') and the reporter will hear that via the earpiece, and ad lib over the pictures. This requires good communication between gallery and location, and an understanding from both ends of exactly how long the pictures are and what they show.

➤ The key to a successful throw is good communication between the studio and the location

➤ Know your in and out cues.

EDITORIAL JUSTIFICATION FOR THE 'LIVE'

While live reporting has added immediacy and freshness to television news coverage, there has to be an editorial justification for it. Let's inject a note of caution from BBC broadcaster John Humphrys. He summed up the dangers of being too obsessed with 'going live' in his 1999 book *Devil's Advocate* (Hutchinson).

Television news does too many things because they are possible rather than because they are necessary. I have never understood why we must 'go live' to a reporter on the scene two seconds after we have seen the report. You know the sort of thing.

'Over now to Kate for the very latest. Kate, what's happening?'

'I've just told you what's happening in my report, cloth ears, and if you weren't listening properly I'm buggered if I'm going to tell you again.'

Sadly they never do say that, but I live in hope.

Unknown to the famous and famously irascible Mr Humphrys, a version of his imagined scenario had taken place a couple of years earlier in a lesser outpost of the very organisation for which he works. A reporter left standing in front of a camera after nightfall in a snow storm at a crime scene was asked the ubiquitous: 'What's happening now?' on a live outside broadcast for *BBC Midlands Today*. His accurate reply: 'Not a fat lot!' earned a serious rebuke from the editor.

THINKPIECE

WHEN LIVE COVERAGE DISTORTS THE STORY – AN ETHICAL QUESTION

The role of the journalist as an interpreter of information is thrown into sharp focus in war. Pictures – and opportunities for 'lives' – may be available from one side of the conflict and not the other. This dilemma arose during the first Gulf War, and was underlined by the invasion of Iraq 12 years later.

In 1991, for the first time in an international conflict, press conferences – by Allied commanders – were broadcast live. Viewers saw live reports from correspondents in war zones, including those in Baghdad, though never from the Iraqi front line. The absence of an accurate Iraqi perspective, and the inaccuracy of some of the reporting meant the picture was never complete.

A reporter for CNN in Tel Aviv appeared live, wearing a gas mask, saying there had been a Scud missile gas attack. In fact, there had been no gas in the missile, which carried a conventional explosive warhead. This was misleading and dangerous reporting. The Israeli government had suggested it would respond with nuclear weapons if there were chemical or biological attacks on its citizens. US President George Bush had already said he was getting some of his information about the war from CNN before it was confirmed by the Pentagon. If the Israeli Prime Minister had been watching CNN, might he have pressed the nuclear button? We know of course he did not, but the thought that he might have done surely brings into the sharpest focus the need to check facts – even in the heat of a major incident.

During that war, a newspaper reporter, appearing on CNN's *Larry King Live*, remarked that it was all very well showing live press conferences, but exposing the mechanics of journalism did the viewers no favours. He said it would be like giving his notebook to his paper's readers and telling them to make sense of it for themselves.

There was precious little interpretation as American generals proudly showed video of laser-guided bombs destroying military targets – and scrupulously avoided any pictures that suggested real people were being killed. The role of the journalist – either during or after those news conferences – should have been to put the 'smart-bomb' pictures in context, pointing out that most of the Allied ordnance was not smart at all. Conventional weapons were being used to carpet-bomb Iraqi troops on the ground. But there were no pictures of that. So, the military successfully commandeered the airwaves – with the consent of the broadcasters.

During the Invasion of Iraq in 2003, embedded journalists moving with US and British forces were able to report live from the battlefront. But again there were few pictures from the Iraqi side. (BBC correspondent Gavin Hewitt discusses his role as an 'embed' in Chapter 9: *Foreign reporting*.)

It is an abiding criticism of war coverage that journalists show the 'bang-bang' – the guns and missiles being fired, but not the consequences of the weapons on human beings. There are two reasons for this. One is practical – if the camera crew is with an army firing weapons, they are unlikely to be able to cross the lines to gather pictures from the other side. There have been few recent conflicts where the media on both sides have had equal access to the military. The second reason for not showing the carnage of war is an unwillingness to offend viewers. Judgements of taste and decency are made all the time by editors and producers, and they don't always get it right. Strong writing can allude to what the viewers are not seeing without showing the most gruesome images.

THERE HAVE BEEN FEW RECENT CONFLICTS WHERE THE MEDIA ON BOTH SIDES HAVE HAD EQUAL ACCESS TO THE MILITARY.

Broadcast journalists have an ethical responsibility to report impartially, independent of external pressures, and a legal responsibility to be politically neutral. That is difficult to do and harder to maintain. Facts, we are told, are sacred. 'Opinions,' Clint Eastwood says as the San Francisco cop Dirty Harry, 'are like assholes. Everybody has one.' But inevitably, opinions come into play when journalists select which facts to report and which sources to quote.

Presenters of rolling news programmes, particularly on radio, often find themselves commenting on the news, but they have to be careful not to be involved in political controversy. Shelagh Fogarty, BBC Radio Five Live breakfast presenter says: 'We make our feelings known on subjects, but not political subjects, not subjects that are sensitive. We make our feelings known about lifestyle things, because that's what people want to hear.'

Challenging facts, and their sources, and separating them from propaganda and spin are among the first duties of any journalist. Establishing the 'truth' of any situation is a near-impossible goal. Truth is almost always subjective. But striving for an accurate and balanced account is fundamental to the job.

PRESENTING LIVE

Just as reporters have had to learn the traditional presenter's skills of talking live and unscripted, so today's presenters have to be accomplished live reporters. Interviewing contributors and linking to reporters and packages are only the beginning of it.

Jeremy Thompson has reported live from wars in Kosovo and Iraq, from the devastation of the 2004 Tsunami, and from the middle of the Mall during the Queen's Golden Jubilee parade in 2003. Sky News uses a digilink – a radio link to the camera, freeing it from the need for an umbilical cord to the satellite dish. It also frees the presenter to be much more ambitious, as Thompson explains:

Jeremy Thompson of Sky News: 'Look there's some people over there. Let's go talk to them.'

If you get it right and you get the kit in place and you've got the right people out there telling the story and you've got a good story to tell, it works. As long as you tell people what you're doing. As long as the audience know – don't worry about the cameraman, he's got to come with me – talk to the audience. The key thing about the presentation business is as long as you're not fazed by it, as long as you're not bothered, they won't be. The one thing you don't want to do is to embarrass the people who're watching or make them feel uncomfortable. My view is if you cock it up, just say: 'Sorry, bit of a mistake.' Just get them along with you. I'll say: 'Look, there's some people over there, lets go talk to them,' and go. That might not always work, but take people with you, take people on the ride. As long as they're on a voyage of discovery with you, as long as you know what you're doing and you're confident about it and you're not fazed, they won't be. And I think people like the idea of 'bloody hell we're there, wow', and peering round corners, picking our noses and finding out what's going on. When there's a big story it clearly is hugely compelling. The number of tales I've had back, we all have, of people who said they had no intention [of watching], but suddenly a big story comes up and they're sat there rooted, and it's actually better drama than fictional drama on telly.

Julie Etchingham presented with Thompson from the disaster relief centre in Phuket after the 2004 Tsunami:

Most of the presenters here have had experience as reporters. If you are in the field as a presenter, you naturally use a more fluid language. If you are describing a scene and you're doing much more stuff live, then the language used is inevitably different. If you look at the way a link into a carefully crafted package is written for the 10 O'Clock News on the BBC, it is in very different terms to the way I would read a link or say a link into a package if I was in the field. It's much more driven by the spoken word.

That has big upsides and big downsides, because it can get much more woolly and can get very sloppy. But at the same time if it's done well, and you're in the field where the story's happening, it can be far more compelling. So actually you think much more about the spoken word and the way it's expressed, rather than crafting beautiful sentences if you've got all day with just one link to write for a package. So it's a different approach totally.

The 2004 Tsunami presented particular problems of tone and content. Etchingham was on air 'living the story', gathering information as teams of reporters in the field uncovered the enormity of the event:

Julie Etchingham of Sky News: 'The language evolves, because you're finding out the facts the whole time.'

The language evolves, because you're finding out the facts the whole time, and actually finding the right language to describe it, particularly something like that where it is so harrowing. It's very easy to suddenly start talking about a disaster in glib terms, frankly, because you're saying it hour in, hour out, and you're talking about the endless figures of the death toll rising. It's very easy just to get glib about it, and you have to make sure that you're always conveying the scale of the story, without slipping into anything that becomes a cliché.

3G PHONES

Mobile phones can be used for the first live television reports from a breaking news story. Although the technology has revolutionised the ease with which a reporter can go on air, using it is a comparatively primitive experience. There will be no talk back or clean feed. Instead the telephone screen shows a tiny thumbnail picture of whatever you are pointing the phone at (yourself, if it's a piece to camera) and the wider screen shows programme output. As soon as you see yourself on the bigger screen, start talking. The system is rough round the edges, but it works.

REMEMBER

➤ New technology allows you to be more ambitious

➤ Don't make the audience feel uncomfortable

➤ Apologise if there's a mistake – then move on

➤ Take the audience with you

➤ Find the right language for the story

➤ Don't use clichés.

CASE STUDY 10.2   EVENT TELEVISION – WHEN ONLY LIVE COVERAGE WILL DO

Some news events so grip the public imagination that live coverage is the only way to watch them. They become a shared audience experience. Mobile phone updates or downloading video-on-demand cannot compete with live viewing.

These events are rare. A survey by Cardiff University researchers of the three British rolling news channels that were on air in 2005 said that the phrase 'breaking news' is often little more than a device for maintaining a sense of drama. They showed that, even if we accept the channels' definition of breaking news, it forms only a small part of their content (3.6 per cent during their two-week survey).

But when there is massive public interest, the battle between Sky News and BBC News 24 is fiercely competitive. After the ITV News Channel closed at the end of 2005, the two big fish were left in the sea. And, appropriately, it was a huge sea creature that provided their first head-to-head encounter. The appearance of a northern bottlenose whale in the heart of London was a once-in-a-lifetime story.

The whale, normally a deep sea creature, found itself off course and stranded in the River Thames. On Friday, 20 January 2006, the story was presented as a

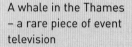
A whale in the Thames – a rare piece of event television

great novelty. But it soon became clear that the mammal was in distress and in danger of running aground. Readers of the next morning's newspapers, and people who'd heard about the whale on radio or seen it on TV the night before, tuned into rolling news channels on the Saturday morning to see what was happening – and they witnessed an extraordinary day-long rescue attempt.

Events unfolded within a timescale that almost perfectly fitted a leisurely Saturday afternoon's viewing. By lunchtime the volunteers from British Divers Marine Life Rescue had succeeded in approaching the whale in shallow water, calming it and surrounding it with inflatable pontoons – all viewed live from helicopters and cameras on the bank of the river.

Teams of BBC and Sky News presenters and reporters offered running commentary and interviewed experts and people involved in the rescue. Sky News talked to people watching from the river bank, while the Skycopter provided live pictures. The flexibility of the aerial coverage – from a thousand feet up, but with a long lens gyroscopically stabilised to provide remarkably close pictures – proved the winning element in their programming.

The BBC had a helicopter too, but it was refuelling when the most dramatic moments of the afternoon took place. News 24 was showing a loop of rushes from earlier in the day, as the Skycopter, broadcasting live pictures, tracked two inflatable boats, with the whale sandwiched between them, gingerly heading a few hundred yards downstream to a waiting barge. They were live on air, shortly after 2.30 p.m., as rescuers strapped the whale into a giant cradle and lifted it onto the barge. And the live shots continued as the whale on the barge was taken out to sea, past the Houses of Parliament, the London Eye and other landmarks.

It was almost an hour after it happened that the BBC showed – at 3.32 p.m. – recorded rushes of the whale being lifted from the water. That their helicopter was grounded during the key moments was bad luck (the Skycopter was refuelling later in the afternoon as the barge made its 40-mile journey to the sea), but a graphic on that evening's BBC1 news was bad journalism. It said the whale was lifted on to the barge at 3.30. That was when the BBC showed the pictures – an hour after the event.

The value of live coverage on a fast-moving story was underlined late in the afternoon. Sky News packaged the events of the day in a recorded report at the top of the hour at 5 p.m. Even as the report concluded, on an optimistic note about the whale being ready for transfer to a deep sea vessel, the breaking news strap across the lower third of the screen announced that the whale had taken a turn for the worse and was unfit for the transfer. The mammal had developed breathing difficulties. It suffered convulsions, and died just off Gravesend in Kent at 7 p.m.

The plight of the whale had been reported worldwide. It was a story of little political significance – although it helped reopen a debate about conservation of marine mammals. But it captured the public imagination in a way few 'hard' news stories do. It was not a story that merited interruptions to mainstream programmes – although presenter Clare Balding on the BBC's *Grandstand* advised viewers that live coverage was available on News 24. Many viewers took that cue to switch over.

The whale story happened less than a week after a feature on the front page of the media section of the *Guardian* headlined 'Rolling news RIP'. Paul Mason, BBC *Newsnight*'s business correspondent, argued that downloaded video-on-demand exposed the inadequacies of rolling news channels. Mason's arguments were well-reasoned, suggesting 'that the concept of "story" – an editorial process whose outcome is a narrative with a beginning, middle and end and hopefully a meaning' had been lost. The 'day the world prayed for a whale', as the *Mail on Sunday* put it, showed that reports of the death of rolling news were greatly exaggerated.

LIVE RADIO REPORTS

Radio reporters are often required to report live. It might be from your mobile phone, from a remote studio, from a radio car, or even using a portable microwave link on a back-pack. The advantage of a radio two-way over its television equivalent is that nobody can see you reading your notes. So, make plenty. As ever, preparation is all.

NAMES ARE EASILY FORGOTTEN WHEN THE ADRENALINE STARTS TO FLOW. PRESIDENTS AND PRIME MINISTERS HAVE BEEN KNOWN TO BECOME ANONYMOUS WHEN THE EXCITEMENT OF GOING LIVE ADDLES THE REPORTER'S BRAIN.

Some reporters, confident of their conversational writing style, will write out their whole answer, knowing they can deliver it in a way that sounds natural. This may be essential if the material is legally contentious. Others will jot down key words and phrases, with particular attention to names they need to include. Names are easily forgotten when the adrenaline starts to flow. Presidents and prime ministers have been known to become anonymous when the excitement of going live addles the reporter's brain. Remember, although the two-way sounds like an interview, it is not. The questions you are asked will have been agreed beforehand, with the producer and the studio presenter. So, that gives you time to concentrate on the technical side. That means making sure you are in a comfortable position where you can see your notebook.

If you are in a crowded street, take a look around and make sure nobody is hanging about waiting to spoil your moment. A shouted 'hello mum' will disrupt your flow and sounds insensitive and inane in the middle of a serious report.

Remember that the most annoying, inarticulate youth has as much right to be in a public place shouting inanities (though obviously not swear words) as you do to be broadcasting. Never lose your cool. Just as you need a certain charm to encourage people to be interviewed, you may need to charm any potential live 'audience' to behave while you are on air. Most passers-by are intrigued by live radio. Those who are determined to get in on the act can often be 'bought off' with the offer of a quick recorded interview, after you've done your report. Explain that you need to talk to people with strong opinions on the story. If they agree, their contribution could even work as part of a vox-pop. Or it might just buy you time to get the job done. Either way, you don't have to use it.

SATELLITE PHONES

The satellite phone is an invaluable tool for international reporting. The first casualty of war is no longer truth. It's communications. An aggressor has to destroy an enemy's communications. And a frequent consequence of natural disasters like earthquakes and hurricanes is also the destruction of communications infrastructure.

The satellite phone is a vital tool for reporters

So, reporters in war zones and places blighted by nature's excesses cannot rely on getting a decent mobile phone signal. That is where satellite phones come into play. Sat-phones are a vital tool for international reporters. They communicate directly with satellites rather than mobile phone masts. Some also provide your exact position using sat-nav technology. They are a must-have accessory for reporters.

REMEMBER

➤ Try speaking from key words and phrases rather than writing everything down

➤ Two-ways are not like other interviews – you can prepare your answers

➤ Use tact and charm to prevent interruptions in public places

➤ Satellite phones are essential tools for foreign reporting.

THE 'AS-LIVE' REPORT

Such is the modern obsession with live reporting that, when resources are not available to go live, news editors may want 'as-live' reports instead – recorded inserts that look live. This is often achieved by a reporter on a single camera walking through a location, conducting interviews on the move. It is an opportunity to be more ambitious than you might be in a live situation where your mistake or a slip by a guest could ruin the piece. You can choreograph the camera to give a series of different shots, moving gracefully from one to the next by tracking or panning.

Sometimes overlay or cutaway shots will be added later – perhaps to give the impression of a two-camera shoot. The editing of an 'as-live' report will be minimal – often no more than 'top-and-tailing' – and the time saved in the edit can be put to good use on location making sure you achieve the best possible take.

'As-lives' can be effective, and are sometimes the best way to tell the story. Often, though, the 'as-live' is a cosmetic device to make the story appear more immediate and interesting.

UNDER NO CIRCUMSTANCES SHOULD YOU CLAIM THAT A RECORDED REPORT OR INTERVIEW IS LIVE.

Under no circumstances should you claim that a recorded report or interview is live. It is dishonest and your sins will find you out. It's not just that play-out systems can fail you – tape grinding to a halt or computers going down – events can overtake you too.

For example, a report on Central News in the West Midlands about a fatal stabbing in Rugby was introduced: 'For the very latest we cross to Rajiv Popat in our newsroom.' When the reporter had finished, presenter Michelle Robinson continued: 'Rajiv, thank you for the update from the newsroom, and in the last few minutes Warwickshire police have named the man they believe was killed . . .' Who had the very latest?

REMEMBER

> ➤ Never pretend that an 'as-live' report is live.

A CLOSER LOOK

MR COOL – THE LYNAM TOUCH

Calm under pressure is the trademark of the finest live presenters. Des Lynam made his name as the coolest of sports presenters. In a world noted for frenzied over-the-top reportage, trying to capture the excitement of sporting action in the language of hyperbole, Des was Mr Cool.

Nowhere was this exemplified more than in his announcement of the most sensational story of the 1988 Seoul Olympics. During a live broadcast on the BBC's *The Olympics Today* he announced: 'I've just been handed a piece of paper here that, if it's right, it'll be the most dramatic story out of these Olympics or perhaps any others. It says Ben Johnson of Canada has been caught taking drugs and is expected to be stripped of his hundred metres gold medal, according to International Olympic Committee sources.'

Lynam's expertise enabled him not only to present the information in a calm and authoritative way, but to interpret the significance of the event live on air. The drug-taking of the 'world's fastest man' remains one of the greatest scandals in modern sport.

CONCLUSION

Live reporting and presenting are core broadcast journalism skills. Nobody can work on air for a network outlet without a fluent live presence. It has never been so easy to broadcast live from anywhere in the world, and the technology is getting cheaper. So, the demand for live broadcasters will only increase.

It is a skill worth practising constantly, at home, in the car or whenever you are alone. Try ad libbing from research notes, and then from memory. Only with practice will your confidence improve, and with confidence comes fluency.

FURTHER READING

Ray, Vin (2003) *The Television News Handbook*, London: Macmillan. Advice from top professionals on the pitfalls of live reporting and presentation.

Trewin, Janet (2003) *Presenting on TV and Radio*, Oxford: Focal Press. Excellent advice on the best preparations for live broadcasting.

CHAPTER ELEVEN

THE PACKAGE

In this chapter, we'll look at the art of structuring and writing the recorded report – the wrap or package. The aim is to tell the story in a way that offers the most impact and is clearest to the viewer or listener.

The well-honed package is still the best way of telling a story concisely and directly. And the skills of packaging news have enjoyed a renaissance because more and more packaged news is available on a variety of media.

Video-on-demand is available on broadband, mobile phones and other hand-held devices. Interactive news services offer stories in packaged easily digestible form. The latest set-top boxes offer packaged content from news organisations. And the local TV service introduced by the BBC in 2005 consisted entirely of packaged reports with no live content.

In the rolling news environment, the skills of live reporting are particularly prized, and for a while in the 1990s it looked like fluency on air would become the defining characteristic of successful broadcast journalists. But reports of the death of the package were greatly exaggerated. Packaging skills are essential both for on-air reporters and for the far greater number of news journalists working as behind-the-scenes producers and on broadband and interactive services.

Multimedia packages, using software like Macromedia's Flash, extend the boundaries of the traditional package. Journalists can combine text, audio, video and graphics in revolutionary treatments of stories. The traditional time restrictions no longer apply. Interviews can be viewed at length, as well as used in edited form. Linear story-telling can be augmented by non-linear techniques, allowing users to explore parts of the story that interest them.

We'll show how to enhance the package when appropriate with music or graphics. The abilities to 'think in sound' and 'think in pictures' – where the musical phrase or graphic image becomes an integral part of the story-telling – are the hallmark of the best reporters. These skills are especially invaluable whenever journalists stray from hard news into feature and human interest territory.

It has been said that hard news writes itself. This is true when broadcast journalists reach a certain level of competence. Creative use of graphics and music requires another level again of production expertise.

A CLOSER LOOK

THE RISE OF THE PACKAGE

In July 1954, BBC TV presenter Richard Baker announced: 'Here is an illustrated summary of the news. It will be followed by the latest film of events and happenings at home and abroad.' British television news was born.

On that first evening, there was an illustrated news summary, read by radio announcer John Snagge, with still photographs and maps. That was very much 'radio with pictures' – a phrase still used as a criticism of weak television reporting. The spoken summary was followed by the newsreel – moving pictures of events in the news. The use of filmed footage set the tone for the next half century. Film, and later videotape, of events became the staple of any TV bulletin.

The first BBC bulletins suggested the corporation didn't trust television as a news medium. Moving pictures were considered far too exciting for the viewers. The early Television Service ended its evening transmissions with a recording of Home Service radio's nine o'clock news, over a caption. Richard Baker remembers it being described as 'news for the blind'.

MOVING PICTURES WERE CONSIDERED FAR TOO EXCITING FOR THE VIEWERS . . . ITN BURST ON TO THE SCENE, WITH NEWSCASTERS PROMOTED AS PERSONALITIES AND A NEW BREED OF THRUSTING REPORTERS.

The revolutionary *News and Newsreel* was a response to the threat from independent television, which was due to start in 1955. Sure enough, ITN burst on to the scene, with newscasters promoted as personalities and a new breed of thrusting reporters. Its most enduring legacy was a less deferential approach to interviewing politicians.

Melvyn Bragg in his series *The People's Channel* celebrating the fiftieth anniversary of ITV said: 'ITN blew away deference and insisted that the newsmakers explained themselves . . . but more than anything, at home and abroad, ITN put people and their stories at the heart of the news.'

Bragg's programme showed a clip of the foreign correspondent Michael Nicholson reporting from camps in East Pakistan in 1971. Children were dying of malnutrition. The veteran reporter explained his technique: 'You don't look at hundreds of thousands. Numbers are meaningless to the viewer. But you hold a dying child in your arms and say: "By the time I've finished my commentary this child is dead." And that has impact . . . Call it melodrama. Criticise it if you like, but it gets to the heart of the viewer and that's what you're after.'

If you watch old TV packages (old reports from the BBC and Independent Television News are viewable online), you will see that they appear slow by comparison with today. Shots are held for longer and longer interview clips are used. Documentary story-telling techniques influenced early TV news reports. The rise of music video in the 1980s means modern audiences are more comfortable with rapid cutting, but in a factual report too much editing can be a distraction.

The wrap or package is an important part of radio news too. Although radio might think of itself as the Senior Service – it was around years before television – sound editing was the younger relation of picture editing. Editing sound recordings on the old wire recorders had not been possible, but film had been cut into story sequences since before the earliest days of Hollywood. In Britain and the US, magnetic recording tape was a post-war phenomenon. Indeed the first tape recorders used in the English-speaking world were seized by allied troops from defeated Germans in World War Two.

So, the package became not only the preferred way of telling a story in pictures and sound throughout the latter half of the twentieth century; it has survived into the modern era as both the most useful way of delivering news in downloaded formats and as a staple of rolling news.

Nick Pollard, the Head of Sky News until 2006, explains: 'We generate an awful lot of non-live picture content, far more, I suspect, than any one person would ever be interested in seeing in the day. The other fascinating thing with online and video-on-demand offering is that it does to a large extent potentially cut out the editorial management as a filter. It does allow a customer – a viewer – to say: "I want a lot of that and none of that. I want lots of stuff about Victoria Beckham and football and *The X-Factor*. I don't want any of that rubbish about foreign news and Europe and finance and politics. It doesn't interest me at all." Or the reverse.'

Statistics from BBC News Interactive suggest users of online news *are* more likely to go for the 'dumbed-down' option – sport and celebrity rather than politics and international affairs. The early users of new technologies are usually younger people, and more of them are men. As the technology spreads, the interests of the wider population will be represented – though don't bet against sport and celebrity leading the news download charts for many years to come. Any editor will tell you they are modern obsessions.

DON'T FORGET THE INTRO

Although this chapter focuses on the package, remember that it will almost always be introduced by a link or cue – whether the words are read by a newsreader or appear as a few lines on a website. As we said in Chapter 5: *News writing*, you need to avoid repeating what the audience already knows.

VIN RAY:
'THE CUE, OR INTRO,
SHOULD "SELL" YOUR
STORY RATHER THAN
"TELL" IT.'

Vin Ray, who runs TV masterclasses using the BBC's top correspondents, says in *The Television News Handbook*: 'As far as it's possible – and it isn't always – the cue, or intro, should "sell" your story rather than "tell" it. Nothing will kill your piece quite like a cue that says it all and leaves you to repeat what's already been said. A good cue will leave the viewer ready and anxious to hear more.'

Ray points out that many correspondents don't write their own intros – an editor, producer or presenter does it. But the correspondent needs to know what's being said and how it sets up the piece so the two flow seamlessly together.

REMEMBER

➤ Don't repeat in the package what the audience has already been told.

RADIO

THE FEATURE

A packaged radio feature may contain several voices – reportage, interviews, commentary – actuality sound recorded on location, and music, sometimes for background or impact, sometimes featuring the words of a song. Shorter wraps – a voicer with interview *clips* or *cuts* – are mini-features.

MAKING AN IMPACT

The opening words or sounds in any report have to grab the audience's attention. Should it be a snappy soundbite or an imaginative use of actuality sound? Should it be voiced on location or in the studio? Whatever you choose it has to make an immediate impact.

If you have recorded gun-shots, explosions or screams at the scene of an incident, these would almost certainly be the most dramatic actuality in the report. But to use those sounds at the top of the piece, without clear explanation in the presenter's cue, would almost certainly be to waste them. The sound of sirens works as a dramatic scene-setter, but other noises need to be put in context. Establishing the context need not take too long, though:

'This was the moment police negotiators knew they had failed.' [sound of gunshots]

'Three anxious hours came to an end with a controlled explosion.' [loud bang]

Having grabbed your audience's attention, it's then possible to backtrack and tell the story chronologically.

LISTENING FOR AN 'IN' AND AN 'OUT'

In Chapter 4: *The interview*, we highlighted the importance of listening to your subject's answers. Remember: *two ears, one mouth; listen twice as much as you speak*. You are not listening for content alone. You are listening for the grammatical sense of what is said, and for speech patterns and rhythms. These will help you identify the 'in' and 'out' points of any clip – the points at which the edited item will start and end.

THE BEST SOUNDBITES ARE SELF-CONTAINED AND SELF-EXPLANATORY.

The clip must make complete sense in the context of the piece. A scripted introduction can set up an idea to clarify what is said, but the best soundbites are self-contained and self-explanatory.

You are looking for comments that are lucid and jargon-free. If someone uses a jargon term, you have to waste valuable seconds explaining it.

As a general principle, you should be looking for emotion and opinion in interview clips. Facts can be explained by the reporter. Sometimes an expert will be offering factual information, but you still want it explained in an engaging way.

SOUNDBITES

During an interview, and later while listening back or reviewing rushes, you will be waiting to hear the clip you want to use. Sometimes the soundbite will jump out at you – and at everybody else.

When the US-manned space programme was relaunched two years after the loss of the orbiter Columbia, Wayne Hale was deputy programme manager of the Discovery mission. As astronauts prepared to inspect the heat-shield on the shuttle, to see if it had been damaged by foam breaking off the fuel tank during the launch, Mr Hale answered questions from journalists about the risks involved. He said: 'The Columbia accident made us realise that we'd been playing Russian roulette with the shuttle crews – that we had been very, very fortunate in the past that the foam did not cause critical damage.'

The 'Russian roulette' comment made it on to every bulletin, and was being quoted in discussion of the mission for days afterwards. Those two words summed up the dilemma that NASA had faced for years.

Tony Blair announced new anti-terrorist measures after the London bombings of July 2005. He said: 'Let no one be in any doubt. The rules of the game are changing.' That quote was used as a headline on most of the coverage of the story. It was used, as audio only, behind pictures of police on the street, as the opening of a BBC TV News report – an unusual and effective story-telling technique. The quote was repeated days later in follow-up stories. We know that politicians and their advisers think long and hard about the language they use. Journalists will be given advance copies of their speeches with key phrases – the day's 'soundbites' – highlighted. Not since his (or Alastair Campbell's) 'the People's Princess' had a Blair comment received such wide currency.

Sometimes the soundbite is spontaneous and worth using on its own merit. Staffordshire University's Dr Mick Temple on the BBC's 2005 election coverage was asked why the collapse of car maker MG Rover, with the loss of 4,000 jobs, did not appear to have had an effect on voting patterns in the West Midlands. His reply: 'It's like Sherlock Holmes. The curious case of the dog in the night-time. It didn't bark.'

Unlike the Russian roulette remark, this was not a major admission by a key player in the story. It did not mark a change in government policy like the Prime Minister's carefully prepared comments. But it was a memorable piece of political analysis and worth quoting.

LINKING TO AUDIO

When you are linking to pieces of audio (soundbites or 'grabs'), your script should introduce the interviewee or set up their opinion. Normally that means naming them before they are heard, and explaining their role in the story.

QUESTIONS SHOULD BE EDITED OUT OF INTERVIEWS UNLESS THEY ARE SHORT AND CHALLENGING.

Bridging between clips of sound also requires special thought. The idea is to carry the narrative forward. Setting up a new clip with a question is usually a lazy, and therefore unacceptable, way of doing it. Questions should be edited out of interviews unless they are short and challenging. Otherwise, introduce what is about to be said with a statement.

Here's an example from a BBC report into the takeover by HMV of the bookshop chain Ottakar's:

The author, Antony Beevor, was one of the leading critics of the takeover: CLIP OF BEEVOR: *I think the outcome is entirely expected . . .*

This is from a BBC Radio Sheffield report of a gas explosion in Chesterfield:

Pat Kerry, who lives next-door-but-one, says there was an almighty explosion: CLIP OF KERRY: *It was completely out of the blue. Blew out the boiler. Blew out the pilot light.*

WHO'S INTERESTED?

Choosing what to put into a story means choosing what to leave out. This is harder than it sounds, and usually harder than deciding what to put in. When you are selecting clips of interviews, which facts to include in your script (or which pictures or sequences to put into a television package), harsh decisions have to be made.

The rules of thumb should be: if it's interesting to you, then it's interesting to the audience. If in doubt, leave it out. But to follow these rules you need to be honest. And brutal.

Just because you enjoyed the company of a particular interviewee does not mean that what they said on tape helps tell the story. It's easy to be blinded by the personal charm of someone who turns out to be incapable of speaking in coherent sentences in front of a microphone. You probably told them they'd be on the six o'clock bulletin, so you have to include them, don't you? Well, no.

IT'S A BIG MISTAKE TO PROMISE, OR EVEN SUGGEST, TO ANYBODY THAT THEY WILL BE APPEARING AT A CERTAIN TIME, OR AT ALL.

It's a big mistake to promise, or even suggest, to anybody that they will be appearing at a certain time, or at all. The news agenda changes. Stories move on or get overtaken by events. Most of what you do in your career will be at risk of being dropped by the editor and may never be transmitted. In a small local radio station, where it's all hands to the wheel, almost everything does get used. Otherwise you'd never fill the bulletins. But the larger the organisation for which you are working, the greater the chances of your story being dropped. A handful of reporters will be repeatedly entrusted with the lead package on the biggest stories. Only technical failure will prevent those getting to air. But most of the time, you will be putting your best efforts into something that may be dismissed at a programme editor's whim. This is not because you have done a bad job. It may be that the story simply does not fit the programme mix – 'There are already two crime stories; we don't want a third,' or 'We've had too much sport this week.'

Living with rejection is one of the hardest lessons for trainee reporters. It's not usually personal but it always feels like it. The aim must be to have a reputation for being so good the editor doesn't want to miss out on your work. Producers want your piece in the programme because they know it will make the programme better. That's why you have to be brutal when choosing the content of your report – it has to be of the highest standard because it has your name on it, and you want your name to be a benchmark of quality.

Treat the contributions of interviewees as you would your own script. Are there unnecessary words? Can they be edited out? Does the clip summarise the speaker's position accurately? Are they speaking with passion? What is the most interesting or enthusiastic part of their contribution?

KEEP IT CLEAN

BACKGROUND SOUND IS ESSENTIAL WHEN YOU ARE ON LOCATION. OTHERWISE, WHAT IS THE POINT OF BEING THERE RATHER THAN IN THE STUDIO?

The value of **clean sound** cannot be stressed enough. Noisy backgrounds and interruptions make editing a nightmare. It is best not to link from pristine studio-quality voice to an interview with heavy background noise. It jars on the listener's ears. It can take a second or two to adjust to what is being said and in that time the sense may be lost. Nonetheless, *some* background sound is essential when you are on location. Otherwise, what is the point of being there rather than in the studio? The background helps paint the audio picture for the listener. Remember, the pictures are better on the radio. It's been said so often that it's a cliché, but it's only true so long as there is an artist with a microphone to paint those pictures.

On location, unplanned interruptions may occur: someone comes into the room; a car drives past; an aircraft passes overhead. Sometimes, background sounds will add to the sense of being there: an ice-cream van at the seaside; a helicopter at an army base; a school bell in a playground. At other times, disruptive sound will put your interviewee off their stride and you may need to break off the interview. There may be occasions when you accidentally speak over your interviewee. You may think they have finished making their point. You start your next question before realising your mistake. You shut up too late and have spoken over the most exciting thing they've said. In these cases the solution should have been to record that part of the interview again. It's no use thinking you can make up for poor recording in the edit. It is unlikely you will be able to.

RUNNING WILD

One important aid to editing, which is often overlooked in the haste to get a story on air, is the recording of **wildtrack**. Taping 30 seconds of 'atmos' (short for atmosphere) in the location where you are recording can save precious minutes back in the newsroom, and even salvage otherwise unusable audio. The wildtrack, which has no speech on it, bridges gaps in edited sound. It is particularly useful when there are jumps in background level between one clip and the next. You might even want to record enough wildtrack to lay behind the whole of your voice report.

USING MUSIC

A MUSICAL PERFORMANCE RECORDED ON LOCATION IS ALWAYS A SURE FIRE WAY OF TRANSPORTING THE AUDIENCE TO THE SCENE OF THE STORY.

Music can liven up any radio feature, either to create an atmosphere or to make an editorial point. A few seconds of music can set the tone of a piece. You need to use enough of it for the audience to recognise the tune, and then you can fade it beneath interview or voice-over. It is never a good idea to use music as a bed beneath the whole of a package.

A musical performance recorded on location is always a sure fire way of transporting the audience to the scene of the story. Make sure you have permission from the performers to use it. There is a news access agreement drawn up by the Musicians' Union which means MU members have to give permission for unpaid use of their work in news programmes.

Recorded music can add flavour to features. You can use music to punctuate or underline the content of a story. Popular songs do this particularly well. If you want to highlight the words of a song, fade into and out of those words rather than playing the whole of a verse or chorus. Even if you are featuring the very first words of a song you will probably want to edit out the musical intro.

Try to be original in your choice of music. For decades, Rod Stewart's *Sailing* was overused on features about boats. Pink Floyd's *Money* was a similar cliché on financial reports.

And remember that recorded music is not free. Your station will have to pay a royalty to the performer and composer of the piece, just as if it were played in a music programme. The use of music has to be logged so that the payment can be made.

REMEMBER THAT RECORDED MUSIC IS NOT FREE. YOUR STATION WILL HAVE TO PAY A ROYALTY.

CASE STUDY 11.1

PULLING IT TOGETHER – USING ACTUALITY

Here's an example of a radio package from the reporting of the Indonesian earthquake of May 2006. Rachel Harvey's piece for BBC Radio 4 News uses actuality sound and an interview to paint an audio picture of the relief operation. Note how the two separate pieces of actuality are explained in the script.

CUE: The United Nations has said that 'enormous progress' is being made in getting aid to those affected by the earthquake on the Indonesian island of Java. However, congestion on the roads is still said to be hampering efforts to get supplies to more remote areas. Up to two-hundred-thousand people have been made homeless by the disaster, in which more than five-thousand-eight-hundred people are now thought to have died. Thousands more were injured. The epicentre of Saturday's earthquake was near the city of Yogyakarta, from where our correspondent, Rachel Harvey, reports:

SOUND: CHILDREN SHOUTING; HELICOPTER NOISE

HARVEY: Helicopters are a welcome distraction for traumatised children. They're also the quickest way to deliver aid across the stricken region. Heavy traffic is clogging the roads, so taking to the air is often a better option. Emergency supplies are reaching main distribution points, but the rural villages which were hardest hit by Saturday's earthquake are only getting a trickle. So, as Kendar Subroto, of the United Nations Children's Fund, explains, some survivors have decided to take the initiative:

SUBROTO: Instead of waiting for aid workers to go to these villages, they came to us. And this morning, for example, we have stands of people, representing various villages, saying how bad the situation is there, and we provide support to them.

HARVEY: Accurate information is crucial to ensure that the right help reaches the right places. Shelter remains a priority. Thousands of people are still without tents and must now face a fifth night in the open. It'll be easier to create temporary camps once the rubble is cleared. The Indonesian military is making a start on that.

SOUND: SHOUTING; COLLAPSING NOISE

HARVEY: A damaged house pulled down with a few ropes and a lot of brute force. Things are moving forward here – but there's a long way to go.

BBC Radio 4 1800 bulletin, 31 May 2006

TELEVISION

PICTURE POWER

While devotees of radio will tell you it is a more powerful medium than television because the pictures are better, that old chestnut is a tribute to the power of the human imagination rather than Marconi's technology. But it can't be denied that radio is usually more immediate – all you need is the human voice to tell the story. You don't have to wait for camera crews and satellite trucks. New technology is making it easier to report live on TV – reporters can be on screen using mobile phones – but it is still the case that television works best when the pictures tell the story.

The power of pictures can never be underestimated. If a picture paints a thousand words then 25 frames a second – 25 different pictures to make up a moving image – equals 25,000 words a second. One second's video is obviously not worth *that* much, but it's pretty powerful nonetheless.

The art of television reporting is to make sure that it never becomes simply radio with pictures. Strong images lead the story-telling. And pictures should never be used as 'wallpaper' just to cover the cracks in poor scripting.

Kevin Bakhurst, Controller of BBC News 24 and a former editor of the *Ten O'Clock News* on BBC1 explains the value of picture-led stories: 'This is TV news not radio news. The two years I was on the *Ten*, it was really important to the programme – picture power and the story-telling with packages – as well as lives – it's good to mix them. Some bulletins can stray too far away from that. You think at the end: "I didn't really see a good picture story in that programme."

'Look at any of the most memorable TV news stories of the last couple of years, and you'll remember them because they were picture stories, not because they were live correspondents.'

Every package should start with a strong image, but not necessarily the strongest image. Often the narrative flow is more important than putting the strongest or the latest pictures first. The defining moment of a story – the picture that sums it all up – will probably already have been used as a headline. But your audience wants to know how that moment has been reached.

Consider a football match. You might show a spectacular winning goal or a controversial sending-off as a headline, but in the package you almost always tell the story of the match in chronological order. Chronology is the most straightforward way of telling a news story too.

Kevin Bakhurst of the BBC: 'Picture power and story-telling with packages are really important.'

Sometimes the most dramatic pictures *are* the story. The coverage of a triple suicide bombing in Baghdad in October 2005 inevitably started with the most dramatic pictures, because the explosions happened within sight of the hotel used by the foreign media. They had been caught on video. Caroline Hawley's report on the BBC began with shots of the explosion followed by the commentary: 'A strike in the heart of the city. A massive bomb captured on camera.' Pictures of the inside of the journalists' hotel followed. Hawley concluded with a piece-to-camera cradling a 'razor sharp piece of shrapnel', which had landed near the BBC offices.

> ### REMEMBER
>
> ➤ Television is not radio with pictures
> ➤ Start with a strong image
> ➤ Tell stories chronologically whenever possible
> ➤ Never use pictures as 'wallpaper'.

MAKING IT RELEVANT – THE VISUAL METAPHOR

DOES POPULARISING IMPORTANT ISSUES DEVALUE THEM? OR IS IT THE BEST WAY OF INVOLVING MORE PEOPLE IN COMPLICATED DEBATE?

Sometimes, the story is seen by broadcasters as important but potentially boring. They don't want it to be 'worthy but dull' so they use gimmicks to engage the audience. This kind of treatment is at the heart of the debate over 'dumbing down.' Does popularising important issues devalue them? Or is it the best way of involving more people in complicated debate?

ITV News used a metaphor from reality television to report the 2005 Conservative Party leadership contest, borrowing the music from *Big Brother*, and describing the elimination process, as MPs voted to reduce the number of candidates, as 'evictions from the Big Brother house'. When the field was reduced to two, David Cameron and David Davies, Tom Bradley reported: 'Big Brother now becomes Love Island as Tory members decide who is their ideal partner.' Daisy McAndrew's report, on the night of the final vote by MPs, used a graphic, blending the face of David Cameron, the favourite in the race, with that of the Prime Minister Tony Blair, pointing out the similar backgrounds of the two opponents. Deborah Turness, the editor of ITV News, has strong views on making stories relevant: 'You see on other news channels and programmes what I call process journalism. It's lazy. It's a story because it's around and everyone else is doing it. "How shall we do it? Well, a few GVs, a bit of a graphic, piece-to-camera, sign-off, Bob's your uncle!" No!

'I always say to people, when they say it'll be fine: "Fine isn't good enough to make it into an ITV News programme."

'We've got half an hour to distil the entire world, surely we can make it exciting, gripping and dramatic. I think news is the best drama on TV, because it's real, it's completely unpredictable and when you turn on your TV, you do not know what you are going to get.'

But Turness is clear that some reporting – notably from foreign correspondents – does not need elaborate treatments: 'Our films from people at the sharp end are never going to have graphics in them. Those are eye-witness reports and those are always going to be the most important things we do, but elsewhere we need to be creative.'

Patrick Burns, BBC Midlands Political Editor, is proud of the way *The Politics Show* on BBC1 sets out to popularise issues of the day:

Any old fool can take a complicated story and render it complicated. It takes someone who's really on top of the issue to simplify it so an audience can understand it and still keep to the truth of the story and what's really going on.

It's quite Reithian [*a reference to the BBC's first Director General Lord Reith, who is identified with the public service aims to inform, educate and entertain*]. We're bringing complicated stories to the greatest number of people.

Our political coverage changed with *The Politics Show*. It used to be enough to take the pictures of a debate in Westminster, show a few pictures of industrial decline in West Bromwich or wherever, and get a couple of MPs into the studio for a debate. That's easy to do. But what could be caricatured as 'dumbing down' takes a hell of a lot more intellectual rigour, doing it so you don't insult the intelligence of the committed viewer and so that you engage the interest of the less committed viewer.

I call it 'cool television' using the sort of visual devices you see on programmes like *Watchdog* and some of the old *Holiday* programmes.

BBC Midlands Political Editor Patrick Burns: 'I call it cool television.'

You try to find something that isn't obvious but becomes a visual metaphor for the story. Looking at Wyre Forest before the local elections, most people knew that they had this independent MP Richard Taylor who won two general elections campaigning on the health service, but hardly anybody knew where this place was. It's a shame that it's named after a forest because the defining feature is the River Severn. It would have been easy to dig out the library pictures of the hospital protests and Dr Taylor's election win, but we thought it was important to let people know about the area. So we started the piece at Bewdley, which is an attractive riverside town. They were pretty pictures. If you're going to use a river as your theme, pick part of it that's attractive. And it let me say things like for Labour to recover from their collapse it was like pushing water uphill.

Another piece asked whether the West Midlands had lost its political clout at Westminster because we didn't have local MPs at the cabinet table and in positions of power. We went to a boxing gym and did lots of close-ups of punch bags and used that as a metaphor for political clout. Add that to popular examples of things where the Midlands has missed out, the supercasino, the national stadium and the city of culture. Attached to those popular examples, the clout, the boxing shots were a very clear image, a recurring theme to talk about this issue.

My colleague Sarah Thackray did a piece about whether new drugs should be prescribed for Alzheimer's sufferers. She used a recurring image of a cinema projector showing an Alzheimer's patient's old cine footage of his family holidays. She said his memories were as transient as each frame of this home movie footage. Once they were gone they were forgotten and looking at them was the only way he could rekindle these memories. The piece kept returning to these cine shots – an ingenious recurring image.

Video journalist Robin Punt: 'When you get a story that's good enough, it makes your job a lot easier.'

REMEMBER

➤ Think imaginatively

➤ Think pictures.

Sometimes a visual metaphor is inappropriate to the story, but you still have a lack of pictures. Here's an example of making the most of what you have from BBC Midlands video journalist Robin Punt, reporting in June 2006 on the story of a paralysed man determined to visit Switzerland for an assisted suicide. All that was available was a single interview with a subject who couldn't move.

The interview with Noel Martin was shot entirely in his own home. Mr Martin was unable to walk or feed himself after a racist attack ten years before.

Pictures	Sound	Robin Punt's comments
	Actuality sound of electric wheelchair Mr Martin: 'You're not living, you're existing . . .	This shot [of Mr Martin being helped through a door by a carer] was just a grabbed shot. It was what he was doing at the time. He'd agreed to do the interview, and I wanted to make the whole experience as easy for him as possible. So there weren't a lot of set-up shots.
	because in order to live you have to be able to feel.'	After a shot showing how difficult his life is, underlined by his own words, you've got to see him. So this is the main interview shot.
	Voice-over: And he can't feel . . . he can't move . . . he can't drink – or do anything unassisted.	This is a cutaway, a pan up as he sits gazing into the garden.
	Paralysed from the neck down after a racist attack in Germany, Noel Martin from Edgbaston in Birmingham wants to die.	Somebody lighting a cigarette for him just shows his dependence on others.

Pictures	Sound	Robin Punt's comments
	'It's my decision. God gave me a free choice,	This is a really tight close-up. It serves as a cutaway too but the intimacy is everything. If you go for lots of medium shots there's no involvement.
	. . . made me in his own image and he gave me a free choice to what I want. And I'm making that decision. I'm not saying it's best for other people, but for me that's the decision.'	Cutback to the interview. You want to see him saying this.
	Question: 'What do your family feel about this decision?' 'I don't know, I've never asked them. It's up to them what they feel.' Question: 'They haven't tried to stop you?' 'They can't stop me. Each person is supposed to . . .	A wider shot from a different part of the interview. I was able to zoom in and out as we did the interview. Most of us are just used to turning up and asking questions, but when you've only got one interview it helps to vary the shot size. The wide shows him in his home, a very nice home, with ornaments on the mantelpiece, and you can see he's quadraplegic. I was able to butt the two clips together, because he doesn't move and so there's no jump. I trailed the question in over the outgoing shot (the original question is on the wider shot). If you can do that even by 12 frames, or half a second, it's so much smoother.
	If you're a man or a woman, you're in charge of your own destiny.'	This shot is really close. Any closer and the camera would have been in his ear.
	V-O: Noel Martin planted this garden,	This shows the controls of the chair, obviously, and two close-ups together work well. It's better than a close-up then a wide, which just looks like an obvious cutaway.

Pictures	Sound	Robin Punt's comments
	restored his beautiful home, with his own hands years ago.	The silhouette from the rear shows his isolation, and the natural light lets you look at his garden. I like doing silhouette shots because they put people in the context of their surroundings.
	From his chair, he can see the memorial built in honour of his wife Jacqueline – she died from cancer six years ago.	This is the POV [point of view] shot. We get to see what he sees, and it gives us a sense of then and now: the man who built the garden, but who can't work on it any more. This is the killer fact, and the shot underlines it. You don't know until this point that his wife died. He has no close family. It's terribly sad.
	Question: 'So you know what you want now?' 'I know what I want, simple as that.'	I pulled focus from the memorial back to the leaves, which brings us back to him in his chair. It was easy to use his sound out of vision because he was such a clear talker. Sometimes you need lip sync to tell what people are saying.
	Question: 'Even when you're sitting there and they're going to administer a fatal injection, you really want to go through with it? You're not going to stop anyone at the last minute?' 'I'm not afraid of dying. Dying isn't a problem. Living is a problem.	The light has changed on this shot, so it's not quite so moody somehow. When you're relying on natural light you have to live with that.
	Dying is no problem. I'm just moving on.'	The reverse two-shot. I'm not a particular fan of putting myself into stories like this, but I'm sitting there able-bodied and I think it makes a point.

Pictures	Sound	Robin Punt's comments
	V-O: On the 23rd of July next year, his 48th birthday, Noel says he'll end his life with the help of two doctors at a clinic in Switzerland.	In a way this shot doesn't work at all technically, because his position in the room has changed. But it's a different angle and I think it does the job. He reverses out of frame to end the piece. Simplicity was the key throughout.

LIBRARY PICTURES

Sometimes there are no new pictures to tell a story. The story could be the latest development in a long-running saga or a follow-up to an earlier report. It is then that you rely on the archive or library. A well-kept library, with a searchable computer database, is a great asset to any news organisation. Huge resources have been spent in recent years converting tape libraries to digital storage systems.

Whenever you use library footage, or file tape as the Americans call it, it is important the viewers are aware they are not looking at new pictures. You can do this by using an on-screen caption or in voice-over.

Sometimes pictures are used as a generic example of something you can't film on the day: a particular model of car or aircraft; the production line of a factory threatened by industrial action or closure; shots of a celebrity who's in the news but not making public appearances. In these cases a simple 'library pictures' caption will do.

Other pictures from the library are shots of well-known events: the September 11 attacks; the 2004 Tsunami; the London bombs of July 2005; the invasion of Iraq; the 2005 General Election. In these cases it is obvious to viewers what they are seeing and the script will explain why they are looking at familiar images.

Other specific events are not as well-defined in the public consciousness, and it is important to explain the context. Shots of the tornado which hit Birmingham in 2005 might be used in a feature about extreme weather conditions. A date caption would help, although plastering dates all over the screen is no substitute for proper scripting. You should write to library pictures as precisely as to any others.

Many agencies keep libraries of pictures which broadcasters can buy. The broadcaster pays a licence fee to use the shots. The Imperial War Museum has an extensive resource of images from the First and Second World Wars and other conflicts, which regularly appear in news reports and documentaries. A word of warning – they can be expensive.

Wherever you get your pictures from, you should take the same care in editing them as pictures that have been shot for your piece. You obviously have no control over the way library pictures are shot, but you have total control over the way they are used.

➤ Script library pictures with as much care as any others

➤ Label library shots clearly – do not deceive your audience

➤ Beware the costs of agency pictures.

USER-GENERATED CONTENT

Contemporary broadcasting makes increasing use of content from users of the media. Americans talk of the new journalism being 'a conversation not a lecture'. Most British journalists would like to think they have never lectured their audience, but you get the point.

MIKE WARD: 'WE ARE IN A USER-DRIVEN ENVIRONMENT RATHER THAN A PRODUCER-DRIVEN ENVIRONMENT.'

Mike Ward, who teaches online journalism at the University of Central Lancashire, says we are in a 'user-driven environment rather than a producer-driven environment'. Users – the audience – can scrutinise and challenge traditional news providers. Major news organisations become facilitators, or even partners, for content providers, the so-called citizen journalists.

He says one of the ways forward is to integrate user-provided content into our coverage, rather than boxing it off as a blog and separating it from our own reporting.

For example, in July 2006, BBC special correspondent Richard Bilton interviewed a Briton, Tony Lteif, at his home in Surrey after he fled Israeli attacks on Lebanon. The report included video from Mr Lteif's mobile phone of his taxi ride from Beirut into Syria, and of the chaotic scenes he saw at the border crossing.

The war artist story on the next few pages is an example of user content contributing to a well-crafted video package. The story ran as part of the ninetieth anniversary commemorations of the Battle of the Somme on BBC local and regional TV.

The story is that of an artist, Rob Perry, who specialises in painting and drawing the landscapes left by First World War battlefields. Regional BBC had featured his exhibitions before, but had never followed him to France to see him working from his mobile studio. In 2006, though, the BBC lent Rob Perry a camera to take with him. They also interviewed him at home in Stourbridge in the West Midlands. The interview and the artist's shots from France were combined to produce two feature-length pieces.

For the first item, the trained artist's eye produced some captivating images. A chance meeting with a former professional cameraman (visiting the battlefield with a group of military history enthusiasts) meant he also had someone to help with some of the shots.

The journalist who edited the piece left in a sequence where Rob jokes about the problems of talking to camera. Paul Myles, a trainer with the BBC, advises video journalists to use humour in their work whenever possible. It can show another side to the subject, even on the most serious stories.

WAR ARTIST

Tracking shot

Music: Bach Suite for Cello No. 1 in G.

Music fades under Rob Perry's voice: 'As you drive through the battlefield area you just can't help but notice how many cemeteries there are dotted about.

Interview

War and its effects are something we should just never forget.'

Cutaway tracking shot

Voice-over: 'For 15 years artist

Rob driving

Rob Perry has toured and painted the battlefield of the Somme in northern France.

Rob in trench

He's made over 40 trips from his home in Stourbridge to these fields, the farmland where ninety years ago this weekend

Tilt up to show landscape

20,000 soldiers died in a single day of fighting.

| Slow zoom on still | Inspired by his cousin, a private in the Royal Warwickshire Regiment who was killed here, this is Rob Perry's video diary.'

Music fades |

| Walking piece to camera | 'Actually I hate doing this, don't you, do you hate talking on the television?

Voice off mic: 'Well, I'm behind the camera mostly.'

Rob: . . . 'especially when you don't know what to say and you find yourself going, well, er, arr, um, err . . .' |

| Wide in woodland, Rob walking. He clears frame | 'It's not a very easy subject to tackle, this, because the ground cover is so even.' |

| Tilt down to Rob working | Pause.

'So I now start working back into it with pen, making all these very fine hatching lines to try to bring a bit of character into this rather bland surface cover of grass.' |

| Close-up of hatching | Upsound of pen scratching paper.

'The grass of course follows the profiles |

| Low angle of artist | of the remains of the shell holes and the ridges.'

Music fades up: Mozart Piano Concerto No. 23 in A Major |

Close-up of sketch	'So there is interest there, but it is quite difficult to find.

Albert street – tracking shot	Birmingham's very closely tied to the town of Albert. Albert was

Albert street scene	the epicentre of the Battle of the Somme.

Tower	But after the war the city of Birmingham

Albert street	adopted the town of Albert and helped with the

Rue de Birmingham sign	reconstruction, raised funds

| Interview | and helped the rehabilitation of the population.' |

| Rob in cemetery, walking to camera | Music rises. 'Now here's a headstone to an unknown soldier |

| Close-up of headstone | of the Royal Warwickshire Regiment. My grandmother had three cousins who were all killed on the Somme, |

| Wide of cemetery | two of them with known graves, but one Bob Dean, with no known grave, |

| Rob kneeling pats the headstone | so who's to know if this isn't Bob here?' |

| Rob rises and clears shot | Music |

Start of tilt	Voice over: 'Tomorrow, Rob meets the historians attempting to find
End of tilt – Rob with historian	the site of one of the biggest tunnel networks on the Somme.
Rob working on large canvas by night	And in the dark and the pouring rain trying to capture a unique image of this massive World War One battlefield 90 years on.' Music fades

REMEMBER

➤ Integrate user-provided content into your coverage.

VOICE-OVER

We've already described how to write for broadcast in Chapter 5: *News writing*, but great scripts only work if they complement the rest of the package – the pictures, natural sound and interview clips.

Writing into interview clips is an art in itself. On TV – unlike radio – there is usually no need to introduce the speaker by name. A caption will do that. As in radio, there is almost always no need to repeat the question. Some clips need no introduction at all. One speaker may follow naturally from the one before, either because they are continuing the narrative (in a hard news story, perhaps) or because they are offering an opposite point of view (a political item).

You also need to avoid repetition. The reporter's first words should not repeat the words in the link. The first words of an interview should not repeat the reporter's introduction to the speaker.

Here's an example of how not to do it:

Reporter's voice: Examinations of the house have revealed what investigating officers are describing as a significant degree of violence.

Clip of Detective Superintendent: Something has occurred in there with some significant degree of violence . . .

Central ITV

And here are some better examples:

Reporter's voice: Two men are dead. It could so easily have been many more.

Clip of surgeon: We had people brought in with stab wounds to the chest . . .

BBC Midlands

Reporter's voice: Well-off schools will be obliged to help others.

Clip of education specialist: A third of the extra money of a specialist school has to be spent helping neighbourhood schools, and that's the whole point of the initiative . . .

ITV News

Reporter's voice: Two weeks ago his parents were called to collect the 14-year old from school because his hair was the wrong length.

Clip of boy's mother: Too short, and it wasn't in the school prospectus.

BBC Midlands

LINKING TO SOUNDBITES

When you link to soundbites, let your words carry the story forward. Remember, a caption will probably be the best way of naming the speaker.

The Conservatives' health spokesman says the government's policy will lead to longer waiting lists for patients . . .

One expert, who's studied the background of successful asylum seekers, says the approach is misguided . . .

This man has lost his home and all his belongings in the flood. He's still searching for his missing wife and child. He's desperate . . .

NATURAL SOUND

One of the greatest failings of beginners to TV reporting is using too many words of voice-over and not enough actuality sound from the pictures. Whenever possible, use the actuality to set the scene. Let the pictures breathe, and give the viewer time to take in what you are saying.

VIN RAY: 'WE DON'T LIVE IN A SILENT WORLD, YET YOU WOULDN'T KNOW IT TO SEE SOME TELEVISION PACKAGES. USE AS MUCH NATURAL SOUND AS YOU CAN.'

Vin Ray, the first director of the BBC College of Journalism, says in *The Television News Handbook*: 'We don't live in a silent world, yet you wouldn't know it to see some television packages. Use as much natural sound as you can. Natural sound really helps the pace of a television package and helps viewers assimilate the pictures and the words they are looking at and listening to.'

How to judge the pace of the package is summed up by Ray in the old saying from broadcast newsrooms: 'It can be as long as you like as long as it's quick.'

A well-paced piece will appear to fly by, whatever its duration. It leaves the audience keen for more. Plenty of natural sound draws the viewer into the piece. It reinforces the sense of 'being there' – the old, but still relevant, idea of television as 'a window on the world'.

THE PIECE-TO-CAMERA

Sky News' Laurence Lee – a PTC from a report about the drugs trade in Tajikistan: note the action in the background and the use of a prop by the reporter

Many packages will include a piece-to-camera, or stand-up (when to use them is covered in Chapter 6: *Location reporting and production*). It's worth remembering that these should be treated like any other shot in the package. If it doesn't fit, drop it or change it.

When you record your PTC (or stand-up) on location, you obviously have a clear idea how it will fit into your piece. By the time you come to put the package together you may find the story has changed or the stand-up is less relevant. Don't feel you have to include it just because you spent time recording it. You need to apply a ruthless second opinion to all your shots, and the PTC is no exception.

Longer pieces-to-camera may benefit from shortening. Some will work better if they are partly covered with pictures or cutaways.

REMEMBER

➤ A package can be 'as long as you like as long as it's quick'
➤ Words should complement the pictures
➤ Avoid repetition
➤ You don't need to name interviewees in voice-over
➤ Use actuality sound – let the pictures breathe
➤ Treat stand-ups critically, like any other shot.

THE ONLINE PACKAGE

The non-linear online package is the closest thing to a new form of journalism since the advent of broadcasting. Traditional broadcast journalism is a linear form. Stories have a beginning, middle and end. You want the audience to stay with your story, so you give it a narrative arc, based on old-fashioned story-telling skills. Viewers and listeners should want to know what happens next. If they stay till the end, you've done your job. When your story has finished, the audience is presented with a new one.

But graphics-based online story-telling can be different. Online, using a programme like Flash, different story-telling elements can be linked. Video, still photographs, sound, text and graphics can all be used to tell the story. And because of the way they are linked, users can decide how much or how little they want to see or hear. There's a linear thread, but the user controls the length of the experience. It's similar to skipping from one story to the next in a newspaper – except it's much more exciting.

Some of the best online treatments of stories are on US websites. Many UK newspapers have seen broadband as an opportunity to train their reporters as video journalists. Most of their early efforts looked amateurish (although they will obviously get better), and UK newspaper companies have largely overlooked the potential of a medium that marries broadcast and newspaper skills.

For examples of great non-linear story-telling, visit www.newsday.com, the site of a Long Island-based newspaper. Their report, the 'Cost of War', achieved 12 million hits in a day and won a Batten Award for Innovations in Journalism. The in-depth account of the impact of the war in Iraq has audio commentary, video footage, top quality news stills, interviews with Iraqis and Americans, personal testimony, blogs, cutaway graphics of weapons systems, diaries, traditional reportage and much more. It demonstrates how a non-linear package can appeal to different audiences. Its content could just as easily satisfy an opponent of the US invasion as a paid-up member of the National Rifle Assocation.

Video-journalist and educator David Dunkley Gyimah, who blogs at www.viewmagazine.tv, says the use of Flash for online journalism is a revelation: 'Broadcasters have finally awoken to a piece of kit only recently the preserve of animators and designers.'

Flash is being used too to deliver video on Sky News Interactive. Deputy Editor Adam Harding says: 'The great thing about using Flash video is you don't get annoying pop-up messages asking if you want to view using Real Player or Windows Media Player. It just plays.'

For links to other professional Flash packages, visit the website www.flashjournalism.com. This is the site of Mindy McAdams' book *Flash Journalism: How to create multimedia news packages.*

INTERACTIVITY

The most successful online packages have a high level of *interactivity*. It's a broad concept. A conversation is interactive. So is playing a game. Reading a novel is not.

USERS CAN SKIP WHAT THEY'RE NOT INTERESTED IN, OR DELVE DEEPER INTO WHAT FASCINATES THEM, PERHAPS ACCESSING ARCHIVE OR EXTERNAL LINKS.

Interactivity in online journalism takes several forms. If a story is constructed in a modular form, with a lot of different elements, users can choose their own path through it. They can skip what they're not interested in, or delve deeper into what fascinates them, perhaps accessing archive or external links.

Users may be able to interact with the technology – bookmarking points they can return to later, or changing the screen layout, to make text easier to read or images easier to view. They might be able to enter their own preferences so that the presentation is tailored to their interests. The package 'learns' things about the user, and offers, for example, the option of restarting a piece of video from the point at which the viewer left off.

Interactivity might also mean the user interacting with other users and the creator of the package – the journalist. Pop-up e-mail boxes and the 'have-your-say' features on BBC web content are the simplest forms of this. More complicated versions might be the opportunity for content from the user (user-generated content) to be added to the treatment, and the creation of online communities around the story.

When you are planning an online package you will probably be unclear what features might be added as the story develops. Some might be suggested by feedback from users. Then your content will be truly interactive.

➤ Online story-telling can be non-linear – the user chooses a way through the content

➤ Combine text, stills, graphics, video, audio and user content

➤ Online packages can appeal to different target audiences at the same time

➤ Use graphics programmes like Flash

➤ Make your package interactive for users.

CONCLUSIONS

The traditional TV or radio package is probably as good a way of telling a linear story as has ever been devised. All the elements can be edited and crafted into an easily digested form that's convenient for viewers and listeners to understand.

But there are new horizons and new challenges. The limits of non-linear story-telling have yet to be explored. There is clearly an appetite for the new form. Many young people prefer playing video games to watching TV. They still use TV, but fewer are engaged by scheduled news programmes. Interactive journalism offers a way to attract that audience, and the opportunity to expand the limitations of traditional broadcast journalism.

FURTHER READING

Chantler, Paul and Stewart, Peter (2003) *Basic Radio Journalism*, Oxford: Focal Press. Expertise on producing wraps and features for radio.

McAdams, Mindy (2005) *Flash Journalism: How to create multimedia news packages*, Oxford: Focal Press. The definitive guide to using Macromedia's Flash in web journalism.

Ray, Vin (2003) *The Television News Handbook*, London: Macmillan. TV reporting explained with many examples from senior practitioners.

WEB LINKS

www.flashjournalism.com. Mindy McAdams' site.

www.newsday.com. A first-class example of Flash Journalism.

www.viewmagazine.tv. David Dunkley Gyimah's web-based magazine *The View* with examples of packaged TV reports.

CHAPTER TWELVE

EDITING

Story-telling is at the heart of journalism. Shakespeare used a quill pen. George Orwell used a typewriter. J. K. Rowling uses a word processor. Broadcast journalists use computer systems to manipulate words, pictures and sound.

The hands-on craft skills of putting together news packages have been practised for years by radio reporters. Now, increasingly, television reporters have to perform the same techniques in their medium. Online journalists need to know how to assemble a web page and input media – text, graphics, stills and edited audio and video.

Editing is the process of selecting information for broadcast. It means leaving out what is unwanted, and choosing the material that best helps tell the story. It is an electronic process that replicates the role of the sub-editor in newspapers. The 'sub' cuts unwanted copy, checks the grammar and content of what has been written and orders what remains into the final story. In modern broadcast journalism, reporters are required not only to write, but to select pictures and audio clips and present them in a narrative structure that will tell the story.

WHAT SOFTWARE?

There are dozens of digital editing software programs for both radio and television. Trade names include Avid, Quantel, Adobe Premiere, Final Cut Pro (in television) and SADiE, Adobe Audition, RadioMan, Audacity, Burli, Pro Tools (in radio).

Whatever the name, the programs have much in common. Most involve assembling the picture or sound information on a computer screen in a sequence from left to right – the *timeline*. Raw media clips may be collected in folders known as clip boxes or bins – a term from film editing. (Each shot, on a strip of film, was hung from a rack, with the trailing end dropping into a large bin, like a dustbin. Waste material ended up literally on the cutting-room floor. On a computer, deleted material is more likely to end in a wastebasket, which isn't a basket at all. Emptying the computer's wastebasket means deleting files.)

Most edit programs can be run on laptops – giving you the flexibility to take them into the field. Extra disk space on removable hard drives may be needed to cope with large amounts of video. Typically an hour's video of broadcast quality will take 14 gigabytes (GB) of disk space.

Which are the most user-friendly editing programs? That depends on the user. Picture editors trained on Avid systems may swear by them. Journalists usually prefer systems designed to make the edit process as simple as possible.

A typical state-of-the-art set-up, the Quantel system at the Sky News Centre in West London, controls ingest (the input of video material from every source), output (the playout of video into programmes) and editing. There are three different levels of editing software.

- **Qview** lets producers and reporters view pictures, with sound, and make simple decisions about *ins* and *outs*, the points at which the shots start and finish. This is ideal for choosing headline shots
- **Qedit** is used by Sky News interactive journalists and their library to re-edit picture sequences for online use and to archive material. It includes simple digital effects
- **Qeditpro** is the high-end professional application used by craft editors to put together news reports and programme material.

Edit systems will be linked to news production systems. MOS (media object server) protocol allows video, audio and graphics to be played out according to the running orders prepared on newsroom computers.

NON-LINEAR EDITING

Digital editing systems are non-linear. This means that sound and pictures do not have to be laid down in a strict chronological sequence. In modern non-linear systems, the raw audio or video has to be transferred to the edit program. This takes time, particularly if the source is tape rather than a computer file. But once it is ingested, manipulating the pictures or sound is comparatively simple.

Some journalists see editing as a chore; others see it as a creative challenge and a chance to enhance their story-telling.

A CLOSER LOOK

LINEAR EDITING – THE WAY WE WERE

Analogue video editing – the technique used for nearly two decades after electronic news gathering took over from film – involved pictures being dubbed across from one tape to another. That meant a news report had to be assembled from the start to the finish in strict linear order. Each shot was dubbed across in the order and at the exact length it was to be used in the final report. Changing shots was tricky because a new shot or shots had to be chosen to fit exactly the same space as what it replaced. If major structural changes were needed, the edited sequences had to be dubbed on to yet another tape, with a consequent loss of picture and sound quality. The audio and video on each copy, or generation, of analogue tape was of poorer quality than the last. Too many dubs and the material became unbroadcastable. Dubbing digital tape holds no such danger, as each copy is technically identical to its source.

Editing analogue audio tape was also complicated. Each length of quarter-inch tape had to be stored on separate reels before they were joined together. Sound was usually recorded at a tape speed of seven-and-a-half inches per second (ips) for speech, or 15 ips for music. A ten-second clip of interview would therefore cover 75 inches of tape. That's nearly two metres. So, editing long features required great discipline and organisation, managing huge lengths of tape and switching reels frequently. And that was just for a single track. For a multi-track edit, you needed the equivalent of a small recording studio.

RADIO EDITING

Sound editing systems present sound as waveforms. You need to get used to the idea of 'seeing' your sound. The peaks and troughs in the wave make it really easy to see where words start and finish. Editing is much more straightforward than in the days when you had to spin the spools of an analogue machine by hand, running quarter-inch tape across the playback head and listening for the beginnings and ends of words.

Layering sound and multi-tracking have also become easier in recent years. You can put commentary, interview clips, wild-track sound and music on separate tracks and then adjust the level of each in turn. Or you can play back material through a mixer and adjust the levels as you go along.

With a system like Radioman, you save your audio files into a clip-box which appears on the desktop, and then move them on to the timeline. Then the fun begins as you cut and shape your package.

MULTI-TRACKING

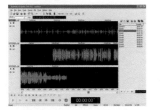

Anisha Shah, of BBC Radio Stoke, using RadioMan

RadioMan editing – multiple tracks show on the timeline

Multi-tracking – laying down several tracks on top of each other and then adjusting the sound of each track to the right levels for the finished project – is comparatively simple with software like RadioMan and Audacity, which is free to download.

The limitation on its practical use is how many tracks you can comfortably view on screen. Most professional broadcasters suggest that three or four tracks are the most you can use quickly in a news production environment. Anisha Shah, a broadcast journalist with less than a year's professional experience at BBC Radio Stoke, says: 'I've used up to five tracks. That's about the maximum. Any more and I can't see what I'm doing.'

SADiE, which is used for longer-form radio programmes like documentaries, is a little more sophisticated. It takes longer to master, but more tracks can be viewed comfortably on screen.

If you want to record music, use a program like Pro Tools, which can be found in many professional recording studios. Editing music is straightforward in most programs – the rhythms of the music can be seen on screen.

The principles of most systems are broadly the same and, if you have learned on one, you should be able to pick up any other fairly quickly.

REMEMBER

➤ Editing software is non-linear – you can move audio to anywhere on the timeline
➤ Multi-tracking – layering your sound – is limited only by what you can see on screen.

MAKING AN EDIT

You should edit first with your brain, then with your ears, then your eyes. The sound is the most important thing. On playback make sure you can hear everything clearly. The timeline helps you to 'see the sound'.

Each track can be edited separately. You isolate the playback sound on the track you are working on, so it is all you can hear on the speakers or in your headphones. You can see the peaks and troughs in the waveform and zoom in for more detail. A continuous series of peaks represents a word. The low points, or troughs, are the gaps between words. This is the point to which you move the cursor to make an edit.

Make sure, when you remove words or phrases, that you maintain the sense of what is being said. Allow pauses between the words you join together to maintain the natural breaths or gaps in everyday speech.

LEVELS

Sound levels have to be balanced before your edit is complete. You need to ensure that all speech is distinct and understandable, and not obscured by the background sound on other tracks.

You also need to make sure that the level of your finished edit is not too low or too high for station output. You should not rely on engineers, or the newsreader in a self-op studio (who has enough to think about), to 'ride' the levels because you haven't done your job properly.

Overall sound levels should peak between 5 and 6 on a PPM (peak programme meter) for speech output. On a digital LED (light emitting diode) meter, you don't want to see too many red lights flashing.

In a busy newsroom, you will almost certainly be using headphones. They make it easy to hear every nuance of the sound, which is great for editing accurately, but does not bear much resemblance to how most people use radio. Most people listen while they are doing something else and your broadcast is competing with background noise, which can be anything from traffic noise to screaming children. If your station broadcasts on an AM frequency, the sound will be even more indistinct.

If you get the chance, play your finished piece back through domestic speakers. Can you hear everything that is supposed to be there? This is how most people will hear your work at home or in the car.

USING MUSIC

As we explained in Chapter 11: *The package*, it is never a good idea to lay a bed of music beneath the whole of a package. Instead, you should feature it where appropriate. You can lay a long piece of music down as a single track and then lift it to audible levels in the mix, but this is not usually the best way. It's usually better to edit out the musical phrases or the bits of a song you want, and drag them to the appropriate place on the timeline.

Unless there is a hard 'in' or 'out' to the music you are using, always lay down a few seconds before and after the phrase you want so you can fade in and out. How long the fade should last depends on the pace of the music and the impact you want it to have in the piece. A rapid fade-in will be punchier; a slow fade-in can build expectation.

➤ Edit first with your brain, then your ears, then your eyes

➤ Get used to 'seeing' your sound

➤ Check your levels (sound should peak slightly into the red)

➤ Monitor the edit on headphones

➤ Play back through small speakers.

TV EDITING

Editing pictures on Final Cut Pro, one of the edit systems used by video journalists

TV editing on modern software is extremely versatile, and elaborate effects can be achieved relatively quickly.

Pictures can be frozen, slowed down or speeded up; they can be reversed or re-sized (to allow 'zooming-in' on a point of interest); the shot can be 'flipped' so that left becomes right; colours can be 'corrected' (if the camera person's white balance was wrong) or changed for dramatic effect (sepia tones or black and white, for example). You can add all manner of fancy wipes, fades and mixes and even do your own graphics.

Split-screen editing – showing more than one moving image on the television screen – is a simple task. All you do is make your picture smaller to fill the part of the screen you want it to occupy. Then do the same with the shots you want to appear in another part of the screen.

INGESTING OR DIGITISING

In computer editing, video from tape or media file has to be transferred to the computer on which it will be edited. This is known as digitising or ingesting. The most important discipline in this process is to label the medium so you can find it again. When video clips are ingested on to a computer they can be selected one at a time, and then digitised, or you can view the material in lengthy sequences, marking *ins* and *outs*, and *batch digitise*. Batch digitising means you can choose your material and then leave the computer to wind the tape and transfer the shots to the hard drive. Just make sure there are no breaks in the time code to confuse the machine while you're away taking a coffee break.

Whether you digitise single clips or a batch, labelling the clips as you go will be the only way you can guarantee finding them again quickly. Make sure the title of a clip gives enough information so that someone other than you can work out what it is. Producers and editors may need to access the material for a headline shot. Other reporters or sub-editors might take over the story later in the day. So 'man walking' is not as helpful as naming the man walking. Words like 'cutaway' and 'interview' may help *you* put a package together, but they're not much use to anybody who is coming to the material fresh and doesn't know what pictures are available. The single word 'interview' could apply to anybody. If it's an interview with the football manager Arsene Wenger, then 'wenger interview' or just 'wengerint' would be better. Similarly, shots of Wenger in the dugout might be labelled 'wenger dugout' to distinguish them from 'wenger presser' or 'wenger training'. You might also want to mark 'CU' for close-ups, 'MS' for mid-shots and so on.

The same applies to transferring material from a hard drive or memory card. Label your clips as you download them. If you are editing direct from a hard drive, name them as you use them for the first time.

TIP BOX

KEY LEARNING POINT – LABEL YOUR STORIES

It is always worth taking time to label clips and stories properly even in the excitement of late breaking news. The bigger the story, the more important the labelling. Huge amounts of video are shot on big stories. Retrieving the right shots from the archive when there is a new development in the story, days, or even years, later, becomes almost impossible without proper labelling. Correct spelling is more important in the computer age than ever before, because a search of an archive will not show a misspelt name or catchline.

TIME CODE

Professional video tape carries a signal, alongside the picture and sound, which records the duration of the recording. It is presented in hours, minutes, seconds and frames usually across the bottom of the picture on a playback machine (UK TV pictures have 25 frames per second). This is timecode. It restarts every time the camera records. So, a shot that starts three minutes, ten seconds and four frames into the tape will appear as 00.03.10.04 on the timecode. If several tapes are to be used on the shoot, the camera can be set so that the 'hours' reading on the timecode begins with a different number for each tape. Tape one will be set to 01.00.00.00; tape two to 02.00.00.00. And so on.

Timecode is essential for editing. When you mark the in and out points of a clip into the edit program, it is the timecode which gives the computer information about where the shot begins and ends. The computer doesn't make rational decisions like ending a shot when the subject has left the frame, or stopping an interview at the end of a sentence. The computer just reads the numbers.

A warning. As well as continuous timecode, cameras can record 'time of day' code, so that the information on the timecode is the time of day at which the shot was recorded. This presents problems for edit systems, which don't like a 'break' in the timecode. When they are trying to ingest material from tape, any break in the code (i.e. if the numbers are not continuous) will stop the digitising process. That includes breaks in the code just before the shot you want to use, because tape requires a brief pre-roll time to get up to speed. If the numbers on the timecode during this pre-roll are not continuous, the edit system will not be able to ingest the material. For news reports, make sure you are recording continuous timecode.

TIMELINES – A REMINDER

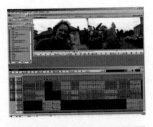

Pictures on a timeline on Avid Express Pro, as used by BBC video journalists

The programme information on digital editing systems is presented on a timeline. Pictures and sound can be added at any point on the line. The media – the clips of raw footage or audio – are stored on a hard drive, either within the edit computer itself, on a separate drive linked to the terminal, or on a server linked to the whole newsroom.

The medium is not stored on the timeline, which means cuts made on the timeline do not affect the raw data, which is still stored on the server. Cutting the end off a shot on the timeline does not mean you have lost the end of the shot. It does not show in the edited piece, but it has not been deleted.

This means there is an almost infinite opportunity to change the edit. Resisting the temptation to tinker endlessly is one of the disciplines experienced broadcasters learn quickly.

REMEMBER

➤ Allow time to ingest media
➤ Label your shots clearly
➤ Make sure your tapes have continuous timecode
➤ Material cut from the timeline is still stored in the system.

PICTURE ASSEMBLY

FANCY WIPES AND DISSOLVES ARE ALMOST ALWAYS A DISTRACTION FROM THE STORY. A STRAIGHT CUT FROM ONE SHOT TO ANOTHER MAINTAINS THE NARRATIVE FLOW.

Edit systems will give you dozens of options of how to go from one shot to the next. By all means, experiment with them, but, as a rule of thumb, *don't use them*. Fancy wipes and dissolves are almost always a distraction from the story. A straight cut from one shot to another maintains the narrative flow. You need a strong editorial justification to depart from this.

CUT OR MIX?

In news reporting, as in feature films, the rule has always been that video mixes, or dissolves, should be used only sparingly. The dissolve – fading in one image as another fades out, rather than cutting from one to another – usually denotes a passage of time. So, it is a useful story-telling device. It is also a way of editing within an interview to show the audience that something has been cut out. It is an alternative to cutting within an interview and then using a separate shot, a cutaway, to disguise the join. Used this way, the mix is an honest device, letting the viewer know what is going on: the televisual equivalent of [. . .] in the middle of a print interview, a device which allows readers to know that some words have been omitted from the published quote.

The increased use of the mix on television is as much a product of technology as a development in the traditional rules of film-making. Editing can be much more creative thanks to digital non-linear editing. In the days before videotape, pictures were literally cut from a length of film and taped together. Then video arrived and pictures were assembled by recording them, one after another, from a rushes tape on to a second tape. Both film and video required extra equipment to do anything other than a simple cut between shots. To mix between shots on film, two separate reels had to be prepared, known as A and B rolls. They were played back simultaneously through a vision mixer and the resulting image was recorded. In videotape editing, a third recording machine was needed at a cost of thousands of pounds in each edit suite.

Mixing between pictures in a news report

Nowadays, computer edit programs include the capability to add dissolves automatically. The only extra time taken is the few seconds to drag and drop the dissolve on to the timeline, and perhaps another few seconds to render the image. So, it is much easier to apply a dissolve or a more complicated video transition between images. A single operator can do the work of a TV gallery.

So, have the rules changed? Probably not. Even though it is easy – and cheap – to apply a dissolve or a wipe to a sequence of pictures, it does not necessarily mean that is the best way to tell a story. Often, technical effects are a distraction from the story-telling. You *can* do it, but that doesn't mean you *must* do it. Watch feature films, or documentaries, and you will see very few vision mixes. They are used only for dramatic effect. There is very little reason to apply them to news reporting.

FADING TO BLACK

Some picture editors will include a brief fade to black within a piece as a pause for thought or to denote a change in mood. This device should be used with caution, if at all. It invariably slows the pace of the piece, and can suggest the item has come to an end. It can upset output engineers too. They watch the programme as it is broadcast to check the technical quality of the signal. They are not necessarily concentrating on the detail of the story. So, if the screen goes black they think the signal has been lost. A 'do not adjust your set' graphic might be flashed on to the TV screen before you have time to explain the black was meant to be there. You should warn the gallery in advance about any black moments in your piece, but it's easier not to have to bother. Ask if the black was really necessary.

Many producers will ban the use of black within a piece for the above reasons.

For most TV output it is unnecessary to fade to black at the end of an item. Just make sure there is enough video at the end of the piece to allow the gallery to mix back to the studio. Extending the last shot by one or two seconds is enough. And don't have an edit point less than three seconds from the end of an item. If the vision mixer cuts out sharply, there will not have been enough time for the viewer to take in the final shot.

When you are cutting streamed video or web inserts, you may want to fade to black at the end. There is no vision mixer mixing to the next item. From the user's viewpoint the piece is self-contained, so a fadeout, rather than an abrupt end to the pictures, is more pleasing.

VIDEO TRICKS

Most edit systems have a range of effects and tricks that would have had a 1960s TV director drooling over his vision-mixing desk. If they are over-used you are in danger of producing something that looks like the product of a 1960s LSD trip.

There is very little need for elaborate effects in hard news reporting. In features they may be used sparingly, but only if they assist the story-telling. Page wipes run the risk of turning your journalism into a parody of a cheesy 1980s promotional film.

Split-screen is becoming more common in news packages. But remember that, if there are two images running simultaneously, there is twice as much editing to do. Can you still meet the deadline? And will there be too much visual information for the viewer to take it all in? The story-telling has to come first.

Some of the fancy wipes available as standard on Final Cut Pro. You would **not** want to use them in news reports

WHEN TO CUT

The pace of any piece of edited video – the speed at which events appear to unfold in front of the viewer, regardless of the length of the piece – is determined by the edit. Some one-and-a-half-minute items appear to drag, while a five-minute feature can leave the viewer wanting more. 'Any length you like as long as it's quick' is a useful mantra. You should always leave the viewer wanting more, because it shows you have maintained their interest right till the end.

One of the hardest skills to master, even when you are familiar with editing technology, is how long each shot should be. The simple answer is that a shot should run to its natural length. And the natural length depends on the shot. A static shot with not much happening in frame will look tired after three seconds. A shot full of action will sustain interest for ten seconds or longer.

Camera moves complicate the decision, which is why not moving the camera is the easiest option for beginners. *You should not cut on a camera move.* BBC video journalism trainer Paul Myles explains: 'Avoid cutting on a move – a zoom, pan or tilt. It's weird for the viewer. You leave people asking: "Where was that shot going to end?"'

JUMP CUTS AND CUTAWAYS

The transition from one shot to the next may jar, and this should be avoided. It usually means you have made a *jump cut*. A jump cut is usually either a cut between two parts of the same shot – such as sections of an interview – or a problem with the continuity of the action on screen. For example, one shot shows a man reaching for a pen; in the next shot he is already writing.

The way to avoid jump cuts is to use a cutaway – a separate shot showing something different – over the join. In an interview this may be a close-up, such as detail of the hands or face (though not the mouth); a reverse shot of the interviewer (the 'noddy'); a reverse two-shot (so you can't see the lips of the person speaking); or shots of what the person is talking about.

Televisually, cutting to shots of what's being described by the speaker is usually the most satisfying option for you and the viewer. You are using sound and pictures to complement each other. Instead of just hearing someone talking about something, you are seeing it as well. Your interview becomes more than just 'radio with pictures'.

Changing shot sizes during an interview helps avoid jump cuts too. As long as the speaker's head is in the same position, a switch from a wide shot to a close-up will not jar.

REMEMBER

➤ Use mixes and wipes sparingly in news
➤ Be wary of fading to black
➤ Don't cut on a camera move
➤ Avoid jump cuts.

AUDIO MIXING

The sound on documentary and feature films is 'dubbed' after the initial edit. In feature films, that may literally mean actors voicing their words all over again. In current affairs, 'dubbing' does not mean re-voicing the spoken word. But it may mean balancing the sound of interviews, natural sound on film or tape, music, audio effects and voice-over.

In news, a rough sound balance should be carried out as you go along. Dip the background noise so it is still audible but isn't drowning out the voice-over. Mix or cross-fade the sound from one shot to the next if there would otherwise be a clash in the levels.

TRAILING AUDIO

You will often want to 'trail' the audio, fading it out after a shot change, or lead into a shot by fading up the sound before you see its source.

One of the big mistakes beginners make is to assume that, whenever you cut a shot, you cut the audio to exactly the same length as the video. This is not often a good idea. It can lead to a jarring 'stop–start' effect. The change in sound, every time the picture changes, emphasises that you are watching a succession of separate shots.

THE NARRATIVE WILL FLOW MORE EASILY IF YOU OCCASIONALLY INTRODUCE A NEW SOUND BEFORE YOU SEE ITS SOURCE. THIS IS PARTICULARLY USEFUL FOR INTRODUCING INTERVIEWS.

Instead, you will often trail sound in or out of shots, cross-fading using the mixing tools on your edit package. The narrative will flow more easily if you occasionally introduce a new sound before you see its source. This is particularly useful for introducing interviews. You hear a new voice, and, a couple of seconds later, see who's speaking. The technique works nicely over a set-up of somebody doing something. You hear the voice, so you expect to see the speaker in an interview. Unless the framing of the set-up is very similar to the interview, you probably won't need to cut away to anything else before the speaker appears in vision.

Sometimes, you may want to use wild-track or continuous sound off one shot over a sequence of shots. This works over street scenes and wide landscapes. If there is an identifiable source of sound in the picture, though, you will want to hear it. For example, if there's a powerful motorcycle passing down the street, you should be able to hear its engine over the rest of the traffic.

Music will usually be faded in and out too, unless there's a strong start or end to the music itself which you want to feature.

WATCH YOUR 'SYNC'

Interview clips and featured sound are sometimes known as 'sync', or even SOT (sound on tape) or SOF (sound on film). The importance of sync (and where the term comes from) is that the picture is 'synchronised' to the sound. If the sound track is displaced by just a few frames from the picture it goes with, the effect is most disturbing. If you are 'out of sync', people's mouths do not move in time with what they are saying. You must avoid this. It looks unnatural – because it is.

You will usually move the sound and picture from a shot together as linked clips. If you move a track, either audio or video, separately, the displacement will be shown on the timeline as a plus or minus figure (e.g., '+ 00.03' or '– 00.03' if you are three frames out one way or the other). Move the offending clip by the appropriate number of frames and link the pair together again.

THE IMPORTANCE OF NATURAL SOUND

Every shot from a location shoot will have its own natural sound. Natural sound gives the viewer a sense of being a witness to events, of 'being there', without distraction from a voice-over or staged interviews. It can be raised in the mix to highlight what's in the picture and to punctuate the voice-over.

The natural sound from dramatic news pictures should always be highlighted: the explosion; the collapsing building; people cheering or screaming. Don't talk over it. And sound with less obvious narrative impact is important in setting the scene and helping tell a story: the traffic on a motorway; children shouting in a playground; the roar of a sports crowd.

Background sound is important in every shot. No jet aircraft ever took off without making an almighty roar. If you can see people playing music in a shot, let's hear the music.

EVERY PAUSE FOR NATURAL SOUND ALLOWS THE REPORT TO 'BREATHE'.

Every pause for natural sound allows the report to 'breathe'. It lets the viewer take in what the reporter or interviewee has just said. End-to-end words make a report difficult to understand and boring for the viewer.

The most important thing to remember when editing pictures with natural sound is that we do not live in a silent world. Viewers expect to hear the sound appropriate to the picture, even when there is a voice-over on top.

Imagine shots of the outside of two buildings – a Victorian town hall and a stately home. Architecturally they may look similar. But the sound on the town hall shot would probably be traffic noise and the bustle of a town centre; the sound at the stately home might be occasional bird-song or the bleating of sheep. Think how odd the two pictures would seem with the sound transposed.

Background sound is so important that it was once someone's job in the newsroom just to make sure it was right. Before videotape, 'mute' film – that's film without recorded sound – was often used for shooting news. It was cheaper to send a single cameraman with a wind-up film camera than a two-person sound crew. Station assistants had to find sound effects from discs to go with the mute pictures. On transmission, the sound effects were often played out live from a gramophone deck. 'Prov town plus tweet' was a particular favourite – a recording of the traffic noise in a provincial town with a single bird tweeting. Viewers never knew that the same bird was heard in shots of towns and cities up and down the UK.

REMEMBER

➤ Cross fade sound between shots if necessary

➤ Try using audio to introduce speakers before you see them

➤ Watch the sync on clips when people are speaking

➤ Feature natural sound

➤ Always use background sound.

VOICE-OVER

The reporter's carefully crafted voice-over (V-O) has to be added to the timeline at some stage in the edit. But when? And how?

We've already read in Chapter 5: *News writing* that the words should complement the pictures, not fight or contradict them. If you do not have location editing, you will send pictures back to the studio, either on tape, probably with a motorcycle despatch-rider (a DR), or via a satellite or broadband link. What you send is known as 'track and rushes'. The track is the voice-over recorded on location; the rushes are the uncut pictures. As the reporter, you need a clear knowledge of the pictures, even though you may not have seen them before writing the script. It's unlikely you will be able to change the script once it has been sent. You also need to give cutting instructions to the editor or producer, highlighting what shots are available and how they should be used. This can be done on the script itself (tucked into the tape box) or by phone or e-mail.

Editing on location or back at base, either by yourself or with a craft editor, is a much more flexible operation. You can choose whether to lay the words down first or later.

Back at the studio, some news organisations have soundproof booths for recording voice-over. Others rely on microphones in edit suites. Lip mics, of the type used by sports commentators, are often used. They have the advantage of picking up clear sound close to the mouth without 'popping' – the distortion caused by the breath at the end of some consonants. They cut out much of the background noise from sports crowds, so they're ideal for reducing background chatter in a busy newsroom, or traffic noise if you're in the back of a van on a location edit.

WORDS BEFORE PICTURES – OR VICE VERSA?

Should you lay down your voice-track before the pictures, or should you cut a sequence of pictures and then add the words?

There is no right or wrong answer to this question, because deadlines impose time limits on any edit. If the reporter is ready to record voice-over and the pictures are still not available (perhaps they are still being ingested or haven't even been shot yet), then laying the track down and cutting to it is a quick way to get a news item on air.

But, if you put the track down first, even if you have a good knowledge of the shots you are going to use, the pictures become constrained by the words. The edit is less flexible and will probably be less well-crafted. You will have to use your shots in a set order – and more particularly for a set duration. A shot that is probably worth only three seconds will be stretched to four or more to fit the script. An arty camera move will have to be ditched because it takes too long. There's less chance too to use the natural sound on each shot, which as we've heard in Chapter 11: *The package* can help the piece to breathe.

So, as a rule of thumb, cut your pictures before committing the words to the edit. A good writer will be able to tweak their script to fit the shots, trimming or embellishing a word or phrase here and there to match the pictures. If you feel

A GOOD WRITER WILL BE ABLE TO TWEAK THEIR SCRIPT TO FIT THE SHOTS, TRIMMING OR EMBELLISHING A WORD OR PHRASE HERE AND THERE TO MATCH THE PICTURES.

you don't have enough to say to cover every last second of the shots, all the better. Natural sound should fill the gaps.

➤ Laying down pictures before V-O usually produces better films
➤ Sometimes you will need to record your V-O before you see the pictures
➤ You need to know the pictures before scripting.

LAYERING VIDEO

A split-screen effect on Final Cut Pro

Just as digital editing allows multi-tracking of audio, you can also work with any number of video tracks. This means you have options for a series of sophisticated effects. The edit tools enable you to achieve:

• Multi-screen or split screen
• Re-sizing pictures within other pictures
• Moving pictures around the screen
• Text and graphics effects.

To achieve a multi-screen effect you will need to reduce the size of a shot so that it fills a smaller space on the screen. It's surprisingly easy to do (in Final Cut Pro, for example, this is done by applying a 'wire-frame' and dragging the shot down to its new size – a process that takes ten seconds or less). Or you can feature just a part of the shot, by dragging the edges in to change the framing. For example, if you drag the right-hand margin of one shot to the centre of the screen and the left-hand margin of another into the centre, and put the two shots on top of each other on the timeline, you will see one half of one shot and the other half of another. This is a *split-screen*.

It looks sophisticated, but consider when you use it whether the viewer can take in all that is happening on screen. It works best when at least one of the shots is a continuation of what has gone before and is already familiar to the viewer.

Split-screens can produce some quirky visual effects. If you film on a locked-off shot, with a camera on a tripod so that it cannot move, you can film one half of the shot separately from the other and match them later. You would be able to appear twice in the same shot and have a conversation with yourself. You are unlikely to want to do this in a news story, but in lighter features the possibilities are endless.

Overleaf is a more mundane effect that enhanced the storytelling of a video journalist on BBC Local TV in 2006. Laura McMullan was operating out of BBC Radio Stoke, so she did not have access to BBC television's graphics department. She created her own graphics sequence in the edit on Avid Express Pro, by layering video on the timeline.

Talking to yourself – a device to be used rarely, but it shows what the technology can do

The background shot of the man in the garden is the bottom layer of the sequence (a). Others are introduced on top, one by one, to build the graphic effect. The second layer from the bottom is the letter from the council (b). The last three layers are the words that have appeared on top of the picture (c) to (e).

(a) A man on a riverbank. He has cleared the site next to his garden to give him access to go fishing with his grandson

(b) But he has received a letter from the council warning that clearing the brambles was illegal

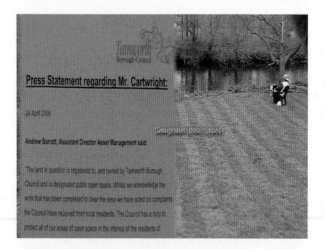

(c) It tells him the riverbank is 'designated public space'. The graphic is animated – the words appear to move out of the letter and on to the right of the screen

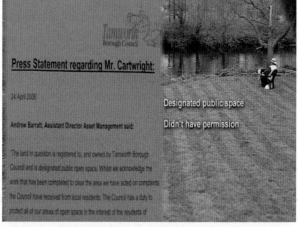

(d) More words from the letter – he's been told he 'didn't have permission' to landscape the riverbank

(e) A final comment from the letter – 'residents complained'

(f) Timeline

➤ Split-screen effects are easy to create

➤ They may be difficult for viewers to follow

➤ Layered video can produce backgrounds for graphics.

THINKPIECE

ETHICAL EDITING

We've suggested ways of using edit systems to enhance your story-telling. You will discover as you practise on edit systems at home, college or work that the possibilities of applying an increasing range of sophisticated and dramatic effects are limited only by your imagination. It follows that you can make things appear to happen that have never happened. Or change the sense of what someone is saying.

As soon as you misrepresent the truth or distort the facts as you understand them, what you are engaged in is not journalism. It is trickery or fraud, and completely unethical.

Sound engineers will claim that, with a long enough audio recording of somebody's voice, they can make them say anything. It's probably true, although it would take considerable skill to make it sound natural. It's not an exercise you would ever want to try in a newsroom.

Some politicians prefer to do live interviews, because there is more chance of getting their views across than relying on the edited version put together by a reporter. But that does not mean the reporter has deceived the audience by leaving out the politician's preferred quote. On the contrary, it means the reporter has chosen the words from the interview that he considers most newsworthy. In a democracy, most voters would think that more important than allowing an unchallenged platform for politicians.

Few people complain that they have been misrepresented by clips of them broadcast on news bulletins. That's because journalists strive to make sure a clip they choose represents an interviewee's view accurately. The charge that someone has been 'quoted out of context' is much more likely to be levelled at newspaper reporters, who can take phrases from separate sentences and write them up as if they were a coherent self-contained quote.

It's harder to distort the sense of someone speaking in a television interview, because chopping the words about would make the picture jump. A clip could be used out of context, but again journalists should attempt to choose a clip that sums up the interviewee's viewpoint.

There are other ways television can mislead an audience. If clips and shots are chosen carelessly, the story can be distorted. Using cutaways to disguise jump-cuts in an interview could be regarded as dishonest, although there are probably very few members of the audience who are not aware that television packages are edited rather than live. Because audiences understand the process, it can be better to leave the edit in, mixing between soundbites so the jump-cut doesn't jar.

If you must use reverse questions, recorded after an interview, you should ensure the wording is exactly the same as it was the first time you asked them. Some American producers have been known to insist that reverses can only be used if the interviewee was present when they were recorded.

WHENEVER YOU USE FOOTAGE FROM THE LIBRARY RATHER THAN NEW MATERIAL, IT SHOULD BE CLEARLY LABELLED.

Another ethical consideration relates to the use of cutaways. When people's reactions are involved, they should be as near to contemporaneous as possible. For example, it would be unfair to show a cutaway of the audience at a press conference sitting stony-faced after the Prime Minister has cracked a joke, if in reality they laughed uproariously. Or the other way round.

Whenever you use footage from the library rather than new material, it should be clearly labelled as such, either in the script or on a caption, perhaps using the date, the title of the event (e.g. 'First Gulf War', 'Ryder Cup 2006') or a phrase like 'library pictures' (the Americans prefer 'file tape'). Sometimes generic footage will be used (perhaps of crowd scenes or particular locations), and there is no risk of deception. It matters if you show old war footage to describe new fighting without making it clear these are not the latest pictures. Does it matter if you show old shots of oil wells in a story about rising fuel prices? Most viewers would think not.

As for fancy video effects, as long as the viewer can tell they are fancy video effects (layered shots, graphics or electronic wipes, for example) rather than a use of the technology to cheat the viewer, that's acceptable. Re-enactments of events by actors should be clearly labelled as such, and you should only show details of which you are absolutely certain. There is no place in journalism for making pictures up, any more than you can make up the facts of a story.

See Workshops and Exercises.

CONCLUSION

Edited audio and video is an important part of radio, TV and online news. The more editing you do, the more familiar you will become with the software and the more tricks of the trade you will learn. The short cuts to working more quickly are the most important for journalists. Deadlines are constant these days. You need to work quickly and accurately. But you will also want to learn how to be creative with your editing.

Editing is one of your key story-telling skills. Remember the advice about being a 'jack of all trades and master of some' (Chapter 1: *Introduction*). The master of editing is in big demand in modern broadcast newsrooms. It is in your interests to become a skilled editor. And it can be hugely fulfilling and a lot of fun.

FURTHER READING

Bordwell, David and Thompson, Kristin (2007) *Film Art: An Introduction*, Maidenhead: McGraw Hill. A well-established film studies guide with chapters on editing.

Kauffmann, Sam (2006) *Avid Editing: A Guide for Beginning and Intermediate Users*, Oxford: Focal Press. Practical advice for Avid users.

Murch, Walter (2001) *In the Blink of an Eye*, Los Angeles: Silman-James Press. A top Hollywood editor's guide to his art.

Weynand, Diana (2004) *Final Cut Pro 4: Editing Professional Video*, London: Peachpit Press. Practical guidance for Final Cut Pro.

CHAPTER THIRTEEN

GRAPHICS

There's been an exponential growth in the complexity of electronic graphics in the past few years. Words and images created in computers have transformed the way television and online journalists can tell stories.

Modern graphics present a whole new range of technical, presentation and writing considerations for broadcast journalists. In television they have led to exciting new ways of explaining complicated stories. Online they have changed the nature of story-telling. Online journalism no longer needs to have a narrative arc created by the journalist. Interactive applications mean you can offer alternative ways for the user to investigate the story, and find out as much or as little as they want. This non-linear story-telling involves providing not just one story-line but layers of story-lines, all accessible through graphics.

We'll look at the guidelines for using graphics and explain how they can enhance television packages and online content. This chapter is about using graphics in journalism. It is not a software tuition manual. There are other books that will help you learn specific programs, like Macromedia's Flash (one of the best tools for creating multimedia packages). A program like Flash will take at least 15 hours of concentrated study to learn. But don't worry if you haven't mastered it at this stage in your career. At most places you work, you will be part of a team, and there will be experts on hand to offer advice.

But remember the guiding principle of successful broadcast journalism – if you are multi-skilled, you will be more employable. It's worth learning picture editing with Adobe Photoshop, a graphics program like Flash and basic web authoring software. Then you can concentrate on the journalism.

TIME IS MONEY

The real cost of graphics is time, not software. What was once available to Hollywood blockbusters can now be seen every night in news bulletins. One reason for this is the increased memory power of computers. Far less kit is now needed to render complicated images within a timescale for broadcast. But the biggest factor determining the use of graphics in journalism is still how long they take to prepare.

Letters and numbers on screen can be animated (made to move) almost instantly; the time taken to render three-dimensional movement is less than it ever was; but it still takes as long for a graphics designer or online journalist to find, draw or import graphical images, to lay out pages, add script and build sequences.

A graphics sequence lasting 15 seconds on screen may take several hours to prepare. Compare that with how long it takes to shoot 15 seconds of video, and you'll see that graphics have to be used sparingly.

Newsrooms have dedicated graphics designers. They will always be busy and demands for complicated sequences should be made as far in advance as the story allows. You might be fighting for their time with a colleague. Documentary programmes have to book and pay for graphics as part of their budget.

WHAT CAN WE DO?

When is it appropriate to use graphics? How complicated should they be? The BBC spent a reported million pounds revamping their weather graphics in 2005. The result was hugely unpopular with audiences, and they had to change them. The Holy Grail of any graphical representation on TV used to be the ability to present information in three dimensions. TV graphics started with 2-D cardboard cut-outs, maps on boards with a graphics operator sliding another piece of cardboard out of the way to reveal place names. In those days – within memory of many senior television correspondents – 3-D would not only have been complicated and expensive; with that technology it would have been impossible.

By the middle of the first decade of the twenty-first century, 3-D was both possible and affordable. So, the BBC weather map became three-dimensional. The map of Great Britain was tilted to allow the virtual camera to sweep across the country and below the cloud line. But tilting the country 'backwards' made Scotland tiny and the Home Counties huge in the foreground. There was an outcry from viewers outside the south of England. The Scottish National Party said the map gave a 'distorted' view of Scotland. BBC managers, hugely conscious of accusations of metropolitan or London bias, had to respond. The map was tilted back to a more traditional upright form. All that was left for the viewers to complain about was the dreary brown colour of the 'green and pleasant land'. That episode showed that viewers notice graphics. Get them wrong and there will be a reaction.

VIEWERS NOTICE GRAPHICS. GET THEM WRONG AND THERE WILL BE A REACTION.

A CLOSER LOOK

BREAKING THE RULES – AND MAKING NEW ONES

It was always a golden rule of television news that words being spoken have to match any words written on screen. Nowadays some news and sports news channels look like particularly confusing web pages, with more words than anyone could take in at one time. But regular viewers soon become familiar with the format. They realise that these stations are telling several stories at once, and you don't have to follow all of them.

For example, most of the screen on Sky Sports News operates like a conventional television programme. There's also a headline strap at the bottom of the screen, and down the right-hand side there are statistics (league tables and results), unrelated to the main story.

For most TV output, though, the graphic is there to help viewers understand the story being told. Expecting somebody to take in one set of words through their ears and another through their eyes is expecting too much. It's not that such a feat is mentally impossible. It's just that it requires an unreasonable level of concentration. Try listening to a radio drama while you are watching a football match on television. The attention wanders.

An exception to this rule has always been the *name super* (see *Captions* below) – people can read captions identifying somebody speaking on screen while they are listening to what that person is saying. In a round-up of locations, a one-word place name is acceptable too – although it is normal to allow a breath for the audience to take in the information. A caption informing viewers that what they are watching is *library pictures*, or in the American idiom *file tape*, doesn't intrude on the viewers' understanding either. Many people will not notice it, but ethically it is important we identify when people are seeing something that is not newly filmed.

Similarly, if events have been recreated and filmed to help tell a story, the word *reconstruction* is used on screen. This is an important ethical consideration. Viewers should never be confused about whether what they are seeing is actual footage of a scene or a re-enactment of it.

Some channels will identify themselves with a 'dog' – short for digital on-screen graphic. It stays in the corner of the screen throughout their output. Because it is always there, it doesn't interfere with the viewers' understanding of what they are watching.

VIEWERS OF ROLLING NEWS CHANNELS WANT MORE THAN THE STORY BEING TOLD AT THAT MOMENT. THEY SWITCH ON THESE CHANNELS FOR A ROUND-UP OF THE DAY'S KEY EVENTS.

The big change that occurred in the era of 24-hour news was the recognition that viewers of rolling news channels want more than the story being told at that moment. They switch on these channels for a round-up of the day's key events. They may have busy lifestyles and cannot wait for an 'appointment to view' the bulletins on other channels. They may be 'news junkies' who want to know every spit and cough of breaking news. Whatever their motive, that audience is there to be served, and different rules apply.

Split screens, breaking news graphics across the lower third of the screen and moving tickertape strap-lines, usually along the bottom of the picture, are techniques pioneered by Sky News and borrowed by the other rolling news stations. It is still important to recognise what information is essential to the viewer, and what might be considered add-ons or 'bells and whistles'. But there is definitely an audience who wants more information than just the main story being told.

There were good examples of the different ways journalists can use on-screen information when the former Conservative Prime Minister Sir Edward Heath died in July 2005.

Sky News ran library pictures of Sir Edward and had a 'Sky News Flash' strap across the bottom of the screen with the caption 'Former PM Sir Edward Heath has died aged 89.' The first moments after such a story breaks are frantic. News crews and satellite trucks are mobilised, but it is too early to expect to see pictures from them. The station relies on telephone interviews. When Sir Edward died, people who knew him were interviewed. A caption identifying the telephone interviewee briefly replaced the headline. The phrase 'Former Cabinet minister voice Lord Brittan' appeared on Sky News for just over five seconds – about the same duration as a caption on an in-vision interview.

The ITV News channel had different library shots, but an almost identical caption to that on Sky: 'Breaking News: Former Prime Minister Sir Edward Heath has died at 89.' Their telephone interviewees were not so easily identified by viewers. A caption saying 'Lord Tebbit, former Conservative cabinet minister' appeared for less than two seconds. ITV News had a rolling ticker-tape of the rest of the day's headlines – everything from Tiger Woods' win in the Open golf to the movie premiere of *Willy Wonka and the Chocolate Factory*. But for people switching on – perhaps in response to a news flash that appeared on ITV1 moments earlier – there was little to identify the voices they were hearing.

BBC News 24 also ran library shots. Their caption 'Ted Heath dies' assumed a greater level of knowledge on the part of viewers. In a headline, it was reasonable to expect a UK audience to recognise the name of a former Prime Minister. Throughout the BBC's telephone interviews the name of the interviewee, 'Tony Benn, former Labour MP', for example, remained on screen. The ticker-tape offered a potted biography of Sir Edward – bullet points about key moments in his career.

Each channel used their graphics in a different way to support the story. The BBC had the clearest coverage – there was never any doubt who was speaking, and there was instant background detail. Sky News, with a more expansive headline, probably offered younger viewers a better explanation of who Ted Heath was. The ITV News Channel (no longer with us) used the graphics to keep viewers abreast of the rest of the day's news.

REMEMBER

➤ Book graphics as early as you can
➤ Check the house style
➤ Spoken words should normally match those on screen.

Name captions on network television

CAPTIONS

Name captions, identifying a speaker in an interview, are among the simplest types of television graphic. They are also known as 'supers' (short for superimpositions) or 'Astons' (after the machine that generates them). They can be added live on transmission using a caption generator, usually the Aston machine. This used to be done manually by an Aston operator, but now newsroom-control systems like ENPS automatically insert and remove captions, according to instructions typed in by journalists. Captions can also be introduced during an edit.

It is important to know your organisation's house style so that captions produced by different journalists are consistent on screen. Do you use capital letters for people's names, or upper and lower case? How are initials and titles used?

Is it   David Cameron M.P.
        (Con) Witney

Or   **DAVID CAMERON MP**
           (CON) Witney

Or   **DAVID CAMERON M.P.**
           (Conservative) Witney

Or any of the variations in between? We prefer the second of these examples. Your style book will determine which you use. Other examples which need clear guidance include the ranks of police and military personnel, and the titles of religious leaders of all faiths.

GRAPHICS IN LINKS

Graphics in the opening for the *Six O'Clock News* on BBC1

Graphics can be used to point to the content of a story during a studio link. The presenter may have an *inset* box over their shoulder with a picture appropriate to the story – guns for a story about armed crime, a picture of the Chancellor of the Exchequer for a budget report, or a wicket for the cricket scores.

Full-screen CSO (colour separation overlay) is also common. The whole screen is a graphic representation of the story, either a still or moving image. The presenter is superimposed on top of the image electronically. It looks as if they are standing or sitting in front of it.

These images have to be simple to understand and should not detract from the words being spoken. Any written words should match those of the presenter. You also need to round figures up or down in your script.

The opening sequence of the BBC's *Six O'Clock News* became a graphics-rich environment when the programme relaunched on a new studio set in Spring 2006. The technology had an effect on how the programme was written, with multiple screens available to show different images.

Graphics behind the presenters in the opening of the *Six O'Clock News* on BBC1

Presenter George Alagiah says in the early days of the relaunched programme there was sometimes too much information on screen: 'There was one thing where they scrolled up a list of all this criminal legislation. The idea was: "Look how much the Home Office has done." But it went up so fast and so small that nobody ever could read it, and that annoys somebody, because if they think they're meant to be reading it, and they're trying to keep up with it, and they can't, they get frustrated, and they don't hear the corresponding script being read. If they're not meant to be reading it, they're thinking why is that there? All it needed in the script writing, and this is a new thing because there's so much happening behind us, was a sentence to say: "Just to mention all the acts the Labour Party's passed would take half this programme." And that relates it to the screen to say: "Don't worry. We're just trying to show you how much there is. Forget about reading it. That's why it's going so fast."

'That was a classic example of how having the ability to put more stuff on screen means you've got to think more carefully about how you write it.'

The graphics-rich environment of the *Six O'Clock News*

THE 'BREAKING NEWS' BAR

A bar across the lower third of the screen is often used for simple headlines and to explain the story on screen. On 24-hour news stations, it's also used to announce breaking news. The term 'breaking news' is somewhat undervalued by its overuse on these channels. The term 'latest' is often preferred nowadays.

The information on the bar can be changed during an item, summarising the key points of the story. Here's an example from BBC News 24 in a studio two-way about the regulator Ofwat's recommendations on the water supplier Thames Water in July 2006. There was a hosepipe ban in force in the company's area, and the company had failed to meet its targets on repairing leaks from the Victorian pipe network.

During a studio two-way with a business correspondent, the top line heading said 'WATER WASTE'.

The second line changed from 'No fine for Thames Water over leaks'
to 'Firm must spend extra £150m fixing leaks'
then 'Company failed to meet targets on leaks'
then 'Firm loses 894m litres of water per day'
then 'Profits up nearly a third to £346 million'.

The five sub-headings rotated throughout the two-way.

The on-screen look of rolling news in Britain

TICKER-TAPE HEADLINES

Scrolling news across the bottom of the screen, or 'ticker-tape', has a variety of uses. CNN International has an on-air label for its ticker-tape strap. It's called the 'newsbar' when it is presenting news headlines. For sports news it becomes the 'sportbar', and for business news the 'bizbar'. This is probably a little over-the-top for British taste, but the labels sum up the way ticker-tape can be used.

Sky News found a way of providing a public service through their ticker-tape during the aftermath of the 2004 Tsunami, offering holidaymakers in south-east Asia the chance to deliver a message to loved ones at home that they were safe and well. Similar messages appeared in the wake of the London bombings of 7 July 2005.

At other times the ticker-tape, or crawler, is most often used for a summary of the main three or four news stories of the day. Each story will be limited to two sentences, concisely written. Sky News and the BBC punctuate their ticker-tape headlines with invitations to viewers to text and e-mail their comments and news stories.

Ticker-tape headlines perform one of the main functions of 24-hour news. Whenever you switch on, you will get a summary of the day's main news within a couple of minutes.

The 'Breaking News' bar

Ticker-tape during a Sky News report

FULL-SCREEN GRAPHICS SEQUENCES

Graphics can determine the shape of an item – a studio-based graphics bonanza rather than a video package – or a 3D swingometer at election time. When graphics cover the full screen the images need to match the script.

The script needs to be written to match the pace at which the images can be taken in comfortably. Sequences are usually built up as a series of pages. Words can be added as necessary. A graphics page might have a headline ('Prime Minister's statement', 'Troop withdrawals', 'Water shortage' or 'Injury news', for

A full-screen graphic illustrating the biggest story of June 2006 – probably – Rooney's metatarsal

example) but, apart from the headline, any words on screen should be matched exactly by what is said in the voice-over.

If the graphic says: '25% vote for Liberal Democrats', you should not say: 'A quarter of people supported the third party in the poll.' It's unnecessarily confusing. You might say '25% voted Liberal Democrat' or 'there was a 25% vote for the Lib-Dems'.

If the words are a statement from a person or organisation in the news (usually somebody who has not been available for interview), they can be animated, so that they appear on screen as they are spoken in the voice-over. Too many words on screen at one time are a distraction. Three sentences or three bullet points are usually enough.

In television, design is usually left to specialist graphics designers, but journalists should have a creative input too. What background do you want? Should it be a still image or moving pictures? Should the background be 'washed out' or 'knocked back' so any words can be read more clearly?

As the journalist, it's your job to check that any pictures in a graphic are not potentially libellous. For example, if you were doing a story about a possible link between pesticides and cancer, and showed a range of products, you would have to make sure the link had been proven for each and every one shown. You might be using pictures of a tractor for this story: if it was from library tape of an organic farm, the farmer might sue.

Make sure too that you have copyright clearance for any images used. Material that wasn't shot by you is probably not your copyright and you can't use it without paying the copyright owner.

CHARTS

A simple chart in BBC graphics style

Graphics are the best way of explaining numbers on television and online. If you are using a chart – a bar graph or pie chart, say – you need to make it clear what the viewers are looking at, to explain the scale, and to make sure the numbers are simple to read (not too many noughts and not too many decimal points).

Once you know the figures are going to be easy to understand, you can think about embellishing the picture with other elements – stills or video. The numbers will probably be the last thing the graphic designer adds to the image, but the journalist has to think first about how the numbers will look and sound in the context of the story.

MAPS

Maps have always been important in TV graphics. Even before graphics were used within stories, a map would be shown to tell viewers where in the world a particular foreign story was coming from.

Maps can explain the location of a remote foreign province or the distance between the scene of a crime and the street where a getaway car was abandoned. They can show a Parliamentary constituency or a crack house. Explaining the 'where' part of a story can often be helped with a map.

Major broadcasters use software like Curious World Maps which can zoom in to anywhere on the globe, or any UK street. The Curious program, which runs on a separate computer in graphics departments, has revolutionised the speed with which maps can be produced. And they look dramatic too with animated moves between world maps and countries, or between city maps and close-ups of streets.

Maps used to take hours and often involved thinly disguised breaches of copyright, using Atlases, the Ordnance Survey and the A–Z as sources. Now they are almost instant, and legally sound.

GRAPHICS IN THE STUDIO

Television studios have become graphic statements in their own right. The back projections on the BBC1 news programmes and Sky News' video wall both show commitments to strong use of graphics in the channels' story-telling.

Regional programmes do not usually have as much going on as the national outlets where graphics teams are bigger, but they too will have large screens for reporters to stand in front of. And occasionally the temptation to do 'virtual reality' is too much to resist.

Curious World Maps – created almost instantly by software which can find a street name or a postcode. They animate spectacularly too

Sometimes stories will be told in the studio using graphics, including 3-D virtual reality. Sky News presenter Martin Stanford enjoys 'walk and talk, show and tell

3-D graphics from senior graphics designer Sue Keeling at the BBC's Mailbox studio. A look at the height of the Midlands' tallest building (it's not that big after all!), and the moment viewers were led up the garden path

Sue Keeling

Martin Stanford of Sky News: a big wall and big, bold graphics

Sky News: The big graphics wall

Nick Higham

stuff', and has been doing it for more than ten years: 'There are some subjects which lend themselves to "human interactive explainers". When they're great, they're really great.'

But there has to be a reason for explaining something this way. Stanford says: 'If you're going to put a human being in there, there has to be a strong motivation for doing it.

'The best example perhaps was our budget explainer, when we had a supermarket checkout, and a little car came over on the checkout, and it went through the infra-red reader, and "ker-ching" – petrol up 3p. And cigarettes came up. "Ker-ching." People still cite that to me. It was the stuff on budget day – which let's face it is quite dry – that people wanted to know, presented in a slightly more interesting fashion than just a load of charts.

'Economics and things can be really dull and dry, but if you get in there and you actually draw the graph in front of your chest and, as you can now, walk along behind it, and say: "This was the down-point when the budget hit the crisis. Then we had the growth period and look how it goes up," and you make sure it goes right through your face and over your head and then down. Suddenly, I think that's 15 seconds of watchable television.'

Rob Kirk, Sky News Editorial Development Manager, says: 'Martin's very tactile with the graphics, which I think works very well. I like graphics that have a human dimension, because as a viewer I like to be led through the story.'

BBC correspondent Nick Higham often tells complicated stories on News 24 with extended graphics packages. He says the important thing to remember is not to get carried away with what the graphic *can* do, instead of what it *should* be doing: 'Sometimes we err too much on the side of entertainment instead of content, but the trick is to help the content. Graphics are a very good story-telling tool.

'Good television is mostly about showing real things and real people, but these things are very whizzy and get good feedback, both internally [within BBC News] and from outside.'

He says audiences love 3-D graphics when virtual objects appear around the studio reporter: 'There's an "ooh" factor when people see these things appearing in front of you.'

Martin Stanford agrees: 'It's the sort of "wow" factor, or "cor" factor!'

Both Stanford and Higham work closely with graphics designers. Stanford says: 'British television design is mostly staid and broadly quite flat. We've gone quite big – the design team here will use big fonts, but we haven't gone the American route. I can accept they might be over the top for a British eye, but they've got so much richness, texture and depth. Simple typological things. They think nothing of throwing three different fonts on screen, nice bold letters with lots of drop shadow and edge.'

REMEMBER

➤ You need a good reason for putting a presenter into a graphic
➤ Don't get carried away by the technology
➤ Working with blue screen is a difficult performing art.

CASE STUDY 13.1

WORKING WITH BLUE SCREEN – THE VIRTUAL REALITY GRAPHIC

Jeremy Vine became the new king of the BBC's swingometer at the local elections on 4 May 2006. He explained the difficulties of working with 3-D graphics in a virtual studio to DJ Chris Evans on Radio Two. He spoke of the problems of working in a space with nothing there, of working off a monitor (which, unlike a mirror, does not reverse your actions), and the amount of practice needed to get it right. Midway through the conversation, Peter Snow, an old hand at election graphics, joined in.

Evans began by introducing Vine and describing the virtual studio as 'the giant of all visual aids'.

Vine: 'You are in this space with nothing really. It's just a big blue curtain. I'm the only person who can't see anything at all, and these things appear around me, but they're not actually there. If I point my left hand it points on the monitor to the right, so I've now learnt how to do that, but I can't walk down the street. I mustn't go anywhere near a mirror at the moment, because, you know, right-hand left-hand reverses it, and this works the other way round, but I have been practising and I've been practising the numbers . . . and I've suddenly realised that numbers are terribly important. We see politics as being gigantic human drama and all that, but in the end it comes down to how many councillors you've got and how many MPs and how many voters.'

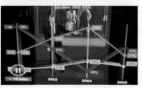

Jeremy Vine in the virtual election studio: trying to tell right from left, and not just in politics

Evans: 'The great thing about the swingometer is that it shows us in the simplest way what is happening in the country. Yet, in order for that to happen, you have to deal with all these massive statistics. Now it used to be a physical thing. Now, you've just described, it doesn't exist, it's a virtual thing. You're just dealing with an invisible piece of technology. So how many hours have you clocked up on this?'

Vine: 'Well, probably 24 so far in front of all these cameras and this blue curtain, because, as I say, I can't actually see anything. The peculiar thing is the really big jump forward. I mean, if you go back 25 years to the first time we saw Peter Snow and a computer, it was the 1979 election, and when Labour won whatever it was in 1979, I think it was 269 seats, the camera came behind Peter, focused on this computer screen, rather like the one you've probably got on your desk, and you saw he typed in 269 and you saw a little blue line. That was it. That was the graphic.

'25 years later, the big change is the graphics don't just happen behind you, they happen in front of you as well. So you need to be aware, like I'm doing at the moment. I'm stepping backwards and forwards on this blue floor. If I walk forward too far, like I've just done, I actually go through a graphic and destroy my own legs, so the virtual and the real must never come into contact with each other.

'We've had a problem with one particular graphic which is Ming Campbell. We've got this thing – Ming Campbell, the new Lib-Dem leader, will he drop the baton? Because he used to be a relay racer, he used to run around a track . . . we need the baton to drop. The first stage has to be a virtual baton, but then a real baton has to drop at my feet. And the only way to do that has been to get somebody into this set area standing near me with a blue sheet draped over them so they're invisible, and then they suddenly throw a baton at my legs. You just look around and you take it all in and you think this is absolute madness. I'm sort of jumping around in an ocean of blue.'

When Peter Snow was introduced, he shared Vine's bemusement – and enjoyment: 'I'm thrilled to hear Jeremy's finding the whole virtual reality scene somewhat bemusing. It is a madhouse . . . It's the best job in television. It's absolutely wonderful . . . You're in that studio and the graphics are telling you for the first time what's actually happening. Up pops a council in blue in Birmingham or something and you have to react to that live. It's terribly exciting.'

Evans: 'What was the most your swingometer swung?'

Snow: 'In the Dudley West by-election a swing of 29 per cent to Labour away from John Major's government, the whole thing blew up, the screen went blank, the House of Commons wouldn't forecast. It was total chaos. Old David Dimbleby, sorry, young David Dimbleby, immediately said: "Peter, I think we'd better come back to me there. We'll come back to you later when you've sorted out your contraption."

'If something goes haywire in the studio, sit back and enjoy it. Have fun. It is just a bit of fun, after all.'

Vine: 'How on earth did you get used to the situation in the monitor where, when you extend your left hand it goes to the left, so it goes in reverse on the monitor? So everything goes the opposite direction to what you're expecting.'

Snow: 'You've said it. It's an absolutely maddening problem. You'll get used to it, Jeremy, in about 30 years' time.'

Evans: 'When I worked with the puppets Zig and Zag, the puppeteers had the same problem. There's a switch on the back of the monitor. You can reverse the monitor picture.'

Vine: 'Yes, but Peter will tell you the problem with that, because then the percentages are all reversed. You can't read the numbers.'

You can see why 'just a bit of fun' became Peter Snow's catchphrase. It *is* fun, but it is also one of the hardest jobs in television. And it is very difficult to practise without a virtual reality graphics studio. While the rest of television technology – cameras, editing, even transmission (via broadband) is within reach of most people's pockets – 3-D graphics studios are not – yet.

See Workshops and Exercises.

ONLINE GRAPHICS

Although TV journalists are unlikely to be asked to operate graphics equipment in TV studios, increasingly sophisticated graphics packages are available to online journalists. Adobe Photoshop has become the industry standard tool for digital image manipulation. Macromedia's Flash allows you to introduce animated graphics into the presentation and content of your online material. Maps and diagrams can be used to help tell the story. An animated map can show the progress of an event; flooding, military advance, or the spread of disease, for example. Video and audio can be inserted.

If you are working online for the BBC, Sky News or most newspapers' websites, inserting still images or simple graphics like quoteboxes is just a question of typing the words into the appropriate window in the software program. You will do very little that could be called graphic design. But if you are given control of web content at a small organisation where there is no house style, or have set up your own web space, then you can and should be as imaginative as you like.

USING MULTIMEDIA GRAPHICS

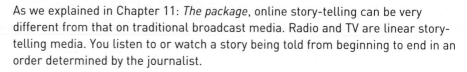

Graphics lead the way in non-linear story-telling.

As we explained in Chapter 11: *The package*, online story-telling can be very different from that on traditional broadcast media. Radio and TV are linear story-telling media. You listen to or watch a story being told from beginning to end in an order determined by the journalist.

Online news can be linear – you can read a story from beginning to end, or play audio and video reports. But there is also the opportunity for non-linear story-telling – for interactivity and for much more user choice in how information is accessed. And for feedback from users.

Non-linear story-telling opens up a whole new world of the imagination. You need to appreciate the strengths of each medium – text, still photographs, video, audio and graphics – and use each to best advantage. Educators talk about developing a 'multi-media mindset'.

The interface – the connection between your different media elements – will almost certainly be graphics pages. Built into the graphics will be links to launch other elements (animations, audio or video, for example) or move to other pages with more interactivity.

Each graphics page will offer a choice of routes for the user. The user chooses their route through the story. For this to happen your project needs to be constructed in modular pieces that are connected. You may also want to add links to external pages or blogs related to the story.

REMEMBER

➤ Graphics lead users through online stories

➤ Construct stories in modular units

➤ Use graphics to enhance interactivity.

GRAPHICS TEMPLATES IN WEB JOURNALISM

Many web journalists working for established media organisations find themselves using prepared templates to put content online. For example, all BBC News web pages look similar. There's a main story with a big picture and other stories beneath, each accompanied by a smaller picture. Sky News Interactive has a different but still distinctive house style.

Journalists fill in templates rather than creating their own graphic design. There's a discipline to working on these sites which is very different from the freedom and flexibility of authoring your own multimedia stories. Headlines have to be a certain number of characters long; teases and stories have to be written to prescribed length. Quotes have to be put in 'quoteboxes', opportunities for user-feedback in 'have-your-say' boxes.

Writing to length is a core journalistic skill. Working on these sites will help you hone your craft. You will learn to upload video and audio and how to link between text and other media. And you will develop an instinct for knowing which stories will attract the greatest user response. These are fundamentals of multimedia journalism.

REMEMBER

➤ Practise writing to exact lengths
➤ Learn to link between different media.

CONCLUSION

Graphics are a vital part of television and online story-telling. From the humble name caption to the virtual studio they provide information to viewers and users. They can make a dull story exciting, and a difficult concept easy to understand. They are particularly valuable in explaining statistics.

So, what are the limits of graphics reporting? It's no use creating *Jurassic Toy Story Lord of the Sith: Part Three: Reloaded* if it won't meet the six o'clock deadline. Three-dimensional graphics are a great tool in modern news programmes. But the time they take to produce means they have to be used sparingly, and only when they improve the story-telling. Sometimes the viewer might wonder if the tail is wagging the dog.

Multimedia graphics packages take time too. They are better used as a growing resource on developing stories, rather than as a treatment for breaking news. Done well, they can be the future of modern journalism.

FURTHER READING

George-Palilonis, Jennifer (2005) *A Practical Guide to Graphics Reporting*, Oxford: Focal Press. Modern and well-informed introduction to the use of graphics in all media.

McAdams, Mindy (2005) *Flash Journalism: How to Create Multimedia News Packages*, Oxford: Focal Press. The use of Flash in web journalism explained.

Quinn, Stephen and Filak, Vincent F. (2005) *Convergent Journalism: An Introduction*, Oxford: Focal Press. Drawing together the disciplines of modern multimedia journalism, including the use of graphics and graphical interfaces.

CHAPTER FOURTEEN

PRESENTATION

TECHNIQUES INCLUDE:

- Posture and preparation
- Delivery
- Timing
- Pitch and intonation
- Microphone technique.

Natasha Kaplinsky: 'You're there as a vessel of information.'

Julian Worricker: 'In TV there are a lot more rules to abide by.'

Showbusiness for ugly people. That's a phrase that was once used to describe politics but could easily have been applied to broadcast journalism. Not any more. Appearance is important, and those who take care over the way they look will get on. But there's much more to news presenting than simply looking good.

This chapter will explain the skills needed for reporters, newsreaders and studio presenters on radio and TV. It covers both studio and location, live and pre-record techniques.

We'll consider what not to wear and even what not to eat the night before a broadcast.

Electronic prompting, or Autocue, in the studio and on location should help make the job simple, but there are pitfalls for those who fail to master it.

Many news magazine and rolling news programmes are presented by two people. Dual presentation offers new opportunities and new challenges. Just what is on-screen chemistry? Who's in charge? And is there such a thing as an ad lib?

We explore the art of talking to time. It's no wonder Political Correspondent John Sergeant's autobiography was called *Give Me Ten Seconds*.

We also cover performing in a virtual studio.

THE VESSEL OF INFORMATION

News presenting shouldn't be about looking glamorous. It's about communicating information. Natasha Kaplinsky, one of the faces of BBC News, is clear about the role of the news presenter: 'You're there as a vessel of information. You're not there to imprint your personality on the bulletin at all. People have turned on to see what the news might be.

'You really are there to be as neat and as smart as possible without even a piece of hair or jewellery being a distraction from the information. It shouldn't matter what you're wearing; you should blend into the background. Of course, there's room occasionally for a smile or some warmth. People like faces they're familiar with and faces they've come to know and trust, but you're not there to have your say, you're there to give them what they want to know.'

Not everyone involved in news presentation is a star. Most, even those on TV, will be pleasantly surprised to meet people who inquire: 'Don't I know you from somewhere?' But for the star names the rewards are great.

Many presenters prefer the flexibility of radio. Julian Worricker, who appears on BBC News 24 and Radio Five Live, says: 'In TV there are a lot more rules to abide by; you're not as free to explore as on radio. You have to look in the right direction, nod at the right moment, make sure you follow the instructions. Otherwise, at least ten people are depending on you doing it, and if you don't, it all goes pear-shaped. Radio is a little bit more relaxed.'

A CLOSER LOOK

THE NEWSREADER AS STAR

Two episodes in the career of newsreader Kirsty Young show how important the presentation of news has become. When Channel Five News started there were hundreds of column inches devoted not to the content of the new channel's bulletins, but to the fact that the newsreader was *standing up.* Later, after a spell sitting behind a desk (most of the time) at ITV News, she returned to Five. The channel's advertising campaign showed her (standing up, naturally) with the caption 'Kirsty' and in smaller letters '5.30 p.m. & 7.30 p.m'. A single name was enough to identify her. She was being given mega-celebrity treatment like Madonna, Kylie or Pele – people who are identified by one name – and the word 'news' was much smaller than the word 'Kirsty'.

Kirsty says: 'You'll never be more important than the story – neither should you be – but if people trust you, that's what counts. Look at Sir Trevor McDonald, who recently retired from the news. People find him a very trustworthy figure. They loved him. If he said it, they believed him.

'As important as beautiful graphics and beautiful studios are, I like to watch people tell me things, if they're people I trust.

'I think when people are younger they can be a little too serious, a little too earnest, because they're trying to have a gravitas they don't have. But we all get older. We get our wrinkles and we get more comfortable in our skin, and we hopefully get better at it, in any job, and reporting and presenting are just the same. So try not to be too po-faced in the beginning.'

Kirsty Young: 'You'll never be more important than the story.'

Nowadays a news presenter standing rather than sitting will not attract headlines (although there was some controversy when the BBC's venerable *Ten O'Clock News* became the last of the major programmes to move their presenter from behind the desk).

Kirsty comments: 'In a way we could reasonably be accused of having started the whole bloody thing, by taking me out from behind the desk. We were trying to have a point of difference, because we were trying to shake the whole thing up a bit, and news, for so many years, was a very, very conservative medium: everybody sat behind a desk; everything was blue; they were usually all men, apart from the odd fragrant lady who was allowed to decorate the set.

'Essentially that's the way it was, and when we went on air, we were trying to say, a little bit naughtily but also with good intent, we wanted to approach it differently. A good way to do that was to take me out from behind the desk.

'When you innovate, sometimes you come a cropper, but you only have to look how much some of the things we did first are now used as a language everywhere to see we didn't get it completely wrong.'

THE PERFORMANCE

All TV and radio presenting is a performance. It requires a lively mind and a cool head. In terms of approach and attitude there is no advantage in distinguishing between live and recorded performance. Experienced live presenters will talk of the buzz of doing a show live and how the butterflies beforehand help them perform. Those remarks disguise the preparation needed to do the job well.

Recording a radio voicer or TV voice-over, doing a piece-to-camera or filming an 'as live' report need to be approached with the same sense of urgency as going live. The chance to retake or to have another go should not detract from the object of the exercise, which is to produce a performance that will be authoritative and polished. Occasionally, the knowledge that there will be another chance if you make a mistake will encourage you to try something more ambitious than when you are on air. Once the mic is live, though, your effort has to be spot-on.

The reporter who wins a reputation as a 'one-take wonder' will earn the respect of colleagues. But dependability is not just about impressing your peers. Getting it right first time buys you valuable minutes as deadlines approach.

POSTURE AND PREPARATION

Speaking is a physical activity. So you have to be physically prepared to speak properly on air. The air from your lungs passes through your vocal cords and sounds are then shaped in your mouth. So you need to have as much control as possible over your breathing.

Nick Pollard, the head of Sky News for ten years, was one of many local radio newsreaders who learned the hard way about reading when you're out of breath: 'The best lesson I ever learned was in local radio. Never, under any circumstances, run if you're late to read a bulletin. I did. I was working at Radio Merseyside. I was sitting there waiting for the clock to tick round to the top of the hour to read the bulletin, and then looked down and realised I'd forgotten to bring the bulletin in with me. There was about 15 seconds still to go, and I legged down the corridor, snatched up the bulletin, ran back to the studio and of course the microphone was already live. You cannot read after you've been running. I sounded like I was having a heart attack. I was gasping for air, unable to get my breath. People were phoning up saying: "Excuse me, I think your newsreader's having a heart attack on air."

'That's definitely my number one lesson. Never, ever run, if you're about to broadcast. Even if you're going to miss it, just miss it.'

Correct posture is the key to good breathing. You must prevent your ribcage from constricting your lungs. So, sit or stand upright and relax. Upright doesn't mean thrusting your shoulders back – your neck and shoulder muscles should not be tense. And relaxing does not mean slumping. If you are seated, place your feet firmly on the ground so they stabilise and balance your body, and don't rely on the chair back for support.

If you are about to read a radio bulletin, don't lean forward to the mic. Take a second to pull the mic towards you. Leaning forwards constricts your abdomen and the diaphragm – the muscles that help you breathe. Tight trousers, a belt or waistband, and even underwear can do the same – dress comfortably.

Nick Pollard: 'Never, ever run if you're late for a bulletin.'

Fizzy drinks or strong curries are never a good idea before a broadcast. The effects on vocal delivery and other bodily functions are well documented.

Whenever you have the chance, and this should mean *always* unless there's a late story breaking, read through your scripts before you enter the studio. Check any difficult pronunciations, and change any tricky phrases. Know your material before you deliver it.

The easiest scripts to read are those you have written yourself. With time, you come to recognise the style that's best for your delivery. Newsreaders will usually have time to rewrite most of the material in a bulletin to suit their voice. Producers and reporters are usually happy to let them do so, just as long as they don't change the sense of what is being said. Or the facts. That is why good newsreaders have to be good journalists.

Huw Edwards of BBC TV News, who writes all his own scripts, says, of being the sole presenter of a programme: 'You can set your own pace. You can put your own stamp on scripts, and deliver in the way you want to deliver.'

In the modern fast-changing news environment the idea of specialist news presenters who have a background as actors rather than journalists is anathema to editors. It used to happen, but simply doesn't any more.

Anyone wanting a job in broadcast journalism because they fancy reading the news – and that includes a lot of potential students applying for college courses – needs to know that the journalism comes before the broadcasting. And it has to be done well. If you need to check facts with a producer or reporter, do so. But be aware that they may not take too kindly to you asking questions as a deadline approaches. Particularly, if all you are doing is changing a script they considered perfectly good when they handed it to you.

THE BEST WAY TO CHECK A SCRIPT FOR FLUENCY AND EASE OF UNDERSTANDING IS TO READ IT OUT LOUD.

The best way to check a script for fluency and ease of understanding is to read it out loud. The weaknesses of words that appear fine on paper or on the computer screen are exposed by the simple test of rehearsing aloud.

Reading aloud also increases your familiarity with the material. If you know what's coming next in most of the bulletin, including the in and out cues of inserts, you are less likely to be fazed by late changes or breaking stories.

In a rolling news environment, there is less chance to check scripts before you deliver them. That's when you come to rely on the professionalism of your colleagues and their ability to write links that are easy to read. It is unlikely that anyone will be so adept that they will write in *your* style, but good writers will produce material that anyone can read fluently. You should aim to be one of those writers.

REMEMBER

➤ You are a 'vessel of information'
➤ Don't run before you read a bulletin
➤ Stand or sit upright, but relax
➤ Don't lean in to the mic
➤ Dress comfortably
➤ Check your scripts.

DELIVERY

Confident delivery is essential to successful broadcasting. Nothing sounds worse than hesitant phrasing and awkward pronunciation. Whether you are reading from a script or ad libbing from background knowledge, you must have confidence in your material.

Chapter 5: *News Writing* explained how good conversational English is the basis of effective communication. If you have checked your scripts and have faith in colleagues who might be writing late stories, you will have fewer nerves in front of the mic.

Much of a presenter's confidence comes from experience. Remember TV presenter Kirsty Young's advice in Chapter 10: *Going Live*: there is no substitute for building up your 'on-air miles'. Get as much on-air experience as you can, whether it's in student radio, hospital radio or local radio. One national radio presenter joked of her co-host: 'You suspect he was making tapes in his bedroom when he was seven years old!' It was a tribute to his fluency on air.

TIMING

The best presenters develop the art of talking to time, condensing what has to be said or filling to meet the time available. No programme format is open-ended. Even rolling news has junctions to meet – headlines on the hour or half-hour, or links to live events, for example.

Continuity announcers have to fill gaps between programmes to the exact second. News presenters have to ensure their bulletin starts and ends on time. Reporters may be given ten seconds to 'wind-up'. Play-out systems automatically record the duration of programme inserts and offer back-timings – the amount of time left before the end of an item or bulletin. The computer has replaced the stopwatch in most galleries, but the human element, the presenter, is still the most important part of getting in and out of a show on time.

ANY PROGRAMME THAT IS PART OF A NETWORK WILL DEPEND ON EXACT TIMING AS YOU OPT IN OR OUT.

Any programme that is part of a network will depend on exact timing as you opt in or out. The local headline sequence on BBC TV bulletins, the tease half-way through the national programme telling viewers what's coming up locally, and the opt-out bulletin itself all have to be an exact length so that viewers will not see the join as different parts of the UK leave the network for their own news and join it again later. The same is true of the regional slots in breakfast TV programmes. Many radio stations take a bulletin, starting exactly on the hour, from Independent Radio News or Sky Radio News. Regional inserts on independent radio's Digital News Network have to be an exact length – a two-minute bulletin or a 40-second summary.

So, how do you develop the art of talking to the exact second? It helps that most presenters deliver at three words a second – slightly faster on BBC Radio One and many commercial stations. But not everything can be precisely scripted – live inserts will overrun or fall short, and technical problems will occur (*'I'm sorry, we don't seem to be able to bring you that report . . .'*). So you need a range of strategies to fill out or cut short your programme.

- In a short radio bulletin the easiest way to fill to time is to take extra, short copy stories into the studio with you. Repeating the main headlines also helps

- If the bulletin ends with the weather report make sure you have three or four paragraphs of weather news, and that the first one or two lines will make sense on their own. *The rest of today will be mostly sunny with temperatures reaching 18 degrees Celsius . . .*

- Keep an eye on the clock from the start, and pace your content accordingly. It's no good linking to a 40-second voice report when there are only 30 seconds of the bulletin left. Don't be afraid to drop material while you are on air

- Have a variety of sign-offs, or closing comments ready. Experienced presenters will not need these to be scripted, but until you have grown in confidence write your closing words on a script and know how long it takes to say them (*That's all for now. We're back with more news in an hour* . . . Four seconds). Some stations will have a standard sign-off (*You've been listening to Smart Radio news – more in half an hour*), so you need to practise that and work out short phrases that will sound right immediately before it (perhaps trailing a news item you know is coming up later in the day)

- On TV, there will be a countdown in your ear from the gallery telling you how much of the programme is left. Get used to talking while listening without being put off.

There's no substitute for practice, of course. So, how can you practise on your own without a studio? To practise talking to time all you need is a watch with a second hand. Or even the counter on a digital music player. Look at your clock and tell yourself you're going to fill for ten seconds. Think about what you're going to say, then as the hand is ten seconds away from the next minute, just do it. Then try 15 seconds or 20. To replicate studio talkback try doing the same thing while you are listening to speech radio. Then try to remember what was said on the radio!

PITCH AND INTONATION

The most important tool of any presenter – and the only tool in radio – is the voice. Emphasis and interest are conveyed by inflection and tone. It may be worth underlining key words in a script so that you can stress them as you reach them.

You have to sound interested in what you are saying. Otherwise why should the listener be? You also have to understand what you are saying. Otherwise what chance does the listener have?

One of the greatest sins of radio presentation is to emphasise the wrong words. We've all heard a strange stress on prepositions in phrases like 'over to our reporter *in* Edinburgh' or 'they've been top *of* the Premiership *since* Christmas'. People don't speak like this, so it is a mystery why some broadcasters feel the need to do it when a microphone is live.

YOU MAY HATE THE SOUND OF YOUR OWN VOICE WHEN IT IS RECORDED AND PLAYED BACK.

You may hate the sound of your own voice when it is recorded and played back. That's because you are hearing yourself as others hear you rather than how you hear yourself. When you speak, the sound of your voice enters your ears by a different route from the way others hear it. Your ears are on the side of your head (hopefully) and you are hearing yourself through your own head – what Andrew Marr has called 'the familiar baffling of bone and flesh'. The recording will be an accurate representation of the way you might sound on air, so live with it. But that doesn't mean you can't improve your broadcasting voice.

REGIONAL ACCENTS

Gone are the days when the news was read in the clipped tones of received pronunciation (RP). 'BBC English' no longer means 'posh English'. Listeners are used to hearing a range of accents on air.

Local radio stations usually have several presenters with strong local accents, although the use of dialect (words and phrases specific to the area) would still be frowned on in a news bulletin.

BBC presenter Adrian Chiles jokes that his West Midlands accent has helped him in broadcasting. He says: 'They assume Brummies are thick, so when you can string two sentences together and ask a sensible question, they think you're a genius.'

FRANK GARDNER: 'IF YOU'VE GOT A GOOD STORY, AND YOU REPORT IT WELL, AND PEOPLE CAN UNDERSTAND WHAT YOU'RE SAYING, IT DOESN'T MATTER WHAT YOUR ACCENT IS AT ALL.'

The encouragement of regional voices has not hampered people with neutral or even 'posh' accents. BBC Security Correspondent Frank Gardner says: 'I got told once by somebody, a colleague who'd been to the same school as me: "Your voice is too posh to ever be on national television." That is just not true. If you've got a good story, and you report it well, and people can understand what you're saying, it doesn't matter what your accent is at all.'

MICROPHONE TECHNIQUE

To get the best out of them, you need to know the technical capability and polar pattern of the mics you're working with (see Chapter 7: *Location Video and Sound*). Put more simply, you need to know how near you need to be to the mic to sound your best.

- In a radio studio, don't be afraid to be almost kissing the microphone (but beware of 'popping')

- On location for radio, with an omni-directional mic, keep it close to cut out ambient sound, or hold it a little further away to add background atmosphere to your piece

- A gun mic on TV will be more directional – ensure it's pointing directly at your mouth

- In a TV studio, the clip mic will be omni-directional, and needs to be secured within six inches (15 cm) or so of your mouth

- Podcasters should recognise that more expensive mics will produce better results. But BBC tests have found that cheap headset mics, with 'noise cancelling', can produce results comparable to professional equipment.

REMEMBER

- ➤ Be confident on mic
- ➤ Learn to talk to time
- ➤ Accents don't matter
- ➤ Know your equipment.

EXPECT THE UNEXPECTED

'We're going to end this programme and we're going to hand over to London where Five Live is going to continue because the BBC's facility which is in the centre of the city centre in Birmingham is being evacuated.'

Jonathan Aspinall, 10.15 p.m. Saturday 9 July 2005

Whenever you are on mic, be aware of what might go wrong. It's not so much that what *can* go wrong *will* go wrong. It's more the case that what can go wrong won't be a disaster if you are prepared for it.

Concentrate to block out distractions. To remain focused when the unexpected happens is easier said than done. There is a famous clip of BBC newsreader Jan Leeming being startled by a studio light bulb which burst above her head and showered her with glass. Who wouldn't be surprised by that? More common are technical glitches within a bulletin – the wrong audio played in, the wrong video, or graphics that suddenly bear no relation to what is being said on screen.

CASE STUDY 14.1   COPING IN ADVERSITY

Perhaps the most famous example of news readers responding coolly when the unpredictable happened came at the top of the BBC's *Six O'Clock News* in May 1988. The top story was a breakthrough in East–West relations as the Cold War drew to a close. But that wasn't what made front page headlines in the *Daily Mirror* next day. Their headline 'BEEB MAN SITS ON LESBIAN' and the subhead '. . . while Sue reads on with woman chained to her desk' summed up one of the most bizarre episodes in broadcast journalism.

Two women in combat fatigues had broken into the studio and handcuffed themselves to the equipment: one to the desk, the other to a camera. They were protesting about Clause 28 of the Conservative Government's Local Government Act, outlawing the promotion of homosexuality in schools. A live broadcast to the nation might seem a predictable target for demonstrators. What made it so unlikely was that the news studio was on the *sixth floor* of Television Centre.

Presenter Nicholas Witchell managed to sit on one demonstrator and hold his hand over her mouth, while Sue Lawley read the headlines and said: 'I am afraid we've rather been invaded by some people, whom we hope to be removing very shortly. In the meantime, if you can avoid the background noise, we will bring the news to you if we can.' Ms Lawley said years later this was 'pompous stuff – but what else was a girl to do?'

Anyone who has visited BBC Television Centre recently will know how hard it is to get past the security at the front desk, never mind into the studios. That did not stop campaigners for fathers' rights bursting into the National Lottery studios in May 2006 and interrupting a live broadcast.

PRONUNCIATION

There's rarely an excuse for pronouncing words wrongly. Check pronunciation as you would facts. The BBC has a Pronunciation Unit, which checks how words are spoken for all outlets from quiz shows to news bulletins. They issue daily checklists of phonetic spellings of names in the news. If you don't have access to pronunciation experts, you can check a word you don't know by asking colleagues, or phoning libraries, language teachers or embassies. Local post offices can be helpful. Add pronunciation experts to your contacts list.

Network news readers often say their biggest challenge is unfamiliar foreign names. When famine struck Niger in Africa, the BBC's pronunciation of the country's name changed. It used to be pronounced like a shortened form of the name of another African country, Nigeria (the accepted pronunciation, incidentally, of the river Niger). The new pronunciation sounded like a shortening of 'knee-jerk'. The modern version (nee-jer) avoids confusion with the river and with Nigeria, and recognises the French-speaking history of the country.

BBC football commentator Guy Mowbray, who encountered dozens of foreign names at the 2006 World Cup, says there is nothing wrong with anglicising names: 'Some commentators try to be too clever. We can't know all about every different language. What matters is that the viewers know who you are talking about.'

IF AN UNFAMILIAR NAME CROPS UP, MOST PROFESSIONALS' ADVICE IS TO 'JUST GO FOR IT' . . . BUT IN LOCAL OR REGIONAL BROADCASTING, YOU CAN'T BLUFF.

If an unfamiliar name crops up, most professionals' advice is to 'just go for it'. If you sound confident, listeners won't think you've made a mistake. But in local or regional broadcasting, you can't bluff. Many listeners will know you've got it wrong, probably because they live in or near to the village you've just mispronounced. Newsrooms need to have pronunciation lists available to all on-air staff.

We've all seen reporters repeatedly fluffing their lines on out-takes programmes like *It'll be All Right on the Night* or *Auntie's Bloomers*, but the novelty has long since worn off. Most are not funny any more, especially when the light is fading and you are on take 47.

Many of the oft-repeated bloopers have one thing in common – the inability to pronounce a particular word or phrase. Everybody has words they stumble over. The trick is to avoid your particular *bête noire*. Use a different word. The thesaurus is full of synonyms for 'phenomenon'. Find another way to say it, or, if the problem word is a proper noun, the name of a person or place essential to the story, break it down into easy phonetic syllables. Visualise it that way rather than the way it is spelt. In a radio script or voice-over write it out phonetically.

Mahmoud Ahmadinejad, the President of Iran, might become *Mar-mood Armour-dinner-jad*.

Paris Saint-Germain, the football club, is usually pronounced *Paris San Jer-man* with the name of the city said the English way, and the rest with the French pronunciation.

Menachem Begin, the late Israeli Prime Minister, whose name still turns up in reports of the conflict in the Middle East, can become *Men-nak-im Bay-gin* – the underlining reminding you the name has a hard 'g'.

A CLOSER LOOK

- ➤ Expect the unexpected
- ➤ Check pronunciations
- ➤ If you're uncertain – just go for it!

RADIO

A GOOD CONVERSATION

Think of live radio as a good conversation, and you won't go far wrong. Some presenters have a mental picture of their listener. It may be a real person (a favourite aunt or grandfather, say) or imaginary (independent local radio's Debbie – see Chapter 2: *What's The Story?*). But almost every radio presenter prefers to think they are talking to one person rather than the actual audience, who are probably too numerous to visualise.

CONCENTRATE ON SOMEONE YOU KNOW WILL BE INTERESTED IN WHAT YOU'RE SAYING – A CRITICAL FRIEND.

The idea of talking to millions, or even hundreds of people, at a time is daunting for most of us. You can't please them all. So, concentrate on someone you know will be interested in what you're saying – a critical friend.

Peter Allen is a Sony-award winning BBC Five Live presenter and a journalist with experience on newspapers and as a foreign correspondent for ITN. He says: 'Radio is just conversation. What makes a good conversation is someone who's got something to tell you. He tells you in an amusing, sharp concise way: sometimes provocative; sometimes a little bit combative; never boring.

'I've worked with Jane Garvey for years, and we got a Sony once where the judge said: "Peter and Jane are in conversation, but it's a conversation that includes the listener." That's the essence of the business – does this help me in a conversation with the listener? Are they understanding what I'm talking about? Am I talking their kind of language? Am I communicating with this person.'

MAKING MISTAKES

PETER ALLEN: 'PEOPLE LOVE MISTAKES. IF YOU'VE REALLY GOT SOMETHING BADLY WRONG AND YOU LAUGH AT YOURSELF, YOU WILL FIND THAT YOU ARE ENORMOUSLY POPULAR.'

Peter Allen says you shouldn't be worried about making mistakes on air. Just apologise. 'If you have done something wrong and you stand up and say, "I think I got that wrong." Anger dissipated. Honour satisfied. People don't even bother to write the letter of complaint.

'Some journalists think if you make a mistake, ignore it, cover it up. No, don't. People love mistakes. If you've really got something badly wrong and you laugh at yourself, you will find that you are enormously popular. If you make a mistake and you sound embarrassed, then they're embarrassed and you've lost. But the bits which people remember are when something goes wrong and you simply laugh and say: "Oh, what a clown, look what I've done." People laugh at you. You laugh at yourself, and on you go. Absolutely no damage done.'

- ➤ Radio is conversation
- ➤ Admit your mistakes, and move on.

DRIVING THE DESK

Most radio bulletins are *self-op*. The reader operates or *drives* the mixer on the desk through which microphone, audio inserts and any jingles or theme tunes are channelled. Nowadays the recorded inserts are likely to be stored on digital hard drives, ready for instant playback. There might also be live feeds from outside broadcasts or reporters on telephone or ISDN lines. There might be up to a dozen channels to control. And sound levels have to be checked on each of them before transmission.

Modern digital desks allow the inputs to be changed to suit the operator. For example, if somebody prefers to have the mic fader on the extreme left of the desk, they can do so by pre-programming the desk. This is helpful for left-handed people. But there is a danger that, unless settings are agreed among station staff, someone called on to read a bulletin at the last minute might find themselves trying to operate a strange desk with all the controls in the 'wrong' place.

The versatility of modern equipment can mean a greater margin for error. Strong studio discipline is required and the station's operating guidelines have to be observed by all staff.

Older studio desks are likely to be hard-wired. The reader's microphone, for example, is always operated by the same fader – usually at the end of a row. It is likely to be alongside the controls for the second mic, which can be used by a separate contributor, perhaps providing a live voice report or presenting a sports bulletin.

REMEMBER

➤ Check the levels on all inputs before transmission
➤ Know the controls on your desk.

NEWS PROGRAMMING

Longer-form news programmes, like BBC Radio Four's *Today* and *The World at One*, the output of BBC Five Live and many speech-based programmes on local radio, have a control room similar to a television gallery. The producer and technical crew are in the *booth* or *cubicle* (or sometimes it's known as just the control room) and can see the soundproof studio through glass. It may be someone's job to answer the phones and put callers on air; someone else will play in audio and dial up ISDN lines. The number of backroom staff will depend on the size of the station.

The producer can talk directly into a presenter's headphones or *cans*.

HEADPHONES

HEADPHONES ARE YOUR LINK WITH THE WORLD OUTSIDE THE STUDIO. YOU NEED TO WEAR THEM TO MONITOR OUTPUT.

Headphones are your link with the world outside the studio. You need to wear them to monitor output – to hear exactly what you and your programme sound like to the audience – and to listen to voices from the control room (your producer or technical operator). You won't be able to hear phone-in callers and other live contributors without your cans, because the studio speakers will be muted whenever your mic is open.

Muting the speakers is necessary to prevent feedback, or 'howl-round', the high-pitched screech produced by sound being picked up from a speaker and re-transmitted through the mic. For the same reason, phone-in callers are asked to turn their radios off. Otherwise, the broadcast suffers from background whistling. Contributors in the studio need to wear cans to hear people on the phone.

Headphone levels are adjustable. Protect your ears by making sure they are not too loud. It might not be your mistake that damages your hearing – it could be a control room error. But it's your ears that will suffer – and they are two of the tools of your trade.

MANY PROFESSIONAL BROADCASTERS SLIP THEIR HEADPHONES OFF ONE EAR; IT MEANS THEY CAN TALK TO PEOPLE IN THE STUDIO WITHOUT SHOUTING.

Many professional broadcasters slip their headphones off one ear; it means they can talk to people in the studio – colleagues or guests – without shouting.

Many presenters develop the art of working on *split-cans*, having one audio source (programme output) in one ear and another in the other ear. The second source may be another station's output or an audio feed from an outside broadcast. A presenter will then be able to link to the second source or relay information from it. You can only do this if you trust the second source. If the second source is something for which your station doesn't have the broadcast rights, but is live on another station (the F.A. Cup draw is a classic example from British broadcasting), an accomplished broadcaster will be able to repeat the information almost immediately.

A variation on this is monitoring TV output while you are broadcasting on radio. On BBC Radio Five Live, for example, a presenter may be watching a TV picture of a press conference on BBC News 24. They will be able to take their cue from the TV and link to the presser at the appropriate moment. This technique also works if you are linking live to events in Parliament – you can watch it live on the BBC Parliament channel – or to a televised sporting event.

> **REMEMBER**
>
> ➤ The presenter's headphones are the link with the production team
> ➤ Practise the art of working on split-cans.

CHECKING FOR ACCURACY

The presenter is at the sharp end of any broadcaster's output – which is why some are so well paid. Contact with the audience brings a responsibility to make sure you get things right.

BBC Five Live's Rachel Burden says presenters need to be constantly aware of the need for accuracy: 'As a presenter you are quite vulnerable to what is being set up for you, and what is being written for you. In the back of my head is the thought: "Does this all make sense to me?" Is there anything glaring that needs to be checked? The next step is: "What's the story?" I look at each story and ask: "What is the key element here? What is the one question people at home will be asking?" And I try and build what we do around that.'

See Workshops and Exercises.

DUAL PRESENTING

Successful presenters are aware of the amount of control they have over the programme. The producer is in charge, but relies on the on-air skills of the presenter.

The presenter will have a close working relationship with their production team. But the presenter who has a strong journalistic input can be 'first among equals', even if a producer is nominally in charge. Working with a co-presenter creates a new set of challenges.

Shelagh Fogarty, who co-presents regularly on BBC Radio Five Live, says mutual respect and a flexible approach to who does what within the programme are keys to a successful on-air pairing: 'You hear all the time about presenters scrapping over stuff, and to me that's like a marriage where you argue about who took the bins out last.'

She explains her working relationship with Nicky Campbell on the breakfast show: 'There's no trick of the trade. We get along. We're both pretty clear on areas of interest and they don't particularly clash that much. If we do bargain it's friendly bargaining, and the editor has a clear idea of how to play to our strengths'.

Presenters need to get on with each other, but it doesn't always have to appear that way to listeners. Peter Allen jokes that his on-air partnership with Jane Garvey began as 'the grumpy old git and the sex-starved spinster'.

Jane Garvey

Garvey is now married (to fellow presenter Adrian Chiles) and has children. Her radio relationship has developed too: 'When we first started we didn't have the contact with listeners we do now. We've got the texts coming up in front of us on our screens. It's not scientific, but it gives you a fair idea of what gets people going. So, increasingly, I can be doing an interview with somebody and someone will text in a question which I will use. That's how fast the interaction is. We're closer to the listenership than has ever been possible before.'

The pair make a point of reading out listeners' comments, particularly the critical ones. Garvey says: 'It's reverse psychology and it actually stops them coming in! But we like it. Any reaction is better than no reaction at all. If it's a boring afternoon, Peter will do a deliberately ridiculous interview just to stir it up a bit. It doesn't do any harm. I don't mean something offensive. He'll just take a slightly ludicrous position.'

Allen says: 'We'll normally argue with each other. There's very little point in us agreeing. It sometime sounds like an old married couple – underlying affection, but quite cross with each other a lot of the time.'

Members of the audience respond according to which side of the argument they're on: 'You get letters which indicate that people look at you as a real friend. They say things like: "I'm very disappointed that you didn't pick up that point, Peter. I really thought you would, because I've always trusted you and you're a mate." It's a very immediate medium, radio. Better than telly. Telly's a bit plastic.'

REMEMBER

➤ Working with a co-presenter involves 'give and take'
➤ Dual presentation on radio can include the listeners in the conversation.

TV PRESENTING

Presenting the news on TV is about communicating and telling stories. When you tell somebody something, all kinds of natural tools help the process: eye-contact, body language, hand gestures. Most of these come into play in TV reporting and presenting, although a deskbound newsreader who started waving their hands and arms about would soon be accused of distracting behaviour.

Viewers are critical of how their news is presented. The letters columns of serious newspapers have been filled with comment about newsreaders standing up rather than sitting to deliver bulletins. It happened when Channel Five's Kirsty Young first stood to read the news; when Sky News and ITV News introduced their 'video walls'; when BBC newsreaders stood up at the start of bulletins.

And then there's the argument about whether one or two people should present the bulletin. BBC presenter George Alagiah, an experienced foreign correspondent with a sense of perspective about these things, says: 'Remember, this is fashion. I won't be very popular for saying this, because every manager comes along and reinvents the wheel. I can remember when they were double-headed, and somebody comes along and says: "We really need the authority that comes with the single voice speaking for the BBC." Then somebody else comes along and says: "Actually we need a bit of warmth, so let's have a double-header." I don't want to sound too cynical, but let's not dress it up too much. Whether it's single-header or double-header, these are as much a function of fashion as they are of journalism.'

Viewers' fascination with changes to traditional news delivery happens at local level too. Ashley Blake, a popular regional presenter and reporter, has a trademark wave to end the bulletin. It started in 2001 when he joined BBC Midlands: 'I was told I had 12 seconds to fill and it wasn't scripted, so I had my words prepared. Then I heard a voice from the gallery screaming: "You've got 18 seconds." I was fumbling over my words and I just waved, as if you were saying to a pal in the pub: "See you later." And I heard the director say: "Did he just wave?"'

'I walked back into the newsroom and the phones were ringing. I thought it was the boss and I'd never work for the BBC again. But it was a viewer saying she loved it and it had restored her faith in human nature. There was another call saying roughly the same, and the third call *was* the boss, saying: "That was lovely."'

Ashley Blake's wave: it prompted e-mails, phone calls and comment in local newspapers

'Now I get e-mails if I don't wave. I even had one from some nurses at an intensive care unit who said they had a 50p bet on which hand I would use to wave.'

When a rival broadcaster, on Midlands ITV, said he was going to wave too, the *Birmingham Mail* called it 'hand-to-hand combat'.

THE PRESENTER AS TEAM PLAYER

One of the biggest differences between TV and radio presenting is that television relies on a team of people to get on air. You can be alone in a radio studio and produce a memorable broadcast. In TV, there are studio and gallery crews (a producer, director and vision mixer, camera and sound operators, Autocue). Everyone in the team needs to know what's going on. If the presenter departs from the script for any length of time, or moves out of shot, everything starts to go wrong.

Producers like to think of their presenters as swans gliding effortlessly across the surface of a pond, with the unseen production team paddling furiously beneath the water.

Star presenters can be a reason for viewers to switch on. They trust them and welcome them into their homes. But the best presenters are more than just the mouthpieces of the news operation. They contribute to the journalism too. That is why almost all the top news presenters are trained journalists. Many of them have been correspondents in the field. Michael Buerk, George Alagiah and Jeremy Thompson were foreign correspondents. Huw Edwards was a political correspondent. Julie Etchingham was a reporter. John Humphrys and Kay Burley began in newspapers.

BBC News 24's Matthew Amroliwala explains how the presenter on a rolling news channel is involved in the journalistic decision making: 'It is a team thing. You're keeping your eye glued to that top line for updates. As well as the information your own team is sending in your ear, there is a relentless stream of factual information from other news agencies and people on the ground, and it's a case of trying to weave all that in.

'It's often the case that you spot something. You whisper it down the microphone to the gallery and suggest we should do this or that, and they make a judgement call on what's around.'

The presenter may be given the go-ahead to deliver information before it has been typed into a formal script. Then the presenter ad libs, perhaps reading from the newsflash on screen or from a print-out. They'll be making sense of the facts as they deliver them.

Amroliwala says: 'Quite often you are aware of the sort of things that might be happening during the course of the day, and in that sense you are able to prepare a bit of the background knowledge and that can sustain you in terms of explaining. You usually only get one line of, say, a Press Association snap on something, and the way you fill in the gaps is through, hopefully, having read into some of the background earlier in the day or knowing some of the background off the top of your head.'

This kind of presenting requires a keen journalistic brain – you are writing the story in your head as you go along.

AD LIBBING

Ad libbing, speaking without a script, on hard news stories is notoriously difficult. There may be legal problems, if you are reporting the outcome of a court case, for example, or considerations of political impartiality. There will always be questions of tone – the right way to deliver information when you are not sure of its significance. Is this significant? How does it fit the bigger picture? These are judgement calls you will become more confident about as you gain experience. The safest way to introduce new information is to attribute it (*according to the Press Association . . . a Reuters report just in . . . our reporters on the ground say*). Sometimes broadcasters get it wrong, but audiences are forgiving as long as they feel they are not being misled. They like to feel they are privy to new and exciting information.

MATTHEW AMROLIWALA: 'AS WELL AS THE INFORMATION YOUR OWN TEAM IS SENDING IN YOUR EAR, THERE IS A RELENTLESS STREAM OF FACTUAL INFORMATION FROM OTHER NEWS AGENCIES AND PEOPLE ON THE GROUND.'

SOMETIMES BROADCASTERS GET IT WRONG, BUT AUDIENCES ARE FORGIVING AS LONG AS THEY FEEL THEY ARE NOT BEING MISLED.

On structured bulletins, there is less need to ad lib. Whenever possible you will want to stick to the script. It's safer to do so. But occasionally an ad lib comment will help fill time. It happens frequently in news programmes with more than one presenter. A cheery exchange brightens up the programme. But the best of these exchanges are thought about beforehand and often rehearsed. The exact words will not be scripted, but you will have discussed with your co-presenter what you want to say and what sort of response to expect. Jokes rarely work unless they have been well thought out. Remember the old one about the secret of good comedy – timing.

AUTOCUE

Most scripts for news programmes, even rolling news, are read from the prompting screen. Autocue is a trade name often used as a generic term for electronic prompting – the scrolling words that appear on a screen in front of the camera lens. The camera looks right through the screen, and the presenter reading the words is looking straight into the lens. This helps maintain eye-contact with the viewer, the surest way of communicating effectively. A reader who keeps looking down at a script is unconvincing – they look as if they are not sure what they are talking about.

Jane Hill of BBC News says: 'I always say a trained monkey could read Autocue.' For presenters like her, who're used to ad libbing as stories break on rolling news channels, reading from the prompt is clearly the easiest part of the job. But how much training does the monkey need? There are several things worth knowing about prompting systems before you use them.

Jane Hill, presenter
BBC News

Most importantly, the prompter follows the presenter, not the other way round. It scrolls at your speed. An experienced operator will ensure that the words you are reading are always towards the top of the screen, so you can see what's coming next. This helps with your delivery. Sometimes on shorter bulletins – like the summaries on BBC News Interactive – you will need to operate the prompt yourself, either with a hand-held control or a foot pedal. This is another discipline to master – but at least you are in control of the pace of the bulletin.

If you are having trouble reading from the screen, the font size can be changed. It's usually best to use the smallest font you can read comfortably, because then more words are on screen and it's easier to make sense of what's written. Technical instructions (e.g. 'Jane on Cam 1', 'VT' or 'OOV') can be included on the Autocue. It's up to you as presenter to ask for the information on the screen that helps you do a better job. You might want a note about turning to another camera, or for a tricky word to be spelt out phonetically.

It is important that you do not become a slave to the Autocue. Some presenters are like rabbits caught in headlights. When they have to leave the safety of the electronic prompt, they're lost. You need to keep your wits about you and your brain in gear. If you have a paper script in front of you, remember to turn the pages even as you are reading from the prompt.

When stories break or late stories come in, the *running order* (the order in which stories run) will change. Autocue will be updated, and it may not be available while that is happening. You need to develop the art of reading from a script, so that you can keep looking at the camera for as long as possible between glances down. This involves reading ahead and memorising the next few words before you deliver them.

See Workshops and Exercises.

THINKPIECE

OVERPAID AUTOCUE READERS

'Let's have a heated debate.' Mrs Merton (Caroline Aherne)

Newspaper journalists appear to like nothing more than writing about their counterparts on television. So, when two of Britain's most respected and experienced broadcasters suggested that television newsreaders were overpaid for doing a very easy job, the columnists reached for their laptops.

Andrew Marr (just before he stepped down as BBC Political Editor) and *Today* presenter (and former TV newsreader) John Humphrys made their remarks at the Hay-on-Wye Literary Festival in 2005. The festival is sponsored by the *Guardian*, so it was no accident that their comments were well reported and sparked a lively debate.

*ANDREW MARR:
'I HAVE NEVER QUITE UNDERSTOOD WHY READING AN AUTOCUE, HOWEVER ADEPTLY, EARNS YOU QUITE AS MUCH MONEY.'*

Marr said: 'Newsreaders, they really do come and go. I must say I have never quite understood why they are paid so much, why reading an Autocue, however adeptly, earns you quite as much money.'

Humphrys spoke from the experience of having read the *Nine O'Clock News*: 'Reading the news isn't work, whatever anybody says. You get paid a lot of money and it requires no brain.'

And then, as if to twist the knife in the injured pride of former colleagues, he continued: 'I have a four-year-old and I think he'll be ready in a couple of months.'

Strong stuff. But were they right? The *Daily Telegraph*'s distinguished radio critic Gillian Reynolds described it as a 'shoot out at the Autocue corral,' reporting that another distinguished name, Michael Buerk, had joined the attack. Reynolds wrote: 'If Fiona Bruce really is on £400,000 a year no wonder he's hopping mad. Buerk was a great television reporter, covering Africa's famines, wars, victims. Which battle has Bruce ever seen, beside the struggle to seem serious?'

Across seven columns of the same page there was an interview with 'a newsreader', who, with the benefit of anonymity, offered an insight into the economics of hiring and firing newsreaders, liberally spiced with industry back-biting.

The *Telegraph*'s Ben Fenton reported: 'There are some presenters whose qualities are not universally respected by colleagues in the television news business, including Natasha Kaplinsky on the BBC and ITN's Andrea Catherwood.' He then quoted the anonymous newsreader as saying: 'And I'm not sure how far Bruce can go, to be honest.'

The story suggested that the advent of Sky News and the value of 'credibility' had driven up the earning power of 'the men and women we invite into our living rooms every evening'.

It included a comment from the 'newsreader' justifying his colleagues' high salaries: 'When you are sitting in the studio and everything's going well then yes, all you are doing is reading from the Autocue.

'It's when the whole thing falls apart behind the scenes and you have to hold it together for half an hour of very complicated live television and not let the viewers know what's happened – that's when you earn the money. And when the BBC says there aren't many people around who can do that, they are right.'

Is it surprising that a broadsheet newspaper should quote an anonymous source so extensively on such an apparently trivial story? Not if you judge the *Telegraph* by the standards of *The Times*, whose treatment of the story was even more tabloid, not to say childish. It read like the script of a 1970s edition of *Blue Peter*. They published a double page feature almost a month after the original 'story' broke with the headline *Here is the news: it's not as easy as it looks*. They sent no less than three reporters to the ITV news studios to 'try the job for themselves', with ITV news presenter Nicholas Owen judging them. The feature offered such glittering insights as:

'Oh well, I thought, I'll just keep pace with the Autocue. I later discovered that the Autocue keeps pace with the newsreader.'

'I'm supposed to ask him questions, only I can't hear a word he's saying. I assume that this is a technical hitch that will sort itself out, and for which I can hardly be blamed. Then I realise my earpiece has plopped out.'

'Now the voices are telling me that we've lost the VT and that I should apologise to the nation. Like it was my fault!'

To quote another comedy chat show host, Keith Barret, it was 'just a bit of fun'.

Charlie Lee-Potter chipped in to the debate, with her column in the *Mail on Sunday*'s magazine *Night and Day*. She was the voice of experience, having appeared on *BBC Breakfast News* and other programmes. Under the cross-head *Never mind the money – reading the news is the silliest job I've had*, she described it as 'a beauty contest for megalomaniacs with more money than brains'.

MICHAEL GRADE: 'WE PAY THEM WHAT WE *THINK THEY'RE* WORTH, NOT WHAT THEY *THINK THEY'RE* WORTH.'

A month later one of the first callers to BBC Chairman Michael Grade, on a Five Live phone-in, asked him if the corporation was 'taking the mickey' with such inflated salaries for newsreaders. Grade said the figures in the newspapers (£400,000–500,000) were greatly exaggerated, but repeated the line that there was a free market for talent. He said: 'We pay them what *we* think they're worth, not what *they* think they're worth.'

The clearest insight into why some newsreaders earn so much came from Chris Shaw, Senior Programme Controller at Five, writing in the media section of the *Guardian*. He pointed out that he has negotiated dozens of presenters' salaries, and some of them earn less than £30,000 a year.

He recognised the unkind view that a presenter is 'basically a gob on a stick and should be paid in lollipops', but said 'authority, fluency and composure in a live studio plus grooming and good looks' are extremely valuable to employers.

Shaw then argued that the main factor explaining why top news presenters can earn up to five times as much as the best-paid correspondents is that they are icons as well as newsreaders. 'They have been picked to represent the value system, the authority and the public service face of the channel on which they work. They are, if you like, the personification of our brands – our own walking talking poster people.'

Five's own Kirsty posters prove his point. Shaw said Trevor McDonald on ITV, Jon Snow on Channel Four and Kirsty Young on Five would almost certainly figure in the top three answers if you were asked who were the faces you most associated with those channels.

So, senior newsreaders have become marketing figures. It might not do much for their journalistic credibility. But it underlines the importance of news to a channel's identity, suggesting there is a bright – and for some highly profitable – future in the television news business.

REMEMBER

- ➤ Presentation style – dual-headed or single-headed – is a product of fashion, not journalism
- ➤ Presenters contribute to journalistic decision making
- ➤ Practise ad libbing
- ➤ Don't be a slave to Autocue.

SCRIPTS

The script, whether it's on paper or in electronic form, is the foundation of any programme. It tells presenters and studio crew where they are and where they should be. It's usual to have a separate page for each story, so a story can be dropped easily when the running order changes.

IF AUTOCUE FAILS, YOU WILL WANT TO READ DIRECTLY FROM THE SCRIPT. SO YOU SHOULD REMEMBER TO TURN THE PAGES AS YOU GO, EVEN WHEN YOU ARE USING THE PROMPT.

If Autocue fails, you will want to read directly from the script. So you should remember to turn the pages as you go, even when you are using the prompt. Then, when you look down, you will be in the right place. You can leave the script on the desk unless you are reading directly from it. If you are standing, holding pages of a paper script can look messy. A clipboard used to be the solution. Now, in a move pioneered in the UK by Sky News, presenters will often be seen with tablet computers in their hand – about the size of an A4 sheet and a couple of centimetres thick. These can be updated electronically, which means changes in the running order do not have to mean awkward shuffling of papers and the risk of losing your place.

TALKBACK

Television presenters are given instructions and can hear what's happening in the gallery through an earpiece connected to the studio's *talkback* system. Comments from the director or producer go directly into your ear without being picked up on your mic.

MOST MODERN PRESENTERS PREFER OPEN TALKBACK, WHERE THEY CAN HEAR EVERYTHING FROM THE GALLERY.

There are two types of talkback – *switch* and *open*. Switch talkback means someone in the gallery has to press a switch to talk to the presenter. The broadcaster only has to listen to instructions specifically for them, rather than any background chatter, which can be a distraction. This means you can concentrate on your performance. But most modern presenters prefer open talkback, where they can hear everything from the gallery. This is particularly useful when news is breaking or running orders are being changed. You will be aware of why changes are being made and can prepare yourself for them. Working on open talkback requires discipline – one of the arts of presenting is to make the on-air communication as smooth as possible, even when there is frantic activity behind the scenes.

Julian Worricker of BBC News 24 explains how open talkback helps a presenter respond to breaking news pictures: 'You can hear everything that's going on – what pictures are coming in – and you're trying to find the right bit of info to come out with. That's when it's at its most satisfying for a presenter. Most times you'll get the warning that you're going to have to do it, and if they get the chance they'll run them by you in the plasma opposite. Sometimes they haven't got the chance and you just pick your way through it as best you can.'

Worricker was on air in the week after the Boxing Day Tsunami of 2004, responding to pictures as they came in: 'Even though you were conscious of the death toll at the time and realised that it was huge, you hadn't necessarily at that point seen pictures that quite tallied with those figures. You knew it was bad but you couldn't quite see why it was so bad. And then one or two pictures began to come in that you were talking over without any advance warning, and as you talked, and you looked, you thought, bloody hell, now I realise why so many people died.'

His BBC colleague Jane Hill says she can't imagine operating without open talkback: 'You've got to know if there's a problem coming up. If you're thinking you're about to talk into such-and-such a press conference and actually they're all screaming: "We've got the pictures, but we've got no sound. We can't hear them, we can't hear them," you've got to know about that, because your brain is filtering that, thinking, right, I'll explain that we've got no sound yet and keep talking over the pictures. If you're on switch, you can't hear that and you're on a hiding to nothing.'

JANE HILL: 'YOU CAN EITHER DIVORCE YOUR BRAIN, KEEP GOING ON AUTOCUE, KEEP LISTENING TO THE DIRECTOR OR THE EDITOR IN THE GALLERY, OR YOU CAN'T.'

She says working with open talkback is a skill some people have difficulty mastering: 'You can either divorce your brain, keep going on Autocue, keep listening to the director or the editor in the gallery, or you can't. You will get better at it with practice and you learn to filter out the things that aren't meant for you the more you do, but the bottom line is you're either born like it or you're not. It's very odd.'

A constant flow of information to the ear of an experienced presenter can be the making of many programmes, especially in sports coverage. For example, Jeff Stelling, the presenter of Sky's *Soccer Saturday*, handles an almost incessant stream of goals, scorers and statistics as he holds together one of the busiest shows in television.

The earpiece

The television presenter's earpiece is their lifeline – their connection to what's being said in the gallery and to the outside world. In a studio, it is usually a wireless receiver, though hard-wired earpieces are still common. Regular presenters will want their own earpiece, moulded to the shape of their ear. They are available from hearing aid specialists and, curiously, high street opticians. Check which ear you prefer before buying – many people have better hearing in one ear than the other. If you have to share an earpiece, make sure there are antiseptic wipes available to clean it before you put it in.

AN ALTERNATIVE TO PAPER

As we've heard the script is the template for the shape of the programme. Printed versions of the script are normally considered essential for presenters to fall back on if Autocue goes down. But paper scripts can be awkward for presenters standing to read the news. A sheaf of papers is unwieldy, and it is difficult to change pages on a clipboard while you are talking.

Sky News introduced an alternative. The idea of presenter Martin Stanford was to use tablet computers, with a wireless connection to the newsroom computers. Not only can scripts appear on the tablet, but he can scribble his own notes, access the Internet or send messages to colleagues.

He says: 'You can be in any one of several locations [in the studio] and yet still have the full functionality which we so live on here, of being able to read an emergency wire or research a quick breaking story straight away. You're not any more disadvantaged than anybody that's sitting in front of a PC.

'Even if I'm in mid-interview, and I can't speak, I can top-line ("top line" is the instant messaging system in our software) a colleague or a producer or a director.'

Sky News presenter Martin Stanford with a tablet computer – the paperless script. He can scribble his own 'sticky-notes' while he is on air

> ## REMEMBER
>
> ➤ The script is the template for your programme
> ➤ Open talkback lets you know what's going on
> ➤ Presenters need to be able to access breaking news information.

WHAT (NOT) TO WEAR

A TV reporter or newsreader's appearance should not distract from the news. But a large proportion of viewers will take notice of what people are wearing. Channel Four News' website had a section devoted to Jon Snow's ties. Peter Sissons was criticised for not wearing a black tie on the BBC when he announced the Queen Mother's death. There were comments from viewers when Jeremy Vine did not wear a tie for Sunday lunchtime's *The Politics Show*. The BBC's view was that most people do not dress formally on a Sunday.

Radio newsreaders used to wear a dinner jacket in the early days of the BBC. The idea is now comical. Today's rule is that news presenters should dress 'appropriately'. For studio presentation that means modern, stylish clothes that fit well. It helps presenters appear warm and engaging to the audience. The BBC stipulates that the announcement of the death of the monarch should be made in a black tie (for a man) or a black jacket or top (for a woman). Otherwise bold colours work well on television for women and formal jackets with collar and

Natasha Kaplinsky

tie are best for men. But think how the colour scheme will look against the studio set.

It is always a good idea to look smart on television. You are appearing in strangers' homes, so it's only courteous to look your best. You will have your own idea of what looks best on you, but remember Natasha Kaplinsky's advice that the newsreader is not there to stamp their personality on the programme.

Patterns that don't work

Some clothing patterns simply do not work on TV for electronic reasons. Herringbone and houndstooth checks and narrow stripes will 'strobe' – wavy patterns appear on the picture. White shirts with no jacket will reflect too much light and cause contrast problems. Too much black will also absorb light and lose definition.

Colours that disappear

If you are working in a studio that uses electronic technology to superimpose images on the set, you will need to be especially careful what clothes you wear. Colour separation overlay (CSO), also known as blue- or green-screen, is used to produce weather maps, insets (a picture within the main picture) over presenters' shoulders, and backgrounds. Some studios are completely 'virtual' – they don't exist in real space and are electronically created, usually against a blue background.

If any part of your clothing is the same colour as the screen on to which the electronic image is projected (usually bright blue or bright green, as the name suggests) the image will appear on your clothes and that part of you will disappear.

MAKE-UP

Presenters may need make-up to help them look natural under TV lights. For women, that may mean wearing more than normal. Powder reduces sweating and glare, noticeably on the forehead or cheeks, and can add definition to your features. Politicians use it. Don't be embarrassed by it.

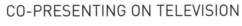

REMEMBER

➤ Dress appropriately – usually smartly if you are in a studio
➤ Avoid herringbone and houndstooth patterns
➤ In front of a blue or green screen, don't wear blue or green, as appropriate
➤ Make-up helps you look natural on screen.

CO-PRESENTING ON TELEVISION

Working alongside a second presenter requires new skills. It can be tougher than presenting alone, where you are reading links and conducting interviews according to instructions from the gallery. Most presenters we've spoken to suggest that, far from halving the workload, co-presenting is harder work than being alone.

Programmes have to be structured so that presenters can share the links. Whenever possible, producers will want interaction between the presenters.

Mark Austin, ITV News

Mark Austin and Mary Nightingale: ITV News 6.30 success story

Jane Hill and Matthew Amroliwala: a successful on-air partnership

ITV News' Mark Austin who often co-presents with Mary Nightingale says: 'Be absolutely clear about who's doing what when. There's nothing worse than both of you starting to speak at the same time, or not knowing where you're going to go next. Real clarity is needed. In a double-header, the most common problem is if there's confusion between the two of you about what you're doing, when you're doing it, who's doing it and that can lead to total disaster. Happily, Mary and I have an understanding that we know that's important, and we don't let it happen.'

In rolling news, it helps producers to be able to give instructions to one presenter while the other is conducting an interview, but the best moments for the viewer can be when both presenters are working together, combining to offer different parts of the story and build the bigger picture.

The BBC news presenter Jane Hill says: 'When there are two of you, there's got to be give and take. When there's breaking news and it's busy and it's really fluid, you've got to understand when the other person's going to speak.'

She's developed an understanding with her regular co-presenter Matthew Amroliwala: 'We just look at each other and do a little hand gesture and we know what that means. It's so instinctive with us.'

ON-AIR CHEMISTRY

Watching television news you will often see a male and a female presenter together. In America, the cliché is an older man (often likened to a favourite uncle) alongside a glamorous woman. Commentators talk about 'sexual chemistry' – the suggestion that the presenters look as if they fancy each other! Is this important? It's certainly a factor when producers put presenters together.

Nick Owen had an on-screen relationship for nearly 15 years with Anne Diamond, spanning the ITV breakfast channel TV-AM, and *Good Morning with Anne and Nick* on BBC1:

Anne and I always used to agree who would start an interview and the other would bide his or her time before nudging the other in the thigh. If Anne was doing the chatting, for instance, she would lean back to let me know I could take over. Or she would keep her position to tell me she was still following a particular line of questioning, so she didn't want me to change direction yet. Or, if one of us was finding it hard going, he or she would lean back without prompting, as if to say: 'Take over, baby, I need help!' A major element of our partnership was based on instinct, which sprang from our close friendship. We instinctively knew, when ad libbing, for instance, the right moment to come in. This applies to our times together at the start of breakfast television with TV-AM, and during *Good Morning with Anne and Nick* a decade later.

More recently, Owen has worked alongside Suzanne Virdee on *BBC Midlands Today*. He says friendship is again the key to success: 'It makes the whole experience really enjoyable if you're working with someone you've become close to, and that's been the case with Anne and Suzanne.

'Working on your own, you're terribly exposed if anything goes wrong. If there's somebody else – and I've been lucky to work for so long with good friends – between us we just get out of it.'

Nick Owen and
Suzanne Virdee on
Midlands Today: 'The
key is friendship.'

The *Midlands Today*
studio is about to
go live

Ad libbing becomes much easier alongside someone you get on with. Suzanne Virdee, who has also worked on *BBC Breakfast News*, says there's an excitement about presenting world events, with colleagues who are 'big players, big names'. But working with Nick has been her favourite job: 'We just do it as it comes. I'm the world's worst actress, so when we fill, it's never scripted. If I've got time, I might say to Nick: "I'll say something coming out of this." Then we just busk it.'

Regional programmes, with less hard news, offer more opportunities for humorous asides than national news. But friendship helps on the bigger stage too. Jane Hill says of her relationship with Matthew Amroliwala: 'We genuinely get on famously, and we're just very lucky. We did nearly five years together on the four till seven [p.m.] slot, which is pretty frantic, and the five o'clock hour is one of the biggest hours for News 24 for audience, so it's an important hour. It was brilliant. We just worked really well.

'It is vital. People call us an old married couple, because we both hate it if the other one's off. The point of the job is, of course, that you have to learn to get on with anyone. But it does make a big difference, your co-presenter.'

REMEMBER

➤ It's vital to have a good working relationship with your co-presenter

➤ Professional respect is key to the relationship.

WORKING IN A VIRTUAL STUDIO

Virtual studios can produce spectacular effects. The space you appear to occupy is created by computer graphics. You are usually working against either a blue or green screen. You may have a video wall behind you on which moving pictures and graphics are projected.

You need to be familiar with the script even if you are reading from Autocue. You will want to turn to the screen, or to your virtual surroundings, and then face the viewers again, picking up seamlessly without interrupting your natural flow. You don't want to sound scripted.

You can read in Chapter 13: *Graphics* Jeremy Vine's account of working with the complicated effects for the BBC's election coverage – complete with an 'invisible' colleague draped in a blue curtain. There is a whole new discipline for news broadcasters working with virtual effects, and wearing the right colour is the least of their worries.

You will have a monitor so you can see what the finished output looks like, but you have to resist the temptation to treat the monitor as a mirror. In a mirror all your actions are reversed (raise your right arm and the mirror image appears to raise their left arm). On a monitor, actions happen as the camera sees them. So, if you raise your right arm, the image in the monitor raises the right arm. Psychologically, it is tricky to overcome years of conditioning caused by looking at yourself in a mirror. You need to practise, particularly if you are required to point to things on the screen or react to objects in the virtual environment around you.

The news bulletins on the BBC's digital interactive service are presented from a virtual studio. It is a tiny single camera operation, set against a blue screen. The reader appears to be on the newsroom set because of the back-projection, and operates their own Autocue. It's another example of multi-skilling – so essential to the modern broadcast journalist.

LINKING TO INTERVIEWS ON A VIDEO WALL

A common technique, used instead of a traditional filmed package, is to stand in front of a video wall, linking to clips of interviews, which will then be mixed to fill the whole screen. At the point at which the interviewee appears in the video wall, they need to be facing towards you, the presenter. If they're facing away from you, it looks odd. So a lot of thought needs to go into filming this type of package.

It's no good coming back from location, deciding you haven't got enough shots to make a package and opting to do the report in front of a video wall instead. Your interviews will probably have been shot with people looking in different directions, so there is nowhere you can stand to make the eyelines look right. Also, video wall sequences take time to set up and involve the whole gallery crew. They need to be planned in advance and shot accordingly.

REMEMBER

➤ Virtual presentations have to be meticulously pre-planned

➤ In a monitor, your actions will be the reverse of looking in a mirror

➤ Interviewees on video walls should face the presenter.

CONCLUSION

Throughout this book, we've emphasised the need for the modern broadcast journalist to be multi-skilled. We've spoken about the range of writing, production and technical skills you'll need if you're entering the business. We also recognise that most (though not all) would-be broadcast journalists want to be on air.

The key to success as a presenter or reporter, particularly in the modern world where many people are on freelance or short-term contracts, is versatility. Within the broad term 'presenter' there is a range of skills to master. Some people will be good at a desk reading a bulletin; others will be happy to ad lib and hold together a breaking news programme; still others will use graphics imaginatively and be at home in a virtual studio or in front of a video wall. If you can become proficient at all these skills and more, you will be much more employable and much more successful in the long term.

FURTHER READING

Chantler, Paul and Stewart, Peter (2003) *Basic Radio Journalism*, Oxford: Focal Press. Solid basic advice for those looking to improve their newsreading and reporting techniques.

Mills, Jenni (2004) *The Broadcast Voice*, Oxford: Focal Press. Even seasoned broadcasters will find something new in this comprehensive book (and CD).

Trewin, Janet (2003) *Presenting on TV and Radio* Oxford: Focal Press. An all-round guide to performing in news and current affairs from a practitioner.

THE PROGRAMME

The range of broadcast news output now runs from brief headline reads on radio to 24-hour news channels on TV, with downloaded news content and podcasts in between. Rolling news changed the agenda of all broadcasters. The availability of video-on-demand through broadband meant another major rethink.

Broadcasters now have to consider not only what to put into a programme, but what *is* a programme. Are we happy to deliver our half hour of news and current affairs, or must it be part of a bigger package, with extras online and web links to outside sources and even other news providers?

Comedy shows like *The Day Today* and *Broken News* have given the conventions of news programmes a thoroughly deserved kicking. Never before has there been so much pressure to offer not only a professional service, but one which avoids self-parody.

We give examples of how programmes deal with breaking news, and give guidance on the production techniques you need to put a programme together:

- Running orders
- Timings
- Bulletin content
- Creating a balanced bulletin.

We canvass opinion on the way news programmes and interactivity will develop in the future, as the public are increasingly able to determine their own news agenda, whenever they want it, through mobile phones and wireless broadband.

THE NEWS AGENDA

Most news programmes are not full of exclusives. Indeed, much of the news agenda is predictable. That is why headlines, teases and striking audio or images have to be presented in a way that will keep viewers watching and listeners tuned in.

Downloadable news and RSS services mean audiences can determine their own news agenda. They become their own editor. But viewing figures suggest traditional news programming is far from dead. Red-button technology was only the first of the interactive options open to news providers.

Nick Pollard, who ran Sky News for ten years, said in 2005: 'We will move towards a genuine on-demand service via the set-top box, because the next generation of set-top boxes will effectively have the hard drive divided in two, one under control of the customer, the other under the control of the company so we can drop things down there. If you had an hour or less available for news, you could drop on to that 12 stories of a couple of minutes long (or longer or shorter or a combination) and a little home-made EPG [electronic programme guide] that allows people just to view things in the way they want. That is then genuinely news-on-demand whereas the red-button offering that we have at the moment, the interactive news, isn't. It's semi-news on demand. It's streamed news.'

His successor John Ryley, writing in the *Independent* in September 2006, explained why traditional news channels, with so much content sitting on servers, were ideally placed to deliver news to mobile phones and other portable devices: 'If you want a service of 20 video clips either sent by broadband to your PC or fired to your mobile, then it's likely to come from the 24-hour news channels . . . in news, anything can be made into anything else and reused on new platforms.'

In the early years of these technologies, news services, from Sky and the BBC, on-demand via broadband or streamed to mobiles, proved to be more popular than longer-form entertainment programmes.

THE APPOINTMENT-TO-VIEW PROGRAMME

Switching the radio or television on at a certain time of day to receive the news is quaintly old-fashioned. News is available at all times of the day, whenever people want it. So what is the role of the traditional appointment-to-view programme?

Chas Watkin, the BBC Editor supervising their pilot project in local TV in 2006, says: 'Journalists are used to working to deadlines, but the deadlines have changed. The programme is no longer the deadline. The story is the deadline. When a story breaks people want to see video as quickly as possible. You do it as fast as you can. We've got to work fast without giving up our commitment to quality and accuracy.'

Chas Watkin on local TV: 'The programme is no longer the deadline. The story is the deadline.'

In the world of instant access to news on broadband and 24-hour news channels, the traditional news programme might seem like a curiously twentieth-century phenomenon. But the truth is that most people are not news junkies – they have less interest in the full range of world events than most journalists. Many people may want to download selected news stories the way they download favourite music tracks, but that doesn't mean they don't want professionally produced digests of all the day's news.

The audience for the main channels' flagship news programmes is still many times greater than that of rolling new channels. The bulk of the UK population still trusts news organisations to present a summary of the day's events in an easily digestible form. Not everybody wants to wait around for stories to develop. Some people make sure they always catch the headlines, but don't bother with much else unless there's something that really grabs their attention. Others will watch the lead story and then switch off. So, there is still an important role for well-presented news programmes that grab an audience.

The Editor of ITV News, Deborah Turness, says: 'The demise of the appointment-to-view bespoke half-hour television news programme is overstated. For quite a long time to come, people are going to want to sit down, not have to click, not

Huw Edwards

Mark Austin

Mark Calvert, Editor of
Five News:
'We're not about, "The
world is going to end.
Hide behind the sofa."'

have to make a choice, just be delivered a news programme that will tell them what happened today in the world.

She says their approach is different from the rolling news channels: 'Our strategy is blockbuster coverage of big stories. Send dishes, helicopters, anchors, everything. Just monster them. The second thing is exclusives from everybody, particularly our specialist units and our foreign bureaux. And the third thing is distinctive ideas like special series that we run, campaigns, features, and if every show has got some of those bits in it, then it's got the stardust that'll make people think: "Whoa, I'm going to watch this every night."'

BBC *Ten O'Clock News* presenter Huw Edwards says: 'I've no doubt there's a long-term future for it. At this stage, I can't foresee a time when BBC1 won't have big structured bulletins on, because they're still drawing five million viewers regularly. We know that people are accessing news on their mobile phones and in different ways, but you've still got five million people tuning in to the *Ten O'Clock News* at night and that should tell you something. There's still a market for it. Looking towards the medium term – the next decade – I think it's inconceivable that these bulletins will disappear from the main channels.'

His opposite number at ITV News, Mark Austin, says: 'We're trying to make quite crafted half-hour news programmes and in many senses it's a dying art now, because all the emphasis is on breaking news and getting it on air as quickly as possible. Of course that has a role, and people want to dip in and out of that, but the real viewing figures show that people still want, and millions of people still watch, so-called appointment-to-view programmes, and only a hundred thousand or so watch each news channel.'

Helen Boaden, the BBC's Director of News, points out that news can increase the audience for the main channels: 'In a digital world where people have far more choice about what they want, the *Ten O'Clock News* actually attracts audiences back to BBC1, and that's because for lots of people it is their opportunity to sit down and say: "These are the most important things that have happened today. I trust the BBC to tell me what they are and tell them in a fair, impartial way," and I don't think that need in people is going to disappear.'

Mark Calvert, Editor of Five News on TV, is cautiously optimistic about the future: 'I imagine that audience figures for traditional appointment-to-view half-hour news programmes, like the one that we produce here for Five, will dwindle over the next decade or so – partly as a result of the dispersing of the audience across a growing number of channels, but also because there's quite rightly a growing number of people seeking out news and information from other sources. But I've no doubt that, within that landscape, there will still be a sizeable appetite for what people like me, editors, think are the key stories of the day.'

For Calvert, it comes back to knowing your audience. News is important to his viewers, but not the most important thing in their lives: 'Watching some channels you think: "Oh, my God, it's the news. The world is about to end. Hide behind the sofa." We're much more interested in making things completely accessible.'

Five presenter Kirsty Young echoes that sentiment: 'I always feel very comfortable saying: "you might remember that" or "let's just give you the background on that", because I think that you should never assume that people remember everything, because I don't and I work in news.'

So, you no longer need an 'appointment-to-view' to keep abreast of the news, but all news broadcasters want you to make that appointment. "All" includes the rolling news channel Sky News. When they revamped their programmes with the move to a new headquarters in October 2005, the trail for *The Sky Report*, the 7 p.m. news round-up, included this line from presenter Julie Etchingham: 'It's going to be fresh, fiery, appointment-to-view television.'

The change did not result in increased viewing figures, however. Sky News revised the evening strands for a second time less than a year later. It was a return to 'core values'.

REMEMBER

➤ Audiences for bulletins are still many times greater than the audience for rolling news

➤ Programme makers need to know their audience

➤ Most viewers and listeners want journalists to be the 'trusted guides' to the news.

CASE STUDY 15.1 THE MICHAEL JACKSON TRIAL

The influence of Sky News on the rest of the UK's news broadcasters could not have been illustrated more dramatically than at the end of the trial of Michael Jackson.

Jackson had been the biggest star on the planet and a mainstay of the red-top tabloids throughout the later part of the twentieth century. The former child star was the self-styled King of Pop. Increasingly bizarre stories appeared about his eccentric behaviour. Tales of plastic surgery, a strange friendship with Bubbles the chimp and an unlikely marriage to Lisa Marie Presley, daughter of the King of Rock'n'Roll, only increased the public fascination in him and did little to harm his record sales. But the 'Wacko Jacko' stories took a sinister turn in the early part of the twenty-first century when he was charged with sexually molesting a 13-year-old boy. The suggestion was that Jackson's Neverland ranch with its funfair, zoo and a bedroom shared with young boys was the ultimate paedophile lair. It was by any standards a sensational tabloid story.

More than 2,000 journalists from more than 30 countries gathered at the court in Santa Maria, US, for the verdict on 13 June 2005 at the end of a 66-day trial. It was the heat of the California afternoon. But, crucially for British broadcasters and for the BBC in particular, in Britain it was approaching ten o'clock in the evening – the time of the flagship BBC TV news bulletin. ITV News flashed – between programmes on ITV1 – that the verdict was imminent. ITV's main bulletin wasn't on air until 10.30 p.m. So, they handed an audience to the BBC and Sky News.

The BBC's editor made a decision to stay with the story live until the jury delivered its verdict. It's a tactic Sky News had used frequently on all sorts of stories. Cynics might argue it helps fill time on a 24-hour channel. But it also guarantees you get the story first – or at worst equal first if some other channel dares to go live at the same time. So it was that the BBC bought into Sky News' philosophy and adopted their tactics – not on their news channel, but in prime time on Britain's most popular television channel. And all for the sake of covering an essentially tabloid story.

The BBC bulletin started conventionally, with titles, headlines and an introduction to the top story, but it soon developed into a waiting game as presenter Huw Edwards and reporter Matt Frei 'filled' until the jury's verdict.

When the BBC decided to devote the first half of the *Ten O'Clock News* to filling airtime waiting for something to happen – not daring to cut to pre-recorded packages for fear of missing something – they were playing Sky's game. Instead of offering an 'appointment-to-view', a digest of the day's news, they were behaving exactly the same as Sky News, the ITV news channel and their own BBC News 24.

It begged the question: 'If this is what BBC1 does, what exactly is the point of BBC News 24?' The truth is it didn't matter to the editor of the *Ten O'Clock News* that the BBC has a perfectly serviceable news channel that could have played the waiting game. The editor – and the channel controller – did not want to lose audience. The decision was taken to give the audience what they wanted, because if BBC1 did not do so, there were at least three other channels – including the BBC's own News 24 – that would. It is a rare news story where such a judgement call is so easy to make.

BBC correspondent Matt Frei spoke – very fluidly and very convincingly – in an extended two-way with presenter Huw Edwards for most of the first 15 minutes of the programme. When viewers were not looking at Frei outside the court, they were seeing a live camera shot of the crowd of fans nearby. The shot was not steady; it panned and zoomed as if the cameraman was not aware he was live on air. We learned later that inside the courtroom (where there were no cameras) the judge spent ten minutes opening envelopes containing the verdicts before the court clerk read them out.

Then the voice of the clerk Lorna Frey delivering the ten verdicts was heard over an exterior shot of the crowd, including a woman releasing a dove for every 'not guilty' verdict. Often the crowd's cheers threatened to drown out the clerk. A caption informed viewers that they were hearing the voice of the clerk, and, apart from brief comments from newsreader Edwards, the viewer was mostly left to interpret the live event for him or herself.

When the verdicts had been delivered, it became clear that Matt Frei hadn't been idly waiting for the court clerk to finish. He'd been making notes of information fed to him from inside the court. He informed us that, as the second 'not guilty' pronouncement was made, Michael Jackson snapped his fingers and was handed a tissue with which he wiped a tear from his eye. Frei observed: 'He has been the ultimate choreographer of his own bizarre lifestyle.'

It was 10.21 p.m., more than two-thirds of the way through the scheduled bulletin, before the BBC ran the first of its pre-recorded packages that evening. It was the 'backgrounder' prepared by reporter David Willis, who'd been following the trial from day one. This was the 'not guilty' version. Other versions, covering various other possible outcomes, including guilty on all charges, would never see the light of day. There followed a biographical piece looking back at Michael Jackson's career and controversial life. The BBC's *Ten O'Clock News* had returned to a more familiar format.

Over on Sky News, where until that point the coverage had been very similar to that of BBC1, a camera focused on the courtroom door. Graphics filled the bottom and left-hand side of the screen: on the left, a fast-changing list of the charges with the words 'not guilty' in bold; underneath, the words 'Sky News Flash: Michael Jackson cleared of all ten charges.' And so it was that Sky News, playing the long game, had the first shots of Michael Jackson leaving the court. That was at 10.28 p.m.

The shots of Jackson leaving court were disappointing. He walked straight to a blacked-out SUV and helicopters tracked him back home to Neverland. The moment was, however, high in expectation. Even the BBC's correspondent had said there was the chance of a news conference on the courtroom steps. But BBC1 was by this time catching up with the rest of the day's news. Before the bulletin ended, a round-up of the Jackson trial by reporter Duncan Kennedy included the shots of Jackson leaving.

The ITV main news started at 10.30 p.m. on terrestrial channel three. They'd missed the main action. Later, ITV News missed the shot of Jackson arriving back at Neverland.

The rest of the evening on all the news channels was taken up by reaction – including an extended press conference from the eight women and four men of the jury. They seemed to be enjoying what amounted to almost literally 15 minutes of fame; Andy Warhol's words – if put to a stopwatch test – had never been truer. It went on so long that Sky News eventually put it on their interactive service, while the main programme returned to the studio for other reaction.

Michael Jackson's press conference never took place. On his website the singer compared the end of his trial to the birth of Martin Luther King, the fall of the Berlin Wall and the freeing of Nelson Mandela. As reporter Ben Ando put it on BBC Breakfast News next day, most people probably think the acquittal of a pop star is not so important.

Two days after the trial closed, a letter appeared in the *Daily Telegraph* asking how much the BBC had spent on its coverage. Why was it necessary to have separate, simultaneous coverage of the trial on BBC1 and BBC News 24, and eventually on *Newsnight*?

The BBC decision was justified (in their own terms) by a paragraph on another page of the same newspaper. It reported that the acquittal was watched by 7.9 million viewers on the *Ten O'Clock News*, two million more than usual.

The BBC itself said the figure was nearly three million more than usual and that they had a 36 per cent audience share – almost unprecedented in the modern multi-channel age. But they received more than 400 complaints. Bulletin editor Kevin Bakhurst appeared on the review programme *NewsWatch*

(BBC News 24 and BBC2), defending the decision to devote so much time to the story. He wrote on BBC Online: 'We knew the verdict was imminent, but that was the full extent of our knowledge.'

As if anticipating the inevitable comparison with Sky News, he continued: 'Obviously we set the threshold for covering breaking news much higher than the 24-hour news channels.'

So, who was the real winner? Arguably Sky News, which not only achieved its fourth highest ratings to that date, peaking at 1,069,000, but seemed to have changed forever the way its rivals covered breaking news.

Bakhurst says the Jackson trial was not a watershed moment. He says the *Ten O'Clock* team were confident about holding for the verdict. Many of them had worked on BBC News 24 and their treatment was a natural response: 'That is the audience expectation now. If there's a story about to happen or happening, they don't expect you to opt out of it and go to something else. People will leave in droves.'

But it was a close-run thing: 'I think it was only two or three minutes away from us saying: "Enough. We can't go on doing this." It was unlucky it went on so long, but it was quite lucky it came when it did.'

See Workshops and Exercises.

ROLLING NEWS – A DIFFERENT DISCIPLINE

Rolling news has changed the way journalists work. The deadline is always with us. The impact of that on reporters in the field is clear, but it also changes the way producers and editors operate.

Kevin Bakhurst edited the BBC's *Ten O'Clock News* (the Ten) and then became controller of BBC News 24. He says there are clear differences in the approach to news programmes and to rolling news: 'A lot of the fundamentals are the same – the basic journalism and so on – but in terms of the skills of the producers and the output editors, it's quite a different set of demands.

'My view was that for too long News 24 was run on exactly the same basis as the bulletins, and actually 24-hour news and the expectation of the audience is different. People rightly expect a bulletin like the Ten to be a kind of bulletin of record, and that, unless there's a big breaking story, what you are told on the Ten is the definitive take on the story.

'On 24-hour news channels, we need to give the audience the latest information that we have, and tell them our assessment of it. Be open with them. You can take the audience along with you and you've got the time to say: "Look, this is the information. This is what we've got at the moment. We're checking it out." And then say if it's right or wrong.'

BBC Radio Five Live is Britain's only true national rolling radio news network. It has a less formal approach than Radio Four – more of a conversation than a lecture, with phone-ins, e-mail and text messages read on air.

Kevin Bakhurst, Controller of BBC News 24: 'Rolling news has different demands.'

Matt Morris, Editor of
BBC Radio Five Live

*VICTORIA
DERBYSHIRE:
'IT'S ALWAYS OK
TO SAY AS A
PRESENTER:
"I DON'T
UNDERSTAND." IT'S
ABSOLUTELY FINE,
BECAUSE, PROBABLY,
IF YOU'RE NOT
UNDERSTANDING IT,
THEN LOADS OF
OTHER PEOPLE
AREN'T AS WELL.'*

Five Live Editor Matt Morris says that audience research from the BBC's Creative Future project suggests how all BBC radio news might sound in future: 'The audience said they regarded us as authoritative, accurate, formal, trustworthy, but they wanted us to be modern, accessible, friendly. Their view was it was a kind of monologue. They wanted a dialogue. Ticking all those boxes, Five Live's there. That's why Five Live's successful. The question is: Do we shift as other bits of the BBC shift towards us, and if we do shift, where do we shift to?

'Five Live has to maintain its conversational tone, but I don't want to drive it downmarket. Our interviews are the kind of interviews you might want to conduct yourself. I'm keen that Five Live is polite, friendly and treats everybody as if they've got something to say, and we're not going to get aggressive with people. On Five Live, you can listen to a conversation not a row.'

He believes Five Live has an important public service role: 'We have to do our journalism in a way that's going to inform people and help them to live their lives, help them to make sense of the world. There's a whole range of things affecting people's lives that are getting much more complicated, and if we have got a role as public service broadcasters, it's got to be helping people to make sense of all that difficult stuff in a way that is not patronising, not paternalistic, but genuinely on a kind of peer basis.'

Morris says Five Live's approach is summed up by presenters saying things like: 'I don't get this. You'll have to explain this to me.' Morris says: 'The audience understands that. Whoah, hang on, let me hear that again. And that's what Five Live should be like. It's not saying people are thick and they don't get stuff. It's about how difficult some stuff is, and on the radio you've only got one bite at it. We shouldn't be afraid of having a second bite at things.

'What we've got to do is concentrate on the audience here. And not on making some kind of perfect product. I don't want perfection. I quite like warts and flaws – not lines going down – but I quite like the sense of "stop a sec, I haven't got that".'

Presenter Victoria Derbyshire says: 'It's always OK to say as a presenter: "I don't understand." It's absolutely fine, because, probably, if you're not understanding it, then loads of other people aren't as well.'

BREAKING NEWS

Breaking news provides the greatest challenge for any broadcast organisation. Just as paramedics talk of the Golden Hour – the time in which casualties have the best chance of being treated successfully – there is a Golden Hour in news coverage. A swift response establishes a lead in covering events that can never be retrieved by reporters late on the scene.

Before 24-hour news channels on TV and radio, news editors and programme controllers would decide whether to break into programmes to provide a news flash or special programmes. That still happens for major incidents. BBC1 and ITV1 both broke into programmes when terrorists bombed London transport targets in July 2005. They shared coverage with their 24-hour services. And, for the first time, content provided by the audience became a major part of the output. Thousands of texts, mobile phone stills and clips of audience video informed the coverage. Viewers' pictures were used on air.

➤ Rolling news programmes can lead the audience through a story

➤ Don't wait for the 'definitive' version of events

➤ Attribute your sources

➤ Use interactive services to encourage user content.

CASE STUDY 15.2

LIVE TELEVISION V. THE INTERNET

The London bombings of 7 July 2005 proved that live television coverage is a more immediate news source than the Internet. Terrorists target high-profile targets. Cities like London, or New York on September 11, are the hubs of major news-gathering organisations. The logistical problems of scrambling news crews to remote locations do not arise. Live links can be established quickly.

In London on the morning of the bombings, news on TV proved infinitely superior to online coverage, despite claims for the Internet that it is the most immediate and flexible of news media. It's a question of resources. When an organisation like the BBC or Sky News throws resources at a story, the range of information being gathered is awesome. Online newsrooms, with a fixed number of staff and no ready pool of extra personnel to call on, cannot match them.

On that summer morning, the BBC news website was reporting at least one person dead and several people injured at a time when the ITV News Channel had a Reuters report of 90 casualties. The Reuters report proved inaccurate, but by naming the source the broadcaster was keeping its audience informed of the way the story was developing without verifying the information and presenting it as incontrovertible fact. The idea of telling the audience what we *don't* know alongside what we know for sure is one of the innovations of rolling news, and particularly of Sky's approach.

Witnesses on BBC News 24, Sky and ITV had already spoken of seeing several bodies in the wreckage of the underground trains and a double-decker bus. The online headline 'Multiple blasts paralyse London' was unchanged and there were few pictures, as eye-witness accounts, political reaction and expert analysis filled television screens. The information deficit for anyone relying on the Web must have been frustrating. BBC insiders say the lack of new information on their online news service was a result of unnecessary caution by duty editors. They clearly did not want to broadcast the untrue Reuters report, but they left out much that *was* confirmed.

The BBC Interactive Newsroom received 8,000 e-mails and 1,500 text messages before eight o'clock that evening. It proved its worth as a means of connecting with its audience, but as a primary news medium it struggled to match the effectiveness of television and radio.

7 July 2005 was the day citizen journalism became a force in British media. Stills and video from mobile phones were shown extensively. TV used material from viewers in reporter packages and in separate items explaining how

people caught up in events had been able to record what went on because of the new technology. On the Web, the mobile phone pictures were mostly an available extra, rather than part of the main reports.

And TV also won on traditional news criteria. It carried the Metropolitan Police Commissioner and the Prime Minister live well before the Web reported their comments.

Sky News' former head Nick Pollard says their plan for big stories is well-honed even though it's not written down: 'You bash the phones, start putting up maps of where these incidents are reported and, most crucially, try to get on the phone somebody who's seen what was going on, whether it's the managing director of London Underground or someone on a mobile phone standing outside a tube station.

'It's an awareness of the importance of chucking all your resources at the stories that really matter and being content to ignore the others.'

Sky launched their Skycopter, with a reporter on board, offering live aerial commentary and scenes of the capital in chaos. They were lucky the helicopter was available. It had been recalled from Gleneagles that day because London had just been awarded the 2012 Olympic Games. Reaction to the winning bid would have been a big story, before events took over. The helicopter was going to be used for aerial shots of the sites in East London due to be redeveloped as Olympic venues. It was soon in the air over Aldgate tube station, showing live scenes.

Sky also used their rolling ticker-tape graphic for messages from people reassuring loved ones they were safe. Sky's impromptu service was in place several hours before the police set up an emergency information line for people worried about their friends and family.

The coverage included mobile phone video footage from inside one of the damaged underground carriages. It was one of the first times this technology had been seen in a major breaking story. It showed how members of the public have become news gatherers in their own right. The wide availability of domestic camcorders has meant viewers' video often turns up on the news. Video on mobile phones adds a new dimension. People carry their phones everywhere, whereas they are unlikely to have the family camcorder with them all the time. It's always a good idea these days to ask witnesses if they have pictures of an incident. Video from mobiles is usually of poor quality, but for the biggest stories any pictures will be highly prized.

Among all the innovations, the London attacks also highlighted one of the weaknesses of 24-hour coverage – the desire to publish any information, however suspect or unhelpful.

Sky News boss Nick Pollard told the *Independent* a few weeks later: 'Our philosophy is that we will tell viewers what we believe is going on. We will attribute every source, claim and figure that we quote. We will also tell viewers what we don't know. I have a feeling that viewers, who are now quite attuned to 24-hour news, understand the rhythm and dynamics of an evolving story and would rather be told what we believe is the detail of an unfolding story, rather than waiting until the whole story is known.'

It was probably this philosophy that prompted both the ITV News Channel and Sky News to run captions almost two hours after the first bombs, quoting a police source saying it was too early to say if the blasts were linked to terrorism. To any reasonably experienced journalist – indeed to any informed viewer – this was clearly not true. Reporting the comments of a cautious policeman or police press officer served no purpose. Within less than half an hour the Metropolitan Police Commissioner said the bombings were probably a major terrorist attack. Within an hour the Prime Minister said it was pretty clear there had been a series of terrorist attacks.

Sky claimed credit for being the first to report a terrorist attack when other stations were still talking about a power surge on the tube system. A Westminster-based producer, Bob Mills, saw the bus which exploded in Tavistock Square and told the newsdesk there was absolutely no question it was a bomb. Sky trusted his judgement and ran with the story. But the early statement from the police seemed to contradict what the station was reporting. The source was, as Nick Pollard says, 'attributed'. But the word 'police' carries an authority that could have misled viewers.

Sky News Crime Correspondent Martin Brunt recalls his approach to covering the story:

If you've been around a few years, you trust your instincts. You go with your urges. When the London bombs went off, I was put on air and all I knew was there'd been six incidents and people were talking about power surges. Inevitably, I started talking about the possibility of bombings and I knew from one phone call there was pandemonium at Scotland Yard. This sort of thing was what they'd been warning about and planning for. You could argue that, if we'd been talking about bombs and it turned out to be power surges after all, we'd be doing the terrorists' job. But we weren't wrong. It's sometimes worth taking a risk. I think if we are a little ragged round the edges it gives us some immediacy. It appears honest. We admit it if we don't know things and I think that's important.

I think that's what 24-hour news has added – much more speculation in the early stages of a story.

See Workshops and Exercises.

SPORTS PROGRAMMES

Sports programmes have similar ingredients to news bulletins, even when the show is devoted to live coverage of an event.

There will almost always be a headline sequence, telling the viewer what to expect, a presenter who anchors the show, usually with the help of studio guests, live reporting and commentary and packaged reports. The packages might be player profiles or reports of other matches in the same competition.

There will be extensive use of graphics, particularly for league tables, performance statistics and for live analysis. Whether it's Andy Gray talking soccer tactics on Sky Sports or an explanation of reverse swing during a cricket

Test, technology is essential to the reporting. The programme close might be a musical montage of highlights of the day.

THE NETWORK BIG BROTHER

The relationship between network TV and the regions, and between national and local radio, is based on co-operation, but fraught with potential conflict. It differs in BBC TV and radio, in the ITV network and in ILR. But the relationship usually comes down to the hunger for exclusives: the desire of individual journalists and editors as well as reporters and producers, to beat others with the stories they cover.

The producer of a regional programme with a national story in his running order has to think of ways to make his treatment different from the network version. This is of particular concern on the BBC where regional news traditionally follows the network bulletin. The instinct is to shut up shop and prevent the network having access to your material, keeping anything exclusive to yourself.

Arguments that 'we're all on the same side', or even as Director General Greg Dyke tried to insist 'one BBC', cut no ice.

But the relationship to the parent organisation means the regional television and local radio newsrooms have the benefit of the BBC's news feeds and access to the network's audio and pictures.

Here's an example of treating a national story differently for a region. A man wanted in connection with failed suicide bombings in London was arrested in Birmingham on 27 July 2005. It was the lead story on the BBC's national news. So, how would the regional TV programme deal with such a big story in their area without repeating what viewers had already seen? *Midlands Today* focused on the impact on the community in Hay Mills. A suspected bomb was left at the scene. Bomb disposal experts were called in, and part of the street was evacuated. Hundreds of people didn't know how long they would be away from their homes. Peter Wilson's report covered these aspects of the story and included shots from an exclusive piece he'd done two weeks earlier on call with the Royal Logistics Corps bomb disposal team – the men brought in to deal with the threat. And there was a telling interview clip which summed up the local angle to the national story. John Bedder, who runs a well-known fish and chip shop just yards from the scene of the arrest, said: 'It's real now.' It's not something you've read in the newspapers or seen on television, serious though that is. It's something on our doorsteps.'

ITV's regional structure has historically been one of its strengths. Regional newsrooms compete with their BBC counterparts and with other ITV companies in areas where the broadcast signal overlaps with their neighbours in the network. They'll also want to provide better coverage of local stories than their network 'big brothers' from ITV News. The ITV companies owned Independent Television News (ITN) but that didn't stop the rivalry at newsroom level. The merging of ITV's major companies into one main player was followed by cutbacks in regional newsrooms. They are no longer as well-staffed (or as well-paid) as their BBC counterparts.

ILR stations subscribe to an audio and copy feed from Independent Radio News or Sky News Radio. The benefit of being part of a network is clear. Local radio stations cannot afford to have their own staff covering national and international stories. So, they buy into a networked service. The network stories appear alongside staff reporters' coverage of local events.

LOCAL TV

Once upon a time in the UK, there was national television and there was regional television. Regional TV was based on the reach of the transmitters set up to deliver analogue television signals across the country. The government offered licences to ITV regional companies to use these transmitters, and the BBC offered regional services based on these transmitters. So, all that followed is a product of the 1950s' TV transmission system. We had programmes like *Midlands Today*, *Central News*, *Calendar*, *Look North* and *South Today*. Now there is a new perspective.

A CLOSER LOOK

Tim Burke, producer, cameraman, editor and a powerful exponent of the value of local TV as a replacement for the traditional regional model

REGIONAL TV – WHO'D BUY IT?

Tim Burke, community content editor of the BBC's local television pilot in 2006, has an amusing, deliberately overstated but compelling argument why regional television is an outmoded idea in the broadband age.

Addressing public meetings to promote the new service, Burke would begin: 'Let's assume the BBC doesn't exist. Let me float you an idea.'

Turning to someone in the front row, he would ask: 'Where do you live?'

As they began to answer, he would interrupt: 'I don't care. Because I'm going to base this service on transmitters. If you live in Cheltenham, you might not be interested in events in Birmingham, but I'm going to give you a service from Birmingham. You might be more interested in events in Bristol. Well, tough. And because of hills, and houses and offices blocking the signal, you might be lumped in with places you're not interested in. I don't care where you live.'

Turning to another audience member, he would ask: 'What time do you get home from work?'

Again, before there was time for a reply, he would continue: 'I don't care, because I'm going to put this service on from 6.30 for half an hour, with a little bit more after the *Ten O'Clock News*. I don't care if you miss it.'

'What are you interested in? . . . I don't care, because I'm going to appoint somebody, probably a middle-aged, middle-class bloke like me, to decide what the most important stories of the day are, and what order they should be shown in. And you won't have any input into that. We'd like you to have a say, so we'll put our phone numbers and e-mail address on screen, but don't try ringing during the programme because we're busy.

'So I don't care where you live, what time you get in or what you're interested in. But I'm going to charge you a proportion of £130 [the TV licence fee] every year for this, and if you don't pay, I'll prosecute you. Now are you going to buy that?'

Put like that, regional television sounds like a very bad deal. Burke says: 'It's like giving somebody an iPod and saying you can only use it between 6.30 p.m. and 7.00. I'll download the tracks for you and decide what order they're in. Now pay me something every year, or I'll prosecute. Who would buy that? Nobody.'

The argument for continuing transmitter-based regional TV looks very thin in an age when satellite, cable and increasingly broadband can be used to deliver television services. After analogue switch-off in 2012, when all TV goes digital, expect it to disappear.

Anita Bhalla, the first woman to be elected President of Circom Regional, the European association of regional television stations, says people are interested in global events and local events. She expects regional television of the kind seen in Britain for 50 years to be squeezed out in time in favour of increasingly local content.

Anita Bhalla: 'People want to know about the places they live.'

She says: 'People want to know about the places they live, to hear their own stories. For example, people in Shropshire want stories about Shropshire; they are curious about their locality. People want news on demand, when they want it and where they want it. They don't want to wait till 6.30.'

The strongest alternative to regional TV appears to be broadband local services with much of the content generated by the users. It means much more localisation of content – almost everything you see is likely to be within a 20-mile radius of your home. This was the model piloted by the BBC in 2006. It was also available on satellite, with six local services on a loop repeating every hour. The local ten-minute bulletins could also be sent to video iPods and mobile phones. BBC producers offered guidance to local people and community groups to help them tell their own stories, sometimes lending cameras and giving basic training to enable them to do it.

There was some opposition to the pilot from local newspaper groups, who saw it as the BBC encroaching on their territory – the provision of local news. Without their role as the main providers of local news, the papers feared sales and advertising revenue would fall. Indeed, many local papers now provide video content on their websites. This offers job opportunities to broadcast journalists within the traditional newspaper industry.

The BBC argued that, as they do not carry commercials, newspapers could still have a near-monopoly of local advertising. Backed by the licence fee, the BBC could democratise local broadcasting, helping people who wouldn't normally have access to the media tell their own stories as part of the corporation's public service remit. It was an extension of the *Inside Lives* digital story-telling project on BBC local radio.

Most business models for local television have struggled to produce quality news content. The BBC model, backed by the licence fee, the corporation's news gathering (including extensive grass-roots contacts through local radio), and access to BBC national and international coverage (and archive) looked, in early 2007, like the surest prospect of a quality local service for viewers.

Ian Johnson is a Midlands-based BBC cameraman, who has covered major UK stories, including the 1984 Libyan Embassy siege, which followed the shooting of WPC Yvonne Fletcher, and stories across Europe and the US for the BBC in the Midlands. He is now a video journalist and was a key figure in the Black Country TV pilot in 2006.

He says: 'It's the way ahead. It's definitely what people want. People want big news – world and national news – and ultra-local news. They want to find out

BBC video journalist
Ian Johnson: 'Local
television is definitely
what people want.'

what's happening on their estate, in their village, in their town, but they don't care what's going on 20 miles away. Today we can deliver the TV equivalent of a local newspaper, whereas in the past you couldn't.'

Chas Watkin, the BBC Midlands News Editor, who supervised the introduction of local TV, says the scheduled bulletins on satellite were successful, but broadband is the way ahead: 'It has to be a totally on-demand service to work.'

Watkin says the broadband service came into its own on local election day in May 2006, when they were able to offer coverage of every local count: 'That was our best day. It's news that drives the hits. The audience wants local news. They may also want something quirky – but they want good quirky.'

REMEMBER

➤ Regional TV is based on signals from transmitters

➤ TV regions are not homogeneous communities

➤ Local TV can provide news from closer to home

➤ Broadband offers news-on-demand.

PODCASTS

*A RADIO PROGRAMME
MAY BE LIVE, AND
A PODCAST CANNOT
BE LIVE, BUT APART
FROM THAT THERE
IS NO DIFFERENCE.*

What is the difference between a podcast and a radio programme? A radio programme may be live, and a podcast cannot be live, but apart from that there is no difference.

There are good podcasts that sound just like radio programmes or features for radio, and bad podcasts that don't. For example, some newspapers tried podcasts with their reporters reading out features they had written for the paper. Adam Harding of Sky News Interactive asks: 'Why would you want to listen for five minutes to a person, who is not a broadcaster, reading something written for print, that it takes you a minute and a half to read for yourself in a paper?' These podcasts certainly bore no relation to Radio Four's *From Our Own Correspondent*.

In 2006 the audience for podcasts in the US was five million – tiny by comparison with radio audiences – but there was exponential growth with a forecast of 45 million listeners by 2010. Podcasts can be important tools for broadcast journalists. RSS feeds that tell users when a new episode has been updated mean you can develop subscriber networks. 'One-hit subscription' is what makes podcasts different from other sound files on the Internet.

BBC Radio Five Live developed some of the most downloaded podcasts in the UK with Mark Kermode's film reviews and the *Daily Mayo*, a cut-down version of Simon Mayo's programme. The station's editor Matt Morris says time-shifting and portability are the attractions of podcasting: 'Time-shifting was already there (you can go on to your computer and listen to output that was on last night streamed on the Internet – we do it all the time) but with portability, if you're a businessman, and you don't want to get up at 5.30, you can get up at 6.30, download *Wake Up To Money*, and listen to it on the way in to work.'

Professional broadcasters can make use of amateur content too. Chris Vallance, producer of the Pods and Blogs spot on Five Live, says: 'One of the things the new digital technologies enable is that, if you buy a computer now, you probably get nearly all the stuff you need to start recording audio, and if you don't have it, you can get it for free.

'In terms of mic technology, if you think about the quality of just those headset mics you can buy now, we did some tests and you can get results that are very similar to very expensive broadcast mics.

Chris Vallance: collecting podcasts from around the world

'There are no barriers to entry in most industrialised countries, and increasingly in the non-industrialised world. Given that that's the case, and given that there are people who are enthusiasts for playing around with sound, be they musicians, be they podcasters, be they bloggers who also do audio blogs, and you've suddenly got a vast pool of people who can send you sound from where they live. They can send you voice pieces, they can send you voxes, they can send you personal viewpoint pieces. We've started exploring that.'

One project involved collecting material from survivors of Hurricane Katrina, which hit New Orleans in 2005. Six months on the BBC broadcast almost 50 minutes of material. Vallance recalls: 'The sound quality of all of them was good, and some pieces were exceptional. There was one beautiful mixed package. He said: "My name is Chris Decker. I'm a trainee Catholic priest," and then he faded up the road noise. Then he said: "When I first moved back to New Orleans, the noise outside my window was absolute silence, and now you can hear traffic." And he used that as a way into riffing about the reconstruction of the city. It was a beautiful piece of radio – very NPR sounding, not BBC at all [National Public Radio is the US public broadcasting service]. Obviously it's coming from his radio culture not ours, and was a very different sound for us.'

Podcasters will occasionally send Vallance unmixed tracks, and he'll do the production work. Most show high production values: 'Some of them don't, frankly. There are breath noises all over the mic, pops everywhere and strange wheezes, pops and crackles – but I've heard one or two of those go out on regular radio.

'There's definitely, among the good people, a high degree of craft skills. They probably wouldn't see themselves as journalists. They see themselves as podcasters.'

Vallance is not sure, though, how long the term 'podcast' will last. 'It just will become radio, if you talk about radio as a device you switch on and talk comes out of it.'

So, podcasting looks as if it's here to stay. It's radio, after all.

REMEMBER

➤ Podcasting is the same as recorded radio programming
➤ RSS feeds mean subscribers can be told instantly when a podcast is updated
➤ Podcasters can provide source material for your own radio programmes.

PHONE-INS

The phone-in is a staple of speech-based radio. It is the forerunner of the interactivity for which many news organisations strive across their coverage.

Text and e-mail messages are part of the mix – but remember, if you are presenting or producing a phone-in, written messages have to be read out by the presenter. According to Jon Gaunt, of Talksport and previously the BBC, reading messages aloud is less likely to attract further callers than a good argument on air.

BBC Five Live strives for conversation rather than argument. Victoria Derbyshire explains her approach to callers to the morning phone-in: 'You've got no idea what they're going to say, it's completely unpredictable, so you just have a normal conversation with somebody you've never met before – courteous, polite, curious, all the sort of basics, what, why, where, when.'

Five Live's editor Matt Morris says: 'For a long time there's been a relationship between a radio station and its audience through the phone-in. We've developed that through e-mails, and then almost unexpectedly into text messaging which taps you into a much wider constituency.

'A typical Victoria Derbyshire programme may get 150 calls on a hot topic, of which you try and get maybe 30 on air. You can get thousands of text messages. You've got to beware of the tyranny of instant public opinion – but there's still something in tapping into public opinion in that way.

'Also text messaging gives you a lot of information about weather, road conditions and all that stuff. Peter Allen, the drivetime presenter, has referred to text messagers as our army of reporters. We've had that kind of interactivity, that relationship with the audience, for some time.'

Five Live's Victoria Derbyshire: her phone-in is 'just a normal conversation'.

THE SPORTS PHONE-IN

A lively sub-genre of the phone-in programme is the sports phone-in. '606' is one of the best known programme strands on BBC Radio Five Live, and Talksport has a similar format on independent national radio.

Although all sports can be discussed, the obsession of callers and presenters since the earliest days has been football.

The sports phone-in began in Britain on local commercial radio. Veteran Midlands broadcaster Tony Butler invented the football phone-in as we know it, when he was sports editor of BRMB in Birmingham in 1974. It started on the new commercial station on a Sunday lunchtime. Butler had four live guests in the studio, in case he didn't get any callers. He needn't have worried. He says: 'I shall never forget it. We had 28 callers in an hour and a half. The most any of the other talk shows had at that time was ten.'

After a 'fact-finding' visit to the US and Canada, where he heard outspoken sports presenters arguing with phone-in callers, he developed his own strident style, delivered in a broad West Midlands accent.

Butler's show moved to a Friday evening, where it became a Midlands institution. He was parodied by the Brummie comedian Jasper Carrott, bringing his show to national attention. When he left BRMB he continued the phone-in on BBC Radio WM, and even for a time on TV, on the cable service Birmingham Live.

He says: 'It hasn't changed over the years. I suppose I've mellowed as the years have gone by, but it's the same show. You don't have to be balanced or anything like that, but you've got to be responsible.'

Butler worked for newspapers including the *Daily Telegraph* and was a regional journalist writing copy for the BBC's regional radio and TV bulletins before he became a local personality. His ethical position on phone-ins is clear: 'I've never set up calls. I won't do that. If they're not calling in, I'm not doing my job.'

Butler says there is a danger on a long-running show that the same listeners call repeatedly, and it can begin to sound too much like a private club: 'We do have regular callers, and I have to be diplomatic, shall we say. I have someone answering the phones, and she'll say: "We've got so-and-so on, and he's already been on this week. Shall I put him off?" The answer is, of course, yes.'

Butler's abrasive style frequently fell foul of the old radio regulating body, the Independent Broadcasting Authority. His catchphrase was 'On yer bike' to get rid of callers. That was deemed acceptable, even in the 1980s, but the IBA complained when he started exhorting listeners to 'get your prayer mats out', whenever Aston Villa were playing in Europe in the run-up to their 1982 European Cup victory. The IBA said it was offensive to Muslims. Butler pointed out that he had received ten prayer mats from Muslim football fans. He says: 'I wouldn't do it today because these are very different times, politically, but in those days the IBA were the bane of my life. They used to drive me spare.'

Tony 'On yer bike' Butler: a Midlands broadcasting legend and the father of the football phone-in

Butler continued his cult status on local radio and regional TV for 30 years. BBC Radio WM sent him to Germany for the 2006 World Cup with sports editor Mark Regan. 'We'd do inserts into programmes throughout the day, starting with breakfast, do the phone-in for an hour in the evening and finish at about ten o'clock. It started as 12 days in Germany. Then they extended it to 24 days. We were running out of clean clothes and booking hotels became a problem. Twenty-four days and I never saw a match except on the telly!'

When he went to Germany, Butler was 71 years old. He says: 'As long as they keep paying me and as long as I've got an audience, I'll keep doing it.'

TIP BOX   **PHONE-INS – THE RISKS**

Any form of live radio involving members of the public carries a degree of risk. Will they use it as a platform for offensive language or views? Will they inadvertently, or even deliberately, libel someone?

Here are the BBC's guidelines on phone-ins.

The live nature of phone-ins means we should be alert to the possibility of contributors breaking the law or causing widespread offence. We should also be careful not to allow phone-ins to become a vehicle for the opinions of the presenter. The following best practice may help to minimise the risks:

- **Contributors to phone-ins should normally be called back and if necessary briefed before they go on air**

- **Content producers should read e-mails and texts before they are broadcast**

- **Presenters should be adequately briefed on BBC Editorial Guidelines and the law and be able to extricate the programme from tricky situations with speed and courtesy**

- When producing a phone-in on a difficult or controversial subject such as child abuse, the production team should be briefed on how to deal sensitively with contributors and support systems should be in place

- When a programme is contacted unexpectedly by someone wishing to share their difficult story, we should consider the implications and refer if necessary.

REMEMBER

➤ Phone-ins are the principal form of audience interaction in radio

➤ They can entertain and inform, and be a platform for public debate

➤ Presenters and producers need to be legally aware and alert to the risk of contributors causing offence.

CASE STUDY 15.3

'It just felt like the whole of London was under attack.'

Jon Gaunt, BBC London

The morning of 7 July 2005 produced some of the most remarkable local radio ever heard in Britain.

What made the suicide bomb attacks on public transport in London an exceptional breaking news story was that it came on a day when everyone was expecting to be covering a huge 'good news' story – London winning the 2012 Olympics.

BBC London, a local station for the capital, had the first eye-witness accounts as the drama unfolded, and in a model of restrained, factual broadcasting, Sony-award-winning presenter Jon Gaunt reported only confirmed information, and insisted on air that the station was not interested in speculation or opinion.

Jon Gaunt: 'I thought it was going to be an easy day.'

Elsewhere in this book you will read the opinions of experienced rolling news journalists who believe modern audiences have a sophisticated grasp of the news-gathering process. They say you can tell people all the information to hand as long as it is attributed. The audience can make their own minds up what to believe. BBC London's approach on 7 July was arguably a more old-fashioned one. The decisions of Jon Gaunt and editor David Robey to stick to the facts as they knew them were informed by the need not to spread panic across the capital.

Here are some of the key moments of the BBC London coverage of the first hours of the story – and an insight into the behind-the-scenes tensions, with Jon Gaunt's comments on what he felt as the story unfolded and what he really suspected was going on.

Gaunt had spoken to his producer as he was on his way in to work on the train from his Northamptonshire home. It was his habit to talk through the content of the morning programme, billed as 'London's liveliest phone-in'.

I just said don't set anything up. Let's just do Olympics, Olympics, Olympics. I thought it was going to be an easy day.

Predictably, the phones 'went crazy' with people wanting to talk about the Olympic victory. After the nine o'clock news, Gaunt went on air with an opening link that summed up the euphoria in the capital.

'There isn't really much to talk about today except one major story. Is this just not the best news ever? When you saw the jubilation . . . it has put a spring in the step. It does make us proud to be British . . .'

At 9.15, travel editor Jules Wilson reported: 'We've got some major travel disruption . . . please stay clear of the whole tube network . . . they've got some incidents taking place.'

Gaunt reacted: 'We've sent reporters to Liverpool Street. If you're in the Liverpool Street tube station area, we need to hear from you now.'

The programme continued with a two-way with a reporter in Singapore, where the International Olympic Committee made its historic decision. There were calls too from ecstatic Londoners.

Then at 9.25, reporter Pete Wilson joined Gaunt in the studio with more on the incident at Liverpool Street.

By then I knew. Pete said they thought a bomb had gone off, but don't say anything on air.

Wilson: 'We've heard a report about a bang.'

Gaunt: 'An explosion?'

Wilson: 'No, a bang. It could have been a collision involving two trains which could have caused a power surge . . . there are reports of walking wounded. The advice is to stay off the tube.'

A trail followed for a phone-in the following Tuesday with the Metropolitan Police Commissioner, Sir Ian Blair. It included a clip of the Commissioner saying: 'My job is to make London safe.'

The 9.30 news headlines led with: 'Emergency services have been called to Liverpool Street station after reports of an explosion. It's thought the incident was caused by a major power failure. The station's currently cordoned off. TfL [Transport for London] are telling people to avoid the entire tube network. British Transport Police have confirmed there are walking wounded, and said paramedics have responded to one report of a person classed as life at risk. More on that as soon as we get it.'

I was of the opinion, surely we've got to say this is a bomb. I was very much in favour of 'Let's go.' I was thinking Ferrari [Nick Ferrari on rival, commercial station LBC] will be doing it. There was a lot of debate with the [control room] cubicle. What I do on air is I produce as I go along. I'd been on air on 9/11 and learnt a lot from that, but a lot of the backroom team didn't have much experience of rolling interactive news. Management weren't in at this stage and we ended up being cautious. You don't want to spread panic.

The travel report repeated the advice to avoid the tube network. Tickets were being honoured by buses.

At 9.32, the first witness was on air. The caller, Tyrone, said there were hundreds of police on the streets. There were loud sirens in the background of the call.

Tyrone: 'Can you hear me?'

Gaunt: 'Yes, carry on.'

Tyrone: 'It seems to be some sort of security alert that has affected the whole of the East London area . . .'

The first witness from one of the bombed trains followed immediately. One of the radio station's staff was on the tube with his wife.

Ian Wade, who was an accountant with BBC London, was on the train, and that's why we had the first witness on air.

Gaunt: 'BBC London's Ian Wade was actually on the underground.'

Wade: 'I was on the train it actually happened to, Jon. We were about 200 yards outside King's Cross and an almighty bang. Lights went out. Soot filled the carriage we was in and then the emergency electricity come on. We was in the actual carriage about 15 minutes. They started filing us out, they shut the line down for the electricity, and officials was walking us down. Now as I was walking out, I asked one of the officials what happened and he said one of the electric overhead lights fell down, he thinks, and hit the front of the train. There's people here crying. We was actually on the train it happened, I've never seen anything like it.'

Gaunt: 'Was there panic on the train when those lights went out? There must have been panic.'

Wade: 'To be honest with you, people were silent for about 15 to 20 seconds. You couldn't believe it. It was . . . some people were saying: "Oh, my God, help me, help me," and all sorts, banging on the doors and others were saying: "No, no, no. Don't open anything. If there's a fire outside we're going to be dead in minutes, if there's smoke coming in." But people were generally very, very good, you know. There's people keeping people calm, and saying: "Look, we're all right. There's no fire, you know, hang on."'

Gaunt: 'How long were you in the dark for?'

Wade: 'I would say 15 minutes but the train was absolutely, which is normal, absolutely packed, so there's . . . it was the busiest train I've ever been on anyway 'cos it was running slow, so it couldn't have happened at a worse time. It was almost like a bomb going off. There was just a boom.'

Gaunt: 'Any injuries?'

Wade: 'I'm just looking over. There's a guy with a short-sleeved shirt on. He's got cuts on his arm, but otherwise that's the first and only one I've seen actually injured, but other than that people are sobbing and covered in soot and all sorts.'

Wade said it had taken 15 minutes to walk along the track to King's Cross.

Gaunt: 'We want you to stay there for the moment until we can get a reporter down. If anything else happens, I want you to ring us back, Ian.'

What I do is produce on air, thinking where the next twist might be or where the next actuality is coming from. Ian Wade wasn't a reporter, but he was great that morning. We needed to have him available to go on air.

Gaunt summarised what they knew so far; the train was on the Piccadilly Line from Cockfosters; people were in the dark for 15 minutes; somebody said it was an overhead light that came down; keep off the tube for now. The next caller was equally dramatic.

Alexa: 'There was a really loud bang and the lights went out and everybody ducked and screamed. We were told to evacuate and we were asked not to run, but everybody ran.'

Gaunt: 'Alexa, you're obviously shook up. Take it easy now . . . We'll talk to the emergency services once they've got the time.'

Pete Wilson returned to the studio and reported the police and fire brigade had been called to Aldgate. It has been declared a major incident, and, yes, there were some casualties.

At 9.43, Gaunt issued a more detailed plea for witnesses: 'It's not helpful to speculate. We don't really know . . . In situations like this, I'll be absolutely straight with you, we rely on you as well. That's why we're an interactive radio station. If you were there, please give me a call now. 020 722 42000. You can also text 07786 200949 or e-mail me gaunty@bbc.co.uk. We are going to do travel bulletins now every 15 minutes.'

The decision to increase the number of travel bulletins was taken by the travel unit, but the rest was all me. There were some people who thought we shouldn't be asking for calls, but I didn't want to just sit there and be a public information centre. We've got this great resource – the listeners – let's use it.

Gaunt: 'Don't bother ringing people back – put them straight through. We need to know what's happening now. As soon as we can talk to the emergency services we will.'

That's me getting annoyed with the cubicle. The normal practice is to ring people back, but there was a chance they'd ring off and be taking a call from a loved one asking if they were safe, and they'd be engaged when they tried to get them. And anyway, the phone lines were getting clogged up. You couldn't get through.

Gaunt: 'We were celebrating a great Olympic victory, but now for obvious reasons we are concentrating on that incident on the tube.'

We were still getting calls about the Olympics. Whether people hadn't heard what was going on, I don't know. We had to clear the lines.

The 9.45 travel bulletin reported King's Cross mainline station was closed, as were several roads. The police were asking drivers to avoid the City of London.

Gaunt: 'Jackie at Kilburn wants to tell me what's happened at Edgware. Jackie, what can you tell me?'

Jackie said she was driving down Park Lane and heard sirens coming from all directions. 'Police bikes, police cars, an ambulance went by, and I thought: "What the hell's going on down here now?"'

She gave more details, and Gaunt thanked her: 'If you find out any more, see any more, give us a call back. We need to go back to Ian Wade in a couple of moments. Can you get him back on the line, Abi, to find out what's going on at Liverpool Street now?'

This is me producing on air, and bossing it. Abi Lewis, my producer, had been with me for years. This is the way we work together. I'm not just a gob on a stick. I couldn't do that sort of radio, being told what to say next. You've got to be involved in your product.

Phil, a cabbie, called from near Russell Square station: 'It's unbelievable. It seems there's a major disaster.'

Gaunt: 'Let's not speculate. We know it's a major incident . . . Come on London cabbies, come on white van men, come on white van women, just tell us what you can see. This is why we have interactive radio like this. Pick up the phone please, and please tell us. Obviously a lot of people will be concerned about relatives and friends who might have been travelling this morning. We will keep you informed and, as soon as we know something, we will tell you. What we will not do on this radio station, let me tell you, is speculate.'

I knew speculation wouldn't help. But I also knew this was a massive opportunity to build an audience. And I was right. The figures went up after this. During a period of terror, people want to know what's going on.

By now, just after 9.50, reporters were reporting from the scenes of the events.

Gaunt: '94.9's Anna O'Neill is at King's Cross. Good morning, Anna.'

O'Neill: 'Extraordinary scenes . . . police telling people to move away from the station and they're starting to cordon off the area. Fire engines, ambulances, police cars and vans. Hundreds of police men and women. Everybody confused. We're not being told very much indeed. We were told there was some kind of a power surge and that we needed to evacuate the station. People are crying, 'cos they don't know what's been happening and they've heard there've been casualties at Liverpool Street. People are shouting: "Get out of the station, get out of the station."'

Gaunt: 'Stay safe, Anna, we'll speak to you later. Ian Wade is back.'

Wade: (alarms sounding in the background) 'I'm in the station, King's Cross station, and I have to retract what I said earlier, Jon. Those who are injured are badly injured, there's a lot of blood in here.'

Gaunt: 'And how many people would you say are injured at the moment, my friend?'

Wade: 'In this room I would say there's probably about 30 or 40 people, but, as I say, it's very bad news. There's a lot of blood.'

Gaunt: 'If you don't mind me asking you, what kind of injuries are you seeing?'

Wade: 'A lot of head injuries. Because it's quite warm this time of year, a lot of people are wearing short-sleeved shirts so you can see a lot of arms cut up and faces cut up . . . this is definitely glass cuts. People are bleeding heavily. People like myself that are covered in soot. I can't fault the police or the ambulance or even London Transport. They're walking round tending everybody that's badly injured, I mean, I'm just slightly shaken.'

By then we knew it was a terrorist attack. Ian wasn't a reporter, but I was just treating him as an eye-witness. I knew he was an intelligent bloke, who wouldn't say anything he shouldn't have. But if he had described really terrible injuries, I didn't care. He was just telling us what he could see.

Gaunt introduced Kevin, another cabbie, at Aldgate.

Kevin: 'I saw a man covered in blood being led by the police. The emergency people are putting on orange chemical emergency suits at Aldgate East.'

Gaunt: 'I'm being told by my research team, that's standard practice.'

Pete [Wilson] came on and said that. He was a good member of the team with that sort of knowledge. I could cut the mic and talk to the people in the cubicle and of course they're telling me lots of stuff. The last thing you want to do is spread panic. But you do want to make it sound exciting, because it is exciting.

Gaunt made another appeal to cabbies, white van men and women.

Gaunt: 'Please don't ring up with comments on the Olympics, please don't ring up to speculate. We want to know what's happening out there in London.'

The 9.58 travel update reported that the whole of town was taking the brunt of road closures. 'Avoid all the roads around the city.'

At 10.01, news reader Max Rushton said a 'power surge incident' had caused a number of bangs. People had been injured, one of them seriously. Clips in the bulletin included Ian Wade and Tyrone talking to Gaunt. It featured the Mayor, Ken Livingstone, on the use of compulsory purchase orders to clear the Olympic site and Sir Ian Blair on Olympic security. There was also George Bush, speaking on climate change at the G8 summit at Gleneagles.

By 10.05, the radio station was reporting the tube network was suspended. British Transport Police had informed them that two trains remained stuck at Edgware Road, but it was not yet known if they had collided. The official police line was that it was 'difficult to know exactly what's happened at the moment'.

Gaunt read out a text message from a listener who said the sound was deafening, there was a lot of smoke and absolute chaos at Aldgate.

Gaunt: 'We are getting a lot of calls about an incident on a bus. If you know anything about that, please get in touch.'

Text messages can be useful in an incident like this. But I don't ask for e-mails. There's no place for e-mails in a phone-in show. They allow people to go on at length and not to join in the debate. If you're an abrasive presenter like me, it lets people avoid being questioned. An e-mail won't get another caller, but an argument will.

On this occasion, Gaunt was not inviting argument. He was after information. Another caller heard a blast from a station platform at Liverpool Street; the travel editor said traffic cameras were showing 'people everywhere' on the streets; the National Grid said they had no reported problems that would have caused power surges; the Royal London Hospital was preparing to take casualties.

There was a kind of other-worldly quality to it all. It just felt like the whole of London was under attack.

Gaunt summed up what was known so far and explained that they had not been able to interview anyone from the emergency services: 'They have many more important things to do than talk to a radio station. We're getting a lot of calls with speculation. I'm sure you'll agree that speculation is not useful at the moment.'

I was a little embarrassed they [the emergency services] hadn't spoken to us. I fully understood their problems, but as a programme we needed to have spokesmen on. You're trying to make it sound authoritative and professional.

Amy, a first-time caller who'd been on the Piccadilly Line train, said she heard a 'very big bang': 'I've heard it might have been a light falling on the train, but it was too big an explosion to have been that.'

It's all about the trust you build with an audience. They might not even like you but they trust you. It's like Pavlov's dog. The reaction is automatic. Something's happened, so ring Gaunty.

At 10.19, reporter Anna O'Neill was on again: 'I've got some rather grim news. One man has actually shown me some footage that he recorded on his mobile phone of a bus exploding a few streets away just near to Euston station . . . some very devastating scenes there. It looks like some people lying on the floor. I couldn't tell you exactly what kind of injuries they've got, people lying motionless on the floor.

'The man who'd been at King's Cross was talking about people covered in soot and blood. We're not sure whether it is this power surge we've been hearing about this morning, or something more sinister is going on.'

Gaunt: 'Of course, but let's not speculate on that. Just tell me about the bus. The bus was in Russell Square, I believe.'

O'Neill reports the man wasn't sure, because he was shocked. He saw the back of the bus explode. He filmed footage of it on his mobile phone. 'He hadn't actually captured the moment the bus exploded. What he captured was the seconds after that bus exploded, and as he gets nearer you can see people lying on the floor, and the bus basically in tatters.'

That footage was all over the Six O'Clock News on TV.

Gaunt reported complete and utter gridlock and advised people not to travel, before taking a call from Steve in Marylebone: 'I was in Tavistock Square, and about six vehicles in front of me, there was a line of buses and then . . . bang! You see the explosion. I don't know what caused it. You see either the side of a building fly across the road, or, as people have been saying, the side of a bus.'

Gaunt: 'How far were you from the incident would you say?'

Steve: 'Probably about no more than 50 metres.'

Gaunt: 'And you're a cabby, obviously, I can hear the meter in the background. What else did you see after that?'

Steve: 'Just chaos. People running across the square, kids on the floor crying, people cowering in the corner and just, basically, havoc really.'

Gaunt thanks the caller and repeats the plea for information: 'All we want you to do is say, "Jon, I saw this or I saw that."'

By this time we were getting calls with anti-Muslim messages. Why can't people express that view? Management were in the cubicle by then. There was a kind of censorship going on, I suppose. But I have to say the editor Dave Robey was spot-on with his news judgement that day.

At 10.18, Pete Wilson was back in the studio with reports from Scotland Yard of multiple explosions: 'It's the first time they've called them that so far this morning – multiple explosions across London. We're told that in the next ten to 15 minutes we'll get a full release . . . It now looks as if there is some kind of pattern, some kind of link as to what has happened across London this morning and that's what we're trying to establish as well.'

I knew then what was happening. The editor was saying we can't say it's Muslims or we can't say it's Al Qaeda, but it sure as hell wasn't the IRA.

Gaunt: 'On a day when we started off so jovial, having a laugh about the Olympics . . . it's turned into something else . . . It's an horrific day for London. There's no two ways about it. It's an horrific day for London, but we will not speculate. We will bring you the facts as we establish those facts.'

Latoya in Liverpool Street told of a big explosion, grey dust falling everywhere, an orange light which they thought was flames and a lot of people who were badly wounded. They were in the front carriages. 'As we walked down the track we saw the full extent of the damage, and it looked like the whole carriage had blown open and they were still rescuing people. There were bodies and er . . . that's it, I guess.'

Gaunt: 'Stay safe. Calm down, won't you?'

At 10.22 Pete Wilson had a full report that had come through from the Metropolitan Police in the last two minutes: 'At approximately ten to nine this morning, police were called to Aldgate station to assist the City of London police and British Transport Police regarding an incident on the underground system.'

Wilson reported a major incident, and that it was too early to say what had happened. Across London there were further reports of multiple explosions. Police were responding to reports from Edgware Road, King's Cross, Liverpool Street, Russell Square, Aldgate East and Moorgate underground stations. Added to this there were confirmed explosions on a bus at Tavistock Place: 'There have been reports of numerous casualties, but again it is too early to say the numbers at this stage.'

Everybody knows these places. Even if you're not a Londoner, the story's made for radio because you don't necessarily need the pictures, because everybody's got a Monopoly board.

Gaunt: 'And every word you've said there was official from the Metropolitan Police?'

Wilson confirmed it was and said it was worth calling loved ones to say you're safe.

Gaunt: 'I've just tried to phone my wife but a lot of the mobile systems are down . . . Please keep the phone lines free, please only ring us if you've got something you can tell us. Let's go straight now to Martin Edwards, who's at Royal London Hospital in Whitechapel. Good morning, Martin, what can you tell us?'

Reporter Edwards said the A and E entrance was closed to the public, there were walking wounded, people on stretchers, and an air ambulance on the scene.

The 10.30 headlines reported explosions in multiple locations: five tube stations and a bus in Tavistock Square.

The travel report said the tube network was closed, trains to King's Cross and Paddington were diverted, and there were road closures, including the Aldgate one-way system.

Off the back of the travel report, Robyn, a witness in Belsize Park, said she saw the bus in Tavistock Square and heard the explosion. There were people running, a number of wounded people. She'd heard on the radio they thought there had been a bomb at Euston station: 'It was a fairly large shock then, to see the bus explode right in front of me.'

Gaunt: 'Hold on. You actually saw the bus explode?'

Robyn: 'That's right.'

Gaunt: 'This is awful to ask you this. Tell me what you saw.'

You have to ask these questions. They'll speak to me because they trust me. People will say things on the phone that they won't say by the time you've got your microphone or your television cameras there.

Robyn: 'Sitting in the car and, of course, the debris of the bus raining down onto the car I was sitting in. I had my 15-month-old daughter sitting with me so of course my first response is to try to . . . cover her and of course praying that nothing's going to seriously damage the car that we're in. Then of course seeing the people in the road and . . . quite a bit of carnage, I suppose, and blood.'

Gaunt: 'How far away were you from it, Robyn?'

Robyn: 'Perhaps a block, if that. There were three or four cars between us and the bus . . .'

Gaunt: 'How's the child?'

Robyn: 'She was, of course, extremely frightened by the explosion, but of course didn't understand anything else that was happening, so . . . she's fine and I'm fine, and we're just, I suppose, in a state of shock.'

Gaunt: 'Of course, Robyn, to be straight, we all are this morning.'

She was great. She ended up on every news broadcast. It's an iconic image. I think in pictures so I could see it all. The explosion on the bus, the mother protecting her baby, and I thought of my kids. I suppose, to be cynical, I was playing the family man card, but somebody who doesn't have kids might not have asked that question.

The broadcast continued with Shep, another cabbie ('It's absolute mayhem here, mate . . . We've just been told there's another two buses blown up'); more eye-witnesses ('they said it was a power surge but a power surge can't do that to a train' . . . 'there were dead bodies on the track'); mobile phone networks jammed; and police and government statements.

Gaunt appealed for video phone footage for 'our TV station', but asked people to avoid the jammed mobile networks and use a landline if possible.

One text message read: 'I've got no words, I'm just crying.'

At 11.39, Gaunt read out internal wire copy: the BBC Security Correspondent Frank Gardner was reporting the explosions had 'all the hallmarks of a planned Al Qaeda attack'.

To be honest, you're thinking, This Is It. A bomb has gone off on my watch. It's the doctor whacking the electrodes on the chest in casualty. This is it. I said let's not speculate, and I knew what LBC would be doing, and I wanted to make our coverage distinctive. A lot of the people on our programme were young kids, and they'd never done a proper story. And a lot of them grew up that day.

As the enormity of the events became clearer, Gaunt's programme was carried across much of the BBC local radio network on 7 July 2005. Gaunt left the BBC soon afterwards to become a columnist for *The Sun* newspaper. The corporation decided his column, with its outspoken and controversial opinions, was inconsistent with working as a BBC broadcaster. He remained in demand as a TV and radio pundit (including contributions to BBC stations), and returned as a radio presenter on the independent station Talksport.

TIP BOX

Jon Gaunt's experience on 7 July highlighted a number of important working practices for broadcasters on live radio.

- You don't have to speculate. Powerful news radio can work without broadcasters or 'experts' speculating.

- Work as a team and put your trust in your team, but when you are on air, yours is the final voice, the final responsibility for the output.

- Somebody has to take control. It can be the producer in the cubicle or it can be the presenter. But you need to know who's in charge. You can't have too many chiefs.

- Be natural and be yourself. Gaunt has a reputation as an acerbic, opinionated phone-in host and commentator, but his professional range included the ability to respond on a human level to events, and to take responsibility for not spreading panic.

- Keep calm and keep a clear head. Think how the story could develop and prepare for those developments.

PROGRAMME PRODUCTION IN TV AND RADIO

SCRIPTS AND RUNNING ORDERS

Every live programme has a script and a *running order*, sometimes known as a *run-down*. The programme goes on air with the production team knowing what to expect. But the thrill of working on news programmes, and the reason most broadcast journalists prefer it to any other form of programme making, is that running orders and scripts will change while you are preparing them, and also while you are on air.

Late news stories appear on the wire services, reporters in the field relay new developments, live interviews overrun, satellite links go down, juries return

A running order in ENPS, the news production system

verdicts, Parliament votes on important legislation, sports results come through. Suddenly the running order you started with is redundant. Then the fun begins.

But programme staff need to go on air with an expectation of what the programme will contain. A producer needs to organise the range of technical resources and the teams of technical and journalistic staff that contribute to modern news output. The running order is the way to do that, even though it may end up as little more than a rough template for what follows.

RADIO BULLETINS

Every station will have its own style guide for bulletins. Many local stations will insist on at least two local stories in the top three. The preferred style may be for a headline sequence followed by a sequence of stories. Or it may be a straight read without headlines.

The content should be flexible. At a time of international crisis, it's not appropriate to stick to 'two local stories out of three'. Normally, the newsreader is the final arbiter of content. The reader drops or adds stories on air to fill to time. On bigger stations or for longer bulletins, the producer will make decisions about content.

A CLOSER LOOK

ELEMENTS OF A RADIO BULLETIN

A radio bulletin will consist of a combination of the following elements.

Headlines	A series of phrases or sentences summarising the main stories of the bulletin. They may include audio clips.
Copy stories	Stories read by the presenter without audio. Usually no more than 20 seconds long.
Voicers	A reporter's voice report, introduced by a cue from the presenter. Voicers can be live or recorded and may be from a location or the studio.
Wraps	A voice report with one or more short clips of audio, usually from interviews. Introduced by the presenter's cue.
Packages	More complex features, with several clips of audio, possibly including interviews, actuality and/or location commentary, and music. Also introduced by the presenter's cue.
Clips	Audio introduced by the presenter. Usually soundbites from longer interviews.
Vox-pops	A series of tightly edited comments from members of the public. Introduced by the presenter as a stand-alone feature, or used as part of a package.

Two-ways	Question and answer sessions, live or recorded, with a reporter or correspondent who's covering a story, either in the studio or down-the-line from a location.
Interviews	Rare in short bulletins, but occasionally a presenter will interview someone in the news.
Weather	Usually in copy form, for use at the end of the bulletin. Weather reports can be flexible in length, so that you can finish the bulletin exactly on time. Write the weather so the first few seconds make perfect sense on their own (*and the weather, it'll be mostly cloudy with sunny spells*). You can then add subsequent sentences to fill to the end of the bulletin.

The content of every bulletin should be varied. The treatment of the lead story, unless it is very recent breaking news, will always include audio, whether it is a voicer, wrap or clip. There should be a variety of treatments available for bigger stories, so that, even if there is no new development, the lead can sound different in successive bulletins. The first version might be a voicer; the second could include an interview clip; the third might be a wrap incorporating elements of both.

Each story should be clearly marked with a catchline (a title for the story, also known as a *slug*), the duration of the cue, the duration of any audio and the out words (the last words) of any audio. On computerised news production systems like ENPS, each story must be identified by a catchline, the length of the cues will be calculated automatically, and the information about the audio can be written in by the journalist responsible.

Some news editors will prefer that a voicer is not followed by another voicer, and that one cue and clip is not followed by another cue and clip. A well-crafted bulletin may follow these guidelines, but it is more important to present the stories in the right order according to your news judgement. Listeners are more interested in the stories than the treatment.

Wherever you work, stick to the rules. But the newsreader who uses their experience to improve the bulletin, by making editorial decisions on air, will rarely be criticised.

LEVELS

All items in the bulletin should be at the same level. The newsreader should be as loud as the voice reports and interview clips.

Output is usually shown on PPMs (peak programme meters), a semi-circular dial registering the peak volumes of the output. You should aim for speech to register between 5 and 6 on the scale. Music, which has a wider dynamic range, and so is easier to hear, should register between 4 and 5. Avoid dropping below 4, because that will be too quiet for many people listening at home. Any speech or music much above 6 will be too loud for the listener and may even distort (this is known

The PPM – always check your levels

as over-modulating or 'over-modding'). The exception is telephone quality voice – which you'll use a lot of on local radio bulletins. *Boost the volume on telephone speech (to over 6 on the scale) to compensate for the poor dynamic range of the audio.*

Some digital desks have a series of LEDs (light emitting diodes) that flash green for acceptable levels and red for over-modding.

EQUALISATION

Equalisation (or EQ) controls on a radio desk change the frequency range of the output, just like a graphic equaliser on a home stereo. You only need to alter the EQ response of a channel if the audio you are playing out is too tinny or sounds muffled. Increase the bass response for something that sounds tinny or too bright; increase the treble for muffled or 'boomy' sound.

REMEMBER

- ➤ Vary the content of bulletins
- ➤ On a local station, ensure local stories are near the top
- ➤ Mark your stories clearly with a catchline and timings
- ➤ Monitor the sound quality (levels and EQ).

TV scripts – divided vertically with technical information to the left and script to the right

TV PROGRAMMES

SCRIPTS

The key to a smooth-running TV programme is teamwork. Working as a team means communication between team members, so that everyone knows what is going on and what part they play in the programme. The information on the programme script is part of that communication.

TV scripts will be divided vertically, so that technical information is available alongside the newsreader or reporter's words. At a glance everyone in the production team can see who is on screen and on which camera or outside broadcast, when VT or graphics should be played in, and the duration and out words of each item.

TIP BOX

TEN-MINUTE TV NEWS BULLETIN – PROGRAMME TEMPLATE

Here's a suggested running order for a TV bulletin in a simple three-camera studio, with two presenters, one for news and another for sport.

Picture and sound sources are listed alongside the content, and the duration, of each section of the programme. Once you've decided on your content, the full script will have a separate page for each story, clearly numbered with a catchline at the top. Camera one is pointing at the main presenter; camera two is a two-shot; and camera three is a shot of the separate sports presenter.

This template has been used by student broadcast journalists as a starting point for bulletins on 'newsdays' when they replicate newsroom practice.
By the end of the day, it will almost certainly have changed considerably.

	Technical Information – Camera/VT/sound	CONTENT	Dur:
1	VT	Titles	15
2	Camera 1 + studio sound	Hello	5
3	VT + studio sound	Headlines	15
4	Cam 1 + studio sound	Lead intro	20
5	VT	Lead package	1 min
6	Cam 1 + studio sound	News Copy	15
7	Cam 1 + studio sound VT	News Copy + OOV	20
8	Cam 1 + studio sound	News Copy	15
9	Cam 1 + studio sound	Package One intro	15
10	VT	Package One	1 min
11	Cam 1 + studio sound VT	Short story + OOV	20
12	Cam 1 + studio sound VT	Wipe story + OOV	20
13	Cam 1 + studio sound VT	Wipe story + OOV	20
14	Cam 1 + studio sound	Package Two intro	15
15	VT	Package Two	1 min
16	Cam 2 + studio sound	Link to Sport	10
17	Cam 3 + studio sound VT	Sport One + OOV	30
18	Cam 3 + studio sound VT	Sport Two + OOV	20
19	Cam 3 + studio sound	Sport Three copy	15
20	Cam 3 + studio sound VT	Sport Four + OOV	20
21	Cam 2 + studio sound	Handback	10
22	Cam 1 + studio sound	Weather link	10
23	GFX + studio sound	Weather	40
24	Cam 1 + studio sound	Finally link	10
25	VT	Finally	1 min
26	Cam 2 + studio sound	Goodbye	10

DURATIONS AND OUT-WORDS

Every link or cue must contain information about the audio or video that follows. The most important technical details for the gallery or control room are the length of the piece – its duration – and the final words of audio – the out-words. These are the cue for the next item in the running order. Directors, vision mixers, sound mixers and presenters await those cues. The information must be accurate if the programme is to run smoothly.

Durations – to the exact second – are easily noted. Stopwatches used to be a common tool in newsrooms. Today's digital editing systems tell you the length of a piece without having to time it for yourself. But it will be the reporter's job to tell the rest of the production team. If scripts have already been prepared as a deadline approaches, typing the duration into the newsroom computer system may not be enough. There may not be time to distribute revised scripts to the gallery and studio. Someone has to make sure people are told.

The out-words are usually the last three words of a script or interview. If a news organisation has a style which involves reporters signing off with a standard out cue (SOC) – for example: 'John Simpson, BBC News, Kabul' – then the letters SOC may appear on the script. Sometimes the 'out' is a repeat of words that have been heard only a few seconds earlier, so it is a good idea to make that clear. For example, if there is an interview clip in which someone repeats the phrase 'in my opinion', and those are also the out-words, then the script should read OUT: 'in my opinion' (second time). If the final audio in a piece is not words at all, but actuality or music, then that should be noted on the script, e.g. OUT: music fades.

REMEMBER

➤ Communication and teamwork are the key to smooth-running programmes

➤ A running order is your programme template

➤ The running order should change in response to events

➤ Mark your scripts clearly with technical information (the source of the VT or graphic, duration and out-words).

CONCLUSION – THE FUTURE OF NEWS PROGRAMMING

So what is the future of news programming as we have come to know it? Industry professionals we have spoken to agree there is a need to embrace change and new ways of delivering news. But the consensus appears to be that we are in a period of evolution, not revolution. The Internet has changed global communications, but core journalistic skills remain.

Kevin Bakhurst, Controller of BBC News 24, says the traditional bulletin is still going to be important for the next five years: 'The Six and the Ten still get five and a half million viewers for a given programme and that's still a sizeable audience, but the fact that News 24 now gets six million viewers a week is a mile ahead of where we were two years ago. The audience is already shifting to some extent.

'As audiences become more sophisticated, as the rollout of digital and Freeview continues, News 24 is going to be a more and more important proposition for the BBC.'

Nick Higham, the BBC's longest-serving Media Correspondent, says we have to accept continuing change. We are not moving from a stable past to a stable future. 'Transition is the stable state.' Here's his assessment of the state we have reached.

Nick Higham, BBC Media Correspondent: 'Transition is the stable state.'

The audience or a section of it is getting its news from a much wider range of sources – especially electronic. We know that newspapers are in long-term decline. We know that people increasingly want and can get news updates on the move from mobile phones, and we know that the audience for conventional news programmes on television is declining, along with the audience for the channels on which those programmes appear, BBC1 and ITV, and we know that, although these things have made something of an impact, the combined audience for Sky and News 24 is still not that great, so there is, you could argue, a kind of looming crisis for television news as a whole.

I don't see any other way of dealing with that than confronting it and continuously trying to reinvent ourselves. The BBC has always been, institutionally, very good at reinventing itself. It sometimes takes an outside stimulus. If you go back to the 1950s, the BBC was dreadfully set in its ways and was given a huge kick up the arse by ITV, and responded in a dramatic and remarkable way. More recently the BBC has been very good at responding to changing audience behaviours and changing technologies. Our position online is extremely strong as a result of being early movers and doing it well.

So, news has got to find ways of re-presenting itself, reconfiguring itself, redefining itself in ways that are going to be meaningful to people who have new and different technologies.

There are two reservations. The audience itself does not move into the new technologies consistently. There are still very large numbers of people who still have only five terrestrial channels, particularly older people who don't want and are not interested in all these new technologies. And the other problem you have is that the pressure of doing news in new ways on new technologies – the competition that is implied in all that, because lots of other people are doing this – all of that means a danger that you do things differently not merely in a cosmetic way, but in a fundamental way. And if you're the BBC that's a problem, because you undermine the brand and the promise and the service that we traditionally deliver.

If you're not careful, you forget that our position in the marketplace is that we're trustworthy, in broad terms, and we mustn't forget that because we're trying to provide a new service for mobile phones.

Nick Higham's view is that the democratisation of the media – the fact that anyone can get access to the Internet – strengthens the position of journalists, particularly with organisations – like the BBC – that have a reputation for trustworthiness.

Our stuff's reliable, so if you want to know, reliably, what is going on, if you want an authoritative statement, then the BBC is the place to go – and news organisations like that – because, although there is all this stuff around, and a lot of it may be very current and very new, judging its accuracy, is a problem. The Internet is a huge great rumour factory, and it produces all kinds of fascinating stuff, but can you believe it? You've no way of knowing what you can believe and what you can't believe. Our job is to say: 'This much we know and you can believe this much.' If you then want to go off and swap gossip with someone online or blog or whatever, that's fine, but bear in mind that what you're seeing there may not be reliable. It may be hearsay. It may be half-truth. So there's a very important role for us, for the BBC and for other news organisations which have built their promise to the audience and promise to the readership on trustworthiness and reliability.

He says there is a potential mismatch when news providers offer a forum for hosting blogs. There needs to be a clear separation between an authoritative news station and something that provides a forum for comment and exchange of views – just as there is on radio between a news bulletin and a phone-in.

This debate is at the heart of the future of broadcast journalism. Journalists are certainly all content providers in a converged multimedia age. It doesn't follow that all content providers are journalists. They never have been, and it is unlikely they ever will be.

There is a clear technological argument that anyone with access to the means of distributing media is in the same position as a traditional broadcaster. That is not the same as being able to command an audience and earning the trust of viewers and listeners.

Journalists have become used to dealing with new technologies, and learning new software. Nick Higham's argument that 'the stable state is change' is a compelling one for anyone operating in a modern newsroom. But the key skills of authoritative story-telling within a legal and ethical framework are a constant.

REMEMBER

➤ Journalists have to be jacks-of-all-trades, and masters of *some*
➤ Content is king.

PARTTWO NEWSDAYS

Newsdays

In this part of the book, we present a unique look behind the scenes in newsrooms across the UK. Some of the broadcast organisations will be familiar to you, and you'll be learning from top professionals; others will be unknown to you unless you live in their broadcast area. Some may be places you aspire to work at one day; others the kind of place you'll look for your first job.

Each Newsday is a snapshot, a moment in time capturing what happened on a typical shift in a particular organisation. If you were able to visit them tomorrow, you might find much the same happening. The stories and the personalities will have changed but the process rolls on, relentlessly responding to issues and events, and the interpretation of events by professional journalists.

Working practices vary hugely across the industry. Here we give you a chance to experience what happens in different workplaces, how decisions are made about what goes on air, and how producers and presenters cope with breaking stories. You'll see the importance of forward planning and the restraints that resources – equipment and manpower – put on the news-gathering process. If there is a theme common to all the newsrooms we visited it is that the driving factor behind every decision is to meet a deadline, whether it is in the next minute, the next hour or next week.

We wanted to show the exciting range of jobs in broadcast journalism, and reflect the enthusiasm of the people working in them. We are grateful to the organisations who let us behind closed doors. There were no 'no-go' areas and nothing we perceived as 'spin' – just busy people getting on with their work. The opinions expressed are not necessarily those of the organisations people work for, though every workplace has its own ethos and we found that successful newsrooms have a strong sense of team spirit. Almost without exception, none of the people we feature would be where they are without dedication and a love of the job.

Sky News

Sky News was the UK's first rolling 24-hour news channel. Part of Rupert Murdoch's News Corporation, it has regularly won awards as Britain's top rolling news channel. It is on satellite, cable and digital terrestrial TV. It has interactive and mobile phone services too.

In late 2005, Sky News moved to a purpose-built studio complex across the road from its original base on a trading estate in Osterley, West London. The move coincided with a redesign of the channel, and a switch to widescreen broadcasting. The programme schedule was refreshed, with dedicated shows aimed at different audience demands throughout the day.

The channel's unique selling point (USP) is that it is first for breaking news. Channel head Nick Pollard, who ran the operation for ten years, asserted: 'We can't afford to be on background or analysis when there's a breaking story.' So, each programme was constructed so it could be broken into at any time to deliver major news.

The programmes changed when John Ryley took over from Pollard in summer 2006, but the commitment remained to build on the reputation for breaking news with specialist correspondents delivering more original journalism.

When we visited Sky, ITV had announced the closure of its rolling news channel, leaving Sky News and BBC News 24 competing head-to-head. According to a senior Sky News manager, the two big players had their tanks parked on each other's lawns.

0600

Sunrise, Sky's breakfast programme, goes on air. It is co-presented by Eamonn Holmes, one of the UK's most popular broadcasters, famous as the host of GMTV's breakfast show and of the lottery, quizzes and factual light entertainment on the BBC. Lorna Dunkley co-hosts, with Jacquie Beltrao on sport.

The opening story is a Sky exclusive about the rescue of a Midlands woman from a forced marriage in Pakistan. The film, following a foreign office rescue team backed up by armed police, is the result of nine months' investigation, research and persuasion by reporter Eve Richings.

At the home news desk next to the studio, Senior Home News Editor Kirsty Thomson has just come on shift. She's been briefed about overnight developments on stories the channel is covering. She'll keep track of crews and reporters across the UK, and keep an eye on what the opposition is doing on a multi-screen display on her desktop. Nick Toksvig is on the foreign desk, co-ordinating input from correspondents around the world.

| **0700** | The first **newsroom meeting** of the day. Head of News Nick Pollard is briefed by Kirsty and Nick. Also at the informal gathering in a glass-fronted conference room are Head of Home News Phil Wardman, and the executive producers of the programme 'belts' which start at 0900 and 1200. They discuss the prospects. |

Kirsty reports that the top stories of the day will include Britain's first 'gay marriage' – the civil partnership of Grainne and Shannon in Northern Ireland, apparently to the strains of Dolly Parton's 'Touch Your Woman'. Sky will be live outside but not allowed into the ceremony. Nick Pollard asks when the 'royal wedding' takes place – Elton John and David Furnish will 'marry' when the law comes into force in England later in the week.

Another highlight should be the unveiling of Rolf Harris's portrait of the Queen.

In politics, Prime Minister Tony Blair will be talking in the Commons about the latest EU budget deal, and the Education Secretary Ruth Kelly will be defending government reforms in front of a Parliamentary select committee. Live feeds of both are available from Bowtie, the company that provides the Parliamentary service to broadcasters.

There's talk of doorstepping Deputy Prime Minister John Prescott, who's criticised the education reforms in the weekend papers.

In foreign news, George Bush is to make a speech from the Oval Office admitting mistakes over the Iraq war and the Israeli PM Ariel Sharon is due to leave hospital after a minor stroke.

| **0740** | Eamonn and Lorna are interviewing an art critic in the studio about the Rolf portrait. David Lee is predictably sniffy, describing Rolf as a 'talented amateur' and saying the portrait looks like something you might see on a tea towel. |

| **0812** | The 'breaking news' caption across the lower third of the screen reveals that 14 people have been arrested in Spain over links to Islamic terrorism. This is one of a number of 'breaking' stories that will not be followed up in great depth but which are seen as integral to the Sky service. Editorial Development Manager Rob Kirk explains: 'You heighten expectation. There's a psychological dimension. People watch Sky News because they don't want to miss anything. They feel that if it's going to happen, it'll be on Sky.' |

| **0824** | Another 'breaking news' strap: Al Qaeda have broadcast video of the execution of a US contractor in Iraq. Nick Pollard mentions at the next newsroom meeting that the word 'killing' should be used instead of 'execution' in this type of story. Sky News editorial guidelines state: 'An "execution" suggests the killing has some kind of legal sanction.' |

Nick Pollard

Kirsty is busy photocopying the day's prospects for the daily 0830 meeting. Nick has the foreign prospects prepared.

0832

Eve Richings

The main newsroom planning meeting, in the same conference room as the 0700 but with more production staff involved, gets under way. There's discussion about the weekend's political developments and their implications for today's stories. Is Blair going to get a 'big kicking' over Europe? Do Prescott's comments mark the return of 'real Labour'?

Nick Pollard enthuses about Eve Richings' forced marriage report: 'It's an excellent piece. Fantastic journalism and it shows. You can tell that we've spent months getting it. And it's infinitely variable in length.' A 3'56" version is running this morning. There's an extended version of over ten minutes for the 7 p.m. *Sky Report* (which will be followed by an interview with a victim of forced marriage who now campaigns to help other women), and a half-hour programme 'Finding Sadia' to be shown tomorrow.

And Rolf's portrait prompts a mini-debate on 'what is art?' – the very talking point they hope will engage the viewers.

0900

The *Sunrise* team come off air. In the studio, presenters Martin Stanford, Anna Botting and Anna Jones take over. In the gallery, Executive Producer of *Sunrise*, Neil Dunwoodie, hot-seats with his replacement Tim Cunningham, who takes over for the 0900-1200 'belt' *Sky News Today*.

0904

Martin Stanford

The *Sunrise* team hold a debrief. There's agreement that the show had excitement and energy, and the art critic was probably the highlight. Neil Dunwoodie says some of the headline writing did not match the pictures; there was a picture of actress Scarlett Johansson while the words referred to Woody Allen. Eamonn Holmes, in jovial mood throughout, notes: 'Nobody's interested in the director. She was the shot.'

Martin Stanford is on air introducing details of President Bush's latest speech from the Oval Office.

0925

The latest official portrait of the Queen has just been released. A live voice-over explains that it's been painted by Rolf Harris to celebrate the Queen's eightieth birthday, and that the public can see it from tomorrow.

0926

Kirsty Thompson

Kirsty is discussing crews and satellite links with Assignment Editor Mark Paterson, who sits opposite her. It's his job to assign London-based crews and the channel's Satellite News Gathering (SNG) vehicles. He can also call up the Skycopter. The Twin Squirrel helicopter – on annual charter – has a gyro-mounted external camera with a powerful zoom and the facility for a reporter/presenter to broadcast live. There's disappointment this week that flight restrictions round Heathrow Airport will prevent them using it on the 'royal wedding', Elton John's civil partnership ceremony in Windsor.

Mark Paterson

0945	Producer Jack MacDonald, from the *Lunchtime Live with Kay Burley* programme, is setting up a 'disco', a discussion, on 'gay marriages'. He asks Mark and Kirsty if a crew and SNG can get to Oxford for 12.30. He's told that would be pushing it, but 1.30 is possible.
1010	There's a problem covering the 'gay wedding'. The satellite truck is at the front of the register office in Belfast. The lesbian partners have gone in through the back door. There are moving pictures and an interview, but reporter Orla Chennaoui has been live on air and the crew hasn't had time to feed the shots. Kirsty sums up the dilemma: 'As we're live 24-hour news, we've got to stay on air, but we have to move the truck. We have to get the pictures and then move the truck round the back, but the couple could come out at any time, and we want to be live when they do.'
1012	Kirsty advises the Belfast team they should have fed the pictures before they went live. Pictures of the couple going into the ceremony have started to appear on other channels.
1014	The live output has switched to Parliamentary correspondent Glen Oglaza, who's talking about the controversy over education reforms. Mark tells Kirsty the arrival pictures from Belfast are coming in on Digi 9, one of the channels for taking in, or 'ingesting', video. Kirsty is thinking ahead: 'To salvage this we've got to get them coming out live.' As she speaks, shots of the arrival are showing on BBC News 24. *Ingest and output are controlled from a communications room a few yards from the newsroom. All incoming video is ingested on to a server-based system from Quantel, a company that made its name with digital TV graphics, but now offers full editing and play-out systems. Reporters and producers can view the material on any desktop. Producers cut headlines using a program called Qview, a simplified editing system. There's also Qedit, used by Sky's video library and for versioning material for the interactive services, and Qeditpro, the top-of-the-range software for cutting reporter packages.*
1020	Chris Birkett, the Executive Producer of *Lunchtime Live*, has decided to do the 'disco' at 1.30. He says he enjoys the flexibility of rolling news, adapting the running order to the availability of technical facilities and guests: 'If you can't do it one hour, you can do it the next. It means you don't often miss things.' He contrasts the experience at Sky News with the BBC, where he was a senior editor on Radio Five Live, News 24 and the *One O'Clock News*: 'When I was editing the One, I was often scrapping with the Six for resources. People here are all pulling in the same direction and it makes a real difference.' [Since Chris left the BBC, the corporation's executives have declared there should be no competition between programmes.]
1040	Grimsby MP Austin Mitchell is interviewed live from Parliament about fishing quotas. As a former TV presenter, he is a regular contributor to live TV debate on all channels. This time he's talking about something that directly affects his constituency.

1055	A live camera shows the rear exit of the register office in Belfast. The lower third caption reads: 'First civil partnership has taken place in Northern Ireland.'
1056	A crowd of guests emerges from the building, followed by the happy same-sex couple. There are no 'traditional' wedding photographs on the steps. Instead they head towards the assembled media, pausing briefly to raise their hands. Grainne says: 'We're going to show you our rings.' Asked how they're feeling, Shannon says: 'Delighted, and to many more.' And with that they turn and get into a cab, apparently followed by a documentary film crew.
1140	Another art critic is being interviewed live, this time down-the-line. Rachel Campbell Johnston says Rolf's portrait is 'safe' but 'appealing': 'It's the nation's most popular painter, painting the nation's favourite granny in the nation's most popular style, impressionism . . . There's a childlike simplicity about it and it becomes almost churlish to criticise him.'
1200	*Lunchtime Live with Kay Burley* comes on air. The 0900–1200 programme has featured very few packages but has a high demand for live pictures and rushes (uncut news footage). The lunchtime show is a round-up of the day's news so far. The best stories will be packaged, and there's a premium on human interest stories and interviews, anchored by one of Sky's most experienced presenters.
1202	A High Court judge has ruled that property tycoon Nicholas Van Hoogstraaten, who was cleared on appeal in a criminal trial, *was* behind the killing of a business rival. The victim's son Amjad Raja is speaking live outside the court. The family are making a civil claim for damages. Mr Van Hoogstraaten is apparently out of the country. Library pictures (also known as file tape) of him are run in a split-screen alongside the live shot of Mr Raja.
1209	A reporter package about the first 'gay marriage' is broadcast.
1211	A live interview follows from Belfast. The Reverend Ian Brown, a Free Presbyterian minister, argues that same-sex unions are against the will of God. He has been chosen from a crowd of protestors by reporter Orla Chennaoui. Planning News Editor Clive Kerfoot explains that, while the planning desk sets up as much as it can for location crews on diary stories, there comes a point when reporters take over and make the story their own: 'We can't see round corners. You can only control so much from this end. That's when reporters start using their talents.'

1228	The lower third strap announces that the hospital in Israel hopes to release Ariel Sharon on Tuesday.
1237	Kay Burley walks along the *newswall* trailing the main stories of the day against a backdrop of giant pictures. *The newswall is a giant video screen 13 metres long and three metres high, made up of more than 250 'tiles'. It is twice the length of the wall in Sky's old studio. The studio itself with a floor space of 7,500 square feet is twice the size of the old one. It features a rotating presentation desk at its heart, one of at least eight different presentation points around the studio.*
1238	Kay breaks off from the *newswall* for breaking news. Crime correspondent Martin Brunt is at the Old Bailey where verdicts have been returned in a high-profile case. Elliot White has been found not guilty of the attempted murder of Homeyra Monckton, the widow of financier John Monckton who was stabbed to death. But he's guilty of wounding with intent. The live two-way explains that sentencing will take place in a month's time after reports have been compiled for the court.
1241	Kay throws live to Glen Oglaza for the latest from Parliament on the education reform story.
1245	There's a headline sequence of three top stories: first same-sex weddings; tycoon responsible for killing; Rolf's portrait of the Queen; and a trail for Sky News Active. *Sky News Active was the UK's first interactive news service, offering a choice of eight channels at the touch of the red button on the TV remote. The active team also provide material for Sky's broadband services and mobile phones. Sky News is available live on mobiles with just a few seconds delay. The Sky News website is the second most popular news site in the UK, after the BBC.*
1246	Eve Richings' exclusive report on forced marriages airs again.
1304	The same-sex marriage package runs again. Sky News is running a text vote. In answer to the question: 'Do you support gay weddings?', 22 per cent of voters say Yes: 78 per cent say No.
1305	Martin Brunt is live again from the Old Bailey explaining the delays in the Monckton court case. The verdicts have come out in 'dribs and drabs' and it's taken three days to get to the end of the trial.

1335	The 'disco' takes place. Peter Tatchell, the gay rights campaigner, is live from the Westminster studios at Millbank. He's pitted against newspaper columnist Anne Atkins, live from her home in Oxford, courtesy of the SNG truck based in the West Midlands.
1358	In cricket, Pakistan beat England by 13 runs to win the one-day series.
1400	Mark Longhurst, Ginny Buckley and Steve Dixon present *Sky News Today*. The use of three presenters in the morning and afternoon 'belts' is a talking point. It breaks with UK convention, but allows lively use of the studio, including the newswall and the positions known as the pod, the pulpit and the mezzanine (a platform reached by a flight of stairs).
1406	Martin Brunt reports live from the court (again). Brunt is one of Sky's most accomplished live reporters. He has never been a glamorous on-screen presence, but he typifies Nick Pollard's commitment to 'accuracy, accuracy, accuracy'. Court reporting has, by law, to be fair and accurate. That is difficult enough to achieve in a scripted report, but in extended live two-ways the pitfalls are obvious. Brunt masters the key facts, and sticks to them.
1530	Live to the House of Commons for Tony Blair's defence of his deal on Britain's EU budget rebate.
1607	More Parliamentary coverage – Education Secretary Ruth Kelly in the select committee, answering questions about the government's proposed reforms.
1642	George Bush has delivered his speech about Iraq. Correspondent Andrew Wilson is live from Washington offering reaction and analysis.
1700 Jeremy Thompson	Jeremy Thompson takes over in the studio for *Live at Five*. The presenter is a veteran of 30 years on the road as a foreign correspondent for ITN and Sky. He brings that experience and an enthusiasm for live TV to the studio, and comes into his own whenever Sky News sends presenters to the scene of live stories like the Tsunami at the end of 2004.

1715	Head of Home News Phil Wardman is in an edit suite reviewing a report from Far East Correspondent Dominic Waghorn. It's due to air tomorrow. The story has elements in common with Eve Rushings' forced marriage report – investigation, secret filming and an insight into an under-reported Asian phenomenon. It is a hard-hitting exposé of China's fur trade. It includes shots of animal cruelty, including dogs and foxes being skinned alive and hung up to die. Wardman has to decide what can be shown, what must be cut and how to treat the rest. Some close-ups are cut. Much of the rest is pixilated to obscure the detail. Wardman says: 'We're not about sanitising the real world, but we don't have to be gratuitous. We're showing enough for the audience to know what's going on.' The next day's news prospects will carry instructions in bold type that the fur trade report should not be broadcast without a 'health warning' – an on-air announcement that some viewers might find the content of the report upsetting.
1732	Bristol reporter Andy Moore has reacted to a Press Association story that appeared earlier in the afternoon. A dying hospital patient had live maggots on her face. He has set up an interview with the woman's daughter. Nyree Ellison Anjee talks live from her home to Jeremy Thompson. Later, Moore will cut a package, including interview clips and a statement from the hospital.
1736	A Martin Brunt package on the Monckton case is aired. It includes interviews with the family's solicitor and a senior policeman.
1743	Andrew Wilson appears in another live two-way from Washington.
1803	The Sky Active vote has been running all day. Do you support gay marriage? 20 per cent say Yes: 80 per cent say No.
1820	Kirsty is about to end her shift, more than 12 hours after she started. She's talking on the phone to Professor Colin Pillinger, the space scientist behind the Beagle Two probe which crashed on Mars two years ago. He thinks a new photograph from the red planet shows wreckage which could be his missing craft. He agrees to come in for a live interview next morning, but, frustratingly for Kirsty, won't agree to a crew visiting him for a recorded interview tonight.
1830	Kirsty hands over to another Senior Home News Editor, Roger Protheroe. He's already aware of the evening's prospects. Kirsty passes on the result of her conversation with Professor Pillinger. There's Andy Moore's report from Bristol due in, and a crew is waiting for celebrity guests outside the venue of Elton John and David Furnish's stag night. The news rolls on.

BBC RADIO FIVE LIVE

BBC Five Live is BBC Radio's 24-hour news and sports channel. It is available on 909 and 693 medium wave, on digital radio and TV and online.

Most of the staff are based at Television Centre in West London. Their office space and studios are on the same floor as the rolling news television channel, BBC News 24, making it easy for London-based reporters and correspondents to appear on both channels in the same day. There are two main studios – each with a 'cubicle' or control room – which are used for alternate programmes.

The channel aims at a younger audience than BBC Radio Four News, and has a more relaxed style. Research shows, though, that the average listener is in their late forties. The audience is predominantly male, because of the emphasis on sport. The channel has commentary rights to Premiership, European and international football. It offers comprehensive coverage of Wimbledon, the Open golf and the Olympic Games. One question for audiences is whether Five Live is a rolling news channel, the radio equivalent of BBC News 24 or Sky News, or is it a news channel only when there is no sport?

The channel is complemented by Five Live Sports Extra where commentary on sports fixtures not on the main channel, including Test cricket, can be found.

0845

Shelagh Fogarty

Matt Morris

Nicky Campbell and Shelagh Fogarty are approaching the end of another three hours co-hosting the breakfast show. Nicky, an experienced host of live television shows like *Watchdog*, is a devotee of Scottish sport. He announces 'some sad news' – the death of the former Celtic and Scotland winger Jimmy Johnstone, 'known as Jinky, one of the Lisbon Lions, Jock Stein's great side'.

Matt Morris, Five Live's Head of News, has made his regular early-morning visit to the gym and is about to start the morning editorial meeting, looking at the prospects for the day with programme and planning editors.

0848

Robin Britten

Nicky links to one of the main stories of the morning. The cue begins: 'Britain's most senior police officer Sir Ian Blair is under more pressure after he admitted secretly taping a private phone conversation with the Attorney General, Lord Goldsmith.'
A recorded clip of Shami Chakrabarti, director of the civil rights group Liberty, follows. She says: 'It is bizarre. I'm speechless, which is not very helpful on the radio. It really does beggar belief.'

After the clip, Nicky interviews Richard Barnes, Tory leader on the Metropolitan Police Authority. Barnes says Sir Ian 'should certainly be considering his position'.

Sir Ian is the main talking point at the editorial meeting. Matt Morris asks if he can survive this latest controversy. Breakfast Editor Richard Jackson points out that what he has done is not illegal, but it is still surprising. Planning Editor Robin Britten says the BBC Home Affairs unit will have an 'obit' ready – a brief history of Sir Ian's career including 'gaffes'.

'Obit' is short for 'obituary', a report prepared prior to the death of a prominent person. In this case it will be ready if Sir Ian resigns. This type of backgrounder is trickier to compile than a true obituary, because there is a risk of defaming someone who is still alive.

It's a Monday morning, so there's discussion in the meeting of the weekend's coverage of big events. There's agreement the death of former Serbian leader Slobodan Milosevic was well covered, even though it happened during sports programming. But there's concern that the South Africa–Australia cricket international when the South Africans reached a record one-day target of over 400 should have led the sports bulletins.

0900

Victoria Derbyshire

The morning phone-in with Victoria Derbyshire is underway. Today's topic: 'Whose job is it to talk to children about sex?' It's a response to the Prime Minister's admission in an MTV interview that he was embarrassed teaching his children about sex. A clip of Tony Blair starts the debate.

In the meeting, there's a swift round-up of what today's programmes have planned. Comedian Johnny Vegas is coming in. Film critic Mark Kermode and the director Spike Lee will be on Simon Mayo's afternoon show. In news, funeral arrangements for Milosevic will become clearer; political correspondent Mike Sergeant is with the Education Secretary Ruth Kelly ahead of a vote on school reforms; two men have been shot in Salford; Dan Brown, author of *The Da Vinci Code*, is due in court accused of breaching the copyright of two other authors; there's an afternoon press conference about the causes of migraine, and a reporter will be trying to 'doorstep' Sir Ian Blair.

Also, it's the tenth anniversary of the shooting in Dunblane of 16 schoolchildren and their teacher. Matt Morris advises his editors: 'We are not going to Dunblane. Do what you like if you think it's appropriate but don't start hassling people in Dunblane.'

0912

Among Victoria's phone-in guests are a sex education teacher, a mother of three, and the editor of *Cosmogirl* magazine.

It is important the phone-in remains topical. The subject is pre-planned, but it's an early morning producer's job to completely revamp the agenda if a new talking point emerges from the overnight news.

0915

Matt Morris attends the BBC Radio News morning meeting. It is usually chaired by the Head of Radio News, and is attended by senior editors with contributions on a broadband video link from the BBC World Service at Bush House and Radio One's Newsbeat at Yalding House. Sir Ian Blair again prompts the longest discussion. It's a 'good yarn', 'a terrific story'. but what he has done is 'absolutely not illegal'.

0941	The Radio News meeting breaks up. After a brisk run through the day's news prospects, the editor of Radio Four's *The World Tonight* suggests that the story of the day is the death of Jimmy Johnstone.
1000	Victoria previews what's coming up before 12.00. 'Ten years after the Dunblane killings, we investigate whether schools are any safer.' There's a ten-second teaser clip, talking about knives, bayonets, machetes and handguns, followed by: 'How do you sue a suicide bomber?' There'll be an interview with a father fighting for compensation. And Victoria asks: 'Tell us what you think about Britain's top cop secretly recording phone conversations with a member of the government. Does it matter?'
1001	Andrew Fletcher reads the news. Sir Ian Blair leads. There's an appeal for calm in Iraq. Four men are being questioned in connection with the shooting in Greater Manchester: two men are dead and two injured. A British couple have been found dead in Crete, and schools minister Jacquie Smith comments on the Education Bill.
	Candles are to be lit in Dunblane in commemoration of the tragedy of ten years earlier. The Queen is in Australia ready for the opening of the Commonwealth Games.
1005	Rob Stewart reads the sports news. India have beaten England by nine wickets on the final day of the second test. Jimmy Johnstone's death is reported. Jose Mourinho, the Chelsea manager, wants to buy Germany's Michael Ballack. England rugby star Matt Dawson is commenting to Five Live on the performance of coach Andy Robinson. Golfer Luke Donald is in the world's top ten, and racing at Plumpton is off due to frost.
1007	Victoria links to an interview with Billy McNeil, Jinky Johnstone's captain when Celtic won the European Cup. Sports presenter Rob joins in.
	After linking to a clip of captain Andrew Flintoff, Victoria talks to cricket correspondent Jonathan Agnew in India.
1010	Victoria links to reporter Linda Kennedy in Glasgow, who has been investigating school safety. Her report includes a recorded insert of a visit to a school in Prestwich, demonstrating how it was possible to walk around the site for 30 minutes despite an eight-foot perimeter fence. The gate was unlocked.
1012	In the 'cubicle', the control room next to Victoria Derbyshire's studio, producer Simon Peeks is trying to find out when the Attorney General will make a statement about Sir Ian Blair. On the talkback unit he liaises with the newsroom. The programme editor tells him: 'We can't get an answer. We'll keep trying out here.'
1018	In the cubicle, they're trying to line up an interview with Simple Minds singer Jim Kerr, who recorded a charity single with Jimmy Johnstone for Motor Neurone Disease, the illness which killed Jimmy. Kerr is on his mobile phone. 'Are you free in ten to 15 minutes? Have you got a landline there?'

1020	Victoria is talking to a primary school governor about the problems of school security. Linda Kennedy reports that there is no pressure from the government to increase security, and it is not measured in league tables. The reporter links to recorded inserts from experts. Victoria talks to phone-callers on the issue.
1023	There's a landline available in Jim Kerr's hotel. They're trying to trace Home Affairs Correspondent Danny Shaw for the Sir Ian Blair story.
1030	Victoria links to Phillip Eden for the weather. It's cold for the time of year.
1031	Headlines with Andrew Fletcher. New stories include the body of Milosevic being released to his family, and the latest on the search for a rapist in Leamington Spa.
1033	Sport with Andrew Fletcher includes a report from Jonathan Agnew and a Flintoff clip. There's a report on Jimmy Johnstone and a clip of Billy McNeil from earlier in the programme. *The McNeil interview is on the BBC server available to all programmes.*
1037	More phone calls on school security.
1040	Victoria links to an archive clip of Jimmy Johnstone speaking on Five Live to Eamonn Holmes. The Jim Kerr interview follows. Kerr, a Celtic fan, speaks with passion about being part of a generation that grew up with Jimmy, and of his great talent as a footballer – and singer. He recalls the Celtic side 'ripping apart' the Manchester United team of the Sixties. An Aberdeen supporter calls in to praise Jinky.
1052	On talkback, the cubicle hears that the Attorney General has accepted an apology from Sir Ian Blair. 'This just in,' Victoria links to the news flash.
1053	Victoria interviews the parents of Luke Walmsley who was stabbed to death at school in Lincolnshire. Linda Kennedy contributes from Glasgow. Jayne Walmsley says her son died in front of CCTV cameras that weren't being watched. She and her husband Paul want airport-style scanners in schools. Victoria introduces John White, president of the National Union of Headteachers. During the interview she reads out e-mails from listeners.

1054	The team have fixed up an interview with the father of Jeremy Lakin, who was killed by a suicide bomber. They're reading the newspapers to get background information.
1100	News and sport. Victoria mentions the Blair apology, which is Andrew Fletcher's top story. The Attorney General Lord Goldsmith says the matter is closed. Danny Shaw reports. Also Thames Water is explaining why a hosepipe ban may be necessary. The employers' organisation, the CBI, is urging the Chancellor to cut taxes.
1104	A backlog of guests is building up. Two people have come in to talk about brain injury, the biggest cause of death and disability in young people. They're waiting in reception.
1105	Victoria reads out text messages on the Sir Ian Blair story, and then takes more calls on school security.
1108	Victoria talks to Danny Shaw, who says the Attorney General was disappointed and cross when he found out about the phone-tapping, but he has accepted the apology. The phone conversation had been about the use of wire-tap evidence in court. Shaw says the fact that Sir Ian apologised suggests he did something wrong.
1115	'Are we saving enough for the future? It seems some of us don't have ready cash to get our hands on.' Interviews with a young Londoner who says he doesn't earn enough to save and an adviser from a building society.
1123	Travel – preceded by a trail for Trevor Lakin, whose son was killed in the Sharm el Sheikh bombings.
1126	'How do you sue a suicide bomber?' Trevor Lakin talks of being 'abandoned, isolated and ignored' by the Foreign Office. When Victoria asks: 'You sound incredibly brave, but is that just because you're on the radio?' Mr Lakin confesses: 'I just feel like crying.'
1128	Sally Abrahams, Editor of the Midday show, discovers they have no time to pre-record an interview with the guests talking about brain damage. The Simon Mayo show can't take them either. Sally hands them back to Victoria's show.
1130	Weather from Phillip Eden, followed by news and sport.

1137	More on the Blair story, with phone contributions from former senior detective John Plimmer and John Falding, who lost his girlfriend in the July 7 bombings in London. Plimmer says he's disappointed, but not surprised. A text messager says: 'Perhaps Sir Ian was just recording his phone calls for training purposes.' John Falding says any more gaffes and Sir Ian will have to consider his position.
1149	The contributors from the charity Headway are introduced, to talk about brain injury. Chief Executive Miriam Lantsbury and assault victim Dean Harding are interviewed for more than five minutes and the charity has the opportunity to publicise its website.
1155	Another gear change, as Victoria reports that Downing Street has issued a statement saying the Prime Minister still has confidence in Sir Ian Blair, and the matter is regarded as closed.
1156	A light-hearted piece about the late arrival of spring closes the programme. Phillip Eden says it's a throwback to the weather we used to have. A dairy farmer from Shropshire says it's the latest spring he's known in 20 years. Might we have a longer summer? Victoria apologises for asking daft questions.
1159	Defence correspondent Paul Wood is advising BBC News outlets using the ENPS system that an announcement about reductions in the number of British troops in Iraq is due this afternoon.
1200	The midday news with Allan Robb. After the news and sport summary, the lead story is the Prime Minister's confidence in Sir Ian Blair. There's a two-way with Danny Shaw, live from Scotland Yard, and an interview with a former firearms officer, who says the story has the feel of a witch hunt.
1210	The Milosevic story is next with a two-way from Five Live Euro News' Paul Henley, including clips from a spokesperson in the Hague, where the former Serb leader died while on trial for war crimes, and a Serbian woman in Belgrade.
1214	The Thames Water hosepipe ban is covered with an expert from an independent water consultancy. Allan's first question: 'A lot of people will be saying for goodness' sake, it was raining at the weekend. Is this really necessary?'
1220	After travel and a trail for FA Cup replay coverage, Allan turns to cricket and a pre-recorded three minute as-live interview with Five Live summariser Geoff Boycott. Boycott says England could have batted better. When Allan says that's easier said than done, Boycott retorts with vintage self-confidence: 'Don't you analyse your performances in your job and try and improve each day or each week. I certainly did . . . I've got to make sure I don't do the same damn mistake [again]. That's what made me a very fine player.' The script for the item offers advice about 'potting', or cutting short, the last answer: *Please avoid unless desperate – the last answer is funny!*

1224	On the Dan Brown *Da Vinci Code* story, Andy Gallagher's two-way explains Dan Brown's courtroom account of his writing and research methods.
1225	PA, the Press Association, confirms on the wires what Paul Wood has told the BBC already – that an announcement on troop reductions is due this afternoon.
1226	There's a pre-recorded interview with a Leeds University professor, who's discovered boys want to learn how weapons work in science lessons, while girls want to study dreams.
1231	Simon Mayo joins Allan to trail his show. News and sport with Andrew Fletcher and Rob Stewart.
1237	Pre-recorded interview with Liberal Democrat MP Nick Clegg about Sir Ian Blair, who says there's a pattern of controversy in what he does and says.
1240	Allan back-refs Nick Clegg and links live to another pre-record – with a government minister on the abuse of the elderly in care homes. That's followed by a live interview via ISDN with a British Gas spokesperson about cuts in council tax for people who insulate their homes.
1247	The story of a British couple killed in Crete. Live two-way with reporter Richard Galpin in Athens.
1250	Andrew Fletcher reads the headlines followed by travel. Five Live Money – Pauline McCole reports on how shares in the London Stock Exchange are rising on reports of a takeover.
1253	A live two-way with reporter James Shaw at Celtic's Parkhead stadium. Shaw has vox-popped fans leaving tributes to Jimmy Johnstone. Scottish football correspondent Roddy Forsyth offers his assessment.
1257	Laura Trevelyan reports live from New York on the start of work on a memorial to the victims of September 11.

1300	Simon Mayo is on air trailing his star guests Spike Lee and Johnny Vegas. Lee's appearance is a coup for broadcast journalist David Braithwaite, who arranges interviews with whatever stars come to town. Usually they are recorded in a hotel room or live via an ISDN line for a few minutes – the time strictly limited by press agents. But Lee is coming into the studio, his first interview after arriving from the US that morning, and is scheduled to stay for half an hour.
1305	Simon asks sports presenter Vassos Alexander to see if he can find a story about the New York Nicks basketball team for Spike Lee. Political correspondent Gary O'Donoghue is two-wayed from Millbank, the Parliamentary Unit, about a row over cash-for-peerages, which will be the main talking-point this hour.
1312	Sir Ian Blair has issued a statement. Danny Shaw is on the line saying Sir Ian recorded the phone call with the Attorney General because he thought they would be discussing a complicated issue and he had no note-taker available. Simon asks Gary O'Donoghue for a comment on Sir Ian Blair, before linking to the travel.
1317	'Now let's look at the funding of political parties . . .' Contributors to the discussion include a politics lecturer Dr Justin Fisher, political commentator Anthony Howard, a Labour peer Lord Berkley, and the Liberal Democrat constitutional affairs spokesman Simon Hughes. Simon Mayo links to a clip from a previous interview on the programme with Stuart Wheeler, the largest donor to the Conservative Party, but it doesn't play. Simon laughs off the mistake: 'Let's turn to Anthony Howard in a moment of desperation.'
1331	Before the news, Simon thanks his guests and announces that the Foreign Secretary is due to make an announcement on Iran's nuclear programme in a few moments' time. The news leads on another expected government announcement – about the withdrawal of British troops from Iraq.
1336	Simon links to the live feed of Jack Straw at the International Institute for Strategic Studies in London.
1338	The 24-hour TV news channels viewable in the cubicle and the studio are still running Jack Straw, but Mayo's editor decides to cut to a two-way with correspondent Gordon Corera.
1341	'We'll stay listening to what the Foreign Secretary has to say and we'll report back later.' Simon trails a pre-recorded interview with British swimming coach Bill Sweetenham, who's in Australia for the Commonwealth Games.

1343	The 16-minute Sweetenham interview is 'self-contained' on the VCS playout system. Self-contained means it includes Simon's cue, so it has to be played off the back of a trail for Five Live Sports Extra.
1359	Simon 'back-annos' Sweetenham and trails Johnny Vegas. He also promotes the podcast of the programme – the Daily Mayo. The new lead on the news is a report from defence correspondent Paul Wood on the troop reductions in Iraq – perhaps as many as 800. The presenters of *Drive*, Peter Allen and Rachel Burden have arrived in the newsroom. *Drive's presenters turn up for work at about 2 p.m., giving them a couple of hours to record any interview inserts. They will have made sure they are well briefed on the day's news agenda before they leave home, and may have been in contact with the editor by e-mail or on the phone. The production team has been working since early morning setting up interviews and programme items.*
1404	Simon thanks Vassos for the sport and tells listeners Johnny Vegas isn't here yet, 'so this could be an extremely long money news or an extremely brief one'. He links to a live Pauline McCole report about Thames Water's hosepipe ban, which includes live interviews with the chief executive of the Consumer Council for Water and the director of Water Wise, an organisation dedicated to reducing water waste.
1409	Johnny Vegas is live with Simon, apologising for being late. He'd been 'getting my hair cut at Blue Peter . . . I went over to the make-up department. I was a bit cheeky.' The interview is wide-ranging: the critical panning of his film *Sex Lives of the Potato Men* (described by Five Live critic Mark Kermode as 'vile, misogynistic, infantile – not in a good way, depressing, unfunny and should not have been funded from the Lottery'); his new BBC3 TV series *Ideal*; and his stand-up routine (he says his recent efforts were 'dire'). Vaughan, a text messager, says Johnny could read from the *Financial Times* and be funny. Simon says the interview is over-running, 'but we have 30 seconds to test that out'. Vassos in the cubicle dashes to the hospitality area, grabs the *FT* and rushes it into the studio. It's taken 15 seconds to find a copy of the paper and ask the comedian to test the theory.
1435	News with Andrew Fletcher, previewing the Defence Secretary's announcement on Iraq troops in about an hour's time.
1437	Sport with Vassos Alexander includes Celtic boss Gordon Strachan on Jimmy Johnstone: 'He lived life to the full, on and off the pitch. I lived life to the full with him one day in Dundee, and my liver's still recovering now.' There's also a clip from Simon's Bill Sweetenham interview with the swimming coach admitting he considered resigning over allegations he was a bully.
1440	Simon trails Spike Lee, and talks to Dave Barry and Ridley Pearson, the authors of *Peter and the Starcatchers*, a new prequel to *Peter Pan*.

1450	Spike Lee has arrived. During a trail, Simon is told this by the cubicle, who also mention the film director is wearing an Arsenal shirt. Simon, a Spurs supporter, is caught on air, saying: 'You're kidding me. That's terrible news.' He instantly shares the joke with the audience and his guests: 'It's ten to three, I've just been told some terrible news. Spike Lee's here, and he's wearing an Arsenal shirt!'

Broadcast journalist
David Braithwaite with
film director Spike Lee

1500	'After the news, Spike Lee in an Arsenal shirt.' During the sport, Vassos stumbles. He's written the name Graeme Souness instead of Gordon Strachan, and laughs about it on air.
1504	Simon introduces Spike Lee and film reviewer Mark Kermode. Vassos talks about the New York Nicks. Lee admits they have the worst record and the highest payroll in the NBA, and the season has been a 'disaster, a debacle, a fiasco and a travesty'. And the Arsenal shirt? 'Thierry Henry is my man and the Gunners are my team.' They move on to talk about Lee's new movie *Inside Man*, and a documentary series he's making about Hurricane Katrina, which will attack the US government for its handling of the crisis in New Orleans the previous summer. Lee says the administration's attitude was malicious, and his film will include allegations that the city's levees were blown up by the government to save some areas at the expense of others. He also says US troops should be brought home from Iraq.
1529	Defence correspondent Paul Wood is in the studio. He has just finished a sandwich outside, between live two-ways on News 24 and Five Live. He previews the Defence Secretary's statement.

Paul Wood

1530	Simon asks Spike Lee if he wants to stay a further ten minutes. 'Can you stay? What are you looking for?' Lee doesn't have his schedule. Simon thanks him and links live to the Commons where 'the Defence Secretary is on his feet. Here's John Reid.'

1532	Spike Lee leaves the studio with David Braithwaite, who thanks him for coming in.
1535	As John Reid's statement continues, the team in the cubicle are discussing what will be put on the podcast of Spike Lee, and if his comments on the US government's role in the Katrina relief effort should be publicised through the BBC press office.
1536	Dr Reid announces a reduction of 800 British troops in Iraq – the figure predicted by Paul Wood.
1538	The editor decides to cut out of the John Reid statement. Asked by Simon to comment, Paul Wood says: 'It's always nice when you go out on a limb and you don't fall off it. The Defence Secretary was kind enough to confirm what the BBC's been reporting exclusively.' News and sport.
1548	'Still, I think recovering from Spike Lee and his story about the levees in the Katrina story, so that documentary series, four hours of it for HBO, is going to be making a few headlines, one imagines.' Simon links to Mark Kermode's movie reviews.
1559	Simon signs off, announcing that for the rest of the week his show is being replaced by coverage of the Cheltenham Festival: 'pounding hooves, sweaty fetlocks, and that's just John Inverdale'.
1600	Drive with Peter Allen and Rachel Burden. Rachel's presenting work includes breakfasts at weekends. Peter Allen is the veteran on the Five Live team. He's a journalistic heavyweight – a former newspaper man and ITN Foreign Correspondent – and teams up with regular co-presenter Jane Garvey who now works a three-day week since becoming a mother.
1605	After the news and sport, Peter links to the opening item about the defence cuts and introduces a clip of John Reid, but the clip played is Trevor Lakin from the morning phone-in show talking about the loss of his son. 'I'm sorry about that. Not quite sure what it was, but it certainly wasn't John Reid . . . Let's talk while we wait to sort that out to Amyas Godfrey, former captain who completed two tours of Iraq . . .' The seamless link has been aided by the script on the screen in front of him where the guest's unusual name is in capitals with the pronunciation explained AMYAS (pron a-MEE-us) GODFREY.

1610 Peter Allen	'Thank you. Interesting stuff. A little earlier, I tried to play you the thoughts of John Reid, the Defence Secretary. I think we can now hear what he had to say in the Commons.' This time the clip plays. Off the back of it, Peter reads a text, pointing out that at this rate the troops will be in Iraq until 2014, and then has fun with the latest army recruiting drive. 92 years after the British Army produced the most famous recruiting poster ever – Lord Kitchener pointing, with the slogan 'Your Country Needs You' – there's an advert for a £50,000 a year marketing manager to 'act as the key interface between the central network and the regional delivery structure' in 'one of the most advanced holistic marketing networks in the UK today'. 'I wonder what Kitchener would have made of that?' The advert warns that the post is 'not for the faint-hearted – and it's spelt F-E-I-N-T – perfect!'
1611 Rachel Burden	Rachel's first interview of the programme is a two-way with Danny Shaw. Paul Stephenson, the Deputy Commissioner of the Metropolitan Police, is supporting Sir Ian Blair. The two-way includes a clip of Stephenson expressing his confidence in Sir Ian, but ducking the question about why phone calls were recorded – 'that's for Sir Ian to explain' – and saying it is not inevitable Sir Ian will have to resign. Peter picks up off the back of Rachel's interview to ask Danny about police recruitment in response to a text from a serving officer.
1618	Rachel reads the headlines. 'Well, the bubble burst . . .' Peter talks English cricket with a clip from coach Duncan Fletcher, followed by a live interview via ISDN with former captain Alec Stewart.
1623	Peter reads a story from PA about a survey of Premiership footballers' cars. Rachel observes that most of their choices are 'naff' and 'tacky': 'I'm quite happy with my Ford Escort.' She links to a pre-recorded interview with a cardiologist about the link between migraines and holes in the heart.
1628	Peter and Rachel introduce the Trevor Lakin clip, some of which had accidentally been played at the top of the programme. It's written as a split link, PRES1 followed by PRES2. Peter then interviews the Lakins' MP Quentin Davies live from Millbank.
1634	Another listener's joke via text: 'I'm not surprised, Peter, that Chelsea players have 4x4s. Have you seen the state of their pitch?' A second text complains that Five Live hasn't mentioned the South Africa v. Australia cricket – 'the greatest game of all time'. Vassos and Peter discuss the game and agree it was extraordinary – with one ball and one wicket left South Africa hit a four to win, finishing on 438.

1636	Traffic news; Rachel reads the headlines; then Vassos reads the sport, which includes the 'what made me a very fine player' clip from Geoff Boycott.
1640	Rachel reads a listener's e-mail about Iraq, and then links to an item about the Thames Water hosepipe ban. Her interviewee is a man who works in water conservation in Asia, but now finds himself affected by the ban at home in Gloucestershire. *Text messages and e-mails arriving at Five Live are sifted by the programme editor. Presenters can see texts in front of them on screen but rarely have time to access e-mails. Drive's editor Jon Zilkha, in the newsroom, reads incoming texts, and filters them for legal problems and content. He can tick a box alongside the message to 'green-light' it for transmission.*
1643	Peter links to the Milosevic story and his lawyer's appeal for the funeral to be held in Belgrade. Correspondent Matt Prodger is on the line from Belgrade.
1646	Headlines and travel news, a trail, then more on Sir Ian Blair. The chairman of the Metropolitan Police authority has said it was 'wholly unacceptable' for Sir Ian to have recorded phone calls. Pete reads out the chairman's statement. Rachel links to the Shadow Home Secretary David Davis at Millbank.
1653	Peter issues a warning: 'If you're listening with small children, or you're offended by bad language, you might not want to listen to the next item after the money news.' The warning was marked MUST READ on the running order. Peter adds: 'You may, however, be one of those people who are desperate to hear what it is.' Peter reads the money news and links to Philippa Busby from Five Live Money.
1656	Rachel repeats the bad language warning and introduces an item about a TV advert for Australian tourism, which closes with the line: 'Where the bloody hell are you?' Peter links to a pre-recorded interview with Paul Denham of the Broadcast Advertising Clearance Centre, who've banned the ad. Fran Bailey, the Australian Tourism Minister, is in the Millbank studio. Peter asks her: 'What are you up to bringing us all this bad language? We are an easily upset bunch.' She replies that the ad is 'cheeky, warm and friendly'. Peter asks: 'This is not another Australian complaining about umpiring decisions, is it?'
1700	Headlines read by Rachel: the troop withdrawals; Sir Ian Blair; and the son of a British couple found dead in Crete has been charged with their murder.
1704	Vassos has the sport.
1706	Peter interviews the former army commander Colonel Tim Collins about the troop withdrawals.

1711	Peter interviews the Defence Secretary, live from Millbank, and asks whether troops withdrawn from Iraq will be going to Afghanistan. Dr Reid admits that's a possibility. The cue for the John Reid item has a note that 'he is doing N24 and will be off air by 7 mins past'.
1717	Rachel two-ways Andy Gallacher, the reporter at the High Court on the *Da Vinci Code* hearing.
1721	There've been 'loads of texts' on the Australian 'bad language'. Rachel says it's hard to read them "cos I'm not supposed to repeat the phrase'. She continues, without repeating the phrase: the phrase is in the Harry Potter movies; the advertising standards people are being prudish; but someone asks if Peter has children, and says he shouldn't assume everyone has standards as low as his. He responds: 'If my children confined themselves to swearwords like that, then I would be relatively grateful. But, unfortunately, they don't.' *Five Live encourages this banter. Head of News Matt Morris says they have a friendly relationship with their audience.* Drive *editor Jon Zilkha says: 'If our core proposition was just to tell people three hours of all the main news stories of the day, people would soon switch off. It's not just about a diet of headlines. We try to offer analysis, entertainment and stimulation.'*
1724	The presenters discuss England's poor rugby performance against France in a defeat at the weekend. Peter interviews former French captain Phillipe St Andre.
1726	The Mayoress of Keighley has been sacked from her apolitical role for joining the British National Party. There's a clip of Rose Thompson, saying she won't stand down as a councillor, a vox-pop from Keighley, and then Rachel interviews the mayor who sacked her, Tony Wright. *The* Drive *team had decided not to interview the sacked mayoress, because her performance at her press conference that morning suggested she wouldn't be a fluent live interviewee.*
1730	There's confusion about where Slobodan Milosevic will be buried. Peter interviews Mirko Klarin, who's covered events at the Hague. He says being buried in Belgrade would be Milosevic's 'final revenge'.
1733	Rachel reads the headlines.
1735	Vassos' sports bulletin includes Jonathan Agnew's report of England's cricket defeat, and a clip of Billy McNeil talking about Jimmy Johnstone from the interview earlier in the day. It has been re-edited to include a clip of commentary of Johnstone in action.

1737	The team discuss their sporting allegiance. Rachel has an Irish passport so supports Ireland in the rugby, but would celebrate if England won football's World Cup. Vassos supported Greece when they won Euro 2004. Peter wonders if you can support two football clubs because Tottenham never win anything.
1738	Peter interviews Professor Mansour Farhang, a former Iranian ambassador to the United Nations, about Iran's controversial nuclear programme. He's live by phone from the US.
1743	Rachel interviews Minnie Crutwell, a nine-year-old footballer who was told she couldn't play in a boy's team when she reaches the age of 11. She's been to meet the Chief Executive of the FA, Brian Barwick, who told her the rule is based on physical ability. Minnie says her brother plays with boys twice his size but never gets hurt. Peter says he doesn't know how good she is at football, but she put her case very well. *Minnie's father Greg was standing by to contribute.*
1747	'Here we are talking rubbish again on Five Live . . .' Peter and Rachel link to an item about waste disposal and recycling.
1750	Five Live Money with 'our old mate Micky Clarke of the London Evening Standard'. Takeover bids for the pub chain Mitchells and Butlers and the London Stock Exchange are the main talking points. The Footsie finished at a five-year high.
1756	Rachel reports that there are now 144,000 mini motorbikes in the UK but the Local Government Association says they should be seized and crushed if they're driven illegally. They're not licensed for roads, but can reach 40 mph and four people have been killed riding them. Trish O'Flynn from the LGA is live by ISDN.
1759	A text says some mysterious force stops you changing football teams, and challenges Peter to try it. 'I support . . . aha, can't be done.'
1800	Peter stumbles over the first headline. 'I apologise for that awful beginning but my computer suddenly stopped.' At the end of the headline sequence, he says: 'Computer now working properly, so here we go.'
1801	The final hour of the programme starts with extended coverage of the big story of the day. Today it's the Iraq troop withdrawal. There are clips of John Reid in the Commons, Shadow Defence Minister Gerald Howarth, John Reid on *Drive*, Colonel Tim Collins and Dr Haider al-Ebadi, an adviser to the Iraqi Prime Minister. The BBC's Security Correspondent Frank Gardner is in the studio to be interviewed by Peter. He gives the bigger picture, including the fact there are 40 kidnaps a day in Iraq but we never hear about it. Britain is seen as being a neo-colonialist power, and is part of the problem.

1808	Rachel picks up with the latest on Sir Ian Blair, including a clip of David Davis from earlier in the programme, and the rest of the day's news. The final item is about the protection of habitats for rare species – including the natterjack toad. Rachel asks: 'What does a natterjack toad look like, I wonder?' Peter says: 'You'll get a text telling you.'
1811	Vassos' sports headlines.
1813	'Councils have become so obsessed about safety that they're designing boring playgrounds that put children off using them.' Professor Lamine Mahdjoubi of the University of the West of England is on the phone and tells Peter children are ignoring playgrounds and playing in more dangerous places instead, and parents are becoming paranoid about children playing outdoors.
1816	Peter reads a text: 'Frank Gardner's great. The only man who can put Iraq in plain English.' Rachel has been given a description of the natterjack toad and reads it out: 'Fairly flattened bodies, apparently.' Peter: 'Sounds like they've already tried to cross the road.' When Rachel says their mating call makes them Europe's noisiest amphibian, Peter says we need to hear one: 'In the good old days the BBC library would have immediately produced the sound. These days I suspect you have to find the charge code before you can get hold of it.' In the newsroom, the team accept the challenge.
1818	Mark Saggers is in the studio to preview *Sport on Five* at 7 o'clock. He refers back to the chat about footballers' cars and reveals that the interior of Claude Makelele's car is Louis Vuitton. They introduce golf expert Jay Townsend to talk about England's Luke Donald entering the world's top ten. It's a three-way chat – Peter, Mark and Jay. Mark says they're trying to get hold of Luke Donald for an interview.
1822	Peter tries a natterjack toad impression. Rachel offers the opinion it's not rasping enough: 'I could teach you how to rasp.' Rachel links to the German author of *The Teacher Hater Book* which has upset the teaching profession. Gerlinde Unverzagt accuses German teachers of failing to teach basic literacy and numeracy. Peter chips in to ask if that's because they can't be sacked. Yes, she says, and she also accuses teachers of dressing sloppily, wearing open-toed sandals, with yellowing in-growing toenails. Peter defends his own friends who are teachers, and says he's sure they don't have in-growing toenails.

1825	Peter introduces Rob the Rubbish, who clears litter from Snowdonia and Ben Nevis and has offered to tidy up Everest. Robin Kevan says it's pretty bad around the base camp, though 'nothing as bad as yellowing, in-growing toenails'. *Every interview in the programme will have been researched, and the presenter will be provided with briefing notes and suggested questions. Often, as with Rob the Rubbish, the notes and questions are barely needed.*
1829	Peter tells a listener's natterjack joke. 'How deep is the water, little froggy? Knee-deep, knee-deep.' After the travel, Rachel reads out a text from a driver who says his progress has been impeded by female natterjacks looking for a mate.
1830	News and sport. Vassos has a clip of the India cricket coach Greg Chappell talking about England's performance, and a Gordon Strachan story about Jimmy Johnstone. On international duty, Jinky had to be rescued by the coastguard. He went for a drink, ended up in a rowing boat without oars going out to sea, singing heartily. There's an as-live chat with racing correspondent Cornelius Lysaght previewing the Cheltenham Festival.
1836	Peter trails Ben Fenton of the *Daily Telegraph* who's due to talk about what's in tomorrow's papers. But first there's a clip of George Bush, who's been talking in the last few minutes about Iraq, admitting the situation is tense. Peter two-ways correspondent Justin Webb in Washington.
1838	Ben Fenton is on the line and offers his opinion on Iraq, Sir Ian Blair – who 'maybe has got another chance' – and the rage in China for nude wedding photos – just brides not couples: 'I've only seen pictures of nude Chinese ladies.' Peter responds: 'This is the BBC. If you want to admit to looking at nude Chinese men, that's fine.'
1844	There's been a text about the German teacher book. The ugliness of people's feet provides an offbeat link to late-night presenter Anita Anand, who says she has a deep psychological issue about them. Her brother has 'extraterrestrial feet – they are too long, too thin and too bony. I can't bear it.' She trails the content of her show which starts at 10 p.m.
1848	Rachel reads the headlines. Peter adds that George Bush has just said in his speech that components from Iran increasingly make up the bombs for Iraqi insurgents.
1850	Peter reads out a text: 'Can you tell Sean Gatting that his wife has just gone into labour. If it wasn't a joke, it's probably a public service we should perform.'
1852	Rachel interviews Philippa Busby about the impact of healthier eating on food producer Northern Foods. Her report includes a live telephone interview with Jon Sopher, 'a company doctor', about their disappointing sales of pizzas, biscuits and ready meals.

1855	Peter and Rachel introduce an item about natterjack toads. Adrian Hughes in the newsroom has found the sound of the toad on a website, and tracked down a licensed handler, who's on the phone from Cumbria. Helen Annan says they're Britain's rarest amphibian and quite attractive with a yellow stripe down their back.
1857	Peter links to entertainment reporter Colin Paterson who's live via radio car outside the Empire film awards. He introduces a clip of Roger Moore talking about the new James Bond, Daniel Craig (Moore says he looks very good). Colin then interviews *King Kong* actor Andy Zerkhis live about the event.
1859	Rachel explains that Andy Zerkhis played both King Kong and Gollum in the *Lord of the Rings*. Peter decides to end on 'a really, silly joke: what do you call a French man in beach footwear? Phillipe Phillope.' Rachel: 'Hurray. A good end to a really serious news programme.'
1900	Mark Saggers introduces Sport on Five. The programme will include a live interview with Luke Donald in the first half hour. Head of News Matt Morris is preparing to go home.

INDEPENDENT TELEVISION NEWS

Independent Television News (ITN) is the main supplier of news broadcasts to two British television channels: ITV and Channel 4. It also provides content for radio bulletins to many UK commercial radio stations through IRN (Independent Radio News). Its flagship television news programme is the ITV News evening bulletin at 18.30. The programme team for the bulletin works closely with the lunchtime and 10.30 teams at their headquarters in central London. They share stories and reports. Their state-of-the-art studio has been called a 'theatre of news'. Deborah Turness, the Editor of ITV News, has been with the organisation 16 years, which has included spells abroad. She says: 'It's a real kind of family. It's a big enough place to do very different things and get lots of different experience.'

0530  Arti Lukha	Arti Lukha, the foreign news editor at ITN for today, arrives at ITN's newsroom in Gray's Inn Road, Central London, to start her shift. The newsroom is located on the ground floor of the modern building. She uses her pass to open the newsroom door. The large open-plan newsroom is relatively quiet with the skeleton nightshift going about their work. Down the left-hand side there are small offices for senior editorial staff, and a small meeting room. On the opposite side of the newsroom is the gallery and studio for the localLondon ITV regional news programme. The newsdesk for the London programme is on the other side of the newsroom. Arti walks up to her 'hot seat' for the day and sits down. She always watches ITN's 10.30 p.m. programme before she goes to bed, so that she is aware of any stories that may have broken late in the evening. Her first task of the day is to check with the overnight team manning the Foreign Newsdesk. She then checks the agency wires to see what the new top lines are. She checks what American stories have happened during their evening while she has been asleep. Arti then liaises with Reuters and AP to find out where the safest places are to film at the moment around the border of Israel and Lebanon.
0630	Arti starts to check in with the crews working in the Middle East. They are two hours ahead of London. They should have finished breakfast by now and be about to leave their hotels. There are three foreign correspondents today in the Middle East: James Mates is in Beirut with a Senior News Editor, Geoff Hill, working as his producer; Martin Geissler is on his own in Northern Israel; and Julian Manyon is in Tyre in Lebanon with ITN's Westminster News Editor, Toby Castle.

0730	Deborah Turness, Editor, ITV News, arrives in the newsroom. She's been keeping up-to-date by flicking between Radios Four and Five Live while driving in. Her office, one of the small ones off the newsroom, is dominated by a large chintz sofa. In May 2004 she became the first female editor of a major TV news network in the UK. She has worked as a journalist for ITN since she graduated: she was part of the launch team for Five News, where she famously introduced 'perching presenters'.
0735	Head of Foreign News, Tim Singleton, rings in from home to talk to Arti. She briefs him on what the correspondents are planning. Julian Manyon is doing a piece about a curfew on the use of vehicles in Tyre. He'll report on how locals are managing to carry on with their lives.
0800	Arti attends the first editorial meeting of the day with the lunchtime programme editor, Channel 4 News, IRN and Multimedia. This is a prospects meeting where the stories for the day are being discussed.
0830	Arti returns to the Foreign Newsdesk, and checks in with the correspondents on their mobiles. The newsroom is still quiet – there are only about 30 staff in the large open-plan office.
0900	The newsroom begins to fill with journalists and production staff drifting in to start their shifts.
0915	Editorial staff squeeze into Deborah's office for the 9.15 meeting. This is usually the main editorial meeting of the day. Deborah likes to be able to discuss each of the stories in detail. There are ten editorial staff at the meeting, sitting on the sofa and perched on chairs around the room. They include three programme editors (the lunchtime editor, the evening news editor, Faye Nicholds, the 10.30 editor), the Home News Editor, Tim Singleton, the Head of Foreign News, and Arti the Foreign News Editor for today. They're chatting about the curfew and the fact that the Israelis have said nobody can drive around. Deborah starts by discussing the previous night's 10.30 programme. 'Angus did an excellent job . . . great to get the PTC where he did . . . How did he manage it? Well, he'd been waiting ages and tried one of the doors into the room, but it was locked. One of the policemen said: "Oh, that door's always locked." He then asked: "Well, which is the door that isn't always locked?" and the guy showed him and they snuck in and did a quick piece-to-camera and got out again! Terrific stuff. Anyway, that is yesterday's news – on for today . . . There's loads of stuff around but it has all gone a bit pear shaped.' Deborah explains a 'slight staffing crisis' – due to holidays and sickness, including one senior programme editor who broke a foot over the weekend, they are short of senior programme editors. Deborah says she'll have to be much more hands-on than usual. She normally gets involved in programme planning and often helps with fine-tuning scripts, but today she'll need to do even more.

Beirut is top of the list – 'the pictures were amazing last night – the attack happened just as we went on air, people digging with their bare hands – 18 dead so far'.

'Mates is just doing the evening news today; he had editing problems yesterday working on Avid, transferring it to tape, plus the computer program on the Avid computer was malfunctioning.'

Deborah warns: 'It is the only kit they have out there, so we mustn't have late direction or late changes.'

She then asks: 'Did we get any pics of the explosion?'

'No it was dark.'

'What about a fireball?'

'No.'

'He's pulling out tomorrow.' (Correspondent James Mates and producer Geoff Hill are leaving Beirut to return home.) Deborah says she wants the story for the flagship evening news programme, and there is an 'explainer' to be done.

Deborah gives a run-down of the situation in Beirut, and asks if they should have a big 3-D experience from Graphics. She asks the Head of Foreign News, Tim Singleton, how he thinks the Beirut story should be developed. He says: 'You've got to wait and see what the Arabs have to say. We may not know by the evening news.' Hezbollah are meant to have only fired 20 per cent of their rockets.'

Deborah asks: 'How do you know that? Where has that come from?'

It is not a rushed meeting. Deborah likes to go into detail on the stories. Members of the team come and go depending on deadlines.

The discussion about the Middle East continues . . . and a discussion over staffing. 'Alastair [Stewart] is not available, he's doing London.' (*London Tonight* is the regional opt-out) . . . 'We could record him maybe?'

Deborah Turness

Arti explains to the meeting: 'Manyon is in Tyre. He's doing a piece now. He's filming now on the curfew in Tyre.'

Deborah is concerned that the piece sounds a bit samey. There is a suggestion they could do a comparison piece with somewhere else in the region.

Tim says: 'I spoke with Toby (Toby is the producer with correspondent Julian Manyon in Tyre) late last night, about 1.30, and he was aiming to do a piece with multiple PTCs. He was furious about the situation there last night.'

Someone says: 'He was only furious because of the curfew; he couldn't get to his restaurant!'

Deborah waits for the laughter to subside: 'A mirror image – both sides of the border – I like that. Keep them both quite tight. We're not going to do 2.30 on them both. We'll need some wipe or other to highlight the symmetry between the two places. We'll ask Martin [Geissler in Northern Israel] to replicate the two towns.'

0940

The discussion moves to an oil slick in the Mediterranean. Deborah says: 'There are some good stills in the papers. This is the biggest environmental disaster to hit the Med.'

The meeting says it's very much a picture-led story, and that aerial shots of the slick are needed, but with the problems in that part of the world they wouldn't be able to get any. Deborah suggests satellite pictures: 'What can be seen from space? Can we see if we can get some satellite images today?'

Deborah then moves the meeting on to discuss a story about a former landscape gardener serving a sentence for paedophilia. The police are planning to dig up a garden in Croydon looking for the remains of children's bodies from 35 years ago. Deborah asks: 'Can we get a chopper up? It's not a Fred West yet, but could we talk to the policeman from the Fred West trial maybe? Can we get a copy of the original newspaper? Who was the reporter on the original case? There's lots of ideas to go on there – some logistics to sort out – this could be the lead.'

A discussion develops over which reporter should be assigned to the 'paedo' story. Deborah says: 'This is just the sort of story Paul Davies would do really well. Paul is the best.' He has been following the Damilola Taylor trial, but it's thought the jury will not return a verdict today. They risk sending Davies to Croydon with a crew to film the police digging up the garden.

0950

Correspondent John Ray pops his heads round the door to join the meeting. Deborah asks: 'John, what have you got?'

He replies: 'I have a double source story about MI5.'

'Is that two different people giving the same story?'

'Two people have been given the same information from the one source – but it is from the horse's mouth.'

'OK. What's the story?'

Still standing in the doorway, he explains: 'MI5 do not have enough people to monitor the terrorist suspects in this country. These are people who are . . . what can I say? They're more than Internet surfers; they are one step away from terrorism. There are over 1,200 bad guys, and MI5 can't monitor them all.'

Deborah says: 'I don't want to do the security service's propaganda for them. Whose fault is it? How do they liaise with Special Branch?' John replies: 'It's a good line. Not maybe the top story, but if I told someone in the pub that, they'd say "F***ing Hell!"'

The meeting discusses other stories. An eight-year-old boy has been held down by some teenagers and stabbed with a needle. Someone suggests that's a good summer holiday story. Deborah says: 'There's a whole swathe of good stories.'

One of the team then mentions the Princess Beatrice story. She is 18 today. 'Have you seen the footage?'

'It's vomit making.'

Deborah says: 'We're not the Royal Information Service. She's page seven of the tabloids – a minor royal princess.'

Then they discuss a story that is a 'must do'. Charles Allen, the Chief Executive of ITV, resigned yesterday, and Alastair Stewart is booked to do a sit-down interview with him upstairs in his office mid-morning. Deborah explains to the meeting: 'For the evening, we'll do an in-house, colourful, background piece about the problems of ITV, and then go into the interview.'

Other stories include an exclusive sit-down with the mother of quads (pictures were shown of the babies in last night's programme); an exclusive with Gail Sheridan (the wife of a Member of the Scottish Parliament involved in a libel action against the *News of the World*); a story about the dangers of speeding; and a row between a childcare expert Gina Ford and mumsnet.com, a website for expectant mothers.

1000	Tim, the Head of Foreign News, leaves the meeting. The discussion drifts back to the Charles Allen item. Deborah says: 'We'll run VT for lunchtime, and take a bite of Charles Allen for the evening. We must address *Love Island*. We can't avoid it.'

ITV News staff are concerned about the poor audience figures they inherit at 10.30 p.m. from Love Island, *the celebrity dating show on ITV1.*

Deborah continues. Last night they showed footage of conjoined twin baby girls due to have an operation to separate them later today in America: 'Twins – I want to keep an eye on this. Needle won't make it. And we can't do both – we'll either do Gina or Beatrice. We have to get Gina for that story to run. But Beatrice and Fergie is car crash telly!'

Faye Nicholds

1010	They discuss the running order for the 6.30 p.m. programme. Deborah suggests: 'We'll have paedo at the top, then Beirut, then New York, then Charles Allen followed by Twins underlay. Have we got room for Gina or Beatrice and Fergie? To me, we're missing something. Charles Allen is a duty story . . .'

Further discussion takes place over John Ray's MI5 story, and he goes to ring his source for clarification and an update. They then discuss cricket. They no longer have a dedicated sports slot on the programme, and sports stories have to stand on their own merit. They discuss the Beirut oil story: 'It's very much picture-dependent of the oil slick. It could be a massive story by tomorrow.'

Assistant programme editor Faye Nicholds adds a few more stories to the list: 'There's that story in the papers this morning about that lorry driver/dangerous driving/mobile phone story . . .'

Deborah remarks: 'We'll end up biffing something out. It's too tight.'

1015	The editorial meeting breaks up.

1018	The assistant programme editor, Faye Nicholds, moves straight into another meeting 'The Huddle', in the small meeting room next door but one to Deborah's office. There are four monitors in the room, switched to CNN, BBC World, Sky News and BBC News 24, and seven chairs. The aptly named 'huddle' is when the early evening production team gather to plan the programme in detail. Faye is programme editor for the evening news tonight, and chairs the meeting. At 28, she's one of ITN's high-flyers. She starts by giving a quick run-down of the running order discussed at the editorial meeting a few minutes ago. Faye then allocates the stories to the two producers: 'Laura, you do paedo and MI5, and Angela, you do all the Beirut stuff.'

Laura Holgate is another high-flyer. She works only on the flagship evening news programme; she is reliable and has lots of good creative ideas. She is very well respected. Angela Saini is a freelance producer brought in because of the staff shortages.

They discuss graphics ideas with Kojo Boateng, the graphics designer assigned to the programme. They start with ideas for the MI5 report. They discuss treating the sequence as if the pictures are on CCTV, and then Laura remarks about the reporter: 'John Ray may not like a graphics sequence. He's quite fussy what he likes.'

They then go on to discuss the Beatrice/Fergie story. The team are not enthusiastic, but Faye explains: 'Deborah is quite keen for us to do this.'

One of the team says: 'Yes, it is Beatrice's birthday, you know. Maybe we're being rather unkind.'

The Charles Allen story is next for discussion. Faye says: 'The ITV press office are really funny about us slagging ITV, but we must do *Love Island*. Otherwise it's the elephant in the room that no one mentions.'

There'll be a complicated virtual reality (VR) graphics sequence for the Charles Allen piece, with the reporter starting off on the *Coronation Street* set, and then walking out of the TV monitor.

'Don't do the interview in a boring place, because it won't match the chromakey multi-screen idea we have going.'

And then a word of warning about VT acquisitions: 'Don't cut the clips too tight. There has to be room to be able to put the Astons for each clip in. Some places are refusing to let us use their clips if their Aston is not up for long enough!'

1050

The meeting ends. Faye goes over to reporter John Ray to find out how his MI5 story is developing. He says: 'I've just checked with my sources, and we're OK to run, but all the plots are sub judice.'

'Can you do a PTC outside the Houses of Parliament?'

'Yes, but we'd better say that they were alleged plots. I'll have a word with the lawyers about some of these cases.'

Faye mentions the CCTV graphics ideas. He says: 'It's a nice idea, but slightly misleading.'

Faye tells him Laura is his producer. They discuss his PTC ideas, and Faye asks if he could get a visual sweep from the MI5 offices to the House of Commons. John remarks: 'We can't do Canary Wharf because of the trial coming up. We can't do Heathrow, and the other terror targets like Bridgewater and Ministry of Sound, because they're all sub judice. We could always go to the MI5 website and film the "highly-likely" category rating. Whereabouts are you running this?'

'Top of part two. We want to tease them with something good.'

1058

John Buckle, one of ITN's lawyers, walks into the newsroom. Faye and John call him over. John briefs him on the story and they then discuss the careful wording for the script: 'We can't say there were four foiled plots. We'll have to say there were four alleged foiled plots.'

John mentions a fifth plot: 'Can we say anything in the PTC alluding to this fifth plot?'

The lawyer asks: 'When is the case coming up? Is this the first time it has been mentioned about the House of Commons? As long as we say alleged plot we'll be OK. Is this live or a package for this evening?' John then talks him through the planned package. The lawyer is concerned.

John says: 'I'll ring up the cops and check it out.'

The lawyer says: 'Never take MI5 at their word.'

John Ray picks up the phone. Faye asks: 'Can we call it an exclusive?'

He replies: 'I'd be happier with "ITN have learnt . . ."'

He gets through to the police: 'I just need to check a few details for the lawyers . . .'

1104	Faye discusses the paedo story with the lawyer.
1107	Arti comes to Faye and says: 'We've just got new pics of the twins being separated. One of the surgeons is holding one of the girls up. It's amazing.' Faye replies: 'Oh! Let's not do Beatrice.' Arti briefs Faye on what is happening in Tyre. She's spoken with the producer Toby, and he's happy with 1.30 as the duration for their piece. Faye comments to Arti: 'I think the death toll will have to go. I won't be able to fit it all in.'
1110	Faye returns to sorting out the running order. She sits at one of the output production desks. *After the lunchtime news, she and her team will move over to the 'current output' desk to be nearer to the foreign news input desk and the home news/planning desk.* Faye logs on to the ENPS system to start her running order. She calls out: 'Who's presenting this evening? Does anyone know? Is it Mark?' No one replies. She turns to Laura next to her: 'It can't be Alastair [Stewart]. He's doing *London Tonight*. It must be Mark.'
1113	John Ray comes over to Laura and Faye with news from the police. 'The trial starts today.' Faye says: 'That's good news for us.' John continues: 'Channel Four have been down. I'm not sure if they've filmed anything.' He returns to his desk to find out more. Faye goes back to her running order on ENPS: 'Oh, no! I've got a three-and-a-half minute ad break! How am I going to fit it all in?' *The evening news does not usually have an ad break. Faye has no say over it and her transmission time is reduced.* Faye inputs all the items for the evening show with their expected durations into the running order. The system automatically adds the timings together to give a final duration. 'How did that happen? We're eight seconds light. Laura, check me, will you?'
1120	Faye advises the reporter working on the Charles Allen item: 'Don't go into too much detail for the early evening. Keep it really simple.'
1125	Faye calls reporter Paul Davies on his mobile: 'Have you a second to chat about the evening news?' They talk through ideas for the paedo story, including using newspaper archive: 'Maybe the library is the best place to go to. A good location for your PTC as well. Any idea when they plan to dig up the garden? . . . It's a cracker of a story. I hear you've got nice shots from next door's balcony. We need road signs. I think we'll go live at the top and then have your package. At the moment you're top story. Your producer here is Laura.' Laura interrupts: 'Tell him it says in the *Sun* there's a letter.' Faye suggests: 'Can you get hold of the letter, Paul?'

1130	Faye comes off the phone and does a quick search on the ENPS system to see if there is any archive footage to go with the paedo story. She can't find anything, so goes over to the home news desk to ask them to look a bit more for some archive.
1140	Faye chats with Alastair Stewart. He's just returned from filming the two-camera sit-down interview with Charles Allen.
1143	Laura has called up on ENPS an item she worked on a few years ago about spying. She wants to use a similar look for the MI5 piece. She and Faye look at the piece on Laura's desktop and discuss the look. Laura says: 'Kojo [the graphics designer] would do that really stylishly. John did talk about maybe a graphics sequence showing how many MI5 officers they have. Shall I commission that with graphics then?' 'Yes, that's a really nice idea.'
1146	Faye pops into Deborah's office to keep her up-to-date.
1150	Deborah goes over to the main output newsdesk to check how things are going for the lunchtime bulletin.
1159	Faye is back at her desk and calls over to Parminder Sandhu, one of the two news writers working on the evening news. She checks some details with him on the graphics explainer on the UN story.
1204	Faye calls Julian Manyon on his mobile in Tyre: 'Hi, Julian, it's Faye. I'm doing the evening news today. What are you up to? I've heard it's amazing up there . . . We'll go for live top and then you . . .' Deborah is standing by the main news output desk, helping with the scripts for the lunchtime bulletin. Faye calls over to her: 'Did we do the death toll last night?' Deborah calls back: 'No. We won't do it tonight either. Let's drop it tonight as well.'
1210	John Ray sits with Laura and Faye discussing the MI5 piece in detail. He says: 'I tend not to use set-ups.' They talk through ideas. He teases her when she gets pans and tilts mixed up.
1215	The lunchtime team gather round a screen to rewrite a script.

1220	Faye writes notes in a notebook. She finds it useful, writing handwritten notes on each story, keeping her focused and up-to-date.
1222	The lunchtime programme editor calls over to Faye and asks her to pop round to an edit to check a package before it goes out on air at 12.30. *ITN have a rule that each package must be viewed editorially by one of the programme editors before it goes out. They help each other when they are up against a deadline.* As Faye walks in, the reporter and VT editor are putting the final touches to the piece. Faye watches the package and advises that she thought the death toll from the bombing had increased. The reporter quickly changes her voice-over.
1228	Faye returns from viewing the package. She calls Angela, the freelance producer, to discuss the draft script of the ITV piece she has been working on. Faye suggests some changes.
1233	Faye swops the TV monitor on her desk from Sky News to the ITV News lunchtime programme. The lunchtime news uses different reporters from the evening news. The lunchtime reporters are on the early shift. The lunchtime news is leading with paedo.
1236	Faye returns to her running order and takes another look at her timings. She asks Laura: 'Will John be able to fit everything into one minute 40 seconds?
1237	Faye watches the piece she viewed ten minutes earlier go out on air.
1240	Faye goes round to Graphics. They're tucked away just off the newsroom past the edit suites. She walks into a discussion about a 3-D map of the Israel/Lebanon border and problems over precise wording.
1246	Faye talks with Kojo, the graphics supervisor, about a graphic showing the conjoined twins now separated. They decide it might be a bit tasteless, and they are concerned they don't have enough information to give an accurate medical account. They drop the idea.
1251	As Faye walks back into the newsroom past the foreign news desk, Arti stops her: 'Manyon has a corker. I've just been speaking with him and Toby on the mobile from Lebanon. They've filmed a seven-day-old baby . . .' As Arti is trying to explain, Faye is called to the phone. Toby is calling to speak to Faye from Lebanon. Faye gives them longer for their piece: 'I don't think we want the live top now.' Arti says: 'There's loads of new stuff around from NBC.' Faye says she won't be able to fit it in with a three-and-a-half ad break. 'You're kidding. They're normally only one-and-a-half minutes!'

| 1310 | Laura and Faye decide they need some fresh air and lunch. They go out into the bright sunshine of central London. Laura goes off for a quick shopping spree; Faye walks 50 yards up the road to a small sandwich shop and orders a takeaway salad. |

| 1323 | Faye returns to her desk and eats her lunch watching the BBC lunchtime news. She writes more notes in her notebook. |

| 1330 | The lunchtime programme comes off air, and the staff return to the newsroom. |

| 1333 | Behind Faye at the output desk, Deborah gives a post mortem on the lunchtime programme: 'There was a terrible buzz on Damien on the line from Croydon. The paedo story felt a bit scrappy and underdeveloped. With hindsight you could have put it lower. It just felt a little thin as the lead. Julian's piece was stunning. The mumsnet piece got into legalese too much. Twins was nice – I could have taken loads more of that. We need to do a cut-down of that and put it out as a pool.'

A 'pool' is a pooled item shared with ITN's affiliates in other broadcasters around the world.

Faye is viewing fresh pictures on her desktop of the bombings in the Middle East. 'The world is going to the dogs,' she says to herself. Laura comes off the phone and says to Faye: 'John Ray says we can't mention the House of Commons.'

The post mortem continues behind them. Deborah enthuses: 'Beatrice was lovely in all its gooeyness. It felt a very live show. Live and lively – thank you very much.' |

| 1341 | The lunchtime post mortem finishes. |

| 1350 | The lunchtime team depart, and Faye and her team move across to the production output desk. |

| 1354 | Faye prints off the updated running order. |

| 1358 | Faye rings TX [transmission control] to check that the ad break really is three-and-a-half minutes long, and there hasn't been a mistake. They confirm the three-and-a-half minutes. |

| 1400 | Faye calls for a meeting. The team of seven gather back in 'The Huddle' to discuss updates on the running order. |

| 1412 | The meeting ends. |

| 1413 | Arti asks Faye if she still wants a live top from Lebanon: 'Tim [the foreign news editor] doesn't want to spend the money on a line if we don't need it. A live costs £500 for 30 seconds. He says we ought to save the money if we can.' |
| | Faye replies: 'I'm just going into a meeting to discuss. I'll let you know.' |

1415	The 2.15 editorial meeting gets under way in Deborah's office. Presenter Mark Austin arrives in the newsroom and pops his head round Deborah's door. He gets a warm welcome from everyone in the meeting. He's just returned from Beirut; he got back last night. He decides to join the meeting – and grabs a seat on the sofa.
	The home news editor keeps the meeting up-to-date with the paedo story: 'Paul Davies and the cameraman are stuck behind a police cordon on a neighbour's balcony – so they're staying there. They're not going to get to the library. The police are talking in half an hour. There's not much to look at. There's lots of SOTs and a chopper's gone up for aerials – so we've done quite well.'
	Deborah says: 'Well done. Thank you. It just feels a bit loose to me. This piece has no beginning, middle or end. Has he got a producer with him that could go off and check the Land Registry for the deeds?'
	There is no producer with Paul, but the Land Registry is online. Someone in the newsroom can help with the research. Deborah is told that Paul is confident he's got lots of stuff.

| 1429 | The meeting discusses the Middle East. Mark Austin asks: 'Is this not a better story than some crackpot in suburbia?' |

Mark Austin

	They discuss Angus Walker reporting at the UN in New York. Mark continues: 'There are grounds for a possible deal here . . . Julian's piece sounds amazing – they're back in the dark ages, no vehicles.'
	Deborah suggests editing the two items using the same style and editing techniques. She asks Faye if she's asked the network for extra time. She hasn't – so Deborah, sitting at her desk during the meeting, sends a message: 'I'll message her now – two minutes would save our bacon.'
	Faye continues to go through the running order. Deborah checks and asks: 'Is it MI5 or MI6? We must make sure we get the right building!'
	Deborah continues: 'We need to take possession of this security story. Can we call it an exclusive?'

1448	The meeting debates what the lead should be.
	They discuss the latest pictures from Reuters of bombing. There is some talk of a funeral procession being bombed, as people buried their dead from the bombings of yesterday.
	Deborah moves the discussion on. 'The twins are a lovely pull-through – it's a picture piece. Gina's not talking. The Damilola jury's out. Should Lebanon be top?'
	As the debate continues, Deborah says: 'Let's see what happens with paedo. If they start digging . . . Mark, what do you think? Others, what do you think?'
	Mark Austin says he likes to be involved in decisions about what the lead story should be: 'I like to have a say or I wouldn't do the job. I'd go back to being a foreign correspondent, where you can have control over your one bit [of the programme].'
	The meeting is about to break up. Deborah turns to Faye and says: 'You're not going to like this. Last night, we didn't do the death toll. I think we need to do it tonight.'

1500	The meeting ends and everyone leaves Deborah's office. Faye takes a call from Paul Davies, trapped behind the police cordon in Croydon.
1501	Faye pops back to brief Deborah on the latest from Paul. Mark (Austin) pops his head round Deborah's door and asks: 'Beirut is still top for the 10.30, isn't it? If not, it'd be the first time we've not led on it since it first started. This is not a Fred West investigation. We've lost the Blair SOT from the evening, OK?'
1503	Deborah's office is full again – this time it's the meeting for the 10.30 news. They start by discussing the UN vote. Deborah asks: 'Shouldn't we be asking: "Why are they dragging their feet?" Is there a sense of life and death at the UN? There's not. I've been there enough times. They were stalling yesterday. Twenty people died. They're still waiting. How many more are to die? Why are they dragging their feet?'
1545	Deborah has finished her meeting with the 10.30 team, and she's locked in discussion with Faye and the foreign news editor, Arti, about the pieces from both sides of the border. Faye has been on the phone to Lebanon and Israel. Following long conversations with the reporters, she realises their two pieces won't marry together.
1548	Mary Nightingale arrives in the newsroom, sits at the desk and starts checking stories. Deborah, Arti and Faye are still talking. Deborah says: 'Let's drop one of the pieces. Leave it for tomorrow. We'll run James.' Deborah and Faye turn to the running order. Faye says: 'Everything is changing by the second.' Arti leaves to ring the reporters.

Mary Nightingale

1554	Faye takes a call from Julian Manyon on his mobile in Lebanon. Faye explains the decision to drop his piece. Faye talks him through the funeral bombing footage: 'They're great pictures. They're pedestrians, they're not in cars, and you see and hear the explosion.'
1557	Faye comes off the phone to Julian, and tells producer Laura that he is watching the top of the hour on BBC World, to see if he can see the pictures for himself. Laura is viewing the pictures at her desk, and says: 'They're not as amazing as they've been billed to be.'
1610	There's confusion about where the agency pictures are from and who shot them.

1620	Faye and Deborah continue to juggle the running order. Faye tells John Ray that his MI5 piece will now be in the 10.30 – things are developing too fast in the Middle East.
1643	Deborah comes over to the desk, and asks what the police have said at the presser in Croydon: 'What is the furthest we can say on that? I think that's the lead. What would make me watch more – more pictures from the Middle East or police digging up children's remains in a back garden in Croydon?'
1646	The calm atmosphere of the newsroom changes, as excited staff notice that film star Patrick Swayze has just walked through (he's appearing in *Guys and Dolls* in the West End, and is pre-recording an interview for the London programme). One male staffer comments: 'The last time this happened was years ago when Michael Jackson came in!' A young production assistant picks something out of a waste paper basket: 'Patrick Swayze's chewing gum. I wonder how much this is worth on eBay?'
	Deborah and Faye return to the question of the lead. Faye calls over Alastair Stewart: 'Alastair, what would you lead with? Funeral or paedo?'
	Mark Austin joins them: 'What are the pictures like?'
	Someone calls out from the foreign desk: 'There are more dead in that bombing. There's an update on that story. The death toll is going up.'
1652	John Ray walks back into the newsroom. Faye calls out: 'You might be back in, mate. It keeps changing by the second!'
1655	One of the home news team approaches Deborah. ITN's exclusive with MSP's wife Gail Sheridan is due to run the next day. But Sky News are apparently not aware of ITN's deal: 'Just before the exec meeting, Sky flashed up there would be an interview with the Sheridans at 4.15 this afternoon. I immediately got on to the agency and got it pulled from Sky. STV have an interview with Sheridan, and we bid for Gail. Should we hang on till this time tomorrow with our Gail exclusive or go with it tonight?'
	Deborah makes a decision: 'Let's go with it tonight. I'll tell Harry.' [Harry Gibson is today's 10.30 programme editor]
	A new story arrives from the Home News desk: a man has died from Legionnaires' Disease on the day he was due to be discharged from hospital. Faye changes the running order again, and asks for stills of the dead man.
1740	Faye is viewing the reports from the Middle East correspondents on her desktop.
1744	Faye tries to call correspondent James Mates and his producer Geoff Hill in Beirut, but can't raise either of them. Their mobiles don't seem to be working. She tries to call Julian Manyon in Tyre, but that call fails as well.

1749	Faye goes back to her script and puts the final touches to the Legionnaires script. She asks Arti to keep trying to contact the correspondents in Lebanon. Deborah arrives at the newsdesk and starts checking through the scripts for the evening news.
1754	Faye rings John in the legal department but he is engaged. Someone asks for her on the phone. She calls out: 'I can't take that call, I've got to write the bongs.' [The 'bongs' are an ITN trademark – the bongs of Big Ben. Staff use the term for the headlines voiced between the bongs.]
1755	Faye and Deborah bounce ideas around for the wording of the bongs. Faye is told: 'They're asking for the underlays [scripts to go with the headline pictures] downstairs [the studio gallery].'
1759	John Buckle, the lawyer, comes into the newsroom to check the scripts. Arti tries to call the teams in Lebanon again. Deborah rewrites the bongs as John Buckle and Faye go through the top story – paedo.
1805	The lawyer visits the edit suite round the corner from the newsroom to check the Charles Allen item is legally OK for transmission.
1811	Geoff Hill calls in to the Foreign News desk from his hotel room. Arti asks: 'Have your phones all been down?' He replies that he thinks all the mobile networks in Lebanon are down.
1824	Laura arrives in the newsroom from the gallery. She tells Faye and Deborah: 'Paul Davies hasn't fed yet.' Faye says: 'It may well have to be a live roll down-the-line. Is he going to make his slot?' Laura replies: 'He's not said that. He's just said it'll be tight. I'm going back downstairs – but we've got to come up with a Plan B.' Paedo is the top story, but Paul Davies still has not finished editing his piece in Croydon.
1828	Faye is still in the newsroom putting the finishing touches to the scripts, but her main worry is if her top story will arrive in time: 'We've got one-and-a-half minutes to air.' The input desk call back: 'They're running to the truck now, and they'll send it unmixed.' ['Unmixed' means sound levels will have to be adjusted as the piece is played out live.]
1830	The evening news is on air. The headlines read by Mary Nightingale and Mark Austin announce the paedo story and then the bombing of the funeral.

1831	After the bongs, Mark and Mary lead into the funeral story. Faye races downstairs to the studio gallery, quickly followed by Deborah. The paedo story still has not arrived in the building.
1832	Laura dashes up to the newsroom from the studio gallery and speaks with the input desk: 'We need to resend the paedo piece – there are lots of glitches on it.' On air, Julian Manyon does a live two-way, and then leads into his package filmed earlier that day about the seven-day-old baby.
1835	On air – a graphic comes up, 'Death in the rubble', and James Mates' piece from Beirut goes out.
1837	On air – Mark announces the death toll with a graphic sequence.
1839	On air – Mark and Mary link into Angus Walker's live report from the UN in New York.
1840	On air – Mark and Mary link into the paedo story.
1841	On air – Paul Davies' paedo report goes out.
1843	On air – Paul Davies' report ends, and Mark and Mary trail the next half of the programme (Legionnaires and the twins separation): 'Still to come . . .' The evening news breaks for three-and-a-half minutes of ads.
1844	Deborah comes out of the studio and returns to the newsroom. As she passes the foreign news desk, she asks Arti: 'The BBC didn't have those foreign pics, did they?' 'No.'
1847	Back on air – Mary links into the Legionnaires' story.
1849	On air – Mark and Mary link into the ITV package.

1851	On air – Mark and Mary link into the Beatrice 'mini mummy' story.
1852	On air – Mark and Mary present the news round-up and link into the opt-out. *[The regional stations have a short headline sequence near the end of the bulletin.]*
1853	On air – Mark and Mary link into the final story – the twins.
1854	On air – Mark and Mary trail a story on Paul McCartney's divorce which will run at 10.30.
1855	Off air.
1856	The team begin to drift back into the newsroom for the post mortem. Thirty people gather around the production desk for the post mortem. Deborah says: 'The programme was clean and not messy. We had very good bongs – but not in the right order. Lessons have been learned all round. We needed stand-by bongs. If the paedo piece looked like it wasn't going to make it, we should have done some stand-by bongs in a safer order. The graphics sequence should have been pre-recorded – we slightly missed in places. Can we review it for the 10.30? Paedophile story – very good news gathering on that. We managed to get the graphic done at the last minute. Thanks. That'll be in tomorrow's papers – visually it was stunning. All in all, a very good programme – a very busy day.
1907	End of post mortem.
1913	Deborah chats with Harry Gibson, the 10.30 programme editor, and the 10.30 team to discuss their running order. Presenter Mark Austin joins them.

1914	Tim, the Head of Foreign News, chats with correspondents in the Middle East. They're planning on moving their armoured vehicle from Damascus to Beirut safely. Tim comments: 'We may never get it back, of course. Give us a ring when you get there.'
1916	Deborah Turness leaves for the day. She's off to a dinner with *The News of the World*. A car is waiting for her outside – she needs to be in W1 for 7.30.
1920	Arti, the foreign news editor, is getting to the end of her shift. She rings producer Geoff Hill in his hotel room in Beirut to give him some feedback on their item and to say thank you.
1932	People start drifting off home for the day and the newsroom quietens.
1939	Harry Gibson, the editor for the 10.30, chats with the reporter on the paedo story over the phone: 'We'll do a live top and tail . . .'
1943	Harry checks through the running order and makes some timing alterations. There is an extra two minutes of airtime in the programme tonight, and the programme is on air eight minutes later than usual at 22.38 due to a Champions League game. He's made the decision with Deborah before she left that Manyon is still the lead. He'll run a float in and two-way off the back.
1948	Harry has another chat about the paedo: 'You'll need to have a conversation with the lawyer, before you start scripting and cutting this story, so that you know what the ground rules are.'
1951	Tom Lowe, home/foreign news editor for the evening shift, checks with Harry what he wants at the top of the programme: 'Do you want Manyon live? Because I haven't booked the line for that – I'll need to move the booking earlier.'
1958	Harry prints off the latest running order for the 8 p.m. meeting. Mark sits in one of the offices along the side of the newsroom. He's been away in Beirut, so he's catching up on his e-mails, and checking the scripts for tonight's 22.30 programme.

2000	Tom talks to Harry about a new line for the Lebanon story that has just appeared on Ceefax. There is a problem with aid getting through.
2002	The 10.30 news team (nine of them) gather round the input desk for a meeting chaired by programme editor Harry Gibson. Harry announces that on-air time tonight is eight minutes later than usual at 10.38 due to the Champions League game, and they have an extra two minutes of air time. Harry continues: 'Sheridan must get legalled. John [duty lawyer] is available at home, and we'll need to legal the Macca story as well.'
2004	The team discuss the Lebanon/UN story and consider various wall images for the studio. The new line on aid not getting through to Southern Lebanon is mentioned. They discuss the UN story, and mention that in the early evening news the script changed so they had Israeli soldiers on screen when the script was talking about Lebanese troops. Harry then explains the evening news' problem with the line from Croydon: 'There was a problem with glitches on the line. We need to feed in with more time to spare.' Harry mentions there is a fresh 3-D package on Charles Allen to give more of a business angle on the ITV story for the 10.30. The Macca divorce story is discussed. Stills have appeared in the London evening newspaper of Heather Mills being locked out of her London home. Harry reports: 'It's £100 for every still we use and £60 after the first still. So it's costly, but I think there are only three usable stills – so it won't be too bad.' Tom reminds the meeting that there is a fresh line about Heather intending to use the same lawyer as Princess Diana. They talk about the Sheridans. ITN have an exclusive, the first television interview with the MSP and his wife since the trial. Harry says: 'It's a good pull-through. We'll have a shot in the bongs, and a shot in the bump throw. We'll need to get the exclusive bug up.' Arti has left the building and is on the train home.

BBC TEN O'CLOCK NEWS

The BBC's **Ten O'Clock News** is regarded by many people in broadcasting as British television's most prestigious and authoritative news programme. It draws on the best of the BBC's reporting and news production talent for a nightly half-hour digest of events and analysis. It regularly attracts five million viewers – more on big news days. It is shown on BBC1, the main television channel, and on News 24. For many years the BBC's main TV news programme was at nine o'clock, with ITV traditionally showing *News at Ten* an hour later than the BBC. When ITV moved their programme to a later slot – to allow full-length movies in peak viewing time – the BBC Director General Greg Dyke seized the opportunity to change 'the Nine' to 'the Ten'.

Each story has a producer assigned to it. The producer works with a reporter or correspondent and technical staff (cameras/picture editors/graphics).

The Ten has a different agenda from the One and the Six. It has a reputation as a 'journal of record', reflecting the main political and foreign stories of the day. The Ten has one main presenter. BBC nations and regions opt out for their own headlines at the top of the programme and for their own bulletin near the end. The BBC news studio, which is used for all the BBC1 news programmes, has a sophisticated graphics capability with video projections on the walls behind the presenters. This usually means the presenter of the Ten is standing for the lead story and seated for later items. The Ten's production desk is at one end of the vast, open-plan BBC newsroom at Television Centre in London. There are similar areas nearby for the other bulletins. Forward planning is at the centre of the room. News 24, Sport and Radio Five Live are upstairs.

1100

Kate McAndrew

Production staff are beginning to arrive for their shift on 'the Ten'. They open post and read e-mails, to get up-to-speed with the day.

Kate McAndrew, one of three assistant editors on the programme, is at her desk completing a list of prospects for tonight's programme. She has been at work since 7.30 in the morning. She's producing the bulletin, but will have input from the Editor, Craig Oliver, and, if there are broader policy issues involved, the Head of TV News, Peter Horrocks. At this early stage in the day, Kate has a clear idea of most of the programme content. The BBC's newsgathering and forward-planning operations are across the main stories of the day, with reporters and producers already assigned. On-the-day stories are assigned as they break.

1120	Kate checks staff arrangements with the *Six O'Clock* – they share some producers.

| **1130** | Kate calls out to the team: 'Right, guys, shall we meet?' The first planning meeting of the day is held in a corner of the Ten's area. |

At the meeting are Kate McAndrew (today's output editor), Gwenan Roberts (the output editor yesterday and tomorrow), Emily Tofield (senior producer, Ten), Chris Partridge (senior producer, Six and Ten), Ian Atkinson (producer, Ten), Abbie Dobson (producer, Six and Ten) and Nicola Owen (graphics).

Graphics produce inserts for packages, and also the content of the video walls. The default backdrop is a panoramic London skyline. Graphics behind presenter Huw Edwards will be projected on to the centre section. Other parts of 'the wall' are referred to by the area of London they show. Reporters on live locations will be shown on 'Battersea wall'.

The meeting begins with a brief post mortem about last night's programme. There was an item that failed to make it to air. Producer Ian Anderson and reporter Rory Cellan-Jones had been trying to feed a story from Scotland about a conference on the future of the Internet. It had been edited in a hotel room on a laptop editing program, but they could not get it off the computer in time.

The previous night's output editor Gwenan Roberts says: 'We kept on being promised it, and then at 17 minutes past, I said: "We're not going to get it, are we?" and had to go with the Postman Pat piece from the *One O'Clock News*. It was the right length.'

Kate comments: 'Not much choice at 10.15.'

The Postman Pat piece (by royal correspondent Nick Witchell) was a light item about the children's character Postman Pat delivering invitations for the Queen's birthday party – not typical Ten O'Clock fare. (Audience research later showed it did not go down as well with viewers as the rest of the programme – 41 per cent of those surveyed said it did not interest them.)

Kate said the Editor, Craig Oliver, had been 'very pragmatic' about the decision. He told her: 'Think of it as an experiment.'

Rory Cellan-Jones' piece will probably run tonight.

Kate goes through today's running order: 'There's stacks of stuff around.'

She expects the lead story will be one of two – the government's announcement of a major revision of pensions, or an exclusive about compensation payments for the victims of chemical warfare experiments at Porton Down in the 1950s.

The pension story means the age at which many people draw their pension will rise. It's likely to affect most of the viewers and their families. Kate says: 'Our audience are going to think pensions will be at the top. It's so important.'

But pensions will have been covered on earlier bulletins, and there will be little new to say. The Porton Down story – a government climb-down after half a century, which could lead to 500 further cases in a class action – is politically important *and* exclusive. Kate says: 'It could be a unique lead, and it's ours.'

Evan Davis, the economics editor, will be doing the main pensions story, produced by Rob Stevenson. There'll be a second piece too. Kate says: 'We've done some nice filming of a small firm in Ipswich – different individuals and families. We must make sure the two pension pieces don't clash and overlap too much.

'We've got to talk about what we're going to have on our wall. I quite like the *Dallas* approach with three main characters in three columns.

'We'll do Robbo live.' [a reference to business editor Robert Peston]

There'll be a trail for Cellan-Jones' online piece, and a report from Gavin Hewitt in Oldham, the scene of riots he covered five years ago. Kate says: 'We'll mix from Gavin then to Gavin now.'

All the stories have a lot of graphics content. Kate explains the graphics will need to be done early, as the main graphics designer is off sick: 'It's a terrible day for someone who's new. Anything that doesn't need graphics won't have graphics.'

1150	The meeting continues with discussion of a pay dispute involving university lecturers. Today they're at ACAS, the arbitration service. Kate feels the programme ought to cover the talks, but says: 'The trouble with these stories is they're pictorially awful. The Six are going to give a student a camera to do an authored piece. 'How can we treat this? Get a vice-chancellor? On a different kind of day, I'd get Peston to just strip out the madness of this pay claim. I think 23 per cent over three years is nuts.' As they move to the rest of the day's agenda, Kate comments: 'I hate that story!'
1155	Kate is coming to the end of her run-down: 'The ill-fated Rory Cellan-Jones' Internet piece will get on. It needs a 15-second top and tail. Ian's trapped in Scotland, but he'll be back at one o'clock with his tears dried to see it through. Anything else, anyone?'
1200	The meeting breaks up. Ian Atkinson and Chris Partridge start researching pensions. Abbie is filling in a time sheet.
1210	Chris is on the phone, checking details for the second pensions story, and double-checking the points being covered by Evan Davis: 'If he's got it, we can't have it.'
1218	Chris has decided the pensions story is as complicated as doing a Rubik's Cube, and that this would make a powerful visual metaphor. He's been looking for a Rubik's Cube expert to film. UK Champion Dan Harris calls back, but apologises and says he's not available.
1220	Craig Oliver, the Editor, visits the team. Chris suggests a meeting at 2.00 for everyone involved in the pensions story. Craig discusses staffing and production for the day with Kate. Chris rings *Newsround* to see if they know a Rubik's Cube expert. No luck.

Craig Oliver

1235	Ian is on the phone 'chasing' the Porton Down story. Chris reports to Kate and Craig (at Kate's desk) about progress on the pensions story. Kate tells him to take care of 'the heads, wall and pensions'. Craig calls Abbie over. Kate tells her a reporter and a producer are on the way to Loughborough University to film students and lecturers. She returns to her desk to think about graphics for the story.
1240	Gwenan is in the viewing area, looking at a Feargal Keane report for tomorrow's programme about the Pope's visit to Auschwitz. She asks Abbie what she's doing. Abbie replies: 'Quite a bit. I've got to think of a motif for the universities piece.'
1244	Gwenan has finished watching the Auschwitz report, and Ian takes over the tape machine to view archive Beta tapes. He's looking through David Shukman's previous reports on the Porton Down story. He needs to find exteriors of buildings and black and white Ministry of Defence footage for tonight's piece.
1305 Ian Atkinson	Ian has found archive footage of Porton Down in the '50s to go on the wall. He's delighted by the MoD pictures – with quaint voice-over and actuality sound suggesting soldiers are not being harmed by the chemical experiments: 'These are good.' He returns to his desk.
1310 Staff cameraman Ingo Prosser	Chris returns to his desk with a sandwich. Staff cameraman Ingo Prosser has arrived in the newsroom, with a full camera kit and lights, to shoot a sequence for the pensions story. Chris gives him a black backcloth – he wants a series of faces against the black background. Ingo explains he's already shot some pictures for the Six – close-ups of people's eyes – and suggests Chris views them before they carry on. The pair go round to graphics to look at the pictures.

1315 Chris Partridge	Chris and Ingo are back in the newsroom. The Six's treatment is similar to what he'd planned for the Ten. Chris suggests Ingo goes for lunch while he discusses with Kate what they need to shoot. Chris returns to the Internet and finds a Rubik's Cube expert who's in London, and able to come in later. He arranges for her to come in at 6.30 to film a sequence. He also asks her to measure the squares on a Rubik's Cube, so he can get graphics to make up stickers to cover the sides: 'I wonder if we might stick up a picture of Gordon Brown on one of the sides?'
1330	Senior producer Ian Anderson arrives back from Edinburgh, with the horror story from last night: 'We were at BH [broadcasting house] in Edinburgh and just couldn't download off a Mac.'
1345	Chris phones Ingo to ask him to be ready to shoot at 2 o'clock.
1400	Chris is running his script by the producers working on the pensions packages to make sure there are no overlaps.
1407	Craig, Kate and Chris are in Craig's office with Robert Peston and the producers assigned to the correspondents. Craig Oliver explains their approach: 'There's a sea of information, and people need big life rafts to hold on to.' He says the Rubik's Cube idea might work as a chapter heading for each of the sections.
1411	Ian Anderson arrives late into the meeting (he'd been on the phone to Edinburgh where he'd left some equipment behind at BH). He says the pensions story is just right for the Ten: 'It's a classic public policy thing which we have to explain. Traditionally, it's the sort of thing we do well.'
1414	Evan rings the newsroom. Ian Atkinson answers and tells Evan: 'Everyone's in a massive meeting.' Evan leaves a message about the Rubik's Cube idea. Cameraman Ingo has finished setting up the black screen.
1415 Abbie Dobson	Abbie rings Loughborough University to get an old university exam paper for use in a graphics sequence. (Her idea is that questions about lecturers' pay will appear on screen as if they are part of an exam.) The press officer says she'll talk to the examinations department and get back to her. Abbie wants them to e-mail it to her. She says the producer Jeanette Long and reporter Sophie Hutchinson are just arriving in Loughborough, and gives the press officer the producer's mobile number. Then she calls Dan Ashley, the press officer of the higher education union, the AUT, to get the 'low-down' on the universities' pay structure.

1425	Ingo has begun filming a series of faces in the newsroom. He's asking production staff if they mind having their picture taken. He's looking for a good mix of ages and ethnic backgrounds. They'll be used in the pensions story.
1431	Ian Atkinson tells Kate that reporter David Shukman is driving down the M1 and should be here within the hour. He also tells Chris that Evan has decided against using the Rubik's Cube motif. Chris observes: 'The Rubik's Cube idea has been bished. It's been bished quite spectacularly.'
1440	Abbie phones producer Jeanette in Loughborough to brief her on what she's found out from the AUT: 'I think you need to chase this yourself now, 'cos I've been chasing this for hours, and I've got to go and sort the graphics.' They discuss the ideas for the graphics. Chris is in Ingo's 'hot seat' having his own face shot for the graphic sequence.
1445	Evan Davis arrives. Chris, Evan, Kate and Craig discuss the Rubik's Cube idea. Evan wanted to spike it. Five minutes later, there's been a change of heart. Chris comments: 'The Rubik's Cube is back on.'
1450	The Jerusalem bureau rings and offers a DTL (down-the-line). Palestinian leader Mahmoud Abbas is considering a referendum to solve a dispute between the political parties in Palestine. It's the time when Washington usually call. It's when they wake up and let the duty editor know what's happening. Kate knows they'll be on tomorrow because the Prime Minister is visiting the US (he'll land soon after they go off air tonight).
1500	Kate and Craig go to an editorial meeting outside the newsroom with senior producers of other BBC news programmes. They share stories, running orders and treatments. The editor of one programme observes of the proposed 'authored piece' by a student (about the lecturers' pay dispute): 'It'll either be good, or compellingly terrible.' Kate confides to the meeting that Sophie Hutchinson's trip to Loughborough may be in vain: 'With everything else going on, that may be lost.'
1505	Ingo has finished filming faces. He packs his gear and leaves the newsroom.
1510	Abbie liaises with Sophie about the wording of the questions on the mock-up exam paper. She checks some of her facts with Dan Ashley at the AUT before getting back to the reporter to finalise the words, and explain the rostrum camera shot she has in mind. Each shot (panning from a screen on a calculator, with moving pictures on it, to the words on the exam paper) will last eight to ten seconds. Sophie will have to script to that length over the pictures.

1515	David Shukman arrives to cut his Porton Down piece. He chats with Ian Atkinson about which library shots they're using. It's a nuisance that the library pictures are on Beta, an outdated format.
1518	The editorial meeting breaks up. Craig and Kate return to the newsroom. A producer from the Six is talking to Abbie about using the shots from Loughborough.
1525	David Shukman chats to Kate about his piece. Abbie goes round to graphics to sort out the exam paper.
1545	Abbie and the graphics team are reviewing the rostrum camera shot. It's a computerised camera move, panning across a typical student's desk to an exam paper. She's delighted with the result.
1555	David Shukman and Ian Atkinson are ready to start editing. They're agreed that the upsound from the archive Ian found earlier will be a dramatic part of the piece.
1615	Special correspondent Gavin Hewitt calls in to say he has nearly finished editing his report on Oldham. It has been completed at his home on a portable editing system, because there wasn't an edit suite available at Television Centre.
1621	Guto Harri, the North American business correspondent, calls Kate from the US. America's biggest fraud trial – the Enron case – has just ended. He can do a live top and tail into his report. Kate decides to change the running order.
1630	Sophie's piece on the universities' pay dispute will include students and lecturers, but not the employers. Abbie is trying to fix up a spokesperson to give the universities' side of the pay dispute.
1700	Huw Edwards, presenter of the Ten, goes live on News 24, with his daily hour-long sequence. It is part of a BBC policy of putting well-known news presenters and correspondents on the 24-hour channel to increase its credibility and kudos. Edwards says he enjoys the extra responsibility, but it means his working day starts on the newsroom mezzanine – upstairs with News 24. He can't join the Ten O'Clock team till after six.
1730	Guto is editing a package for the Six about Enron. After this has been fed, he will have time to talk to the Ten about whether they want a different version.

1740	Chris goes up to the business unit to see Evan, to discuss the shape of his piece on pensions.
1745	Gavin Hewitt is on his way in to Television Centre, where the final touches will be applied to his report from Oldham.
1755	The team from the Ten switch the output of the screens on their desks to BBC1 for the Six. *The Rolec, the small screen on each desk, allows access to 18 TV channels, 20 radio stations, and news feeds from within the building, outside broadcasts, the Parliamentary studios at Millbank and foreign feeds.*
1800	The Six is on air. The team watch intently. Cameraman Ingo is back in the newsroom to set up for the filming of the Rubik's Cube champion Chris has found. She's an Australian expert living in London.
1810	Huw Edwards arrives at the Ten desk. He jokes with the team, takes a seat on the end of the desk opposite Kate, and logs on to ENPS, the news production system, to start looking at the running order. Enron has moved up to the second lead.
1825	Kate says Guto's piece on Enron was fine, but it needs a different emphasis in his live link: 'All we need to do is big up that it's the biggest trial in American corporate history.'
1829	Graphics call Chris and ask him to go and see them in 20 minutes about the Rubik's Cube pictures.
1830	Ian Atkinson returns to the newsroom from the edit suite. He says the Porton Down piece should be finished within the hour. Kate says: 'You can't go over on time. We're very stretched for time. Today is not the day to go over.'
1832	Guto calls from Houston, Texas. Kate says: 'We're just about to have our meeting. Can I call you back?' There's a 15-minute production meeting. Producer Ros Anstey has been monitoring the ITV News. They've headlined the story of an alleged Al Qaeda cell plotting to blow up the Ministry of Sound nightclub. Home Affairs correspondent Daniel Sandford has been covering it for the BBC, and has been trying to get permission to use audio of secret MI5 recordings of the gang. The way the ITV headline is written it suggests they have the audio already. Ros watches the ITV piece: 'It's actors' voices. They haven't even got it. Our lawyers said we mustn't use actors' voices. We could mislead the jury.'

1835  Chris Partridge and Rubik's Cube champion	The Rubik's Cube champion has arrived in reception and is ready to be filmed. On the way up to the newsroom, Kevin Bakhurst, until recently the editor of the Ten but now Controller of News 24, sees her playing with a cube. He's so impressed he wants her on the 24-hour channel as well as the Ten.
1838  Daniel Sandford	Daniel Sandford announces the judge has ruled the MI5 surveillance tapes from the anti-terrorism trial *can* be broadcast: 'I think that we'll have the audio before eight. What we can do is get the words ready before that.' The audio is quite indistinct, so there will be subtitles. Sandford is excited by the judge's ruling: 'It's a real first. We get to hear surveillance tapes during a trial. Evidence of MI5 listening to terrorism suspects is about as high octane as it gets.'
1845	The production meeting ends.
1848	Abbie returns from graphics and announces: 'The university piece is done. It's really good. I've just got to edit it.' Kate says: 'We're dropping the university story.' Abbie says: 'But the guy from the university is already on the train.' She's booked the vice-chancellor of Luton University to go to Millbank for an interview.
1850	Abbie rings the vice-chancellor's mobile. He doesn't answer. She leaves a voice message, explaining the story has been dropped. She then rings the producer and reporter to let them know Enron has taken their place in the running order: 'Sorry, Sophie. It's a big story.'

1900	Ros checks the Channel Four news at her desk. Will they have the surveillance audio? Daniel says: 'No, they won't have it. We'll be first with it.' Daniel and Ros start to write up the transcript for the subtitles. According to the judge's ruling, they have to be faithful to the context of the original. They're relying on the police producing a copy of the audio. Daniel says: 'We should get it, but we've got to have a back-up plan if it doesn't happen.'
1910 Gavin Hewitt	Gavin Hewitt arrives in the newsroom. He hands his tape to Emily. Daniel says to Ros: 'I don't know when to call the Yard. How often can you ring the Yard without upsetting them?'
1920	Daniel checks with the police: 'Have you got it yet?' He discusses logistics.
1924	Daniel is off the phone. He says to Ian Anderson: 'I think it's going to work, but I don't quite believe it.'
1934	Abbie is talking to Guto: 'Hallo, I'm looking after you tonight. I've not been around because I've been working on another item that's been dropped . . . Everything in hand? . . . Good.'
1945	Ros talks to Daniel about the logistics of getting the audio quickly, bypassing the normal procedures. They then prepare their script, stressing this is the first time during the course of a trial that they can broadcast what the jury heard in evidence.
1953	Abbie watches Guto's Six package to get up-to-speed. Kate has asked for some changes. He's going to recut it.
1955	David Shukman walks past Craig's office and tells him he's 'almost done'.
1957	The Rubik's Cube expert is on News 24. Huw arrives back in the newsroom with a hot supper from the nearby food bar. Huw resumes work on his scripts. He asks if the Shukman piece starts in vision. Nobody knows.

2003	Craig Oliver comes over to Kate's desk and checks in before he leaves for the night. He'll be available on his mobile and watching the programme from home. He checks with Huw and then calls out 'Goodbye' to the rest of the team. He's wearing fluorescent cycle clips, a cycle helmet and carrying a fluorescent waistcoat.
2015	David Shukman's piece is ready for air.
2040	The audio from Scotland Yard has arrived in the building. A CD has been delivered by despatch rider.
2055	Craig rings in from home to check that all is well. There's a brief discussion with Huw about the audio quality of the Scotland Yard material, and also about the running order.
2056	Craig rings off. Huw has written the link, and calls out to Daniel: 'The first line, Daniel. Does that do the job?' Daniel can read Huw's script on his own terminal.
2058	Huw reads his script out loud to himself to check it. Kate asks Abbie: 'Have you heard the latest on Enron?' Abbie replies: 'No, do you want me to check anything?'
2059	Craig rings Daniel to ask whether he thinks the terrorism story should be the lead. Daniel says: 'I think it's powerful. There's a man discussing blowing up your younger sister and laughing about it. I feel it's strong and unique. I've never heard of it before.' He reads Huw's top line to Craig. 'Huw, it's Craig on the flashing line.' Craig then speaks to Huw.
2104	Daniel says: 'I need to talk to the lawyers.' He's concerned about the possibility of contempt of court. He needs to ensure his script puts the surveillance audio in its proper context. He asks Kate: 'Is there a possibility of a two-way?' Kate responds: 'Only if we lead on it, and at the moment we are.'
2108	Daniel discusses with Kate and Huw the importance of the story and its implications. Huw reads his script out to Daniel to check it. Daniel speaks to staff lawyer Chris Hutchings on the phone, and reads him the script. Daniel says: 'It's absolutely amazing, groundbreaking stuff. Because we're probably going to lead on this, they want me to do a two-way in the studio. To what extent do we let the jury know this is unusual?'

	The lawyer's advice is that the script should not hint at questions of innocence or guilt. Daniel tells him: 'The rest of my piece is uncontentious. We've swapped some script around due to your earlier advice.' *The staff lawyer sits in the newsroom during the day, and is available on his mobile during the rest of his duty shift. There's 24-hour cover.*
2114	Kate takes a call from Craig. She puts the phone down and turns to Daniel: 'We're not going to lead with it. We'll go second. But I still want to do a two-way.'
2120	Abbie rings Guto: 'I just want to check how you're doing. What time do you think you'll file?' He hands over to the American producer Kari Browne. Abbie asks: 'Can you give me any Aston guides? Are they similar to the Six?' She gives an e-mail address to send the Astons to. 'So you think you'll file at five to ten? It won't be any later than that, will it?'
2135	Huw asks: 'Is this Horrocks' decision?' Kate: 'Yes.'
2139	Abbie says: 'My Astons have just arrived.' Kate calls Daniel, who's in Graphics: 'Can you come round so I can check your two-way?'
2140	Daniel arrives. He says: 'It's one question and it's around how unusual is this?' Kate says: 'You have one minute fifteen seconds.'
2144	Huw checks his scripts with the producers and makes final changes: 'OK, guys. Shall I go in?'
2146	Kate goes into the gallery. She's told Gavin Hewitt's piece is now ready.
2152	Huw discusses the exact wording of the headlines with studio director Ian Blandford. It is a paperless gallery. Huw is still logged on to ENPS in the newsroom, and someone has to log him off before he can access the studio PC. He rewrites the top of the programme – the pensions intro.
2155	Political Editor Nick Robinson is outside 10 Downing Street, but nobody can speak to him: 'Does anybody have a mobile number for Nick Robinson? We might need it for the clean feed to him.'

2158	Ian calls: 'Two minutes to air. Can we rehearse the headlines?'
2159	Rehearsal is complete. Ian says: 'Back to top. Thirty seconds to air. Here we go everyone. Have fun.'
2200	The programme is on air. There are five cameras in the studio, all operated by remote control, and one floor manager. The opening sequence includes the faces filmed earlier in the day projected on to the video wall. The opening piece about pensions by Evan Davis includes a recurring motif of a Rubik's Cube.
2203	Ian points out: 'We've got no microphone for Daniel Sandford. We've got three packages to sort it.'
2208	Nick Robinson reports from Number 10. He says the pensions crisis is *more* complicated than the Rubik's Cube, and explains why.
2211	As Daniel says a few words for sound level, the floor manager is lowering his chair, so that he's the same height as Huw in the studio. Producers walk in and out of the gallery, to be present when their item is broadcast. The programme runs smoothly. Guto Harri delivers an accomplished live from Houston. Gavin Hewitt's piece includes the mix through from him in Oldham during the riots to the same location now.

2230	During the six-minute regional opt-out, Huw is revising his closing headlines on the studio laptop. The director cues Huw three seconds early. For viewers around the country his first few words are cut off. The bulletin is also 30 seconds over.
2238	The phones are ringing in the newsroom. Some of the regions are unhappy. Kate is very apologetic. Huw remarks that the junction almost always goes smoothly and comments: 'The Welsh will forgive me.' He's in a good mood because he's about to go on holiday.
2239	Kate begins a debrief. She thanks Ian Atkinson for getting the Porton Down piece cut so quickly; the Guto piece had a strong top and tail: 'Thanks everyone.' Huw says: 'Thanks Kate, you can come again.'
2243	Craig rings Kate to offer feedback. She says: 'I think we slightly underestimated Enron. We could have said more in the heads, like "facing prison for 400 years" or something.' Huw says: 'I think pensions was the right lead. Most people watching would think it affects them, so it passes every relevance test we've got.' He picks up the goody bag he'd received at the BAFTA awards a few weeks before, and leaves for his holiday.

100–102 CENTURY FM

Century FM is a regional commercial radio station in the north-east of England, covering an area from the Scottish borders to North Yorkshire. It is owned by GCap Media, the company formed by the merger of GWR and the Capital Radio Group. Most of its output is play-listed pop music with hourly news bulletins and a half-hour news round-up at 5.30 on weekday evenings. There is a nightly football phone-in *The Three Legends* presented by three former stars of the region's top clubs, Newcastle United, Sunderland and Middlesbrough.

The station's six newsroom staff are based in Gateshead, just over the famous Tyne bridge from Newcastle. As well as Century's output, they are responsible for recorded bulletins on a series of digital stations, including Smooth, the Arrow and X-FM. This digital bulletin and a headlines sequence are also aired on DNN – the rolling news service on the digital multiplex. The recorded bulletins for the digital stations have to be timed to the second. The Century bulletins are more flexible in duration ranging from three minutes to a minimum of six minutes at 6 a.m. and 1 p.m. The newsroom can also break into programmes for a newsflash if a big story breaks.

The station has a news booth for recording the digital bulletin, and a separate news production studio, both adjoining the newsroom. Bulletins are read in the main studio, with the presenter driving the desk and playing in cuts (pieces of audio) and beds (music stings and pieces to play under the newsreader's voice).

Journalists also update a scrolling headlines ticker on the station's website.

0400

Rik Martin

GCap regional head of news Rik Martin comes on shift. He will prepare and read bulletins during the breakfast show, and then stay on station for most of the day running the news operation.

This morning he has had just a couple of hours' sleep because of a management meeting with GCap in London the previous day, which meant he didn't get home till after midnight. Rik comments: 'Weekends are for sleeping, I've found you can build up a sleep bank – your body equals out over a period of time.'

Rik started in radio at Trent FM in Nottingham in 1989, as a part-time runner on sports programmes. He was 14 years old. Now he says what he does is not a job: 'You do it because you love it.'

Century FM's first news bulletin of the day goes out live at 6 a.m. but he also has to write copy and read for the digital rolling news network DNN that runs from 6 a.m. until midnight. Rik's local news needs to be on the DNN server by 5.30 a.m. for the 6 a.m. transmission.

He logs on to the GCap intranet, checks his e-mails and the overnight file which should contain local stories, left from the day before. Unusually, there are none. All he has been left is the 'Issue' – a story which can provide a talking point for phone-ins and further coverage later in the day. It's a story about children being affected by the 'winter blues'. Rik decides it is too much like an earlier story they did on Seasonal Affective Disorder, and decides to look for another one.

The Issue is Century's way of meeting Ofcom's requirement for the station to provide challenging speech content. If the Issue is too 'soft', the station's bosses become concerned that they are not fulfilling their remit.

Rik comments: 'The Issue is a bit of a nightmare. You have to find one every day and be topical, but it has to appeal to our audience of mid-thirties mums. We've done heavy subjects like the death penalty and domestic violence, but the presenters are involved in this too and they find it hard to change gear.'

0415

Rik begins rewriting national stories from Independent Radio News to give them a local flavour. He comments: 'I very rarely use IRN copy as is – I give it a little bit of a twist. The UK desk in Leicester Square also rewrites copy for the group; you often see your top story locally break nationally the next day.'

The top story is about a British man who is facing extradition to the US accused of murdering his wife and baby. It's a running story and Rik has background knowledge which allows him to write 'Former York University student Neil Entwistle . . .'

There's a story too about library books. For the first time the romantic novelist Catherine Cookson is not among the top ten most-borrowed authors. Rik writes: 'We're falling out of love with north-east author Catherine Cookson . . .'

And the author who is now top of the list is localised with the phrase: 'Jacqueline Wilson, who opened the Centre for Children's Books in Newcastle last year . . .'

The sport gets similar treatment. Newcastle United are without a manager at the moment, so when it's reported that Alex McLeish is leaving Glasgow Rangers, Rik writes: 'What are the chances of him taking over at Saint James' Park?'

Century's reporters write their copy in a program called BiNG. It was the in-house system devised for Capital Radio. It has feeds of IRN copy, the Press Association and Sky News Radio. It calculates the duration of written stories and adds the length of any audio, so readers will know how long each story will be on transmission. There is an archive with a search facility, a group-wide contacts lists, and short-form keys to send and receive scripts and audio to and from other parts of the group, or publish a bulletin to the Web.

0440

Rik has started listening to IRN audio cuts on the *Brian* system on the computer next to him, before transferring them to the playout system.

Century has two audio systems – Brian which takes in the IRN audio cuts, and RCS where material is edited and played out. RCS handles all the station's songs, promos, advertising and jingles as well as news cuts. The system presents each separate item as a cartridge on a 'cartwall'. Tape cartridges were the favoured analogue way of playing in jingles, commercials and news cuts, so the computer system offers a graphic representation of a system that older broadcasters are familiar with. Each cart has its own serial number, and all the news material has the same prefix so it is kept together on the system.

Rik has identified a possible legal problem. The report of the extradition story includes audio of the District Attorney in Massachusetts and a clip of a 'family friend'. It is highly prejudicial and would be contempt of court in Britain. There is also no doubt that if Neil Entwistle were to be found not guilty he would have a *prima facie* case for libel. Rik decides to edit the IRN package.

0450	Rik listens to another IRN story – a survey on how people keep their children occupied on long car journeys. He decides this will make a better Issue for the day. It is not a particularly challenging topic, but Rik considers that the station can afford to be a bit more light-hearted today as it is a Friday and coming up to the weekend and half-term.
0500	Rik has nearly finished editing the Entwistle story. Breakfast presenters Scott Makin and Lisa Shaw have arrived to prepare their show.
0502	Rik starts to call the four police voice-banks that cover their area – North Yorkshire, Cleveland, Durham and Northumbria. He types the day's weather report as he listens to the recorded messages giving details of recent incidents. Rik doesn't have shorthand. There are only two stories filed at 04.30 – neither of them major – a road accident near Richmond where a car collided with a tree and police are appealing for witnesses, and a nightclub assault in York last Saturday night – six days ago. 'That's North Yorkshire police for you – it's *Heartbeat* country,' says Rick. The idea that a Saturday night assault should be news on a Friday morning amuses him, but in the absence of much else the story will make the bulletin.
0515	Rik has finished writing the copy from the voice-banks. It's the second time today he has checked them. The first time was on the way into work; he normally checks them as he drives in, to save time and to see what sort of day he is going to have. The numbers are programmed into his mobile and he has a hands-free kit in the car. He goes over to check with breakfast presenters Scott and Lisa that they are happy with the Issue being about keeping children happy in the car.
0525	Rik assembles the stories on his computer for the two-minute digital bulletin.
0530	Rik prints out his bulletin. He doesn't trust reading directly from the computer, in case it crashes: 'I've known too many people caught out by reading off screen.'

0532	Rik moves into the booth next to the newsroom to record the digital bulletin. A flawless two-minute read is followed by a separate 40-second headlines sequence, also delivered to the second without fluffs. There are two cuts in the longer bulletin – Rik's edit of the Entwistle material and a cut from the winner of a by-election in Dunfermline and West Fife.
0536	Back at his desk Rik loads the bulletin into the 'Play' file which means it will be transmitted automatically on digital stations across the north-east. He says: 'It's clever, but it's frightening, that you can actually run a radio station out of a box.'
0545	Rik moves to the news studio for some post-production and to load material into the playout system. Each cut will have a number, a title, a duration and out-words, the last words spoken on the cut. The same information appears on the cartwall and the reader's script. Rik has decided to add some music to the bulletin. There's a story about Britney Spears being photographed driving with her young child on her lap. Rik introduces it with the singer's hit 'Oops! . . . I Did It Again', manually riding the sound levels on a simple mixer desk while he reads the story. Then he mixes in Gary Numan's 'Cars' to link to the Issue of the day about keeping your children occupied in the car.
0550	Rik writes the 'tease' – the headline sequence which will begin the programme in ten minutes' time.
0556	Rik records the headline sequence in the news studio. The sequence is recorded, like the Britney Spears story earlier, to ensure levels of voice and background music don't clash.
0559	Rik walks upstairs to the main studio and sits at the mic opposite presenter Lisa Shaw.
0600	Rik goes on air with the first Century FM local bulletin of the day. Longer bulletins are branded 'The Way It Is', with their own jingles. The cuts (audio inserts) Rik prepared in the newsroom earlier are played in by Lisa. They include 'Tease' (the headline sequence with very short clips) and 'Britney and Issue'. Lisa also plays in the news 'beds' (musical themes chosen to suit the mood of the story being read). The final item is a light story about Barbie's boyfriend Ken being redesigned to have a more rugged appearance. Lisa and Rik banter on air about the new-look doll being modelled on her co-presenter Scott Makin.

0606	Rik comes off air and returns to the newsroom.
0610	Rik starts writing the sports bulletin for tx at 0630.
0612	The Digital News Network (DNN) bulletin Rik recorded earlier is just being aired and is monitored on a portable DAB radio next to the main newsdesk.
0613	A digest of the news bulletin on BBC Radio One appears on the information service from the group's UK News desk based at Leicester Square in London. Rik notes that their running order is similar to his own.
0615	Rik continues with the sports summary. He checks the football club websites – Newcastle United, Middlesbrough, Sunderland and Hartlepool.
0622	The IRN report about the Entwistle case (which Rik edited for legal reasons for his own bulletins) is being broadcast on DNN. Rik has no control over DNN output – the station is part-owned by several commercial radio companies. *DNN output 'sweeps' – or repeats – four times an hour. The idea is that anyone listening for 15 minutes will get a digest of the news. Century try to update their bulletins – the regional content – every couple of hours, or sooner if a story breaks.*
0624	Rik is still writing the 0630 bulletin. He checks the clock.
0626	Rik checks the clock again and listens to Scott and Lisa on output.
0627	Rik prints off the sports news. He leaves the newsroom and heads for the studio again.
0631	Rik is back in the studio to read the headlines and sport. There is no audio in the bulletin this time, although normally they would try to include at least one sports cut. He signs off: 'Century FM News, I'm Rik Martin. There's more at seven.'

0634	Rik collects the newspapers from reception. They've been pushed through the letterbox; reception isn't open until after half-past eight. There is a full set of national titles, plus *The Journal* (Today's Voice of the North) and *The Northern Echo* (County Durham's Great Daily). He checks the local papers first. Rik comments: 'I try and update DNN every two hours unless anything breaks. I'll next update just after seven – the 0730 headlines will be very much based on the 0630 headlines – therefore I should have more time after seven to update DNN.'
0650	An advisory note from the GCap UK News desk appears on Rik's screen: 'Please beware – some of the audio on the Entwistle case suggests his guilt.'
0652	Rik hears one of the 'guilty' cuts go out on DNN. Rik considers talking to the DNN editor and warning him of the legal problems with the cut.
0658	Rik prints off the script and checks it. He goes into the studio with a bulletin timed at 6'16" – a little too long for the time slot. He may decide to drop something while they are on air.
0701	The seven o'clock news starts a minute late. Timings are flexible within Century's programmes – unlike the digital slots which have to be timed to the precise second.
0706	The bulletin ends. It is more than a minute over the normal duration of three or four minutes. It included only one fresh local story – the six-day old assault in York last Saturday.
0708	Back in the newsroom, Rik takes calls from colleagues Ian Haslam and Dan Entwisle about the news agenda for the day.
0714	Scott and Lisa are taking their first phone call on the Issue of the day – Martin, a security guard, is explaining his family's version of the TV show *Countdown* using car number plates.
0718	Rik hears himself on DNN and decides the bulletin needs updating, but says he'll have to do it after 7.30.
0720	Rik edits down his script for the front page of the website. He takes out any audio references. It was last updated at nine last night.

0724	Rik tries to upload the script-only bulletin to the website. It should be a simple matter of pressing Control W on his keyboard but there seems to be a problem with the server.
0726	He prints off his script and listens off air.
0730	Rik is back in the studio. Reporter Anne Garrick arrives in the newsroom. Before she has had time to take her coat off, the phone rings and she answers it. It's not a call for the newsroom; the caller wants the studio number.
0735	Rik is back in the newsroom.
0740	Another update of DNN. Rik freshens up the audio on the stories. He uses the Harry Smith clip on Entwistle and an alternate clip of the Lib Dem's Willie Rennie.
0748	Rik sends his DNN bulletin to the server – it should get there for 8 a.m. He changes the audio cuts on the Issue about car games; he puts in local chap Martin, the security guard who rang in earlier, instead of the cockney voice that came from IRN.
0752	Rik tries and fails to update the website again. It's still reading the same as nine o'clock last night.
0753	Anne goes into the DNN studio to read an updated DNN bulletin. Rik goes into the small booth off the newsroom to mix the new audio for the car games item.
0754	Rik comes out of the booth and rechecks and updates his script. He puts the new cut on car games into the system to be played during the bulletin at eight.
0757	Rik prints his script off and goes up to the studio.

0801	The bulletin starts late, but it's a flawless read.
0802	Reporter Charlotte Foster arrives in the newsroom. She picks up the Marantz audio recorder and checks it's working. She's on her way to cover Sunderland manager Mick McCarthy's press conference. Sunderland are bottom of the league and heading for relegation. He doesn't know it, but McCarthy is in his final weeks in the job.
0811	Charlotte leaves the newsroom in Rik's company car, which doubles as a news car. On the road, she'll listen to Century's rival Metro radio to see what stories they have.
0812	Rik checks the voice banks again. Anne hears her DNN radio read on air.
0815	Anne and Rik start their handover. Rik is still 'on desk' so he is sitting at the newsdesk next to the operational computer where the cuts are prepared. They discuss the legal issues surrounding the Entwistle story. Anne asks: 'What standpoint are we taking?' 'We're taking the normal standpoint. The Americans are so blatant – you'll say: "Hey, hang on there!"' The handover continues. Anne asks: 'Have you run the Britney one to death?'
0827	Rik prints off the headlines. He goes to the studio and Anne continues to update the scripts.
0829	Anne moves across to where Rik has been sitting to take over on desk. Rik goes on air.
0833	Rik returns to the newsroom and sits at the workstation where Anne had been sitting. They resume their discussion about Entwistle, and Rik helps Anne with the legal wording for the script. *Rik explains: 'I think it's right that we change the newsreader with every show. You've been at the desk for four hours, and then the new newsreader comes on desk and suggests leading with a new story, because they are fresher and have a fresh eye. You've been leading with the same story all morning, and you've been head down, and possibly missed the fact that your lead shouldn't be the lead any more.'*

0836	Anne checks the police voice-bank. She checks with Rik it is OK to drop one of the stories.
	Charlotte arrives at the Sunderland training ground, The Academy of Light, on South Tyneside.
0840	Rik checks Century's website. The front page now has today's news on it.
0844	Anne checks the voice-banks again.
0845	Anne checks the sport stories with Rik.
0846	Anne checks with Rik about what stories to drop. They drop the Freddy Laker story and the broken leg story. Rik suggests they keep the Corrie story for the next hour or so.
0848	Rik asks: 'Is there a statue for Catherine Cookson or a street or a roundabout named after her in the area? There are loads of fluffy stories around this morning by the way.'
	He picks up one of the papers and starts reading.
0854	Charlotte rings the newsroom from Rik's mobile. The oil warning light is on in Rik's car. He tells her not to worry.
	Anne prints her script.
0855	Anne checks the pronunciation of Joe Flaghterley's name with Rik. Rik is on the phone researching the local angle on the Catherine Cookson story.
0857	Anne goes up to the studio. Mick McCarthy's news conference is under way. He's doing television interviews first in a separate room. The sound is relayed to the waiting print and radio media in the main conference room. The manager is unhappy about reports suggesting he's fallen out with the chairman. He says his comments were taken out of context.
0858	Rik answers the newsroom phone. It is the local library. They're returning Rik's earlier call. Rik asks if they are free to do an interview, but they're not available when Rik wants to do it.

0901	Anne Garrick takes over from Rik as newsreader and goes on air. The story off the voice-bank of a missing teenager goes out for the first time. Anne personalises the car games story by saying her favourite car game used to be 'Dr Bob's Monkey'. She makes a slight fluff reading the sport.
0906	Anne comes off air. Mick McCarthy comes into the press conference room and three radio reporters surround him. Charlotte is at the front of the desk with her arm stretched over the desk. He says hello to her. All the questions are asked by BBC Radio Newcastle's Nick Barnes. The third reporter is Sun FM's Stephen McCabe. BBC Five Live's Peter Slater is there too, but he's waiting for a one-to-one interview with the manager.
0908	Anne is back in the newsroom. She explains: 'A lot of things will change now in the next hour – new press releases will come in, the mood changes, people are now getting to work and so it is a good opportunity to freshen the bulletin up'.
0910	Steve Close from Century's promotions team arrives for a quick chat with Rik, letting him know about a quit smoking campaign they are planning to run next week to coincide with the House of Commons debate. Steve tells Rik he has contacts for speakers if Rik wants.
0916	McCarthy has finished his radio interviews. Broadcasters are asked to leave while print journalists ask their own questions. BBC Radio Five Live's Peter Slater leaves with the other radio reporters, even though he has not yet recorded anything. He checks his MiniDisc recorder. He'll be the only reporter at the press conference to get an exclusive interview.

Peter Slater checks his MiniDisc

0923	Charlotte takes a call from the newsroom. Rik wants her to go to South Shields for reaction to the Catherine Cookson story.

0924	Anne checks the voice-banks. She then starts cutting a voice piece on gossip about Madonna being apart from her husband. Anne explains that they may decide not to cover a showbiz story if the artist's music is not played by the station. But even though they don't play Babyshambles' music, they would do a story on singer Pete Doherty because listeners know him from the tabloid papers.
0925	Rik continues to chase someone from a local library to comment on Catherine Cookson. He locates someone on the phone willing to comment and transfers the call through to the small newsroom studio. He goes into the studio and records an interview. Anne continues to update and rewrite the script for 10 a.m. There are no headlines at 9.30 – the next half-hour headlines are at half-past four.
0942	Anne checks the local geography. She needs to know if Easington is big enough to name on its own or should she put the county in the script. Rik checks the cut he's just recorded and writes a script to wrap round it for the 10 o'clock bulletin.
0945	Charlotte and the other radio reporters are interviewing Sunderland player Danny Collins in what's described in a sign on the door as a television studio. It has noisy air-conditioning and the reporters have to work with their mics close to his mouth.
0947	Anne checks the voice-banks. She double-checks with Rik the location of a road accident.
0953	Anne checks the voice-banks again. 'I normally check the voice-banks at least twice between 9 and 10 – a lot usually happens during that hour.'
0955	Anne prints off the script and checks her cuts with the script. 'I check it 20 times,' she laughs.
0957	Anne leaves the newsroom for the studio clutching her script. Charlotte checks in with Rik. He suggests she visits some warden-controlled flats called Catherine Cookson Court: 'I want some good local reaction.'

1000	Anne reads the ten o'clock bulletin.
1005	Anne comes off air.
1015	Charlotte arrives at Catherine Cookson Court. There's nobody around. A sign says 'Private property. No entry.' An elderly resident appears and explains that the warden is on holiday. She calls Rik but he's not available, so she decides to try elsewhere.
1017	A call comes in to the newsdesk to say that the ISDN line is ready from Radio Lincoln. Rik goes into the small newsroom studio to do an interview with the marketing manager at a well-known florists. It's a pre-record for an item for Valentine's Day the following week.
1020	Journalist Ian Haslam arrives in the newsroom to start his shift.
1026	Rik comes out of the studio and is told Charlotte needs him to call her.
1028	Charlotte has just parked outside the central library when Rik calls back. He wants the Cookson vox and another about the Issue: 'Knock off a vox for kids in a car and a Catherine Cookson vox – but not the same people.'
1042	Rik and Ian discuss yesterday: 'You missed the busiest day of the year yesterday . . .' Anne checks the voice-banks.
1043	Anne chats with Rik about getting interviews on a missing girl story from the police voice-bank: 'There's a press conference at 10.30 so nothing will be available yet.' She asks if they should still be leading with the Entwistle story. There is nothing else. He says: 'He's due in court this morning so it will change.' She checks on the Group computer to see what time Entwistle is in court. 'They don't know either,' she tells Rik.

1044	Charlotte is in the car and on her way back to base. She's had no trouble getting vox-pops – she approached people in queues for a bus and at a bank's cash machine.
1050	Journalist Dan Entwisle arrives in the newsroom for his shift.
1056	Anne prints off her script and checks the cuts with her script very carefully. She leaves the newsroom and heads for the studio.
1059	Anne goes on air slightly early with the 11 o'clock news.
1103	Rik takes part in the regular Group conference call with other news editors around the country. He runs through his stories.
1105	Ian takes over the newsdesk. Rik continues his conference call and is asked what packages Century are doing. One by one the news editors explain their stories. This is an opportunity for them to share and pool stories. Beacon Radio mention that they have some fresh audio from Glen Hoddle. Rik says he'd like to use that.
1113	The conference call ends.
1115	Rik asks Anne to check with the police about the missing girl.

1116	Charlotte has returned, but there's no room in the station's tiny car park, or the parking bay at the front of the station. She leaves the car on the road.
1117	Anne hands over to Ian. Ian checks the voice-banks.
1125	Charlotte plays back her audio to record it into the system. Anne will edit the voxes. Charlotte has 7 minutes 55 seconds of McCarthy and a little bit less of Danny Collins.
1127	The TV in the corner of the newsroom is tuned to Sky News with the sound down. They turn the sound up when they realise there is breaking news on the Entwistle case. Entwistle has agreed to be extradited to the US. They turn the IRN live link up to hear the IRN audio.
1140	Dan and Rik discuss the stories from the local paper.
1142	They notice on Sky that Entwistle's lawyer is giving a statement. IRN had pulled the plug on the audio feed and missed the very beginning of the statement. The statement finishes and the lawyer answers reporters' questions.
1145 Dan Entwisle	Dan starts to research a story from the local paper about Newcastle being voted top of the league by bosses and makes a few calls.
1148 Ian Haslam	Ian cuts the IRN feed of the lawyer's statement and plays the cut to Rik, who says: 'How long have we got? I'll wrap around it.' Ian: 'Can you do it?' Rik: 'Yeh, I can do that.' Ian checks the voice-banks.

1152	Charlotte checks with Rik about the cue for the Mick McCarthy cut. Ian checks the inserts and cuts, including the Hoddle cut from Beacon Radio.
1154	Ian continues his ring round the voice-banks.
1155	The McCarthy story is nearly ready. The link reads: 'Sunderland boss Mick McCarthy has spoken to the press for the first time since his apparent war of words with chairman Bob Murray.'
1157	Cleveland Police ring for Anne. They can do an interview about the missing girl. Rik finishes writing his script on Entwistle.
1158	Ian gets the cuts ready for Rik's script: 'Which way round do you want the two clips?' Rik prints his script off.
1159	Ian runs to studio 1 to read the 12 o'clock bulletin. Rik follows. Sky News has a breaking story – a judge has refused an application for a private prosecution of the entertainer Michael Barrymore over the death of a man in his swimming pool.
1201	Rik reads his Entwistle script live on air. Dan starts the ROT [record off transmission] but misses the very beginning of the bulletin.
1203	IRN 'snaps' the Barrymore story. Dan Entwisle races to the studio and hands the copy to Ian.
1206	'And some news just in . . .' Ian reads the Barrymore story on air.
1210	Terry Lubbock, the father of Stuart Lubbock who died in Barrymore's pool, is live on Sky News.

1215	Anne tells Ian she has a long 35-second cut of an interview with the police about the missing girl. Ian says it's too long for a bulletin, but if it's good and can sustain it, that's OK. Justin King, Head of Group News, rings for Rik but he's still in the studio.
1220	Dan goes into the DNN studio to record the interview he set up earlier about Newcastle being voted top of the league by bosses.
1221	Anne has cut the Cookson voxes. She'll have the Issue voxes ready by one o'clock. Rik plans to alternate the two stories in future bulletins. Rik asks Charlotte to update DNN.
1230 Fran Read with Comrex	Late reporter Fran Read comes on shift.
1234	Ian checks the voice-banks.
1236	Charlotte Foster goes into the DNN studio to record the updated digital bulletin.
1247	Charlotte sends her bulletin to DNN from a PC in the newsroom. It's taken her several takes to get the timing right.
1249 	Ian prints his script off and checks the cuts with the script.

1250	Rik comes off the phone from Justin King. He announces to his team: 'Make sure you send the right script to the right slot. We had an incident yesterday where we sent the headlines to the news slot and we were very short.'
1252	Rik goes into the small newsroom studio to record and mix a package on Entwistle for the one o'clock bulletin. They pre-record the tease and opening.
1258	Ian leaves the newsroom for the studio.
1300	Ian goes on air with the lunchtime bulletin. It is a 10-minute programme that allows for more packages. They use their own interview with Cleveland police about the missing girl, an IRN package on kissing, and then play a Catherine Cookson package Charlotte has worked on, and the car games package.
1310	Ian comes off air and returns to the newsroom.
1324	Ian rewrites and updates the scripts and checks the cuts.
1348	Ian asks Rik to voice up the Entwistle story. Rik goes into the studio.
1351	Rik comes out of the studio and tells Ian the number entry for the newly voiced Entwistle cut on the system. Ian takes the cut and puts it into his script for the two o'clock bulletin.
1400	Ian leaves the newsroom for the studio.
1402	Ian goes on air.
1409	Ian is back in the newsroom. Anne asks Rik for some help downloading off the Internet in the newsroom studio.

1411	Charlotte is about to take over at the newsdesk, and asks Ian for a handover. They discuss how many times some of the stories have been used and what should be dropped.
1419	Charlotte goes on to the local BBC website to see what is on other networks.
1426	Rik asks Dan what packages he is planning for the five o'clock bulletin. Dan explains: 'I like to have something that resembles a programme at this stage, lots of material, and then I'll go and listen to what I've got and then decide what I'll keep and what I'll chuck out. I don't like to put padding in. Every story should be in there on merit so I don't like chucking anything out.'
1430	Dan discusses with Ian how long he wants his sport report to be.
1436	Ian asks Charlotte to check the fixtures for tomorrow. There is some confusion over when Sunderland are playing. Their list, published in the *Sun* last August, says Sunderland are playing Spurs on the 11th, tomorrow (Saturday), but Mick McCarthy this morning said it was Sunday 12th – Charlotte suggests Ian checks on the website.
1440	Rik checks the prospects for next week. He needs to find an Issue of the day for Monday.
1447	Charlotte checks the voice-banks.
1452	Charlotte finishes updating the website and prints off the script for three o'clock.
1454	Charlotte checks the cuts with her script. And leaves for the studio.
1500	Charlotte goes on air. The top story is Rik's Entwistle piece, a package with three cuts. The next story is a new cut on the missing girl. The new cut is a separate part of the police interview Anne recorded earlier in the day.
1503	Charlotte stumbles over her read on air. She laughs and says: 'I'll have to restart that again.'

1506	'I'm Charlotte Foster. That's Century FM News.' Charlotte comes off air.
1513	Charlotte is back in the newsroom, and she answers calls and checks stories. The Sky News strap has breaking news. Entwistle has told police he didn't murder his wife and small daughter. Charlotte checks with other sources. She checks PA and the local BBC website, and keeps an eye on the TV monitor.
1523	Charlotte asks Ian to do a wrap for the four o'clock bulletin on Entwistle.
1535	Anne has now finished her two-minute package on Catherine Cookson.
1545	Fran updates DNN.
1550	Charlotte checks the voice-banks.
1555	Charlotte prints off her script and checks the cuts against her script. Ian comes out of the studio after voicing the new Entwistle package.
1558	Charlotte goes up to Studio 1.
1600	Charlotte goes on air with the four o'clock bulletin.
1610	Rik leaves the newsroom for home at the end of a 12-hour day. 'People question my loyalty and hard work for a radio station. They say: "They'll buy you a wreath for your funeral and that's about all." But they don't understand. It's not a job. You do it because you love it.'

BBC NEWS 24

BBC News 24 is the BBC's 24-hour rolling news television channel. It shares some output with the BBC TV channel BBC1. Most of *Breakfast News*, the *One O'Clock News*, *Six O'Clock News* and *Ten O'Clock News* are simulcast – shown at the same time – on BBC1 and News 24. News 24 offers signing for the hearing impaired during the lunchtime bulletin, and can provide a separate service if there is a pre-planned live event, an unexpected breaking news story, or if the *Ten O'Clock News* is late because of a live football match over-running. In 2006 it was named Best News Channel by the Royal Television Society. This RTS Award had previously been dominated by Sky News. Unlike Sky News, reporters and correspondents appearing on News 24 are not all working exclusively for the channel. Most are part of the BBC Newsgathering operation with commitment to other outlets, including the main bulletins on BBC1, BBC World, Radio 4's news programmes, Radio Five Live and the BBC World Service.

0630

Simon Waldman

BBC News 24 is sharing output with BBC Breakfast News, presented by Dermot Murnaghan and Sian Williams. News 24's Editor Simon Waldman comes on shift. His Assistant Editor Marion Fountayne has been in since 6 a.m. preparing the early prospects. Her list of stories to cover includes a House of Lords ruling on divorce law, the start of a five-week knives amnesty by the police, the announcement of the shortlist of towns that might be chosen for Britain's first super-casino, the news from the World Health Organisation that six Indonesians have died from bird flu, and an interview with Sir David Attenborough on climate change. Marion knows that Sir David, the television wildlife presenter, is to appear live on Breakfast News. The prospects ask: 'Can he come to us afterwards?'

0715

The prospects meeting is under way. Twenty-three people gather around the production desks or perch on the low windowsills of the curved building to discuss the day's news agenda. Simon starts the meeting with a few 'parish notices' – operational details on the day – and hands to Marion. The divorce ruling is due at 9.45, with reporter Claire Marshall outside awaiting the verdict. There are judgments on two separate cases – the Millers and the McFarlanes, both wealthy couples. The suggestion is that the Law Lords could penalise the husband in one case for his adultery – and so end the long-established principle of 'no-blame' divorces, potentially affecting thousands of people. There's a suggestion that the EV, or 'early voice' reporter, should package the material that comes in.

Simon wants to make the story accessible to the widest possible audience and suggests that they 'number crunch and work out how many people are involved' and 'get Joshua down there'.

Joshua Rozenberg is the Daily Telegraph's *legal affairs correspondent, who used to work for the BBC. Simon believes he is the best in the business at unravelling legal jargon, and jokes: 'We get him on air more often now than when he worked for the BBC.'*

The knives amnesty story may include a package by Home Affairs Correspondent Andy Tighe and a studio discussion. Reporters are live in Birmingham and Blackpool to respond to the casino announcement.

Andy Tighe

0730	As Marion asks for further suggestions, Emma Brannam, the news interactive presenter, says: 'There's something going off in Manchester. There's a drop on the wires – six people arrested. Five hundred police involved.' Home news organiser Helen Miller adds: 'We've got something from Birmingham. Something went off overnight. Someone rang up with footage from their mobile.' Simon says: 'We'd better stick somebody on the terror stuff.' Among other stories discussed is a report that the Bishop of Cheltenham is stranded in a remote part of Africa, after the Archbishop of Kenya withdrew his hospitality. The Kenyan Christians objected to the British bishop's liberal views on homosexuality. Can the bishop be contacted on a mobile phone?
0735	The meeting breaks up, and Simon and Marion review how they're going to cover the breaking story.
0745	The discussion centres on moving the truck (satellite link) in Birmingham. Should they leave the casino story (correspondent Philippa Thomas is at a Birmingham casino) to chase the terrorism arrests in the Small Heath area of the city? Simon checks Sky News and sees that both they and Breakfast News have flashed eight arrests. *Simon observes: 'Maybe it's not as big as we thought. Just eight arrested. But 500 police were involved. It's a newer story. It's a breaking story, and if we have to, we can do the casino "as-live".'* Simon decides to send the truck to Small Heath for the start of the programme at 8.30, but doesn't know if the Midlands correspondent Rajesh Mirchandani will be there in time. He tells Marion and Helen: 'It's touch and go if the truck will be there.'
0750	Simon is told that Security Correspondent Gordon Corera can do a phone from home. He just needs to do some calls to get background. He has 40 minutes. Home Editor Mark Easton has been catching up on the story already and is in the building. Simon says he'd prefer to do Easton on set rather than Corera on the phone.

0755	In the middle of discussing with Marion how they're going to approach the half-heads (the half-hour headlines at 8.30) Simon rings Breakfast News to ask what they're doing before the opt-out at 8.30.
0758	Simon leaves for the regular 8 a.m. meeting with Newsgathering and the network TV bulletins.
0805	Presenter Julian Worricker is checking the number of arrests in the anti-terrorism raids and briefing himself on any background he can find on the wires.

Julian Worricker

0815	Simon returns from his meeting with a coffee, fully briefed about what the rest of the BBC's TV news outlets are covering, and with a clearer idea of how they can share resources.
0825	Simon arrives in the gallery. Director and vision mixer Roger Webster and senior broadcast journalist Tanya Hines are already there. The presenters Julian Worricker and Carrie Gracie are in the studio. Simon tells them via talkback that they'll have to ad lib while they get the guest in. Roger says he wants the guest, Mark Easton, on the seat next to Julian.

Roger says the role of director on News 24 has become more complex (and more stressful) as the channel has grown in confidence. He's assisted by automatic counts on VT packages (a recorded voice counts down to the 'out' and to Astons – graphics used to name people on screen), but has to count out of the live sections of the programme himself. He directs, vision mixes and operates the remote cameras in the studio. He says: 'When News 24 was first launched, the shots stayed the same, but now the shots are more ambitious, more people are watching. The role is very complicated.'

News 24 is sub-titled. This is now done 'out of house' and the technology enables the process to take place hundreds of miles away. Aine Aughney-Macdonald (pictured below) has been doing the sub-titles for BBC News for over six years. She lives in rural Ireland and does the early morning News 24 shift from her home. The equipment she uses is very different from a normal keyboard.

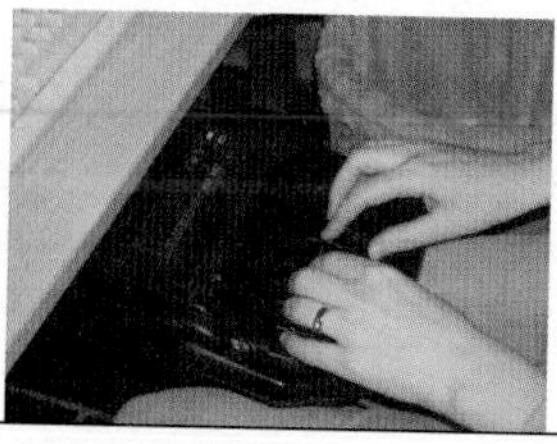

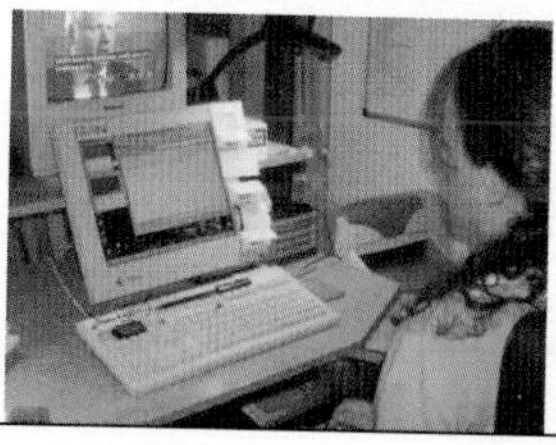

0830	News 24 goes live. The strap reads 'Breaking News' and 'Terror Raids'. Julian introduces Carrie and himself. She reads an OOV (out of vision read) over pictures from Manchester, about the terrorism arrests. Julian introduces and interviews Mark Easton in the studio. He explains that the arrests are believed to be linked to the plotting of terrorism overseas.
	Simon has a talkback unit in the gallery and a telephone, which means he can speak to the presenters and floor manager, his team outside in the newsroom and other parts of the BBC. He's told that Frances Lawrence, the widow of Philip Lawrence, the London head teacher who was stabbed to death outside his school, is available for the studio discussion on knife crime. She's already been on Breakfast News. News 24 asked them to see if she'd stay on for another studio spot.
0834	Carrie links to North of England correspondent Mark Simpson, who's live in Manchester at the scene of one of the anti-terrorism raids. He explains that 500 police officers from at least five forces were involved.
	Roger, on talkback, asks the floor manager if the two guests have arrived for the knives 'disco', and suggests they should be brought into the studio during the summary. The presenters ask whether they should both ask questions, and it is decided that they should.
0839	Frances Lawrence and Shaun Bailey, a community worker, discuss the knives amnesty.
	On the banks of monitors in front of them, everyone in the gallery can see their own output and other channels, including Sky News, BBC World and incoming domestic and international video feeds.
	Simon notices the former Iraqi Deputy Prime Minister Tariq Aziz on one of the screens, and rings BBC World to ask if they're going to be translating what he's saying: 'A minute would be lovely for us.'
	Declan Curry, the business reporter, is on another monitor at the London Stock Exchange. He can hear gallery talkback, realises how busy the programme is, and offers to cut a minute off the business report. The gallery declines the offer.
0843	Thirty seconds after he'd offered to cut back his report, Declan is on air. The report includes an interview about pensions with financial planning expert Christine Ross.
0846	The 'quarters', the headlines on the quarter hour, include the terror arrests, divorce and the knife amnesty. There's more on the arrests with the presenters ad libbing over live pictures from Moss Side in Manchester, and the news that Cleveland police have confirmed a house in Middlesbrough was among those raided.
	Paul Grey, the senior duty editor from sports news, arrives in the gallery to supervise the sports bulletin. Simon has left the gallery to liaise with Breakfast News. Both networks have news bulletins on the hour and both want live contributions from correspondents on location for the main story.

0848	Sports presenter Dan Walker starts with the news that Michael Owen will captain an England 'B' side playing Belarus tomorrow.
	Simon returns to the gallery and announces: 'Breakfast will do Manchester at the top and we'll do Birmingham.' He comments on the Michael Owen interview, which came from a much-publicised visit the previous day by England players to Wembley Stadium: 'Not too much of this later in the day. The pictures say yesterday.'
	Paul Grey says: 'We'll just do it this morning.'
0851	Word comes through to the gallery from the newsroom that the Metropolitan Police's anti-terrorist squad have been involved in the overnight raids. Simon says: 'That ups the ante a bit. We'll do a new line on the Met now.' Simon speaks to the presenters on talkback. After sport has reviewed the newspaper back pages, Julian will say, 'More from inside the papers in a moment . . .' and go straight to the breaking line about the Met.
	Seconds later, Julian links to the breaking news with an almost verbatim repeat of Simon's words: 'More from the papers in a moment . . .'
	The on-screen strap reads 'TERROR RAIDS Met anti-terrorist squad involved.'
0853	The paper review resumes with a mention of Sir David Attenborough who's on the front of *The Independent*, and trails his appearance on News 24 at 0915.
0855	The Birmingham pictures appear on a monitor for the first time. The reporter is Phil Mackie (not Rajesh Mirchandani). Simon speaks to him: 'It's News 24 here. It's going to be a bit rock'n'roll, Phil, 'cos we'll have a bit of you and a bit of Mark. I heard you talking to Mr and Mrs Cameraman. Any pointing and hand-waving you do, we love all that.'
0856	Simon tells the presenters: 'Tease Birmingham before the weather.' Phil leaves the camera position temporarily.
	The director cuts to the live shot from Birmingham.
	Carrie says: 'Let's take a look at what's been happening in Birmingham . . .'
0858	During the weather report, Simon and Roger decide how the top of the hour will look. Roger's still calling the shots ('one minute on weather', 'one-thirty to headlines, everybody'), and others in the gallery offer encouragement: 'Going very well, Rog.'
	Tanya is told by the crew in Manchester that one of the sequences of shots from Moss Side can't be used because it shows a 'sensitive' number plate. She deletes it from the system and chooses another sequence.
0900	Simon tries to help Roger through the complicated headline sequence. As the presenters appear back in vision, he chips in: 'Well done, Rog.'
	Julian says: 'This is the scene in Manchester . . .' and the OOV is followed by a 'double box', a split-screen effect with the reporters in Manchester and Birmingham side by side. Mark Simpson is clearly talking (he's already being interviewed down the line by Breakfast News on BBC1); Phil Mackie stands still ('a listening shot') as he waits to talk to News 24. Mark Easton is in the studio, and he's interviewed first.

0902 LIVE BIRMINGHAM BBC NEWS 24 09:03 TERROR RAIDS	When Phil responds to his question from the studio, he points down the road and the cameraman zooms in to a house raided by the police.
0906	Simon talks to Phil. He's already asked the reporter: 'Can you do us at 9.30?' and adds: 'Anyone you would normally vox-pop and can string two words together, get them ready to be live.' Simon comments: 'Do we know what's happened? Not really. A lot of speculation, but hey, it looks good. This is going very well.'
0908	There's relief from the breaking story as the preview package on the divorce ruling runs. Simon leaves the gallery to get the latest from Mark Easton, who's been keeping on top of the terrorism story in between live studio spots.
0910 Tanya Hines	Off the back of the divorce package, there's a live with reporter Ben Ando outside the Houses of Parliament where the Law Lords will soon deliver their verdict. In the gallery, Tanya says: 'We'll do latest pics from Birmingham for ad libs after quarters.' Sir David is in the studio and getting his mic on. Roger suggests: 'Before the quarters, can we tease David sitting on set?' Tanya notices a spelling mistake on a cricket caption and changes it.
0916 BBC NEWS 24 CLIMATE CHANGE 09:21 David Attenborough speaks out HEADLINES BBC THE JUDGEMENTS CONCERN WHAT FACTORS	The quarters include an ad lib over Birmingham pictures. They're followed by a VT promo of Sir David's climate change programme, and his interview. He's already been on Radio 4's *Today* programme, Five Live and Breakfast News. Tanya tells the presenters: 'Plenty of time for this.'
0923	'Let's leave this and go to breaking news. There's been a ninth arrest. Eight in Greater Manchester and one in Merseyside.' Tanya advises the presenters to be careful about the wording. The arrests were led by Greater Manchester police, but they are not necessarily in the Manchester area.

0928	The presenters ad lib over the latest Birmingham pictures. As the programme cuts to the weather, Simon tells the gallery: 'That was a good half hour, wasn't it?' Tanya is checking whether reporter Claire Marshall, who's at Westminster for the divorce story, has a guest with her. There is no guest, so she tells the presenters and gallery: 'Claire Marshall is a DTL, not a throw.' *DTL is short for 'down-the-line' – a two-way. A 'throw' is a live report with the studio 'throwing' to the location reporter, who then delivers a self-contained report, usually with an interviewee and with no input from the presenters. The gallery will remind the reporter about timings.*
0931	The DTL with Claire Marshall is under way. Simon tells Carrie: 'Mention the Miller case again, and we can bring in the stills.' He checks with Tanya that the picture in the preview monitor is definitely the Millers. Carrie's next question begins: 'As we were saying, Claire, this Miller case is . . .' The picture of the Millers appears in a box next to the reporter.
0934	Julian links to the casinos story. The announcement is previewed with a package that has already been used on Breakfast News. Philippa Thomas' live contribution from Birmingham has been delayed while the truck is in Small Heath for the terror raids. Roger talks to Declan at the Stock Exchange advising him they'll be coming to him in four minutes.
0937	There's a live interview in the studio with Anthony Jennens, of the charity GamCare, about the dangers of gambling. 'Coming to you, Declan, live off the back of this interview.'
0941	Declan is live. Tanya has noticed some activity on the monitor of the Westminster camera: 'Who is that getting into screen?' Before she can find out, Roger asks Tanya if Declan is running up to the quarters. 'Yes, because there's no sport yet. Shall I give them a ring?' She calls and is told they're on their way.
0946	Sport goes live. Roger asks: 'Have we got anyone to cover this Lords thing?' They have a choice of taking the live feed from inside the House of Lords and risking a lengthy announcement in legal jargon, or they can use reporter Claire Marshall to interpret the information. Simon listens across the feed from inside the House. Tanya speaks to Claire and confirms they'll come to her after the ruling.

0951

Julian OOVs the pictures from the Lords. He says: 'That's the scene now inside the House of Lords where a decision is expected in a few moments . . . they don't just stand up and give a neat and tidy press conference for the likes of us . . . let's just dip into what's being said.'

The live feed is confusing. Each Law Lord stands in turn to give the reasons for his ruling.

Simon, listening to the feed on headphones, says: 'They've dismissed the first and allowed the second. I don't know what that means.'

Simon quickly works out that the winners in both cases have been the ex-wives and tells the presenters. Glancing at the monitor, he observes: 'Sky have messed up. We didn't.'

Simon tells Tanya: 'You need to brief Claire – she can't hear,' and then calls for quiet as he listens to the Law Lords.

Simon later comments: 'I probably didn't know as much as I should have done about the details of both divorce cases. Our job is to simplify and clarify. We spend a lot of time interpreting complicated stories.'

0955

Simon says: 'Lose the pictures of the Lords and we'll go straight to Claire.'

Claire Marshall, underneath a canopy outside the Lords in pouring rain, talks to a family lawyer for interpretation of the verdict.

Just a few feet from the News 24 set, broadcast journalist Tory Milne and freelance presenter Emma Brannam are preparing the short bulletins for the BBC Interactive services, on satellite, Freeview and broadband. Their summaries are updated regularly, with new stories and updates slotted into the sequence whenever they break. The bulletins are recorded in a tiny virtual studio in another part of the building. With the aid of blue-screen it looks as if Emma is reading the news from the News 24 set.

Tory Milne

Emma in the virtual studio

0958

During the weather, there's a change of director. Roger is replaced by Gordon Findlay.

1001

The Security Correspondent Gordon Corera is live in the studio. Rajesh, the Midlands Correspondent, is now at the Birmingham live point.

1003 	Rajesh is on air off the back of Gordon's interview. During Rajesh's two-way, Tanya sees some people on a monitor emerging from the entrance to the House of Lords. Simon asks: 'Who are they?' Tanya explains that it's Julia McFarlane and her solicitor. The solicitor, James Pirrie, has agreed to talk to the BBC. Carrie cuts the two-way short: 'Sorry, Rajesh. I'm going to have to break in there. We'll come back to Birmingham later. Right now we go to the Lords.' The gallery take a live feed of Mr Pirrie standing alongside his client. A technician is putting an earpiece in Mr Pirrie's ear as he speaks to reporters outside the House.
	Julian summarises the divorce ruling and throws to Claire Marshall, who has Marcus Dearle, one of the solicitors for Mrs Miller in the other case. Over talkback to the outside broadcast, Simon tells Mr Pirrie: 'Stay there. We're coming back to you.' And in an aside off talkback: 'We've got both solicitors. This is very good. We're having a stonking morning.' Carrie interviews Mr Pirrie, who is still fumbling with his earpiece.
1011 	As James Pirrie talks live to the studio, Tanya says: 'I'm going to keep this going till we go to the quarters.'
1014	The newsroom tells Simon that Elton John has been awarded £100,000 in libel damages. He asks: 'Do we have a still of Elton John?'
1016	Gordon, the director, warns the studio that the Elton story is breaking. A still is now available. The presenters joke about how happy Sir Elton looks in the picture. The headlines, and sports headlines from Dan, follow.
1018	There's a report on the knives amnesty by Home Affairs Correspondent Andy Tighe.
1021	Mark Easton is live in the studio again. Simon calls Claire to thank her for her previous live on the divorce cases. *Simon comments: 'Think of a swan. The presenters are the serene beings with long necks, and we're paddling like mad under the water behind the scenes.'*

1026	Philip Hammond, the Shadow Work and Pensions Secretary, is live from Westminster talking about pensions reform.
1030	The studio links to a recording of the earlier knives amnesty 'disco' but the cue refers only to Frances Lawrence. Carrie, on talkback to the gallery, says: 'I don't know who wrote that, but we must intro both guests on a disco.' An Aston (caption) – 'Shaun Bailey, community worker' – explains who he is. And Carrie asks if he should be 'back-anno-ed'.
	The back-anno or back-announcement is a reference back to something when an item has finished, usually the reporter or contributors.
1035	Carrie back-annos Shaun Bailey. More recorded items follow – the set-up film of Sir David Attenbough, and the Attenborough interview from earlier. It's a time to relax for a few moments. Simon enters the gallery and comments: 'Oh, we're on tape, I can go away again.'
1039	Karen Bowerman is about to present the business news from the studio, but she's told that her guests at the Stock Exchange are not ready. They arrive with seconds to spare. She interviews a market analyst about the poor profit results of DIY stores.
1046	The quarters are followed by a pregnant pause – a minor technical glitch of about two seconds on the wrong camera shot, which the presenters laugh off. During the sports bulletin which follows, the news presenters tell the gallery they don't know what went wrong, but Carrie couldn't hear her talkback.
	Simon leaves the gallery to check with the production team what the divorce verdicts will mean for people other than high-earners.
1052	Divorce lawyer Helen Marriott is live from Manchester discussing the morning's verdicts. The gallery is told Mark Easton is on the phone. He wants one minute before the weather. Tanya says: 'It's Mark Simpson, not Mark Easton – tell Aston.' The reporter in Manchester has been to a police press conference.
1056	Fresh from the press conference, Mark Simpson confirms the number of arrests and the police forces involved. He reveals the arrests were linked to alleged terrorism in Iraq.

| 1057 | Roger, the director, returns after his hour's break. Tanya leaves the gallery – her time in charge ends with the programme strand. Julian and Carrie are replaced in the studio by Matthew Amroliwala and Jane Hill. |

| 1100 | Jane is seated and Matthew standing across the studio as they read the headline sequence – 'A win for the First Wives Club . . .' |

| 1107 | After another throw to Claire, who this time is interviewing a divorce lawyer Alan Kaufman, Matthew, now seated next to Jane, ad libs over the latest pictures from Manchester – live pictures from a helicopter of the Moss Side area of the city, including shots of a police van on the road. He also introduces shots from the police press conference. A senior officer is being interviewed – it's the Chief Constable Michael Todd. But before Mr Todd can be named, the interview ends abruptly. Matthew is suddenly back in vision: 'Well, apologies for that. That's just part of the latest police briefing. What we'll do is take that in full and bring you the key extracts.' |

He links instead to Rajesh Mirchandani who has now moved to another live location in Birmingham outside an Islamic relief agency that was raided as part of the police operation. Then he speaks to a fresh Manchester correspondent, Nick Ravenscroft, who's on the phone. The gallery play in the aerials and other Moss Side shots.

Matthew explains his approach to this type of presenting: 'When things that are clearly important break, you go into a sort of sustaining mode where you're trying to weave in pictures, facts, interviews, developing lines that are coming in all the time. It's that sort of juggling that's going on and that hopefully you do without dropping the ball.'

| 1113 | The appearance of former Iraqi Deputy Prime Minister Tariq Aziz as a defence witness in the trial of Saddam Hussein is mentioned over pictures of him in court. |

| 1114 | Matthew reads from a Home Office statement, handed to him on a printout, which says five foreign nationals have been detained with a view to deportation during the morning's police operation. Andy Tighe's knife amnesty report follows. |

1119	After the news and sport headlines, Matthew returns to the latest from the Manchester police briefing 'we saw a glimpse of earlier'. In his interview the Chief Constable says 18 addresses across the UK were targeted and there have been seven people arrested in connection with terrorist offences abroad. While the VT is running, Jane is told to throw to Claire Marshall outside the Lords next.
1121	Jane ad libs the throw into the latest on the divorce rulings, summarising the story so far. Kenneth McFarlane's lawyer Jeremy Levison is interviewed by Claire Marshall.
1126	After a brief read of some viewers' comments on the divorce rulings, split between the presenters, Jane links to the news that six people have died from bird flu in Indonesia. World Health Organisation spokesman Peter Cordingley is on the phone from Manila. He describes the outbreak as 'the mother of all clusters', and says there is the possibility of human-to-human transmission. Jane asks if people should be worried. He says: 'This is not the start of a pandemic.'
1130	Weather is followed by a short promo VT and the headlines.
1133	Jane throws to Philippa Thomas at a casino in Birmingham. She interviews Annette Fleming from the counselling service Aquarius about gambling addiction.
1137	Simon looks at the Sky News monitor in the gallery, and notices a story about the anti-cancer drug Herceptin. He asks: 'What is the line on Herceptin?'
1139	There's a package from Washington Correspondent James Westhead, reporting on the meeting of Israeli Prime Minister Ehud Olmert and US President George Bush.
1142	The business news includes a report from Shanghai about the importance of branding to China's biggest companies, and how they want their names to become internationally known.
1147	Just as the sports news begins, with a story that a Welsh rugby tour of Argentina is under threat because of a strike by Argentine players, the shortlist of towns that will compete for the super-casino is announced. Presenter Dan Walker is just beginning a down-the-line interview with correspondent Wyre Davies in Cardiff. The lower third strap across the bottom of the screen announces: 'Breaking News: shortlist released for first super-casino.' The names of the shortlisted towns are included on the super, but Roger and Simon in the gallery want to get the reaction to the story.

	Roger asks: 'Any more on this before we do the breaking news?' Simon decides: 'Hand back after this, and say we'll have the rest of the sport in just a minute.' Dan finishes his interview and says: 'We'll get more sport in a moment. Let's go back to Jane and Matthew first of all.' The news presenters link to reporter Jayne Barrett, windswept against a backdrop of Blackpool Tower. Blackpool is on the list and she reports local feeling that they must be favourite to win the bid.
1152	Sport continues with football and cricket news.
1153	The Bishop of Chelmsford's chaplain Rev. Chris Newlands is interviewed live from Chelmsford. He explains how a party of 20 British Christians is trying to get out of Africa after being snubbed because of objections to the bishop's tolerance of gay people. During the interview, Simon asks for a map of Africa to be shown. Roger tells Matthew: 'That's the last question. Quick out.'
1156	Health Correspondent Branwen Jeffreys is in the studio to explain a European ruling that the drug Herceptin has been approved for use in treatment of the early stages of breast cancer. There's a minute of weather before the top of the hour.
1200	Roger takes another break from directing and vision-mixing, and is replaced by Julie McKie. It's a Wednesday, so the next half hour or so will be coverage of Prime Minister's Questions (PMQs) in the House of Commons. But first they take the headlines, and miss the very start of proceedings. Simon says: 'I want to get through the heads before PMQs.' *Julie, who previously worked at the ITV regional company Tyne Tees, explains her role: 'You don't have a formal hand-over, you just take over. You need editorial awareness, but you never know what pictures you've got and what's coming in. We don't decide what comes next. That's up to the broadcast journalists. Often we take a lead from the presenters as to how they want to play things.'*
1204	The Prime Minister and the Leader of the Opposition are locked in their weekly exchanges – a mainstay of News 24's weekly coverage and a guide to the political mood in Westminster. But there's breaking news from Afghanistan, and it looks big. The strap reads: 'Breaking News: Attack on British Troops.' Simon is patched through from the gallery phone to correspondent Alastair Leithead in Lashkar Gah, who's called London with the story. Simon asks: 'What can you see, dear boy?' Alastair's answer prompts a quick decision from Simon: 'We're going to break out because Alastair Leithead can see flames [he listens again] . . . bloody hell.' Simon starts taking notes. 'Can you come on the videophone or not? . . . Right . . . so we'll take you via traffic straight away.' *'Traffic' is the BBC communications centre where lines and satellite feeds are patched through to programmes.* An aircraft has crashed, and Alastair has been briefed off-the-record. Simon tells the gallery and studio: 'The British Ambassador was on board, but do not say that to anybody, on air or out there [pointing to the newsroom]. He says the plane might have been brought down by small arms fire, and he thinks, but he can't say so, that the British Ambassador was on board, so it's going to be big.

'Can we get a map of Afghanistan – Helmand province? South Afghanistan if necessary. Ask Alastair how and where pictures are being fed.'

Simon explains: 'It's one of those where we've got to do it. I'm being given off-the-record guidance, so we can't tell the viewer the whole story yet. We know it's big.'

1211	Jane interrupts PMQs and tells viewers coverage will continue on the BBC Parliament channel. Alastair is on the phone. There's a still of him and a map of Helmand. He explains that he's been watching a column of thick smoke for the last half hour and that it's been confirmed a British aircraft has been involved in an 'incident'.
	Simon tells Jane over talkback: 'Put it in the context of high levels of military activity in the last few days. Lots of civilian casualties.'
	Jane picks up the theme immediately: 'There's been an increase in violence over the last week or so . . .'
1213	A breaking news strap on Sky News announces the Ministry of Defence has confirmed an incident with a British military aircraft in southern Afghanistan. Simon knows Sky have no reporter in Helmand and he's determined to press home the BBC's advantage.
1214	News 24 returns to coverage of PMQs.
	Simon says: 'We need to repeat this again when we come out of PMQs. We won't break in again.'
	Rachael Kennedy, the assistant editor, comes into the gallery to explain that Alastair is going to set up a videophone and he might be able to point it 'in the vague direction of the plane' to get a shot of the smoke.
1224	The channel leaves PMQs with another reminder from Jane that coverage continues on the 'sister channel BBC Parliament'. There's a summary of what's known about the Afghan plane crash, with Jane and Matthew ad libbing throughout. There's a new line from the MoD that there are no UK casualties. Library pictures of British soldiers in Afghanistan are played in.
	The next story will be the casinos announcement. Jane confirms with the gallery that Philippa is expecting a throw, not a question, to start.
	Simon says: 'As soon as Alastair Leithead comes up, that's our priority.'
1228	Jane introduces the casino story over a split-screen of reporters Philippa and Jayne, and throws to Jayne in Blackpool.
1230	Chief Diplomatic Correspondent Paul Adams arrives in the gallery to brief Simon. He's been checking the Afghan incident with Foreign Office sources. The plane crashed on landing – a burst tyre may have been responsible rather than insurgent activity. Everyone on board escaped injury, including the Ambassador, who, he can confirm, was definitely on the flight.
	All is not going well with the super-casinos item. There's interference on Philippa's mic.
	Julie says: 'Get her to wrap. The sound quality is awful.'

1233	Alastair appears on videophone. His piece-to-camera includes a pan to the plume of smoke behind him. The picture is pixilated, but clear enough to see what's going on. Simon says: 'These pics will do for the 12.45 heads.' Paul Adams is in the studio to explain what he's learned from his sources. He confirms that all on board escaped injury. Simon is thinking ahead to the business news: 'What's the footsie [FTSE] doing?' He's told the index is down 102 points. 'We must do it.'
1243	Jane says: 'Let's return to domestic politics . . .' Clips of the exchange between Tony Blair and David Cameron are played in. The presenters throw to political correspondent James Landale, who has two commentators to interview outside the House of Commons, Julia Hartley-Brewer of the *Sunday Express* and Michael Settle of *The Herald*. Matthew in the studio has spotted something on the wires – the agency feeds on his computer. He whispers to the gallery: 'Guys, do you want to do this Foreign Office statement?'
1248	Matthew reads from the Foreign Office statement, confirming some of the details of the plane crash. He points out that Paul Adams had already given most of the facts.
1249	After the headlines, Karen Bowerman has the business news, linking to Henk Potts of Barclays stockbrokers in the City. The line is lost and the screen goes green during one of his answers. 'Oh, dear me, we seem to have lost Henk Potts, right in the middle of his flow.' Karen mentions the falling market.
1251	Correspondent Nick Higham is in the studio to explain the impact of the landmark divorce rulings. He uses a series of graphics, and also refers to the possible impact on Sir Paul McCartney and Heather Mills, who have recently announced their separation.
1255	The sports slot is cut short. It's been a busy hour.
1300	News 24 simulcasts the One O'Clock News presented by Darren Jordon. Simon Waldman has finished his shift. Today he's taking his presenters to lunch.

STAFFORDSHIRE NEWS

Staffordshire was one of the first parts of the UK to be served by three distinct local broadcast services. The BBC local radio station, Radio Stoke, covers north Staffordshire and south Cheshire. The commercial radio station, Signal 1, part of the UTV group, has a similar transmission area. In December 2005 they were joined by BBC Local Television for the county of Staffordshire, run from the Radio Stoke studios.

Radio Stoke (indicated in roman type throughout the section) has a news editor and nine journalists including three district reporters in Leek, Stafford and Crewe. The station is on air 24 hours, with speech-based radio from six in the morning until seven in the evening.

Signal Radio (indicated in italic type) has a news editor, a sports editor and an early morning newsreader. The early shift runs Monday to Friday from 04.30 a.m. until 12 noon and the news editor and sports editor flip-flop their shifts 9 a.m. –5 p.m. and 10 a.m. –6 p.m. They have freelance cover over the weekends and for holidays. Signal Radio has two stations, Signal 1 and Signal 2. Signal 1's main target audience is 15–44 year olds with a 'best variety of hits' format, and Signal 2 aims itself at the over 35s with a mix of music from the past four decades. Signal 1 goes on air at 6 a.m. and runs through until 10 p.m. and Signal 2 goes on air at 6 a.m. and runs through until 6 p.m. Both stations then go on to an automated service taking national IRN (Independent Radio News) bulletins throughout the night. There is no local news overnight.

BBC Local TV (indicated in bold type) has seven full-time video journalists, including a community-content producer and a faith producer. They produce short video reports which are available on broadband and on digital satellite TV. There's a ten-minute bulletin, which runs at ten to the hour on the same digital satellite stream as five other local services for other parts of the West Midlands region.

Here we look at a day's broadcasting, comparing the output and the editorial decision making of all three services.

| 0320 | *Signal's morning newsreader, 28-year-old Tom Cooke, leaves home in Coventry to drive to the studios in Stoke-on-Trent. He's been home for the weekend. He rents a small flat just opposite Signal's newsroom where he lives during the week, but today is Monday so it's an early start.* |

0420	*Tom is driving through Fenton in Stoke-on-Trent, when he sees about five cars with blue flashing lights drive past him.*
0430	*Tom arrives at Signal. He is the first in. He unlocks the front doors into reception and turns the alarm off. He then re-locks the front doors and enters the code to get into the newsroom. The newsroom is long and thin. The news team share the room with the mid-morning show on Signal 1. There are three news work-stations at the end of the room. Tom sits at the main operational work-station. His first bulletin is at 6 a.m. Waiting for him is a handover note left by the freelance journalist who did the Sunday shift. She informs him there was a major crash locally on the A53 at Endon on Saturday evening. A car carrying four young men had careered off the road and hit a tree. Two men died and a further two had been taken to the main hospital critically ill.* *His next job is to check overnight feeds from IRN. Tom says: 'IRN churn out stuff from the paper; they don't check the figures. IRN overnight staff are even younger than me – much less experienced.' He rewrites some of the IRN copy, and takes some of the figures out of the stories. He needs to write a three-minute bulletin using some of the IRN stories and audio, and his own local stories which he needs to find. Signal has its own style for a three-minute bulletin: Tom is looking for a maximum of seven local stories and a maximum of three national stories. Signal's (and UTV's) policy is that 70 per cent of the news must be local.*
0455	*Tom pops to the kitchen to make his first cup of tea of the day. He then looks for audio cuts for the bulletins. Signal's policy is to have a maximum of three clips, unless they are really short. The normal maximum length for an audio clip is 15 seconds – 16 seconds at a push, but never 17 seconds. Tom says: 'You get rid of all the breaths, and all the ums and ers, you can take 40 seconds of audio and knock it down to 15 or 16 seconds easily.'* *The minimum length of an audio clip is five seconds. Tom says: 'I've heard Paul [Sheldon, Signal's news editor] use short stabs of audio at the beginning, and it has worked really well. The hardest thing is to identify cuts. You want the cuts to add to the story, but so that it isn't going to take too long to say it.'*
0500	BBC Radio Stoke's early reader Lizzie Meek arrives for work. A bulletin has been left for her. The lead story previews an announcement later in the day of revised plans for the rebuilding of the city's main hospital. The University Hospital of North Staffordshire's trust recently announced a thousand job cuts. Senior managers have resigned. The new management team have to stop losses of £3 million a month. Cuts of £40 million are needed over three years. Two men are critical after a car crash at the weekend in which two people died. There's a police appeal for witnesses. Early presenter Den Siegertsz is on air. He'll be available to report for the breakfast programme when he finishes at seven.
0515	*In the Signal newsroom, Tom is continuing to prepare his bulletin for 6 a.m. He checks the latest weather and celebrity news, writes them up for the early morning show presenters, and takes the scripts into their studio.*

0520	Tom rings the local police about the blue flashing lights he saw on his way into work. The Signal news team have an excellent relationship with the police in Stoke-on-Trent, and Tom charms his way to getting the information he wants for his bulletin. He is told three people have been arrested in the Birches Head area of Stoke, and three vehicles recovered, over the suspected theft of a vehicle. Tom asks: 'Oh, did you use a stinger? I like those . . . Very helpful. Right then, mate, is that the lot?' He checks on the two people in hospital from the car crash on Saturday night: 'Are you still appealing for witnesses?'
0525	Tom comes off the phone to the police and checks an e-mail from Staffordshire Ambulance Service updating stories from last night. A microlight crashed yesterday in the Staffordshire Moorlands, near Leek.
0530	Tom starts writing up the Birches Head vehicle theft story. He's hoping this will be an exclusive for Signal. The news editor, Paul Sheldon, has been at Signal since the station opened in 1983 – he thinks he's the second-longest-serving commercial radio news editor in the country. Tom says: 'Paul's taught me so much here. One of the main things is to get to the point. The Beeb say if you've two lines for a story, you've not got enough in that story. Paul says you've got too much in that story!' When Tom finishes writing a story, he saves it on the computer: 'I must save the stories in the right place on the computer. It's all well and good me knowing where the stuff is, but when Paul gets in he must know as well.'
0535	Tom rings the Cheshire Police voice-bank. The recorded message gives details of a misper – a man from Nantwich has gone missing.
0540	Tom rings Staffordshire Fire Service's voice-bank. A horse has been rescued by the fire brigade at 2100 last night near Leek. The horse was trapped in mud by a stream. It was rescued using ropes and slings. Tom comes off the phone and starts to write the story. He comments: 'Everything has gone out of the window this morning. It is so busy.'
0548	Tom rings the Cheshire Newsline again to double-check the facts of the misper. He then writes up the Nantwich missing person.
0551	Tom rings the Cheshire Newsline again. There's something else he needs to make sure of.
0552	Tom finishes writing the misper and decides to drop the microlight crash: 'Nobody has died.' He checks the timings, generated by the scripts in the computer. He has two minutes 52 seconds for his three-minute bulletin – seven seconds under. Tom usually reads slightly more slowly than the computer's estimate, so he reckons he should be OK: 'You must always read your script out live when you're writing it. It helps you to get the right feel.'

0555	Tom puts an audio cassette into the cassette recorder on the floor of the newsroom to record Radio Stoke's bulletin at 6 a.m.
0556	Tom throws sports headlines into his script on the computer.
0557	Tom leaves the newsroom and goes through into the tiny studio next door. He double-checks his handwritten prompts are in place. There are three scraps of paper propped up on the desk – each one reading slightly differently: 'The latest at six. I'm Tom Cooke.' 'That's the latest. It's three minutes past six.' and 'That's the latest news and sport on Signal 1. It's . . . (TIME CHECK).' He has no paper copy of the news stories he's written. He reads the scripts he wrote on the newsroom computer direct from the computer screen in the studio. Tom checks he has his cuts (audio) in the right place.
0559	Tom reads the stories out loud. He finds a typo error and quickly changes it, using the keyboard in the studio.
0600 Tom Cooke Lizzie Meek	Tom goes on air, broadcasting live on both Signal 1 and Signal 2. He checks timings as he reads and plays out audio clips. He decides he has no time for the horse story and drops it. As an audio clip is playing, one of the presenters from the early morning breakfast show, Andy Goulding, buzzes through from another studio to say hello. (He'd arrived at Signal while Tom has been working in the newsroom, but hasn't disturbed him because he knows what a busy time Tom has before he goes on air with his first bulletin.) With just seconds to go before the audio finishes, Tom quickly says: 'Hi. No time,' and continues to read the bulletin. The early morning show is pre-recorded from 6 a.m.–7 a.m. So Andy is under less pressure than the newsreader. Radio Stoke breakfast presenter Janine Machin, producer Ros Chimes and sports presenter Phil Bowers start their day. Lizzie is in the NPA (news production area) in the corner of the newsroom, reading the bulletin.
0603	Tom comes off air but stays in the studio to pre-record the heads (headlines) for later. He goes through the script and changes the wording where he fluffed reading the script live a few minutes earlier.

0606	Tom records the heads for 0630 for Signal 2. He says: 'When I first arrived here at Signal, I was thinking: "How am I going to get it all done?" Now, I look at the clock and I think: "Oh, I've got plenty of time." You only learn by going through it. No matter how many newsdays you do at university, nothing can prepare you for the times when you ring up the voice-bank and the police say they're investigating four deaths from arson, or you're on your own in the newsroom and the London bombings kick off.'
0610	Tom finishes his pre-record for Signal 2 and rehearses the heads for Signal 1.
0617	Tom pre-records his heads, using different music beds for the different sponsors.
0622	Before leaving the studio Tom writes himself a prompt to remind himself what to do at seven. The 7 a.m. bulletin will probably be the same as the 6 a.m. depending upon any breaking news. Tom returns to the newsroom.
0630 Janine Machin	Radio Stoke's team discuss the lighter material for the show. There's a feature on the decline of working men's clubs, and talking points in the papers include the return of K9, the mechanical dog, to *Doctor Who*, and a survey which suggests women prefer housework to sex.
0632	Tom listens back to the cassette of Radio Stoke's 6 a.m. bulletin. He discovers that over the weekend someone has changed the station, and he's recorded Virgin Radio instead!
0633	Tom rings Staffordshire Fire Service's voice-bank. It hasn't been updated. He rings the fire service direct to find out more about the microlight crash. He learns that nobody from the fire service attended the crash. He rings the ambulance service.
0646	Tom takes a call from Staffordshire Police. He is asked if he knows anything about the Home Secretary, John Reid, coming into Signal Radio. Tom says he knows nothing about it: 'He came in just a couple of weeks ago, so I doubt if he'll be in again. But I'll ring back after nine if I find anything out.'

0650	Tom collects the newspapers from reception. He starts checking through them.
	Clutching a handful of newspapers, scripts and an orange, Janine makes her way to the studio downstairs. Ros is still in the newsroom, editing some vox-pops from the boy band Take That's first reunion concert the previous evening. Local interest is reduced because the band's most famous member Robbie Williams, who's from Stoke, is not on tour with the others.
0657	Tom checks his script for seven o'clock. He has nine stories. Two are national; one of them is about the boy band Take That, who are re-forming for a tour. There's a Robbie Williams line in the story, but Signal still class it as national, even though Robbie Williams is from Stoke-on-Trent.
0658	Tom sets the cassette recorder to record Radio Stoke's 7 a.m. bulletin. As Tom walks into the studio, he hears Louise Stones, the early morning presenter, reading the weather he put in her studio before she arrived.
0700	Tom reads the news live. When he finishes his read, he listens to the live output of Signal 1: 'They sometimes speak to me after the news and we have a bit of banter. The ad libs keep it real.'
	Mick Tucker, a young freelance, arrives for work. He'll be doing a live outside broadcast in just under an hour from some allotments in the Longton area. The story is that local people are taking over the management of allotment sites from the council. There's a briefing sheet Mick can print out from ENPS. He'll read it when he gets to the location.
0710	Tom returns to the newsroom and listens back to the Radio Stoke bulletin he recorded. He discovers their running orders are very similar, and comments: 'Maybe they're leading from me!' Radio Stoke have used different wording and have more detail in some of the stories.
	The first news feature of the day is a two-way with reporter Stuart Fear about the hospital crisis. It was recorded three days earlier. It was decided to take the unusual step of recording the contribution so Stuart wouldn't have to get up early. He has to be at the trust meeting that afternoon to find out which of the plans for a new hospital is chosen. The meeting is expected to run late and Stuart will then have to report live into evening programmes and prepare material for the next day's breakfast.
	When the scale of the hospital's financial difficulties became clear, news editor James O'Hara changed Stuart's shift pattern so he could concentrate on the story. James explains: 'It would be a big story if a thousand jobs were cut at any of our big local employers, Michelin, Doulton or Wedgwood, but this is in the public sector *and* we know that health is a big driver for our target audience. Now Stuart knows more about it than anybody else here, producers know he's the specialist on the story, and he's usually available to broadcast live at a moment's notice.'
	Stuart is normally the station's South Cheshire reporter, working from an office in Crewe. He welcomes the challenge of tackling such a big running story: 'It's very rare in local radio these days to have the time to get your head round such a complicated story. I have to boil it all down and present it in a way that isn't going to be a turn-off.'

0724	Tom looks at his scripts for the 8 a.m. bulletin and rewrites a few words.
0727	Tom goes into the studio for the live headlines at half past. He listens to output: Andy and Louise are in full swing with their show.
0731	Tom reads the 7.30 headlines live. They're the same news headlines as at 6.30, with sports headlines as well.
0734	Tom finishes the news and sport and then ad libs with Andy and Lou about what he's done over the weekend, and about pub quiz questions. They also ask Tom how happy he is on a scale of 1–10.
0735	Mick has arrived at the allotments, but parking the radio car is a problem. He has to be on the highest point of the site, near the entrance, to ensure his radio transmission will work but has to waste valuable seconds driving the length of the site before there's a turning place. The lead story in sport is an exclusive. Stoke City football manager, Johan Boskamp, has told Radio Stoke he's not prepared to wait to resolve his contract dispute with the club. The suggestion is he'll quit. In the ops room (studio control room), Ros is trying to call Nina Flemming, a staff nurse from the University Hospital. She's due to be interviewed on an ISDN line from the Royal College of Nursing's conference in Bournemouth. Ros can't get through on her mobile. Janine fills time on air chatting about working men's clubs.
0737	Tom comes out of the studio and returns to the newsroom. He begins to rewrite the stories for the eight o'clock news with new lines. Tom's worked at Signal for nearly a year: 'I've worked at stations as a freelance, where the Internet has gone off because they haven't paid the phone bill, or there's no loo roll and you have to go to the loo in the pub opposite. But you're a freelance, so you have to learn to bite your lip.'
0738	Mick has started to put the radio car's mast up, and introduces himself to his three interviewees. Nurse Nina Flemming has arrived at the ISDN point in Bournemouth and is live on air. Clips from her interview will run in later bulletins.

Mick and the radio car mast

0742	*Tom rings Cheshire Newsline to check the details on the misper. He rewrites the story.*
0745	The computer in the ops room crashes. The screen freezes. As Ros restarts the computer, Janine copes on air, linking to the traffic report. Her style is chatty with plenty of ad-libbing. She reads most of her links from the screen, but has hard copies in front of her. 'The screen controls ENPS, e-mails and text messages from listeners, and I switch between them, so it makes sense to have a script in front of me.' *Tom rewrites the Endon crash story and puts in a new line about the police appealing for witnesses.*
0748	*Tom rewrites the Birches Head story.*

0750 Mick at the allotment	Mick Tucker is live on air. With a script in one hand, microphone in the other, and headphones through which he hears talkback and programme output, he has a radio link to the radio car parked on the other side of an allotment shed. He enters the plot, clanking the gate behind him as he sets the scene. He chats in turn to members of the local Community Gardens Association.

0751	*Tom finishes his rewrite and starts to build the eight o'clock bulletin. The eight o'clock is Signal's main bulletin of the day when most people are listening. Tom says: 'You have to keep across all the national stories as well as the local ones. I missed a big local story in Cheshire the other week about Volkswagen losing jobs. I didn't know that Volkswagen own Bentley, who are obviously based in Cheshire and Paul (Sheldon) said: "Ooh you've missed a big one." And I thought: "Well, if I don't know Volkswagen own Bentley, then who else will?"'*
0758	*Tom checks the police newslines and puts a cassette in to record Radio Stoke's bulletin.*
0759	*Tom arrives in the studio.*

0800 	*Tom starts speaking at exactly eight o'clock: 'The latest at eight o'clock . . .'* *Tom knows Signal's news editor, Paul Sheldon, will be listening at home. The early bulletins are usually pre-planned from the day before. Paul says: 'If Tom hasn't rung me, I know nothing big has broken.'* *Paul makes the executive decisions: 'I tell him what we're doing.'* News Editor James O'Hara has arrived and pops in to the ops room. The bulletin lead is the hospital story, with the car crash second.
0803	*Tom comes off air. He had been worried that he wouldn't have time for the Take That story – so he cut the last paragraph during the live read.*
0809	There's another interview on the health story: a recorded piece with Ian Syme, from the pressure group North Staffordshire Healthwatch. Clips from this interview will also run in later bulletins.
0812	*Tom starts to update the website. He plans to have it all updated by nine o'clock: 'If someone hears a story on their way into work, and they want to know more about it, research shows there is a spike on the website hits when people get into work and log on to their computers.'* *Tom copies and pastes his news scripts on to the website. He doesn't rewrite the stories, he just puts the numbers into numerals and loses the back announcements. Tom says: 'This is my favourite part of the day – I get to come up with puns for the website story headlines.'*
0820 Ros Chimes	A live interview down the line to Westminster correspondent Paul Rowley focuses on the Health Secretary Patricia Hewitt's comment that it has been 'the best year ever' for the health service. How can she say this with thousands of jobs being lost? Rowley explains that she was talking about targets for the number of operations performed, but her comments have not gone down well with the unions representing health workers. Station manager Sue Owen is in the ops room discussing programme content. Ros is unhappy with a two-minute package in the *Inside Lives* series. This is user-generated content, part of the BBC's commitment to engage listeners in digital story-telling. Ros thinks today's piece is poorly made, and doesn't even make it clear where the story-teller is from. If it was by a reporter, she would have dropped it or asked for it to be re-edited. But the 'producer', a listener, is not available to do that. Ros is concerned that there is a 'three-line whip' to run *Inside Lives* pieces even when they're not very good. Sue reassures her that she can drop it if she wants to.

0827	Dave from the Police rings with information about thefts from cars. Tom says he'll ring him back after the 0830 headlines. Tom goes into the studio and listens to Signal 1 output. He looks at the TV monitor in the news studio which is tuned to the BBC regional news from Birmingham. He notices that they're using the wrong pictures of the A53. Tom recognises the pictures as being the Leek to Buxton stretch of the A53, not the part of the road at Endon where the fatal crash happened. But he learns from BBC Midlands that the police are due to release the names of the two dead young men later today.
0830	Radio Stoke's breakfast show becomes less speech-based once it it assumed people are arriving at work. The first record after the news and sports bulletin is Michael Jackson's *Thriller*. The production team do not control the play-list, although they are free to include relevant tracks, such as Take That to go with the reunion story.
0831	Tom reads his headlines and ad libs with the presenters.
0836	Tom returns to the newsroom. Simon Humphries, Signal's sports editor, has arrived.
0842	Tom checks for anything breaking and has another look at the eight o'clock bulletin to see if he needs to change his script. He decides to use some fresh audio, and deletes the audio he used in the earlier bulletins.
0855	James, the news editor, asks Mick to check out who the RCN reps are for other hospitals in the transmission area. They may want to comment on the health debate from the conference in Bournemouth. Later he'll ask Mick to check another health story, the closure of Westcliffe Hospital, a geriatric unit with about 30 patients.
0856	Tom goes into the studio to read the nine o'clock bulletin. He reads the same bulletin as at eight.
0903	Tom returns to the newsroom as news editor Paul Sheldon arrives. They catch up on the morning's stories. Tom does 'a bit of housekeeping' with his scripts on the computer to help Paul and Simon access the bulletins. He goes through the draft bulletins for the day, dragging over any filler stories that haven't been used already: 'I can remember when I first left university, making the calls to the voice-banks, and saying to myself: "Oh no, please don't let anything have happened," because I was worried about being able to write everything up in time. I would panic thinking I had to get all the details in. These days I can do my police check calls at three minutes to the hour, and if there's anything, I'll jot it down and say, "Breaking news . . . We'll bring you more in the next hour". I've learnt to drip-drip the detail of the information over the bulletins using the carrot-and-stick method, keeping the listening audience interested.'

0930	Tom sets about doing his police check calls.
0940	James meets Ros for a de-brief and to talk about tomorrow's prospects. Radio Stoke have a good relationship with the University Hospital, not least because the hospital's press officer is the station's former news editor. The trust's new chief executive, Antony Sumara, who's been brought in to sort out the financial mess, will come in to tomorrow's breakfast show live.
0942	Tom starts to re-work his script. The bulletin goes down to two minutes at 10 o'clock.
0950	Tom takes a call from the police press office about the possibility of the Defence Minister coming in to Signal. He discusses it with Paul. Paul keeps an executive eye on the day: 'I have to live and die by the decisions I make. You're making hundreds of decisions each day on the hoof – what stories to go with, what stories to ditch. You have to be really careful and sometimes you get it wrong.'
	Tom's last read of his shift will be the 12 noon bulletin. Paul is preparing to take over the read at one o'clock, and starts checking stories.
0958	Tom goes into the studio for the 10 o'clock bulletin.
1000	Most of the local television team are now on shift. Their working day has different deadlines from the radio stations. Their content can be uploaded onto the broadband site at any time, but in practice most of it has to be ready by the early evening. Bulletins for the whole of the Midlands local TV service are loaded on to the digital satellite stream from the BBC's regional centre at the Mailbox in Birmingham. The video feed to the Mailbox only operates one-way. So, if they want to access library pictures from Birmingham they have to plan ahead and have them sent in the post.
1012	Paul asks Tom to check the voice-banks.

1015

Sue Owen

Radio Stoke meeting

Sue Owen leads the morning news meeting. James and nine other staff, presenters, producers and reporters contribute. Sue says their audience will want whatever they can get on the health story. Janine, who has just come off air, is worried about holding listeners' attention if there is too much in one chunk. Sue suggests interviewing the chief executive Mr Sumara, then giving him 'a cup of a tea and a croissant' and asking him back into the studio later to deal with the listeners' comments that are bound to follow the interview. Other available contributors include Ian Syme from Healthwatch and Greg Hopkinson, a consultant, who went on the record about the hospital's difficulties in a letter to the *Daily Telegraph*.

There's a discussion of the double-fatal accident on the A53. It involved two young drivers. Were they racing each other? Lizzie, the newsreader, says she has been told off the record that they weren't. She's been checking with the police and the names of the victims are about to be released.

Other topics include the large number of dead badgers on local roads. Are they all the victims of road accidents, or are some of them being shot by farmers and dumped on the road? The idea has been mooted by a vet, but he won't go on the record as he relies on farmers for his livelihood.

Everyone in the meeting seems certain that the Stoke City football manager will be 'gone by the end of the week'.

On the Local TV desk at the other side of the office, video journalists are editing packages using Avid Express. Stuart Ratcliffe asks VJ Laura McMullan to check out a story that has appeared on GNS (the BBC's General News Service) about a disabled Tamworth man who has been told by the council he'll be prosecuted unless he puts back brambles and other rubbish that he's cleared from the banks of the River Tame near his home. She's also trying to set up a story about a transport café that's been named in a 'Michelin-style' guide as among the best in Britain. Stuart suggests taking a restaurant critic to the café.

1045

Tom asks Paul about the correct way to word his script. He's having trouble with the wording on the Endon crash story and naming the two people who have died. Paul suggests 'believed to be . . . but not formally identified.'

1046

Radio Stoke's morning news meeting has finished. Lizzie has the names of the road accident victims and they'll be in the next bulletin. During the meeting there has been little if any mention of what other local media are reporting. Sue Owen's philosophy is clear: 'If we've got stories that are on the first three or four pages of the *Sentinel* [the local paper], we've failed. What's the point of two local media organisations covering the same stories with the same interviewees. That's not what we do'.

Laura, the VJ, has spoken to the agency News Team International in Birmingham, who supplied the Tamworth brambles story to GNS. They don't have the man's phone number. She knows the road he lives in and is trying to call neighbours, using the computer database of information from the electoral roll and telephone directories.

1055

Tom checks through his script and goes into the studio to read the 11 o'clock bulletin.

1100	*Tom reads the 11 o'clock bulletin live.*
1102	James, the Radio Stoke news editor, liaises with Stuart from Local TV and tells him the best times to interview the contacts the radio station has lined up for the afternoon's announcement of the plans for the new hospital. Using the radio station's research and contacts, Local TV will be able to put together a package with the chief executive Antony Sumara, the consultant Greg Hopkinson and campaigner Ian Syme.
1103	*Tom returns to the newsroom and starts looking for new stories for the 12 noon bulletin.*
1115	*Tom discovers that a marshal who died at Oulton Park race track has been named. He discusses with Paul how he should write it. Paul says: 'Write it differently from the Endon crash story. Often Cheshire police will only give out the name of someone when the inquest has been opened and then adjourned. Check that, and then that can be your line.'*
1125	*Paul continues writing the one o'clock. He decides to use just the marshal story for this bulletin. He checks through the draft later bulletins Tom has prepared. He checks the writing and discovers some word repetition. One story has the word 'makeover' twice. He changes one of them to 'facelift'. He changes another story to the present tense to make it more immediate, cuts out some unnecessary words and adds some geographical tags. Paul explains: 'All intros have a geographical tag because the patch is so big. We need to signpost for all the stories.'* *The lead story is about the local hospital. He tightens and hardens it by changing the tenses ('will pose' becomes 'are to pose') and cuts out some words: 'I rewrite everything from IRN. It is not as short as I would like, so I cut two paragraphs down to one.'* *Paul has a skeleton bulletin ready for one o'clock: 'If a big story breaks now, I have a skeleton ready, which allows me to concentrate on the breaking story.'*
1130	The public spending watchdog the Audit Commission has issued a press release criticising the Stoke hospital management for not balancing the books. James asks Paul Stanworth, a reporter who's acting as producer of the afternoon drive time show, for a voicer for the 1200 bulletin.
1133	*Tom checks for new stories to update his script for 12 noon.*

1136	Ian Syme from Healthwatch is in reception. James asks Phil, the morning sports presenter, to go and see him. Phil is keen to gain more news experience. He spends nearly 15 minutes with Mr Syme. The health campaigner asks if the newsroom has seen the Audit Commission report, but that's not the reason for his visit. He provides background information about a forthcoming inquest into the death of a 17-year-old in hospital, apparently from the effects of the MRSA bug. Phil is given the phone number of the victim's mother. Lizzie's seven-hour early newsreading shift is coming to an end. She leaves a handover note for the afternoon newsreader Helen Thomas, explaining which stories have been used and how often.
1145	*Paul continues adding to his script for one o'clock. He decides to drop the audio on the Unison story and rewrites it as a straight read: 'I've hacked it to pieces and left it as a back anno – because there is little new news. We're tabloid in style, but we don't use the language of tabloids – people who overwrite get a sound slapping! A lot of journalists are guilty of kite-flying. I always say: "If it's a good enough story, it will stand on its own two feet." Please excuse the two metaphors!'*
1148	*An e-mail has arrived, timed at 1135. This is the new lead story. The District Auditors have gone public on the hospital story.*
1155	*Paul goes through the report from the Audit Commissioners with a highlighter pen.*
1158	*Paul considers rushing through the report and breaking the story for the bulletin at 12 but decides against it. He wants to get it right and decides to break the news at 12.30. He wants time to digest and understand the report before he writes it. He then notices an embargo until 3 p.m.*
1200	*Tom reads the 12 noon bulletin with no reference to the report from the Audit Commissioners.* Lizzie reads her last bulletin as Helen arrives. A clip of the nurse Nina Flemming from the breakfast show leads the bulletin, followed by Paul's voicer on the Audit Commission report. James monitors Signal News, notes they have nothing worth following up and begins a ten-minute lunch break.
1205	*Paul writes the headlines for 12.30. He studies the report carefully and discovers that the Audit Commissioners' report is not embargoed until 3 p.m. – it is the response that is embargoed.* *Simon Humphries is sitting at the desk next to the main newsdesk where Paul is sitting. Simon has been in since 08.30 and has been working on tomorrow's news, writing draft bulletins from press releases and diary stories. He is now working on the financial news and sports bulletin for today. Signal's one o'clock and 5 p.m. bulletins are nearly six minutes long and contain a full sports bulletin.* *Simon and Paul discuss whether they can say that Boskamp is going – Sky News have said he is going.*

1215	*Paul has written the headlines for 12.30. He gets the weather off IRN's website and writes it into a script. He takes it to the studio for the presenters.*
1220	*Paul starts writing the Audit Commissioners' story from the press release. He says it's his job to make the press release understandable, without oversimplifying the story. He wants to get an audio clip from local Labour MP Paul Farrelly. He checks his contacts book and rings the number he has for Farrelly's local assistant. He discovers she changed her job four years ago. He rings the MP's mobile phone direct, but gets no reply.*
1224	*Paul rings the MP's office at the House of Commons. He explains who he is and how he has already tried his mobile. The MP's assistant in London says she'll try and locate him, and will ring Paul back. He explains he wants him for the one o'clock bulletin. Paul knows the MP well, and expects he will be critical of the hospital management.*
1225	Mick has not had any success tracking down relatives of elderly patients at Westcliffe hospital. So, an appeal goes out on air asking anybody with relations in the unit to get in touch with the station.
	Stuart phones engineers at the Mailbox to send a package from the previous week to BBC South Today. A dog that went missing from Staffordshire four years ago turned up in part of South Today's region. The story emerged when the dog was reunited with its owner in Tamworth, after a vet discovered it had an identification chip. BBC Radio Five Live also want to hear the audio before arranging an interview with the dog's owner.
	Laura has spoken to a neighbour of the man being accused of unlawfully clearing brambles, but he wasn't too helpful. She suspects it might be same neighbour who complained to the council. She can't find a restaurant critic for the café story either. She decides to drive the 45 miles to Tamworth to find the brambles man. And she'll try a different tack with the café story – she'll ask a friend who's an award-winning restaurant chef to sample the café's menu.
1230	*Tom reads the 12.30 headlines.*
1236	*The Sentinel, the local evening paper, has arrived. Paul checks through it and ticks off the stories they've already covered. He turns to the births, deaths and marriages: 'I always go though the hatched, matched and dispatched – just in case.'*
1244	*Paul checks the Staffordshire and Cheshire police voice-banks. He then rings Mark in police control for more detail on one of the stories. Somebody has forced their way into a flat in Crewe. Mark says he'll ring back with the answers to Paul's questions.*
1245	*Tom leaves for the day.*

1248	*Paul checks through the latest news from IRN and decides to use a story with the Prime Minister Tony Blair commenting on the NHS above the Unison story.*
1249	*Paul changes his mind and decides to use Blair as a back anno on the hospital story.*
1250	*Local MP Paul Farrelly rings. Paul rings him back immediately and records him directly off the phone on to the computer system on his desk. Paul knows the soundbites he wants from the MP, and poses the question he expects will get the right response. Referring to the Audit Commissioners' report, he says: 'They're having a right good go on the hospital – what's your take on that?'* *Paul gives a thumbs-up to Simon.* *'What's your position on the managers' response, then? You're saying what, then?'* *'Should managers lose their jobs?'* *'You're not very impressed then?'*
1254	*Paul continues questioning the MP. He keeps looking at the clock. He has to edit the soundbites ready for the bulletin in six minutes' time.*
1255	*The call ends. Paul has already chosen the clips he wants to use as he was recording. He edits them, and saves them in the system ready to play in the bulletin.*
1257	*While Paul is editing the soundbites, Mark from Cheshire Police rings back with the answers to Paul's questions. Simon takes the call: 'No to any injuries, and no to anything stolen.'* *Simon gives Paul the message.*
1258	*Paul rushes into the studio to read the one o'clock bulletin.*
1305	*Signal's mid-morning presenter rings the newsroom to say he couldn't hear the last audio clip on digital.* *Paul returns to the newsroom and changes the script. He has repeated himself and rewrites to avoid the repetition. He has problems making sense of the difficult language in the report.*
1340	**Laura arrives in Tamworth. She finds her way down to the river, but can't get through the brambles and household rubbish. Then she notices a clear area, half of it turfed, further along the riverbank. A man is in the back garden of an adjoining house. She makes her way back to the road and discovers that the man in the garden is the son of the man she's looking for. He's out but will be back soon. She promises to return in just under an hour, and goes off to find some lunch at a local shopping centre.**

1345	*Paul continues to work on the wording of the report.*
1350	*Paul checks the voice-banks, and rings round the local emergency services' press officers. Paul has been the news editor at Signal for so long he is on very friendly terms with the press officers.*
1358	*Paul makes final checks on his script and asks Simon to listen to Radio Stoke's output at two. He is aware that Patricia Hewitt, the Health Secretary, is due to speak at the Unison conference in Gateshead, and so also puts Sky News on in the newsroom. He asks Simon to keep an eye on what happens. Paul goes into the studio for the two o'clock bulletin.*
1400	*Paul reads the two o'clock bulletin.*
1403	*Paul returns to the newsroom and monitors Sky's output.*
1410	*Patricia Hewitt starts speaking at the Unison conference and Paul takes notes for the next bulletin.*
1415	*Paul does his police check calls. He discovers that the Crewe flat break-in story happened a week ago.*
1420	James is told by the BBC Parliamentary Unit at Millbank that Patricia Hewitt, the Health Secretary, has been speaking about the Stoke hospital at the annual conference of Unison, where she's been heckled by the union's members. The speech is live on BBC News 24. James can access the audio on the BBC's 'autorot' system. Autorot is short for 'automatic record off transmission'. It means material from the BBC's radio networks and its main TV channels can be accessed by other parts of the organisation. It's stored digitally in half-hour segments. James listens to the Health Secretary saying the hospital's managers should apologise to the thousand workers losing their jobs. This is an unexpected new angle. **In Tamworth, Laura returns to the riverside house and meets Garry Cartwright, a 60-year old disabled man, who has spent £1600 improving his access to the river at the foot of his garden. He shows her the letter from the council threatening him with criminal and civil action, unless he reinstates the land to its former condition.**

1425	Paul asks Simon how tomorrow's bulletins are shaping up. Simon replies: 'Pants, mate!' Paul decides to lend a hand looking for stories for tomorrow. He writes up the Crewe break-in story. Paul says: 'Journalism has got to be a vocational call. When I started it was hot metal and newspaper presses. You've got to be a nosey bugger and not give up. Someone who is half hearted just won't make it – a lot of young people just can't be bothered. You have to want to do it. If you think you want to do it, then it is not to be.'
1442	Paul checks the voice-banks. He then calls Carol Evans, who works in the press office at Staffordshire Police. He knows her well and puts on his 'charm': 'What have you been up to this weekend then?' They chat about decorating and domestic life. Paul then asks: 'Anything happening?' Paul then rings Mark at the Cheshire Police press office. They laugh and joke, but when Paul asks the same question, the reply is: 'Nothing happening, mate.' Paul's relationship with the police has been built up over his 23 years as the news editor at Signal: 'I know I'm trusted. I have the best job in the country – for my style. Stoke-on-Trent is a great patch and the people are just amazing here – it's just a great city.'
1443	Laura is busy filming Garry Cartwright. He's told her he wanted access to the river bank to teach his grandson fishing. It's not the fishing season, so she can't film him with a rod in his hand. Instead she settles for set-up shots of him on the newly-laid turf with his dogs. Laura filming Garry Cartwright
1445	Paul decides that, with nothing happening locally, Patricia Hewitt will have to go into his next bulletin at three o'clock. He takes the IRN audio clip from the Unison conference, and rewrites the IRN copy to make it much shorter.
1448	Paul checks the latest IRN stories on his computer. The stories appear in red when they are local to Signal's area. He notices one about a teacher's body being found and can't understand why it is red. He reads further and discovers the teacher was from Macclesfield, which means it is a local story. Paul has a new lead story. He rewrites the IRN copy.
1450	Stuart, BBC Stoke's health story specialist, arrives at the hospital site in Hartshill to cover the trust meeting.

1458	*Paul asks Simon to monitor Radio Stoke's bulletin and goes into the studio and reads Signal's three o'clock bulletin.*
1500	A clip of Patricia Hewitt leads the Radio Stoke bulletin, followed by the Flemming audio.
1510	*Paul returns to the newsroom. Simon tells him that Radio Stoke had a story about the Ivor Novello songwriting competition with mentions of Coldplay and James Blunt. He starts updating the stories for the four and five o'clock bulletins and writes the Macclesfield teacher's body story for tomorrow morning.*
1512	**Laura continues her filming in Tamworth.**
1525	*Paul answers the phone. Mark from Cheshire Police has information about a court appearance a few weeks previously.*
1532	*Paul continues writing fresh lines on the Macclesfield teacher, and checks how the other police stories start to make sure he's not repeating the same opening words.* *'I've heard stations that are still running stories that first went out at ten in the morning, using the same wording and the same audio clip eight hours later at six in the evening. You can run the same stories, but you need to freshen them. People listen traditionally in 20-minute bursts. You can often leave the same bulletins running for two hours. In the mid-morning and mid-afternoon, you can even leave them running for three hours.'*
1548	*Paul rings Carol at Staffordshire Police press office for another friendly chat: 'Is it quiet? . . . Good. OK, talk later.'* *He rings Diane at Cheshire Police press office, but nothing is happening.* *'You have to be everyone's mate as a journalist.'* *Paul checks the draft bulletins ready for Tom in the morning. There are already six stories written for him: 'We're 60 per cent done – that'll give him a good head start.'*

1559	Paul goes into the studio and reads for level.
1600	The second hand reaches the top of the hour and Paul starts his bulletin. He finishes two minutes later as the second hand hits two minutes past. Two clips of Patricia Hewitt lead the bulletin, both about the University Hospital. She'd spoken about its problems for several minutes, saying the mess the hospital is in is entirely of its own making. Off the back of the second clip, Helen announces: 'The former chair of the hospital Calum Paton will be talking to Tim Wedgwood on BBC Radio Stoke later this evening. He says he's unhappy at being made a scapegoat.'
1602	Paul is back in the newsroom. He starts writing new headlines for five o'clock. He has a dilemma. Does he stick with the Ivor Novello music awards just after the headline about two people dying in a car crash? 'Yes, we do.' He changes his mind: 'No, we don't.' He checks with the police on the condition of the two young men in hospital after the Endon crash. Paul says: 'We don't have enough manpower to be ringing hospitals checking on their condition. Also, should we be bothering hard-working medical staff on patients' conditions?'
1615	Paul checks on the weather update off IRN and takes it round to the presenters on air. He goes into the small news studio and records the headlines and weather for overnight for the various outputs.
1618	Laura has finished filming. She has recorded 22 minutes of video, which she'll edit into a two-minute package. The council have told her they won't offer a spokesman for interview, but they have issued a press statement in an e-mail that's waiting for her when she returns to the office. She pulls in to the roadside to call her friend Simon, the chef, who agrees to meet at the transport café the following morning. She decides to drive back to Stoke via the A515 which will take her past the café, so she'll know how to find it tomorrow.
1624	Paul returns to the newsroom and checks his e-mail for any new press releases.
1643	Paul takes a call from a listener about a stolen item. Paul says he is sorry, but he can't read it out on the news.
1649	Paul rings the voice-banks and makes his regular police check calls. He picks up details of a family's tribute to one of the victims who died in the Endon crash. The drive-time audience is traditionally a much lower audience on Signal than the breakfast audience, and Paul decides not to use it for the five o'clock bulletin. He wants to keep something fresh for the morning: 'I don't want to use all my eggs today. I won't waste a fresh update on a smaller audience this afternoon. I'll save two or three eggs for an eggy dip in the morning!'

| 1650 | The hospital trust has agreed a revised scaled-down design for the new hospital, with more than a hundred fewer beds than first planned. Stuart is having trouble with interference from a taxi firm on the radio car's link to the studio. He does a 40-second voicer on his mobile phone. It will run in the next two bulletins. A 'phono' voicer can be filed straight onto the station's auto-recorder – a high-quality answerphone. The reporter reads his cue, records his voicer and the report can be top-and-tailed in Radioman, the edit system. If a producer in the newsroom is expecting the reporter to file, there's not even a need to phone in. |

Stuart Fear at the hospital OB

| 1657 | *Paul goes into the studio to read Signal's five o'clock bulletin.* |

| 1700 | The Radio Stoke bulletin includes the two clips of the Health Secretary and Stuart's voicer. |

| 1706 | *Simon leaves the newsroom for the day. Paul returns to the main news desk in the newsroom and starts writing the tribute story for tomorrow morning. He files it on the system under Tuesday 6 a.m. He then writes another version of the story for the 8 a.m. bulletin, saving a line about the 'lessons learned' for the larger audience at eight.* |

| 1715 | Stuart does a live two-way with presenter Tim Wedgwood. He returns to the meeting for the rest of the business and to collect audio for later bulletins. |

| 1756 | *Paul checks the voice-banks. There are no new stories.* |

| 1800 | *Paul reads the same bulletin as he read at five o'clock.* |

1805	*Paul leaves the newsroom for the day.* Immediately after the news, there's an interview with Calum Paton, the former chair of the hospital trust. He's unhappy at being made a scapegoat by the Health Secretary.
1850	Local TV's 10-minute bulletin includes a report from BBC Midlands Today, the regional programme, about villagers in Gnosall who've bought their own speed gun to catch speeding drivers. There's a NIBs (news in brief) bulletin of three items read by Rupinder Bahra, the community content producer; an item presented by Chris Campbell-Brown who does ghost walks in Burton-upon-Trent (complete with 'spooky' camera tricks); and pieces about breakdancing classes and the Paralympic sport of goalball. The NIBs include the names of the A53 car crash victims. Laura's brambles story will run tomorrow. It will also be shown on the regional programme Midlands Today.

RADIO 1 NEWSBEAT

BBC Radio 1 Newsbeat is in audience terms the biggest news station in BBC radio. Their remit is to make sense of the news for a mostly young audience with highly crafted packages. Based on the second floor of Yalding House in Clipstone Street, near Broadcasting House in London, Newsbeat staff work alongside the news team on their digital sister network 1 Xtra, who are based one floor above on the third floor. There are about 60 staff on both networks, with 36 on Newsbeat. Most staff stay a maximum of just two years on Newsbeat. The staff is 60 per cent female, and 30 per cent are from ethnic minorities. The journalists all have to be highly able technically (there are no studio managers).

Newsbeat's audience is 50 per cent male, 50 per cent female, a higher proportion of female listeners than most other BBC News output. Most of the audience are in their twenties, working as sales reps, in supermarkets, the building trade, and the armed forces. Ten per cent of the audience are students. Newsbeat staff write as if the audience are 'mates, who know a lot'.

The Newsbeat newsroom is long and thin, with the editor Rod McKenzie's office at one end and the studio and control room at the other. There is a large plasma screen near the studio, and each work-station has a small screen tuned to either BBC News 24, GMTV, Sky News or CNN. Radio 1 plays constantly in the background.

There are news bulletins on Radio 1 hourly from 4.30 a.m. until 6.30 a.m. After that, they are every half-hour until 9.30, when they revert to hourly. At noon, there is a short entertainment news bulletin, and at 12.45 the 15-minute lunchtime Newsbeat programme. From 1.30 the bulletins are every half-hour until 5 p.m., when there is a short bulletin/trail for the evening Newsbeat. The evening programme runs from 5.45 until 6 p.m. There is an entertainments bulletin at 6.30.

0700

Newsbeat's duty editor for today, Kevin Silverton, arrives and has a brief handover from the overnight team. He starts researching the main leads for the day. Kevin is one of six or seven duty editors on Newsbeat, and is duty editor roughly once a week. The first editions of the morning papers arrive around midnight, and the overnight team have been researching stories. Newsbeat's main rivals are commercial radio and the IRN website. They aim to get a 'national' feel to their output, using BBC regional reporters and sending Newsbeat staff around the country rather than keeping them in London.

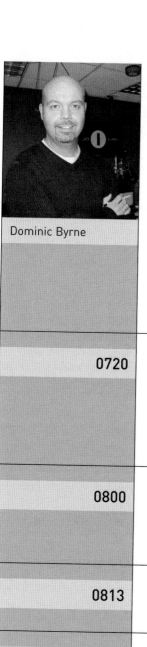

Dominic Byrne

In the basement of Yalding House, Chris Moyles and the breakfast team are on air. At this time of day there are between eight and ten million listeners. The early news team is based next to the Chris Moyles studio in the Live Lounge. There are three in the early news team: the news producer, the news presenter and the sports presenter who writes and produces the breakfast sport. Duty news editor for Breakfast today is Adrian Pearce, who has been in since 4 a.m.

The Live Lounge sits in the middle of the four Radio 1 studios with a large window looking into each studio. It is a versatile area used for production, with three newsdesk computers for the early news team. It can also be used – by folding away the desks – as a studio to record bands and acoustic sessions later in the day.

Adrian sits at his work-station and researches and writes the bulletins. Dominic Byrne, Breakfast's newsreader, spends 70 per cent of his time in the studio. He reads the copy Adrian has written (all Newsbeat presenters prefer to read from a paper script). Carey Davis is on sport today. Chris Moyles presents his show standing up, and, when in the studio, newsreader Dominic is perched on the opposite side of the desk with other contributors to the show.

0720

Kevin spends his first hour talking to the reporters already assigned to stories. Hannah Morrison has been sent to Wales where the number of Welsh students staying in Wales to study has increased. He also talks with the political reporter, Rajini Vaidyanathan, who is in Manchester all week for the Labour Party Conference. This is usually the time the duty editor sends reporters out on 'obvious stories' – the ones they don't need to decide upon at the morning meeting. Kevin says waiting till the meeting would be a waste of time, with the first main programme on air just four hours later.

0800

Most of the Newsbeat staff are now in. They are busy catching up on the news, reading the morning papers, checking facts on their computers and watching the breakfast news output on the TV screens on their desks. Radio 1 is playing in the background throughout the newsroom.

0813

The majority of the team start to move downstairs one floor to the meeting room, for their daily morning meeting. It is a large room with black sofas.

0815

The meeting gets underway. It is chaired by Kevin Silverton as today's duty editor. Twenty-three staff from both 1 Xtra and Newsbeat attend, including Rod McKenzie, Editor, Radio 1 Newsbeat and 1 Xtra.

Kevin begins by listing what has already been planned: 'Heather has filed a report from the US on the Colorado siege. Hannah is in Aberystwyth; she went yesterday. New figures show that more Welsh students are applying to Welsh universities. Fifty per cent of freshers in Wales are Welsh because of the tuition fees. Simi is in New York looking at the Virgin Galactic Explorer Spaceship mock-up.

'The Ents team went to the Borat film last night; there'll be a piece on at lunchtime. There's Rio Ferdinand's book launch; the hip-hop weekend on 1 Xtra; Michael Knowles – Beyonce's father – is releasing a hip-hop rap album for kids – with no profanities. And Gordon Ramsay is on Moyles. Steve Irwin's wife, Terri, is speaking – there's some really lovely audio. And finally Pete Doherty and Kate Moss are back in the news.'

0820

Rod McKenzie at the morning meeting

Kevin opens the meeting up, and asks for other stories. Ian offers two technology stories: Microsoft's high-definition DVD drive, and film director Peter Jackson going to work on computer games with Microsoft. He tells the meeting: '*Newsround* are there and I was talking with them late last night co-ordinating with them over the audio.'

A dangerous criminal escaped in transit near Worcester yesterday lunchtime. Audio is available from West Mercia Police.

'The problem with this story is that he'll be found just before we go on air at lunchtime.'

'How dangerous is dangerous?'

'He's an armed robber.'

'I play football with a couple of prison officers and they say . . .'

The meeting is relaxed with a lot of good humour. Rod and Kevin take a back seat allowing the junior members of the team to chip in, discuss stories and pitch their ideas. Rod McKenzie wants others to have an equal voice: 'They argue passionately for their ideas. It's a creative, free-flowing process. It's as non-hierarchical as possible – the orthodox editorial comes later. It needs to be quite open, a safe environment to bounce ideas.'

They discuss a new poll on the best road-works in Britain.

'It's so British – we get something positive out of it!'

'It's so predictable.'

'It would be great for the 5.45 with people driving.'

They move on to discuss a new cure for hay fever – Dr Hilary Jones had been on GMTV earlier discussing it.

They are looking for stories that provoke reaction. A 17-year-old has given birth to triplets and already has a child.

'Do we want it as a positive story?'

'How would the listeners react?'

A discussion takes place about whether their audience would view it as a positive story.

The meeting turns to John Prescott's swansong at the Labour Conference. He is due to give his final conference speech as Deputy Leader at around 12ish. Editor Rod asks the meeting: 'Is it accessible for our audience?'

One of the team says: 'But who knows he is still the Deputy Prime Minister? The story is he's retiring. Oh, sorry, didn't realise you were still there!'

'I think we ought to spend 20 minutes today trying to get the first interview with Richard Hammond [the presenter of *Top Gear* was injured in a 300-mph crash eight days earlier]. He's moving to a general ward today. The BBC have put a bid in. It'll never happen if we go through the BBC Press Office.'

Rod McKenzie says: 'If the BBC have already put a bid in, this comes under the "Big Bid Rules", and we can't do that.'

They discuss a new ring that heats up to remind the wearer of important dates. More jokes.

The lead on TV's *Ten O'Clock News* last night was about the Chinese harvesting organs. Ten thousand people are executed in China every year, and 95 per cent of transplants in China are from prisoners on Death Row.

'Would our audience be interested?'

'We know that ten thousand people are being executed in China, what's new?'

'We might know that, but do our audience know it? Not that we have that many Radio 1 listeners in China!'

They discuss cricket and bungs in football.

'I couldn't give a shit about bungs. It doesn't affect me – I'm not interested.'

'If bungs are a scandal, then the fees are a scandal as well.'

'Is it affecting fans out there rather more than it affects the news team?'

'I'm with Toby on this – it might be big with football fans, but what about the non-football fans?'

'It's rather gossipy.'

They bounce the bung story around until someone says with a laugh: 'Moving on from the football bung story . . .'

'Citizenship classes. These lessons are failing. The majority of our audience would have gone through them. Ofsted officials say that some of these lessons may be dangerous.' Lots of laughter . . .

0848	Kevin closes the meeting. The teams move back to the two newsrooms. 1 Xtra is based on the third floor of Yalding House. The 1 Xtra news team is a scaled-down version of the Newsbeat team situated in a corner of the 1 Xtra production area.
0900	Back in the Newsbeat newsroom, Kevin and Rod discuss the stories they will cover. *Rod explains: 'We are very audience focused – it's what the audience care about we'll cover. Texts are important to us. We have a fantastic level of interaction with our audience. They're very interested in sex. We have a lot of ordinary soldiers from the armed forces listening to us.'*
0905	Newsbeat planner, Karlene Pinnock, leaves to go to Television Centre at White City. She is on the rota to sit on the news planning desk. Newsbeat has a representative on the planning desk each day in the main BBC newsroom in west London. Rod comments: 'They're not really interested in what we're doing; they're telling us what they're doing, but we're not really interested.'
0915	Rod goes into his office for the daily conference video-link with the BBC Radio planning meeting at Television Centre. He dials in.

0918	The video conference call begins. Also on the video-link is World Service News at Bush House. On the large plasma screen in a corner of his office, Rod can see the meeting room at Television Centre, where radio editors and Newsgathering are seated around a large conference table. On the left of the screen, he can also see the news editor from World Service at Bush. The meeting has already started as Rod joins on the video-link. The discussion is about the output over the previous 24 hours. The tone is one of praise.
0920	A voice over the video link asks: 'Rod, how was yesterday with you?' Rod says: 'The best story for us was the sex scandal with the judge.' The reply comes with a smile: 'It was the best story – I reprimand anyone who didn't do that story yesterday.' 'It was a very funny day yesterday – we were looking for leads. The China transplant story was pulled forward. It was a stockpile feature that was brought forward because there was no lead. The secret filming in Beijing was good.' 'Let's talk about today . . .'
0925	Home Newsgathering go through a list: 'Labour Party Conference. There's the Reid speech this morning and John Prescott's at around 12. Musharraf – no usable audio is expected with Blair. Accident rates are going down. Universities – we've some commissioned stuff there. Seasonal flu preparations, what to expect. Not very exciting, quite boring. New jobs at Swindon are expected to be announced today. There's a presser on the 14-month-old savaged by a Rottweiler, nothing live and we're looking at the anti-Pope demonstrations.'
0931	Foreign Newsgathering are invited to go through their list. 'There's been a possible tsunami. The ball-tampering ICC ruling is expected later today. There's a spy row over Russia and Georgia. In St Petersburg, the body of the mother of the Tsar is being buried – some nice audio is expected out of that. At 12 o'clock our time in New York, there's the unveiling of the spaceship. And there are lots of Irishmen in Paris for the Derry match.'
0935	'Rod, what are you up to today?' 'We're going to mop up the Colorado shooting. We're doing Terri Irwin. We're in Aberystwyth with some Welsh students – we have Glyn from Big Brother with us. Prescott's in Manchester. We're doing the "best road-works" story.' Rod is told that Five Live have already done some stuff this morning from the M42 near Birmingham. He might want to have a look at it. Rod thanks them and continues: 'We went to the Borat screening last night and will be covering that. There are also two technology pieces, one on HD DVD and Peter Jackson is getting into computer games. And then we're covering the Virgin Galactic spaceship.' It is then Radio Two's turn: they're covering the judge, coughing, dangerous dog, and John Simpson is on the Jeremy Vine show. World Service list what they are covering and then leave the video meeting. Radio Four are then asked what they are up to. The *World at One* (or WATO as it's known) will be covering Prescott's speech and doing a piece on prisons. *PM* will be at the Labour conference in Manchester and covering Pakistan, the Zambian elections and the citizenship story. *The World Tonight* will be covering the conference, and they're doing a piece on Brazilian crime.

0940	The end of the conference meeting. Rod comments: 'Our agenda and the agenda for the rest of BBC radio news is a chasm apart. There was an enormous breadth in that meeting – the complete world of journalism. We are so diverse on coverage.'
0955 Maddy Savage	Georgina Bowman, Newsbeat's presenter, arrives in the newsroom. She starts getting up to speed with what is happening. Her first bulletin is in 35 minutes at 10.30. Sitting at the next work-station to Georgina is senior broadcast journalist Maddy Savage. Maddy is writing all the bulletins today. It is her job to write fresh scripts and to get fresh audio for each hour. The bulletins are two minutes long and she writes six stories for each hour, with three audio clips. Each clip is no longer than 12 or 13 seconds. Voicers on Newsbeat are under 20 seconds, but if they are political they might be a bit longer. Most copy stories are just a couple of lines, and there is sport in every bulletin.
1010	Kevin hears from Newsgathering that Richard Hammond is expected to leave hospital in Leeds within the next hour to go to a general ward in Bristol.
1020	Georgina is busy putting the finishing touches to Maddy's 10.30 bulletin script. One of the team is trying to find out which hospital Richard Hammond is moving to. Frenchay Hospital say they are not expecting him.
1025	Georgina prints off the script, and goes into the studio to read the bulletin.
1027 Georgina Bowman	Georgina has no technical help for this bulletin today; she has to self-op. Normally there is a studio broadcast assistant to operate the desk for the bulletins during the day. They concentrate on the sound balance, allowing the presenters to concentrate on their read. Georgina tries to contact Jo Whiley on talkback. Jo's show is now live from one of the basement studios. She is not sure which studio Jo is broadcasting from. 'I don't know what studio Jo's in – I don't normally do this.' She calls through on talkback to one of the studios, and asks if Jo is there. She is told she's got the wrong studio. 'Who was that?' she asks. 'It was Chris Moyles,' says a BJ (broadcast journalist), who is collecting something from the studio. 'No, it wasn't,' Georgina sounds shocked. 'Yes, it was. Look at the camera.' *All the studios are linked by webcams.*

1029	Georgina finds Jo Whiley's studio and lets her know on talkback she's reading the bulletin. The 10.30 bulletin is often read by Dominic Byrne, who has been on the Chris Moyles show. He and Georgina work out between them who will read this bulletin, depending on their commitments during the morning.
1030	Music fades and Jo Whiley cues Georgina. She opens her fader and starts reading.
1032	Georgina finishes the bulletin and comes out of the studio. *Working practices on Newsbeat have changed enormously in the past ten years. They no longer have studio managers or producers. The production and technical operation is done by senior broadcast journalists. Journalists are not only expected to write, research and report; they are also expected to be able to edit their pieces and self-op in the studio to a high level of creativity and competence.* Newsbeat use a different editing system from the rest of BBC Radio News. They use Cool Edit (now called Adobe Audition) to edit, and Cool Play to play out. Everything is designed to be as simple as possible for the journalists to self-op. They have an Instant Replay system on the studio desk – it plays audio clips and music stabs at the touch of a button.
1040	Kevin and Georgina are reading texts from listeners. 'Texts are very, very important to us,' Kevin explains. 'They show listener feedback.' They like to be able to read some of them out, but they discover a lot are abusive comments about the prisoner who has escaped. They won't be able to use them.
1043	Dominic Byrne is checking a story with the Entertainments team.
1050	News breaks on PA, and the Sky Breaking News strap appears across the plasma announcing that Richard Hammond is due to leave hospital.
1051	Kevin rings Anna Lee, the BBC reporter who is meant to be covering the Hammond story in Leeds.
1052	Georgina and Maddy return to writing their scripts. Georgina says: 'That's the lead for half eleven then.'

1055	Georgina is trying to write the Prescott story for the 12.45 lunchtime programme, but she's struggling. The top line of PA is not written in a way the Newsbeat audience will go for.
	'It's hard to write when he hasn't spoken yet. Our audience loved the Prescott fling story,' she says, as she writes: *Who could forget those photos of John Prescott during his fling with his secretary? Or him parading round that posh ranch . . .*
	She deletes it all and tries again:
	It's one of those images from the papers that stick with you . . .
	She deletes the lot and goes to the university story instead.
	Well, its Freshers' week . . . she presses 'delete' again.
	He might not have won Big Brother but he's still doing his bit for his country . . .
	'If you can grab them like that – they'll want to listen.'
	Sitting next to Georgina, Kevin adds: 'The Newsbeat style is a difficult style to crack. It's basic, but not simplistic, and not patronising. Often the way stories work best for Newsbeat is as eye-witness accounts from reporters.'
1105	Georgina is asked if she has time to take a call from Hannah, the reporter in Wales. Hannah wants to discuss her cue. Georgina goes into the Cool Edit program and checks the out-cue with Hannah over the phone. She then returns to her script and continues writing.
1110	*There's been yet more amazing news about Richard Hammond and his recovery . . .*
	Georgina calls to Kevin sitting next to her: 'I've put a cue in for Richard Hammond – but it might all change.'
1114	Georgina starts writing the John Prescott story again.
	It might be hard to look at John Prescott and think politics, and not about that affair he had with his secretary. But the Deputy Prime Minister's just been speaking at the Labour Party Conference in Manchester. He's just . . .
1116	Francis from the Entertainments team calls out: 'There's Richard Hammond sitting up in the helicopter.'
	The first shots of Richard Hammond leaving hospital are on the plasma. People in the newsroom stop what they are doing and watch these first pictures. Francis says: 'Wow. That's amazing.'
1119	Kevin has written a trail for the lunchtime programme to be read in the 11.30 bulletin. Maddy calls across to Kevin: 'Kev, does that cue work, if we say we'll have a report from our reporter at the hospital after Richard Hammond has left the hospital?'
	Kevin starts to rewrite the trail.

1126	Georgina picks up her bulletin script and goes into the studio.
1130	Georgina goes on air. This time Derek Knight, one of the technical broadcast assistants on Newsbeat, is there to sort the sound levels out for her. All Georgina has to worry about is her read.
1133	Georgina returns to writing scripts for the lunchtime programme.
1150	Frances Cronin, the duty editor for the Entertainments team, comes off the phone and laughs with Georgina sitting opposite her in the bank of work-stations: 'My friend has just become Janet Street-Porter's PA. Janet's having a party tonight to launch her autobiography, and she wants us to mention it. But she won't tell us what stars are going, or where it is going to be, and we can't go. It is going to be star-studded, but she won't tell us who is going.'
1155	'Hannah on two for you, Kevin.' Kevin and Hannah go through Hannah's university script over the phone.
1200	Kevin and Georgina watch Sky's report on Richard Hammond and then discuss what wording to use – they decide upon 'sitting up and smiling'.
1203	Kevin asks one of the team to record the John Prescott speech on their terminal, because he wants to edit the speech on another terminal as it happens.
1205	Kevin and Georgina discuss the timing of the Prescott speech. Georgina says: 'We'll just have to busk it. They'll want to get it in before the one o'clock news, won't they?' Kevin says: 'Blair was half an hour late yesterday with his speech. Keep an eye on the TV screens . . .'

1215	In the studio cubicle, Derek is top-and-tailing some clips. He checks the sound levels. He takes the Borat clip and 'builds' it using music: 'It's a bit of a frantic programme, so I like to get as much down on "tape" before we start, but when you're getting near to the wire, it's often best to take it live.'
1220	Georgina has rewritten her Prescott script again. *Deputy Prime Minister John Prescott will be gone from his job within the year. A fling with his secretary and visits in cowboy boots to a posh ranch in the States. It's been more about the scandal than the politics for John Prescott this year. But the Deputy Prime Minister's just been speaking at the Labour Conference. He says he's going to quit . . .*
1226	Kevin comes into the studio cubicle. Traffic buzzes through. Derek is told that regional news reporter Anna Lee from Leeds is coming through on OS2 (outside source 2) for a pre-record. 'OK. I'll go and get the presenter. I assume it's a two-way.' Georgina arrives in the studio and starts speaking to Anna down the line: 'I've just listened to you on Five Live.' Georgina and Anna run through the questions for the two-way. Anna says: 'I don't want to say he's still in the air, because he might well have landed by the time we go on air.' They start recording. Anna fluffs and they restart.
1234	Georgina asks Kevin if there is anything she can do. John Prescott gets to his feet to start his speech. Georgina is monitoring it on the screen in the studio. Prescott says he is sorry.
1235	Maddy pops her head round the studio cubicle door: 'I've taken in road-works for you.' Kevin takes a clip from the start of John Prescott's speech: 'I just want to say sorry.'
1239	Kevin comes into the studio to say that there's a new Hammond clip now. He has just added a quote from the doctor to Anna's piece.
1240	Kevin says: 'We've nearly got everything in now. Hannah's piece has a nasty end.' He asks Derek: 'Can you do anything?' Derek listens to the end of the piece.

1243	Broadcast Assistant Sophie Donaldson hands out the script to everyone. Georgina quickly says: 'Sophie, we have a different news to this one. Has no one told you?' Sophie prints off the new scripts. Jo Whiley buzzes through to the studio op talkback and asks: 'Are you there?' Derek replies on talkback: 'Yep. Standing by with George for you . . .'
1245	The red light goes on, and Newsbeat is on air. Derek thanks Jo on talkback. As each item runs, Derek discards his script page by page on to the floor behind him.
1246	'Out of this at 47.45,' Sophie tells Georgina over talkback. Georgina replies: 'I'm dropping the line after the dog clip.'
1248	'Colorado in ten,' Sophie calls. It's her job to do the on-air timings. Georgina is watching Prescott on the TV screen in the studio. She calls through to the cubicle on talkback: 'Is it too late to put Prescott earlier?' Derek says: 'Yes.' He asks her if she's seen the cricket news on the screen. The ICC have made their ruling about ball-tampering in the England–Pakistan test.
1249	Sophie dashes out of the cubicle to alert David Garrido at the sports desk in the newsroom. She returns to carry on the timings, and says: 'He hadn't seen it.'
1250	'It's ten to one,' Georgina says on air. 'Prescott in ten,' calls Sophie. 'Standby.' Georgina finishes her link into Prescott and cues in Rajini, the political reporter live in Manchester.
1253	David Garrido pops into the cubicle with his sports script for Sophie, and then goes through into the studio to join Georgina. The best road-works package is playing.
1256	Georgina introduces the sport with David Garrido.

1258	Georgina cues in the Borat package that Derek mixed earlier. Georgina quips on talkback to Derek: 'Love the music!'
1259	Georgina is advised by Derek on talkback: 'You've only 20 secs at the end.'
1300	They come off air, and move out of the studio into the newsroom for the post-mortem. Kevin stands outside the studio door, and talks to the whole newsroom: 'Prescott was still talking when we went on air. Well done on Borat. It was all good really, well done.'
1303	The post-mortem ends.
1332	Kevin takes a call from Rajini in Manchester. She tells him she has the chance of a one-to-one with Prescott. She asks Kevin: 'If I have one question for John Prescott, what would it be?' He opens it up to the other journalists around him. Sitting opposite him, the Entertainments duty editor Francis suggests with a naughty laugh: 'Did he use a condom?' Kevin suggests another question: 'Do you think anyone will take you seriously?'
1336	On the plasma, Richard Hammond can be seen on News 24 walking from the helicopter in Bristol. Kevin is still giving suggestions to Rajini over the phone: 'You could ask: "Why did you decide to say sorry? What do you regret most? Our audience find it difficult to take you seriously."'
1338	Kevin is told that Georgina wants to do a pre-record with Rajini in the studio. He says: 'She can't. She's got a one-on-one with Prescott.' In Manchester, the Deputy Prime Minister is ready for the interview. Rajini rings off.
1341	Rajini rings Kevin back. 'Blimey, that was quick,' he says. 'What did you ask him?'
1345	Kevin grabs some lunch at his desk, and takes a look at the lunchtime edition of the *Evening Standard*.

1400	Becky Clarke arrives in the newsroom. She is a freelance masseuse. She regularly comes in to give some of the staff a neck and shoulder massage at their desks. Entertainments duty editor Frances Cronin is second on her list. The journalists – not the BBC – pay for her visit.
1405	Broadcast Assistant Sophie Donaldson has a technical training session booked with broadcast journalist Gabby O'Donnell up on the roof.
	Sophie is in charge of the portable technical equipment for Newsbeat staff. They have 12 laptop computers that reporters take out. They record onto MiniDisc recorders and use a GSM card, like a large SIM card from a mobile phone, in the side of one of the laptops to send their reports. The recordings are saved as MP3 files and can be sent via wireless broadband. There are Wi-Fi hotspots around the country: Newsbeat reporters tend to use McDonald's and Starbucks to send their reports. BBC Traffic has a massive server that takes the reports in. To file a one- or one-and-a-half-minute piece on the mobile network it takes about ten minutes.
	Gabby's training session is on the satellite and ISDN phone kit. Newsbeat have four M4 Sat kits that reporters can take out. Sophie is busy checking through one of the M4 Sat kits for one of the Newsbeat team to take to the Middle East tomorrow.
1525	Back in the newsroom, Maddy prints off the 3.30 bulletin she has just finished writing.
1526	Georgina goes into the studio. Mark Chapman (Chappers) is already there for the sport. He's dressed in a pinstripe suit today.
1529	Radio 1 DJ Edith Bowman comes through to the cubicle on talkback and checks who's doing the news and sport. Derek tells her Mark is looking very smart in a suit today. She can see him on the webcam, and in her cue into the bulletin says: 'Here's Georgina and a pinstriped Mark Chapman . . .'
1530	Georgina goes on air: 'Two Jags, a few shags and that famous punch during an election campaign. A video montage of John Prescott's most embarrassing moments has just been shown to Labour's Party Conference . . .'
1542	Frances and Georgina go through the entertainment news for 5.45.

1545	Georgina is busy writing her scripts for the 5.45 programme. She asks Maddy next to her: 'What's another word for space?' 'Universe,' she suggests.
1548	Kevin asks Debbie, one of the broadcast journalists, to help out: 'Can you write a cue for Anna's piece on Richard Hammond? Listen to Anna's piece and make sure you don't repeat what she says!' Debbie starts listening.
1553	Debbie is busy writing the cue. She asks Kevin what Anna Lee's surname is. He says: 'That's it! Anna *Lee*!' 'Oh no,' says Debbie. 'She must think I'm a right div. I've been calling her Anna-Lee, as if it's her first name, all day! How embarrassing.' Everyone laughs.
1606	Kevin is on the phone. Sitting next to him, Georgina draws Kevin's attention to the TV screen. So Solid Crew's Megaman has been cleared of murder. Georgina calls to Debbie about the Richard Hammond cue: 'Nice one, luvvy.'
1607	Kevin comes off the phone. Newsbeat reporter Toby Sealey calls out as he passes Georgina and Kevin's desks: 'You've seen Megaman's been cleared.'
1630	Georgina is on air again. Prescott is the lead with fresh audio. There's new audio on the Richard Hammond piece as well.
1635	Kevin and Georgina discuss the So Solid rapper's acquittal: 'He's a little bit off the radar now . . .'
1640	Frances and the Entertainments team move downstairs for their weekly Entertainments planning meeting. She has prepared a 12-page list of forthcoming events. 'Kylie has her book launch this weekend. Can we go on Saturday? Rod is happy for us to bend the rule about submitting questions beforehand if we need to. 'Gary Barlow – well, we'll have to bid for that – I'll do it tomorrow. 'Russell Crowe interview? Nat, that's for you, I think! 'Jack Osbourne – we've got to bid for him . . . 'Peter Kay is a "no" now. '*Dr Who* set visit. We'll actually get to see real Daleks! We've got to go to that . . .'

1730	The weekly Entertainments planning meeting draws to a close.
1732	Kevin goes through the rotas for the next couple of weeks.
1736	The techno fair in New York (with the Virgin spaceship) is on News 24. Georgina asks Kevin: 'Have you seen this on 24?'
1739	Maddy prints off the 5.45 script. Georgina's mobile rings. 'You've done it again,' she laughs. 'I'm going on the radio in five minutes!'
1740	Georgina walks into the studio.
1741	In the cubicle Derek comments: 'We've loads of time ahead of ourselves. Give me some level.'
1742	'I'm just going to listen through the Prescott package again – 'cos I'm paranoid!'
1744	'Here's Georgina Bowman . . .' Newsbeat is on air.
1745	Toby Sealey's cricket-ball-tampering package is the top story in Newsbeat's running order. Georgina reads the cue: 'Such a gentlemanly game – men in white – leather on willow . . . cheating and sit-in protests? It was one of cricket's biggest scandals when Pakistan was accused of ball-tampering last month. Their captain Inzamam-ul-Haq has been cleared of that charge. But he will still be banned for four one-day games for bringing the game into disrepute. Newsbeat's Toby Sealey has more . . .' The ball-tampering package lasts one minute 22 seconds.

1749	During the Prescott package, sports presenter David Garrido comes into the studio cubicle to speak with sports reporter, Nigel Adderley, down-the-line in Italy. He checks the in and out words and the pronunciation of the local stadium in Italy. He then pops back into the newsroom. David comes back into the cubicle and checks with sports reporter Andy Gilles down-the-line in Prague. He gets him to read the script out and checks the out-cue: 'That's fine. I'll speak to you on air.' He joins Georgina in the studio.
1755	Derek double-checks the sound levels on Nigel Adderley in Italy and Andy Gilles in Prague.
1756	Georgina cues in David on air: 'Sport now with David Garrido . . .'
1757	Nigel Adderley comes off air, and Derek gives him a quick 'thanks' over the line. Georgina cues in Andy Gilles.
1758	Busy doing the timings, Sophie comments on Georgina's heavy use of sarcasm in the script today.
1759	Sophie calls 'ten' for the headlines and weather.
1800	Off air.
1801	The Newsbeat team meet in the newsroom for the regular de-brief. Kevin starts it off: 'There was great scripting in Toby's piece. Generally, a well-rounded programme. I can't think of anything negative to say!' There is a discussion over the placing of the So Solid Megaman story in the running order [it was low down, just before sport]. Editor Rod McKenzie joins in: 'It would be a great story for 1 Xtra, but he's been off our radar recently, so I think it was right to run it where we did. I'd just like to say I think today's programme was absolutely f***ing brilliant!'

PARTTHREE
THE ESSENTIAL GUIDE

PART LIST
THE ESSENTIAL GUIDE

GETTING A JOB

THE JOB APPLICATION

Typically there are two ways of applying for jobs in broadcast journalism – a letter or e-mail accompanied by a CV (curriculum vitae) and possibly a showreel, or an online application form.

You can prepare a letter, CV and showreel that would fit any job. But it is not the best idea. Your application should be tailored to the job you are applying for. The worst sin in any application is to show no knowledge of the organisation you are applying to and its output. You are unlikely to be invited to interview.

Online applications are tougher, because you have to fill in all your details, including all that boring stuff you repeat every time about your education, qualifications and experience. This is a chore, but it helps you focus on only including the details that are relevant to the job and will make a positive impression. Most organisations that use online forms (like the BBC) allow you to store the information and go back to it later. Don't rush it. Fill in the basics, then return to the form later when you have given serious consideration to the sections where you have to write creatively about yourself and the job.

If you are applying for a job in journalism, there is no excuse for an application with spelling or grammatical mistakes. Use of language is a core journalistic skill, so many employers will use a spelling mistake or grammatical error as a reason for rejecting an application. It's an easy and sensible way to reduce the number of applications to a shortlist for interview.

BBC presenter Huw Edwards, who looks at a lot of job application forms, says: 'I've got to the stage where I just bin lots of stuff. I really am quite hard-line about it. If somebody can't be bothered to get their stuff up to scratch if they're applying for a job, you just think, well, do I really want to take this on? You may be dealing with somebody who's got a really good aptitude, a really good journalistic approach, but the fact is they will be really badly let down by how they present themselves on paper. It's what the job's about.

'If you can produce good writing, you will stand out from the crowd and you are going to advance more quickly than other people.'

THE COVERING LETTER

Your covering letter, which may be an e-mail, should also be concise – rarely more than a page, grammatically accurate and with correct spellings. One journalism student had an offer of a work placement withdrawn because she made a spelling mistake in her e-mail accepting the offer. Imagine how much more important it is to be accurate in a job application.

It is fundamental that you spell the names and titles of people in the organisation you are applying to correctly.

Your letter should focus on why you are suitable for the job in question. Try to avoid clichés like 'I am an enthusiastic, hard-working team player.' It's better to give brief examples of why you are a special candidate.

- Ask other people to describe your best qualities – it's better than trying to describe yourself.

- Have you achieved something of which you are particularly proud?

- Did you lead a team to success?

- Have you produced an original piece of journalism?

- Can you find a story?

- Have you been involved in a successful broadcast or website?

THE CV

When you apply for a job, you will include your CV, whether it's a prepared document or something you do online. So how do you prepare a CV for maximum impact?

You need to keep it brief and to the point. Few editors will want to look at more than one or two pages. You will find CV templates in most word-processing packages. There is nothing wrong with these. It's how you fill them in that matters. Don't use fancy fonts. They are distracting and difficult to read.

A CV for a job in journalism should:

- Be concise – most jobs in journalism are hugely over-subscribed, so editors faced with hundreds of applications will not be impressed by anything over two pages

- Emphasise your *relevant* experience – three weeks in a local radio station, even if it was unpaid, will carry more weight than two years' part-time work on a supermarket checkout

- Stress your key skills – any technical skills (camerawork, editing, software skills, shorthand) and legal training (the NCTJ law exam, for example) should be listed

- Contributions to any broadcast or journalistic output – including hospital radio, student radio, websites and local newspapers – must be included.

Never lie on a CV. You will be found out. Maybe not the first time, but eventually. It may be on an application for your dream job that your lies are discovered.

Simon Cole, Deputy Head of Sky News, is looking for that extra something – but admits it boils down to a subjective decision: 'These days Media courses, I think,

Simon Cole, Deputy Head of Sky News: 'What it boils down to is me – whether I like you or not.'

are totally oversubscribed and what you get is a whole raft of really bright youngsters – they've all done a gap year, they've all done good works abroad, they've all done something interesting. They've done a post grad, or a journalism degree, they've had work experience at CNN or the Beeb, or whatever – they've done a movie which is on DVD and all nicely set out for you, and they are all absolutely bloody fantastic – and so you think: how do I choose?

'And what it boils down to, to me, is – if you're sitting there – whether I like you or not. Whether I think you've got some character; whether you're going to have development potential to be whatever; whether you're a news editor or a reporter – because everyone wants to be a reporter, don't they? We all did – but these days the competition is so fierce, they've got to have something a bit different on the CV to get into my door and then they've got to sit on the couch and I've got to like them.

'For example, one person was very clever and they'd done some homework, and they'd heard that I'd got fridge magnets and so they brought in a fridge magnet that plays a tune. That person didn't get a job, but they got a second interview. You've almost got to use a gimmick – you've got to be a salesman or a saleswoman because what you are selling is yourself. It's not a car; it's not a Ducati motorbike; it's not a Fender Stratocaster – it's yourself. This is your big chance because if you get a job at Sky, you've made it. Whether you stay with the company, or whether you move, you're going to have that on your CV and you are in the business.'

REMEMBER

- ➤ Correct spelling and grammar are essential in a job application
- ➤ Keep your CV concise, with relevant experience near the top
- ➤ Know the output of the organisation
- ➤ Never lie.

SHOWREELS

A good showreel – an edit of highlights of your best work – can be the difference between getting an interview and not. It can also be the difference between getting the job and not, even if you do not perform your best at interview.

It's best to make a showreel that's geared to the job for which you are applying.

Here's an unfortunate fact – most showreels are not viewed beyond the first minute. So, give the first minute the most attention. A montage of pieces-to-camera (stand-ups) or studio presentation is a good idea. Try to make it entertaining and varied, with a mix of hard and light stories. It lets the prospective employer know how you perform on screen. They can judge your voice, presence and whether the camera likes you. TV professionals talk about the 'magic box'. Some people who are attractive in real life do not necessarily look good in two dimensions. Others, who are not conventionally good-looking, come across as strong and engaging personalities on screen.

After the montage, you should include a full-length package or two, so the employer can consider your writing skills, and use of pictures and sound. They will be asking if you can write to pictures, and tell a story.

You may want to include a hard news story, and a lighter piece. Don't make it longer than ten minutes and five will usually be enough.

A DVD presentation with a title page giving choices of shorter or longer content can help. The best option is to make a showreel for each job, tailored to the job description. Freelances looking to increase their portfolio of employers apply the same principle.

- If it's a reporter job, show your best reporting and any exclusive stories

- If the job is for a presenter, show your best studio work

- If you are applying to be a producer, include stories that show imaginative production techniques – graphics, perhaps, or visual metaphors.

Don't worry if all you have is student work. Professionals looking for someone suitable for a first job will recognise talent, even if the production values are not quite up to broadcast standard.

For a radio job, a CD or an MP3 file attached to your e-mail application does the same job as a showreel, and the same rules apply. Start with impact, then give examples of bulletin reading and crafted packages. Many broadcast journalism students will return from work placements in local radio with examples of their broadcasting skills, either off air or recorded as a demo in the studio.

REMEMBER

- ➤ Keep a showreel brief
- ➤ Make it entertaining and varied
- ➤ Most editors only view or listen to the first minute
- ➤ Tailor your showreel to the job description.

THE INTERVIEW

There are books and websites devoted to job interview techniques. Look them up, and we won't bother replicating their advice here. They'll tell you about dressing well, making a good first impression and showing confidence.

But what are the questions interviewers ask when they are appointing people to jobs in broadcast journalism? They can be divided into four broad categories:

- Awareness of our output
- Story ideas
- Treatment
- Knowledge of broadcast law and ethics.

AWARENESS OF OUTPUT

Interviewers will want to know you have listened to or watched enough of the broadcaster's output to judge the content, treatment of stories and how it compares with the opposition. It is never good enough to claim a vague knowledge of what the broadcaster does. There is no excuse for not having heard or seen the latest bulletin. Listen in the car or on the train on the way to a radio interview. Watch on satellite or online if you don't live in the region where the TV station broadcasts.

STORY IDEAS

You should enter any journalism interview with at least three story ideas. There is no excuse for not having knowledge of the station's transmission area. It's easy enough to research online. And better still, if you can find local contacts, call them and ask what's going on. Don't just think about blockbuster exclusives – you'll be lucky to find those. Think about areas of local activity that are under-reported. Ask community leaders what they think is missing in local coverage. Then ask for contact details of people you can use in your treatment of the story.

Treat stories you want to use at interview like stories you are researching in the newsroom. An interview panel will be impressed by comprehensive research.

TREATMENT

The treatment of stories can be as important as the story idea itself. Interviewers may ask you how you would treat themes, trends and issues in the news.

Personalising a story is always a good idea – find somebody affected by the issue. Reeling off a list of potential interviewees is not so good. Your idea has to be achievable within the organisation's deadline and budgets.

You will also need to have an awareness of forthcoming stories in the diary and how you would deal with them.

LAW AND ETHICS

Most interview panels (at the BBC they're known as 'boards') will want to know you can operate within legal and ethical guidelines. Study the Ofcom Code and BBC Editorial Guidelines. Make sure you know about defamation and contempt of court. An employer does not want the nagging doubt that the person they have appointed could land them in legal trouble.

For more on journalistic ethics and the regulatory framework, read Chris Frost's book *Journalism Ethics and Regulation*, published by Pearson. It should help you answer the tricky ethical questions that interviewers love to ask.

INTERVIEW EXERCISES

Many selection processes will include group exercises. These are designed for you to show leadership, teamwork and your personal problem-solving qualities.

There may be personal tests too. It might be a live two-way exercise, in which you are briefed on a story and then expected to deliver a 'live' report. Or it may be a reporting exercise. A favourite on BBC reporter interviews has been to send people out with a digital recorder and expect them to come back with a story. A tip – if you are sent into an unfamiliar town to find a story, look for a market. Market traders and their customers can have extraordinary stories to tell.

USING NOTES

There is nothing to stop you taking notes into a job interview as a prompt in case you forget the points you wanted to make. It's always worth jotting down three or four main points you want to get across, no matter what you are asked. The main points should be about your personal qualities and how they will fit into the job description. You don't have to look at the notes, but they can be a confidence booster and help prevent you drying up.

DUMMY INTERVIEWS

Before an important job interview, you would probably like some sort of rehearsal. Try and get a couple of people with experience of interviewing for journalism jobs to form a mock panel. Journalism tutors, or people you know from work experience, are the best option.

They should enter into role play and assume they have not met you before. After the interview, they should give you honest feedback. We regularly carry out these mock interviews, and students have benefited by getting the job.

REMEMBER

- ➤ Know the organisation's output
- ➤ Prepare story ideas and treatments
- ➤ Take brief notes into the interview if it boosts your confidence
- ➤ Set up a dummy interview
- ➤ You can never prepare too much for an interview – more knowledge gives you more confidence.

THE LAW AND BROADCAST JOURNALISTS

Broadcast journalists operate within a legal framework, regulated by the statutory bodies which govern broadcasting (in the UK, Ofcom) and the laws of the land (which differ in Scotland from the rest of the UK).

This is a guide to the areas of law and court practice of which journalists have to be aware. It is not a substitute for the law modules run within accredited broadcast journalism courses, or the information found in specialist books (*McNae's Essential Law for Journalists*, the core text, runs to over 500 pages).

Law comes from a variety of sources:

- Custom – established practice (known as common law)
- Precedent – the application of earlier decisions to a current case (case law)
- Statute – Acts of Parliament (statutory instruments)
- European Union regulations
- The European Convention on Human Rights.

In Scotland, there are also 'writers', institutional texts from respected writers on Scots law, mostly from the seventeenth, eighteenth and nineteenth centuries. Equity, the concept of natural justice and fairness, informs all the UK's legal systems.

DEFAMATION

Defamation is probably the biggest risk faced by working journalists. Whenever you write about someone, there is a danger you will damage their reputation, sometimes unwittingly. A spoken defamatory statement is slander, except where it is spoken in a broadcast (or in a public performance of a play). Then it has the same status as a statement in print and is defined as libel.

Civil actions for libel in pursuit of damages may be taken out against a broadcaster by anyone who considers they have been defamed. There is also, much more rarely, a risk of criminal libel, where the publication might lead to a breach of the peace.

Juries have to decide if reasonable men and women would consider a statement defamatory. Does it:

1 expose the person to hatred, ridicule or contempt?
2 cause him (or her) to be shunned or avoided?
3 lower him in the estimation of right-thinking members of society generally? *or*
4 disparage him in his business, trade or profession?

A corporation (usually a business whose trading reputation has been damaged) can sue for libel, but most frequently actions are taken by individuals. A claimant has to prove the statement is defamatory, that it refers to him and that it has been published to a third party. He does not have to prove the statement is false. It is up to the defendant (the journalist) to prove it is true, or offer another defence.

DEFENCES AGAINST LIBEL

Knowing the defences available in a defamation case helps you decide what can and cannot be broadcast. The defences are:

- **Justification** – meaning that the words complained of are true. This is a difficult defence to sustain because you have to be able to prove facts are true. Unless you have proof to hand when you broadcast, this can involve a costly investigation to collect evidence. (The *Guardian* newspaper's investigation to successfully defend a libel action by the former Cabinet minister Jonathan Aitken took four years.)

  You also have to be able to prove not only the literal truth of a statement but also any inference or innuendo behind the words. For example, calling somebody 'a thief' might imply somebody is an habitual thief. If the claimant had a conviction for shoplifting the words would be literally true, but the defence might fail if it were proved the offence was a one-off lapse by an otherwise honest person. Sticking to a defence of justification and failing can result in the courts imposing higher penalties.

  Under section 5 of the 1952 Defamation Act, it is not necessary to prove every fact in a defamatory report. The Act says: 'a defence of justification shall not fail by reason only that the truth of every charge is not proved, if the words not proved to be true do not materially injure the claimant's reputation'.

  The exceptions to truth being a defence in a libel action are references to convictions covered by the Rehabilitation of Offenders Act 1974. It allows people with minor convictions (anything less than two-and-a-half years in prison) to live down their past.

  So, after ten years, sentences between six months and two-and-a-half years become 'spent' and cannot be referred to. A sentence of less than six months (or dismissal from the armed services) is spent after seven years, and a fine or other sentence is spent after five years. These periods are halved for offenders under 18.

- **Fair comment** – means comment made honestly on a matter of public interest. The comment has to be based on provable facts, or on privileged material.

- **Privilege** – usually laid out in Acts of Parliament – is a legal understanding that in some instances freedom of speech is more important than protection against defamation and untruths. Courts are covered by Absolute Privilege; a fair and accurate, contemporaneous report of proceedings in open court will not be the subject of a successful libel action. This is so that the media can report the often highly defamatory content of court cases. The law applies to UK courts, and to the European Courts of Justice and Human Rights and international criminal tribunals established by the Security Council of the United Nations or by an international agreement to which the UK is party.

Qualified Privilege is a more limited defence, but applies to more than just courts. Qualified Privilege covers a wide range of matters of public concern, provided they are published or broadcast without malice (i.e. ill-will, spite or an improper motive). It applies to reports of legislative bodies, courts, public inquiries and meetings of international organisations anywhere in the world, and to extracts from their official publications.

Some statements only have Qualified Privilege 'subject to explanation or contradiction.' In other words, if a defamatory statement has been broadcast, 'a reasonable letter or statement by way of explanation or contradiction' must also be broadcast. This condition covers notices issued for the information of the public by a legislature in any member state of the European Parliament, by the government of any member state and by any authority performing governmental functions. This last category includes the police, so official police statements are covered by Qualified Privilege. Statements which are privileged subject to explanation also include reports of the meetings of local authorities, statutory tribunals, public companies in the UK (including documents circulated to their members) and also 'public meetings'.

A 'public meeting' is defined as 'a meeting bona fide and lawfully held for a lawful purpose and for the furtherance or discussion of a matter of public concern, whether admission to the meeting is general or restricted'. *So, a public meeting does not have to be open to all of the public.*

Another public interest defence is the Reynolds Defence, which recognises for the first time in law the importance of matters of public interest being broadcast, whether or not they can be proved to be true. It arises from a 1998 case when the former Irish Prime Minister, Albert Reynolds, sued the *Sunday Times* over allegations that he misled the Irish Parliament. The newspaper lost, because they'd failed to represent Reynolds' side of the story properly. The Reynolds Defence relies on a series of tests, which challenge the rigour of the journalistic process, including the reliability of sources, the steps taken to verify the information and whether comment was sought from the claimant.

- **Accord and satisfaction** – is a plea that the matter has already been dealt with – by the broadcast of a correction or apology, for example, which has been accepted by the claimant. If the claimant does not accept an apology, publishing a correction *may* make matters worse because it acknowledges a mistake was made. A broadcaster may make a payment into court – a sum of money the claimant can accept instead of pursuing the action. If the eventual damages prove to be less than or the same as the amount paid into court, the claimant will usually be expected to pay both sides' costs in the case.

- **Offer of amends** – is a written offer to pay damages and make a suitable apology and correction. This defence can only be used where someone has been accidentally defamed. If it is rejected it is up to the claimant to prove the defamation was not 'innocent'.

COURT REPORTING

It is a general principle of the law that courts should administer justice in public. There are exceptions, including matters of national security and where the welfare of children is concerned. Usually, though, the press are admitted to courts. But that does not mean you can report everything that is said. It is important to understand the functions of different courts and the restrictions on reporting from them.

Civil courts deal with the rights and duties of individuals towards each other. In a civil case a claimant sues a defendant who might be held liable. The civil courts include tribunals, and county and High Courts.

Criminal law deals with crimes against the state. A defendant is prosecuted by the state and will be found guilty or not guilty. In Scotland (where the law developed separately prior to the Act of Union in 1707 and has continued to be separate), a third verdict of 'not proven' is available. The state enforces law and order through the magistrates' courts, youth courts, and crown courts in England, Wales and Northern Ireland. In Scotland, the courts are the district Court (presided over by a Justice of the Peace or magistrate), the sheriff court and the High Court of Justiciary.

The decisions of the lower courts can be overruled or reversed by the Court of Appeal, and after that the House of Lords.

Courts can refer cases to the European Court of Justice, although this is not a formal stage in the appeal procedure. The European Court of Human Rights in Strasbourg hears allegations of breaches of the European Convention on Human Rights. The convention is incorporated into British law. Of particular importance to journalists are Article 10, Freedom of Expression, and Article 8, the Right to Respect for Privacy.

Ninety-seven per cent of criminal cases are heard by magistrates (also known as Justices of the Peace or JPs). They do not have to be legally qualified. The maximum sentence they can give is 12 months in prison for a single offence or a fine of £5,000, except in cases of customs and tax evasion. Sentences can be suspended for a length of time – the guilty party does not have to go to prison unless they re-offend within that time. It is wrong to say someone given a suspended sentence has been jailed.

Outside Scotland, magistrates deal with three types of criminal offence:

1 those which can be tried only on indictment at crown court (e.g. serious offences like murder, rape and robbery)

2 'either-way' cases which can be tried at crown or magistrates' court (e.g. theft, indecent assault)

3 summary offences (including motoring offences and drunkenness) which are usually only tried by magistrates.

The Crown Prosecution Service (CPS), not the police, is responsible for criminal prosecutions in England, Wales and Northern Ireland. In Scotland, the Crown Office and the Procurator Fiscal Service perform the same function (the Lord

Advocate or an Advocate Depute presents the case in the High Court against the accused). Lawyers can represent people in court. Solicitors deal with members of the public and brief barristers ('advocates' in Scotland). Solicitors serve as advocates in the lower courts and in some higher court cases, but usually they 'solicit' the services of a barrister to put the case in higher courts.

Magistrates can send people to the crown court for sentencing if they think their own powers of sentencing are not harsh enough. They also commit people on serious offences for trial at the crown court.

There are restrictions on reporting committal proceedings, to prevent a potential juror being influenced. The Magistrates Court Act 1980 limits reports of preliminary hearings on offences triable by jury to 10 points, which include a summary of the offences and the names, ages and addresses of the accused and witnesses, but no details of the alleged crime beyond what is on the charge sheet. In Scotland there are no committal proceedings, but once a person has appeared before a sheriff on petition for judicial examination, they cannot be detained longer than 110 days or, if given bail, they must be tried within 12 months.

What the English call 'indictable' cases are known as 'solemn' cases in Scotland. In England (and Wales and Northern Ireland) a judge sits with a jury of 12 people, and will usually prefer a unanimous verdict (all 12 people agreed). In Scotland, a judge or sheriff sits with a 15-strong jury, and will expect a majority verdict.

CONTEMPT OF COURT

Even if you are not attending court to report on proceedings, you need to be aware of the dangers of contempt of court.

The contempt law is designed to ensure trials are conducted fairly. You should not broadcast any material that might influence a potential juror, unless it has been presented before the jury in court. This means you have to be especially careful before a trial has started.

Under section 2 of the Contempt of Court Act 1981, strict liability contempt applies where:

1 the publication creates a substantial risk of serious prejudice or impediment to particular proceedings; and

2 proceedings are active.

So, you need to know whether criminal proceedings are 'active' or not. According to the Act, proceedings are active if a person has been arrested, a warrant for an arrest has been issued, a summons has been issued or a person has been charged orally. If you are not certain any of these things have taken place, you should be very cautious. Be wary of the phrase 'helping the police with their inquiries'. If someone is at a police station against their will, they are under arrest.

Proceedings cease to be active when:

1 a person is released without charge (except on police bail);

2 no arrest is made within 12 months of the issue of a warrant;

3 a case is discontinued;

4 a defendant is acquitted or sentenced; or

5 a defendant is found unfit to be tried, unfit to plead or the court orders the charge to lie on the file.

The proceedings remain active until sentencing, not just until a guilty verdict. After sentencing, even if a lawyer says his client will appeal, there is a so-called 'free-for-all' time before proceedings become active again when the appeal is formally lodged.

The court has powers to limit reporting under the Contempt of Court Act 1981. Under section 4, a court can order postponement of the reporting of a case, but only if there is a substantial risk to a fair trial. Under section 11, a court can order a name and address to be withheld; usually this is to protect a blackmail victim or a member of the security services. Both types of order can be challenged in court by the media.

This type of challenge happened in September 2006 in a high-profile and highly unusual case involving two immigration judges who had been lovers. A Brazilian cleaner was accused of blackmailing them by threatening to make public a video of them having sex. The cleaner, Roselane Driza, was found guilty of blackmailing the female judge, but not the male (she *was* found guilty of stealing two tapes from him). The media argued that, as there was no blackmail involved in his case, the male judge should be named. The Recorder of London, Judge Peter Beaumont, agreed. He said: 'The finding of the jury in respect of the allegation of the theft of his property does not in my judgement entitle the court to continue the protection over his identity. I can find no justification in doing so in light of the evidence given in this trial.' So, Mohammed Ilyas Khan was photographed and named across the media while his former lover remained anonymous.

Sometimes, a warrant for an arrest will be issued, but the police will still want help with a case and they will issue an appeal for information. To publish that information could be a contempt of court. But the Attorney General made it clear in 1981 that the press have nothing to fear from publishing such information, and there has never been a prosecution.

An area where broadcasters in particular run a risk of contempt is the definition of the precincts of the court. You will want to take pictures of people involved in a case arriving at and leaving court, but it is an offence to take pictures within a court's precincts. The definition of 'precincts' is left to the discretion of the court. So, it is worth checking with the court officers what is allowed. Incidentally, photographing jurors could be contempt, even when they are outside the court visiting a crime scene.

YOUNG PEOPLE AND THE LAW

Youth courts deal with people under 18. In law, a child is anyone under 14 and a young person is a 14–18-year-old. A child under ten (under eight in Scotland) cannot be charged with a criminal offence.

Under the Children and Young Persons Act 1933, *you cannot identify a person under 18 who is a defendant or witness in a youth court*, although the court may lift that anonymity in the public interest or the interests of justice.

There is no automatic ban on naming a minor in an adult court. Under section 39 of the 1933 Act, the court can make an order preventing identification of a child involved in the case, but the judge or magistrate must have good reason and these orders can be challenged. The court has no power to prevent the naming of dead children.

According to the 1933 Act, a child or young person can be identified by their name, address, school or any other particulars. So, you need to be particularly careful. In a small village, for example, there would be comparatively few 12-year-olds. Obviously, recognisable photographs or moving pictures of children in court are forbidden, though pixelated images obscuring the face can usually be used (although there have been cases in Scotland where 'no picture' means literally that).

When a child is subject to a section 39 order, there is a danger of 'jigsaw identification' – where one news organisation names a defendant without giving their relationship to a child and another gives the relationship but not the name. The pieces of information fit together like a jigsaw to identify the child. The Code of Practice adopted by the Press Complaints Commission is also followed by broadcasters. Adults should be named but their relationship to a child should not be given (the word 'incest' should be avoided if it would identify a child victim).

Often ASBOs (anti-social behaviour orders) are granted by magistrates against young people. These are civil proceedings (although breach of an ASBO is a criminal offence) and there is no automatic ban on naming the defendant. Similarly, there is no automatic ban on naming the defendant in an ASBO application before a youth court.

You cannot identify a child as a ward of court (i.e. a minor who is under the care of the court), and it is contempt of court to publish information about court proceedings in private relating to children.

SEX OFFENCES

Victims of most sexual offences are granted lifetime anonymity by the law. As soon as an allegation has been made you cannot name or show pictures of the alleged victim. You must also avoid mentioning their place of work or any educational establishment they attend. The only exceptions are if the mention of a sexual offence comes in a report of a trial other than for a sex offence; if the judge or magistrates remove the anonymity because it imposes an unreasonable restriction on the reporting of the case; or, on the application of the defence, anonymity is lifted to bring witnesses forward.

Because the anonymity applies during the victim's *lifetime*, you *can* name a victim of rape who has been murdered.

Victims over 16 can agree to be identified. They need to give consent in writing, and the court needs to be satisfied no-one 'interfered unreasonably with his or her peace or comfort to obtain that consent'. There is no anonymity for those accused of sex offences and the courts have no power to prevent their being named.

BREACH OF CONFIDENCE

Journalists often deal with leaked documents or information from whistle-blowers – people disclosing information about their employer or workplace. So, it is important you understand the principle in law that a person given information in confidence should not take unfair advantage of it.

The laws on breach of confidence are used by individuals and governments to try to keep information secret and to preserve their privacy. There is also a right to privacy under the Human Rights Act. Courts nowadays may be asked to weigh privacy against the public interest and the right to freedom of expression.

Breach of contract also covers the image rights of personalities. 'Snatched' wedding pictures of Michael Douglas and Catherine Zeta-Jones in *Hello!* resulted in *OK!* magazine being awarded more than £1 million in damages.

There are three elements to breach of confidence:

1 the information must have the necessary 'quality of confidence';

2 it must have been imparted in circumstances imposing an obligation of confidence;

3 there must be unauthorised use of the information to the detriment of the party communicating it.

The law is often enforced by applications before judges to impose interim injunctions preventing the publication or broadcast of confidential information.

COPYRIGHT

Every broadcaster must understand the law of copyright, because every time you use a photograph, video clip or piece of music that is not your own, you risk breaking the law.

Copyright is a branch of intellectual property law designed to protect the products of people's work and time. Facts, ideas and information (the 'news', for example) cannot be copyrighted. Copyright exists after someone has put time and original effort into presenting the information.

Copyright in a written work lasts till 70 years after the author's death; copyright in a broadcast lasts 50 years.

Copyright belongs to the 'author' of the work (e.g. the photographer if it is a photograph) unless the work is carried out in the course of employment, when the employer owns copyright. Freelance work belongs to the author unless there is agreement to the contrary.

A person who commissions a photograph for private purposes has a right not to have it made public under the Copyright, Designs and Patents Act 1988. Reporters should be wary if borrowing a wedding photograph (taken since 1988) from a relative of someone in the news.

Copyright work (apart from a photograph) can be used for the purpose of reporting current events, as long as it has been made public and the author is acknowledged. This is known as 'fair dealing'. It also applies to review or criticism of a work. The courts decide if the dealing is fair, based on whether the use competes with the commercial interest of the copyright owner.

A broadcast work can have a number of 'authors'. The broadcast organisation transmitting it and the company that produced it will have copyright in the whole of a programme, while it may contain elements with different authors.

Copyright can be wholly or partly assigned to a third party, usually in the form of a licence. An exclusive licence would limit the material to one outlet. An 'all rights' agreement would mean the licensee could do what they wanted with the material, and the owner has effectively lost control of it. Whenever you use third-party material, you should be clear of the terms under which it is used.

THE REGULATORS

Broadcasting in the UK is regulated by Ofcom. The Ofcom Broadcasting Code can be found at www.ofcom.org.uk/tv/ifi/codes/bcode.

The BBC Editorial Guidelines, which perform a similar function within the BBC, are available at www.bbc.co.uk/guidelines/editorialguidelines/edguide.

FURTHER READING

Bonnington, Alistair J., McInnes, Rosalind, McKain, Bruce and Clive, Eric M. (2000) *Scots Law for Journalists*, Edinburgh: W. Green.

Frost, Chris (2007) *Journalism Ethics and Regulation*, Harlow: Pearson.

Welsh, Tom, Greenwood, Walter and Banks, David (2007) *McNae's Essential Law for Journalists*, Oxford: Oxford University Press.

GLOSSARY

A

Accreditation Clearance to attend and cover an event. May involve special passes.

Actuality Sounds recorded as they happen – sometimes used to refer to interviews (a.k.a. wildtrack, atmos).

Ad Advertisement or commercial.

Ad lib Unscripted, improvised speech.

Adobe Audition A digital radio editing system (trade name).

Agency copy Story that has come from a news agency.

ALC Automatic level control. Electronic device to reduce or boost the incoming sound signal automatically.

A-listers Top celebrity guests.

AM Radio frequency on the AM waveband.

Ambush interview American term for forcing someone to speak with you on camera against their will. (editorial guidance needed)

Analogue A signal which has a continuous wave form.

Analogue recording Recording that is not digital – normally used when referring to magnetic tape.

Anchor American term for main news presenter.

And finally Item (often off-beat) at very end of a bulletin.

Angle The point in a story that the journalist wants to emphasise. The new angle would be the latest development in a story and the local angle would be pointing up the relevance to the local audience.

AP Associated Press, one of the major wire services in America.

Appointment to view The decision to make a mental note to watch a particular programme at a particular time.

Archive Previously broadcast material.

ASBO Anti-social behaviour order – a civil order by magistrates (or in Scotland the sheriff court) to stop someone causing alarm, harassment or distress to others.

As-live Recorded inserts that look/sound live. (Remember, never claim that a recorded report or interview is live.)

Assault In legal language, assault is a hostile act which threatens an attack on another person.

Assignment editor Journalist who assigns stories to reporters and camera crews.

Aston Brand name for electronic caption on TV (a.k.a. super).

Atmos Atmosphere. Background noise that provides a sense of location to interviews or voice pieces (a.k.a. wildtrack).

Audacity A digital audio editing system (available as free shareware).

Audio Sound.

Audio feed Sound sent to other studios and stations.

Audio mixer Control desk (or control panel) for mixing sound sources.

Autocue TV prompting device which allows the presenter to read a script while looking at the camera. Autocue is a trade name – like 'Hoover' it is often used as a generic term (a.k.a. teleprompter, Portaprompt).

Avid Digital video editing system (trade name).

B

Back anno Back announcement. A final piece of script giving extra information (usually read by the presenter at the end of an item).

Backlight The light used behind an interviewee to pick them out from the background. It adds depth, softens shadows and highlights the hair.

Back projection Pictures projected onto a screen behind the newsreader.

Band A separate piece of quarter-inch audio tape used on a reel-to-reel player.

Barn door Adjustable flaps on a studio or location light used to direct the beam.

BBC British Broadcasting Corporation.

BCU Big close-up.

Bed A music bed or a sound bed is audio played underneath a voice or actuality.

Berliner A newspaper size used by the *Guardian* in the UK, smaller than a broadsheet.

Bi-directional mic A mic (microphone) that will pick up sound from the front and from the back.

Biff To drop an item (a.k.a. spike).

Bi-media TV and radio operation.

BJ Broadcast journalist.

BJTC Broadcast Journalism Training Council. An accrediting body providing guidelines for university and college broadcast journalism courses.

Black Control track on a videotape. Also, a complete fade from a TV picture – 'fade to black'.

Blind lead-in A general lead-in to a report from location, used when you do not know what the reporter will say at the top of the report.

B-listers Celebrity guests who are not as well-known as those on the A-list.

Blog A regularly updated website. A blog can be a personal diary, a political soapbox, a breaking-news outlet, opinion articles, private thoughts, memos to the world.

Blogger Someone who writes blogs on the Internet.

Bongs The headlines at the top of the ITN News.

Boom A long telescopic pole for holding a microphone.

Boom mic Microphone held on a pole or boom.

Box Used to indicate that a picture, freeze-frame video or graphic will appear in a box on screen.

Breaking news A news story that is happening now and developing throughout the day (a.k.a. a spot story in America).

Bridge Words that connect one piece of narration or soundbite to another (a.k.a. link).

Brief Instructions given to a reporter on how to cover a story.

British Broadcasting Company What the BBC was called before it became a public corporation in 1927.

Broadsheet A newspaper format that is the larger of the two standard UK newspaper sizes, characterised by long vertical pages. Broadsheet newspapers are usually more serious in content than tabloid newspapers.

B-roll A film term often used to describe the use of video to cover narration or an interview.

Bug An on-screen graphic.

Bulk eraser Powerful electromagnet used for erasing tapes for reuse.

Bulletin A report providing the latest information on a topic such as news, weather or travel.

Bumper The short sting before and after the commercial break (a.k.a. bump).

Bumper tease A short headline with video, used before commercials in a TV newscast, to hold the audience's attention (a.k.a. bump tease).

C

Camcorder Hand-held video camera with a built-in recorder.

Camera desk The desk in a newsroom that assigns camera crews.

Cans Headphones.

Capacitor mic Small battery-operated mic (often used as a tie-clip mic).

Caption A graphic with written information (a.k.a. Aston, super).

Carrier wave A frequency modulated to carry a video or audio signal.

Cart Cartridge used for recording and playing inserts into TV and radio programmes.

Catchline A one- or two-word name used to identify a story (a.k.a. slug).

CBI Confederation of British Industry. The UK's leading independent employers' organisation.

CCD Charge-coupled device. A solid-state sensor used instead of tubes in cameras.

CCTV Closed circuit television.

Ceefax BBC's Text pages on TV.

Character generator Electronic caption machine.

Check calls Regular calls from the newsroom to the emergency services.

Chequebook journalism The form of journalism where a news organisation pays a subject money for the exclusive right to publish their story, often outbidding other organisations.

Child The legal term for a person under 14 years old.

Chroma key See CSO.

Citizen journalists Members of the public who send in pictures from their mobile phones or video recorders of a news event they've witnessed, or who contribute news content to Internet sites.

Claimant The person who takes an action to enforce a claim in the civil court (previously known as plaintiff).

Clean feed A special feed of the programme output that lets a remote contributor hear the presenters and other guests, without being distracted by hearing a delayed version of their own voice off air (a.k.a. mix-minus in America).

Cliché A hackneyed and over-used expression.

Clip Insert. Short extract (a.k.a. cut or grab).

COI Central Office of Information.

College Green The stretch of lawn opposite the public entrance to the House of Commons, often used for interviews with politicians.

Commentary booth Small studio in which a journalist records script or broadcasts live.

Contact Source of news information.

Contacts book Usually laid out alphabetically, a book containing names, addresses, phone numbers (particularly mobiles) and e-mail addresses of anyone who might be a source of news.

Contemporaneous Originating, existing or occurring at the same time. To attract absolute privilege a court report must be contemporaneous, usually meaning at the earliest opportunity.

Continuity Network presentation studio – the place/person introducing programmes on a large network like Channel 4 or BBC Radio 4.

Maintaining the appearance of continuous action in a recorded item.

Contribution circuit Network of linking landlines along which news material is sent and received.

Contribution studio Small studio used for sending material down-the-line (DTL) or for DTL interviews.

Cool Edit Pro Digital audio editing software (renamed Adobe Audition in May 2003).

Copy Material written for broadcast.

Copy story News story which is just script, with no accompanying audio or pictures.

Copytaster Journalist who sifts incoming stories to select items worth running.

Coroner An official responsible for investigating sudden or unusual deaths (and also treasure trove).

Cover footage Pictures shot at the scene of a news story, used for the reporter's V-O.

Crash Colloquialism for serious problems in a broadcast.

Crawler Tickertape graphic across the bottom of a TV screen.

Cross-fade Mixing or overlapping of one sound with another.

CSO Colour separation overlay. Method of electronically replacing a single colour with a second image or graphic (a.k.a. chroma key).

CU Close-up.

Cue Written introduction to a report either live or recorded (a.k.a. in-cue).

The instruction/signal given to a presenter to start or stop speaking, either visual (hand or light) or verbal.

Sound of continuity or the programme played into a person's headphones to introduce or indicate when they should start broadcasting (e.g. in a live studio, on an outside broadcast or on a telephone).

Cue (feed) Cue, as opposed to clean-feed, sends output down the line to the remote guest. When the remote guest talks, they will hear themselves as part of the full programme mix. There may be audible delay, especially if the contributor is on a satellite link.

Cue-light Light on top of a studio camera indicating the camera is live. In radio the cue-light is a small, normally green, light that sits on the studio table and lights when the presenter is cued to speak.

Cut Short extract of an interview to illustrate a story (a.k.a. grab or insert).

The term used to signal the end of filming a shot. It can also be used to describe the sort of edit required. Most news items use cuts rather than mixes.

Cutaway A shot used in TV to cover a jump-cut edit.

D

DAB Digital audio broadcasting. It uses a sound signal made up of discrete electronic units, rather than an **analogue** signal which has a continuous wave form.

DAT Digital audio tape.

DB Decibel – unit of loudness.

Death-knock Calling on the recently bereaved to request an interview or pictures.

Delay A recorded delay of several seconds in playing back a 'live' phone-in programme to prevent defamation or obscenities being broadcast.

Delayed lead Keeping the most important information in a story until the middle or end to create suspense (a.k.a. drop intro).

Demographic The profile of a station's listeners based on age, gender, income, profession, race etc. Important to advertisers who target particular audiences.

Demos Demonstrations.

Desk The control panel in a studio that mixes sounds and/or pictures for transmission.

An operational unit in a newsroom (e.g., newsdesk, home desk, foreign desk, camera desk).

Diary Usually electronic – the future story file in a newsroom. A breaking story may be off-diary.

Digital radio Radio transmission system offering high-quality sound requiring a special receiver (a.k.a. DAB).

Digital recording The storage of sound and/or pictures digitally (as a series of noughts and ones in computer systems). Copies of digital recordings can be made with no loss of quality.

Digitising The process of playing tape into a digital editing system.

Directivity pattern Area over which a mic can pick up sound (a.k.a. pickup).

Dissolve A video effect that mixes from one image on the screen to another (a.k.a. mix).

DOA Dead on arrival. Term used by the emergency services for a victim who has died either before help could arrive or before the ambulance could reach the hospital.

Dog Digital on-screen graphic.

Dolby system A system which reduces audio noise.

Doorstep To knock on a person's door unannounced or approach them in the street for an interview. Normally used when someone has refused to be interviewed previously, and is subject to editorial approval.

Double-header Item or programme presented by two people.

Down-the-line An interview or report from a location conducted via an electronic link (a.k.a. DTL).

DR Despatch-rider.

Drive To drive a desk is to operate a radio studio desk.

Drive-time The time of day when a lot of the radio audience is driving. Usually the late afternoon/early evening.

DTL Down-the-line.

Dubbing Duplication of a recording from one recorder to another.

Laying a voice down over pictures, or mixing sound on to a TV programme (a.k.a. dub).

Dubbing theatre The studio where presenters record their voice-overs for television and audio dubbing takes place.

Dumbing-down Over-simplification. The theory that media audiences are being fed an increasingly mass-produced, poor-quality and populist diet leading to an ever-decreasing audience attention span.

Duration The length to the nearest second of an item or programme (a.k.a. dur).

E

Earpiece Small device worn in the ear that enables a presenter or reporter to listen to talkback from the studio gallery.

Edit To prepare an item or programme for transmission by cutting out unwanted material.

Editor The person who edits audio or video.

A senior journalist in charge of output.

Embargo Request not to release information until a specified date or time. Used to control the publication date and time of a news item.

ENG Electronic news gathering with portable video cameras.

ENPS Electronic News Production System (trade name). Networked newsroom computer system used worldwide.

EPK Electronic Press Kit.

EQ Equalisation. Improving audio quality by altering the frequency characteristics.

Establishing shot A wide shot to set a scene.

Evergreen An American term for a story which is timeless and can be used at any time (a.k.a. shelf item).

Executive Producer A senior figure who oversees producers.

F

Face-to-face When two people are facing each other.

Fade out Used in TV when a picture fades to black. In radio when the volume of an audio signal is reduced until it disappears.

Fader Slide mechanism on a studio desk that opens an audio channel and controls its volume.

Feature An edited item for a programme. Also used to describe softer news stories.

Feature opener An introduction to a soft news story, designed more to arouse curiosity and to entertain than to inform (American term).

Feed A supply of audio or video from an outside source.

Programme output to a contributor at a location other than the programme's originating studio (e.g. a phone call or an interview down-the-line from a remote studio). Most studios offer a choice of Cue (programme output) or Clean Feed.

Feedback The effect produced when the signal from a mic is transmitted through a nearby speaker. The mic picks up the speaker sound producing a high-pitched howling sound. It can also be caused by a phone-in contributor having their radio on, tuned into the same programme, too near to the phone (a.k.a. howl-round).

Fibre-optic Cable system composed of hollow fibres which carry light. Fibre-optic cables are used for telephone calls, computer data and TV signals.

Fill Lamp casting a soft light to fill in shadows.

Fillers Items of secondary importance (often without a peg) used to fill out a programme.

Final Cut Pro A digital editing system for TV (trade name).

Fish eye A special camera lens that gives an extremely wide angle (nearly 180 degrees) like the eye of a fish.

Fishpole Hand-held sound boom.

Fixed spot An item that is regularly in a programme at a particular time, like the weather, or travel news on a drive-time programme.

Fixer Someone (often a local person in a foreign country) who uses their contacts and local knowledge to 'fix' and organise filming and recording schedules.

Flash A graphics editing package (trade name).

Flats Boards used as a backdrop to the studio set.

Fly-on-the-wall A documentary style. In television the camera watches the action apparently unnoticed; in radio the mic eavesdrops on the action, like a fly on the wall.

FM Radio frequency on the FM (frequency modulation) waveband.

FO The Foreign and Commonwealth Office, more commonly known as the Foreign Office. British government department responsible for overseas relations and foreign affairs (a.k.a. FCO).

FOI Freedom of Information Act. Act which enables anyone to have access to information held by public authorities.

Format The structure and presentation of programmes in an agreed style. The format will dictate how often time-checks are given or station idents used. It provides uniformity of sound across a station's output.

Freelance Self-employed journalist who works for more than one employer and gets paid for the job or for the day.

Freeze-frame A still video image.

Frequency Rate at which a sound or light wave or an electronic impulse passes a given point over a specific time. A station's frequency denotes its position on the dial. Frequencies on the AM waveband (amplitude modulation) are expressed in kilohertz (KHz) including medium- and long-wave transmissions, and on the FM waveband (frequency modulation) in megahertz (MHz).

Front projection Pictures are projected from in front of the newsreader on to a screen alongside.

Futures file File in which stories and news events that are known to be happening on a certain date are placed, so that coverage may be planned in advance (a.k.a. diary).

FX An abbreviation for sound or video effects.

G

GFX Graphics.

Glitch Technical error.

GNS General News Service. The BBC service to all its news outlets.

Google A widely used search engine (trade name). To 'Google' means to look something up on the Internet.

Grab Soundbite. Bit of an interview or a piece of actuality sound.

Graphics Graphs, photos, maps and other stills used in a TV news story or online.

GTS Greenwich Time Signal. Now no longer from Greenwich but generated by the BBC. Six pips broadcast at the top of the hour to give an accurate time-check.

Gun mic Directional microphone for picking up sound at a distance (a.k.a. rifle mic).

GV General view.

H

Handling noise Unwanted clicks and bumps picked up by a mic as a result of handling and moving the mic.

Hard disk Computer disk for the permanent storage of material.

Hard lead A lead that places the most important information at the top of a story.

Hard news Information of importance about events of significance.

Hard news formula A hard news story will cover most of the basic facts by answering the questions: Who? What? Where? When? Why? And How?

Head The moving top of a tripod.

Heads Headlines. Short summary of the main news stories.

Hertz (Hz) Frequency of sound measured in cycles per second.

HD High-definition TV system of more than a thousand lines resulting in excellent picture quality.

HGV Heavy goods vehicle.

Holding copy The first version of a story left by a reporter to be run in their absence while they collect more information.

Hot desking Practice of workers not having their own desk, but logging on to work-stations as needed.

Human interest Soft news item. Of interest to the audience, but often of no great news significance. Background stories following major news events are human-interest stories; also stories about animals and celebrities.

I

Ident Piece of recorded music, or a simple announcement by the presenter, used to identify a particular programme (a.k.a. stab, sting, jingle).

ILR Independent local radio.

In-cue The first few words of a report.

Information overload Putting too much information in a story.

Ingest The input of video and audio material from external sources.

Input The news-gathering operation of a newsroom.

Inquest Formal process of investigation. An official inquiry (presided over by a coroner) into the cause of a death.

Insert Item inserted into a bulletin or programme.

Internet Global network of computers.

In the field On location.

Intro Introduction. The first paragraph of a script written to grab the audience's attention. It gives the main angle of the story and the main facts. The lead or cue of a report.

Investigative reporting Developing news reports in depth. Investigation uncovered by a reporter usually about something that someone is trying to hide.

IPCC Independent Police Complaints Commission.

ips Inches per second. Refers to the speed of tape going past the recording head of an analogue tape machine. Rarely used today. The two most common speeds were 7.5 ips and 15 ips (faster speeds mean a higher recording quality) (a.k.a. inps).

IR Independent Radio – all non-BBC radio covering national, local and regional stations in the UK.

IRN Independent Radio News. Company that supplies national and international news to many independent radio stations in the UK.

ISDN Integrated Services Digital Network. High-quality digital audio signal sent through telephone lines.

ITC Independent Television Commission. It used to regulate independent TV in the UK. It ceased functioning in December 2003 and its duties have been assumed by Ofcom.

ITN Independent Television News. Company supplying news to networks including ITV and Channel 4.

IV In vision. Instruction on a script to indicate a TV presenter should be on camera.

J

Jack plug A connecting plug used to route or reroute sources.

Jigsaw identification Identification of a person who should not be named in court proceedings, by combining details from different sources. For example, one station broadcasts a person's name; another suppresses his name but gives details of his relationship to a child. If the two reports are heard, together they form a jigsaw identifying the child.

Jingle Piece of music used to identify a certain programme (a.k.a. ident, sting).

Journalese The jargon of bad journalism.

Judicial review Review by the Queen's Bench Divisional Court of decisions taken by a lower court, tribunal, public body or public official.

Jump-cut An edit in a sequence of video, where the subject appears to jump from one position to another.

Juvenile A young person below the age of 18.

K

Key Main lamp providing a hard light.

To impose one image over another electronically (see Chroma key, CSO).

Key words One or two words which sum up the most important part of a news story. Also used by search engines to search for information.

Kicker American term for a light story used at the end of a bulletin.

L

Landline Cable transmission for audio and/or video. The cables are capable of carrying a high-quality signal (used for radio outside broadcast before the introduction of ISDN).

Law Lords Lords of Appeal. They sit in the House of Lords, not the Court of Appeal.

Lead First and most important item in a news programme.

The written cue to a news report.

An electrical cable from one piece of equipment to another.

Leader Leader tape is coloured tape used to show the start and end of a piece of audio on analogue reel-to-reel tape. The leader tape cannot be recorded upon and the correct colours must be used: yellow for the start and linking bands and red for the end. Rarely used today, but useful if listening to archive tapes.

Leading question A question during an interview that tries to elicit information the reporter wants to hear.

LED Light emitting diode. Low-powered light used for electronic displays. Used on desks and other equipment for on/off indicators, level meters etc.

Level The volume of recorded or broadcast sound as registered on a meter.

Level check Pre-recording check on the volume of a speaker's voice.

Lighting grid Construction suspended from the studio ceiling to support lights.

Linear editing Editing where sounds and/or pictures have to be assembled in order.

Line-up The arrangement of stories in a bulletin (a.k.a. running order or rundown).

Links Any speech between items that introduces or sets up the item. Narrative linking or bridging interviews in a report.

Links vehicle Motor vehicle used as a platform for a microwave transmitter or satellite dish.

Live Broadcast in real time.

A live report from the scene of a story.

Local news Stories relevant to a local community.

Log A recording of all of a radio station's output on slow-speed audio or video or computer.

A register of music played for notification to the PRS (Performing Rights Society), so that royalties can be paid.

To note down the content of recordings in preparation for an edit, usually involving logging timecode.

Lords of Appeal Law Lords. They sit in the House of Lords, not the Court of Appeal.

Lower third The bottom third of a TV screen. This is where most Astons and name supers appear.

LS Long shot. Usually showing somebody full length.

M

Man-in-the-street American term for vox pops.

Marantz A portable recording machine (trade name). The make was popular for audio cassette machines, and more recently solid-state audio recorders.

Marking up Marking a story with important details: the catchline, who wrote it, and when it was written.

Masthead The front page title logo of a newspaper.

MCPS The Mechanical-Copyright Protection Society collects and distributes royalties for the use of recorded music.

MCU Medium close-up. The standard interview shot in television.

MD MiniDisc. Digital audio recording medium using small discs. Popular during the bridge between analogue tape and solid-state recorders.

Media Channels of communication for transmitting information to the public (e.g. the 'mass media' – newspapers, television, radio and the Internet).

Recorded data (e.g. audio files, video files).

Media conference A stage-managed event designed to impart information to journalists (a.k.a. news conference, press conference).

Menu Script explaining what is coming up later in the bulletin or programme, including sound or video clips.

Meter Device for measuring audio level. The VU (volume unit) meter gives an average reading of the audio; the PPM (peak programme meter) measures the peaks of audio.

Mic Microphone (a.k.a. mike).

Mic rattle The noise caused when a mic cable is moved during recording.

Microwave System for relaying audio and video signals on very short wavelengths.

Minicam A lightweight video camera.

Mini DV A digital video tape format.

MiniDisc Digital audio recording medium using small (miniature) compact discs (a.k.a. MD).

Mini-jack Jack plug with a small connection.

Mini-wrap Brief package.

Misper Missing person.

Mix Transition from one audio source to another or from one picture to another (a.k.a. dissolve).

Mixing Combining two or more audio or picture sources. Used in making packages when interviews and/or links are played over music or special effects.

Mix-minus A special feed of the programme output that lets a remote contributor hear the presenters and other guests, without being distracted by hearing a delayed version of their own voice (a.k.a. clean feed).

MS Medium shot or mid-shot. Usually showing the head and upper body.

Multimedia Working across all media (usually TV, radio and Internet).

Multi-track Laying down several audio or video tracks on top of each other. The level of each track is adjusted for the finished project.

Recording technique in a music studio to record different voices and instruments on different tracks to mix later.

N

Nagra A portable recording machine (trade name).

Natural sound Location sound.

Needletime The amount of time a station may use to play commercially produced music.

News agency An organisation that provides news stories on a commercial basis for use by other news media.

News bed Music played under the reading of news.

News booth Small studio where bulletins are presented on air or recorded.

Newsclip Short extract of an interview to illustrate a story (a.k.a. cut, insert, grab, soundbite).

News conference A stage-managed media event designed to impart information to journalists (a.k.a. press conference, media conference).

News copy News story.

Item in radio news with no audio, or TV with no pictures.

Newsflash Interruption of normal programming to give brief details of an urgent breaking news story.

News judgement Ability to recognise the relative importance of news.

Newsmix A mixture of different types of news in a summary (e.g. national and local, hard and soft).

News release Publicity handout from an organisation or PR company informing the newsroom about a possible news item. Traditionally these were received through the post but increasingly newsrooms receive them via e-mail (a.k.a. press release or media release).

Newsroom conference Discussion between journalists about what stories to run and how they should be covered.

Newsroom diary A diary, usually electronic, in the newsroom listing all the known stories and news events by date (a.k.a. prospects).

Newsworthiness The qualities that make a story worth telling.

NIB News in brief.

Noddies Shots of the reporter nodding or listening, recorded separately from a television interview to be cut in later to cover edits.

Noise reduction The electronic reduction of interference induced by the transmission system.

Non-linear editing Editing out of sequence using digital storage of audio and video data.

Nose Angle. A journalist asked to give a story a new nose is expected to give it a new angle.

NUJ National Union of Journalists.

O

OB Outside broadcast.

Obscenity button Switch used for taking a programme instantly out of delay to prevent an obscene caller from being heard on air (a.k.a. profanity button).

O/C On camera.

Ofcom Office of Communications. A statutory body that sets standards for the content of TV and radio broadcasting in the UK.

Ofcom Code The Ofcom Broadcasting Code came into effect on 25 July 2005. It is available in printed form or available online from the Ofcom website www.ofcom.org.uk.

Off-diary Off-diary stories are stories which break during the day, or exclusives uncovered by correspondents.

Officialese The use of official jargon (often from government offices) which is difficult for the public to understand.

Off-mic Noise not fed directly through the microphone but audible in the broadcast. If someone does not speak directly into the pick-up area of the mic, they may sound 'off-mic' and their sound will not be as crisp and clear as when they are 'on-mic'.

Off-the-record A term used when talking with sources. There are varying interpretations:

1 The informant does not mind the information being broadcast as long as they are not identified as the source.
2 The story can only run if it can be confirmed by somebody else.
3 The information should merely be guidance to the reporter in the pursuit of a story.

It must be made clear to the informant exactly what 'off-the-record' means.

OMB One-man band. Single-person camera crews – a single operator works the camera and monitors the sound levels.

Omni-directional Term used for a mic with a circular pick-up pattern.

One-to-one A one-to-one interview is when a reporter or presenter speaks to one interviewee.

On-mic When someone is positioned correctly and speaking into the pick-up area of the mic.

On-screen streamer Text that scrolls from right to left across the lower third of a TV screen (a.k.a. tickertape).

Open talkback When the presenter can hear everything that is going on in the studio gallery through an earpiece.

Opt-in The process of switching between local and network transmissions. Opting-in occurs when a local station goes over to a live network programme.

Opt-out To return to a local programme from a network.

An early point at which a report may be brought to an end (a.k.a. pot cut, early out).

A regional TV programme that opts out of a network.

OOV Out of vision. Instruction on a TV script to show the narrator is not to appear in vision while reading the script (a.k.a. voice-over, VO, underlay).

Out cue Last words in a sound bite (a.k.a. out).

Out of sync If video is 'out of sync', the sound and video do not match. People's mouths do not move in time with what they are saying.

Output The sound that is heard by radio listeners.

The programme-making operation of a newsroom.

Out-take Part of any recorded media that is not used.

P

PA Press Association. The UK's biggest news agency.

Package An edited report.

Padding Items used as fillers. Non-essential stories. (a.k.a. pad copy, fill copy)

Paintbox Electronic graphics machine (trade name).

Pan A horizontal camera move.

Pan handle Handle on the camera to turn the head. (a.k.a. panning handle)

P as B Programme as broadcast. A written record of everything used in a programme, including music, ads, jingles. (a.k.a. log)

Pay-off The last words of a programme or item.

Peg A reason (date, anniversary, event) for using a story.

Phone-in Programme where listeners ring in with their comments.

Phono Report or interview made by telephone (a.k.a. phoner).

Phono lead A lead used to connect one piece of equipment to another.

Photo-calls Stage-managed media events similar to news conferences with the emphasis on the picture opportunities they offer the media.

Picture store Device for electronically storing pictures.

Piece-to-camera Reporter talking to camera on location. (a.k.a. stand-upper, stand-up)

Pixel Single dot of information on a video screen. They combine to form a television picture. The more pixels on a screen the higher the quality.

Pixelate To distort part of a TV picture to obscure the identity of something like a face or a car number plate.

Planning board Large board in a newsroom to show the stories that are being covered and which reporters and crews have been assigned to them.

Popping Harsh sound distortion during speech when saying the letters 'p' and 'b', usually caused by the speaker being too close to the mic.

Portable hard drive Portable computer hard drives used for storing digital audio and/or video clips for editing.

Portaprompt Electronic prompting equipment (trade name). (see Autocue)

Pot cut A rapid fade-out of a radio programme.

PPM Peak programme meter. Meter for measuring peak audio signal level.

PR Public relations/press relations.

Precincts Area around a court. Defined by the court, not by reporters. No photography (including moving pictures) is permitted within the precincts of a court.

Pre-fade Facility on a sound desk that enables you to listen to a source while on air, without transmitting it. Used to check levels and in-cues.

Press conference A stage-managed event designed to impart information to journalists (a.k.a. news conference, media conference).

Press pass A special pass for media representatives issued by the organisers of an event.

Press release Publicity handout from an organisation or PR company. (a.k.a. news release)

Presser Press conference.

Pressure group An organisation that campaigns for change, usually on a political issue.

Prima facie At first sight (legal).

Primary source The initial source of a story.

Primetime The time when radio and TV have their highest audiences.

Producer A person in charge of a production – either a programme or an item within a programme.

Profanity button Switch used for taking a programme instantly out of delay to prevent an obscene caller from being heard on air (a.k.a. obscenity button).

Promo Promotional trail (a.k.a. trail).

Prompter Electronic device that projects scripts onto a screen in front of the camera lens so they can be read by presenters (a.k.a. teleprompter, teleprompt, Autocue, Portaprompt).

Prospects The stories from the newsroom diary likely to be covered.

Proximity Closeness to home. A concept defined by people's perception of themselves and how they fit into the world around them.

PRS Performing Rights Society. Collects and distributes licence fees for public performances and broadcasts of musical works.

PSC Portable single camera.

PTC Piece-to-camera. Reporter talking to camera on location (a.k.a. stand-upper, stand-up).

Q

Q & A Question and answer. Often used for reporter two-ways.

Quango Quasi-autonomous non-governmental organisations – loosely used to describe non-elected public bodies that operate outside the civil service and are funded by the taxpayer.

Quantel A company producing TV transmission systems.

R

RadioMan A digital editing software program for audio (trade name).

RAJAR Radio Joint Audience Research. The body that measures audiences for all radio stations in the UK.

Reach The percentage of total listeners in the TSA (Total Survey Area) who tune in during a specified period.

Recordist Member of camera crew who operates sound and/or video recording equipment.

Red tops Populist tabloid newspapers usually identified by a red title or masthead.

Reel-to-reel A tape recorder that uses quarter-inch magnetic tape.

Remote studio Small, unmanned studio where guests can be interviewed.

Reithian Values ascribed to Lord John Reith, the first Director General of the BBC (he had strong Scots Presbyterian values). Associated with the mission to 'inform, educate and entertain'.

Reuters An international news agency.

Reverse A shot of the reporter looking at the person being interviewed (to be used in the editing process).

Reverse question Shot of the reporter repeating questions asked during the interview.

Reverse two-shot Shot of two people with the interviewee's back to camera.

Ribbon mic Sensitive directional microphone, frequently used in recording studios.

Rifle mic Directional microphone for picking up sound at a distance (a.k.a. gun mic).

Rip and read Radio wire copy written for broadcast without any rewrite.

Robbery Theft by force, or threat of force.

ROT Record Off Transmission. A recording of the output.

RSL Restricted Service Licence.

RSS Really Simple Syndication is the system that allows web users to choose topics they want to know about and be alerted when stories on those topics are available to view or hear.

RTA Road traffic accident.

Running order The arrangement of stories for a bulletin. The order the stories will run in (a.k.a. lineup, rundown).

Running story A story that develops and is repeatedly reported over a period of time.

Rushes Raw shots prior to editing.

S

SADiE A digital radio editing software system (trade name).

Safe area Central area of the TV screen where pictures and captions will not be cut off on domestic television sets.

Satellite phone A telephone using satellite technology rather than the phone networks.

Scanner An OB vehicle.

Telecine machine.

Caption scanner.

Device which copies pictures into a computer.

A radio which automatically tunes in to broadcasts by the emergency services.

Schedule A sequence of radio or TV programmes.

Scoop An exclusive story.

Scrambler Device for scrambling satellite TV signals so only authorised viewers can view them.

Segue A sequence of two or more pieces of music broadcast without interruption (a.k.a. seg).

Self-op Self-operation – a presenter operates without technical assistance.

Sexy story A story with instant audience appeal – not necessarily about sex.

Share A radio station's audience measured as a percentage of the total amount of time spent by people listening to radio in the survey area.

Shelf item A story that is timeless and can be used at any time (a.k.a. evergreen in America).

Signposting Headlining and trailing within a programme to keep the audience interested.

Simulcasting Broadcasting the same output on different services (e.g. radio and TV, or two radio channels).

Single-header Item or programme presented by one person.

Skeleton Incomplete programme script with gaps.

Sky News A 24-hour rolling news channel.

Sky News Radio A national and international radio news service for independent stations.

Slug Catchline. A word or two written at the top of the script to identify the story.

SMS Telephone text messaging.

SOC Standard out cue. An agreed form of words used by a reporter at the end of a story: e.g. 'Gary Hudson, Midlands Today, at Stafford Crown Court'.

SOF Sound on film.

Soft lead A lead in which the most important fact is not given immediately.

Soft news Feature-type stories, as opposed to hard news.

SOT Abbreviation for sound-on-tape. Actuality (a.k.a. SOF, sync).

SOTUP Upsound – short for 'sound on tape up'.

Sound bed Natural sound played under voice or other sound.

Soundbite Bit of an interview or snatch of actuality sound (a.k.a. grab, cut).

Sounder Ident, jingle.

Sound under Keeping the natural sound low under the voice of a reporter or newscaster.

Source Someone who provides information used in a news story.

The source of a line feed.

Spent conviction A conviction that can no longer be reported safely after a specified time.

Spike A metal prong on which unused or old copy and other pieces of paper are kept. To 'spike' a story is to drop it and not run it (a.k.a. biff).

Spin In PR, spin is giving a heavily biased portrayal of an event.

Spin doctors PR people who apply spin to stories.

Splicer Device for manually joining pieces of film or quarter-inch audio tape (a.k.a. editing block).

Splicing tape Sticky tape used to join edits on film or audio tape. Seldom used today.

Split page The standard TV news script. The left side of the page is used for video directions and the right side is for the script.

Split screen Showing more than one moving image on the television screen at the same time.

Spoilers Stories designed to spoil the impact of a rival's scoop.

Spot story American term for an item of breaking news (e.g. a fire or air crash).

Stab Short jingle used for emphasis.

Staging Unethical practice in which a reporter asks people to behave in a contrived way on camera.

Standbys Items available for use if others are lost.

Stand-up A report on camera on location (a.k.a. PTC, piece-to-camera, stand-upper).

Stereo A recording using left and right channels to separate and spread the sound.

Stills Still images (like photographs) used in TV programmes.

Stills store System for storing stills.

Strap Caption or Aston.

Streamer Text that scrolls from right to left across the lower third of the TV screen (a.k.a. ticker-tape).

Stringer Freelance reporter covering an area where there is no staff reporter available. Term often used for overseas freelance reporters.

Subpoena A court order compelling a person to attend court or submission of evidence.

Sub judice Literally 'under law'. Often applied to the risk that may arise in reporting forthcoming legal proceedings.

Frequently and incorrectly used by authority as a reason for not disclosing information.

Summary Round-up of the most important news.

Summons An order issued by a magistrate to attend court at a stated time and date to answer a charge.

Super Title or caption mechanically superimposed or electronically generated on a TV picture. Used mostly for the names and titles of people being identified in a news package (a.k.a. Aston, font in America).

Suspense lead A lead that keeps the most important part of the story until the very end (a.k.a. drop intro).

Switching pause Short pause in transmission before and after the network bulletin to permit local stations to opt in and out clearly.

Switch talkback Talkback limited by the use of a switch so the presenter can only hear instructions intended for them.

Sync Interview clips and featured sound (a.k.a. actuality, SOF, SOT).

Syndicated material Recordings sent out to radio stations by PR and advertising agencies to promote a company or product.

T

Tabloid A newspaper format that is the smaller of the two common formats in the UK.

Tabloid press Newspapers focusing on less 'serious' content, especially celebrities, sports and sex.

Tailpiece Light-hearted story at the end of a bulletin (a.k.a. And finally, kicker).

Talkback Off-air communication system linking studios, control rooms and OB locations. Commonly used for presenter, producer and technical staff to talk between studio and control cubicle.

Talking head A single shot of someone speaking on camera.

Taster Snappy, one-line headline which may include a snatch of actuality. Often used before a commercial break (a.k.a. teaser, bump tease).

TBU Telephone balance unit. Device used when recording telephone interviews. Permits the interviewer to use a studio mic and balance the levels of the two voices.

Teaser See Taster.

Tech op Technical operator. Someone who drives a radio programme from outside the studio.

Teleprompter Electronic device that projects scripts onto a screen in front of the camera lens so they can be read by presenters (a.k.a. teleprompt, prompter, Autocue, Portaprompt).

Teletext A text and graphic information service on TV.

Theft Dishonest appropriation of property with the intention to permanently deprive another of it.

3G phone Third-generation mobile phone capable of video.

Throw To link to a reporter, who picks up the story and runs with it, without relying on questions from the studio.

Ticker-tape Text that scrolls from right to left across the lower third of the TV screen (a.k.a. on-screen streamer, crawler).

Tilt A vertical camera move.

Time-code A numerical code recorded on videotape as it is shot, used in editing. Shows on edit monitor but not on the finished story.

Tip-off Call from a stringer or member of the public about a story.

Tone A constant sound signal used by audio engineers to check sound levels are the same on recording and playback machines.

Top and tail To edit a piece to ensure a clean start and end.

Top line The first line or main point of a story. A new top line would be the latest development in a story.

Touchscreen Equipment controlled electronically by touching part of the screen of a computer.

Trail To tell the audience about items coming up.

A promotional item for a forthcoming programme (a.k.a. promo).

Transmission area The geographical area served by a station.

Tribunal A special court or committee appointed to deal with particular problems.

Tripod Portable, collapsible, three-legged stand used for mounting a camera.

TSA Total Survey Area – the area surveyed by RAJAR.

Two-shot Camera shot of two people.

Two-way An interview between a presenter and a reporter to provide information and analysis of an event or story (a.k.a. Q and A).

TUC Trades Union Congress.

TX Transmission.

U

UCAS University and College Admissions Service. The university applications body.

U-Lay Underlay. Pictures laid under a voice (a.k.a. OOV).

Umbrella story A single story incorporating a number of similar items under one link.

Underlay See U-Lay.

Uni-directional mic Microphone that responds mainly to sounds directly in front of it.

UPI United Press International – a news agency.

Update New information in a news story that requires a rewrite.

V

VCR Videocassette recorder.

VJ Video-journalist. Journalist who reports with a videocamera and shoots and edits on their own.

Video phone A phone that transmits video.

Vision mixer Operator in a studio gallery who cuts between pictures.

The equipment a vision mixer uses.

Visuals The visual element of a TV report: stills, film or video and graphics.

Vlog A blog using video content.

V-O Voice-over. Commentary over pictures by an unseen speaker.

Voice-bank Recorded information from the emergency services accessed by journalists by phone.

Voice-over V-O.

Voice-piece Voicer.

Voicer Voice-only report (with no soundbites).

Vox pops Street interviews with members of the public. From the Latin *vox populi* or voice of the people (a.k.a. voxes).

VTR Videotape recorder or videotape recording.

VU meter Volume unit meter. Meter for monitoring recording and playback levels.

W

Wallpaper Derogatory term for TV pictures which are simply there to cover the narrator's words.

Waveform Digital image for audio displayed on a computer in the form of zig-zag waves. These can be edited on screen.

WHAT formula A formula for story construction: What has happened? How did it happen? Amplification. Tie up loose ends.

Wildtrack Recording of ambient sound for dubbing later as background to the report (a.k.a. atmos).

Windshield A foam 'sock' used over a mic to prevent wind noise.

Wipe Crossing from one picture to another, giving the impression that one is wiping the other off the screen.

Wire copy Material written for broadcast distributed by wire services like AP and Reuters.

Wire service News agency which sends copy to newsrooms along landlines (wires). News agencies increasingly send copy online or via satellite, but are still known as 'the wires'.

WMD Weapons of mass destruction.

WPB Waste paper bin.

Wrap To wrap is to end a shoot (according to film buffs the term is short for 'wind reel and print').

A radio news item including an interview clip: the reporter 'wraps' their voice around a soundbite. In some newsrooms a 'wrap' is interchangeable with a package, but it is usually shorter and only features one clip.

WS Wide camera shot.

WTN Worldwide Television News.

WWW World Wide Web. Graphical interface of the global network of digitised information stored on the Internet.

Young person In law, a person 14 years of age or above, but below 18.

PARTFOUR
WORKSHOPS AND EXERCISES

WORKSHOPS AND EXERCISES

CHAPTER ONE: INTRODUCTION

- Track the progress of a news story on different platforms from the same news organisation (the BBC and Sky News offer TV, radio, online and mobile phone services). How do the length and treatment of the story differ on:
  1 Terrestrial television news
  2 Rolling news
  3 Radio bulletins
  4 The website
  5 Broadband services
  6 Mobile phones.
- Visit the website of a major news provider. How many different types of job do they offer in broadcast journalism? Find out the roles of:
  1 A field producer in TV
  2 A foreign news editor
  3 A TV researcher
  4 A regional TV programme producer
  5 A radio reporter in commercial radio.
- Prepare a background file on a running story – e.g. conflict in the Middle East, the next US presidential election, the London Olympics. Select stories that are new developments or related to the same issue. Order them in a folder (preferably electronically as downloads or weblinks, or, if not, in the form of newspaper cuttings). Whenever there is a new angle on the story, consult your files and see how that helps your understanding of the story.

CHAPTER TWO: WHAT'S THE STORY?

- Who do you think is the typical listener to the radio station nearest to your home? Now do a bit of research into the profile – average age and social background.
- Ask somebody at the station if they have an imaginary listener in mind when they broadcast.
- Imagine a commercial radio station playing your favourite music. What might be the profile of the imaginary listener?

  Now think of a station playing your parents' favourite songs. Would the target audience just consist of older people? Or would they have to broaden the appeal to attract advertisers?

- Think back over your lifetime. Can you recall five big stories and remember where you were when you first heard the news? How did you receive the news? Were you on your own or in company? How did you react?
- Look at the table on *Theories of News Production* (page 23) and decide which model most closely represents the way news is produced on:
  1 BBC News 24
  2 Sky News
  3 Your local commercial radio station
  4 A tabloid newspaper
  5 A Sunday broadsheet newspaper.
- Consider the **news values**, as defined by Harcup and O'Neill (pages 24 and 25). Watch a TV news bulletin, listen to news programmes on radio, or consider a half-hour segment of any rolling news programme – Radio Five Live or Sky News, for example. Now ask:
  - Did all the stories fit into the categories outlined by Harcup and O'Neill?
  - If not, what were the factors that made other stories newsworthy?
  - Does the requirement for balance and impartiality in broadcast news affect the news agenda?
  - Where does sport fit into this list?
  - Is broadcast news becoming more or less like newspaper news?
- How could you make the following stories relevant to the core audience for an independent local radio station in Scotland:
  1 House prices in the Home Counties are rising by 20 per cent a year.
  2 London's congestion charge is going up again.
  3 A budget airline has announced more flights from Edinburgh airport.
  4 Andrew Murray is promoting tennis for young people at a photo-call in a Central London car park.
  5 Firemen in Cardiff have rescued an iguana from a chimney.
- Consider whether you would want to use any of these stories at all. Then imagine it is a slow news day – and you *have* to use them. How would you treat them? And what order would you put them in?

- Look at the ingredients that made some of the biggest stories of recent years so important to audiences worldwide.

    1 The death of Princess Diana – royalty, celebrity, death, sex, intrigue.

    2 The events of September 11, 2001 – high death toll, terrorism, religion, world-famous landmarks, global politics, dramatic TV pictures.

    3 The 2004 Tsunami – huge death toll, shock, natural disaster, holiday destinations affected, charity, global politics, dramatic TV pictures.

    4 Michael Jackson trial – celebrity, pop music, sex, crime, courtroom drama.

    5 Hurricane Katrina – natural disaster, high death toll, tourist destination, political bungling, allegations of racism, environmental problems, dramatic TV pictures.

- Watch a TV news programme or listen to the radio news. List the factors that made each item in the bulletin newsworthy. Now compare it with another programme or bulletin. Does your research suggest that different organisations have different news values?

- Next time you meet up with your friends, analyse the conversation: do you discuss the news at all? If you do, what are the news stories that you talk about? Do the same exercise with your family. Are the types of stories you discuss with them different? Why? Have you ever discussed a news story with a complete stranger, maybe someone you've sat next to on a bus or train? What was the story? What was it about the story that you felt able to discuss with a stranger?

CHAPTER THREE: FINDING THE NEWS

- Start your own **contacts book**. Buy a small notebook with an alphabetical index. Begin by listing public and private bodies likely to figure in news stories (courts, councils, the emergency services, hospitals, airports, rail companies, major employers, chambers of commerce, trades unions, community groups, sports clubs). Find their numbers and e-mail addresses from the Web or the phone book. Ring the switchboard of larger bodies and ask for the press officer. Then ask the press office for the names of contacts and their direct line numbers.

    Add friends and family to your contacts book if you think they have specialist knowledge or personal experience that might come in handy. Transfer numbers from your mobile phone. Cross-reference your entries so that people are found under their name and the subject

heading (e.g. a friend who works on the railways might offer useful background to stories about train delays or a rail crash).

- Call the local police, fire service and ambulance services and ask for their voice-bank numbers. Check the **voice-banks** regularly and see how many possible news stories they contain. Is there enough information on the voice-bank to write a convincing version of the story? What extra information do you need?

- Visit your local magistrates' or sheriff **court**. Look at the court list. Which cases appear to offer interesting copy? Sit in court (you may be allowed onto the press bench; otherwise use the public gallery). Pick the most interesting case and write about it. Did you manage to get down all the relevant facts? Have you been able to check names, addresses and their spellings?

- Make an application (in writing) to your local council under the **Freedom of Information Act**. Pick a subject you have heard people complaining about – waste collection services, for example, or the state of local parks. Ask for statistical information that should be easy to provide. Analyse the response. Do the figures suggest a story?

- See how many factual **inaccuracies** you can spot in established news outlets over the period of one week. This may involve comparing the same story in different newspapers, websites or radio and TV programmes. Do they all contain the same facts? What does this tell you about the journalistic process?

- Prepare a **diary of forthcoming events** you would want covered if you were the editor of a local radio station. See if you can find enough future events to fill bulletins for a period of three successive days, without resorting to new or breaking events.

- Listen to a radio news programme or watch a TV news programme and analyse what stories are diary stories.

CHAPTER FOUR: THE INTERVIEW

How would you go about controlling your nerves before an important interview? Do you have your own relaxation techniques to cope with stress at work? Do you think you would be able to control your opinions?

- Take another look at Jeremy Paxman's interview with George Galloway and consider these questions:

    - *What does the interview tell you about George Galloway's relationship with the media?*

    - *Did Paxman achieve anything by being so adversarial?*

    - *What does it say about Paxman's attitude to politicians?*

- Watch any TV interview or listen to an interview on radio. Has the interviewer prepared well? How would you have prepared differently? Draw up a list of questions you would have asked if you had been the interviewer.

- Record and listen to an extended interview on the radio or a television chat show. Note any **soundbites** that could be used in a short news bulletin. What are the in and out points of the clips? What is the story?

- Carefully watch or listen to a **political interview**. Who is in control of the interview – the interviewer or the interviewee? Have ground rules been agreed beforehand? Are there any no-go areas? Does the interviewer give the interviewee a hard time or an easy time?

- Watch or listen to a news programme and study how **vox pops** are used. Are they predictable? What do they add to the story?

- Watch a current affairs programme like *The Politics Show*, *Newsnight* or *Channel 4 News* and analyse the choice of guests interviewed. Are they all treated in the same way? If not, why not? Are guests in the studio given an easier ride than someone who is in a remote studio?

CHAPTER FIVE: NEWS WRITING

Here's some sound advice and an exercise in concise writing. It is worth trying because using words accurately and not vaguely is a vital discipline. It is tempting to use words that make a story sound important but which have no exact meaning. The BBC correspondent Allan Little, in an online guide to writing for radio, says: 'Choose words whose meaning you know. Don't use words like "substantial" or "considerable". These seem to me to be meaningless and their frequent use always suggests to me a writer who isn't sure what he means to say, and is therefore choosing a word which leaves the meaning of the sentence vague or obscure.'

Little suggests a lesson in news writing. *Try writing a news story in words of one syllable.* 'It's hard,' he says. 'But it makes you think about the way you're using the language.'

- Try writing a story in words of no more than two syllables – this is arguably more realistic, and an easier exercise to do.

- Research and collect different companies' **style guides** – compare them to see how they differ

- Listen to news reports on Radio Four. Do they differ from reports on Radio Five Live? List the differences.

- Just after eight o'clock in the morning retune your radio (without looking) and try to decide what station you are listening to from the style of the writing, the running

order and sound clips used. Rapidly repeat the exercise a number of times within the first couple of minutes after the hour. How many did you get right?

- Take a story from a newspaper. Assume the interview quotes are available as audio clips. Write the story (including a cue) in the style of:

  1 A BBC Radio Four 1.15 package

  2 A 40″ wrap for commercial radio

  3 A 20″ copy story

  4 A two-minute network television report for Sky News.

- Pick a story from the front page of a newspaper. Now write the following **headlines** for the story:

  1 A two-sentence programme opener (e.g. BBC Ten O'Clock News, ITV News at 10.30)

  2 A five-second headline for use in a menu (second or third story)

  3 A tease (for use before a commercial break)

  4 A closing head.

- Pick a page lead story from a newspaper. Write a cue or link for broadcast in the following styles:

  1 Hard news formula – the most important facts first

  2 Soft feature-style introduction

  3 Drop intro – saving the key facts for impact.

- Listen to the output of one day on radio. Listen to a range of output – a local commercial station, Five Live, a local BBC station, Radio Four, Radio One – and analyse what stories each station covers. Are they the same? Have they been treated the same? How does the writing change? Is audio used? Is music used? Are headlines used?

- Listen to radio news reports and see if you can apply the Christmas Tree theory to them.

CHAPTER SIX: LOCATION REPORTING AND PRODUCTION

- Try watching a TV news programme and working out whether a story was pre-planned or one that broke on the day. How did you tell? What proportion of stories in the bulletin were planned in advance? Does the proportion surprise you? What does that tell you about whether it is a slow news day?

- Visit a location where you know broadcast journalists work (e.g. you will have seen TV reporters outside courts, football grounds, in local shopping centres). Do a **recce** by making notes about the location under the following headings:

  1 Health and safety – What are the risks to safe operation of broadcasting equipment?

2 Permissions – Can you work here without permission from the landowner or other authority? If not, find out who you need to ask and whether they are likely to agree.

3 Interview locations – Is the environment suitable for conducting interviews? What are the background noise levels? Can they be reduced if necessary? Are there backgrounds useful for a TV interview?

CHAPTER SEVEN: LOCATION VIDEO AND SOUND

• Take a portable sound recorder and microphone on location with a friend to act as an interviewee. Pay particular attention to setting your levels and the distance you hold the mic from the speaker's mouth. Using headphones to monitor the results, compare the sound recorded in the following environments:

1 A field or park

2 A shopping centre

3 A car park

4 A crowded café or bar.

• Repeat the above exercise using a camera. Pay particular attention to what your shots look like. Does a tree appear to be growing out of the top of your interviewee's head? Can you see your reflection in a shop window? Is the background too distracting?

CHAPTER EIGHT: SPORTS REPORTING AND COMMENTARY

• Call a local sports club. See what criteria they apply to offering access to the media. What **accreditation** is needed? Are there sports rights agreements in place? What facilities do they have for the media? Is the venue divided into different levels of access for different media representatives? Do they accommodate student journalists or beginners?

• Study the sports pages of a newspaper. With a marker pen highlight all the examples of cliché and journalese (all the phrases you have seen many times before). Rewrite two or three stories without using the clichés.

• Research a televised sporting event using newspapers and the Web. Prepare lists of key facts about the fixture and the competitors. Turn the sound down on the broadcast and deliver your own **commentary**. Start with television commentary for ten minutes at a time. Build up to longer stretches. Then try radio commentary.

CHAPTER NINE: FOREIGN REPORTING

• Visit the FCO (Foreign and Commonwealth Office) website, follow the links, and find out what special preparations or permissions you would need to work as a broadcast journalist in the following countries:

1 US

2 Turkey

3 Israel

4 Iraq

5 Kazakhstan.

• Watch a TV news report from a foreign conflict. Apply a risk assessment to what you see on screen. What **health and safety** issues are there? Were the reporter and camera crews in danger? Did the report use agency material or was it all shot by the TV channel's own crews?

CHAPTER TEN: GOING LIVE

• Take a newspaper story that has few interviews in it and is unlikely to offer picture opportunities. Now rewrite the story as a series of questions and answers for a **two-way**. Practise answering by consulting notes (as if for radio) and then without notes, speaking for up to 30 seconds at a time. Start with two questions, and build up to five or six.

• Practise **talking to time**. Try talking on a topic of your choice, but preferably something in the news – for exactly 20 seconds. Now try 30 seconds. Now repeat the exercise on a topic you know little about and have researched in the past hour.

CHAPTER ELEVEN: THE PACKAGE

• Listen to radio reports on Radio Four (World at One and PM) and identify the techniques used in their reporters' packages. How have they used the sights and smells of a story in the audio? Have they painted pictures with the words that have been used? Which specific words and phrases worked well?

• Watch the television news with the sound turned down. See if you can tell what the story is about without hearing any speech. It is a very useful way to analyse how a story is told visually.

• Pick a story from a newspaper and work out what audio and interviews you would need for:

1 A two-minute radio package

2 A 40″ wrap

3 A five-minute feature.

Would the piece be enhanced by archive sound or music? What would you use? How would you order the material for maximum impact?

- Listen to coverage of a personality-based political story on BBC Radio Four or another speech-based radio station. How would you tell the story in an engaging and entertaining way for television? Can you think of a **visual metaphor** or motif to explain the story to as wide an audience as possible?

- Watch a feature package on a television news programme and study the use of **music**. Why was it used? How was it used? Was the choice predictable? Did it add to your understanding and enjoyment of the package?

CHAPTER TWELVE: EDITING

- Listen to a news package on BBC Radio Four and analyse the pace and structure. How many audio clips have been used? How have they been combined or separated? Is the piece strong on actuality, or is it mainly the reporter's voice? Can you work out how many different audio channels were used in the edit?

- Record a short interview in a dead acoustic – like a studio. Then record an interview in a live acoustic – like a corridor or a room with background noise – and also record wildtrack at the second location. Now edit the first interview. Try adding some of the wildtrack to your studio recording. Does it match the sound of the second interview? Are the sound levels the same? What are the differences?

- Watch a TV news programme and see how often the reporter packages include **layered video** (split-screens or pictures within a picture). Are they successful in helping tell the story? If you have access to editing software, try replicating the effects.

CHAPTER THIRTEEN: GRAPHICS

- Count the number of characters (letters and spaces) in the on-screen graphics of a rolling news channel. Then pick a newspaper story and write it in the style of:
  1 A ticker-tape streamer
  2 A breaking news bar.

- Find a story with a series of statistics in it. Decide which are the most important facts and figures. Now script them to be accompanied by a **graphics sequence**. Write the sequence as a series of reveals or separate pages disclosing fresh information. What background images would you use behind your graphic?

- Imagine you have access to 3D graphics in a **virtual reality** studio. Devise and sketch out a graphics sequence for each of the following stories:

1 A national housing shortage
2 Global warming
3 The widening of the motorway between Birmingham and Manchester.

CHAPTER FOURTEEN: PRESENTATION

- There is no substitute for practising reading aloud. When you have got used to writing and reading your own bulletins, add the following factors:
  1 Always practise reading exactly to time – a three-minute bulletin should be three minutes long to the exact second, not five seconds over or seven seconds under.
  2 To replicate an unexpected change to your programme timings, set an alarm clock to ring towards the end of your bulletin – at that point you have ten seconds left to wrap up and end.
  3 Pick up a newspaper story that you have not read before halfway through your bulletin. Try to present it in a broadcast style.

- Practise **ad libbing** by adding extra information and your own comments at the end of each story. The ad lib should be unscripted and should always be relevant to the story that preceded it. Set yourself target times to fill: 5 seconds, 10 seconds and so on up to 30 seconds.

- Even if you do not have access to a professional studio, you can replicate working with talkback by practising reading a bulletin while you have the radio on. Keep it loud enough so that you can hear everything that is being said. Try to recall what was said on the radio at the end of your read. To replicate switch talkback, try turning the radio on for up to 10 seconds at a time (until you can understand the sense of what's being said) and then off again.

CHAPTER FIFTEEN: THE PROGRAMME

- Watch an hour of rolling news on TV. Make a note of the main headlines, the packages, interviews and two-ways. Draw up a running order for a half-hour **appointment-to-view** programme based on these elements.

- Using the **programme template** prepare a TV bulletin based on the content of a local radio station's news output. Now do the same with stories from a newspaper.

- Compare two news programmes on rival channels (TV or radio). Which stories, if any, could be described as exclusive? Were there elements of the same story that were exclusive to one channel or the other? What does this tell you about the nature of news gathering?

INDEX

The Longman Practical Journalism Series

ISBN-10: 1-4058-3536-2
ISBN-13: 978-1-4058-3536-7

'Given the endless controversies around privacy, ethics and media regulation this book is a timely, comprehensive and indispensable handbook for journalists and a rallying cry for all those who believe ethical journalism is not just possible but an essential part of a free media in a democratic society.'
Jeremy Dear, General Secretary of the National Union of Journalists (NUJ)

Journalism, Ethics and Regulation provides journalism students and trainee journalists with the tools to make informed ethical decisions in their working lives. The text provides detailed coverage of the main codes of practice and regulatory bodies – PCC, Office of Communications, BBC, NUJ – in the UK and beyond.

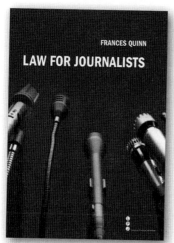

ISBN-10: 0-582-82311-0
ISBN-13: 978-0-582-82311-2

Containing essential information for newspaper, magazine, broadcasting and online journalists, this book is an invaluable guide for all journalists and students of journalism. Whether you are – or plan to be – a news reporter, feature writer, sub-editor or editor, it is packed with useful advice to make sure that you stay on the right side of the law and do your job even better.

Written by an award-winning journalist and experienced author, the book covers the content of most journalism courses including those accredited by the NCTJ.

Available from all good bookshops or order online at
www.pearsoned.co.uk/practicaljournalism

 Longman Practical Journalism

Licensing Agreement

This book comes with a DVD. By opening this package, you are agreeing to be bound by the following:

The files contained on this DVD are, in many cases, copyrighted. **THIS DVD IS PROVIDED FREE OF CHARGE, AS IS, AND WITHOUT WARRANTY OF ANY KIND, EITHER EXPRESSED OR IMPLIED, INCLUDING, BUT NOT LIMITED TO, THE IMPLIED WARRANTIES OF MERCHANTABILITY AND FITNESS FOR A PARTICULAR PURPOSE.** Neither the book publisher nor its dealers and distributors assume any liability for any alleged or actual damages arising from use of this DVD.